SECRECY IN THE SUNSHINE ERA

SECRECY IN THE SUNSHINE ERA
The Promise and Failures of US Open Government Laws

Jason Ross Arnold

UNIVERSITY PRESS OF KANSAS

Published by the University Press of Kansas (Lawrence, Kansas 66045), which was organized by the Kansas Board of Regents and is operated and funded by Emporia State University, Fort Hays State University, Kansas State University, Pittsburg State University, the University of Kansas, and Wichita State University

Library of Congress Cataloging-in-Publication Data

Arnold, Jason Ross, author.
Secrecy in the sunshine era : the promise and failures of U.S. open government laws / Jason Ross Arnold.
pages cm
Includes index.
ISBN 978-0-7006-1992-4 (hardback)
1. Freedom of information—United States. 2. United States—Politics and government—1989– 3. United States—Politics and government—1945–1989. I. Title.
KF5753.A765 2014
342.73'0662--dc23

2014019779

British Library Cataloguing-in-Publication Data is available.

Printed in the United States of America

10 9 8 7 6 5 4 3 2 1

To Stephanie: from Chinese Christmas to
Duxbury cliffs to . . . *this*?

CONTENTS

PREFACE AND ACKNOWLEDGMENTS

This is not the book I intended to write. I began the project in 2010 with every intention of comparing how democratic governments have complied with their transparency obligations. The idea was to track the globalization of freedom of information laws and then compare how they fared in practice. After gathering data from a range of cases—including the United States—I sat down in May 2011 to start writing. For reasons I cannot remember, I first dove into the US chapter.

By Memorial Day, the chapter had grown large and unwieldy, pushing 100 pages and filled with too many sections. The book obviously needed two US chapters, I thought, maybe divided between pre- and post-9/11 periods. As I continued, the two-chapter restraint seemed increasingly pointless. So did the narrow focus on the Freedom of Information Act (FOIA). So I kept going where I was going, points unknown. The global secrecy project needed to wait.

The book's structure soon took form. I wanted to compare administrations and understand why some seemed more secretive than others, despite all of them having to operate under more or less the same information policy framework. As I collected stories about abuses of executive secrecy powers and officials' clever and cynical (and clumsy) efforts to evade transparency laws, I realized that too many episodes came and went with the barest of traces. To my surprise, no one had put it all together before, at least not in the way I envisioned. The book I wanted to read during that first summer didn't yet exist.

I faced the same problem as anyone else studying secrecy—at any rate, those of us without top security clearances. How would I construct a comparative political history of executive branch *secrecy*? The subject, after all, involved hidden information, exclusive knowledge. Clearly, we cannot document the secrecy system in full, observing and measuring every secret, knowing every transgression, every overclassification, every circumvention around open government laws. But because of those powerful laws, as well as leaks, lawsuits, journalism, and other secret-spilling mechanisms, hundreds of pieces of evidence have made their way into the public record.

As I gathered the pieces and stacked them up into piles for each presidential administration, I noticed some conventional wisdom–busting patterns. Most interesting was how Bush-Cheney secrecy started to look less and less "unprecedented," as many have alleged. To be sure, Bush and Cheney ran one of the most secretive administrations in history. But along several of the dimensions examined in this book, not only did the scale and scope of their secrecy have historical precedents but other administrations sometimes proved to be worse (the normative word *worse* flowing from the conceptual framework sketched in chapter 2). When they did exceed their predecessors in scale, they often did so by using tools and tricks those earlier officials had invented and developed. And then came Obama-Biden officials, promising "the most transparent administration in history" and ending their first term still trumpeting that promise despite the evidence.

The book therefore is a comparative historical analysis of administrations during the sunshine era, the period following the game-changing series of open government laws passed in the 1970s (the Federal Advisory Committee Act, the Government in the Sunshine Act, and the Privacy Act, as well as crucial FOIA amendments). I strove to make the analysis as comprehensive as possible, all the while recognizing the inherent problems of studying secrecy and the impossibility of including everything relevant. I was especially drawn to the intense drama of many of the secrecy conflicts. Hence, I didn't shy away from telling stories, despite what some of the hegemonic norms in political science say about that. Like Percival Godliman in Ken Follett's *Eye of the Needle,* I rediscovered how much I "liked the unraveling of mysteries, the discovery of faint clues, the resolution of contradictions, the unmasking of lies and propaganda and myth." Like Iowa Bob in John Irving's *Hotel New Hampshire*, I got obsessed and stayed obsessed.

The book was hatched and developed at Virginia Commonwealth University (VCU), where I have many wonderful colleagues who offered continued support and encouragement even after the project changed shape. For that and other reasons, I thank the core political science faculty: John Aughenbaugh, Deirdre Condit, Herb Hirsch, Bill Newmann, Chris Saladino, Faedah Totah, and Judy Twigg. Extra thanks go to Deirdre for just being awesome. I also thank David Gompert, who read the entire manuscript, offered many valuable criticisms, and reminded me of the important differences between bunting, balking, and punting. VCU also afforded the able research assistance of Cindy Cors and Jessica Zielonis, as well as the dogged and resourceful librarian Bettina Peacemaker (thanks also to Bettina's colleagues Gail Warren, the state of Virginia law librarian, and Gail Zwirner, law librarian at the

University of Richmond). I am also grateful for the students in my Political Institutions and Processes seminars who provided extensive comments and criticisms on earlier drafts. Thank you Cindy Cors, Kevin Harris, Grant Rissler, and Mona Siddiqui.

I often found strangers I contacted with random questions to be unexpectedly generous with their time. From their posts in government agencies, universities, advocacy organizations, and other nongovernmental organizations, the following people helped fill in missing pieces, share data, or confirm facts: Gavin Baker, Robert Chesney, Greg DeCarolis, Bette Farris, David Grimes, Stasia Hutchison, Christian Lee, J. William Leonard, Beth Lyon, Andrea Johnson-Stewart, Jacob Sullum, Peggy Ushman, Maggie Weber, Charles Weisselberg, and Nina Wilson. Thanks also to any others whose names I've forgotten to include. Although I did sometimes encounter grumpy, uncooperative (and probably underresourced) FOIA officials, overall I was surprised and pleased with the level of responsiveness at government agencies.

Every author should be so lucky to have an editor like Chuck Myers. I realized my good fortune right away when he responded to my proposal with an incisive comment that helped me reframe the project. All along the way, he seemed to be an enthusiastic backer, and he was always a significant contributor and critic, identifying and helping to correct problems and thereby improving the book (blame any remaining errors on me). Thanks, Chuck, for all of this and for our many intellectually stimulating conversations. I am also grateful for the anonymous reviewers whose extensive comments and criticisms improved the book in many ways. Thanks also to Michael Kehoe, Larisa Martin, Becca Murray, Joan Sherman, and others behind the scenes at the University Press of Kansas for all of their hard work and patience as we transformed the manuscript into a finished product.

There are dozens of others whose words and actions have been sources of inspiration and insight. I probably would not have even started the project if Chelsea (née Bradley) Manning had not leaked the Apache helicopter video to Wikileaks, which published it as "Collateral Murder" in April 2010. Other courageous individuals—Daniel Ellsberg, Edward Snowden, Jesselyn Radack, Sibel Edmonds, and Thomas Drake, among others—forced me and the rest of the world to reconsider what counts as necessary and unnecessary secrets and to never forget how crucial an informed citizenry is for high-quality representative democracy. I am also grateful for the tireless research and advocacy work of the following organizations (and the people inside): the National Security Archive, the Federation of American Scientists, the American Civil

Liberties Union, the Union of Concerned Scientists, the Electronic Frontier Foundation, the Government Accountability Project, the Sunlight Foundation, the Project on Government Oversight, and the Center for Effective Government (formerly OMB Watch). In addition, I would like to acknowledge the late Meg Greenfield, who wrote about a "sunshine era" long before I did. Though I came across her reference after I had already completed and named the book, Greenfield nevertheless beat me to it.[1]

Finally and perhaps most of all, I thank Stephanie and the little family we grew over the course of this project. Thanks, Steph, for managing crowd patrol and noise reduction duty when I had to close the door to the office. (Thanks as well to Brian Eno and other musicians for counterbalancing some of those noises with other ones that better facilitated writing.) Steph, thanks also for just about everything you've done over the past eighteen-plus years; I am eternally grateful. Penelope and Charlotte, I cannot wait until you can read what I was always working on in that stuffy office (Pen, it wasn't just about the headphones). I also cannot wait to hear what you have to say about it.

1

INTRODUCTION

Three days into a 1975 diplomatic tour of the Middle East, Secretary of State Henry Kissinger sat down with a group of American and Turkish dignitaries in Ankara for a conversation about two nagging political problems: Cyprus and the US Congress. Turkey had invaded Cyprus seven months earlier, in response to a Greek-sponsored coup d'état on the small sovereign island nation. Both countries believed Cyprus was rightfully theirs, and both paid a heavy price for disrupting the status quo. For Greece's coup, the US Congress cut off military aid to the right-wing junta leading the government, still a North Atlantic Treaty Organization (NATO) ally despite its unabashed and repressive authoritarianism. For Turkey's invasion and ensuing human rights violations against Greek Cypriots, Congress cut off aid and took the unusual step of imposing an arms embargo on its other longtime NATO ally. Although Congress had overlooked ethnic cleansings in the past, atrocities that happened to occur in Europe rarely went unnoticed.[1]

After earlier refusals to meet with Kissinger, a peevish group from Turkey agreed to see him on March 10, 1975. Senior Turkish officials changed their minds about a meeting once he and the Ford-Rockefeller administration sent signals they strongly opposed Congress's vote on the embargo. Kissinger underscored the point as soon as the two sides sat down, saying the group was meeting at a "time that is not easy in our relationship, when the U.S. Congress has taken an action which is totally wrong and with which we totally disagree." After discussing the ways the administration was working to restore aid and arms to Turkey through legal channels, Kissinger and Turkish foreign minister Melih Esenbel began to discuss alternative, not so legal plans, some of which seemed already well hatched. When Esenbel began to speak a little more explicitly about the ideas, US ambassador William Macomber piped in to remind the secretary, "That is illegal," just in case anyone there forgot about the appropriateness of violating an official US embargo. Kissinger's reply was, well, vintage Kissinger—bracing, with a charming wink: "Before the Freedom of Information Act, I used to say at meetings, 'The illegal we do immediately; the unconstitutional takes a little longer.' [laughter] But since the Freedom of Information Act, I'm afraid to say things like that." If Esenbel missed the underlying point, Kissinger continued, in his distinctive slow, guttural voice, "We'll make a major effort [to send you arms illegally]." Kissinger's joke, which recognized the power of the Freedom of Information Act (FOIA) while simultaneously mocking it, illustrates all too well the promise and pitfalls of FOIA and the other truly radical transparency laws of the 1970s.[2]

The Promise

In a country where policy change is usually incremental at best, the "sunshine laws" passed in quick succession in the 1970s were, by comparison, revolutionary, a rare example of punctuated change. The Federal Advisory Committee Act (FACA) (1972), the Privacy Act (1974), FOIA's strengthening amendments (1974 and 1976), the Government in the Sunshine Act (GITSA) (1976), and the Presidential Records Act (PRA) (1978) all passed Congress in a six-year period. The potential impact on US political processes—and on the quality of US democracy more broadly—was enormous. For the first time, citizens would not need to rely on officials' beneficence to access information about government actions. FOIA authorized citizens to demand unclassified information from government agencies, which had to comply, with limited exceptions. FACA and GITSA allowed ordinary citizens to literally sit and watch private interests try to influence government officials on presidential task forces. After meetings adjourned, people could read the transcripts and any other unclassified task force documents. Through the PRA, citizens could review all nonclassified presidential documents that had once been immune to FOIA, after a twelve-year delay. And the Privacy Act empowered citizens to demand dossiers the government had collected on them—or at least some of the unclassified parts.[3]

Earlier open government laws, such as the Federal Records Act (FRA), had edged the government toward transparency, but much was left to officials' discretion, leaving citizens with a spotty, highly selective record of government action—not exactly ideal for democratic citizens trying to monitor and evaluate their representatives as well as government processes and performance more generally. The separation-of-powers system also created some natural incentives and opportunities for competitive parties to rat each other out. For example, members of Congress can hold hearings, issue press releases, publish letters written to senior officials, and push for reforms (such as the State Secrets Protection Act). But governing norms and credible threats of retaliation, on top of the closed government legal framework, greatly limited information disclosure to actors outside the executive and nurtured a culture of secrecy in Washington, DC. Information flowed to citizens, but presidential administrations selected each drop.[4]

FOIA and the other sunshine laws thus empowered citizens like never before. Officials could withhold information or otherwise block access, but they had to justify doing so within an explicit set of parameters. Sensitive national security, law enforcement, and other types of information could be withheld but only under specified conditions. Otherwise, the laws said, the information should be accessible to anyone who was interested. Plus, if agencies rejected a FOIA request or if presidents failed to comply with FACA, citizens could contest the decision in court, taking final decisions away from the executive branch, which, after all, might have illegitimate reasons (and questionable motives) for its secrecy. Overall, the sunshine laws offered citizens a radically more open government, and in so doing, they promised to constrain elite behavior, improve democratic accountability, and possibly even hasten the end of DC's secrecy culture.

The advent of powerful and relatively cheap information technologies in the 1980s and 1990s sweetened the deal for citizens even more. They could click a few buttons and immediately wade through thousands of declassified and unclassified government documents published online. They could read a Central Intelligence Agency (CIA) propaganda plan from the 1961 Bay of Pigs operation in which the author reminded officials of the agency's ability to plant news stories "directly on international wire services." They could learn in 2003 about the detailed maps of Iraq's oil fields, refineries, and pipelines that Vice President Dick Cheney and his secretive energy task force examined in 2001. Thousands of other declassified, unclassified, and leaked classified documents have streamed out of the government since the 1970s, revealing truths many political and economic elites would much rather have kept hidden.

Given these changes, the post-1970s period was distinct from all earlier periods of American political history. The laws and the new technologies together helped usher in what we might call the sunshine era, in which the ever-watchful eyes of citizens simply became a fact of life, forever influencing policy making and elections, for good or ill. Everything not classified in the new "floodlit society" would be open to scrutiny, scorn, and electoral punishment. At least, that was the promise.[5]

Although most citizens embraced the transformation, the new political calculus drew its fair share of skeptics—with Cheney being only one of the most prominent. Transparency sounds nice and noble on paper, they warned, but the passionate, often misguided gaze of the electorate could easily warp the political process. The country thus faced the danger of *too much transparency*. All that monitoring, if haphazard and driven by easily manipulated emotions, might lead citizens to false impressions, steering them toward pettiness and irrationality. Politicians, worried for their political futures, would refrain from making the hard but ultimately correct choices. Finally, though leaks had always been an issue, the new technologies made leaking even easier, multiplying the risks to national security. The techno-legal information revolution was promising, they argued, but it had gone too far.[6]

The Pitfalls

However much the new laws promoted transparency, the sunshine era also has had a huge, underexplored dark side. It is not only a matter of the enormous and growing "national security state," although that is something that can hardly be ignored. The system before the 9/11 attacks was already huge, shrinking only minimally after the end of the Cold War in the 1990s (see chapter 3). After 9/11, it grew to staggering proportions, with a dizzying array of acronymed institutions packed with secrecy workers. In the counterterrorism–homeland security–intelligence matrix alone, millions of individuals in 2010 worked in 1,271 government agencies and 1,931 private companies in some 10,000 locations across the country (plus thousands abroad). About 854,000 of those individuals, in both the private and public sectors, had top secret clearances, the highest-known level. Millions of Americans with security clearances made hundreds of thousands of decisions to classify information every year—tens of millions of decisions if we include derivative classifications, as we should (see chapter 3).[7]

Overly optimistic arguments about the sunshine era also buckle under the weight of decades of government insiders' repeated admissions, before and after 9/11, that the classification system "has grown out of control," as one Defense Department review concluded in 1994. Panels commissioned by presidents and congresses across the post–World War II era have consistently found rampant overclassification and, more generally, "excessive secrecy" within the federal government. President Ronald Reagan's National Security

Council (NSC) executive secretary, Rodney B. McDaniel, for example, concluded in 1991 that 90 percent of classified secrets were not legitimately held. The post-9/11 period brought, at a minimum, more of the same. The chair of the 9/11 Commission, Thomas Kean, estimated that 75 percent of government secrets were unnecessary. ("Three-quarters of what I read that was classified shouldn't have been.") Even former defense secretary Donald Rumsfeld conceded, "It may very well be that a lot of information is classified that shouldn't be." As Richard Nixon's former solicitor general Erwin N. Griswold put it in 1989, "It quickly becomes apparent to any person who has considerable experience with classified material that there is massive overclassification and that the principal concern of the classifiers is not with national security, but rather with governmental embarrassment of one sort or another."[8]

To grasp the full scale and scope of the secrecy system, we must also factor in all the hidden *unclassified* information, though we would almost surely underestimate the size of those secret libraries. For one, the government does not track all of its "sensitive but unclassified" (SBU) information—or if it does, it does not share the details. Just about anything can be trapped by SBU and similar designations, from documents about dual-use nuclear materials and heating and air conditioning systems to scientific data about Agent Orange's health effects and antibiotic-resistant bacteria leaking out of midwestern hog farms. There are dozens of other cases, some involving national security, many not. Indeed, this book documents case after case of presidents and their administrations contorting themselves to hide unclassified information, not always for self-interested political gain or to please private interests but often enough.

When we sift through all those examples, which include historical fights over particular pieces of information as well as abstract categories of information (such as SBU), it becomes apparent how much the secrecy system has *grown* during the sunshine era. If one thing is consistent, it is presidents' efforts to weaken the system's legal foundations. Sometimes the efforts were deliberate. Top Bush-Cheney officials, for instance, worked from day one to restore what they saw as the proper balance of interbranch power that prevailed before Congress and the country overreacted to Watergate and Vietnam. Cheney's protracted fight over his energy task force—in which he refused to comply with FACA's requirement to publish the names of the group's private sector members and details of their meetings—was more about his governing ideology than about the gory details of energy policy, although that was also a factor (see chapter 4). Though Bush-Cheney officials attracted a lot of criticism after openly defying sunshine laws like FACA and pushing hard against the PRA, they also followed their predecessors in circumventing laws in quieter and subtler ways—often for short-term, more pragmatic reasons that had little to do with principled stands on presidential power. Sometimes it worked, sometimes not. When it did, precedents were set, giving future administrations more secrecy tools to use as they pleased. The quantity of carved-out exceptions to the sunshine laws grew through both deliberate strategy and unintended consequences.

What remains underexplored—and underexplained—is this extensive shadow history of presidential resistance to the new legal regime. Indeed, a complete history of the era reveals episode after episode of evasive maneuvers, rule bending, clever rhetorical gambits, and outright defiance, under Republican and Democratic presidents alike. Effective means of evasion accumulated over time, kept in a virtual secrecy toolbox that presidents could use when in a pinch. Other presidents used the tools and added to the toolbox for more ideological reasons. Administrations gradually chipped away at the legal regime, leaving it still standing but poked full of holes.

Any history of America's information revolution thus requires a history of information policy retrenchment in counterpoint. It is a strange paradox. Although many government operations were more transparent in the sunshine era thanks to the new legal framework, the secrecy regime circa 2014—with its medley of rules and precedents gutting the letter and spirit of the sunshine laws and with its millions of secrecy workers and blacked-out pages—is at least as excessive as it was in the 1970s, when Washington promised something new. What escapes most citizens is how resistant the system is to change, with moves toward transparency infrequent and, when initiated, often abandoned. This has occurred no matter which party presidents have belonged to and no matter how noble their intentions have seemed.

Comparing Sunshine-Era Administrations

Still, some administrations appear more secretive than others. This was certainly the case during the Bush-Cheney years, when the president was accused of running an exceptionally secretive administration. After 9/11 and especially after the invasion of Iraq, accusations that the administration was governing with unprecedented secrecy became increasingly common:

- Bush-Cheney secrecy was "unprecedented and deprives the public of information it is lawfully entitled to receive." (*Center for National Security Studies et al. v. Department of Justice*, December 2001)
- "The Bush administration has taken secrecy to a new level. They have greatly increased the numbers and types of classified documents. . . . They have made it far more difficult and time-consuming to obtain documents under the Freedom of Information Act. And they have imposed 'gag rules' on an ever-widening group of government employees." (Steven Aftergood, director of the Project on Government Secrecy at the Federation of American Scientists, 2004)
- "George W. Bush and Richard B. Cheney have created the most secretive presidency of my lifetime. Their secrecy is far worse than during Watergate, and it bodes even more serious consequences." (John Dean, White House counsel during the Nixon administration, 2004)
- Bush-Cheney led "the most secretive White House in modern history." (David Sanger, *New York Times*, 2005)
- "The Bush administration . . . has consistently demonstrated an extraordinary mania for secrecy. . . . Public recourse has become more difficult: enforcement of the Freedom of Information Act has become slower and more burdensome. The one thing the administration has made no secret [*sic*] is its antipathy to government transparency. The secrecy fixation is a threat to democracy and an insult to honest history." (*New York Times* editorial board, 2006)
- "The current administration has exercised an *unprecedented* level of restriction of access to information about, and suppression of discussion of, the federal government's policies and decisions." (OpenTheGovernment.org, 2006)
- "More than any other administration in recent history, this administration has a penchant for secrecy." (Sen. Russell Feingold, 2008)
- Bush-Cheney led "the most secretive administration we've ever had, at least in the modern era." (Dan Metcalfe, who directed the Justice Department's Office of Information and Privacy [OIP] for over twenty-five years, 2009)

It is not a stretch to say the "unprecedented" claim became the conventional wisdom, shared not only by partisans but also by more objective analysts like Aftergood and Metcalfe.[9]

However obviously true the conventional wisdom might seem, impressions can often be misleading. Frustrated partisans whose candidate lost the last election are apt to complain about the incumbent's shenanigans. Republicans on the floor of Congress, on Fox News, and all over the Internet complained bitterly about Obama-Biden secrecy before White House officials could even put their family pictures on the wall. My favorite was an article that appeared on the popular right-wing website Newsmax *six days* after Obama's first in-auguration, entitled "Obama, Most Secretive President Ever." Though that may have been an erroneous and premature accusation, the Obama-Biden administration's frequent boasts about being "the most open and transparent administration in history" were also premature and probably unfounded, as chapter 10 shows. Indeed, the *New York Times*'s David Sanger, who called Bush-Cheney "the most secretive administration in modern history" in 2005, described Obama-Biden in even harsher terms: "This is the most closed, con-trol-freak administration I've ever covered."[10]

Scholarly conclusions, like Aftergood's and Metcalfe's, are usually more circumspect than partisan jabs, heat-of-the-moment complaints, and govern-ment public relations claims (for example, "most open and transparent"). They likely contain elements of truth. Still, we lack systematic comparative historical analyses of the sunshine-era administrations' secrecy records. Was Obama-Biden the most open and transparent administration in history? (Through the end of the first term, probably not.) Was Bush-Cheney secrecy unprecedented in scale and scope? (Yes but only along some dimensions.) In certain areas, Bush-Cheney clearly did expand the secrecy system—for in-stance, by relying more frequently on "secret law" within the executive branch to circumvent inconvenient laws. However, in other areas, including those in which the administration appeared to be vying for a world record in presi-dential secrecy, Bush-Cheney had close competitors. In several of those areas, such as the suppression of proprietary scientific information, Reagan-Bush and Bush-Cheney battled it out for the gold medal. (Did open government advocates and liberal Democrats in the 2000s *forget about* the 1980s?) Bush-Quayle also earned a few records for its efforts, and Clinton-Gore did not run far behind (for instance, in FACA violations). At the very least, the historical evidence, when stacked up and compared, suggests a more subtle conclusion than popular assessments, such as the widely accepted, unqualified one about unprecedented Bush-Cheney secrecy.

Organization of the Book

This book provides a comprehensive history of the sunshine era's dark side, told through a comparative historical analysis of presidential administrations from Reagan-Bush through Obama-Biden's first term. There are other books about US government secrecy, but none offer systematic comparisons, none explain how officials have resisted sunshine laws to make excessive secrecy happen, and none explain why presidents and their teams got away with it. We have, among others, books that focus on specific administrations (Mc-Dermott, Shulman), secrecy tools (Rozell), and issue areas (Fisher, Gup, Pallitto and Weaver, Roberts, Schoenfeld, Stone). But we lack studies that systematically compare administrations across issue areas. *Secrecy in the Sunshine Era* therefore gives historians, social scientists, and curious general readers the first comprehensive, comparative analytic history of sunshine-era secrecy.[11]

The book is organized thematically rather than chronologically. The structure works well for several reasons. First, it highlights the often surprising continuity across sunshine-era administrations. Second, the thematic format illuminates the often sharp contrasts between administrations in each issue area. Although there was continuity across administrations, there was also a lot of variation—surely not a linear increase in secrecy over time. Third, with a straight chronological approach, readers would lose each chapter's depth of focus on specific issue areas. For instance, if the FACA cases were divided and distributed across separate administration-specific chapters, readers would finish the book with less of an understanding of the nature and importance of that law.

After the brief introduction, chapter 2 poses and begins to address the questions that drive the analysis. Which government secrets are legitimately held? What is the nature and scale of America's "excessive secrecy" problem? What are the costs and consequences of excessive secrecy—for democracy, the economy, and national security? Why so much secrecy, despite the sunshine era's legal framework and promises of openness? How have administrations circumvented the laws? Were the tactics mostly implemented piecemeal, for pragmatic purposes, or were they usually tied to broader strategies aimed against the legal framework? What consequences did administrations face for violating laws? What does it mean for American democracy that few senior officials suffered *any* costly legal consequences? Why have administrations had such varied records?

Through the process of answering those questions, chapter 2 outlines a conceptual framework that balances a functioning democracy's need for open government against its need for security and rights protections. It also shows how recent advances in historical institutionalism, particularly in research on institutional change, can help explain why presidential administrations have such varied records. Related work by constructivist institutionalists, who have emphasized how political actors' ideas and rhetoric shape institutional change, also sheds light on the ways administrations have defied, dodged, and reconstructed sunshine laws.[12]

Chapter 3 focuses on statutes and administrative rules governing classified and unclassified information, during settled and unsettled times. Using the September 11 attacks as an empirical starting point, the chapter first examines how officials in the Bush-Cheney administration developed and interpreted new and old secrecy rules during the national security crisis and the subsequent critical juncture. Most of the time, they built atop precedents or revived older ideas and circumvention tactics from earlier administrations, especially Reagan-Bush. They also made distinctive policy choices based on a governing ideology that predated 9/11. A Gore-Lieberman administration just would have handled (some) things differently, due to its different governing ideology, all else being equal. Chapter 3 further highlights the role of ideas in institutional change by tracing the gradual application of "mosaic theory" as a conceptual and legal basis for secrecy. Finally, the chapter compares administrations' classification and declassification records, as well as their FOIA response records. Overall, the chapter shows how a real or perceived national security crisis can create political space for policies tilted toward secrecy. However, there was plenty of secrecy before Bush-Cheney and 9/11, caused by forces more enduring than a particular governing ideology or exogenous shock.[13]

Chapter 4 compares sunshine-era administrations on their FACA-defying behavior, finding none deserving of praise but with Bush-Quayle emerging as the most laudable. Indeed, presidents have flouted FACA more brazenly than any of the other sunshine laws. Upset citizens filed lawsuits, but through a variety of circumvention tactics—playing word games, running out the clock, and pretending nothing wrong happened—administrations often got away with it, letting their task forces continue uninterrupted and in secret. Each unpunished violation demonstrated to successor presidents how weak and unenforceable FACA could be. The chapter pays special attention to chapter 2's "How?" question, with the circumvention tactics front and center in the case histories. Indeed, FACA seems to draw out officials' most creative and cynical word game efforts. "Members" became "consultants," "guests," and "visitors"; public "participation" became "consultations"—all to escape FA-CA's requirements. When citizens did sue, FACA case law allowed administrations to finely hone their running-out-the-clock tactics. By exploiting and creating delays in the legal process, officials learned to complete task forces' work before judges could rule, accomplishing the groups' goals with a speed and efficiency unknown to most government work. When judges finally did rule, the FACA defiance continued: officials complied halfheartedly with orders to disclose records. By the time Obama-Biden took power, FACA had been poked so full of holes that senior officials learned they could simply pretend the law did not exist, whenever they deemed it necessary.

Chapter 5 examines the historical development of so-called secret law in the executive branch and catalogs all known efforts by administrations to use secret legal memos to contravene statutes. The issue first became a major source of controversy during the Bush-Cheney years, after news broke about the "torture memos" written by Department of Justice (DOJ) attorneys in the Office of Legal Counsel (OLC). It more recently reemerged as a major political issue during the Obama-Biden administration, when many citizens demanded the immediate declassification of OLC memos justifying the extrajudicial assassination of US citizens. Although the history of secret law centers on the OLC, the chapter analyzes the use of binding, immunizing secret legal memos written by officials in other executive branch units, such as the National Security Council.

Chapter 6 looks at how sunshine-era administrations have used and abused secrecy tools in court cases, focusing on the state secrets privilege and the use of "secret evidence." The state secrets privilege involves executive branch efforts to exclude (usually) classified evidence from trials, often with the goal of persuading judges to dismiss plaintiffs' lawsuits. Secret evidence involves administrations' efforts to *include* sensitive information—but only when it stays concealed from defendants and their lawyers. The chapter compares administrations broadly and examines the use of both evidentiary tactics through several case studies of lawsuits, including those involving Maher Arar, Sibel Edmonds, and Hany Kiareldeen, as well as the Truman-era case of Ellen Knauff. In each case, executive branch officials insisted that the country's national security needs demanded government secrecy. Only later did judges, litigants, and litigants' relatives and supporters learn that many of those insistent declarations were baseless, used to protect officials from embarrassments, not to protect citizens or the Constitution. (Thus, in these cases, the excessive secrecy did not emerge from bureaucratic conservatism or related impulses—

the forces officials usually blame for overclassification.) For those and other reasons, chapter 6 again brings us face to face with the politically constructed nature of "national security" and the problem of trusting executive branch officials to judiciously base their secrecy claims on the concept.

Though the state secrets privilege gets a (half) chapter of its own, the book covers executive privilege only in relevant cases throughout the pages ahead. The main reason for this relative lack of attention is that executive privilege is one of the few secrecy-related topics that have already received abundant scholarly attention, as in Mark Rozell's comprehensive book on the subject. As defined in chapter 4, executive privilege is a Supreme Court–sanctioned authority allowing senior White House officials to resist demands for information by the other branches, under certain conditions (determined by the courts).[14]

The two chapters on "secret science," chapters 7 and 8, compare sunshine-era administrations in terms of their efforts to conceal proprietary scientific information, whether produced by government scientists or otherwise held exclusively held by the government. Because so few of the cases involved national security or anything close to it, administrations did not have the luxury of making security-related appeals when forced to justify their secrecy. They certainly offered excuses, making tenuous claims about privacy protections or citing their obligation to protect private sector trade secrets. When possible, they said nothing at all, especially if the secrecy seemed to clearly benefit corporate interests (producers of asbestos, aspirin, dioxin, meat, and so on) while harming specific groups (for example, Vietnam veterans) or the public health more generally. Whereas other chapters focus more on circumvention tactics or on the misuse of national security claims to conceal misdeeds and embarrassments, these chapters return to the initial question from chapter 2: which secrets are legitimate? The case studies deliver a clear answer: *not these*. On top of the harms done to American democracy, secret science has had enormous public health consequences. As for the comparisons across administrations, Bush-Cheney deservedly attracted criticism, but there are many reasons why Reagan-Bush needed a chapter of its own.

Chapter 9 catalogs and describes in narrative detail every known effort by senior officials to illegally shred, burn, delete, or otherwise destroy secrets. For instance, the analysis revisits Oliver North and friends' shredding party to get rid of Iran-Contra documents. It also covers the legal fight over White House e-mails that stretched across three administrations, which ultimately added another layer of institutional secrecy to the US government courtesy of Clinton-Gore's unilateral action. In all cases, government officials went beyond mere sunshine law "circumvention tactics" and instead reverted to crude acts of destruction, usually done during (secretive) fits of desperation. Given how unlikely it is that the public record contains the full universe of cases, the chapter generally refrains from making comparative conclusions.

Chapter 10 evaluates the unfinished Obama-Biden administration on each of the relevant dimensions (for example, FACA and secret law). In most categories, Obama-Biden began by taking important steps to rein in excessive secrecy, but officials soon retreated or else abandoned the mission along the way. The analysis shows that despite their frequent boasts about being the most transparent administration in history, Obama-Biden officials have a mixed record, one that does not support their rhetoric—at least not through the first term.

Why does the Obama-Biden administration sit alone, apart from the others covered in the thematic chapters? When I wrote this book, the Obama-Biden administration was a work in progress, with new data and stories appearing daily. Every comparative measure (such as the number of FACA violations) needed constant readjustment; each still deserves an asterisk. Every case history was a current event, subject to twists and corrections. In short, it was an incumbent administration with years to go, an ever-changing case. Incorporating the half-finished presidency into the other chapters would have sapped the strength of the comparative historical analysis.

2

EXCESSIVE SECRECY AND INSTITUTIONAL CHANGE

Necessary and Unnecessary Secrecy

Few would dispute John F. Kennedy's rhetoric about the tension between government secrecy and democracy: "The very word 'secrecy' is repugnant in a free and open society; and we are as a people inherently and historically opposed to secret societies, to secret oaths and to secret proceedings. We decided long ago that the dangers of excessive and unwarranted concealment of pertinent facts far outweighed the dangers which are cited to justify it." But should we have openness about *everything*?[1]

Very few go that far, including Kennedy, who pitted justified versus "excessive and unwarranted" secrecy. Even the most dedicated open government advocates tend to recognize the need for some government secrecy. But what counts as a legitimate secret? What is an acceptable level of risk? What is the proper trade-off between keeping secrets and letting citizens make informed choices? The boundaries are not always so clear.

Let us start with an easy one: most would agree the government should safeguard the procedures and passwords that launch nuclear-tipped missiles or shut down the electric grid. Though *you* might not do anything malicious with the information, that creepy guy across the street—or the cyberwarrior in Tehran—just might. How about active law enforcement operation details? An undercover team is about to raid a terrorist cell's hideout—should we publicize that in advance? Broadcasting the location and future movements of one's army in an ongoing war is also widely considered a bad idea, for obvious reasons. So is revealing an intelligence agency's sources and methods.[2]

Most of us would probably accept other broad categories, including some not involving national security, such as citizens' personal privacy rights. Full disclosure would mean easy access to names, addresses, Social Security numbers, medical records, credit card numbers and purchases, and other personal data held by governments. All citizens deserve these basic privacy protections to reduce vulnerability to crime and other abuses. The risks from disclosure are higher for some groups, such as women fleeing stalkers and abusers as well as mob informants hiding in witness protection programs from their vengeful old comrades. Overall, each privacy protection entails more secrecy.

In short, few would deny there are government secrets worth keeping. Legitimate secrets are essential to the operations of a sovereign, rights-protecting democratic state. But accepting that fact does not require us to accept secrecy claims writ large, including those based on the categories just listed. Take the classic "troop movements" scenario. A state that publicizes its army's location and trajectory during an active war is a state primed for defeat. And Fox News's Geraldo Rivera clearly erred in showing viewers the location and likely movement of the US Army's 101st Airborne Division in a sand map on live, international television a week after the American invasion of Iraq. Yet not all troop movement secrets should be treated as equals. For example, for seventy-five years the government concealed an army document describing troop movements that was drafted nine days after the United States entered World War I. Steven Aftergood's persistence through the FOIA process finally forced the army in 1992 to release the document from 1917. At the same time, the government held on to three other army documents from April 15, 1917.[3]

There are also reasons to reject or at least question the unconditional acceptance of the other information categories. For instance, strict privacy protection laws from the 1970s have prevented the Internal Revenue Service from sharing information that could help parents find missing children. Parameters must also be placed around law enforcement operations, including the terrorist arrest example cited earlier. It would obviously be self-defeating to let a terrorist cell know that its lair is about to be raided. However, publicizing news of a raid and arrests after the fact might cause the terrorists' accomplices to rethink their plans. As the official 9/11 Commission report noted, "Publicity about ['twentieth hijacker' Zacarias] Moussauoi's arrest [on August 16, 2001] and a possible hijacking threat might have derailed the plot." Ramzi Binalshibh, another Al Qaeda detainee, told interrogators on February 14, 2003, that Khalid Sheikh Mohammed would likely have called off the 9/11 attacks if he had known about Moussauoi's capture. Of course, Binalshibh might have strategically lied, hoping to lead the government to discount the risks of disclosing that kind of news to Al Qaeda (for example, news of a capture might signal to terrorism plotters to relocate). However, news of Moussauoi's arrest might have caused Al Qaeda to delay its plans or hastily and clumsily move the operation to an earlier time. Then, a more vigilant government on high alert—one that actually investigated Moussauoi's belongings, as Minneapolis Federal Bureau of Investigation (FBI) agents Harry Samit and Coleen Rowley (among others) had begged their supervisors to do—might have had a chance to prevent the attacks. Surveillance of flustered Al Qaeda members on the move would probably have produced other operational details. A vigilant public, armed with at least some of that information (such as pictures of the suspects' faces), would have generated a flurry of tips. Only one needed to be credible. Overall, as former Republican governor and 9/11 Commission chairman Thomas H. Kean concluded, "We're better off with openness. The best ally we have in protecting ourselves against terrorism is an informed public."[4]

Additionally, though some forms of diplomatic work might merit secrecy, should all State Department communications be concealed from the public? Clearly, the ins and outs of sensitive diplomatic negotiations deserve secrecy, at least some of the time. There would have been no reason for the Reagan-Bush administration, for example, to reveal its arms control negotiating strategy in advance of summits with Soviet leader Mikhail Gorbachev. But it does not logically follow that all State Department (DOS) communications should be classified. To put it somewhat differently, what percentage of the diplomatic cables obtained and released by Wikileaks should have stayed secret? For how long?

What about Department of Defense (DOD) documents? Should the government conceal evidence of interrogation methods or military operations that violated human rights and any associated laws and treaties? Should it conceal and thereby obstruct the prosecution of potential war crimes just because a military action could be filed in typically excused categories, such as "national security"? Consider the 2007 helicopter attack video that PFC Bradley Manning leaked to Wikileaks, which showed US Army troops in AH-64 Apache helicopters attacking mostly unarmed men, including journalists, on a Baghdad street (two carried weapons, but this was Baghdad in 2007, after all). Altogether, the Apache pilots killed at least twelve, among them two Reuters journalists, and injured several others, including two children. Forced to respond because Reuters publicized the story, Bush-Cheney officials refused to accept responsibility, alternately blaming the victims and the alleged insurgents. Perhaps the journalists, both Iraqi nationals, were hanging out with insurgents for a reason, the military suggested. ("There is no question that coalition forces were clearly engaged in combat operations against a hostile force.") The insurgents provoked the gunfight with the Apache helicopter flying above, the government added. Perhaps they also killed the journalists. Reuters filed FOIA requests for the attack video to verify those claims, but the army rejected them on national security grounds. Ultimately, the leaked, classified video strongly challenged many of the government's claims.[5]

Why was the video classified in the first place? An accurate but insufficient answer is that the army classifies all videos of that sort because they contain sensitive national security information. Because national security is a contested, subjective, socially constructed concept, that answer requires additional scrutiny (see the later discussion). The video might have indeed contained legitimate military secrets, such as attack criteria or communications about counterinsurgency surveillance, but those sensitive bits could have been redacted or spliced out.[6]

A more practical justification for the classification might have emphasized the potential dangers to US forces resulting from disclosure. For instance, Iraqis or their sympathizers might have vowed revenge against the United States for killing unarmed children and firing on civilian buildings and vehicles. Secrecy would prevent that violence. But how defensible is the argument for keeping potential war crimes (such as firing on civilians and journalists) secret in a democracy because disclosure might have negative effects? An overall less secretive military might have even prompted commanders to be more careful about their targets, sparing so-called collateral damage and preventing new enemies from forming. Moreover, in a democracy, public opinion should carry some weight. Most Americans—even in the post-9/11 era—felt strongly about their government killing civilians in their name. In early 2007, five months before the Apache helicopter attacks, 77 percent said there had been an "unacceptable" number of Iraqi civilian casualties. At least that many likely would have objected to killing Reuters journalists.[7]

Determining the bounds of what governments should be able to do and then conceal in the name of "national security," "law and order," "personal privacy," and other elusive notions is at the heart of our debate about justified versus excessive government secrecy. The Church Committee raised some of the same questions in its 1976 Senate investigation:

What is a valid national secret? Assassination plots? The overthrow of an elected democratic government? Drug testing on unwitting American citizens? Obtaining millions of private cables? Massive domestic spying by the Central Intelligence Agency (CIA) and the military? The illegal opening of mail? Attempts by the agency of a government to blackmail a civil rights leader? These have occurred and each has been withheld from scrutiny by the public and the Congress by the label "secret intelligence."

The next few sections begin to examine how democracies might balance the need for secrecy with the need for transparency, given the contested nature of the central concepts.[8]

What Do You Need to Know? What Do You Need to *Not* Know?

To define the boundary between necessary and unnecessary secrecy, it is helpful to start with two simple questions:

- *What do you need to know?*
- *What do you need to* not *know?*

What you need to *not* know—that is, what kinds of things should stay secret—is arguably the better starting point for the discussion because we can enumerate the specific categories based on the previous section. Table 2.1 lists those and other categories from the official FOIA exemptions, not all self-evidently legitimate (such as "bank reports" or "oil and gas well" information). As argued previously and as most would likely concede, secrecy decisions require case-by-case evaluation—recall the difference between Geraldo Rivera's sand diagram and the World War I troop movement documents. Given the amount of information the government produces and receives, careful case-by-case analysis is unquestionably a difficult task for information officers. For the present purpose, we can acknowledge the fact of legitimate secrets, thus recognizing that there are some secrets citizens need to *not* know.[9]

After acknowledging the fact of legitimate or "necessary" secrets—each independently evaluated in good faith, based on democratically validated rules and categories—the answer to "What do you need to know?" is clear: everything else that citizens believe to be relevant to their role in the democratic process. Because citizens have different perceptions of what they need to know, the second question could be rephrased as "What could you learn if you wanted to?"[10]

Using the two broad categories, we might visualize the boundary between

TABLE 2.1

Types of Secrets

Type	Description/Examples	FOIA Exemption
National security	Military plans, weapons systems, or operations; intelligence sources, methods, and activities; scientific, technological, or economic matters "in which release would harm national security"	1
Intelligence sources, methods, activities, and cryptology	Information about government espionage and surveillance activities	1
Internal agency memos, deliberations	Within and among agencies, including information "related solely to the internal personnel rules and practices of an agency"	2, 5
Other kinds of information explicitly exempted by other laws	(Hundreds of examples, see chapter 3)	3
Trade secrets	Trade secrets and commercial or financial information, obtained from a person, that is privileged or confidential	4
Personal privacy	Confidential identifying information that could be used maliciously (e.g., personnel and medical files)	6
Law enforcement operations	Records whose release would interfere with an investigation or create an unwarranted invasion of privacy	7
Bank reports	Federal government records of banks "contained in or related to examination, operating, or condition reports"	8
Oil and gas well data	Geological and geophysical information and data, including maps, concerning wells	9

necessary secrecy and unnecessary secrecy as the point between the two ovals in Figure 2.1. The oval on the right symbolizes all necessary secrets. The larger oval on the left represents the universe of information citizens should be able to easily access to hold politicians and governments accountable or otherwise make informed choices. The ovals are not drawn to scale, although the relative sizes reflect the assumption that citizens should have access to most political information flowing through a democracy. It is hard to imagine a functioning democracy where that would not be the case.

In an ideal system, the two ovals would meet at a single point, at which

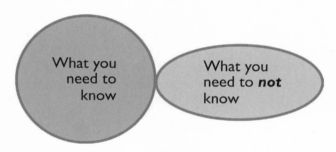

FIGURE 2.1
The Boundary between Necessary Secrecy and Unnecessary Secrecy

the secrecy system (the right oval) does not intrude into the open society, concealing legitimately free information. Alas, we don't live in an ideal world. Towering stacks of documents awaiting official markings pile high on bureaucrats' desks. FOIA officers and classification authorities make mistakes and face hard choices every day. (*Should I classify this potentially sensitive information, which might harm the country if released, or should I discount that risk?*) Even following clear administrative rules demanding a presumption of openness (see chapter 3), information officers have some discretion, and they sometimes make the wrong choice. The occasional error is to be expected, even accepted. Though we need not tolerate secrecy that serves individual or organizational interests at the expense of the public's right to know as a general rule, we must recognize that real errors and bad choices sometimes occur. Therefore, democratic citizens might reasonably yield a little bit, allowing a slightly less than ideal arrangement, as in Figure 2.2's depiction of an "acceptable world."

The problem comes when the secrecy regime intrudes deeply into the open society, sucking up a great deal of information that should have remained free. The intrusion results not from occasional errors but from a combination of maximal, institutionalized risk aversion and decisions made against the public interest for specific individuals or organizations (say, to avoid embarrassments and lawsuits or to maximize agency budgets). The universe of secrets in this case includes the legitimate secrets and the occasional errors, plus illegitimate secrets. Figure 2.2 depicts this world of excessive secrecy, what many of us would call reality.

That American democracy suffers from a systemic problem of excessive secrecy is not a new idea—not even close. Just ten years into the development

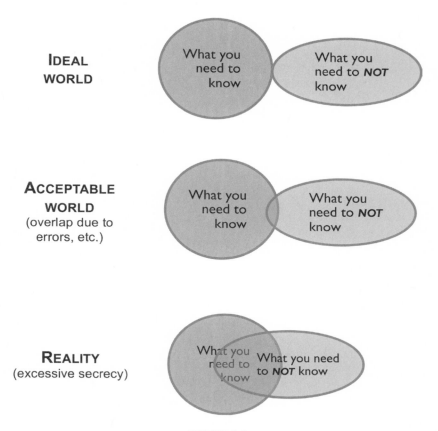

FIGURE 2.2
The Boundary between Necessary Secrecy and Unnecessary Secrecy in an Ideal
World, an Acceptable World, and Contemporary Reality

of the post–World War II national security state, former assistant secretary of defense Charles Coolidge and his internal DOD Committee on Classified Information concluded that overclassification had already "reached serious proportions." Congress's Commission on Government Security (the Wright Commission) warned in 1957 about "the danger to national security that arises out of overclassification." By 1970, the DOD Science Board Task Force on Secrecy (the Seitz Task Force) estimated "the amount of scientific and technical information which is classified could profitably be decreased perhaps as much as 90 percent." The DOD's 1985 Stilwell Commission said little had changed in fifteen years: "Too much information appears to be classified and much at higher levels than is warranted." Nixon's former solicitor general, Erwin N. Griswold, reported in 1989 that "it quickly becomes apparent to any person who has considerable experience with classified material that there is massive overclassification and that the principal concern of the classifiers is not with national security, but rather with governmental embarrassment of one sort or another." The Joint Security Commission surveyed the post–Cold War landscape in 1994 and reported to the DOD and CIA that "the classification system, largely unchanged since the Eisenhower administration, has grown out of control," leading to "unacceptable levels of inefficiency, inequity, and cost." Three years later, the Commission on Protecting and Reducing Government Secrecy (the Moynihan Commission) recommended ways to end still-rampant overclassification and, more generally, excessive secrecy. When he tried to estimate the size of the problem, President Reagan's National Security Council executive secretary, Rodney B. McDaniel, concluded that 90 percent of (classified) government secrets were not legitimately held.[11]

And that was all before 9/11! After the attacks, little changed. The 9/11 Commission chair, Thomas Kean, estimated that 75 percent of government secrets were unnecessary. ("Three-quarters of what I read that was classified shouldn't have been.") Carol A. Haave, former undersecretary for defense and intelligence, was more generous: only half were unnecessary. J. William Leonard, who ran the government's Information Security Oversight Office (ISOO) out of the National Archives and Records Administration for decades, agreed: "Over 50 percent of the information . . . , while it may meet the criteria for classification, really should not be classified." Even former defense secretary Donald Rumsfeld conceded, "It may very well be that a lot of information is classified that shouldn't be." The problem continued through the Obama-Biden administration. The president took the unusual step of publicly identifying "the problem of over classification" on several occasions. "We do overclassify," agreed Obama's director of national intelligence (DNI), James R. Clapper, Jr. In short, overclassification—just one type of excessive secrecy—continued across all post–World War II administrations, despite all the investigations and commissions and despite congressional action, such as the 2010 Reducing Over-Classification Act.[12]

This chorus of top-level officials, confirming and condemning excessive secrecy across a half century, said nothing that would surprise well-informed observers of American politics. And for each of the government insiders cited here, we could easily find hundreds of attentive outsiders making similar claims. We could also find apologists, some with self-interested motives for preferring the status quo. Richard Nixon's attack on Daniel Ellsberg in 1973 is one example. ("I think it is time in this country to quit making national heroes out of those who steal secrets and publish them in the newspapers.") Nixon, of course, was referring to Ellsberg's successful leak in 1971 of the Pentagon Papers (*United States–Vietnam Relations, 1945–1967: A Study Prepared by the Department of Defense*), a collection of historical analyses and narratives documenting the evolution of American involvement in the Vietnam War, revealing lies politicians like Nixon told along the way. Other apologists without clear self-interested motives appear from time to time, denying the fact and scope of excessive secrecy and defending the status quo despite the evidence. The DOD's Office of the Inspector General (OIG) in 1995, for example, declared the department's process "fundamentally sound" and concluded that "the present size of classified holdings is not the result of too much information being needlessly classified." Most of the time, however, people who feel the need to defend secrecy tend to make some version of the uncontroversial argument that legitimate secrets should be protected.[13]

Policy recommendations that would bring the system closer to our acceptable world come and go by the dozen, rarely finding enough traction in Congress or in the executive branch. Positive changes do sometimes occur, forced by social movements, willful leaders, or historical events. Thus, President Clinton's major post–Cold War declassification program and his attorney general's "maximum responsible disclosure" rule for FOIA requests (the "Reno Memo," in chapter 3) had materially important consequences that, for a time, brought us closer to the acceptable world's more open society. Yet for every reform, there has been at least equal and opposite backtracking, keeping the secrecy regime consistently huge. Moreover, Clinton's declassification program may have freed forests of documents, but most of those were older and of largely historical interest. They were not terribly useful for real-time democratic accountability. Plus, as agencies complied with Clinton's executive order, they still classified hundreds of thousands of documents every year, actually increasing the number steadily after the initial 1995 order.

The Consequences of Growing and Excessive Secrecy

An analysis of the ways in which excessive secrecy undermines democratic governance could easily fill a book on its own. Before briefly identifying some of those ways, it is worth noting other negative consequences.

CHAPTER 2

Economic and Social Costs

Keeping secrets—and paying people to work the secrecy regime—can get quite expensive. The annual cost to taxpayers from "salaries, safes, locks, security training, records management, computer programs, and the like" is itself a secret, but the ISOO in 2011 estimated classification programs alone cost about $11.36 billion. Keep in mind that number omits the CIA, the Defense Intelligence Agency (DIA), the Office of the Director of National Intelligence, the National Geospatial-Intelligence Agency, the national Reconnaissance Office, and the National Security Agency (NSA). Those are big exceptions. The number also omits money the government paid to private contractors, who increasingly handle classifications, FOIA requests, and other information policy work. The ISOO does periodically provide private sector secrecy costs (for example, $1.25 billion in 2011), but it uses only the dollar amounts some industries volunteer in an unspecified "sampling method." The estimation method clearly has reliability problems. Back in 1992, Rep. Lee H. Hamilton (D-IN), then a senior member of the House Intelligence Committee, reported that private contractors alone spent about "$14 billion per year to meet government requirements for the handling of classified material." Given the growth and privatization of the national security state after 9/11, it is hard to square Hamilton's $14 billion from 1992 with the ISOO's $1.25 billion from 2011. Other classification data problems abound (see chapter 3). Alas, the data presented in Figure 2.3 are the only data we have.[14]

Along with the substantial costs of keeping secrets, there are all the costs of creating secrets via surveillance and intelligence gathering. The publicly announced intelligence budget in 2009 was $75 billion, although that does not include an array of domestic and foreign counterterrorism and military programs. The real budget has always been a secret. Dana Priest and William Arkin did their best to survey the immensity of the national security state in *Top Secret America,* discovering, for just one clearance category alone, that "every day across the United States, 854,000 civil servants, military personnel and private contractors with top-secret security clearances are scanned into offices protected by electromagnetic locks, retinal cameras and fortified walls that eavesdropping equipment cannot penetrate." During Nixon's presidency, approximately 700,000 individuals in and out of government had top secret clearances, not much less than the 854,000 in 2009. Altogether, approximately *4.2 million* Americans in 2011—1.4 percent of the popu-

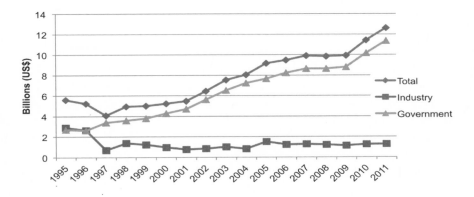

FIGURE 2.3
Estimated Secrecy Costs (incomplete), 1995–2011.
Source: ISOO Cost Report 2011; the totals do not include amounts spent in the
CIA, DIA, DNI, NSA, National Geospatial-Intelligence Agency, the national
Reconnaissance Office, and the National Security Agency, as well as funds
transferred to private contractors

lation—were cleared to access classified information, including top secret, secret, and confidential levels. Many others had clearances for protected, unclassified information (for instance, "for official use only" and "sensitive but unclassified").[15]

In addition to the monetary costs (under)estimated here, there are the immeasurable opportunity costs of misallocating all the dollars, skilled labor hours, and useful knowledge as a result of the excessive secrecy. Those resources could be put to more productive uses, including other public investments such as physical infrastructure or public education. Moreover, excessive secrecy impedes scientific progress by stifling free information flows. The downstream effects are enormous, since unnecessary secrecy removes information from scientific communities that could use it to improve health and prosperity, including inventing or refining welfare-improving technologies, stimulating economic activity, or otherwise expanding human knowledge. On top of the substantial indirect effects, there are direct ones. For example, the government frequently issues "secrecy orders" on patents, which has kept thousands of inventors from commercially developing their unique ideas. Sometimes, the government just assumes control over the inventions for intelligence or military purposes.[16]

Undermining National Security

Defenders of the American secrecy system often justify its enormity and excesses by citing national security needs. The risks and harms from excessive secrecy, they argue, pale in comparison to those that would result from disclosing information potentially useful to malicious enemies. We may not even know what information would be useful, they argue, and therefore, the government's heavy hand is warranted.

The latter point is an expression of the "mosaic theory," an increasingly common information policy framework, found in court opinions and executive branch rule making. The argument is, at first glance, compelling: because clever enemies can string together bits of "seemingly innocuous," seemingly unrelated information into more legible wholes (or mosaics), they can indirectly view state secrets. That outcome is probably even worse than more direct leaks of classified information to media organizations. Leaks might hurt, but governments at least know when they happen and which bits of information have spilled out. When secrets trickle out unnoticed, whether via enemies' mosaic methods or espionage, a country faces unique security vulnerabilities from the resulting information asymmetries. Mosaic theorists therefore defend overprotection of sensitive information, and they advocate secrecy even when transparency rules require openness. "Better safe than sorry," as the conservative advice goes. Any other considerations—civil liberties, a "right to know," and the like—become subordinate to risk aversion. Secrecy policies generally exist to minimize risks to national security, privacy, law enforcement operations, and so on. Mosaic theory focuses on the subset of risks that are difficult to conceptualize and measure.[17]

An information policy framework guided by extreme risk aversion, however, is not necessarily ideal for national security, notwithstanding the substantial costs to informed democratic decision making. For one, it assumes that protecting potentially sensitive information is always worth the costs: every time we keep a secret, we become safer. Whenever governments are more secretive, enemies do have a more difficult time pinpointing vulnerabilities or running counterintelligence programs. But the problem is that excessive secrecy (motivated by mosaic theory or other ideas) produces its own risks to national security.[18]

By concentrating information and decision-making power atop hierarchies in centralized political orders, societies assume the large risks of what Josiah Ober calls the "cloistered expert approach" (CEA) to policy making: "Gather the experts. Close the door. Design a policy. Roll it out. Reject criticism." Supporters of a CEA, including well-intentioned apologists for excessive secrecy, assume smart insiders with strong analytic skills can make the optimal decisions. (*Who needs outsiders or the "wisdom of crowds"?*) Those with pointier heads might reference Marquis de Condorcet's jury theorem, which does not require experts but works just as well with them. Condorcet argued that even a small group of individuals—say, a jury or Ober's cloistered experts—can, on average, make good choices (that is, at least half of the time). With a larger number of individuals, the probability of getting it right increases, ultimately reaching 100 percent as the group's population swells. CEA defenders, citing Condorcet, could reasonably argue that a large enough group of experts could perform well enough. But there are several strong criticisms of the CEA.[19]

First, Condorcet's theorem itself has important limitations, including its assumptions that there are only two decision options and that decision making is completely individualized and independent (in other words, that there are no social influences). Second, when a society leans too heavily on cloistered experts, it cannot fully utilize the outside world's diverse ideas, and it thus fails to access knowledge, skills, and modes of thinking not available to the cloistered set. Though experts can read outsiders' books and policy papers and reflect on past conversations, they have limited knowledge bases, including a bounded familiarity with the important ideas and texts on an issue. They might fail to identify and evaluate the likely risks and benefits of alternative options. They might miss important ideas, criticisms, and theoretical frameworks. They forfeit the power of what James C. Scott calls *metis,* or "local knowledge." Members of the group might simply lack the creativity needed for the task, or their insulation might limit their creative potential, given the restricted ideas and analytic tools on hand. Outsiders might also identify faulty assumptions and other oversights. The problem is especially pronounced when the cloistered experts are a homogenous bunch. With these ideas (and more), Scott Page updated Condorcet's theorem with his own, which demonstrates that "diversity trumps ability" in most collective decision-making environments.[20]

The size and diversity of cloistered sets typically shrink with the perceived sensitivity of an issue. As David Halberstam famously documented in *The Best and the Brightest,* so many of the errors Presidents John Kennedy and Lyndon Johnson and their supposedly brilliant advisers made in the early years of the Vietnam War came from their limited perspectives and their immunity from outside criticism. Halberstam was struck by the tragic irony:

"What was it about the men, their attitudes, the country, its institutions and above all the era which had allowed this tragedy to take place?" The answer, he argued, was that "they had, for all their brilliance and hubris and sense of themselves, been unwilling to look and learn from the past," discounting the little they knew of Indochinese history and resorting to misleading analogies, including domino theory and the Munich Agreement with the Nazis. As the Vietnam War grew increasingly unwieldy and unwinnable, the isolation at the top also grew. James C. Thomson, Jr., an East Asian expert who advised the Kennedy and Johnson administrations until he resigned in protest in 1966, recounted the self-defeating "closed politics" of Vietnam policy making in an influential 1968 essay:

> A recurrent and increasingly important factor in the decisionmaking process was the banishment of real expertise. Here the underlying cause was the "closed politics" of policy-making as issues become hot: the more sensitive the issue, and the higher it rises in the bureaucracy, the more completely the experts are excluded while the harassed senior generalists take over (that is, the Secretaries, Undersecretaries, and Presidential Assistants). The frantic skimming of briefing papers in the back seats of limousines is no substitute for the presence of specialists; furthermore, in times of crisis such papers are deemed "too sensitive" even for review by the specialists. Another underlying cause of this banishment, as Vietnam became more critical, was the replacement of the experts, who were generally and increasingly pessimistic, by men described as "can-do guys," loyal and energetic fixers unsoured by expertise. In early 1965, when I confided my growing policy doubts to an older colleague on the NSC staff, he assured me that the smartest thing both of us could do was to "steer clear of the whole Vietnam mess"; the gentleman in question had the misfortune to be a "can-do guy," however, and is now highly placed in Vietnam, under orders to solve the mess.

Many of the decision-making failures within the Bush-Cheney administration on Iraq policy were also caused by Thomson's "closed politics," as historians of the period have exhaustively demonstrated.[21]

Defenders of a CEA to US government decision making might counter those arguments by noting an obvious workaround: invite outsiders whenever necessary, giving them the requisite security clearances. Agencies might even incentivize insiders to be honest about their limitations and homogeneity, pushing them to draw from Page's "power of diversity." Indeed, if you go to planning meetings at, for example, the Defense or State Department, you are likely to stumble upon "consultants"—academics or other nongovernment experts invited to provide outside information or offer policy criticisms. There are at least two problems with this workaround. First, it assumes governments can identify the right outsiders, given the insiders' limitations. They might choose correctly, but that is by no means assured. How likely is it that a group at, say, the Defense Department would invite like-minded, "inside the Beltway" defense intellectuals to consult on a project? Second, the "consult when necessary" workaround assumes insiders would know *when* to draw from the power of diversity. If it is up to them, how often will they get it right? The cloistered set also might not be able to resolve other common problems in small-group dynamics, such as groupthink or succumbing to the charms or strong will of a dominant personality.[22]

The *general* problem, as Ober, Elizabeth Anderson, Friedrich Hayek, and others have noted in more comprehensive theoretical treatments, comes from relying on a centralized order, which concentrates critical information and decision-making power at the top of a hierarchy. Decentralized orders are messier and less controllable, but there are clear knowledge benefits in relying on the collective brainpower and local experiences of what insiders might simply see as the seething rabble outside the door. Just as centralized economic planning lacked the requisite knowledge to manage Communist political economies, centralized national security policy making comes with an important, possibly self-destructive set of information problems.[23]

Though governments have an obligation to protect some secrets, as argued earlier, overprotecting secrets has significant costs. It was a significant cause of the US government's failure to predict the collapse of the Soviet Union, as Sen. Daniel Patrick Moynihan and his "secrecy commission" concluded several years after the collapse:

> Too much of the information was secret, not sufficiently open to critique by persons outside the [US] government. Within the confines of the intelligence community, too great attention was paid to hoarding information, defending boundaries, securing budgets, and other matters of corporate survival. Too little attention was paid to ethnic issues, both domestic and foreign. The Soviet Union, after all, broke up along ethnic lines. And *much* too little attention was paid to the decline of Marxist-Leninist belief, both here and abroad. The Red Scare was far

less fearsome than many would have had us believe. . . . As the secrecy system took hold, it prevented American government from accurately assessing the enemy.

Excessive secrecy and the associated information problems were also major contributing factors in the government's failure to thwart the 9/11 attacks, as the 9/11 Commission, the Senate Intelligence Committee, and other official groups concluded—along with all of the smart, unofficial outsiders.[24]

After 9/11, the problems continued. Information flows across government agencies improved with post-9/11 reforms, but, as anyone would guess, bureaucratic information hoarding persisted. And few would laud the Bush-Cheney administration for increasing transparency; quite the contrary, as this book makes clear. Jack L. Goldsmith, who helped lead the DOJ's Office of Legal Counsel during 2003–2004, argued in 2007 that "there's no doubt . . . the extreme secrecy . . . not getting feedback from experts, and not showing it to experts, and not getting a variety of views, even inside the executive branch, led to a lot of mistakes" in the government's counterterrorism campaign. The costs of excessive secrecy in the post-9/11 period were "measured in lives as well as dollars," as former congressman Christopher Shays (R-CT) said in early 2005: "Somewhere in the vast cache of data that never should have been classified, and may never be declassified, is that tiny nugget of information that if shared, it could be used to detect and prevent the next deadly terrorist attack."[25]

There is a real attractiveness to the CEA. Cloistered experts have a better chance of blocking out several undesirable influences: fickle, myopic public opinion; the frequently trivial, inane, and similarly myopic news media; pundits' fake expertise and proven inability to predict outcomes "better than dart-throwing chimps"; and the self-interested demands from special interests, often at odds with wider public interests. However, the CEA fails to utilize a society's widely dispersed knowledge, which is arguably a greater problem.[26]

Finally, increasing the size of the cloistered set and the secrets these experts sit on might generate a new group of problems. A government with too many secrets—in which the necessary ones drown in piles of the unnecessary ones—will have a difficult time protecting the truly sensitive secrets from unauthorized disclosure. And as the number of insiders with security clearances has grown in recent decades, the risks of unauthorized leaks or espionage have concurrently increased. The surge of insiders pales in comparison to the exponential growth of information captured and stored by ever-improving surveillance technologies. The enormity of the problem can be illustrated by DOD's planned "global information grid." The DOD is working to build, in the medium term, a system that can hold and process a *yottabyte* (a septillion [10^{24}] bytes) of data, which roughly translates to "500 quintillion (500,000,000,000,000,000,000) pages of text." Eric Schmidt, Google's former chief executive officer (CEO), once guessed that all the world's human knowledge, from the first hunter-gatherers until the year 2003, equaled five *exabytes*. If the DOD's plan succeeds, that department alone will soon have the capacity to hold and process a million exabytes (Internet traffic is now producing about 970 exabytes a year). Some of that information will be publicly available, since many of those bytes will be drawn from the public Internet. But much of it will not, as it will be produced by government satellites, cameras, microscopes, telescopes, biometric systems, and so forth. Despite the growing number of insiders, analysts and decision makers will have a mighty difficult time going through those quintillions of pages. Their computers will fare better, but millions of diverse brains, dispersed across society, might arguably find patterns and needles in haystacks—threats to the nation—that even the best government employees and machines cannot.[27]

Corroding Democracy

At least as important as excessive secrecy's negative effects on national security are the ways it corrodes democracy. The founding fathers, who disagreed about so many things, almost to a man believed free information flows were central to the democratic process. James Madison argued in the Virginia Resolution of 1798 (against the Alien and Sedition Acts) that government transparency, along with First Amendment freedoms, was a *core* right, underlying all others. The "right of freely examining public characters and measures, and of free communication among the people thereon," he asserted, were "justly deemed the only effectual guardian[s] of every other right." Thomas Paine, six years earlier, insisted democracy required free information flows and citizen political awareness: "A nation under a well regulated government should permit none to remain uninstructed. It is monarchical and aristocratical government only that requires ignorance for its support." Railing against the Stamp Act back in 1765, John Adams struck a similar chord: "Liberty cannot be preserved without a general knowledge among the people, who have a right, from the frame of their nature, to knowledge. . . . They have a right, an indisputable, unalienable, indefeasible, divine right to that most dreaded and envied kind of knowledge, I mean, of the characters and conduct of their rulers." Radical, '60's era Adams continued: "The preservation of the means of knowledge among the lowest ranks is of more importance to the public than all the property of all the rich men in the country." And therefore, he urged, "let every sluice of knowledge be opened and set a-flowing."[28]

Words are cheap. Some two hundred years later, Republicans in Congress similarly lambasted secrecy as "the first refuge of incompetents," arguing that it had to be kept "at a bare minimum in a democratic society, for a fully informed public is the basis of self-government." "The power to withhold the facts of government," they proclaimed, "is the power to destroy that government." Meanwhile, the Republicans supported their party leader, President Dwight D. Eisenhower, as he expanded the national security state into a behemoth, most of it hidden behind opaque walls. It surveilled "subversives" at home (through the FBI's COINTELPRO program and other means), experimented on unsuspecting citizens with radiation and LSD (as in Project MKUltra), and overthrew democratically elected foreign governments abroad (including Iran and Guatemala)—all in the public's name but without public knowledge. The Democrats, of course, continued many of the same practices under Kennedy and Johnson. Nixon did the same, although the peculiar ways he wielded the executive's secrecy powers, with the distinctly Nixonian mix of arrogance, political paranoia, and clumsiness, contributed to his downfall and helped create the political space for the flood of new transparency laws in the 1970s.[29]

The main reason why excessive secrecy is so corrosive to democracy is that it very likely deprives citizens of the ability to make informed choices, as Madison et al. argued. The consequences are well known. Under- and misinformed citizens cannot effectively enforce democratic accountability. They might not punish representatives who deserve it. They might not push for change when change is needed. Their influence on critical policy choices is restricted. Excessive secrecy also affects citizen preferences. For example, Americans who learn about coups their government supported against democratically elected foreign governments tend to revise some of their preferences and predispositions about US foreign policy.

The problems remain even if we accept the premise that voters can make reasonable choices despite lacking a great deal of political knowledge. Political and cognitive scientists have demonstrated repeatedly that citizens can often effectively overcome their information deficits by taking "information shortcuts"—cues from better-informed and trusted elites or social network members. Imagine that Alice and Bob were traveling to their respective polling places on Election Day 2012. They shared a similar civil libertarian political philosophy, but only Alice devoted much time to following current events. Bob, acknowledging his ignorance, skimmed the headline and abstract of the annual "report card" put out by the American Civil Liberties Union (ACLU) on his smart phone as he approached the high school gym filled with voting machines. Alice checked the ACLU's site too, but she also had read it nearly every day for four years. As they voted, both had the same general judgment of the Obama-Biden administration's civil libertarian record. Thus, similar individuals can make similar political choices in line with their similar preferences, even if they are not equally informed.[30]

However, with excessive secrecy, even cue-*givers* are deprived of electorally relevant information, disrupting the entire chain connecting cue-givers and cue-takers. When legitimately free information is withheld, even exceptionally attentive citizens like Alice and the staff at the ACLU cannot evaluate and share. And people like Bob become even more informationally disadvantaged. Secrecy is not the only factor involved in public ignorance, but it is elemental. Even if citizens all of a sudden reached levels of awareness only dreamed about by democratic theorists, they still would fail to realize the ideal of an informed citizenry—or anything close to it—if their government routinely and illegitimately concealed truths.

In addition to preventing citizens from making informed choices, excessive secrecy corrodes democracy in three key ways. First, it undermines interbranch relations, the checks and balances so vital to the US presidential system. Legislators cannot effectively perform their oversight functions, including detecting and disseminating information on administrative incompetence and abuses of power, if they are kept in the dark. Litigants, lawyers, and judges similarly starved of relevant but illegitimately concealed information cannot gather evidence and make effective judgments about executive branch actions.[31]

Second, excessive secrecy affects citizens' trust in government. If citizens believe they are unnecessarily deprived of real-time, electorally relevant information, they will likely have less confidence in their capacity to make informed choices. Once those experiences begin to accumulate across lifetimes, many of those citizens begin to question the legitimacy of the regime. *What kind of democracy based on popular sovereignty keeps its citizens in the dark to such an extent?* Distrust left to fester breeds cynicism and fear, prompting

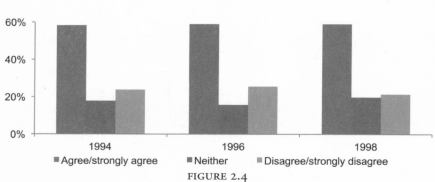

FIGURE 2.4
"Does the Government Classify Too Many Documents as Secrets?"
Source: General Social Survey

more apathy and abstention from the public sphere than would naturally occur. A democratic regime can survive for a while under those conditions, but
few would argue it would be a high-quality democracy or even a functioning
one.[32]

That many Americans believe their government is secretive is backed by
public opinion evidence. Large majorities, for instance, believe the government is "somewhat or very secretive" (70 percent in 2010, 73 percent in
2009). When asked point-blank whether there is *too much* secrecy, a smaller
but still substantial majority says *yes*. In three surveys in the 1990s, 58.3
percent (1994), 58.9 percent (1996), and 58.9 percent (1998) either agreed
or strongly agreed that the government classified "too many documents as
secrets" (see Figure 2.4). About ten years later (after 9/11), participants in another national sample of Americans were asked whether there was "too much
secrecy" at the federal level. An almost identical number—59 percent—
thought there was. Though we should hesitate to generalize too broadly from
these numbers, given the limited number of surveys available and the public's
tendency to express potentially contradictory beliefs on surveys (for example,
majorities also said they thought the government "definitely should" maintain
a high level of secrecy surrounding military operations and counterterrorism
policies), the public opinion evidence is clear and consistent: democratic citizens believed there was "too much secrecy."[33]

Third, excessive secrecy's corrosive effects also work on political elites, the
people entrusted to work as public servants. A late 1968 (pre–Pentagon Papers) conversation between Daniel Ellsberg and Henry Kissinger captures
what happens at the top end of the information divide. Ellsberg, who worked

in the Defense Department, shared his experiences with insider access as Kissinger and the rest of the incoming Nixon administration prepared to take office:

"Henry, there's something I would like to tell you, for what it's worth, something I wish I had been told years ago. You've been a consultant for a long time, and you've dealt a great deal with top secret information. But you're about to receive a whole slew of special clearances, maybe fifteen or twenty of them, that are higher than top secret.

"I've had a number of these myself, and I've known other people who have just acquired them, and I have a pretty good sense of what the effects of receiving these clearances are on a person who didn't previously know they even *existed*. And the effects of reading the information that they will make available to you.

"First, you'll be exhilarated by some of this new information, and by having it all—so much! incredible!—suddenly available to you. But second, almost as fast, you will feel like a fool for having studied, written, talked about these subjects, criticized and analyzed decisions made by presidents for years without having known of the existence of all this information, which presidents and others had and you didn't, and which must have influenced their decisions in ways you couldn't even guess. In particular, you'll feel foolish for having literally rubbed shoulders for over a decade with some officials and consultants who did have access to all this information you didn't know about and didn't know they had, and you'll be stunned that they kept that secret from you so well.

"You will feel like a fool, and that will last for about two weeks. Then, after you've started reading all this daily intelligence input and become used to using what amounts to whole libraries of hidden information, which is much more closely held than mere top secret data, you will forget there ever was a time when you didn't have it, and you'll be aware only of the fact that you have it now and most others don't . . . and that all those *other* people are fools.

"Over a longer period of time—not too long, but a matter of two or three years—you'll eventually become aware of the limitations of this information. There is a great deal that it doesn't tell you, it's often inaccurate, and it can lead you astray just as much as the *New York Times* can. But that takes a while to learn. In the meantime it will have become very hard for you to *learn* from anybody who doesn't have these clearances. Because you'll be thinking as you listen to them: 'What would this man be telling me if he knew what I know? Would he be giving me the same advice, or would it totally change his predictions and recommendations?' And *that* mental exercise is so torturous that after a while you give it up and just stop listening. I've seen this with my superiors, my colleagues . . . and with myself.

"You will deal with a person who doesn't have those clearances only from the point of view of what you want him to believe and what impression you want him to go away with, since you'll have to lie carefully to him about what you know. In effect, you will have to manipulate him. You'll give up trying to assess what he has to say. The danger is, you'll become something like a moron. You'll become incapable of learning from most people in the world, no matter how much experience they may have in their particular areas that may be much greater than yours."

Ellsberg's advice reiterates some of the problems identified earlier, such as the danger of insiders rejecting outsiders' ideas. But his conversation with Kissinger also shows how the gigantic secrecy regime can distort the relationship between citizen and state and why insiders might be reluctant to listen and be responsive to citizens. Information elites simply live in a different world, where common truths are laughable and ostensibly sophisticated outside analyses are devoid of value because they are based on half-truths at best. The starkness of the information inequality makes even well-informed outsiders seem like fools, with insiders part of a relatively small club.[34]

Explaining Excessive Secrecy

The undesirable "reality" depicted in Figure 2.2 is not inevitable. Multiple forces push democracies toward excessive secrecy. Some are more or less constant. Others fluctuate with different agents and shifting structures across space and time. We could probably take for granted, for instance, that government bureaucracies will always place expansionary pressure on the right oval in Figure 2.2. Bureaucracies might strive to get ahead of other agencies in the budgetary pecking order. Or they might simply try to maintain last year's budget allocation. Either way, keeping secrets deprives other agencies—and, by implication, citizens and other government branches—of valuable information. Why should we value and continue to fund the Super-Secret

Intelligence Agency if another one across town, the Super-Special Intelligence Agency, has the same information? Legislatures often fund both, of course, and we can point to lots of bureaucratic redundancy in reality (not all of it bad). However, fears of the budget ax are rampant, and the bureaucratic impulse to hoard information is well documented.[35]

Max Weber identified a related impulse—the bureaucracy's "sure power instinct"—in his *Wirtschaft und Gesellschaft* (Economy and Society):

> Every bureaucracy seeks to increase the superiority of the professionally informed by keeping their knowledge and intentions secret. Bureaucratic administration always tends to be an administration of "secret sessions" in so far as it can, it hides its knowledge and action from criticism. . . . The pure interest of the bureaucracy in power, however, is efficacious far beyond those areas where purely functional interests make for secrecy. The concept of the "official secret" is the specific invention of bureaucracy, and nothing is so fanatically defended by the bureaucracy as this attitude, which cannot be substantially justified beyond these specifically qualified areas. In facing a parliament, the bureaucracy, out of a sure power instinct, fights every attempt of the parliament to gain knowledge by means of its own experts or from interest groups. The so-called right of parliamentary investigation is one of the means by which parliament seeks such knowledge. Bureaucracy naturally welcomes a poorly informed and hence a powerless parliament at least in so far as ignorance somehow agrees with the bureaucracy's interests.

We might quibble with specific points, such as Weber's use of *always* to describe bureaucratic behavior (are there no exceptions?) and his claim that the "official secret" was "the specific invention of bureaucracy" (since kings, queens, and other authoritarians had earlier kept lots of official business from their subjects). However, those flaws do not diminish his main point: government bureaucracies have incentives to be excessively secretive, "far beyond those areas where purely functional interests make for secrecy." Individual bureaucrats have reputational concerns and other self-interested motives (such as career-oriented ones) that might come into play. Rocking the boat thus does not pay. Moreover, Weber's "power instinct," the bureaucracy's self-interested push to increase relative or absolute power and size within the government, is a driving force. Whistle-blower Sibel Edmonds's experience at the FBI is just one example, though it is a particularly shocking one. After

Edmonds volunteered after 9/11 to help the FBI translate documents from Turkish and Farsi, she encountered supervisors who allegedly told her to let the work "pile up" because her division could then ask for "more translators and expand the department" (see chapter 6). A related impulse is the abuse of secrecy powers to protect individuals and organizations from embarrassment, as former solicitor general Erwin N. Griswold noted in the quote introduced previously—"It quickly becomes apparent to any person who has considerable experience with classified material that there is massive overclassification and that the principal concern of the classifiers is not with national security, but rather with governmental embarrassment of one sort or another." There are hundreds of examples, such as the CIA's legendary failed prediction in 1950 that the "Chinese Communist intervention in Korea . . . is not probable in 1950." Two weeks later, 300,000 Chinese soldiers entered Korea.[36]

Self-interest, however, takes us only part of the way there. Obama's director of national intelligence, James R. Clapper, was probably partly right when he said overclassification is "more due to just the default" position in federal agencies. "It's the easy thing to do," he argued, not "some nefarious motivation to, you know, hide or protect things for political reasons. That does happen too, but I think it's more of a—more of an administrative default or automaticity to it." The bureaucrat's default position on classification and other secrecy matters is driven by many of the same factors that shape administrative behavior in general. Rules and norms, for instance, sometimes push bureaucrats toward risk aversion, depending on the agency and administration. To cite one example, compare Attorney General Janet Reno's "maximum responsible disclosure" rule for FOIA requests with the rule used by her successor, John Ashcroft, which essentially called for minimal possible disclosure (see chapter 3). Even with rules like Reno's, many bureaucrats have discretionary powers, especially when administrative rules in general are poorly enforced. Thus, the Stilwell Commission in 1985 found bureaucrats routinely overclassified despite the existing rules designed to stop them from doing so. The problem was "primarily a matter of inadequate implementation of existing policy, rather than a matter of deficient policy." Some bureaucrats keep secrets to hide embarrassments or promote their agencies or careers, but others do so for more noble reasons. Bureaucrats, like everyone else, face uncertainties about the consequences of their actions, which leads them toward risk aversion more often than not. (*If I don't classify this information, it is possible enemies might use it against the nation. Better safe than sorry.*)[37]

Overall, many of the causes of excessive secrecy—including the power instinct, the compulsion to hide embarrassments, or other factors—are inherent to bureaucracy and cannot be expunged no matter what new administrative rule is implemented. New rules, like Reno's, might cause some positive behavioral changes, but fairly constant incentives and cognitive biases as well as lax enforcement limit their impact. Other causes of excessive secrecy examined throughout the book, such as business power over government officials, are not necessarily inherent to bureaucracy—bureaucratic autonomy can and sometimes does happen—but are widespread enough across the American system to appear as permanent as the power instinct. Still, history shows significant changes in the scale and scope of the secrecy system, almost always moving the nation further away from our "acceptable reality." In other words, the relative sizes of the ovals in Figure 2.2 are not fixed. For this reason, we cannot say Weber was right and walk away.[38]

Explaining Change in the Secrecy Regime

What changes the nature, scale, and scope of the secrecy regime? As Steven Aftergood notes, there are a multitude of forces:

> The secrecy system does not exist in some kind of abstract isolation. It is an ordinary bureaucratic artifact that is subject to pressure on many levels—political, legal, sociological, international, and others. It is constantly undergoing changes due to press reporting and leaks (unauthorized disclosures), budget appropriations and congressional oversight, [FOIA] requests and lawsuits, and foreign government disclosures, errors, whistleblowers, financial pressures, and—not least important—an ideological or tactical preference for disclosure—or the opposite—on the part of senior officials.

All of Aftergood's pressures are important, although the list is heavily weighted toward forces exogenous to sitting administrations. Leaks and lawsuits matter, as do wars, terrorist attacks, and FOIA requests (and more). Senior officials' "ideological and tactical preferences" also matter, as the book makes clear, but there are also other endogenous forces shaping the secrecy regime that rarely attract scholarly attention. This section outlines a theoretical framework that identifies and connects exogenous and endogenous forces of change. In the process, it brings what is largely an atheoretical enterprise in political science into contact with prominent theoretical traditions. Because ideology is as important as Aftergood argues, we can begin there.[39]

Governing Ideologies

Every sunshine-era president has faced a similar core legal framework, spelled out in the sunshine laws (for example, FOIA or FACA), along with any relevant statutes, judicial decisions, and administrative orders. Each president, however, has navigated the resulting set of opportunities and constraints with a distinctive governing ideology, a belief system about how best to rule and what governments should do. Some ideologies, most famously the one dominant during the Bush-Cheney years, have contributed to presidential efforts to tweak the policy framework. When institutional or other political constraints (such as voters' attitudes) forbade formal rule changes, administrations instead used a variety of tactics to defy or otherwise circumvent the offending rules. This section examines governing ideologies hostile to transparency, and the next section examines the methods administrations have deployed to tweak the system.[40]

Presidents seldom outline anything like a clearly articulated philosophy of government secrecy. Instead, they mostly recycle high-minded protransparency platitudes into their speeches and executive orders. Judging from their rhetoric, presidents have uniformly celebrated America's traditions and laws upholding transparency and open government, while offering almost identical caveats about the need to occasionally keep secrets for national security or other legitimate reasons. For example, Bush-Cheney kept a passage from Clinton-Gore's executive order on classification verbatim: "Our democratic principles require that the American people be informed of the activities of their Government. Also, our Nation's progress depends on the free flow of information. Nevertheless, throughout our history, the national defense has required that certain information be maintained in confidence in order to protect our citizens, our democratic institutions . . . " Clinton-Gore concluded this last sentence with "and our participation within the community of nations." Bush-Cheney, by contrast, chose to conclude with "[,]our homeland security, and our interactions with foreign nations." (Perhaps *community of nations* sounded too "kumbaya" for the more hawkish, blustery administration.) Both also pledged that "protecting information critical to our Nation's security remains a priority," but Bush-Cheney wanted nothing to do with Clinton-Gore's "in recent years, however, dramatic changes have altered, although not eliminated, the national security threats that we confront. These changes provide a greater opportunity to emphasize our commitment to open Government." Reagan-Bush (and Bush-Quayle) preferred a much simpler statement: "It is essential that the public be informed concerning the activities of its Government, but that the interests of the United States and its citizens require that certain information concerning the national defense and foreign relations be protected against unauthorized disclosure."[41]

Most administrations have barely ventured beyond the occasional platitude about transparency, and exactly none have scrupulously adhered to the legal framework underpinning open government. The Bush-Cheney administration was exceptional and in some ways politically courageous in articulating a strong public defense of secrecy on principled grounds, at least when its flouting of rules and traditions was detected and remotely excusable. The prosecrecy ideology described by senior officials was part of a broader belief system about presidential authority and the constitutional separation of powers.

As has been well documented, Vice President Cheney entered office believing in a strong version of the "unitary executive theory," an interpretation of the separation-of-powers doctrine that most constitutional scholars find extreme. The subject is covered extensively elsewhere; therefore, only a brief summary is needed here. First, the strong version of the unitary executive theory (sUET) argues the Constitution's separation-of-powers framework implies a system where each branch controls unique, nonoverlapping spheres of influence. Article II gave "the executive power" only to the president, adherents argue, which essentially means Congress and the courts should back off and let presidents govern as they see fit, especially in the foreign policy arena, ruled by the "commander in chief." Administrations might share information with Congress and the public, but they should only do so on a voluntary basis.

Second, since the president alone heads the executive branch, he (or presumably she in the future) has ultimate authority over every executive branch decision, no matter how mundane. One implication is that presidents should have direct hiring and firing authority over every executive branch employee, including protected career bureaucrats. The positive result, sUET adherents argue, is that all government employees will have incentives to support and follow the elected president's preferences, from soup to nuts. After all, the argument goes, why should unelected bureaucrats subvert the elected president's will? To best achieve a more compliant bureaucracy, presidents should staff governments with like-minded agents or at least those willing to surrender any bureaucratic discretion. Overall, the sUET takes the concepts of separation of powers and organizational hierarchy to logical extremes and minimizes the checks and balances that tend to round out most interpretations of the separation-of-powers system.[42]

Cheney's vision of the unitary executive was multidimensional, but secrecy was a key part, according to his harshest critics and closest allies. I. Lewis "Scooter" Libby, the vice president's close friend and first chief of staff, spoke frankly about Cheney's view of secrecy: "He firmly believes—believes to the point where, when he talks about it, his eyes get a little bluer—that for the presidency to operate properly, it needs to be able to have confidential communications." In addition to particular readings of the Constitution, Cheney and fellow travelers called upon *The Federalist Papers* to support their vision. For example, Alexander Hamilton argued in Federalist #70 that "energy in the executive is a leading character in the definition of good government. . . . It is essential to the protection of the community against foreign attacks." The task, according to Hamilton, was best done with uninhibited executive "decision[making], activity, secrecy, and dispatch." It probably did not bother Cheney or his followers that Hamilton spoke about a constrained executive elsewhere in #70, as well as in #69. For a world leader, a selective reading of something like *The Federalist Papers* usually does the trick—supporting sincerely held ideological beliefs without all the fuss academics make about logical or historical consistency.[43]

Textual interpretations aside, Cheney's push for greater executive secrecy had many practical benefits, a fact that also contributed to the White House's broad governing ideology. First and foremost, Cheney and others often emphasized the need for presidents to receive frank advice from anyone they called upon. The sunshine-era system allowed too much monitoring by Congress and the public, which decreased the likelihood presidential advisers would feel comfortable telling hard truths and voicing unpopular opinions. Too many constraints, including too much monitoring, Cheney wrote in 1989, would keep officials from taking risks, which in turn would keep a president from having the "flexibility or the power to do the job we expect him to do for us." Greater secrecy on internal deliberations also tamps down interest group pressures, especially when groups opposed to the president's policies could more effectively use their resources if they knew the White House's legislative strategies. The practical utility of Cheney's approach was clear to all involved. An anonymous "prominent Republican" close to the White House confided to a journalist in early 2002 that "President Bush and

Dick Cheney are really big on secrecy," partly because it made twisting legislators' arms easier. In addition, as Barton Gellman put it, Cheney knew well that it was "easier to win a battle when opponents did not show up," and one way to make that happen was to hide the fact of the battle from opponents.[44]

It is worth briefly noting the origins and evolution of the vice president's ideology, since this development perfectly overlaps with the time period investigated in this book. Cheney's entry into presidential politics came during the Nixon administration, when he worked as an assistant to Donald Rumsfeld. He impressed enough people over the next several years to wind up as President Gerald Ford's chief of staff while only thirty-four years old. His ascent within the executive branch coincided with growing citizen anger about the many failures of the "imperial presidency." The Watergate scandal and the stalemate in Vietnam were early 1970s tipping points, but previous events, such as President Johnson's war escalations, were also crucial. The emergent bipartisan movement of citizens and representatives demanded major reforms they believed would restore the proper constitutional balance of powers, including the sunshine laws and the War Powers Resolution. Cheney and Rumsfeld, sitting at the center of presidential power in the 1970s, railed against the reforms: they were unconstitutional, they would degrade the presidency, and they would harm national security. Although the changes may have clashed with Cheney's extant right-leaning ideology, much of his opposition sprouted from his position at the heights of presidential power. Graham Allison has described the political condition well: "Where you stand depends on where you sit."[45]

The ideas, however, survived Cheney's departure from the White House in 1977, and they continued to influence him after he won Wyoming's seat in Congress in 1978. Despite working within the legislative branch, he remained a stalwart supporter of unhindered executive power. In 1985, he strongly opposed efforts by the Democratic majority in Congress to constrain the foreign policy–making powers of the Reagan-Bush administration (such as the Boland Amendment cutting off aid to the Contras in Nicaragua), describing his opposition in ideological terms: "I retain strong feelings of the importance of the executive branch, views that were shaped by my time at the White House. But I believe I'm in a minority up here [in Congress]. The President has to have broad leeway to operate. The Congress too often interferes in areas in which he has primacy." In 1986, as his (especially Democratic) colleagues criticized Reagan's secretive decision to bomb Libya, Cheney again waxed ideological:

I am satisfied that I know all I need to know at this point, and I would disagree with what we often hear from the Hill, the cry for consultation in advance, let us in on the decision, we want to share responsibility. It seems to me that this is a clear-cut case where the president as commander in chief . . . is justified in taking whatever action he deems appropriate and discussing the details with us after the fact.

In 1987, Cheney authored the Republican Party's minority report on the Iran-Contra hearings, in which he repeatedly emphasized the need to respect "inherent Presidential powers" and what he considered the wrongheaded "boundless view of Congressional power," especially on foreign policy. ("Congressional actions to limit the President in this area therefore should be reviewed with a considerable degree of skepticism. If they interfere with core presidential foreign policy functions, they should be struck down.") The Democratic majority was "hysterical" in claiming Reagan-Bush had abused powers in any significant way. Just go read Hamilton, Cheney said—he wrote so eloquently about "energy in the executive" and the associated secrecy. In 1989, Cheney again marshaled Hamilton's secrecy argument and wrote that "the presidency . . . was designed as a one-person office to ensure that it would be ready for action." Finally, as is well known, Cheney retained the same views as vice president. In 2005, for example, he observed:

Watergate and a lot of the things around Watergate and Vietnam during the 1970s, served, I think, to erode the authority I think the president needs to be effective, especially in the national security area. . . . Especially in the day and age we live in . . . the president of the United States needs to have his constitutional powers unimpaired, if you will, in terms of the conduct of national security policy.

And in 2006, he stated: "I clearly do believe, and have spoken directly about the importance of a strong presidency. I think there have been times in the past, oftentimes in response to events such as Watergate or the war in Vietnam, where Congress has begun to encroach upon the powers and responsibilities of the President; that it was important to go back and try to restore that balance."[46]

George W. Bush did not articulate a coherent governing ideology as a presidential candidate, speaking only of his intent to be a vaguely defined "compassionate conservative." There is also no evidence he then shared Cheney's plan to restore the pre-sunshine-era balance of power. By Inauguration Day, however, Bush seemed to have experienced a conversion no less influential than having been "born again" a decade earlier. Almost immediately after taking office, he told his head counsel, Alberto Gonzales, to make the expansion of presidential power a top priority for White House lawyers. Either Cheney had succeeded in persuading Bush during the campaign and interregnum or Bush had acquired the views independently, most likely during his father's presidency (although Cheney was there too, as defense secretary). In any case, both men were ready to go on day one, driven by a distinct governing ideology.

Despite their widely disputed, five-to-four Supreme Court–ordered victory in 2000, the men indicated they were "absolutely" certain they should move "full speed ahead" on their agenda to restore Nixon-era levels of presidential authority. They hired a team of fellow travelers in the White House and the DOJ who could be counted on to advance the cause, including Cheney's chief of staff, David Addington, and DOJ attorneys John Yoo, Patrick Philbin, and Jay Bybee. According to Lawrence Wilkerson, Secretary of State Colin Powell's chief of staff, the group walked the halls of government talking about "these incredible theories" and, like *Othello*'s Iago, "stand[ing] behind their principals, *whispering in their ears* about these theories, telling them they have these powers, that the Constitution backs these powers, that these powers are 'inherent' and blessed by God and if they are not exercised, the nation will fall." Administration officials generally kept quiet about the ideas during their first year in office, but by January 2002 they decided to go public. Cheney, in his typical calming manner, announced, to anyone who had not already caught on, that Bush was fully on board with his mission to restore the rightful powers of the presidency. From that moment on, the White House "sent signals to everyone around them that this is the way they judge people, whether they can keep secrets."[47]

Bush and Cheney's governing ideology, the sUET, directly affected the way they navigated and tried to change the system. It shaped the way they responded to public and interbranch conflicts over secrecy, including how they framed their positions after Bush "came out" in early 2002. It also influenced how they handled officials across the executive branch who sometimes had the gall to contest the legality of their actions. The impact was unmistakable, as this book repeatedly demonstrates.

Bush and Cheney's predecessors also challenged and circumvented the same set of laws but without a Cheney-esque belief system (if they shared it, they never expressed it). They proceeded for practical or base political reasons.

Ideology is thus a factor—an important factor—but it is not a necessary or sufficient cause of presidential actions regarding secrecy.

If Gore-Lieberman had taken power instead of Bush-Cheney in 2001, the Democratic administration officials also would have moved the country away from an "acceptable world" after 9/11, all else being equal. But they would not have done so under the banner of a governing ideology with secrecy at its core. As Alexander George and Andrew Bennett remind us, there are "many alternative causal paths to the same outcome." Still, ideology can be a crucial factor, as it was during the Bush-Cheney years.[48]

Another counterfactual example illustrates this point well. In the absence of 9/11, Gore-Lieberman probably would have followed a path charted by Clinton-Gore in the 1990s, one that included the occasional flouting of secrecy laws but also perhaps some substantial moves toward transparency. By contrast, a Bush-Cheney administration absent 9/11 would still have worked to expand the secrecy regime—or, as administration officials saw it, to restore rightful presidential powers—but their strategy and tactics would have been different and their task much more difficult, for reasons that are outlined in the next section.

Changing and Circumventing Laws in Settled versus Unsettled Times: The Case of the 9/11 Critical Juncture

American presidents face multiple constraints just by being executives in a presidential system. No matter how much Bush and Cheney disliked (for instance) FACA, they could not have eliminated the open meetings law unless they convinced Congress to repeal it or the Supreme Court to find it unconstitutional. Executive orders and other administrative rules can do only so much. Even with Republican majorities in both chambers, the administration would probably have still failed, given its party's concerns about electoral blowback, among other things. The extent to which a president, whether ideologically motivated or not, can alter the legal framework of the secrecy regime is therefore limited by the veto-point-studded institutional landscape surrounding the executive branch.[49]

That landscape, however, can change. Although the Constitution and established electoral rules keep the formal structure of the system intact—the United States has always had federalism, presidentialism, bicameralism, and first-past-the-post voting—several variables can alter the relative strength of the veto points, in addition to those mentioned previously (such as partisan control of Congress). Take the extent to which a country is living through a "settled" or "unsettled" period. Ira Katznelson's distinction emphasizes the vastly different sets of opportunities and constraints political actors face during unsettled times (such as those during rare "critical junctures" when big change is possible) compared with relatively settled, longer periods of "normal" politics. During settled times, power holders are constrained by the generally stable set of veto points and policy legacies that accrue and reinforce over the course of path-dependent development. For example, senior Bush-Cheney officials before 9/11 may have wanted to move full speed ahead in their efforts to restore powers enjoyed by pre-sunshine-era presidents, but they knew any efforts would come up against the usual set of institutional veto points working at full throttle. The political actors manning those defenses would likely not have given the administration much leeway if a proposed policy change was seen as too sharp a break from the status quo. Plus, veto holders had their own reform agendas, with their own interest coalitions behind them. Bush-Cheney officials thus knew they had to adjust their strategies and tactics accordingly.[50]

After the 9/11 attacks, the administration enjoyed—and helped shape—a new political environment. For one, the veto points were less obtrusive and easier to get around. The formal institutional structure was still there, but the gatekeepers were more accommodating. Politicians and ordinary citizens backed the administration's new national security agenda, which included fresh ideas about the proper balance between security and liberty and between secrecy and transparency (among them ideas about warrantless wiretapping). Others were cowed by a tough-talking, suddenly popular president, whose public support was no less influential despite resulting from predictable rally-around-the-flag dynamics. Exogenous events like 9/11 that spark national emergencies thus create windows of opportunity, giving policy makers more room to make changes within institutions because political opponents offer less resistance. The ways presidents and other political actors actively work within critical junctures to keep those windows open is addressed in the pages that follow.[51]

That the 9/11 attacks ushered in a critical juncture in American politics is probably uncontroversial, although there are surprisingly few analyses explicitly describing it that way. What remains unclear is the extent to which the attacks removed the political constraints that earlier stood in the way of Cheney's ambitions for the restoration of the imperial presidency. Although hyperbolic statements like "9/11 changed everything" can be swiftly dismissed—the country's two-party system and its formal political institutions remained standing, after all, and even satire eventually returned—the attacks clearly unsettled a relatively stable political environment, where institutional constraints and policy legacies limited what the administration could do. But those restrictions were not absolute, and they did not prevent the administration from challenging and circumventing the sunshine laws, using new and old tools. As this book demonstrates, all of the pre-9/11 administrations tried to wriggle out of the sunshine-era constraints that bound them, to varying degrees. Bush-Cheney officials were merely unique in bursting out of the January 2001 starting gate, already wriggling. The events of 9/11 changed the game by loosening their reins, allowing them to accomplish more than they otherwise would have.[52]

One surprising detail that emerges from the period's history, as shown in this book, is that Bush-Cheney officials, despite the critical juncture, did not qualitatively change their approach to institutional change. For example, they did not even try, at least not in any serious way, to radically alter any of the sunshine laws, even at the height of the 9/11 critical juncture. Instead, they generally used the same tools and tricks developed by their predecessors, albeit more frequently in some realms. Thus, they were not exactly the radical revolutionaries—the "insurrectionaries," in James Mahoney and Kathleen Thelen's framework—that some accused them of being and that Cheney and his followers probably wanted to be. Although 9/11 might have given them the opportunity, they did not work to displace the sunshine-era shackles they seemed to loathe, which would have entailed, according to Mahoney and Thelen, a "rapid, sudden breakdown of institutions and their replacement with new ones." Like their predecessors, Bush-Cheney officials worked to incrementally expand the secrecy regime through "layering" and "conversion" strategies: adding "new rules . . . to existing ones" through "amendments, revisions, or additions to existing ones" and interpreting and administering existing rules in new ways, "by actors who actively exploit the inherent ambiguities of the institutions." They may have been insurrectionaries in spirit and ideology, but in practice they were mostly "opportunists" and "subversives," making and taking opportunities boldly and quietly, depending on the targeted institutions, the anticipated political costs, and the probability of success. Perhaps the world had not changed so much as to let Cheney lead a frontal attack against the sunshine laws he seemed to find so troublesome—that is, despite the critical juncture, the sunshine laws were too deeply institutionalized to be uprooted. Or maybe Cheney and his team were not as extreme as was commonly believed, at least on government secrecy. In any case, they did not significantly alter the sunshine era's legal framework, as we might have expected. The critical juncture probably allowed more—and more rapid—change than otherwise would have occurred, but Bush-Cheney left for Obama-Biden a system that Clinton-Gore would have quickly recognized, even if it was larger and remodeled around the edges.[53]

Overall during the post-9/11 critical juncture, the Bush-Cheney officials did much to change the secrecy regime, but their efforts and reform agenda were always "deeply embedded in antecedent conditions," perhaps more than we might have expected given Cheney's dominant ideology. They may have wanted to scrap FOIA, FISA, and FACA once and for all, but they did not— or could not—do so, even during the critical juncture. Perhaps they were waiting for the other shoe to drop. Addington, for example, angry about the FISA court possibly restricting the White House's secret domestic surveillance program, told DOJ lawyer Jack Goldsmith in February 2004, "We're [still] one bomb away from getting rid of that obnoxious court."[54]

Circumventions, Sometimes with Lasting Consequences

As argued earlier, presidential administrations often attempt to circumvent the existing legal framework governing the secrecy system by not complying with sunshine laws. When they succeed—when they "get away with it"—the action as applied to a specific rule can set a precedent for presidents to use or build on in the future. Repeated circumventions of the same law can thus reshape the secrecy system, even if presidents setting or using the precedent never intended to permanently change it. In many of the examples described in this book, administrations adopted circumvention strategies for mostly pragmatic reasons; they were merely trying to solve problems as they perceived them, to avoid obstructions in the way of effective governance. Yet presidential actions are long remembered, and if those actions entail successfully avoiding compliance with a power-constraining law, then subsequent presidents will naturally see a benefit in using them.

Most circumvention strategies fall into three general categories: (1) running out the clock, (2) playing word games, or (3) simply pretending nothing untoward happened and hoping no one challenges the farce. Only the first two categories require further explanation, although the first is also largely self-explanatory. Running out the clock essentially involves executive branch efforts to use delaying tactics and related evasive maneuvers to reduce by attrition the importance and sometimes the legal relevance of some conflict related to the administration's noncompliance. Several administrations have used the tactic when, for instance, they have faced lawsuits related to FACA, wherein plaintiffs have demanded meeting notes and transcripts as well as task force members' names, as FACA requires. Faced with the lawsuits, administrations have used a variety of legal maneuvers to complete a task force's work before courts can meaningfully act. Many FACA-wielding plaintiffs have found precedent-citing courts unwilling to deal with the relevant complaints at the relevant time. (Thus, in the case against Cheney's energy task force, the DC appeals courted stated in 2001: "If events outrun the controversy such that the court can grant no meaningful relief, the case must be dismissed as moot.") The Clinton-Gore and Bush-Cheney administrations used this circumvention strategy in major fights over secrecy related to task forces working on health care (Clinton) and energy policy (Bush) (see chapter 4). Other examples include fights over White House e-mails during the Reagan-Bush, Clinton-Gore, and Bush-Cheney administrations (see chapter 9).[55]

Circumvention strategies also take the form of what we can call word games—efforts by administrations to challenge legal requirements by claiming a new semantic interpretation of a law. Officials in every sunshine-era administration examined in this book clearly recognized the presidency as a source of great interpretive power, using their semantic creativity to wriggle out of an inconvenient obligation. They were often quite clever and audacious. For example, during several FACA fights, officials sought to avoid the law's transparency requirements by claiming, in effect, X was not X but Y instead. Similarly, as part of a circumvention strategy that also included running out the clock, Clinton-Gore tried to convince a court that its health care task force members were not "members" at all but "consultants." That discursive gambit did not succeed. However, when Bush-Cheney officials later tried something along the same lines, legally redefining their energy task force members as "guests" and "visitors," they were more successful. And when Clinton-Gore officials picked up the long-running legal FOIA fight over White House e-mails, which began during Reagan-Bush, they tried to shut down the lawsuit by declaring that the National Security Council was no longer an "agency" and thus was immune from FOIA requests.

It is probably true that all legal conflicts in the United States involve contending semantic interpretations—word games large or small, most not involving the president. The idea that much of politics involves conflicts over meaning, with each side attempting to construct a hegemonic interpretation, is of course also not new. However, the kind of "discursive institutionalism" sketched here—or, perhaps, a "suitably tailored historical institutionalism"— is absent from previous scholarly work on government secrecy. As noted earlier, officials do not always play word games with the goal of changing the rules (that is, changing institutions). Much of the time, the efforts appear to be part of shorter-term circumvention strategies. Still, sometimes the efforts are precedent setting, and they can change the secrecy system just as much as more direct layering and conversion efforts can.[56]

Rhetorical Coercion and Threat Inflation

One way presidents and their administrations try to weaken the opposition and, in turn, the veto points that block their way is through rhetorical coercion, "a strategy that seeks to rhetorically constrain political opponents and maneuver them into public assent to one's preferred terms of debate and ideally to one's policy stance." Executives use this tactic during both settled and unsettled times, although we would expect it to be more effective during the latter, when opponents are already deterred by the perceived costs of challenging presidents who are enjoying rally-around-the-flag effects. How rhetorical coercion has directly affected fights over transparency and secrecy is unclear because of the difficulties of observing and measuring the extent to which opponents buckle under rhetorical pressure. At the very least, we can say it probably helps to soften veto points or otherwise give executives added leverage.[57]

Examples are not difficult to find. Right after 9/11, President Bush famously declared, "Either you are with us, or you are with the terrorists," in a televised speech to Congress on September 20, 2001. As a way to deter any Democratic legislators or free-thinking judges, it was about as simple and powerful a rhetorical cudgel as they come (or a "frame," as social scientists would call it). It is true that Bush made the threat while describing plans for a broad new strategic security posture, warning states of the consequences of harboring terrorists. At the same time, the remarks came in a speech to Congress; any Democrats in the room heard the hegemonic, Manichean language loudly and clearly. At the least, they left with nagging questions. Who was the president's "us"? Was he directing his remarks only at *other* nations when he said, "Every nation, in every region, now has a decision to make"? They must have realized Bush's speechwriters and advisers were too smart not to understand the speech's multiple audiences.[58]

For much of Bush-Cheney's first term after 9/11, anything with a hint of dissidence, no matter how mild, was open to accusations of subversion or worse. Thus, Attorney General John Ashcroft attacked Senate Democrats who questioned a few parts of the mammoth USA PATRIOT Act (the PATRIOT Act) in this way: "To those who scare peace-loving people with phantoms of lost liberty, my message is this: Your tactics only aid terrorists, for they erode our national unity and diminish our resolve. They give ammunition to America's enemies, and pause to America's friends. They encourage people of good will to remain silent in the face of evil." During more settled times, such accusations are not uncommon, but they are more often seen as extreme and undemocratic. They are also ineffective; the rhetoric is there, but the coercion is not. At various times in the 1980s, for instance, Ronald Reagan's supporters attacked Democrats and other critics as closet communists or for being the Soviet Union's "useful idiots." Those kinds of attacks might have intimidated some, but many (if not most) Democrats pressed on in their fight against Reagan's Central American policy, to cite one example, or his "Star Wars" missile defense plan. However, during unsettled times, like the 9/11 critical juncture when everyone was talking about nuclear dirty bombs exploding in the cities and anthrax in the mail, the accusations carry more weight. Americans were primed to think of Bush's policy opponents as those threatening "us."[59]

An example better illustrates how rhetorical coercion can soften veto points during unsettled times. Like a few other Senate Democrats who (very reservedly) asked Ashcroft about civil liberties in December 2001, Majority Leader Tom Daschle (D-SD) in late February 2002 sheepishly questioned one facet of the administration's "war on terrorism." Before actually voicing a criticism, Daschle felt the need to laud the administration for its successes—something leaders of the minority party in Congress do not tend to do during settled times. Then he admitted it would "do no good to second-guess what has been done to date." Still, he felt the need as majority leader to urge a greater effort to "find Mohammed Omar . . . Osama bin Laden . . . and other key leaders of the al-Qaeda network, or we will have failed. We're not safe until we have broken the back of al-Qaeda, and we haven't done that yet." He also expressed concern about the lack of "a clear direction" from White House officials about how they would accomplish those goals, adding that "we need to have a clearer understanding of what the direction will be." In response to those mildly critical words, Republicans loyal to Bush unleashed a torrent of blistering attacks. "Disgusting," said Majority Whip Tom DeLay (R-TX). Rep. Tom Davis (R-VA) said Daschle's "divisive comments have the effect of *giving aid and comfort to our enemies* by allowing them to exploit divisions in our country," a clear accusation of treason. In the Senate, Minority Leader Trent Lott (R-MS) suggested Daschle's mild criticism of the president's approach would endanger US troops: "How dare Sen. Daschle criticize President Bush and our war on terrorism, especially when we have U.S. troops on the ground. Our country is united, and Sen. Daschle should not attempt to divide us." Senator Daschle did not go hiding in a corner of the Democrats' cloakroom, but after those attacks, he and other politicians, especially those in competitive districts, probably thought twice about criticizing Bush when his administration circumvented sunshine laws in the name of national security.[60]

A second way presidential administrations and their supporters try to gain political leverage is through *threat inflation*—"the attempt by elites to create concern for a threat that goes beyond the scope and urgency that a disinterested analysis would justify." In other words, it is an effort to shape elite and mass perceptions about the nature and size of a national security threat, as well as about the estimated risks and benefits from policy alternatives. As happens with rhetorical coercion, elites inflate threats during both unsettled and settled times, though the tactic is probably more successful during the former (that is, the efforts pay off). During critical junctures, presidents might work to keep populations fearful about threats—more than "a disinterested analysis would justify"—in order to *endogenously keep open the windows of opportunities originally opened by the exogenous cause*. Bush-Cheney after 9/11 again provides an illustrative example. The threat from Al Qaeda was, of course, a real one. The attacks were proof of that. But the extent to which 9/11 should have changed policies and institutions in line with Bush-Cheney preferences was not preordained. The security-related political decisions in the ensuing years were not reflective of objective state interests as identified by impartial analyses, and the administration was not just responding to the functional needs of the nation (the "material conditions of the moment") without any interpretive frames. With their enhanced influence over the marketplace of ideas (due to the unsettled times and the rally effects), including the ability to coerce opponents rhetorically, Bush-Cheney officials had free rein to create the dominant understandings of what security problems the United States faced and what it should do in response. The power asymmetry that landed in the White House's lap after 9/11 thus had multiple uses. Among the most important involved heightened discursive powers, which conferred new opportunities and capabilities to define threats and marginalize opponents.[61]

One reason threat inflators are often successful (in manipulating the perceived costs and benefits of policy options) is because psychology is on their side. Humans have cognitive biases that overestimate risks and favor hawkish views. These are especially consequential when the political environment is filled with unusual levels of fear and uncertainty and opposition voices are quieted. Although some threat inflators are duplicitous, many elites themselves misperceive threats, due to their own cognitive biases and/or interelite persuasion. No matter why they are successful—an important but for our purposes tangential question—if threat inflators are successful in obtaining more hawkish policies or otherwise mobilizing state resources toward the threat, greater government secrecy tends to follow right behind. (*How can we effectively meet those threats if our enemies know our every move?*)

In sum, presidential administrations use rhetorical coercion and threat inflation to weaken the institutional opposition; to propagate hegemonic interpretations; and to endogenously expand windows of opportunity, including during critical junctures. Administrations use the discursive acts during settled and unsettled times, although the latter provide more opportunities and probably increase the chances of success. Before concluding, let us consider how these tools can be used to endogenously extend the *duration* of an exogenously caused critical juncture.

The literature on critical junctures is surprisingly vague on the duration question. Ruth Berins Collier and David Collier clearly thought about it in their landmark 1991 study—just flip to the "How Long Do Critical Junctures Last?" section. Junctures might end relatively quickly, they note, but still might be remembered as "moments of significant structural change." Longer junctures could last through more than one presidential administration or another prolonged "regime period." Historical institutionalist work following Collier and Collier has generally left the duration question to rest. If we are to fully appreciate Katznelson's (2003) point about how the agent-structure equation is flipped on its head during a critical juncture, where political actors momentarily can (to some extent) free themselves from the typical structural constraints, then we are left with the possibility that those same actors can use their enhanced powers to try to extend the critical juncture for as long as possible. And why wouldn't they? Critical junctures give actors a chance to get more of what they want. Therefore, though actors might find themselves empowered initially as a result of a critical juncture they did not create, once in the midst of it they work to keep it going. As we will see in the next chapter, Bush-Cheney officials frequently did just that, including in their explanations for keeping secrets.[62]

3

KEEPING SECRETS, DURING SETTLED AND UNSETTLED TIMES

A "Pearl Harbor Sort of Purple American Fury": 9/11 as a National Security Crisis and a Window of Opportunity

September 11's vivid images were hard to shake. Citizens and officials, glued to their television screens, watched the looped newsreels endlessly replay the moments when terrorists steered two jumbo jets into the World Trade Center. Soon, the skyscrapers smoldered and crumbled, causing hundreds of men and women to jump to their deaths from great heights. In DC, another jet slammed into the Pentagon, convincing anyone who remained doubtful that this was political violence unlike any the country had seen before. The one silver lining of the day occurred when the fourth hijacked plane failed to make its destination in the nation's capital (either the White House or the Capitol building), although the fiery death of all forty-four passengers aboard Flight 93 as it crashed into a rural Pennsylvanian field at 563 mph was hardly something to cheer.[1]

Reeling from the national trauma, many Americans wept and wondered *why.* Others immediately saw grand historical analogies of war and proposed vengence on a massive scale. In "The Case for Rage and Retribution," published in *Time* the next day, journalism professor Lance Morrow demanded that the country snap out of its grieving: "For once, let's have no fatuous rhetoric about healing. Healing is inappropriate now, and dangerous. . . . A day cannot live in infamy without the nourishment of rage. Let's have rage. What's needed is a unified, unifying, Pearl Harbor sort of purple American fury." The historical analogy also crossed the president's mind as he wrote in his diary on the night of the attacks: "The Pearl Harbor of the 21st Century took place today." But the problem in 2001 appeared even more difficult than the one in 1941, since the new enemy was a scattered, elusive, transnational force, not really vulnerable to conventional US miltiary attacks.[2]

President Bush's "Address to the Nation" on 9/11 did not explicitly invoke military action, but it did begin to frame the events as war worthy; it also introduced the concept of a "war against terrorism" and established parts of the inchoate Bush doctrine. "The search is underway for those who are behind these evil acts," the president announced. "I've directed the full resources for our intelligence and law enforcement communities to find those responsible and bring them to justice. We will make no distinction between the terrorists who committed these acts and those who harbor them." In private, Bush was more open about using aggressive military force. CIA director George Tenet wondered aloud in a meeting on 9/11 how this new policy of retaliating against countries that harbored terrorists might work, considering that Al Qaeda operated in at least sixty nations. Bush's reply—"Let's pick them off one at a time"—telegraphed his intention to ready the military for perpetual conflict. The new military plan was even called Operation Infinite Justice.[3]

Eerily, several senior officials—Paul Wolfowitz, Stephen Cambone, and I. Lewis Libby—had published (with others) a Project for the New American Century report in 2000 that proposed "revolutionary" national security policy changes like the ones Bush-Cheney pushed after 9/11. The authors lamented that the pace of change would be slow, "absent some catastrophic and catalyzing event—like a new Pearl Harbor." Although the report retrospectively seemed prophetic or even conspiratorial, it at least reflected an awareness among elites that a massive domestic attack would produce a critical juncture, in which many of the policy-making shackles that constrained politicians during "settled times" would come off. Gripped by uncertainty and fear, filled with rage and bellicose nationalism, citizens would be ready for retribution and big reforms. Almost everyone seemed to support and trust the president to do what he thought was right. Bush's approval ratings shot up 35 percent overnight (from 51 percent to 86 percent), and they generally remained above 60 percent until mid-2004, a number still very high historically. There was also a dramatic surge in citizen trust in the government "to do what was right" always or most of the time. In March 2001, 29 percent of Americans said they trusted the government in this way. By late September, after the attacks, the number had more than doubled to a record 64 percent.[4]

Despite Morrow's insistence in *Time* that Americans reject "healing" and "grief counselors" for "the nourishment of rage," the national trauma of 9/11 was rawly remembered for years, stoked by weepy memorials, flag pins, hit songs, and annual media retrospectives hosted by grim anchors. Unsurprisingly, Bush, Cheney, and other politicians often invoked the memory of 9/11 for persuasive effect, and they frequently tied it to policies they said would help them win the wars on "terror" in Afghanistan and, later, in Iraq. With the country solidly behind the president, White House officials recognized their window of opportunity, and they immediately went to work.[5]

The Rise of Mosaic Theory

In order to win the war of "good versus evil," officials in the Bush-Cheney administration made it clear they would "not talk about any plans we may or may not have." Understandably so, as one of the widely accepted, legitimate bases for secrecy involves protecting deliberations about ongoing military, police, and intelligence actions related to national defense (see chapter 2). But the administration went further, arguing that the "new war" would need to proceed "with unprecedented secrecy." This effort would entail "heavy press restrictions" and a deliberate policy of "clamp[ing] down on even routine information because it could prove of some use to potential terrorists." This perspective was widely shared. The 9/11 plotters proved they were shrewd, well coordinated, and patient, so *who knew* what malicious plans they and their associates might concoct? Indeed, across the country, imagining how Al Qaeda would strike next had become a kind of grisly parlor game in some circles and a nightmare-inducing tic in others. (Would it be a "suitcase nuke" in Chicago? Or maybe Topeka? Or multiple, simultaneous apartment building bombings in the Denver suburbs? Tampa and the military bases?) If little bits of dangerous but "seemingly innocouous information" fell into the wrong hands, the consequences could prove catastrophic. The uncertainty of the times seemed to justify extreme caution.[6]

Though they might not have mentioned it by name in public, Bush-Cheney officials began using a theory of information control that had been kicking around Washington since at least the Truman administration. Officials who argued they needed to "clamp down on even routine information because it could prove of some use to potential terrorists" were following the logic of "mosaic theory," which generally holds that "disparate items of information, though individually of limited or no utility to their possessor, can take on added significance when combined with other items of information" (see chapter 2). Although the idea empowers government executives, federal judges actually embraced the secrecy tool before presidents did. Harry Truman explicitly rejected mosaic theory for guiding his government's classification decisions in his 1951 Executive Order 10290: "Documents shall be classified according to their own content and not necessarily according to their relationship to other documents." President Eisenhower carried Truman's directive forward, as did all presidents until Reagan, who first imported mosaic logic into an executive order (#12356). Reagan was concerned about the KGB's cleverness in aggregating seemingly unrelated pieces of information: "Information that is determined to concern one or more of the categories in Section 1.3(a) shall be classified when an original classification authority also determines that its unauthorized disclosure, *either by itself or in the context of other information,* reasonably could be expected to cause damage to the national security." When the next Democrat won the presidency, the language endured. President Bill Clinton wrote in Executive Order 12958: "Compilations of items of information which are individually unclassified may be classified if the compiled information reveals an additional association or relationship that: (1) meets the standards for classification under this order; and (2) is not otherwise revealed in the individual items of information. As used in this order, 'compilation' means an aggregation of pre-existing unclassified items of information."[7]

Though often overblown, concerns about clever enemies using bits of "seemingly innocuous" information for malicious purposes are not unfounded. Take the case of *U.S. v. Progressive, Inc.*, in which the Carter-Mondale administration sued *The Progressive* magazine—not an "enemy" but a still-clever left-wing periodical—for an article it planned to publish entitled "The H-Bomb Secret: How We Got It, Why We're Telling It." Using unclassified information from a variety of sources, journalist Howard Morland was able to piece together "the essence of . . . the H-bomb secret": "It is a mosaic of bits and pieces taken from employe [*sic*] recruitment brochures, environmental impact statements, books, articles, personal interviews, and my own private speculation. A number of reliable sources have confirmed that the information fragments are correctly assembled." Morland's article was originally scheduled to appear in the March 1979 issue, but it was delayed for eight months after the government convinced the US District Court for the Western District of Wisconsin to issue a prior restraint injunction blocking publication. Ultimately, the government withdrew its case after the *Madison Press Connection* published similar information, but it still maintained its position about the dangers of unguarded, though unclassified, information—not only for nuclear information "born secret" but especially so.[8]

Mosaic theory inspired many of Bush-Cheney's moves toward secrecy after 9/11. Right away, the administration removed large tracts of sensitive unclassified information from government libraries and websites and anywhere else it was located. Some of this was understandable, given the deep level of uncertainty in the government and in the country about potential future attacks. The Nuclear Regulatory Commission (NRC) took down its public website. The Bureau of Transportation Statistics closed off access to its National Transportation Atlas Data Base. The Environmental Protection Agency (EPA) removed from libraries and websites information about toxic chemicals lurking in local communities, as well as corporations' "risk management plans" for industrial chemical accidents. The risks that terrorists might turn factories into chemical weapons of mass destruction (WMD) were apparently just too great to worry about the right-to-know provisions of the 1986 Emergency Planning and Community Right-to-Know Act. A few activists grumbled on the media periphery, but most citizens, including opposition politicians, seemed to cut the president some slack as a result of the unsettled times.[9]

Mosaic theory was also deployed with the zeal of a recent convert in intelligence and law enforcement actions. The "preventive detentions" of hundreds of mostly Middle Eastern and South Asian foreign nationals in late 2001 during the PENTTBOM investigation of the 9/11 attacks were not in and of themselves based on mosaic theory. (PENTTBOM was the FBI's code name for the Pentagon/Twin Towers Bombing Investigation.) However, the theory shaped the way the government handled the detentions, in two different ways. First, the government refused to make the detainees' names available, even though officials held the vast majority of the men for ordinary visa violations and other immigration charges. Only a very small number aroused reasonable suspicion based on circumstantial evidence, among them a Pakistani man named Mohammad Mubeen who had the misfortune of renewing his driver's license at the same Florida Department of Motor Vehicles branch used by 9/11 terrorist Mohamed Atta twenty-three minutes later. Most men were picked up because of their dark skin, foreign names, and presumed religions; indeed, Hindus, Sikhs, and Buddhists were tossed in cells with Muslim suspects detained only because of their religion, which was then a sufficient basis for suspicion. To minimize all possible risks, administration officials decided they needed across-the-board secrecy. A very sophisticated terrorist organization, they believed, might have used detainee data (such as names and arrest locations) to make inferences about the FBI's counterterrorist tracking methods. In some detention hearings, government lawyers explicitly used mosaic language. For example, one FBI affidavit argued, "The business of counterterrorism intelligence gathering in the United States is akin to the construction of a mosaic":

At this stage of the investigation, the FBI is gathering and processing thousands of bits and pieces of information that may seem innocuous at first glance. We must analyze all that information, however, to see if it can be fit into a picture that will reveal how the unseen whole operates. . . . What may seem trivial to some may appear of great moment to those within the FBI or the intelligence community who have a broader context within which to consider a questioned item or isolated piece of information. At the present stage of this vast investigation, the FBI is gathering and culling information that may corroborate or diminish our current suspicions of the individuals who have been detained. . . . In the meantime, the FBI has been unable to rule out the possibility that respondent is somehow linked to, or possesses knowledge of, the terrorist attacks on the World Trade Center and the Pentagon. To protect the public the FBI must exhaust all avenues of investigation while ensuring that critical information does not evaporate pending further investigation.

The FBI used the same language verbatim in other affadavits, such as one justifying the preventive detention of Ali Abubakr Ali Al-Maqtari, a Yemeni citizen first picked up in Kentucky with his army wife on September 15. Officials also drew upon mosaic theory when processing the bounty of information produced by the mass detentions. Actually, it was more like an expression of inverted mosaic theory, since the government worked to connect the dots from bits of "seemingly innocuous information" gathered from detainees.[10]

Closing immigration cases to the public was not new. The government had closed particularly sensitive cases in the past. But the DOJ's new policy, formulated by Attorney General John Ashcroft and written, compliantly, by Chief Immigration Judge Michael Creppy, was novel in making a sweeping claim of secrecy across an entire class of cases. Judge Creppy designated *all* the detainees as being of "special interest" and issued in November 2001 what became known as the Creppy Directive. The guidelines required immigration courts to conceal detainee names, dates of arrest, and prison locations and to forbid the press, defendants' family members and friends, and other interested people from all hearings. To reduce the risk of leaks, the directive also prohibited defendants' lawyers from taking documents out of courtrooms and from speaking about their clients publicly or privately (in other words, they suffered gag orders). The administration even classified the lawyers' own identities, whether they wanted them to be secret or not. And to ensure "deep secrecy"—concealing from the public the fact that something was being kept secret—the directive ordered that no information about the cases would appear in public records, as if they never existed. Mosaic theory guided all these moves, although the government also justified its actions less abstractly on the basis of "privacy laws, judges' orders and the secrecy rules surrounding the grand jury investigation of the Sept. 11 attacks."[11]

CNSS v. DOJ

As the scale and scope of the administration's secrecy became increasingly clear via leaks and then official confirmations, civil libertarians and human rights activists drew upon the powers of the sunshine laws. The Center for National Security Studies (CNSS), for example, filed a late October 2001 FOIA request asking three DOJ agencies—the FBI, the Office of Information and Privacy (OIP), and the Immigration and Naturalization Service (INS)—for information about the detainees and their court proceedings. The DOJ's complete rejection of the FOIA request came admirably quickly (long delays are a recurring problem), and the short rationale was steeped in mosaic theory and related abstractions. Citing the theory by name, along with relevant court decisions, the DOJ claimed disclosure of *any* information would harm its terrorism investigations, even if the government could not offer any details about actual risks from disclosure. Government policy, argued Dale L. Watson, executive assistant director for counterterrorism and counterintelligence, held that "bits and pieces of information that may appear innocuous in isolation, when assimilated with other information that terrorists may or may not have in hand, will allow the organization to build a picture of the investigation and to thwart the government's attempts to investigate and prevent terrorism." A clearer expression of mosaic theory as public policy could hardly be found.[12]

Dissatisfied with the explanation, CNSS, along with the ACLU, the Council on American-Islamic Relations, and several other groups, sued the government on December 5, 2001, alleging that the DOJ violated the FOIA, the First Amendment, and case law precedent. During the still uncertain and unsettled times, the late 2001 challenge to Bush-Cheney was as gutsy as it was unusual. Though explicitly recognizing the legitimacy of law enforcement actions related to terrorism, the plaintiffs challenged the DOJ's sweeping, mosaic theory–driven use of FOIA's Exemption 7(A), which allows the government to withhold information for law enforcement reasons. (The government also cited other FOIA exemptions, but only 7[A] rested on a mosaic argument.) The plaintiffs argued exemption 7(A) required a case-by-case assessment of the risks of disclosure for active investigations and operations; the DOJ needed to cite specific law enforcement risks for each detainee case. Remarkably, given the new political environment, the DC district court agreed with the plaintiffs and told the DOJ it could not use mosaic theory to justify blanket secrecy. Besides, Judge Gladys Kessler argued, mosaic theory fit better with FOIA's Exemption 1, which covers classified or some unclassified national security or intelligence information. The administration's choice to invoke 7(A) instead of 1 indicated the information it sought to protect did not qualify for that kind of protection. For those and other reasons, Judge Kessler ordered the DOJ to release the names of the detainees and their lawyers, within fifteen days. She granted the government two exceptions. First, the DOJ could withhold names if detainees preferred anonymity. Second, courts could evaluate secret evidence provided by the DOJ in camera and rule for exclusion on a case-by-case basis (see chapter 6). The DOJ did win the right to keep secret the dates and locations of the arrests and detentions, but because of the other losses, officials appealed the decision. Things worked out in their favor.[13]

The DC appeals court overturned Judge Kessler's decision, embraced the DOJ's experimental use of mosaic theory, and rejected plaintiffs' other arguments based on the First Amendment and common law. Because some of the "detainees could be acquaintances of the September 11 terrorists, or members of the same community groups or mosques," the court ruled, their anonymity would not only ensure their protection from terrorists but also give them more incentives to "cooperate with the investigation" into the attacks. Even if the detainees did not request anonymity, Judge David Sentelle argued, the government had a compelling interest in keeping their names secret for law enforcement purposes. Otherwise, they might "close up like a clam." Besides, terrorists could use the disclosed information to gain "insights into the investigation they would otherwise be unlikely to have." Based on these and other arguments, Judge Sentelle reversed the lower court's opinion, including its order to disclose the unclassified information. The Supreme Court declined to consider the plaintiffs' appeal. *CNSS v. DOJ,* along with two other cases from the immediate post-9/11 period, made it clear the courts fully accepted mosaic theory as an appropriate basis for information control and, specifically, FOIA administration. Like most others in the still unsettled post-9/11 period, Judge Sentelle seemed content to give Bush-Cheney extra wiggle room, even if that meant letting the executive branch establish a new precedent, thus expanding the scope of the secrecy system.[14]

North Jersey Media Group v. Ashcroft

The Bush-Cheney administration's policy of banning reporters from deportation hearings and preventing them from reviewing the docket information also drew a direct challenge. In *North Jersey Media Group v. Ashcroft*, journalists for the *New Jersey Law Journal* and the *Herald News* challenged the legality of the Creppy Directive on First Amendment grounds, arguing secrecy decisions needed case-by-case authorization, not mosaic theory's blanket approach, which unduly restricted speech. In the District Court of New Jersey, Judge John Winslow Bissell largely agreed, siding with the plaintiffs. But as with *CNSS v. DOJ*, their colleagues at the appellate level overturned the decision, giving Ashcroft and the DOJ another victory. The two-to-one majority actually sidestepped the Creppy Directive, arguing the government's secrecy could be justified based on a long-standing two-part test for open proceedings ("we need not reach the subsequent questions whether the Creppy Directive's closures would pass a strict scrutiny analysis"). At the same time, the court endorsed the DOJ's use of mosaic theory: "The government maintains that these protections would be ineffective given the complexities in combating terrorism. It contends that individual, seemingly innocuous pieces of information, including a special interest alien's name, could be harmful to national security when compiled by terrorists into a mosaic. This seems correct." The dangers and uncertainties of the unsettled, post-9/11 era, the majority continued, made the secrecy even more justified:

> The era that dawned on September 11th, and the war against terrorism that has pervaded the sinews of our national life since that day, are reflected in thousands of ways in legislative and national policy, the habits of daily living, and our collective psyches. Since the primary national policy must be self-preservation, it seems elementary that, to the extent open deportation hearings might impair national security, that security is implicated in the logic test.

The one dissenting judge, Anthony Joseph Scirica, politely called the Creppy Directive's blanket closure rule and, by implication, his colleagues' arguments "constitutionally infirm." As long as "reasonable alternatives" existed—such as case-by-case determinations made in concert with immigration judges—mosaic theory and the resulting blanket secrecy were indefensible in his opinion. But "the logic test" won out over Scirica's First Amendment reading, giving the government more license to expand secrecy categorically.[15]

Detroit Free Press v. Ashcroft

In contrast, in *Detroit Free Press v. Ashcroft* a unanimous Court of Appeals for the Sixth Circuit unambiguously rejected the government's mosaic claims and found the Creppy Directive to be "over-inclusive." The case involved the INS's detention of Lebanese citizen Rabih Haddad, the cofounder of Global Relief Foundation, an Illinois-based Islamic charity the government accused of financially and otherwise supporting Al Qaeda. The *Detroit Free Press*, the *Detroit News,* and Rep. John Conyers, Jr. (D-MI), joined Haddad in suing for injunctive and declarative relief because of the closed trial. Judge Damon Keith acknowledged the possibility of "mosaic intelligence" risks but could not grant the executive unhindered discretion to "speculate" at the cost of core First Amendment rights. It did not help the government's argument that the DOJ actually admitted that none of the information from Haddad's three hearings threatened "national security or the safety of the American people," the primary concern of mosaic theorists. More broadly, the court highlighted the "danger of secret trials" and mosaic theory's potential for endless government secrecy:

> There seems to be no limit to the Government's argument. The Government could use its "mosaic intelligence" argument as a justification to close any public hearing completely and categorically, including criminal proceedings. The Government could operate in virtual secrecy in all matters dealing, even remotely, with "national security," resulting in a wholesale suspension of First Amendment rights. By the simple assertion of "national security," the Government seeks a process where it may, without review, designate certain classes of cases as "special interest cases" and, behind closed doors, adjudicate the merits of these cases to deprive non-citizens of their fundamental liberty interests.
>
> This, we simply may not countenance. A government operating in the shadow of secrecy stands in complete opposition to the society envisioned by the Framers of our Constitution.

Ultimately, Judge Keith argued, "democracies die behind closed doors." The executive might close individual trials, but closing off an entire class of cases was unjustified.[16]

Summary

The conflicting judicial decisions left mosaic theory's status for detention policy uncertain. On the one hand, *CNSS* and *North Jersey* provided support; on the other hand, *Detroit Free Press* forbade it. Because of the courts' different geographic jurisdictions, the rulings freed the administration to continue its policy of mass secret trials—but only in forty-six states; given the Sixth District appeals court's (*Detroit Free Press*) jurisdiction, the policy stopped at the Kentucky, Michigan, Ohio, and Tennessee borders. Finding alternative venues was not a problem. Moreover, because of the protracted judicial process and a strong dose of judicial deference to the executive, Bush-Cheney officials continued their policies, without intrusions or injunctions. By the time the courts ruled, the administration had completed the first wave of sweeps and detentions. For practical purposes, what the court decided no longer mattered. The running-out-the-clock strategy may not have been deliberate, but administration officials ultimately benefited from it. Plus, they could wave around two new court decisions validating mosaic theory for the new war on terrorism and beyond. That the precedents were built atop particular understandings of an abstract concept—mosaic building—makes this an interesting example of constructivist institutional change.[17]

Tightening up FOIA Administration: Returning to Reagan-Bush Rules

The Bush-Cheney administration's use of mosaic theory for detainee and FOIA administration was part of a larger "preventive paradigm" developed after 9/11, touching everything from information security to torture policies (for which the mosaic builders were intelligence analysts). Standing in the way of the new paradigm's path was the sunshine era's strong but already pockmarked legal framework. Though senior officials might have privately loathed that framework, the White House publicly showed a willingness to live with it. Not once did Bush-Cheney officials make an effort to eviscerate it, by pushing Congress to repeal the laws. Instead, they built on the secrecy system they inherited, poking more holes in it and otherwise circumventing the sunshine laws when opportunities arose.[18]

The quest to conceal everything remotely sensitive began with the one-off moves described earlier, such as pulling information out of government libraries and off websites. For instance, it suddenly made little sense for the Defense Department to post real-time updates showing the geographic locations of its warships, which continued even after the USS *Cole* bombing in Yemen in 2000. The administration had a lot of leeway in restricting public access to unclassified information because US presidents faced few clear-cut *proactive* transparency legal requirements (that is, to automatically publish information, without a citizen's request). By contrast, the FOIA set into place a very clear framework for *reactive* transparency. Citizens sent FOIA requests to specific agencies for specific types of unclassified information. Unless the information could be withheld according to FOIA's specific exceptions (Table 2.1), citizens were supposed to receive what they requested.[19]

The administration's problem was that bureaucrats needed to exercise some discretion when evaluating FOIA requests. Whether information needed protection was not always clear. What exactly did Exemption 2 mean, with its protections for information "related solely to the internal personnel rules and practices of an agency"? How broadly should "internal personnel practices" be interpreted? Or what about Exemption 5's protection of "intra- or inter-agency memoranda that would be considered privileged in civil litigation"—especially since people disagree about what counted as privileged information? And as we will see, Exemption 3 is as big as Congress wants it to be. With Bush-Cheney's commitment to the preventive paradigm, nothing would be left up to chance.

The Ashcroft, Reno, and Smith Memos

Although Bush-Cheney officials did not make FOIA discretionary behavior a priority before 9/11, they quickly changed course after the attacks. In a very short but sweeping early October 2001 memorandum about how to handle FOIA requests, Attorney General Ashcroft instructed all federal agency and department heads that "any discretionary decision by your agency to disclose information protected under the FOIA should be made only after full and deliberate consideration by the institutional, commercial, and personal privacy interests that could be implicated by disclosure of the information." To make it clear that secrecy should trump transparency and to ease any resulting concerns about potential legal challenges from information-seeking citizens, Ashcroft continued: "You can be assured that the [DOJ] will defend your decisions unless they lack a sound legal basis or present an unwarranted risk of adverse impact on the ability of other agencies to protect other important records." His central point was clear: if the DOJ could reasonably interpret something as being covered under FOIA's exemptions, then officials should always prevent disclosure.[20]

Ashcroft's memo overturned FOIA rules established by his predecessor, Attorney General Janet Reno, eight years earlier. Reno's "foreseeable harm" standard ordered agencies to release information unless disclosure would clearly cause harm to national security or privacy rights or unless it would unambiguously fall under one of the other FOIA exemptions: "It shall be the policy of the [DOJ] to defend the assertion of a FOIA exemption only in those cases where the agency reasonably foresees that disclosure would be harmful to an interest protected by that exemption." For twelve years (1981–1993), the government had worked under Attorney General William French Smith's more restrictive guidelines, biased toward secrecy. The Reno Memo, by contrast, told information officers to release FOIA-ed information, even if the DOJ could feasibly defend secrecy on technical legal grounds. According to President Clinton, the change in policy reflected the administration's broad "commitment to openness," as he indicated in an accompanying memo. FOIA's effectiveness as a "vital part of . . . government" had been diminished by "unnecessary bureaucratic hurdles." ("The use of the Act by ordinary citizens is not complicated, nor should it be. The existence of unnecessary bureaucratic hurdles has no place in its implementation.") Reno's "maximum responsible disclosure" standard promised to steer the government back toward the letter and spirit of the FOIA. It stipulated that, via "discretionary disclosure," federal agencies could disclose information even if it fell under one of FOIA's nine exemptions. In practice, the Reno Memo created a new default position of openness within the large realm of FOIA administration. The Ashcroft Memo, by contrast, reestablished the Reagan-Bush policy of *minimal possible disclosure* as outlined in the Smith Memo.[21]

The shift toward more closed government, which came as the World Trade Center rubble was still belching smoke across New York Harbor, seemed to attract little public attention or concern. Or perhaps it was that editorial boards for major media companies, which had held their tongues since the attacks, were not ready to challenge the administration on what was a major change in information policy. One of the first public mentions came more than two months after the Ashcroft Memo, when Tom Beierle and Ruth Greenspan Bell of Resources for the Future pleaded with citizens not to let the sunshine law become a "war casualty": "Years of hard-won battles that turned FOIA into a fundamental routine bulwark against government secrecy were undermined in a day. The memo ushered out the principle of 'right to know' and replaced it with 'need to know.' Now, the presumption is that information is inherently risky." The editorial board of the *San Francisco Chronicle* waited two months to alert citizens about the loss of one of "their most precious freedoms": "The President didn't ask the networks for television time. The attorney general didn't hold a press conference. The media didn't report any dramatic change in governmental policy. As a result, most Americans had no idea that one of their most precious freedoms disappeared on Oct. 12. . . . Without fanfare, [Ashcroft] simply quashed the FOIA." Of course, he did no such thing. The change revived the more restrictive approach to FOIA favored by Reagan-Bush and Bush-Quayle. Bush-Cheney officials may have wanted to "quash FOIA," but in reality they sustained it, although they did reset the knobs back to Bush-Quayle settings.[22]

Responding to the critical newspaper writers and a few others (there was barely a peep from congressional Democrats), Bush-Cheney officials actually took a conciliatory approach, offering assurances that FOIA administration would not change much in practice. Dan Metcalfe, then the codirector of the Department of Justice's OIP, argued the new policy would not cause "drastic" changes in practice, although he acknowledged there was "certainly a shift in tone." The director of the Information Security Oversight Office, Steven Garfinkel, also dismissed critics' concerns about a quashed FOIA: "You know what? The Janet Reno memorandum is all but meaningless. The John Ashcroft memorandum is all but meaningless. What you do every day on the job is what is truly meaningful in the area of access to government information." How extensively the Ashcroft Memo actually changed FOIA officers' behavior remained unclear.[23]

In 2003, the General Accounting Office (GAO) stepped in and conducted a survey of 205 FOIA officers across twenty-five agencies. How "drastically" did Ashcroft's memo alter bureaucratic behavior? About half of the respondents (48 percent) reported no changes, whereas about one-third (31 percent) indicated they probably decreased their overall "discretionary disclosures" (6.6 percent said they probably released more information, and 14 percent didn't know or had "no basis" for a response). Because FOIA officers might have changed their behaviors due to 9/11 and not Ashcroft's guidance, the GAO

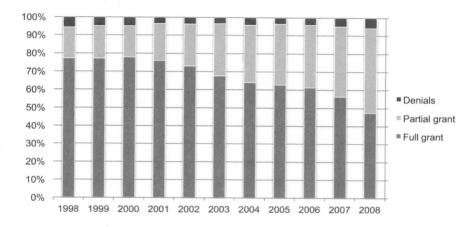

FIGURE 3.1
FOIA Grant Rates, 1998–2008.
Source: Coalition of Journalists for Open Government; FOIA.gov; government
agencies' annual FOIA reports

asked respondents to identify the reasons for any changed behaviors. The vast majority (75 percent) of those who decreased their discretionary disclosures cited the new rule as a primary reason for their new approach. Overall, even though it did not completely nullify FOIA as some feared, Ashcroft's memo appeared to cause immediate and substantial changes to what many FOIA officers did "every day on the job" (as Garfinkel put it).[24]

Data on FOIA administration, published by the government, corroborate the story (see Figure 3.1). On the one hand, full denials—when petitioners received nothing they requested—changed little during the first three years following the Ashcroft Memo (2002–2004). Indeed, full denials were higher during the latter part of Clinton-Gore under the Reno Memo, although Bush-Cheney returned to Clinton-Gore levels by 2008. Even then, however, 94.3 percent of FOIA applicants received at least some of the information they sought.[25]

There was no outbreak of full denials after 2001, but FOIA officers increasingly refused to grant petitioners some or most of what they requested. Full grants decreased markedly (from 76.1 percent in 2001 to 47.5 percent in 2008), whereas partial grants climbed (from 20.4 percent to 46.8 percent). In practice, that meant tens of thousands more petitioners every year received "blacked out" government documents. Whether the redactions covered a few scattered lines or many full pages remains a mystery (that is, partial grants could be anywhere from barely to almost fully redacted). The new politics of national security after 9/11 was obviously a key cause of these changes, although the data reflect decisions across the government (outside security and intelligence agencies), so we should be hesitant in making too much of the connection. In any case, *something* caused a change in FOIA response rates, and the Ashcroft Memo is one likely cause, just as the FOIA officers in the GAO survey said. If the Ashcroft Memo had an impact, the Card Memo was at least as important.[26]

The Card Memo: Everything Is (Potentially) Sensitive

Five months after Ashcroft's memo, White House chief of staff Andrew Card took the preventive paradigm several steps further. In his March 2002 memo, Card notified all agency and department heads that the White House wanted the tightest possible restrictions applied to "sensitive but unclassified" (SBU) information. FOIA already protected much of it via exemptions, but senior Bush-Cheney officials in the post-9/11 environment sought tighter safeguards for information about weapons of mass destruction or anything else terrorists might find useful. A great deal of WMD-related information was already classified, but the large and complex web of production, transportation, and storage processes, involving chemists, biologists, physicists, arms manufacturers, railroad companies, nuclear storage facilities, and the like, may have left some SBU information more accessible than it should have been.[27]

For guidance on how officials should apply this vague new SBU standard, Card attached a memo written by the heads of the ISOO and the OIP, who emphasized the power of FOIA Exemptions 2 and 4. They also outlined new standards by which to reclassify previously declassified information that had not yet reached the public through FOIA requests or proactive measures (for instance, posting on websites). Thus, the ISOO/OIP memo identified methods to protect SBU but kept the information category ambiguously defined. Yes, the memo instructed agencies to look out for any "information that could be misused to harm the security of our Nation and the safety of our people." But in a world governed by the preventive paradigm, that could have meant just about anything. The Card Memo's ambiguity thus helped the cause of maximizing bureaucratic risk aversion.[28]

Perhaps aiming to clarify or to show how wonderfully broad SBU was, anonymous White House officials took to the mass media to provide instructive examples. First, they offered the requisite platitudes about the "cautious balance" between openness and secrecy. Then, they demonstrated how far the Card Memo could go. Beyond the obvious (such as "documents on 'dual use' nuclear materials"), the SBU category might include "information on heating and air conditioning systems," they said, or perhaps "computer maintenance data that might aid hackers in stopping the disbursement of Social Security checks." There were plausible links to counterterrorism, but critics wondered, could *anything* be filed under SBU?[29]

The ambiguity (and breadth) of the Card Memo was exacerbated by a lack of uniform standards for SBU across agencies. This was not a new problem. As statutes referring to SBU information began to pile up in the 1970s, starting with 1977's Telecommunications Protection Policy, affected agencies began to independently define the category to suit their needs (they did the same for similar categories, like sensitive security information [SSI]). The US Agency for International Development (USAID), for example, sent out a memo in 1995 declaring that "'SBU' supersedes the terms 'sensitive data' or 'sensitive information'" and could involve just about anything—"procurement source evaluation and source selection, company proprietary, investigative, restricted scientific/technical information, and travel plans of USAID employees to or through a high or critical terrorist threat environment. The following categories of information are considered potential SBU information: legal, financial, budget projections, medical, contractual, procurement, intellectual property, agency-critical or foreign government." Other agencies' definitions were even broader, before and after 9/11.[30]

Agencies also established their own rules about who made SBU decisions. All 180,000 Homeland Security employees, for instance, could stamp "For Official Use Only" onto sensitive or potentially sensitive documents. No interagency body monitored the rule-making process or the SBU decisions themselves, possibly because what emerged was such a mess. Four years before 9/11, agencies already used fifty-two different types of SBU-related protective markings, such as "Limited Use," "Sensitive Security Information," and "Not for Public Dissemination."[31]

On top of the Card Memo's ambiguity and the overall lack of clear, uniform standards, bureaucrats had to grapple with the tension between the new SBU rules and existing laws. To cite one example, an SBU-related section of the Computer Security Act (CSA) of 1987 stipulated that

nothing in this Act, or in any amendment made by this Act, shall be construed . . . to constitute authority to withhold information sought pursuant to [the FOIA and] to authorize any Federal agency to limit, restrict, regulate, or control the collection, maintenance, disclosure, use, transfer, or sale of any information . . . that is . . . disclosable under [the FOIA] or other law requiring or authorizing the public disclosure of information . . . or public domain information.

CSA supplementary documents were even clearer: "The Computer Security Act did not alter the Freedom of Information Act (FOIA); therefore, an agency's determination of sensitivity under this definition does not change the status of releaseability under the FOIA." Bureaucrats were thus stuck between two opposing political forces—existing laws and their current boss's administrative orders. Bush-Cheney officials ultimately recognized that they needed a new law to resolve the problem. In particular, they realized FOIA needed another layer, another broad exemption.[32]

Critical Infrastructure Information

Tucked deep within the massive Homeland Security Act was a little-noticed provision called the Critical Infrastructure Information Act of 2002 (CIIA), which authorized officials to withhold SBU information from FOIA requests. The CIIA attracted so little media attention after its late November 2002 passage that the only story to appear before the 2004 presidential election was a brief note in the *Wall Street Journal* reporting that the new Homeland Security Department had finally published the corresponding regulations. The new law probably did not seem all that radical to most political observers. After all, Congress had passed laws governing critical infrastructure information before. But a closer inspection of the CIIA's broad definition of *critical infrastructure,* in the context of FOIA exemptions, would have revealed the potent new secrecy tool Bush-Cheney created for itself and all later administrations.[33]

 Although the law's definition of *critical infrastructure information* (CII) expanded on older definitions, the DOJ acknowledged the new one was rather "extensive." For instance, it included information that, if disclosed, might "harm . . . interstate commerce" or threaten "public health or safety." The CIIA also identified the "critical" nature of information linked to "all types of communications and data transmission systems." If picked up by the wrong people, this CII could help enemies plan a "physical or cyber-attack." Given the breadth and ambiguity of the definition, FOIA officers, working under a preventive paradigm, likely started to see CII just about everywhere—hospitals, baseball stadiums, malls, movie theaters, amusement parks, office parks, apartment buildings, and more. Before 9/11 and the CIIA, the proportion of SBU information compared with the entire universe of unclassified information was already large. The DOD's Joint Security Commission in 1994 estimated that up to 75 percent of all government information could be considered SBU. After 9/11 and the CIIA, the number likely increased.[34]

Bush-Cheney officials cautioned agencies not to worry, as they could use more detailed definitions of *critical infrastructure* from previous laws for interpretive guidance. However, many of those were similarly ambiguous. The PATRIOT Act's Section 1016(e), for example, defined the term as "systems and assets, whether physical or virtual, so vital to the United States that the incapacity or destruction of such systems and assets would have a debilitating impact on security, national economic security, national public health or safety, or any combination of those matters." As with the CIIA, FOIA officers were left with a nearly boundless set of possible targets. Which private "systems and assets," if harmed, would hurt national or economic security, they wondered, or public health and safety? Which would not? Which kinds of destruction would only affect local economic security and public health and safety, and which would be national in scope?[35]

President Clinton's definition of CII in a 1996 executive order was more specific, focusing on "telecommunications; electrical power systems; gas and oil storage and transportation; banking and finance; transportation; water supply systems; emergency services (including medical, police, fire, and rescue); and continuity of government." Bush too had developed a list of more specific CII categories, weeks after 9/11:

1. Energy production, transmission, and distribution services and critical facilities;
2. Other utilities;
3. Facilities that produce, use, store, or dispose of nuclear material;
4. Public and privately owned information systems;
5. Major events (at publicly and privately owned facilities);
6. Transportation, including railways, highways, shipping ports, waterways, airports, and civilian aircraft;
7. Livestock, agriculture, and systems for the provision of water and food for human use and consumption; and
8. Other critical infrastructure services and critical facilities within the United States needing protection from terrorist attack

It is difficult to imagine parts of American daily life *not* covered by that list. Bush left it up to "appropriate senior officials" to interpret categories as they saw fit. Which "major events . . . at publicly and privately owned facilities" had "national significance"? People like DHS secretary Michael Chertoff and FBI director Louis Freeh would decide. What kinds of information about "livestock, agriculture, and systems for the provision of water and food for human use and consumption" deserved protections? Senior officials at the US Department of Agriculture (USDA) would decide (see chapter 7 for several reasons why this might be problematic).[36]

The reach of the CIIA triggered one set of problems. The law's designated process for selecting information triggered another. The process at first glance seemed straightforward enough. Individuals or organizations could voluntarily submit threat assessments for information they believed worthy of government protection. DHS then determined whether to make the information "protected critical infrastructure information" (PCII). Federal agencies could also independently submit to the DHS information they had previously received from private interests, with or without the knowledge or consent of those interests.[37]

Ideally, private interests sought protection when they thought, in good faith, that their information would harm national security if disclosed. But private interests often have more self-serving reasons for working with the government. Profit-seeking corporations, for example, routinely try to influence policy-making processes to restrict market competition or otherwise obtain exclusive benefits. The pervasiveness of this rent seeking is widely acknowledged by political observers from across the ideological spectrum. There is no reason why the CIIA would be immune from rent seeking or other unsavory parts of interest group politics. Indeed, the CIIA offered corporations and other private interests an almost ideal mechanism for concealing potentially costly information from market competitors, consumers, activists, and would-be plaintiffs. Sometimes information can reduce monopoly rents, harm reputations, turn off consumers, or trigger lawsuits, so why *wouldn't* private interests have the government conceal that kind of information if they could? A corporation drilling for natural gas with hydraulic fracturing ("fracking") techniques might, therefore, plausibly convince officials that chemicals used in the process needed to be kept secret for national security purposes (since terrorists could steal chemicals for weapons or simply explode drilling sites). Once an energy and drilling company convinced the DHS to make fracking chemicals PCII, the company could better avoid public scrutiny—

and lawsuits—related to what many consider to be a serious environmental health threat. Plus, under the CIIA, private sector interests enjoyed civil liability immunity protections for anything involving the PCII, unless they gave formal consent to litigants. The frackers would thus enjoy the secrecy as well as extra layers of legal immunity. The CIAA also prevented agencies from using PCII to enforce regulations, an added bonus to private interests. Overall, the CIIA offered private interests an invaluable new tool to seek rents and keep information hidden. For self-interested business concerns, the CIIA was a gift that kept on giving.[38]

For all these reasons, the CIIA might indeed have represented "the most severe weakening of the [FOIA] in its 36-year history," as Sen. Patrick Leahy (D-VT)—generally not one given to hyperbole—put it. By contrast, CIIA backers, such as Sen. Robert Bennett (R-ID), accused Leahy and other critics of being "paranoid" individuals who adopted an overly expansive reading of the law. The extent to which an "overly expansive" use of the CIIA contributed to the marked growth in redacted FOIA responses (Figure 3.1) from 2002 to 2008 remains unknown and unknowable. But as this book repeatedly shows, American history is rife with examples of officials exploiting new secrecy tools like the CIIA.[39]

Protecting Avocado Importers, Watermelon Growers, and Tire Companies

The CIIA was just one of many sunshine-era statutes that "protected" new categories of unclassified information from citizens' FOIA requests. FOIA explicitly authorized Congress to designate new protected information categories in statutes—essentially letting politicians fill the open, flexible Exemption 3 with whatever they desired. Shocking as it may seem, presidents and legislators found many uses for Exemption 3. Few citizens noticed when they buried new statutory exemptions deep within bills. Indeed, the process allowed them to expand the secrecy system with relative ease, without the political costs sometimes associated with such efforts. In 2008–2009 alone, agencies used 172 of what the law calls b(3) exemptions (5 USC § 552 (b) (3)), according to a *ProPublica* study. Some b(3)'s are uncontroversial and redundant. For example, one protects intelligence sources and methods, information already classifiable and covered by Exemption 1. But many of the other 171 statutes are more than a little puzzling, among them the Hass Avocado Promotion, Research, and Information Act, which contained a new b(3) exemption letting agencies reject FOIA requests about avocado imports. Another b(3)-wielding law authorized officials to deny FOIA requests about "watermelon growers and handlers." It is hard to escape the stench of ordinary interest group politics covering much of the list of 171 b(3)'s.[40]

When adding new b(3) exemptions proved too politically difficult (due, say, to partisan opposition in Congress), presidents and their administrations used unilateral methods to achieve the same goal. Take Bush-Cheney's efforts to void a popular law's consumer safety reporting requirements. In 2000, Congress passed the TREAD (Transportation Recall Enhancement, Accountability and Documentation) Act, following a spate of deadly automobile accidents caused by faulty Firestone tires on Fords. The accidents killed over 200 and injured thousands. One part of the TREAD Act required motor vehicle manufacturers to provide early-warning safety information to the government, which would then publish it. The TREAD Act also required disclosure when the corporations discovered recurring problems (such as faulty brakes) through customer complaints, warranty claims, or other reporting methods. The law thus promised more public safety as well as real corporate accountability. Ford and Firestone apparently had known about the safety defects for years but decided to keep selling their defective, injurious products. The TREAD Act's disclosure requirements corrected the information asymmetry.[41]

But less than three years after the law passed, a little-noticed regulatory change gutted its disclosure requirements. The National Highway Traffic Safety Administration (NHTSA) quietly announced in 2003 that federal agencies could withhold from FOIA requests the same safety and performance information the law guaranteed. For the relatively few who noticed the NHTSA's announcement, officials framed the move as an effort to increase business competition: consumer access to the information placed companies making dangerous products at a competitive disadvantage. At least they were honest about their priorities. But clearly, the secrecy had nothing to do with national security, personal privacy, active law enforcement investigations, confidential presidential communications, or even legitimate trade secrets—the justifications usually given.[42]

Summary

However potent the FOIA may still be, the sunshine era is littered with political efforts that have effectively weakened it. Although different administrations have tilted the system toward or away from transparency with new discretionary rules (such as the Smith and Ashcroft Memos versus the Reno Memo), all have used various methods to expand the list of exempted unclassified information categories, often with the support of large congressional majorities. FOIA's text is part of the problem. Some of the exemptions are intrinsically ambiguous, giving officials quite a bit of leeway to interpret contested concepts like national security. Exemption b(5) lets officials shield just about anything ("inter or intra agency communication") by citing the *deliberative process* privilege. And exemption b(3), as we have seen, invites Congress to protect altogether new and specific categories. Most Americans would surely be grateful to know that their representatives have been working hard to protect from FOIA requesters the vital secrets of the watermelon and avocado industries. Though the changes to FOIA were numerous and substantial, all kept the basic structure of FOIA intact. None of the sunshine-era administrations, not even the ones claiming to favor secrecy, acted like Mahoney and Thelen's "insurrectionaries," who scrap institutions and start afresh. All instead used existing tools to build atop the status quo, adding and tweaking layers and incrementally expanding the boundaries of the secrecy system.[43]

Given the level of (sincere or cowering) bipartisan support Bush-Cheney officials had during the unsettled times after 9/11 and given their preference for secrecy, their restraint might strike some as surprising. Why just expand b(3)'s and add other layers to the FOIA? Why even play word games or use other circumvention tactics? Why not just eviscerate the laws that inhibited "unitary executive" action (see chapter 2), especially those that related to counterterrorism and Iraq? There are several possible reasons why the Bush-Cheney team never became insurrectionaries for institutional change.

First, as we have seen, previous administrations using a variety of tactics had already reconfigured the sunshine-era secrecy system, giving presidents plenty of leeway and tools to conceal information. Second, tweaking the system was not difficult, especially during unsettled times in the name of national security. Even outside of critical junctures, presidents could count on Congress to grant them more secrecy powers. Legislators did so for a range of reasons: to burnish their hawkish credentials, to serve their benefactors (such as avocado importers or defense contractors), or to sincerely (as they saw it) improve governance and maximize national security. Whatever their motivations, members of Congress have tended to reliably support or at least tolerate new statutory layers added onto FOIA and other parts of the secrecy system, as we will continue to see.

A third reason why senior Bush-Cheney officials probably did not act like insurrectionaries involves the availability of unilateral administrative action. Even when administrations encountered legislative resistance or just did not feel like making the legislative effort, senior officials could issue administrative orders to achieve some of the same ends (such as scrapping the TREAD Act's disclosure requirements). Doing so is typically easier than working with Congress. And it is far quieter, attracting less public notice.

Finally, many citizens in the sunshine era, like their Revolutionary era predecessors (see chapter 2), continued to see open government as an integral part of representative democracy. Even when individuals never personally used FOIA, they tended to recognize it as a cornerstone of the contemporary system. For instance, 62 percent of Americans in a 2006 survey agreed that "public access to government records is critical to the functioning of good government." Only about 5 percent believed FOIA and other sunshine laws provided "too much access." The political costs of trying to roll back the laws—especially FOIA—were high enough to dissuade any rational politician from trying. There is no evidence any of the administrations ever considered it, probably for that reason alone. Any public argument for rescinding FOIA would be deeply complicated by the fact that the law covers a lot of information outside the security realm, from consumer safety to environmental regulations and beyond. Prosecrecy arguments usually rest on national security justifications. Tossing FOIA aside would strike many as throwing the baby out with the bathwater. Plus, unorganized and well-organized interests would have many reasons to oppose such a move.[44]

Overall, senior Bush-Cheney officials—like those from all administrations—probably found their transparency requirements annoying but manageable. Existing secrecy tools were plentiful, and new ones, through legislative or administrative actions supported by the courts, were not politically difficult to construct, especially in the name of national security. All those additions to the sunshine-era legal framework carved out new exemptions and thus new opportiunities for secrecy. And so far, we have barely broached the subject of *classified* information.

Classified Information

Of all the sunshine-era administrations, Clinton-Gore worked the hardest to reform a classification system many believed needed serious repairs. A procession of government committees since the 1950s, staffed by medaled army generals and other entrenched insiders, agreed unanimously about a chronic overclassification problem (see chapter 2). Lawsuits revealed the army stubbornly refused to declassify documents with questionable contemporary military value, like the one from 1917 discussing World War I troop movements. For a variety of reasons—the Cold War's end, an ideological preference for open government—Clinton-Gore took a few strong swipes at the system in 1995. For a little while, the efforts seemed to pay off.[45]

Clinton's Executive Order 12958 was very much a break from the past, revising procedures in place since Reagan issued Executive Order 12356 in 1982. Emphasizing the new national security context following the Soviet Union's 1991 collapse, Clinton announced the time had come for change: "Protecting information critical to our Nation's security remains a priority. In recent years, however, dramatic changes have altered, although not eliminated, the national security threats that we confront. These changes provide a greater opportunity to emphasize our commitment to open Government." This was, for once, not mere rhetoric. For the first time in the sunshine era, the president asked classification officers to adopt a presumption of openness. Like the Reno Memo for FOIA administration, Clinton's Order 12958 asked information workers to flip their risk-averse decision formulas on their heads, focusing instead on why information should *not* be released to the public: "If there is significant doubt about the need to classify information, it shall not be classified." If they followed his directions, classification authorities should have marked fewer documents with the long-concealing stamps of top secret, secret, and confidential.[46]

On top of establishing new decision standards for new information, Clinton launched a major declassification program, ordering departments and agencies to evaluate all their records and to release everything no longer deserving their classified markings. Together with new laws bookending Clinton's two terms—the President John F. Kennedy Assassination Records Collection Act of 1992, the Nazi War Crimes Disclosure Act of 1998, and the Japanese Imperial Government Disclosure Act of 2000—the program led to the unprecedented declassification of millions of pages. Indeed, the initiative likely freed *over 500 million more* pages than agencies would have otherwise released (Figure 3.2). The emergence of the Internet in the 1990s made this avalanche of documents even more significant, by vastly expanding information dissemination opportunities.[47]

Why did the declassification wave begin to wane near the end of Clinton's second term? One possibility is distinctly apolitical: agencies may have just

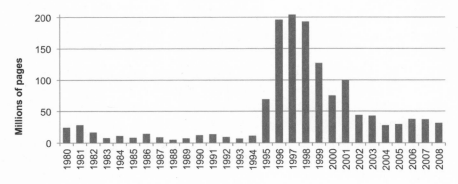

FIGURE 3.2
Declassified Pages, 1980–2008.
Source: 1997 and 2010 ISOO Reports to the President

completed their declassification review processes, releasing all they could by 1999 and 2000. Another possibility might highlight Max Weber's "sure power instinct." By 1999, Clinton-Gore veterans were deeply immersed in the secret world they inhabited, internalizing and accepting its culture of secrecy and enjoying the power it bestowed. Perhaps the White House quietly asked agencies to slow down—to de-prioritize the declassification process, causing the decline shown in Figure 3.2.

Or perhaps Clinton's sense of the "national security threats that we confront" changed substantially after his 1995 order. The administration, after all, was actively waging war in the Balkans, engaging in low-intensity combat in Iraq's no-fly zones, and grappling with the emerging threat from Al Qaeda and Egyptian Islamic Jihad, which bombed the US embassies in Kenya and Tanzania in August 1998, killing 223 and injuring thousands. Back in 1995, the world may have seemed relatively less fraught.[48]

All those reasons probably contributed to the decline. Plus, Clinton faced strong internal resistance to his reformist efforts. Senior officials at the CIA, the DIA, and other intelligence agencies expressed their opposition to the 1995 executive order right away, warning of the dangers of releasing sensitive, sometimes "seemingly innocuous," information. Still, they gritted their teeth and complied, growing increasingly uneasy. By 1999, six agencies had had enough, and they decided to push back. Not content to merely stem the flow, they launched their own *re*classification program, in an effort to scoop some of the secrets back up.[49]

A number of their concerns were understandable. For example, someone along the way had declassified documents instructing readers about the proper use of high explosives. Those documents probably should have remained classified. The same goes for State Department telexes filled with detailed information about the overseas locations of US nuclear weapons from the early 1970s. Other declassifications may have even contributed to a Chinese spying operation at the Department of Energy (DOE). Clinton-Gore officials' fixation on nuclear engineer Wen Ho Lee, whom they accused of spying, turned out to be baseless. Lee was acquitted of 58 of 59 charges leveled against him (the only charge that stuck was for mishandling sensitive computer files). However, *something* seems to have gone awry at DOE, leading Energy Secretary Bill Richardson to close his department's declassification program in 1999. Other agencies followed the DOE's lead, as senior officials wondered what else had slipped through the cracks.[50]

In fact, information officers researched that question and found *a miniscule amount* of sensitive information fell through the cracks. A DOE group examined 700,000 declassified documents (the State Department telexes), finding only 9 (0.0013 percent) worthy of contemporary concern. But those 9 would have been useless to terrorists or other enemies. Instead, they probably just angered allies, who learned the United States once secretly put nuclear weapons inside their borders.[51]

Unsurprisingly (given the system's default overclassification position), quite a bit of the information that was scooped back up should have stayed declassified. ISOO head J. William Leonard closely examined 16 reclassified documents from intelligence agencies and found none deserving of reclassification. It is not unreasonable to generalize from that analysis, given the history of overclassification. The agencies' response to a few declassification mistake—reclassification—was thus out of proportion to the problem, although the program may have only recovered some 55,000 documents. Ironically, as agencies scrambled to reclassify harmless information, other documents probably deserving classification remained available. Thus, technical documents about chemical and biological weapons, how-to guides about making explosives with common ingredients, and World War II–era sabotage manuals all remained on the open shelves of the National Archives through (at least) early 2006.[52]

Examples of Overclassification

On top of its many other benefits, Clinton's declassification program offered further evidence of a long-broken secrecy system. Many liberated documents showed a widespread disregard for presidents' classification guidelines. Some revealed how officials used the system to conceal government mishaps, misdeeds, and other embarrassments. For instance, one 1950 document showed the CIA as a rather unreliable predictor of world events, stating: "*Chinese Communist intervention in Korea* must be regarded as a continuing possibility, a consideration of all known factors lends to the conclusion that barring a Soviet decision for global war, such action *is not probable in 1950*." Of course, about two weeks after the CIA circulated that intelligence estimate, 300,000 Chinese soldiers entered Korea.

One could argue the government has a strategic interest in hiding its bad predictions (that is, its incompetence). The CIA, so the argument goes, must develop a reputation for omniscience and infallibility. However, we must weigh those reputational benefits against the right of citizens to access legitimately free information. Plus, officials could easily use the justification (*Let's hide these embarrassments for the greater good!*) for mostly self-serving and corrupt reasons.[53]

Sometimes, overclassification occurred for more puzzling reasons. Take, for instance, a two-page 1975 DIA biography of Augusto Pinochet, Chile's former authoritarian leader who rose to power in a 1973 US-sponsored coup d'état against the democratically elected president, Salvador Allende. That the biography was generally positive should not have been surprising, given the US role in bringing Pinochet to power. It also made sense, from the DIA's perspective, to keep the admiring biography secret, in light of the Nixon and Ford administrations' attempts to downplay the US role in the coup, as well as their continued support for the repressive dictator. Still, the details were hardly explosive, focusing on Pinochet's mundane habits and preferences. DIA analysts painted a picture of Pinochet as "intelligent . . . widely admired and respected . . . very honest, hard working, dedicated." He was "a devoted, tolerant husband and father," who "live[d] very modestly" and "respond[ed] to a frank, man-to-man approach." Given the biography's twenty-year classification, the DIA apparently believed US national security depended on hiding that Pinochet "like[d] parties," preferred "scotch and pisco sours," and enjoyed "fencing, boxing, and horseback riding." It is puzzling why the DIA believed Pinochet only "reluctantly . . . join[ed] in the military intervention" to oust elected Allende, "forced" by a "deteriorating economic and political situation." Perhaps the DIA wanted to paint Pinochet in a positive light for Ford and whoever would succeed him. Perhaps the CIA failed to share its operational details. In reality, Pinochet's coup coalition, along with its US backers, did all it could to instigate that deteriorating economic and political situation.[54]

Other leaks, lawsuits, and clever FOIA requests revealed examples of inexplicable secrecy. The government refused to release General Eisenhower's World War II weather reports for at least thirty years. The DOD clung to a "top secret" document from Jimmy Carter's failed Iran hostage rescue attempt . . . about milk. The air force told pilots not to pack milk for lunch because it would likely spoil.[55]

Bush-Cheney: Reverting Back to Reagan-Bush, with a Dash of Nixon and a Few New Tweaks

Up until March 25, 2003, the Bush-Cheney administration adhered to Clinton-Gore's revamped classification system. On declassification, they even (given their reputation for secrecy) outperformed most of their predecessors, including Clinton-Gore before 1995. The timing of Bush's Executive Order 13292 was actually a coincidence, despite appearing like a desperate attempt to implement it for the Iraq War.[56]

At first glance, Executive Order 13292 appears not to diverge too sharply from Clinton's order. Indeed, Bush kept much of the structure and language of the older order intact. A closer look at the new rules and definitions scattered throughout, however, reveals some significant differences.[57]

For one, Bush immediately shut down Clinton's declassification program. His administration still declassified, but it released documents much more slowly and selectively and sometimes for obviously self-interested political reasons. That is, Bush officials selectively declassified bits of information to help them win political arguments. For example, during the run-up to the Iraq War, Bush ordered Cheney to declassify and disseminate sections of the October 2002 National Intelligence Estimate (NIE) that appeared to corroborate their claims that Saddam Hussein had ongoing WMD programs. Other parts of the document, less supportive of the official story, were kept classified. After the invasion of Iraq, when former ambassador Joseph C. Wilson IV and others challenged the WMD claims, the White House declassified and disseminated another politically helpful portion of the NIE, leaving sections highlighting intelligence agencies' uncertainty still redacted. On several other occasions—as when they sought to discredit 9/11 commissioner and former Clinton staffer Jamie Gorlick's counterterrorism credentials, to undercut congressional oversight efforts on surveillance policy, and to bolster their arguments in other counterterrorism debates—Bush, Cheney, and National Security Adviser Condoleezza Rice selectively declassified information when it was politically useful. This was not a new tactic; they borrowed from Nixon's playbook. But it clearly represented a break from Clinton-Gore practices, which were at the very least less selective (Figure 3.2).[58]

Bush's order also formalized and strengthened the *re*classification program the intelligence agencies quietly inititated in 1999. Not only did they turn the spigot off, they also tried, often in vain, to reverse the flow. Historians who filed FOIA requests received documents covered with redactions, even though the blacked-out parts had earlier been published. Government officials even tried to reconceal Pinochet's bland biography, redacting some of the most mundane details (Figure 3.3). The public was allowed to (still) know that he "ha[d] a mustache; [wore] glasses for reading; [and was] quiet"; that he was "charming, attractive; socially at ease"; that his "family [was] very close"; and that he had "long been interested in and directed a Catholic assistance program for illegitimate children." But the description of him as "mild-mannered; very businesslike. Very honest [etc.]" was kept from the public. Also too sensitive was the bit about the pisco sours, as well as his penchant for fencing and the fact that he "enjoy[ed] discussing world military problems and would respond to a frank, man-to-man approach." Officials even reclassified his small black-and-white photograph, as if he had a covert identity. Only a few details—such as his alleged slur of another military officer ("lackey")—might be interpreted as remotely sensitive, although that incident happened in 1973 and involved a man who died a year later (Gen. Carlos Prats Gonzales). Anyone with an Internet connection could compare the documents. Rep. Christopher Shays (R-CT) probably put it best, calling the (bipartisan) reclassification program an "absurd effort to put the toothpaste back into the tube." However absurd it was, Bush's reclassification effort was far from unprecedented: the order restored Reagan's policy that had remained in force until Clinton eliminated it in 1995.[59]

Beyond de- and reclassification, Bush's order changed the rules in important ways. It was the first order to grant the vice president original classification authority (through "top secret"), giving Cheney and his successors the power to make new secrets (§ 1.3 (a)(1), (c)(2–3)). Furthermore, it gave vice presidents and selected aides the right to view classified information after leaving the White House (§ 4.4 (a)(2–3)). And it granted CIA directors the authority to veto declassification decisions previously made by the head of the Interagency Security Classification Appeals Panel (ISCAP), a unit Clinton created to evaluate citizens' appeals of classification decisions (§ 5.3 (f)).

In addition, Bush's order added "transnational terrorism" as a specific category of national security threats, and it created two new classification categories: (1) information provided by foreign governments "in confidence," and (2) "infrastructures" and "protection services" relating to national security, which built upon Clinton's similarly vague concern for "vulnerabilities or capabilities of systems, installations, projects or plans" (§ 1.4, § 6.1 (r)(1–2)). Bush's "infrastructures" category was related to the unclassified "critical infrastructure information" discussed earlier, but being a classification category, it obviously involved more sensitive information. Last of all, Bush reversed Clinton's presumption-of-openness standard—bringing the government back to Reagan's 1982 guidelines. It is worth noting that Bush retained Clinton's mosaic theory of classifying unclassified information (§ 1.7(e)).[60]

Comparing Sunshine Era Classification Records

The ISOO has fortunately monitored classification activity for decades, allowing us to compare administrations' records. Alas, data reliability problems truncate the analytical possibilities. The ISOO substantially revised its sampling methodology in 1985, making comparisons with the pre-1985 period problematic. Then, the ISOO announced in 1989 that its data from 1985 to 1988 were also unreliable due to sampling and reporting problems within the DOD, especially the navy. Although leaving the DOD out would bring its own set of reliability problems, that option was not possible because the ISOO released data in aggregated form (that is, not for each agency separately). For these reasons, the figures that follow only display data since 1989, the year when reliable, high-quality data first became available. Also keep in mind that patterns of classification activity have multiple causes, such as changes in the political environment (for instance, new security threats) or new decision guidelines (the executive orders). Administrations also vary in terms of their cooperation with the ISOO. Vice President Cheney, for example, refused to report his office's classification activity to the ISOO starting in 2002. Cheney defended his action by arguing that the vice president was not technically part of the executive branch, given his role as Senate president.[61]

Figures 3.4 through 3.6 trace top secret, secret, and confidential classification activity from Bush-Quayle to Bush-Cheney. Figure 3.7, which combines

SECRET

BIOGRAPHIC DATA

CHILE
Gen Augusto PINOCHET Ugarte
January 1975

(U) NAME: Gen Augusto Pinochet Ugarte
(pee-noh-CHET), Army.

(U) POSITION: President (chief of state since 12
Sept 1973; position officially named President of
the Government Junta, 12 Sept 1973-June 1974;
Supreme Chief of the Nation and Head of the
Executive Branch June-Dec 1974; President since 18
Dec 1974); and Commander in Chief of the Army (since
24 Aug 1973).

(U) 1973

(S/NFD)

He became President and the strongest member of the
Government Junta (composed of the four service commanders) following the
11 Sept 1973 military coup, the first in Chile since 1931, which overthrew
the government of Marxist-Socialist Salvador Allende Gossens (President,
1970-1973). In June 1974, the Junta structure changed and Pinochet became
head of the executive branch of the government, while continuing as head of
the Junta, which became the legislative branch.
(b)(1)

The Junta abolished Congress and all political
parties but claims to be moving towards a return to democracy. It is
most concerned with rebuilding Chile, especially the economy;
(b)(1)

(S/NFD) POLITICS:

(S/NFD) International:
(b)(1)

He shares the common concern of most
Chilean Army officers over the threat of a possible invasion of Chile by
Peru. Pinochet has served as an Instructor at the Ecuadorean Army War
College and has travelled to Mexico and the Canal Zone.

UNCLASSIFIED

NO FOREIGN DISSEM
SECRET

SECRET

(V21)

BIOGRAPHIC DATA

CHILE
Gen Augusto PINOCHET Ugarte
January 1975

(U) NAME: Gen Augusto Pinochet Ugarte
(pee-noh-CHET), Army.

(U) POSITION: President (chief of state since 12
Sept 1973; position officially named President of
the Government Junta, 12 Sept 1973-June 1974;
Supreme Chief of the Nation and Head of the
Executive Branch June-Dec 1974; President since 18
Dec 1974); and Commander in Chief of the Army (since
24 Aug 1973).

(U) 1973

(S/NFD) SIGNIFICANCE: Gen Pinochet, an intelligent,
ambitious, professionally competent and experienced
Infantry officer, is widely admired and respected by
fellow officers. He became President and the strongest member of the
Government Junta (composed of the four service commanders) following the
11 Sept 1973 military coup, the first in Chile since 1931, which overthrew
the government of Marxist-Socialist Salvador Allende Gossens (President,
1970-1973). In June 1974, the Junta structure changed and Pinochet became
head of the executive branch of the government, while continuing as head of
the Junta, which became the legislative branch. Gen Pinochet would have
preferred that the Armed Forces, and particularly the Army, remain in
their traditional role as a professional, apolitical force that does not
involve itself with partisan politics. The deteriorating economic and
political situation, however, forced Pinochet reluctantly to join in the
military intervention. The Junta abolished Congress and all political
parties but claims to be moving towards a return to democracy. It is
most concerned with rebuilding Chile, especially the economy; obtaining
foreign arms purchases and making other preparations against the threat of
war with Peru; and improving Chile's world image regarding human rights.

(S/NFD) POLITICS:

(C/NFD) International: Anti-Communist and anti-Cuban, Gen
Pinochet has always spoken favorably of, and desires to keep close ties
with, the United States. He has twice travelled to the U.S. He favors
the acquisition of U.S. equipment and the training of Chilean military
personnel in U.S. service schools. He shares the common concern of most
Chilean Army officers over the threat of a possible invasion of Chile by
Peru. Pinochet has served as an Instructor at the Ecuadorean Army War
College and has travelled to Mexico and the Canal Zone.

UNCLASSIFIED

CLASSIFIED BY   DI
EXEMPT FROM GENERAL DECLASSIFICATION
SCHEDULE OF EXECUTIVE ORDER 11652
EXEMPTION CATEGORY
DECLASSIFY ON   31 Dec 2005

NO FOREIGN DISSEM
SECRET

Declassified by DIA

CHILE
Gen Augusto PINOCHET Ugarte
January 1975

(S/NFD)

(b)(1)

(C/NFD) PERSONAL DATA:

(U) Birth: 25 Nov 1915 in Valparaíso, Chile.

(C/NFD) Family: Wife, Lucía Hieriart Rodríguez de Pinochet (born about 1926; of French ancestry; Roman Catholic; married about 1943;

(b)(1)
(b)(6)

about 1944 | born about 1946 | Children (5): Lucía (f), born Augusto (m),
1950 | ; María Verónica (f), born about
1957; Jacqueline Marie (f), born about 1959. | Marco Antonio (m), born about

(C/NFD) Description: Caucasian. Large build (5'10", 180 lbs); dark brown hair, green eyes, oval face; fair complexion; has a mustache; wears glasses for reading; quiet;

(b)(1)

Member of Geographic Society of Chile. He is well known as a military geographer and has authored three geography books, at least one of which is used as a secondary-school textbook.

(b)(1)

(U) Languages: Native Spanish, some French and English.

(U) Religion: Roman Catholic.

(U) Decorations: Colombian Order of Merit General José María Córdoba. Ecuadorean Abdón Calderón Star (Gold). Peruvian Military Order of Ayacucho. Chilean Military Star of the Armed Forces (Grand Star for Military Merit, for 30 years' service); Goddess Minerva Medal; Minerva Medal.

UNCLASSIFIED

SECRET

CHILE
Gen Augusto PINOCHET Ugarte
January 1975

(S/NFD) Internal: Gen Pinochet is conservative in his political thinking. It is believed that he remained basically apolitical during the administration of President Allende, viewing the government as legally and constitutionally elected. Pinochet enjoyed the complete confidence of Eduardo Frei Montalva (President, 1964-1970).

(C/NFD) PERSONAL DATA:

(U) Birth: 25 Nov 1915 in Valparaíso, Chile.

(C/NFD) Family: Wife, Lucía Hieriart Rodríguez de Pinochet (born about 1926; of French ancestry; Roman Catholic; married about 1943; charming, attractive; socially at ease; family is very close; has long been interested in and directed a Catholic assistance program for illegitimate children; in 1973 allegedly strongly denounced the then Army Commander in Chief, Carlos Prats Gonzáles, for his "lackey" relationship with President Allende). Children (5): Lucía (f), born about 1944 (married; is an infant-welfare specialist); Augusto (m), born about 1946 (a military officer); María Verónica (f), born about 1950 (married; is a computer programmer); Marco Antonio (m), born about 1957; Jacqueline Marie (f), born about 1959. One daughter lived with her husband, an engineer, in Panama.

(C/NFD) Description: Caucasian. Large build (5'10", 180 lbs); dark brown hair, green eyes, oval face; fair complexion; has a mustache; wears glasses for reading; quiet; mild-mannered; very businesslike. Very honest, hard working, dedicated. A devoted, tolerant husband and father; lives very modestly. Drinks scotch and pisco sours; smokes cigarettes; likes parties. Sports interests are fencing, boxing, and horseback riding. Member of Geographic Society of Chile. He is well known as a military geographer and has authored three geography books, at least one of which is used as a secondary-school textbook. Enjoys discussing world military problems and would respond to a frank, man-to-man approach.

(U) Languages: Native Spanish, some French and English.

(U) Religion: Roman Catholic.

(U) Decorations: Colombian Order of Merit General José María Córdoba. Ecuadorean Abdón Calderón Star (Gold). Peruvian Military Order of Ayacucho. Chilean Military Star of the Armed Forces (Grand Star for Military Merit, for 30 years' service); Goddess Minerva Medal; Minerva Medal.

FIGURE 3.3
DIA Pinochet Biography (1975),
before and after Reclassification
Source: National Security Archive.

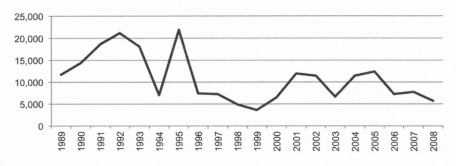

FIGURE 3.4
Top Secret Original Classification Decisions

those categories, shows very clearly that Bush-Quayle surpassed its successor administrations in overall classifications, with 500,000 original classifications per year, across all four years (1989–1992). When Clinton-Gore took over in 1993, the number dropped precipitously, remaining below 250,000 per year throughout both terms. Clinton's 1995 executive order preceded a substantial but comparatively modest drop in 1996, followed by a return to the 1993–1995 status quo and then a slow but steady rise back to 1993 levels. The presumption-of-openness order apparently generated none of its intended effects. If anything, classification authorities moved in the opposite direction. Also notice the unusual spike in top secret markings in 1995 (the year of the order), besting Bush-Quayle's record high from 1992.

Bush-Cheney officials appear to have generally maintained the combined levels from the late Clinton-Gore administration, with 2004 as an obvious

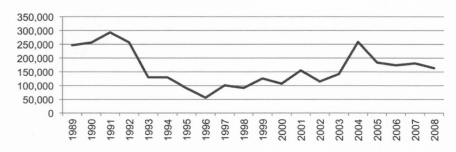

FIGURE 3.5
Secret Original Classification Decisions

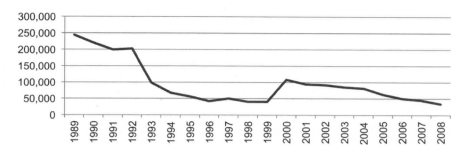

FIGURE 3.6
Confidential Original Classification Decisions

outlier. But notice that the administration steadily reduced confidential mark-ing across both terms, while increasing secret designations. That is, the decline in confidential classifications was partially offset by an increase in secret ones.

Altogether, the averages were as follows: Bush-Quayle classified on average 165,457 a year, compared with Clinton-Gore's 58,760 and Bush-Cheney's 80,526. Far from being "unprecedented" in the scale of its classification ac-tivity, as critics often charged, the Bush-Cheney administration classified many fewer pages than Bush-Quayle and not that many more than Clin-ton-Gore. Even during the first few years of the so-called global war on terror, the younger Bush's administration classified no more than half the number classified by his father's administration, including in 1992 when Bush, Sr., declared victory in the Cold War.

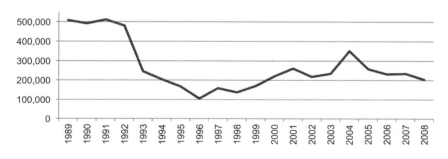

FIGURE 3.7
Total Original Classification Activity, 1989–2008

TABLE 3.1
Original Classification Activity by Agency, 2009

Department of the Army	75,080
Department of State	55,224
Department of Justice	48,950
Executive Office of the President	1,609
Department of Defense	967
Department of the Air Force	665
Department of the Navy	502
Department of Homeland Security	178
Department of Agriculture	25
Department of Treasury	10
Central Intelligence Agency	4
Millennium Challenge Corporation	4
Department of Health and Human Services	2
Office of the Director of National Intelligence	2
US Agency for International Development	1
Department of Commerce	1

Source: ISOO 2009.

Counting Other Kinds of Secrets

In addition to the caveats about data quality noted previously, there are reasons to be cautious when drawing too many conclusions about administrations' overall secrecy records from the original classification data. First, the ISOO does not record other kinds of secrets, such as those in the unclassified SBU category discussed earlier. Second, there is the issue of "derivative classification decisions." The government generally discounts the importance of derivative decisions. The ISOO, for instance, has claimed original classification decisions are "in essence . . . the only new 'secrets.'" However, take a look at Table 3.1, which compares agencies' original classification rates using ISOO data from 2009.

That the CIA classified just *four* documents during 2009 might seem puzzling, possibly even a typo. Yet the following year's report indicated the number was no aberration: the CIA officially classified just *five* documents in 2010. The table also shows strange numbers for other agencies (for example, only ten for Treasury). The explanation—which leaves as many questions as answers—involves the variation in agencies' classification procedures. Each agency compiles a security classification guide (SCG), which becomes a "source document" for derivative classification decisions. But agencies' SCGs vary widely in

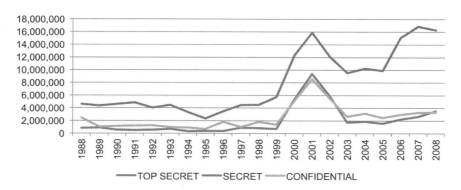

FIGURE 3.8
Derivative Classification Decisions, by Category

their level of detail. The CIA's is exceptionally detailed, which means it covers most of the agency's classifiable information *ex ante*. Therefore, because of its SCG, the CIA makes very few original classification decisions, instead using the guide to derivatively classify most of its secrets. The State Department, by contrast, does not produce a very detailed SCG, which leads it to originate classified information comparatively more frequently and derivately classify information less frequently. So, one analytical problem comes from interagency variation in SCGs. Another results from the fact that agencies can rewrite their SCGs at their discretion, and the ISOO does not publish data about that kind of variation. Thus, we cannot assume stability of SCGs from year to year.

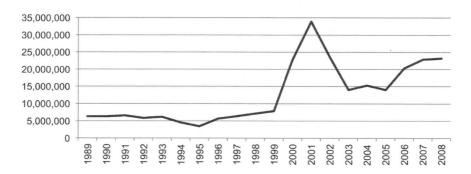

FIGURE 3.9
Total Derivative Classification Decisions

Overall, over-time comparisons using aggregated agency data need to be taken with a grain of salt. Perhaps more important, the ISOO's original classification data do not really include some of the government's primary classifiers, such as the CIA and the Treasury Department. Those agencies rely almost exclusively on derivative classifications based on the SCGs.[62]

The government defines *derivative classification activity* as "incorporating, paraphrasing, restating, or generating in new form information that is already classified and, therefore, are not considered new 'secrets.'" If that is true, we should treat the many millions of classification decisions depicted in Figures 3.8 and 3.9 as an empirical footnote. Consequently, the fact that derivative classification activity soared to record heights during the Bush-Cheney administration should not affect our comparative analysis. The unprecedented *34 million* derivative classification actions in 2001 mean little, according to the definition. Perhaps they just made lots of copies that year.[63]

To put that number in perspective: in 2001, agencies made 92,862 derivative classification decisions on average every day. That is 3,869 decisions every hour, or about 64 every minute. Though the Bush-Cheney administration broke records in 2001, its predecessors started the rally in 2000, with a number (22,744,437) that was more than three times higher than anything Bush-Quayle mustered and higher than most of the totals from the Bush-Cheney years.

Part of the over-time increase resulted from agencies' growing use of new communication technologies for sharing classified information, including "classified web pages, blogs, wikis, bulletin boards, instant messaging, etc." When a piece of information is originally classified in one medium, it needs to be derivatively classified when it appears in another. The growth of new technologies without corresponding governmentwide standards also led to a lot of variation across agencies, with some, for instance, counting all the derivatively classified "reply to" or "forwarded" e-mails and others not. However, technological changes and resulting agency behavior cannot fully explain why the number of derivative classifications spiked in 2000 through 2002, retreated in 2003 through 2005, and then sharply rose again in 2006 through 2008.[64]

Another likely cause of the increase seen during late Clinton-Gore through Bush-Cheney involves the growth of the public-private national security state. Anyone with even minimal security clearances can derivatively classify, including government contractors. For homeland security, counterterrorism, and intelligence matters alone (in 2009), this included individuals working in 1,271 government agencies and 1,931 private companies in approximately

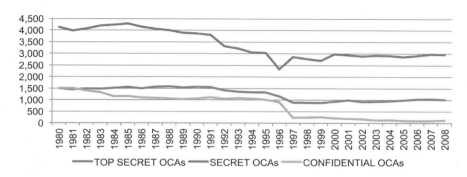

FIGURE 3.10
Original Classification Authorities, 1980–2008

10,000 locations across the country. About 854,000 of these individuals had top secret clearances. Millions more made derivative classification decisions. The ACLU estimated that those security workers made *99.66 percent* of all classification decisions. To the extent that was a problem (see the later discussion), it was not a new one. In 1997, original classification authorities (OCAs) made only about 6 percent of all classification decisions. More than 3 million others, inside and outside government, made the rest. The government does not publish data on what we might call derivative classification authorities (DCAs), but the growth of the national security state, with its associated clearances, is well documented.[65]

One problem with that growth concerns the huge variation in training. Indeed, having millions of undertrained public and private sector individuals making millions of classification decisions has led to millions of classification errors. The ISOO has acknowledged that systemic errors are rife within the system. In one study, the ISOO found 65 percent of sampled documents contained "discrepancies." Of the 1,019 error-ridden documents in its sample, there were 1,805 discrepancies. Some agencies had error rates above 90 percent. Most (three-fourths) had error rates above 50 percent. Though errors took many forms, the ISOO concluded that, overall, 35 percent of the documents were likely improperly classified. A more independent assessment (from outside the government) would probably find even more errors—whether those involved true mistakes; run-of-the-mill bureaucratic risk aversion; or efforts to conceal misdeeds, mishaps, and embarrassments.[66]

Expanding the field of private sector classifiers also exacerbates the secrecy system's inherent accountability problem (see chapter 2). Oversight and accountability mechanisms for public sector officials (such as those established by Congress or by the ISOO) are problematic enough. Monitoring millions of individuals scattered across the world is exponentially harder. So, the relative stability seen in Figure 3.10, which shows the number of OCAs over time, tells us little about how things have changed. For that, we would need to track numbers of derivative classifiers.

Finally, derivative classifications often sweep up information that would not otherwise be classified. Entire documents (reports, e-mails, and so forth) are frequently classified even when only a few pieces of information need protection. Like collateral damage in war, information sometimes becomes secret via derivative classification because it just happens to be in the proximity of the targeted operation. Of course, the potential for that kind of overclassification grows with the expansion of DCAs.[67]

Conclusion

As the preceding sections show, any comparative conclusions about administrations' secrecy records run up against a slew of analytical problems, many caused by the ISOO itself. However, no matter how frustrating the ISOO's shifting methodologies and incomplete definitions have been, the agency has maintained a sterling reputation for nonpartisanship, professionalism, and public service. The fact that the office has irritated power holders with its commitment to transparency suggests it is doing something right. For instance, when ISOO head J. William Leonard in 2007 attempted to audit Cheney's office (a routine function of the ISOO), the vice president refused Leonard's request. When Leonard persisted, David Addington, Cheney's chief of staff, responded with the kind of Bush-Cheney passive-aggressive behavior the next chapter repeatedly documents. To deal with what Cheney and Addington probably saw as Leonard's inappropriate encroachments on an executive branch official, Addington sent an e-mail to the a top administrator in the Office of Management and Budget (OMB), ordering her to eliminate all of Leonard's authorities, including the position of ISOO head itself, in Bush's Executive Order 13292: "Strike 'director of the Information Security Oversight Office' each place it appears." Although Bush-Cheney earned a tarnished reputation for actions like that, the ISOO's official interpretation of classification activity still shows that this administration was less secretive than Bush-Quayle. Clinton-Gore gets the bronze medal.[68]

The analysis presented in this chapter moved beyond mere quantitative comparisons. For example, we tracked presidents' different classification rules, some of which had material effects and lasting legacies. Bush-Quayle kept in place Reagan-Bush's classification guidelines, which tilted toward secrecy. Clinton-Gore, by contrast, introduced a presumption-of-openness standard, which seemed to have little influence over information workers in the trenches (that is, in their cubicles). Even if presidents' orders seemed to have limited effects, Bush-Cheney chose to revive Reagan-Bush rules and added a few secrecy-expanding parts to boot. For instance, Bush expanded the vice president's classification authority, and he gave Cheney, his successors, and their top aides access to classified information after leaving the White House. Bush's 2003 order also defanged Clinton's citizen-oriented Interagency Security Classification Appeals Panel, by granting veto authority to the CIA director on relevant ISCAP decisions. When Obama-Biden officials entered office in 2009, they inherited a system much like Clinton-Gore saw in 1993, with a few more prosecrecy goodies thrown in thanks to Bush, Jr.

The one unequivocal move toward a more acceptable world (see chapter 2) occurred as a result of Clinton's truly unprecedented declassification program, launched in 1995. It released millions of previously (over)classified documents into the public record, most of which remained there despite later, often futile reclassication efforts. Historians, social scientists, and many other citizens benefited enormously from the avalanche of information. Still, however beneficial and admirable Clinton's declassification program was, it mostly released secrets from the distant past. The information was historically significant but not very relevant for contemporary political debates. Classification decisions happening in real political time are more important for citizens actively monitoring their government's actions.

The administrations' different managerial approaches to the classification system mirrored the ways in which they tried to control sensitive unclassified information. Recall how the Ashcroft Memo reversed the Reno Memo's "maximum responsible disclosure" standard for FOIA officers and reinstituted a standard biased toward nondisclosure. The Card Memo continued along those lines by instructing Bush-Cheney officials to withhold as much potentially sensitive SBU information as possible, broadly construed.

No matter how restrictive its approach to information policy seemed, the Bush-Cheney administration clearly built atop precedents developed by pre-

vious administrations—Clinton-Gore included, in the case of SBU information, the emerging reclassification program, and ramped up derivative classifications. Though Bush-Cheney may have reached "unprecedented" levels
of classification in some ways (for example, in derivative decisions), its approach was plainly more incrementalist than insurrectionist (see chapter 2).
The next chapter reaches a similar conclusion and finds Clinton-Gore and
Bush-Cheney with relatively similar records of FACA-violating behavior.

4

VIOLATING FACA FROM THE START
A HISTORY OF PRESIDENTIAL DEFIANCE

The Bush-Cheney Administration

The Energy Task Force

Despite the ample supply of cheap gasoline in the consumer market, the Bush-Cheney presidential campaign in 2000 worked hard to place an "energy crisis" near the top of the political agenda. Naturally, Bush blamed the incumbent Clinton-Gore administration: the Democrats failed to adequately and enthusiastically promote oil and gas drilling in places like the Arctic National Wildlife Refuge, committing the sin of prioritizing environmental protection over energy industry development. For that and other reasons, candidate Bush lamented on *Live with Regis,* "We haven't had an energy policy in this country for a long time." Once in power, he swiftly put his administration to work.[1]

Nine days after inauguration, Bush tapped the vice president to head the National Energy Policy Development Group (NEPDG)—better known as Cheney's energy task force. Like many other groups created within the executive branch, the NEPDG consisted of government officials and non-government advisers who met to discuss potential new policies as well as the performance of existing ones. Given the policy domain, key Republican Party constituencies, and Bush's and Cheney's personal backgrounds as Texas oil men, an oil-soaked guest list should not have been surprising to anyone. However, given energy policy's many other stakeholders, as well the Federal Advisory Committee Act's requirement that groups like NEPDG be "fairly balanced in terms of the points of view represented," environmental and other advocacy groups demanded more than a token seat at the table. After NEPDG's ceremonious launch, environmental groups loudly complained they had not received invitations to join. When they pressed the White House to disclose the composition of the task force, Cheney refused their request.[2]

Cheney's refusal, backed by Bush, struck many as a deliberate violation of the 1972 law. FACA, also commonly known as the open meetings law, was one of the first of the sunshine laws passed in the 1970s, after decades of citizen complaints about how interest groups influenced policy making behind closed doors. Its main contibution to government transparency has been its requirement that any advisory body—including "any committee, board, commission, council, conference, panel, task force, or other similar group"—that gives "advice or recommendations for the President or one or more agencies or officers of the Federal Government" must remain open and accessible to the public. Task forces must announce upcoming meetings at least fourteen days in advance and keep the doors open once the day arrives. They must promptly make transcripts available, as well as meeting minutes, reports, working research papers, and appendixes. But first, they need to obtain a charter from the approriate administrator (General Services Administration [GSA]) or congressional committee, making public the committee's name, mission, meeting frequency, expected costs, and termination date. The only exceptions are when the group and its proceedings are officially classified or when the group "is composed wholly of full-time officers or employees of the federal government." Thus, FACA is triggered whenever outside interests are given the opportunity to share information or otherwise influence the executive branch, with the noted exceptions.[3]

Citizens and members of Congress suspected that Cheney's task force did not quite achieve the requirement of being a "fairly balanced" committee, but these critics were prevented from finding out if that was true. The White House deliberately withheld the group members' names and meeting details, and it did so for a number of reasons. First, Cheney and his head counsel, David Addington, believed strongly that FACA and the wave of open government laws passed in the 1970s had severely constrained the executive branch, which operated best when allowed to fulfill its separate constitutional role without undue hindrances from the other branches, not to mention the fickle, uninformed public. Their dedication to executive branch secrecy grew from their distinctive constitutional interpretation, as well as from a more pragmatic belief that they could only obtain good information when their advisers—whether governmental or not—enjoyed the comforts of confidentiality (see chapter 2). Hard, unpopular truths would only be glossed over as a result of citizen monitoring, since advisers' behaviors would always change under the limelight. Cheney was not shy about his unconventional beliefs or his absolutist tendencies. For example, in early 2002, he asserted it was "important to preserve our ability to get unvarnished advice from *anybody we want on any subject.*"[4]

A second reason why Cheney and Addington (and presumably Bush) felt confident in flouting FACA was that they deliberately designed NEPDG to circumvent the law. FACA covers, as noted, all advisory committees except those composed only of governement officials. Addington's NEPDG plan hinged on a strategic interpretation of the word *member*. Exxon and Conoco executives, American Petroleum Institute lobbyists, and others who participated in meetings were officially branded White House "guests" and "visitors," rather than "members" as similar participants in similar advisory committees had been labeled in the past. Addington's novel rhetorical twist around FACA followed Cheney's order to design NEPDG "beyond the reach" of the law. For extra security, Cheney instructed task force members—ahem, "visitors"—never to speak about their secret meetings.[5]

If the discursive gambit failed to persuade their critics, as they probably expected, White House officials likely took some comfort in knowing FACA carried with it no penalties for violations. For all its protransparency glory, FACA does little to incentivize aggressive, risk-accepting political actors like Cheney and Addington to follow it. Congress can make noises and hold hearings, but that's about it—short of cutting the president's purse strings. The only recourse for interest groups, the press, and other aggrieved or concerned parties is a civil lawsuit. Though the courts can force recalcitrant administrations to open their records, the legal process, with its long-delayed and uncertain outcomes, allows patient, resilient actors to proceed with their task forces as desired, fighting about the details after the fact. Cheney, Addington, and other senior officials might have even deliberately set things up to provoke a legal challenge, giving them an opportunity to use the courts to weaken a law they viewed as illegitimate and unconstitutional. If it was a conflict they sought, they must have been pleased with what transpired next.[6]

As reports swirled around Washington about the task force's one-sidedness and secrecy, Rep. John Dingell (D-MI) and Rep. Henry Waxman (D-CA), ranking members of the House Energy and Commerce and Government Reform Committees, urged the NEPDG director, Andrew Lundquist, to release the information, in a letter on April 19, 2001. (They also asked the General Accounting Office to investigate on the same day.) Lundquist by that time had apparently grown concerned about his professional reputation, since the political conflict had spilled onto national headlines. Critics were calling it a cover-up and lambasting the "Texas oil men" and their cronies for secretly plotting to gut all of the twentieth-century's hard-won environmental laws. It was in that context that Lundquist suggested to Cheney they should comply with FACA. Cheney's gruff reply indicated he was ready for a fight: "*Don't ever suggest that to me again.*"[7]

The White House's official response came not from Lundquist but from Addington, a switcheroo that caught the congressmen by surprise. Why not Lundquist, NEPDG's director? Why did Cheney's lawyer pen the letter, unless the White House wanted to escalate? Also curious was why Addington sent his response not to them but to ranking Republicans on the Energy and Commerce and Government Reform Committees, Rep. W. J. "Billy" Tauzin (R-LA) and Rep. Dan Burton (R-IN). Would the White House refuse to even communicate with Democrats?

Addington's passive-aggressive letters were thick with abstract language about the separation of powers and the unconstitutionality of congressional oversight of executive branch deliberations. Though he paid homage to the "comity between the executive and legislative branches," Addington rejected all requests for information, based on the argument NEPDG was exempt because it was "composed wholly of full-time officers or employees of the Federal Government." Cheney's idea to label the 300-some outside members as guests and visitors was finally put to the test. But Addington's refusals hardly mattered anyway for people who wanted to monitor NEPDG in real time. The task force delivered its final report and disbanded on the same day Addington responded to the GAO's inquiry.[8]

The GAO nevertheless continued its investigation, as was its responsibility following the requests from Dingell and Waxman. What emerged from the process was unprecedented: GAO comptroller general David Walker announced in late January 2002 that he planned to sue the vice president over the NEPDG affair. It was the first time the GAO had sued senior executive branch officials. However, *Walker v. Cheney*, which developed more as a conflict about GAO-executive relations rather than FACA, was dismissed by the DC district court on December 9, 2002. Walker decided against appealing the decision.[9]

A more direct challenge to the administration's FACA interpretation came from the Sierra Club and Judicial Watch (JW), which filed lawsuits after the government rejected the groups' FOIA requests about the task force. The ideologically divergent groups joined forces after the DC district court consolidated their lawsuits into *Judicial Watch, Inc. v. National Energy Policy Development Group.* Despite the administration's best efforts to thwart the discovery process, the groups prevailed, and they managed to unearth some very interesting material that offered clues about why the administration had gone to such lengths to keep NEPDG secret. Following a court order on March 5, 2002, for example, the Department of Commerce (DOC) released NEPDG documents from March 2001, including: detailed maps of Iraq's oil fields, pipelines, refineries, and terminals; and two charts listing Iraqi oil and gas projects; and one document titled "Foreign Suitors for Iraqi Oilfield Contracts"—suitors who of course would only receive Iraqi government invitations after regime change. The emergence of documents did not prove that NEPDG—or the administration—had hatched a plan to invade Iraq for oil two years before the actual invasion. Indeed, there was no mention of war. But Cheney and Addington's insistence on secrecy did raise suspicions about war motives once the documents were released. Such are the hazards of excessive secrecy.[10]

Additional legal victories by the plaintiffs vindicated the argument that the administration deliberately circumvented FACA. The DC district court and later the DC appeals court upheld the groups' requests to obtain documents showing NEPDG members' involvement in task force meetings. If Cheney wanted to keep the information secret, both courts ruled, the administration should have asserted executive privilege—the Supreme Court–sanctioned authority allowing senior White House officials to resist demands for information by the other branches under certain conditions (determined by the courts, following *U.S. v. Nixon*). Judges would need to review the documents to evaluate the assertion against the public's right to know, the courts noted, but they would do so in camera, far away from the plaintiffs and anyone else. Besides, they argued, the lower courts did not have the authority to stop the suit's discovery process via mandamus order without a privilege assertion. But the Supreme Court, hearing Cheney's appeal as *Cheney v. United States District Court for D.C.*, argued in a seven-to-two majority opinion that the lower courts had "prematurely" rejected Cheney's motions to stop discovery, which had already released sensitive information. Though only two in the majority (Justices Antonin Scalia and Clarence Thomas) accepted Cheney's substantive arguments, the court's opinion on the procedural issues was a major victory for the White House's quest for greater secrecy powers—a step toward restoration of the pre–sunshine-era regime. The court argued that the executive did *not* need to assert executive privilege to stop discovery (mandamus relief). As Robert M. Pallitto and William G. Weaver note, "The Court relieved the vice president from the burden of even claiming privilege—it was enough for the vice president to claim merely that the discovery orders interfered with his constitutional duties." The judicial branch thus voluntarily surrendered an important oversight function, in a case that had nothing directly to do with national security, the field where courts usually indicate a need for deference.[11]

The majority, dissatisfied with several of the lower courts' arguments, sent the case back to the DC appeals court for reconsideration of the unresolved substantive issues, including whether NEPDG documents should be disclosed. There, in an unexpected reversal, the court sided with Cheney, accepting his rhetorical twist around FACA. Because none of the 300-some nongovernmental "visitors" had voting or veto authority in NEPDG deliberations, Judge A. Raymond Randolph argued, they were "no more [members] of the committee than the aides who accompany Congressmen or cabinet officers to committee meetings." The appeals court's volte-face decision emboldened Cheney, Addington, and their allies, allowing them to declare another precedent had been set. The court affirmed an absolute "constitutional right of the president and vice president to obtain information in confidentiality," as Cheney's office framed it. Their supporters and critics both wondered: did Cheney kill FACA?[12]

Fortunately for transparency advocates, he did not. But the appeals court ruling poked yet another hole into one of the linchpins of the sunshine-era legal framework. The new precedent boosted the executive's secrecy powers by giving officials an additional legal tool to fend off citizens demanding FACA compliance. As we will see, the FACA-defying toolbox was already well filled when Bush-Cheney took office in 2001, after two decades of court cases and behind-the-scenes experiments in administrative noncompliance.

We can partly blame the law itself due to its ambiguity, which clever officials have exploited with some success (as with Bush-Cheney's "guests" are not "members" word game). However, a plain, noncynical interpretation of the law does not require much straining: advisory committees, composed of private sector members consulting with public sector employees, need to open their meetings and publish their documents, with the usual set of exceptions, such as personal privacy and national security information. (The Government in the Sunshine Act of 1976 clarified some ambiguous parts of FACA and listed the exemptions.) Moreover, FACA's transparency rules apply to all advisory committees, including boards, commissions, councils, conferences, groups, panels, and task forces, as well as subcommittees, subgroups, and so on (Pub. L. 92-463 § (3)(2)). The law thus covers a wide range of executive branch consultations with nongovernment individuals—not just the trumpeted presidential task forces tackling high-profile issues.[13]

In addition to the cynical executive branch wordsmiths exploiting the law's ambiguity, certain federal judges deserve some of the blame for FACA's dispiriting history. Some helped set the precedents that officials later used and developed. Others let the precedents stand and allowed administrations to use running-out-the-clock tactics when citizens sued, refusing to issue injunctions to open or delay advisory committees while evaluating plaintiffs' arguments. Most of the blame, however, should go to the executive branch officials who snubbed the law, one way or another. Much of the time, they committed sins of omission, quietly and deliberately circumventing the law. The Bush-Cheney administration, like most of its predecessors, made ample use of all circumvention tactics.

Beyond the NEPDG

As congressional leaders and the GAO pressed the administration to follow the law for NEPDG, the White House announced another energy policy group, the White House Task Force on Energy Project Streamlining (EPS), which focused on energy production and environmental protection. As with NEPDG, only government employees on the EPS were considered members, even though private sector "guests" would have influence on sixty-eight federal energy projects (managed by the Forest Service [FS], the Fish and Wildlife Service [FWS], and the Bureau of Land Management [BLM], among others). Compared with NEPDG, EPS more closely adhered to FACA. For example, the administration announced open houses where the public was invited to submit comments on selected issues. Nevertheless, the administration kept EPS free from FACA with word games (members were guests), closed-door meetings, and secret records and transcripts. Energy interests involved with EPS enjoyed an easier-than-usual permitting process for oil and gas drilling in western states, as they sidestepped the regular public comment periods and environmental reviews.[14]

Another task force seemingly designed to expedite the energy permit process also operated behind closed doors. The inaugural meeting of the Rocky Mountain Energy Council (RMEC) took place in July 2003 and was attended by federal government "members," state government delegates, quasi-government organizations like the Western Governors' Association, and industry representatives. RMEC's leaders blocked journalists and environmental groups at the door. But at least one concerned insider leaked to the press that the group engaged in a serious discussion of how it might best circumvent FACA. Ultimately, environmentalists, led by the Natural Resources

Defense Council, somehow managed to pressure the administration enough, with public criticism and FOIA requests, that the administration uncharacteristically backed down and disbanded the RMEC.[15]

Altogether, citizens alleged that at least twelve Bush-Cheney task forces violated FACA, covering issues as diverse as Social Security, Medicare, Food and Drug Administration (FDA) regulations, pesticide regulations, judicial nominations, the *Columbia* space shuttle disaster, aviation security, information technology security, and intelligence policy on weapons of mass destruction. Some of the secrecy may have been legitimate, such as some of the proceedings of the intelligence policy task force. When the administration could not avoid FACA's requirements by citing "necessary secrets" and the associated exemptions, it used a variety of circumvention tactics.

The President's Commission to Strengthen Social Security was yet another task force created during the interbranch conflict over NEPDG. For this one, administration officials tried something a little different. They divided the group into two eight-member subcommittees that were immune from FACA's disclosure requirements because they fell short of group-size minimums as outlined by General Services Administration regulations. Only when the full sixteen-member commission met to review the subcommittees' work would the proceedings be open to the public. Rep. Robert T. Matsui (D-CA) and, again, Rep. Henry Waxman, tried without success to open the commission's subcommittees. In an ironic twist, the White House convinced commission member Daniel Patrick Moynihan to fend off Waxman and Matsui, who apparently backed down. Former senator Moynihan had, just a few years earlier, chaired the Senate's Commission on Protecting and Reducing Government Secrecy. Having Moynihan, with his strong protransparency credentials, deliver the message added a potent symbolic element to the administration's "demonstrative use of power."[16]

Another example highlights the administration's institutional creativity. Immediately after the *Columbia* space shuttle disintegrated upon reentry into the atmosphere, killing all astronauts on board, the National Aeronautics and Space Administration (NASA) announced the creation of the Columbia Accident Investigation Board to probe the causes of the accident. NASA said it hoped the participation of outside, nongovernmental experts as board members would ensure its independence and thus help it reach the truth, however inconvenient, for government officials or private sector partners, whose reputations were on the line. Almost as soon as NASA argued for an independent task force, the agency reversed course, making all outside members government employees, with $134,000 annual salaries. On top of new conflict-of-interest issues, the move made the group immune to FACA, keeping all of its deliberations and work protected from public scrutiny.[17]

A final example shows, again, how free the administration felt to disregard FACA. In the wake of 9/11, Bush-Cheney created a fast-track task force on aviation security in the Department of Transportation (DOT)—convened on September 16, with a report expected two weeks later. That the task force, which included private sector interests from business and labor groups, met in secrecy should by now not be surprising. When GSA officials challenged its secrecy, DOT officials said it was "ridiculous" to claim the department had violated FACA. But their arguments did not cite national security considerations, even in the immediate 9/11 aftermath. Baffled by the GSA's criticism, the best DOT spokespeople could come up with was that all of the nongovernment task force members had active contracts with the government. Whether all of them did was unclear, since the member list was kept secret. Even so, FACA contained no "active contracts" exemption. In any case, the task force had disbanded before the GSA or anyone else could try to open it.[18]

Legitimate Exemptions and Questionable Loopholes

Presidents and their administrations do not need to resort to such evasive tactics when task forces discuss and write about so-called necessary secrets. FACA, along with GITSA, specifies acceptable exclusions. All of FOIA's exemptions also apply. FACA gives the president the authority to withhold a "timely" public announcement of a task force meeting for national security purposes (§ 10(a)(2)) and to exclude "any information" from his or her annual report to Congress for the same reason (§ 6(c)). Presidents therefore have a tremendous amount of discretion about what can be excluded from FACA's disclosure requirements.[19]

Courts have also validated four loopholes, allowing even more task force secrecy. The "contractor loophole" allows agencies to legally delegate to private entities the authority to create, organize, and oversee policy advisory groups—essentially, presidential task forces clothed in private sector garb. Bush-Cheney's Office of Management and Budget drew upon the loophole in September 2003 when it explicitly encouraged agencies to contract out their task forces (or "peer review panels") to avoid FACA's requirements. The contractor loophole was by no means used only by Bush-Cheney. For example, the DC district court in 1990 backed a Bush-Quayle FDA decision to

hire the Federation of American Societies for Experimental Biology to create
and manage an advisory panel for food and cosmetic safety issues.[20]

The "strict management" loophole allows agencies to avoid FACA when
task forces are created and run "by joint agreement" with private groups,
when their subgroups lack a "formal structure," and when government agencies withhold "control over who participate[s]" and does not pay any "salaries,
fees, or travel expenses." The "nonvoting loophole" was the one created as a
result of *Cheney v. U.S. District Court*, described earlier. Finally, the "subcommittee loophole" works when task forces create their own subgroups, whose
work upon their creation becomes immune to FACA. Bush-Cheney may have
had this loophole in mind when designing the Social Security Commission's
subcommittees, but there is no direct evidence of that.[21]

Despite the loopholes and the legal protections for necessary secrets, the
administration frequently chose to circumvent FACA through other means,
as we have seen. If we take Cheney, Addington, et al. at their word, the motivation was ideological—a sincere belief that presidents should receive unfettered, confidential advice from whomever they choose. As Cheney put it,

> I believed, and the president backed me up, that we had the right to
> consult with whomever we chose—and no obligation to tell the press
> or Congress or anybody else whom we were talking to. If citizens who
> come to the White House to offer advice have to worry about law-
> suits or being called before congressional committees, it would pretty
> severely curtail the counsel a president and vice president could receive.
> There were plenty of people, including some in the White House, who
> thought we should just turn over the lists [of NEPDG members]. Since
> there were no nefarious secrets hidden in them, they argued, all we were
> doing was creating a real political headache for ourselves by refusing to
> give them up. But I believed something larger was at stake: the power
> of the presidency and the ability of the president and vice president to
> carry out their constitutional duties.

Ideologically motivated action was especially well suited for FACA, given the
law's very limited consequences for violations. The only real option for citizens was to sue the government, in the hopes that a court could force an injunction while the task force was still active. When lawsuits materialized, all
an administration had to do was use delaying tactics to run out the clock and
prevent meaningful judicial action.[22]

Summary

The Bush-Cheney administration developed a bizarre relationship with FACA. Senior White House officials clearly despised it for ideological reasons. More important, they often found it irrelevant, something they could avoid at will, perhaps with a little creativity. They played and won word games, saying NEPDG members were really guests. They helped create and validate gaping new loopholes, such as those involving nonvoting members and FACA subcommittees. They made private sector members government employees to avoid FACA's strictures. Or they just declared, without basis in law, that government contractors did not count as outside advisers.

At the same time, there seemed to be an awareness that it was, in fact, a real law, one that the executive branch was supposed to follow. In the announcement of the President's Commission on Intelligence on Weapons of Mass Destruction in February 2004, for example, FACA was mentioned but mostly to say that it was irrelevant. Still, the administration felt the need to justify the task force's secrecy: "While the Commission does not concede that it is subject to the requirements of the Federal Advisory Committee Act . . . it has been determined that the July 14–15 meeting would fall within the scope of exceptions (c)(1) and (c)(9)(B) of the Sunshine Act . . . and thus could be closed to the public if FACA did apply to the Commission." Bush-Cheney did not concede FACA was relevant for the commission, but it nevertheless cited the proper exemptions.[23]

Coda: Breaking New Records for Closed Task Force Meetings

Task forces can close their meetings for very specific reasons, as outlined in FACA and GITSA and noted earlier in this chapter. Meetings might, for instance, involve discussion of classified information or proprietary data on medical research or from grant applications. From FACA's emergence in 1974 through 1993, task forces closed many of their meetings (20 percent to 30 percent) using the exemptions, but closed meetings were certainly not the norm (Figure 4.1).

Then, starting in 1994, the proportion of closed meetings began rising sharply, reaching nearly 60 percent by the time the Clinton-Gore administration left Washington. Bush-Cheney took the number higher but not by very much (to a maximum 65 percent), especially compared with Clinton-Gore, whose record for closing meetings was truly unprecedented.[24]

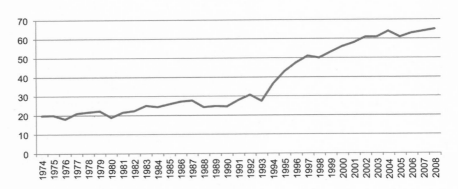

FIGURE 4.1
FACA Meetings (%) Closed to the Public, 1974–2008.
Source: FACA Annual Reports, OpenTheGovernment.org Secrecy Report Cards

The Clinton-Gore Administration

> We've never had any situation where we were absolutely
> stonewalled by a task force of this type.[25]
>
> —David M. Walker, describing the GAO's conflict with
> Vice President Cheney's energy task force (2001)

At every Clinton-Gore campaign stop before the 1992 election, promises to deliver national health insurance were about as common as another spin of Fleetwood Mac's "Don't Stop [Thinking about Tomorrow]." Five days after his inauguration, President William Jefferson Clinton set the wheels in motion. Before all of the boxes were unpacked and the baby pictures were hung on the walls, Clinton formally appointed his wife, Hillary Rodham Clinton, to chair the President's Task Force on National Health Care Reform. The first meeting was held on January 28, 1993. As invited members sat down in a White House meeting room for their first sip of coffee and the launch of the task force, the doors were shut—and Clinton's presidential honeymoon ended as soon as it began.

Reporters and interested citizens who hoped to document the potentially historic reform process were shunted aside, blocked from entering the meeting room. They were told they would also not be allowed in future meetings. This all came as a bit of a shock, especially because the candidates had promised more open government during the campaign.[26]

Under FACA, the task force was supposed to have published a notice in the *Federal Register* fourteen days in advance to alert citizens and the press about the meeting. All printed materials, such as research papers and policy plans, should have been distributed to anyone who wanted them. A charter should have been filed with the GSA, estimating things like overall costs and final deadlines. The GSA received nothing of the sort. Eight days in, the new administration appeared to be breaking the law in numerous ways.[27]

The White House offered a conflicting mess of explanations and evasions, ranging from denials and defiance to feigned ignorance. Communications Director George Stephanopoulos made a reasonable-sounding point, "We don't have to open up every single staff meeting for the press." Task force coordinator Ira Magaziner disingenuously pleaded ignorance, saying, "This is the first time I've heard of it," apparently referring to FACA itself. "I'll look into it," he promised, "now that I've heard about it." To reporters asking why the public could not attend, Press Secretary Dee Dee Myers gave her version of a frustrated mother's "*Because I said so!*" wrapped up in circular logic. Reporters were barred "because the task force meetings will continue to be closed throughout the development of the policy."[28]

Much of the conflict revolved around different interpretations of task force head Hillary Clinton's official status. If the First Lady qualified as a federal employee and if the meetings only involved other executive branch employees, then under FACA the meetings were justifiably closed to the public. White House groups composed solely of government officials are not covered under FACA. If Mrs. Clinton did not qualify as an executive branch official, then FACA rules applied.

Although White House officials immediately acknowledged Mrs. Clinton's quasi-outsider status, since she did not collect a salary and did not sign the ethics pledge the president required of all officials, they still denied that the task force fell under FACA's purview. Their resistance was understandable, given Mrs. Clinton's complicated position in the White House. On the one hand, she performed all of a First Lady's typical ceremonial and symbolic tasks. On the other hand, she was one of the president's top advisers, with an office in the West Wing and a staff of about twenty federal employees. And, of course, she leveraged her legal experience—not to mention her domestic ties—as head of the White House's health care reform task force. Justice Department lawyers stood squarely behind the White House's argument that "the First Lady and the Second Lady are Government insiders, members of the Government who perform true public services in the operation of our

Government. For the purpose of [FACA], the First Lady is really the functional equivalent of a Government employee"—despite never filling out W-2s and signing ethics pledges. Even Republicans like Rep. William F. Clinger (R-PA), who threatened GAO action on the issue, recognized Mrs. Clinton's complicated role, conceding she probably was more of an insider for FACA purposes. The argument also seemed to have the support of the Supreme Court, which had cautioned against overly literal readings of FACA in 1989's *Public Citizen v. Department of Justice*. Thus, with Mrs. Clinton's quasi-official status generally recognized and the White House's declaration that the task force's other members were all federal employees (cabinet secretaries, the OMB director, and a few White House advisers), it seemed Mrs. Clinton's argument would hold. Just to be certain, White House counsel Bernard Nussbaum backed it up with a legal memo justifying the secrecy. To smooth the rough edges, the president appealed to pragmatism. Allowing the meetings "would be like opening the White House at every staff meeting we have. We can't do that . . . nobody ever does that. I mean, we would never—we can't get anything done."[29]

Once it became known that Mrs. Clinton's task force meetings included not just the dozen or so executive branch officials but at least 300 outside "experts," the uneasy truce quickly evaporated. The administration argued the diverse group of policy specialists had unique insights that would help the Clintons reform America's labyrinthine health care system. Critics countered that the outsiders were better seen as special interests, who would use their seats at the table to rewrite the health care bill for mostly self-interested reasons. Because the administration refused to disclose the outsiders' names, citizens could not make judgments about whether they were in fact experts or special interests. In any case, since outsiders—not just First Ladies and cabinet secretaries—were attending the meetings, FACA's rules should have kicked in, making the debate about Mrs. Clinton's role irrelevant.[30]

Faced with these criticisms, the White House offered a new set of rationalizations. Stephanopoulos argued disclosure would make task force members "subject to lobbying, to enormous pressure," distorting the process and possibly killing reform. Flipping her critics' claims on their heads, Mrs. Clinton said the real threat from outsiders would come after disclosure of the task force names. Thus, secrecy was necessary to *prevent* the harmful work of special interests—never mind the interests already at the table.[31]

Less than two months after the inauguration, a federal judge ruled against the administration, arguing it had violated FACA. Judge Royce Lamberth of the DC district court demanded that Mrs. Clinton open many of her meetings to the public and publish all papers produced for and by the task force. He did not buy the First Lady–as-insider argument. Still, he gave ground on the breadth of his ruling. The task force's smaller "working groups," focused on policy development, were immune from FACA, since only federal employees attended those. But Judge Lamberth was mistaken. Outside consultants were often deeply involved in the smaller working groups. Moreover, the White House defiantly interpreted the work of all 500-plus members—newly christened as consultants—as being part of a larger working group. When pressed by the GAO to release the names of the consultants, Mrs. Clinton refused, saying Judge Lamberth's ruling only forced her to disclose the names of cabinet secretaries and other government officials on the task force: "I think it's been very clear and the judge's opinion on this point that the working groups are not covered by that law, and we're going to comply with the law." The White House's defiant interpretation of the court's ruling convinced no one. Despite claiming victory, the White House appealed Judge Lamberth's decision and refused to supply most of the relevant information.[32]

Even before the late April appeals court hearing, the White House lost another round. Lists of task force members had spread around the capital, a sign that at least one member did not agree with Clinton-Gore's aggressive secrecy. The tipping point came when the *Wall Street Journal* published a list of 528 alleged members on its editorial page. Earlier, smaller publications had printed some of the names, but the *Journal*'s move made the administration's position futile. To correct what it called inaccuracies—or perhaps just to admit defeat—the administration distributed what it described as a complete list of all insiders and outsiders on the task force. The list appeared to be hastily compiled, but its dissemination marked a turn toward transparency, however grudging it was.[33]

The DC appeals court ruling was a mixed bag. The White House celebrated Judge Laurence Silberman's decision that the First Lady was the "functional equivalent" of a government official. Any meetings consisting of just Mrs. Clinton and other officials were thus outside FACA's purview. But the appeals court decision hardly mattered anyway, since the task force itself had disbanded in May 1993. A loss would have had a limited substantive effect. Anybody who wanted to attend the task force's meetings no longer had the chance. The administration's legal battles and foot-dragging helped to run out the clock; whether or not it was a deliberate circumvention tactic remains unknown. On the question of releasing the papers, which many citizens still wanted to see, the court punted and sent that decision back to the lower court. To no one's surprise, Judge Lamberth demanded their release and rejected the government's argument revolving around its "working group" interpretation, saying it and related arguments were "preposterous." Moreover, if White House officials did not release the documents in twenty days, he said, he would hold them in contempt of court. Although Clinton-Gore had released "dribbles and drabs of information at its convenience," he stated, "the court condemns this litigation tactic and will not tolerate it in future responses in this case." Everything—working papers, meeting records, travel vouchers, payroll records, and the full list of names and responsibilities— needed to be released by November 29, 1993.[34]

Instead, the White House continued its dribbles and drabs approach. By March 1994, the groups that brought the suit, including the Association of American Physicians and Surgeons, cried foul. They argued many of the working groups Clinton-Gore claimed were strictly composed of insiders were either all or more than half filled with outsiders. Those records had not been furnished. Back in court four months later, the White House argued it could not actually disclose the names of the ostensibly staff-level groups because the 500-plus task force was "an anonymous horde" (and, at the same time, "a leviathan"—take your pick from the mixed metaphor). Senior official and task force coordinator Ira Magaziner pleaded for the court's sympathy, since the group's "membership was fluid, not fixed." The members worked in a state of "creative chaos." The group overall had a confusing structure, with a mix of federal employees and a handful of outsiders. Therefore, he and the DOJ argued, from a position of incompetence and confusion, that the court should just consider the task force FACA free. Of course, as the *Wall Street Journal* had revealed, there were more than a few consultants. It was never entirely clear exactly how many participated—perhaps because of the chaos, perhaps because the White House had in fact *asked employees and outsiders to shred and burn documents.*[35]

In December 1994, after nearly two years of obstruction, Judge Lamberth, a man of apparently limitless patience, ruled against the administration once again, citing its "misconduct." Nevertheless, he offered the White House "one last opportunity" to release everything before he decided on appropriate sanctions. That threat seemed to do the trick, as the DOJ finally agreed to release the last batch of documents. Perhaps trying to convince those who were only following the headlines, the administration said it would release the last batch because it had "nothing to hide"—something at odds with the long legal wrangle and the White House's passive-aggressive stance.[36]

Once the documents were out and other details about what happened had leaked, the gap between rhetoric and reality became even clearer. When it was time for Judge Lamberth to finally impose sanctions on the White House for misconduct, he did not hold back. In 1997, when many Americans had forgotten all about 1993's mini-scandal, Lamberth hurled sharp words toward the executive branch, especially toward Ira Magaziner and the White House's DOJ legal team. The White House and the DOJ had committed "dishonest" and "reprehensible" acts, including lying to and hiding information from the court. The judge was "convinced" that Magaziner had intentionally lied about the composition of the task force's working groups and that administration lawyers failed to correct that statement as the case proceeded—which had led Lamberth years earlier to allow Mrs. Clinton's group some immunity from FACA. Lamentably, he added, "some government officials never learn that the cover-up can be worse than the underlying conduct." He awarded the plaintiffs about $285,000 for their accumulated legal costs. Two years later, in 1999, the DC appeals court unanimously cleared Magaziner of perjury and the administration of acting in "bad faith." Lamberth's accusations, they argued, came "without clear and convincing evidentiary support." Champagne bottles popped in the White House as the conflict that started during inauguration week finally drew to a close.[37]

Comparing Bush-Cheney and Clinton-Gore

All of the talk in 2001–2002 about Cheney and Addington's unprecedented "stonewalling" of the GAO and the general public was a clear reminder of Washington's—or America's—short attention span (or dementia, if you prefer). Less than ten years earlier, the Clintons had done the same thing, albeit in a clumsier, hastily stitched together way, compared with Cheney's bold and patient approach. Instead of pretending outside interests were not involved in the task force working groups—Mrs. Clinton's gambit—Cheney did not deny that energy sector outsiders roamed the West Wing. He and Addington simply labeled them guests and visitors instead of members, part of their effort to deliberately design the energy task force to make it beyond the reach of FACA. The Clinton-Gore administration also played word games—calling the work of all 500-some consultants part of a larger FACA-immune working group—but that attempt fell flat on its face.[38]

No matter the different means, both administrations found ways to conceal the work of their task forces as they proceeded. Both broke the law and suffered few consequences. And both taught future administrations that it pays to do whatever you can to run out the clock. One way to do that is to play word games—with the courts, Congress, and the public. The better you play, the longer you can go without transparency.

As shown earlier, Cheney's energy task force was only one of several his administration tried to hide. From the President's Commission to Strengthen Social Security to the NASA board investigating the *Columbia* space shuttle disaster, Bush-Cheney officials did their best to keep at least twelve task forces beyond FACA's reach, no matter what the law said. Clinton-Gore has been typically seen as leading a more transparent government, sometimes for justified reasons (see chapter 3), but that administration defied FACA almost as many times as Bush-Cheney did. Instead of (at least) twelve cases, Clinton-Gore had at least ten. Indeed, even as federal judges ruled against them in *Association of American Physicians and Surgeons v. Hillary Rodham Clinton*, administration officials deployed many of the same circumvention tactics for other advisory committees.

Beyond the Health Care Task Force

In 1994, following the arrest and espionage conviction of former CIA counterintelligence officer Aldrich Ames, President Clinton ordered the creation of the Security Policy Board (SPB) and the Security Policy Forum (SPF), to advise him on a range of security issues, including classification, counterintelligence tools, and interagency coordination. The problem was that the SPB/SPF advisory groups included nongovernmental outsiders—"security experts" from the private sector, including some selected from industries that might exclusively benefit from new security policies. Because of the involvement of unrepresentative special interests, Clinton's new task force fit squarely within FACA's purview. a fact not lost on senior officials. The administration never argued FACA/GITSA's national security exemptions were applicable to SPD/SPF.[39]

To help SPD Director Peter Saderholm ignore FACA, Clinton's DOJ offered several suggestions. In a (leaked) secret memo, the DOJ recommended that Saderholm:

- "Clearly distinguish the functions of private nonmembers from those of the federal members. The private nonmembers should not have an involvement that is similar, or equivalent, to that of federal members.
- Consider varying the private nonmembers who attend the meetings [so private sector participants] are less likely to constitute an 'organized structure' [. . .] or 'fixed membership.'
- Consider informing the private nonmembers that their presence at meetings is permitted for the purpose of exchanging facts, information and individual advice only, and not for providing consensus advice regarding government proposals.
- Avoid receiving consensus group advice from the private [sector members].
- Avoid officially formulating or adopting federal policies or recommendations in the presence of private nonmembers."

Even if the SPB and SPF used these techniques to circumvent FACA, the participation of nongovernmental actors made the group susceptible to the law. Transparency advocates like Steven Aftergood of the Federation of American Scientists did try to challenge the administration by asking to attend; he was refused entry. But because it takes a lawsuit to force executives to comply with FACA, it really didn't matter (and as we have seen, court rulings can have limited effects anyway). The SPB and SPF continued unabated.[40]

Although executives often enjoy extra leeway in circumventing transparency laws when dealing with national security policy, through exemptions or the overall greater deference given to presidents in that realm, they face more skepticism when it comes to other kinds of policies. The tangle over Mrs. Clinton's health care task force was one example. Another was Clinton's Forest Ecosystem Management Assessment Team (FEMAT). Set up in response to a proenvironmental 1991 ruling by Judge William Lee Dwyer and the District Court for the Western District of Washington, FEMAT was given a mission to develop a new federal timber policy that would win Judge Dwyer's approval. The team's main meeting took place in July 1993 in Portland, Oregon, where the administration organized a forest management conference attended mostly by scientists with expertise in sustainable forestry. The attendees included administration officials as well as "several hundred" others from the private sector. It was exactly the kind of task force FACA was supposed to regulate.[41]

In its suit against the Clinton-Gore administration, the Northwest Forest Resource Council of Portland, Oregon, with help from the Native Forest

Council of Eugene, Oregon—about as odd a couple as you can get in the Pacific Northwest—argued the government clearly and probably knowingly flouted FACA. As a result, they asserted, the secretive FEMAT should not be allowed to submit its forestry plan for Judge Dwyer's review. Judge Thomas Penfield Jackson of the US District Court for the District of Columbia agreed with the plaintiffs that FEMAT "was convened and did its work in violation of" FACA. He also enumerated FEMAT's many violations, including its closed meetings; biased membership (generally "pro-ecosystem management, having minimal sympathy for the forest products industry"); failure to publish notices in the *Federal Register*; failure to let outsiders attend; failure to produce documents and detailed meeting minutes for public consumption; failure to submit a charter to the GSA; and failure to ensure it was "not inappropriately influenced by special interests"—all in all, a grand slam of FACA violations. Judge Jackson capped off his recitation of government abuses with an appeal to common sense: "If [Clinton's] going to appoint something that looks like, walks like and quacks like an advisory committee, he's got to do it in accordance with FACA."[42]

The government's arguments persuaded very few. DOJ attorney Robert Whitman, for instance, suggested that because some FEMAT members were on the faculty of public universities, they were "in effect" government employees. Whitman's argument, although somewhat clever, had limited reach: it did not apply to private sector members who were not public university professors. In the end, whether the administration could defend its illegal actions mattered little. Judge Jackson decided the plaintiffs' requested injunction—delaying FEMAT's report to Judge Dwyer—would be worse than the violation of the law ("such an injunction would exceed the injury presently to be addressed"). Thus, the Clinton-Gore administration faced no consequences for violating FACA, which, as we will see, is a recurring theme. Publicly, officials acted as if the ruling was a vindication of their aboveboard behavior. Kevin Sweeney, a spokesman for the Department of the Interior (DOI), said (perhaps sarcastically) that Judge Jackson "acknowledges the good-faith effort we have made." Under the cloak of anonymity, relevant officials dropped the act. One anonymous official said the ruling merely "slaps us on the wrist and allows us to move forward."[43]

For Clinton-Gore, its successors, and its predecessors, repeated slaps on the wrist did little to induce compliance with FACA. It is no wonder why the act was violated with such frequency and bravado. Just within the realm of forest management alone, the Clinton-Gore administration violated FACA more than once. The second time came near the end of its second term, when US Forest Service officials worked at the White House with representatives of the Audubon Society, the Heritage Forest Campaign, and the Sierra Club to develop a proposal to ban new road construction in national forests. According to Republican senators, governors, and conservative legal foundations, the advisory committee violated FACA by secretly conferring to write the new administrative rule. Wyoming Sawmills, Inc., enlisted the Mountain States Legal Foundation to block the new policy in court, citing FACA violations, as well as the National Forest Management Act, the National Environmental Policy Act, and the First Amendment's establishment clause (the suit involved forests Native American groups considered sacred). Judge Alan B. Johnson of the US District Court for the District of Wyoming ruled against the plaintiffs, saying the "consulting parties" *were* exempt from FACA and citing a broad exemption for "actions in support of intergovernmental communications." It was a puzzling argument because that exemption applies only to meetings "held exclusively between Federal officials and elected officers of State, local, and tribal governments (or their designated employees with authority to act on their behalf) acting in their official capacities." Why Audubon Society, Heritage Forest Campaign, and Sierra Club representatives were considered government officials was never explained. The Court of Appeals for the Tenth Circuit upheld the ruling. Both courts emphasized the need for judicial deference to the executive, which apparently meant allowing executives to defy the law without consequence.[44]

Some FACA conflicts, like the one involving the Forest Service and another involving Securities and Exchange Commission chairman Arthur Levitt, Jr., elicited confident denials of wrongdoing from senior Clinton-Gore officials. Others, like the one about FEMAT, led to weak or mealymouthed defenses but nevertheless proved satisfying enough for the judiciary. Though the administration's arguments did not always prevail in court, the negative consequences were insignificant, as usual. One case involving two task forces at the Department of Energy compelled the administration to send members of Congress a letter clarifying that they may have, in fact, violated the law. But the task forces, as usual, had already completed their work. Another case involved a task force deciding which medical procedures using new technologies should be reimbursed by Medicare. The conflict ultimately forced the administration to admit wrongdoing and promise change—next time around, that is. The medical task force by then had disbanded.[45]

Conclusion

Altogether, the Clinton-Gore administration appeared to violate FACA ten times over its two terms in office (see chapter 7 for the tenth). There were additional allegations, but the aggrieved parties did not sue or succeed in pushing for investigations, leaving little historical information about those conflicts. It is likely there were also cases that drew no accusations, due to the administration's success in keeping quiet. The evidence we do have demonstrates plainly that Clinton-Gore officials found it advantageous to occasionally defy FACA across their eight years in power. What happened under Bush-Cheney was clearly not unprecedented.[46]

Bush-Quayle: The Most FACA Compliant

Although the Clinton-Gore administration is often praised for ending the long, twelve-year stretch of Reagan and Bush government secrecy, its not-so-praiseworthy record, as outlined here, demonstrates a more complicated history. Clinton-Gore undeniably pushed toward transparency in several ways, such as the major declassification program and the "maximum responsible disclosure" FOIA policy described in chapter 3. However, when it came to FACA violations, it pushed the envelope far more frequently than Bush-Quayle, its immediate predecessor, an administration that stands out among the sunshine-era set.

Bush-Quayle officials certainly did not leave office with their hands clean. But their clashes with FACA were often not about secrecy. For example, one EPA task force faced conflict-of-interest allegations. Critics also complained about "unbalanced" task forces, but those kinds of allegations are common, and the conflicts in question dissipated almost as soon as they emerged. The one prominent secrecy-related fight involved national media organizations against the National Endowment of the Arts (NEA), which apparently held secret grant-selection meetings to limit right-wing interest groups' influence in the process. Several social conservative groups at the time were waging an antiobscenity campaign, which targeted painters, musicians, and performance artists, as well as the NEA because of its patronage.[47]

Social Conservatives and the NEA

Aside from the occasional setback (as when Robert Bork was "Borked"), social conservatives during the late 1980s and early 1990s were politically ascendant. Led by groups like Focus on the Family and the Moral Majority and leaders like James Dobson and Rev. Jerry Falwell, conservatives were enjoying the fruits of more than two decades of well-funded organizing. By the Reagan years, they occupied a position within the core of the Republican Party. By the time Bush moved from the vice president's office to the oval one, the relatively moderate Episcopalian had to accommodate his party's traditionalist base, including a large contingent of religious fundamentalists.[48]

Conflicts between provocative artists and social conservatives who wanted to censor them were nothing new. Artists in America had long criticized or lampooned the deep-seated traditions and authority structures conservatives cherished. Or artists simply highlighted what was considered taboo or not fit for public discussion. One need not look very far for examples, especially from the world of fiction (consider Mark Twain's *Adventures of Huckleberry Finn*, Henry Miller's *Tropic of Cancer*, or Lillian Smith's *Strange Fruit*). During some of the more puritanical periods of American history, social conservatives often successfully allied with government officials to ban or otherwise repress art they considered obscene. The National Legion of Decency and other groups, for instance, deftly used antiobscenity laws like the Comstock Act from the 1930s to the 1950s to keep art from reaching large publics. Once the sexual and counterculture revolutions went mainstream in the 1960s and 1970s, social conservative forces were knocked back on their heels. Their resurgence came during the Reagan and Bush era of the 1980s and early 1990s. "Obscene" art was not more common than ever, but once again conservatives finally had the organization—and the connection to institutional political power—to try to do something about it.[49]

Ironically, if not for the Moral Majority and their political allies, edgy artists like Andres Serrano (creator of "Piss Christ") and Robert Mapplethorpe would not have been household names (as impossible as it may seem now, they were). Artists and other button-pushers might have been the ones who pressed uncomfortably against cherished traditions and values, but conservative forces made them famous. Attempts to cajole Hollywood to leave behind its sins and spectacles typically failed, as gigantic entertainment corporations profited handsomely from those sins and spectacles. The NEA, by contrast, was a small federal agency, a budgetary afterthought, subordinate in 1990 to a

Republican president—in short, governmental low-hanging fruit. It was also the only agency using taxpayers' money to fund and promote what conservatives considered prurient, ungodly art. It was bad enough that the government taxed them in the first place; now they were forced to underwrite a photograph of a plastic crucifix in a glass of Serrano's urine. And the people who helped Serrano pay his rent—rather than, say, a nice portraitist or someone like Norman Rockwell—were the men and women on the NEA's grants committee, who had chosen, behind closed doors, pornography and blasphemy over old-time religion.

By the time the Bush-Quayle team was in office, liberals suspected the White House had pressured the supposedly independent NEA to tone things down. Artists like Serrano and Mapplethorpe were finding it much more difficult to get NEA support. The NEA had conducted secret grant committee meetings before, but members' decisions had never been so scrutinized, except perhaps in the art world. Journalists hoping to cover the NEA's meetings amid charges that its grant committee had been "politicized" found themselves shut out. Because the committee included both government and nongovernment members, its secrecy seemed to clearly violate FACA. The *New York Times,* the *Washington Post,* and the *Philadelphia Inquirer* consequently asked the US district court in DC for a temporary restraining order on April 29, 1992, the day before the next round of NEA working group meetings would begin. Judge Norma Holloway Johnson ruled against the plaintiffs on the same day, granting the NEA the right to keep its meetings closed. Judge Johnson argued the plaintiffs failed to show that the groups would discuss "specific grant applications." Even if they would, she continued, the plaintiffs offered no evidence the working groups would not report on their discussion of the cases "before the full Council." As a result of the precedent-setting case, other agencies were allowed to review grant applications without a public audience. It was the one major FACA-related conflict that Bush-Quayle officials faced. And they won without playing the kinds of interpretive games seen during other administrations.[50]

Reagan-Bush: FACA Defiers par Excellence

Compared with Bush-Quayle, Reagan-Bush defied FACA much more frequently. And like all of the other administrations, it often got away with it. The first major conflict occurred soon after inauguration. At issue were six meetings at the Environmental Protection Agency from June to September 1981, at which EPA administrators and chemical industry representatives discussed the regulatory status of two suspected carcinogens, formaldehyde and DEHP (di-(2)-ethylhexyl-phthlate). According to the main participants, the meetings were not at all policy relevant—just serious, "ad hoc" chats about chemistry and toxicology. "The meetings were anything but back-slapping, friendly, cigar-smoking sessions," said C. T. Howlett, Georgia-Pacific's corporate coordinator of environmental health and safety and the Formaldehyde Institute's government affairs committee chair. "This was down in the trenches with scientists. The blood from their rats was still smoking." The participants absolutely did not discuss regulatory reforms, swore the EPA's deputy administrator, John W. Hernandez, Jr., to his congressional overseers. No one had any intention to violate FACA, he and EPA administrator Anne M. Gorsuch promised. The meetings were simply fortuitous gatherings of scientists with differing opinions about the chemicals in question.[51]

For journalists and members of Congress who investigated those heady, ad hoc gatherings, it did seem odd that the chemical industry had brought along teams of lawyers. Most people don't bring lawyers to their informal academic conversations. And when it became clear that the meetings were prearranged and that environmental and public interest groups were not notified, industry participants maintained the magnanimous posture, saying they just assumed anyone interested knew about the not-so-impromptu discussions. Perhaps the environmentalists just didn't want to attend, said the Chemical Manufacturers Association (CMA). Interested groups like the Natural Resources Defense Council (NRDC) strongly rejected that claim, saying that "environmentalists never had a chance to attend" given the absence of public announcements and the meetings' secrecy.[52]

The administration's story grew more and more flimsy. Two EPA officials conceded they failed to publicize the upcoming meetings, as required by FACA. Deputy Administrator Hernandez also admitted he told participants of the secret meetings that no one at the EPA would keep a record of their discussions. "What I wanted . . . was an honest, free-wheeling exchange of scientific information," he later said, apparently not finding the presence of industry lawyers and his agency's deliberate exclusion of opposing viewpoints ironic and antithetical to free-wheeling conversation. As a Carter-era EPA administrator put it, the meetings had a "completely one-sided nature." The CMA assured critics that the industry group was "not at all interested in a one-sided debate." But at the same time, its vice president and general counsel agreed that "it is quite often more effective not to have competing sides attend the same meetings" and that discussions of the dangers of chemicals like DEHP "should be free of political policy debate." The tendency for powerful groups to stifle debate, exert secret influence, and get what they want against the public interest is exactly why Congress passed FACA in the first place.[53]

Years later, EPA officials revised their regulatory process because of a lawsuit filed in 1983 by the NRDC, the American Federation of Labor and Congress of Industrial Organizations (AFL-CIO), and other groups. Because FACA clearly did not support the EPA's "decision conferences"—what the agency eventually called its secret industry meetings—they were forced to settle with the plaintiffs. The EPA officials agreed to make their meetings FACA compliant and to review thirteen pesticides previously approved through the problematic process. Overall, the administration seemed to take a hit and to mend its ways. Indeed, the administration had a much more FACA-compliant record during its second term. But the conflict over the EPA's secret meetings was just one of many during Reagan-Bush's first term.[54]

James Watt's FACA-Defying Bender

The first sign that the secretary of the Department of the Interior, James G. Watt, would defy FACA came in early 1982 when his department's Bureau of Land Management (BLM) quietly announced a new National Public Lands Advisory Council (NPLAC). The announcement itself was kept far away from the capital's burgeoning environmental groups: the BLM circulated its news release about NPLAC only in the West, stopping at the Colorado border.[55]

The council's lack of balance was obvious and uncontroversial. Most of the 21 advisory council members, selected from a pool of 269 applicants, had clear links to extractive and real estate development industries, some more direct than others. The panel was heavily weighted toward oil and gas, mining, ranching, logging, and construction industries. One member, listed by DOI only as a "civic leader," actually ran an oil company and had leadership roles in oil-drilling equipment companies. Another, listed as the chairman of a Utah county commission, also ran an oil company. Only two members appeared to have few or no links to industry—Ben Avery, a conservationist and former outdoors reporter for the *Arizona Republic,* and John E. Butcher, an animal science professor at Utah State University. If the BLM was trying to give the impression of balance, it wasn't trying very hard. Avery served as the only likely counterweight to a group generally hostile to environmental protection and sustainable development. Though his presence might have (barely) slowed down giddy Reagan-era corporate forces hoping to exploit western public lands, Avery was probably not very threatening to begin with, given the fact that Watt's BLM had selected him for the job.[56]

When land-planning activists and other critics challenged NPLAC's imbalance, Watt's subordinates in the BLM offered the kind of tepid response one might expect from an agency expecting little in the way of negative consequences. "We think we've met the criteria of balance," a BLM spokesman said in response to critics. "Just because we might talk to them [council members] about matters of land-use planning doesn't mean we have to have land-use planners on the council." Perhaps the spokesman, Tim Monroe, was trying to be clever or sound counterintuitive. Or perhaps his BLM and Interior Department bosses sincerely believed land-use planners had nothing valuable to offer. Unlike many charters for new task forces, NPLAC's did not even mention the need for diverse perspectives. According to FACA, however, judgments about the relevance of, for example, land-use planners for land-use planning should not be left solely to federal agencies hosting advisory councils. More important, FACA was supposed to prevent private interests with unrepresentative preferences from having exclusive access to rule makers behind closed doors.[57]

Watt's group went ahead, mostly unchanged by the environmental groups' criticisms. NPLAC did invite the public to monitor a two-day meeting in May 1982, but otherwise it worked in the shadows. The council brought another individual on board, but member number twenty-two's only apparent qualification was a personal friendship with President Reagan. Although steel magnate Robert H. Adams seemed like a generous friend—he enjoyed exchanging gifts with the Reagans, such as a $183 crystal bowl (equal to about $439 in 2012)—he appeared to have little expertise in public lands management.[58]

If the stacked deck of Watt's advisory committee wasn't bad enough for environmentalists, the DOI also sought to rapidly accelerate the planning process, sidestepping environmental and health risk assessments and severely restricting public participation. BLM officials suggested, for instance, reducing the public comment period by half (from ninety to forty-five days). More creative was their effort to delete references to *participation* in the BLM's bylaws, inserting *consultation* wherever appropriate. How they intended to use that discursive gambit was not immediately clear, although they seemed to believe changing the language reduced their open meeting obligations.[59]

Watt led the DOI into at least two additional FACA-related tussles. One involved an off-the-books group of hunters who met with Watt and G. Ray Arnett, DOI's assistant secretary for fish and wildlife and parks. The Secretary's Resource Roundtable drew ten leaders from "sportsmen's organizations" to advise Watt and Arnett about less restrictive hunting rules in national parks. Watt probably expected (correctly) that the official DOI advisory group on the subject, the diverse National Park System Advisory Board (NPSAB), would not enthusiastically embrace his ideas. He had failed to persuade many on the NPSAB with his proposals for a hunter-friendly wilderness section of the Everglades National Park, "squatter camps" for hunters in the Big Cypress National Preserve, and widespread offshore drilling and commercial fishing on public property. His FACA-defying group, however, was a more welcoming bunch. He therefore sought support for his plans at Roundtable gatherings and stopped mentioning them at NPSAB meetings. Because wilderness and conservation groups were not invited and, in any case, never knew about the Roundtable's meetings—the DOI did not announce them, as required—Watt did not face many dissenting views. Roundtable meeting minutes, reports, and other member communications also never made it to the public. And to reduce the paper trail, much of the task force's business involved Watt phoning each member, without keeping transcripts or recording the calls. Thus, when information about the group leaked, DOI spokespeople were not entirely lying when they said that there was no evidence of Roundtable meetings and that there was no record Watt even created such a group.[60]

Watt was apparently on a kind of FACA-defying bender in 1982. In addition to his Roundtable and NPLAC, there was POWDR. The secretary created Protect Our Wetlands and Duck Resources in the summer of 1982, ostensibly to find the best way to protect vulnerable migratory bird habitats. To accomplish that goal, he asked those he considered the most relevant private sector individuals to offer advice on crafting a new law—large landowners and corporate executives with personal economic interests in the policy. A traditional task force would be too constraining, too caught up in environmental hogwash. "In order to make this a successful program as quickly as possible," Watt told the group, "we are going to work outside normal government channels." When uninvited groups (such as the Environmental Defense Fund [EDF]) learned about POWDR's existence and mentioned the FACA violations, they were accused by DOI of "snip[ing] at us in the most vicious partisan way possible." DOI representatives framed it this way: POWDR was nothing more than "a group of folks in a position to do something, and they're doing things." Whether "doing things" meant protecting vulnerable bird populations or paving the way to private sector profits by destroying the birds' habitats, the DOI did not say. In any case, Watt and other Reagan-Bush officials knew that defying FACA would bring few meaningful consequences. Perhaps they would get their wrists slapped in the end, but the secretive, exclusive work of the task force would ultimately shape habitat policy. And for officials like Watt, that's what mattered.[61]

Pressure from EDF and others prompted Watt to bring POWDR out into the open, at least for one public meeting. At the January 25, 1983, public forum, he goaded his critics, calling the environmentalists in attendance "outsiders." Meanwhile, the DOI maintained that POWDR should not be characterized as an advisory committee subject to FACA because the group had not spoken about legislation. After someone leaked a letter from Watt to POWDR members, in which he wrote about "the draft legislation" created from "my own ideas based on the conversations we had in Alabama," it was no longer possible to deny the group's task force status. Additional leaks—such as Watt's message to the group in 1982 that "there will be opposition to [the legislation]. I'll deliver the administration if you folks will deliver Congress"— made DOI's characterization even more suspect. In the end, *after* the group had finished preparing the POWDR Act (as it was known in Washington), the Interior Department finally decided to grant POWDR advisory group status. By that time, the deal was done, with a bill written exactly as Watt and his private sector confidants wanted.[62]

Reagan's Other FACA Conflicts

FACA conflicts during the Reagan-Bush years went well beyond Watt's stint at DOI and the EPA's "decision conferences." The administration disregarded or otherwise circumvented FACA—or at least danced close to the edge—ten other times. Some conflicts went to court and were resolved in the administration's favor, such as Public Citizen's lawsuit against the President's Commission on the Celebration of the Bicentennial of the Constitution. The DC district court ruled that the task force could proceed outside FACA, since its work was "primarily ceremonial" and did not contribute to "law enforcement, 'rulemaking,' issuance of 'advisory opinions,'" or resource allocation. Public Citizen also challenged the DOJ's Standing Committee on Federal Judiciary nominations, led by the (nongovernmental) American Bar Association (ABA). The Supreme Court decided unanimously in *Public Citizen v. DOJ* that presidents can essentially nominate judges however they please. As a result, the court made the ABA's nominations committee, used by presidents since 1947, immune to FACA's requirements. Whether those rulings were legally sound is another matter altogether.[63]

Sometimes, the Reagan-Bush administration appeared to defy the law and get away with it simply because protransparency interests failed to mobilize. At other times, FACA violations escaped public notice, disappearing as soon as they appeared in the public record (to the extent they appeared at all). For example, the President's National Productivity Advisory Committee worked as a FACA-compliant group from its official creation in November 1981. Then, inexplicably and without consequence, in 1982 the Treasury Department stopped publishing the group's May meeting records. A similar case involved a special review board examining the role of the National Security Council in the Iran-Contra Affair. The board appears to have been subject to FACA, although presumably some of what its members discussed was properly classified (such as the names of still-covert CIA agents involved in the affair). Nevertheless, the previously FACA-compliant task force board closed all of its meetings to the public, without a peep from critics. "No one . . . complained about the lack of open meetings," said its spokesman Herbert Hutu.[64]

Other FACA challenges fizzled out for unclear reasons, including those involving the Commission on Integrated Long-Term Strategy and the President's Commission on Americans Outdoors. Perhaps Reagan-Bush critics backed down because they realized they had weak legal arguments, or perhaps they recognized the many obstacles in a challenge against the government. The administration might also even have chosen appeasement, opening up the task forces and thereby quieting any media coverage of the conflicts. Whatever happened remains unknown.[65]

The Reagan-Bush administration did actually choose appeasement, occasionally, and usually after a bruising fight. For example, in early 1984, Census Bureau (CB) officials planned to meet with eight economists to discuss statistical techniques for measuring poverty in the United States. OMB director David A. Stockman strongly opposed the way the CB had measured poverty since 1964. In a contentious exchange during a congressional hearing in 1983, Stockman criticized the CB's method, saying it vastly overestimated the number of poor Americans because it did not properly account for noncash government assistance (such as housing, medical, and food aid). From Stockman's perspective, the real number of poor Americans only amounted to two-thirds of the CB's estimate. We can only guess about his motivation. His efforts to change poverty statistics could have been driven by a sincerely held academic conviction, or they could have just been a way to bolster the president's record.[66]

In any case, the CB, with Stockman's guiding hand, put together a panel of eight economists. They planned their first meeting in April 1984 and decided to hold it in secret. When critics cried foul, the CB defended its approach by saying the group, consisting of government employees and outside consultants, should not be considered a FACA-compliant advisory committee. Explaining why was the harder part. According to the CB, the panel would not be an advisory committee mostly because it would not be officially chartered through the GSA. By this logic, FACA only applied to officially sanctioned advisory committees. Officials could avoid the GSA paperwork, and voilà, a group could do what it wanted. Plus, the CB said the members of group would only meet on an "ad hoc basis" and probably would not produce a "consensus" view. Therefore, the CB argued, we should just cut them some slack.[67]

The argument unsurprisingly fell flat. To force the administration to comply with the law, Representative Matsui (D-CA) rallied about sixty of his congressional colleagues, who cosigned letters asking the CB to open the meetings. He and several antipoverty groups also sued the administration. Probably realizing its weak position in the face of the lawsuit, the administration backed down. Instead of opening the May 18 meeting, the CB canceled it and disbanded the panel.[68]

Four years later, the administration tried again to secretly revise its economic statistics with outsiders, indicating officials either forgot what happened in 1984 or hoped this time no one would notice or care. The National Economic Commission's (NEC's) prominent members and broad mandate—to recommend policies for continuing prosperity, with a focus on cutting the budget deficit—attracted heightened scrutiny, making its FACA defiance all the more controversial. Although the NEC planned to invite the public to some of its meetings, interested citizens would not be allowed into what cochairmen Drew Lewis and Robert Strauss apparently saw as the really sensitive ones—the ones that mattered most. For those, Lewis and Strauss jumped through the right hoops, obtaining the GSA's approval for closed meetings. Just before the 1988 presidential election, the GSA's acting administrator, Richard G. Austin, certified that the NEC could proceed with its November and December meetings, including eleven behind closed doors. Austin's decision, however, directly contradicted the intent of Congress, which created the NEC as an entirely FACA-compliant presidential panel in its Omnibus Budget Reconciliation Act of 1987.[69]

The NEC forged ahead with its politically controversial agenda, including a November 28 meeting to discuss "economic assumptions," with a closed session on the "treatment of social security." Why a discussion of the pension program's future was considered a necessary secret was not self-evident; it was not as if members planned to discuss military strategy and the use of nuclear weapons. Perhaps Lewis and Strauss expected the group's economic assumptions—which were themselves contested in academic and policymaking circles—to lead NEC members toward a discussion about shrinking or privatizing Social Security. They must have known that such a discussion was politically dangerous for the administration; there was a reason former Speaker of the House Tip O'Neill called the Social Security issue the "third rail" of US politics—"touch it and you die." One could only guess which popular programs would be on the chopping block when NEC members discussed "budget options" in a closed December 12 meeting.[70]

A December 5 FACA lawsuit by Public Citizen, the *Wall Street Journal,* the *Washington Post, Business Week,* and the Bureau of National Affairs forced the NEC to offer up a defense of its puzzling secrecy. Officials did not say what they were probably thinking: that the great unwashed masses were a bunch of economic illiterates who would ruin their sophisticated plans, plans that would help those illiterates despite themselves. Instead, they constructed an argument that focused on the need to facilitate and protect the group's "deliberative process." The consequences were dire, officials argued; if the veil were lifted, global economic chaos could ensue. The "prestige" of the panel's economists and the heightened scrutiny their comments would thus receive would make jittery financial markets even more jittery. Didn't everyone remember, they argued, when Alan Greenspan's words precipitated a plunge of the Dow Jones average and the value of the US dollar? Because members believed openness would spook markets, they would refrain from offering honest truths. The legal basis of this defense rested on FACA's Exemption 9(B), which says openness might "significantly frustrate implementation of a proposed agency action." The argument failed to sway DC district court judge Joyce Hens Green, who conceded "that it may well be easier to work without public scrutiny and may even facilitate eventual determinations and recommendations by the Commission. But facilitation is not the issue here. The issue is whether opening these Commission meetings to the public would 'significantly frustrate the implementation of a proposed agency action.' This defendants have failed to demonstrate." Judge Green ordered immediate declaratory and injunctive relief and later overturned the GSA's decision. Her rulings thus barred secrecy in any remaining meetings and overall forced the NEC back under FACA, as Congress intended. Once again, Reagan-Bush efforts to shield a task force because it would discuss economic policy were thwarted by the courts.[71]

The President's Private Sector Survey on Cost Control, by contrast, managed to survive challenges from multiple quarters and to set FACA-defying precedents used by later administrations. P2S2C2, as it was commonly known, emerged from a June 1982 executive order, which tasked it with the mission of conducting a "private sector survey on cost control in the Federal Government" and advising the president about "improving management and reducing costs." The need for secrecy was again not obvious; this was not a commission to discuss nuclear bombs or CIA covert operations. P2S2C2, however, was a large and multifaceted group—and a top priority. It included about 1,000 private sector representatives in 35 task forces, working under a 150-member executive committee, staffed by some of the corporate world's leading lights: J. Peter Grace of W. R. Grace and Company, Roger E. Birk of Merrill Lynch, Willard C. Butcher of Chase Manhattan Bank, and Donald E. Procknow of Western Electric Company, just to name a few. The 35 task forces spread out across the government, each targeting an allegedly wasteful agency. Because of its maneuverings around FACA and pretty obvious conflicts of interest, P2S2C2 quickly attracted criticism.[72]

Conflicts of interest were hard to deny. P2S2C2 members from Cargill, Quaker Oats, and other agribusinesses targeted the Department of Agriculture. Most of those in the EPA subgroup came from industries regulated by the EPA. More than half of the group targeting energy policies came from oil and utility companies. To those who worried about political corruption—using government authority for exclusive, private benefits—the White House offered thin reassurances. P2S2C2, they were told, "made every effort to be absolutely certain that there is no conflict-of-interest problem." In reality, this entailed nothing more than asking task force members to fill out a form. Some members offered their own reassurances. Dow, for example, asked critics not to worry about its designs on the EPA, since the chemical company's agents were really only "technical people who were not involved in political or policy issues," as if Dow employees would not tend to favor Dow's interests or environmental policy making could avoid politicization, given all of the competing values, trade-offs, and analytic approaches involved.[73]

The stink of corruption was worsened by P2S2C2's refusal to disclose most members' names. That refusal also set the administration up for one of its biggest FACA fights, and it established a precedent that both Clinton-Gore (in its health care task force) and Bush-Cheney (in its energy task force) would later employ. To ensure P2S2C2's secrecy, Reagan-Bush officials devised this clever work-around: members were not "members" because they technically worked for the nongovernment foundation that funded P2S2C2 (a foundation rich with business corporation donations). That private foundation, they argued, was not subject to FACA's disclosure laws, which allowed P2S2C2 to keep members' names confidential despite repeated requests from Congress's General Accounting Office and citizens' groups. With this defense, Reagan-Bush blocked the release of P2S2C2's work schedule, meeting minutes, and reports, and it prevented outsiders from attending meetings. Members were ordered not to share information with anyone outside the group.[74]

J. Peter Grace, the chairman and public face of the task force—at one point "virtually a household name . . . or as close as any businessman is likely to come to achieving that distinction"—adopted the role of the courageous, benevolent statesman, the good guy fighting a bloated bureaucracy in the public interest. "I'm just down here to help," he earnestly swore. His executive director, James W. "Bud" Nance, could not believe how anyone would object to what he, Grace, and the other corporate interests were doing. Nance accused his critics of ignorance and pleaded with them to trust in the group's authority and benevolence: "This is really a motherhood thing. How could anybody be opposed to making [government] more efficient?" When radical, unpopular ideas from the secretive group did leak out, such as one suggesting the government abolish the Veterans Administration (VA), many people wondered whether blind trust was such a good idea. But Grace periodically took to the media with his good-guy image, riding Reagan's coattails. "This whole [controversy about the VA] is ridiculous," he assured Americans. That thing about abolishing it? It was just the unused product of a brainstorming session, jotted down hurriedly on a "scrap of paper." P2S2C2's public relations strategy boiled down to "Trust us! We're here to help!"—with the group then pretending FACA and widespread antiauthoritarian public opinion did not exist. Public skepticism about private interests influencing government policy behind closed doors was precisely why the law was passed in 1972.[75]

Despite efforts by institutional actors like Rep. William D. Ford (D-MI) and advocacy groups like Public Citizen, P2S2C2's secrecy continued without interruption. Pressure from Representative Ford and his Post Office and Civil Service Committee squeezed some names out of the group but only via a leak—the task force directors gave nothing. The administration then fought off subpoenas from Ford, including one demanding eight secret legal memos from the DOJ's Office of Legal Counsel about P2S2C2's imaginative legal end run around FACA involving the private foundation (see chapter 5). The administration also successfully contested a lawsuit from antihunger groups objecting to P2S2C2's secrecy and unbalanced composition. DC district judge Gerhard A. Gesell rejected the groups' arguments, appealing to the need for efficiency and expediency, even if those values appeared nowhere in FACA: "The attempt to formulate efficient fiscal management of the government would bog down in a plethora of hearings, demands for document access and increasing time-consuming litigation." Judge Gesell later asked Grace's group to refrain from tackling "broad public policy issues" and to make its membership more inclusive, in another lawsuit brought by food stamp recipients. No one could verify whether P2S2C2 complied because its secrecy blocked any monitoring of its actions.[76]

It is possible that every P2S2C2 member acted from pure patriotic impulses, heeding Reagan's call to "work like tireless bloodhounds, leaving no stone unturned in their search to root out inefficiency and waste of taxpayer dollars." But even accepting that unlikely premise—unlikely, given the conflicts of interest—the group operated boldly in defiance of FACA, fending off criticisms and legal challenges with crucial support from deferential judges. The experience, like the other FACA violations, demonstrated to later presidents how easy it was to get away with unlawful behavior, including with large, prominent task forces like P2S2C2. With this experience as well as lessons learned from some of Secretary Watt's efforts, the administration continued to experiment with creative ways of circumventing FACA.[77]

In late 1983, for instance, Reagan put together the Task Force on Food Assistance, growing out of his concern "about the extent to which we have a problem that should not exist in this great and wealthy country. That is the problem of hunger." Apparently fearing the scrutiny of antihunger experts who might disagree with the president on policy details, the administration designed the group so that during its tenure members would only meet one to one with government officials (and keep all information secret). If that proved difficult, task force planners sought to ensure meetings would be kept to a maximum of three members because any more than that would trigger FACA. It was yet another example of the institutional creativity of the Reagan-Bush administration, a way of increasing secrecy despite the sunshine laws that were supposed to move the government in the other direction.[78]

Conclusion

It is possible, though unlikely, that the sunshine-era administrations only violated FACA's requirements in the cases identified and described in the preceding pages. Given all their vigorous FACA-defying efforts, one would need an unshakable faith in government to believe the administrations closed all of the other task force meetings shown in Figure 4.1 for purely legitimate reasons. Add to the list of violations the task forces presidents launched without even bothering with FACA (see, for example, chapter 10 on the Obama-Biden administration).

Still, this chapter's comparative analysis clearly illustrated the administrations' quite different approaches to the open government law. Given Bush-Quayle's less defiant approach, we can conclude with some confidence that it probably was more generally compliant with FACA's requirements than its sunshine-era peers. Those peers, by contrast, more or less equally resisted the law. Given that level of resistance, the administrations also probably defied FACA without prompting fire alarms or formal legal challenges, making our collection of cases a conservative estimate of the actual total.

Most of the time, the administrations tried to quietly circumvent the law, hoping no one noticed. When people did notice, officials sometimes feigned ignorance, as when Clinton-Gore health care task force head Ira Magaziner claimed, "This is the first time I've heard of it [FACA]. I'll look into it, now that I've heard about it." Or they just pretended they did nothing wrong. When citizens sued, the administrations tried their luck with other circumvention tactics.

Running-out-the-clock tactics exploited the delays inherent in judicial processes, including motions to dismiss and conflicts over discovery parameters. Most judges in those cases (as in *Judicial Watch, Inc. v.* [Cheney's] *National Energy Policy Development Group*) believed they could not—or just would not—use injunctions to force administrations to immediately comply with the law. As a result, FACA-defying task forces continued to meet in secret, racing to finish their work before courts could rule. Once the task forces disbanded, judges often refused to apply FACA retroactively (for instance, by forcing disclosure of transcripts or members' names)—a rather convenient case law development for the executive branch.

Administrations also played a variety of legalistic word games to circumvent FACA. It didn't always work, as when Clinton-Gore failed to persuade DC district court judge Royce Lamberth that its health care task force members were really "consultants." But when Bush-Cheney tried something similar—saying its energy task force "guests" were not "members"—the rhetorical gambit did work. That victory and others like it sent a clear message to future presidents: if you're linguistically creative and you land a forgiving judge, you have a decent chance of violating FACA without consequence—if, for whatever reason, you cannot apply the law's already generous statutory exemptions.

Overall, the steady beat of circumventions, plus the increasing use of exemptions (Figure 4.1), did much to diminish FACA's once-great promise. Yes, lots of task force meetings remained open to the public, with their transcripts released and members' names disclosed. And yes, officials felt constrained enough by the law—and by the credible threat of lawsuits and the occasional skeptical judge—to only selectively violate FACA. Sunshine-era administrations clearly did not ignore it outright, violating it with abandon. For those reasons, the sunshine law in practice made American politics relatively more open than it had been before 1972, when Nixon signed it. But how effective is a law that lets officials violate it when they choose, even if they have to be somewhat selective? That they do not *always* violate it without consequence is hardly a reason to uphold the status quo.

Several accountability-enhancing reforms could be deployed to make FACA (or something like it) work better. First, more judges should utilize their authority to issue injunctions for immediate relief to counter running-out-the-clock tactics. (*Comply now with FACA's requirements or suffer legal consequences. And shut down the task force* now.) Judges need not use an injunction in every lawsuit, but a greater credible threat of one would place another much-needed constraint upon the executive. Second, legislators should define the law's words more clearly. For instance, they could define *private sector members* to include anyone who meets with a task force's public sector members, where *anyone* includes individuals not on the government's payroll, without an official government title, and/or without any government authorities. Every contestable word should be clearly defined to limit word game opportunities.

Similarly, the GSA should rewrite and generally tighten FACA regulations to limit circumvention opportunities. For instance, Bush-Cheney got around the law by dividing its President's Commission to Strengthen Social Security into two FACA-immune, eight-member "subcommittees." Stricter standards would reduce officials' opportunities for employing FACA-defying organizational creativity.

5

SECRET LAW
THE "SINISTER TREND THAT HAS GONE RELATIVELY UNNOTICED"

The timing could not have been worse for the Bush-Cheney reelection campaign.[1] Just weeks after *60 Minutes II* broadcast shocking pictures of detainee abuse from the Abu Ghraib prison in Iraq, the *Washington Post* on June 8, 2004, published a front-page story about a secret legal memo that the executive branch used to justify the gruesome acts. Democratic candidate John Kerry was then ahead in the polls, due in part to voter revulsion about Abu Ghraib, and now the administration, facing added electoral risk, had to publicly respond to the allegations after years of assuring the world it had strictly adhered to domestic and international laws banning torture.[2]

The administration argued its secrecy was completely justified, emphasizing the legitimacy—and sometimes the sanctity—of confidential communications within the executive branch. The Department of Justice, the source of the memo, said it would "not comment on specific legal advice it has provided confidentially within the executive branch." The argument appeared reasonable enough. *Of course*, it seemed, the president should be allowed confidential legal advice and enjoy confidential deliberations on sensitive subjects. Besides, it only made sense that legal advice on classified matters should similarly be classified. Should national security secrets not be protected simply because they were filtered through legal logic? Despite the DOJ's reassuring pledge that "it is the policy of the United States to comply with all U.S. laws in the treatment of detainees—including the Constitution, federal statutes and treaties," the *Washington Post* piece contributed to a growing body of evidence that the administration was flouting laws (for example, on torture) with breathtaking regularity. The administration's secrecy surrounding the memo only heightened critics' suspicions.[3]

It would later emerge that the torture memos told the president and his agencies they could in effect *not* comply with "federal statutes and treaties," as the DOJ spokesman insisted. One memo, written by Deputy Assistant Attorney General John Yoo, flatly declared, "Criminal statutes do not apply

134

to the properly-authorized interrogation of enemy combatants by the United States Armed Forces during an armed conflict." Another, written by Assistant Attorney General Jay S. Bybee, infamously asserted that the president's subordinates could coercively interrogate detainees using techniques that inflicted pain up to the point where they caused "serious physical injury, such as organ failure, impairment of bodily function, or even death." As long as the interrogator did not have the "specific intent" to violate domestic and international laws, the "enhanced interrogations" could not be construed as torture, despite the fact that waterboarding and other methods had long been considered as such in the law of war and in US military and intelligence history. Bybee's memo even contained a section entitled "Interpretation to Avoid Constitutional Problems," which could hardly have been more explicit about its cortortions around the Constitution.[4]

The Bybee and Yoo memos were only two of the many written every year by politically appointed lawyers within the DOJ's Office of Legal Counsel. The OLC is charged with giving the executive branch legal advice to ensure the "lawfulness of presidential and executive branch action, including contemplated action," based on the Constitution's directive that the president should "take Care that the Laws be faithfully executed." The president receives plenty of legal advice from lawyers inside and outside the White House, but the OLC's opinions are unique in that they are authoritative, binding, and immunizing within the executive branch. They are authoritative in the sense that their interpretations provide for officials the last word on a congresssional statute. They are binding and immunizing by giving legal protections to officials whose decisions are based on their guidance, if those decisions and subsequent actions are later called into question. OLC opinions are thus not merely advisory. They also directly shape policy; immunize officials; and, if divergent from existing law, create tensions among the branches of government.[5]

The Legality of Secret Law

The first Congress of the United States (convened in 1789) was very clear about what the government needed to do with new legislation. Every "law, order, resolution, and vote, [should] be published in at least three of the public newspapers printed within the United States," and "one printed copy [should] be delivered to each Senator and Representative of the United States, and two printed copies duly authenticated to be sent to the Executive authority of each State." Congress was silent about whether the executive branch should publish its own laws, orders, and resolutions because at that time the executive was not seen as a rule-making authority (that is, Article II envisions a rule-enforcing executive). As the government grew during the nineteenth century and especially during the twentieth following the New Deal and the rise of the "national security state," executives increasingly offered guidance to the bureaucracy, in the form of executive orders and regulations, in order to bring clarity to vague, contradictory, or complex congressional statutes. However, even as executives became more and more involved in rule making, they operated without clear guidelines about publication. Scores of orders, directives, and regulations were pushed through the system, affecting citizens' lives but concealed from scrutiny. The hidden thicket of rules often led to organizational chaos within the executive branch. The inefficiency of the system—not to mention its undemocratic nature—was most evident in interbranch relations. At one point in Franklin Delano Roosevelt's first administration, for example, the president's solicitor general had to admit before stunned Supreme Court justices that an executive order at the heart of a major lawsuit was actually no longer in force. The order had been mistakenly revoked, a fact that escaped the solicitor general until the case had risen all the way up to the Supreme Court.[6]

As a result of that case, along with other embarrassments and revelations, the Congress passed the Federal Register Act of 1935. The measure established the *Federal Register*, wherein the executive branch would need to publish every "presidential proclamation or executive order" and any "order, regulation, rule, certificate, code of fair competition, license, notice, or similar instrument, issued, prescribed, or promulgated by a Federal agency." The Administrative Procedures Act of 1946 expanded the executive branch's obligation to publish, forcing it to also disclose proposed rules for public comment. As the executive branch continued to swell during the post–World War II era, Congress passed the historic Freedom of Information Act in 1966, which, among other things, ordered the government to publish "final opinions, including concurring and dissenting opinions," "statements of policy and interpretations which have been adopted," and "instructions to staff that affect a member of the public."[7]

Over time, all three branches carved out exceptions to the general obligation to publicize rules and legal opinions. The entire classification system, for instance, rests on the widely shared premises that executive branch secrecy is sometimes necessary to protect national security and that government officials are bound, with few exceptions, to shield classified information from the public and enemies of the state. The obligation to protect classified information, including intelligence sources and methods, naturally carries over into realms like OLC memos. There might even be cases where an entire memo would be appropriately classified—say, if it focused on the legality of different troop positions or other actions in an ongoing war (the legalities of which might be in question because of ratified treaties). Short of an entire memo's classification, redactions could hide sections of documents, as is commonplace when OLC memos have been declassified.[8]

If the Bush-Cheney administration had followed the law, its OLC opinions would have been published, with very few exceptions. However, in just over three and a half years after the 9/11 attacks, the administration opted to fully classify at least sixty-four opinions, which dealt with issues like detainee treatment, domestic and international surveillance, international treaties, executive power, and the geographic bounds of the Constitution. Some, like Yoo's, declared presidents have the power to unilaterally abandon international treaties that had been ratified by the Senate. Others authorized surveillance of US citizens without obtaining court warrants as required by law. Many OLC rulings were based on a political philosophy, embraced by Bush, Cheney, Addington, and others, that envisioned very few checks and balances across the branches of government (see chapter 2). The expansive view of presidential power some would deride as monarchist—"unitary executive theory" to its adherents—led Yoo to declare, "Congress may no more regulate the President's ability to detain and interrogate enemy combatants than it may regulate his ability to direct troop movements on the battlefield." Though that might be a debatable proposition, the fact that it and others like it remained secret for years—as the government continued to act upon them—is a major reason why the OLC memos sparked such controversy when they were eventually disclosed.[9]

Defenders of a secretive OLC tended to make several points. First, secrecy in this context is necessary to maintain the confidentiality typically afforded to discussions between lawyers and their clients—in this case, OLC attorneys and presidents. It is simply an application of attorney-client privilege. Second (and related), OLC memos should be seen merely as the kind of valuable advice lawyers routinely give their clients when considering different courses of action. The president and his cabinet, not the OLC, ultimately make policy decisions, sometimes not congruent with OLC memos. Third, OLC memos containing classified information should themselves be classified, including those dealing with secret government programs. Finally, defenders argued, we should not exaggerate the power of this small office within the DOJ because its findings, when adopted in presidential policies, are only binding on one branch of government. Plus, Congress has the authority in most areas to make laws more explicit, to counter problematic OLC memos.[10]

The last argument, about Congress's ability to make its statutes more explicit in order to counteract OLC secrecy, is probably the weakest. As Sen. Russell Feingold (D-WI) argued, it would be mighty difficult for Congress to "exercise that prerogative if it doesn't know what OLC's interpretation is" on an existing statute. In other words, if an administration uses secret law to twist around a statute, members of Congress cannot make appropriate clarifications to the law for the simple reason that they do not know what clarifications need to be made. Likewise, the lack of executive branch transparency about its own orders and regulations hinders legislative action. One Bush-Cheney OLC memo, for instance, gave the president the authority to rescind existing executive orders without notifying Congress or the public. By making these kinds of secret changes, "reversible executive orders" prevented the Congress from legislatively responding to executive branch policy changes and effectively gave the president the right to "actively mislead Congress and the public, who will mistakenly believe that a published order is still in effect when it isn't," as Steven Aftergood put it. Sen. Sheldon Whitehouse (D-CT), who brought the memo to light in 2007, distilled its essence in a speech to Congress: "One, I [the President] don't have to follow my own rules, and if I break them, I don't have to tell you that I am breaking them; two, I get to determine what my own powers are; and three, the Department of Justice doesn't tell me what the law is, I tell the Department of Justice what the law is."[11]

The other arguments defending secret OLC memos outlined above suggest the OLC operates just like any other executive branch lawyer and that its memos serve only as "advisory opinions," covered by long-standing standards of attorney-client privilege. (Some go further, saying executive branch memos can be presumed covered by executive privilege, even when it is not explicitly invoked.) However attractive the analogy with ordinary attorney-client privilege or even ordinary executive branch legal advice may be, OLC opinions in effect operate as binding rules within the entire executive branch, setting parameters, defining concepts (for example, "torture"), and providing legal cover to anyone who might later be scrutinized. As a result, the "mere legal advice" argument is not appropriate. The memos transcend typical executive branch communications because they are authoritative, binding, and immunizing. Lawyerly advice in all other contexts does not have that kind of authority. Concealing advice from OLC lawyers *before* an opinion becomes official might be justified. But once in force, memos are no longer mere communications.[12]

Finally, though redacting classified information from legal opinions is sometimes justified, it is clear from the declassified and leaked OLC memos that no information of the sort appeared in them. None contained information about CIA or NSA agents or operations. None described classified information extracted from detainees. The legal opinions were just that— argumentative essays of the sort one would find in an academic law journal.

Indeed, it likely was the possibility of avoiding any kind of peer or public review process that led the administration to embrace secrecy in the OLC. Bush-Cheney officials had not been terribly successful in persuading many in Congress and in the public to embrace their views about unhindered presidential power during wartime. To be sure, many Americans accepted arguments from politicians and Hollywood producers (as from the show *24*) about the need for executive discretion in detaining and even torturing terrorism suspects. However, figures like Cheney, Addington, and others knew their unconventional views of presidential authority—views that declared the Congress legally impotent with regard to *any* foreign policy decisions, as Yoo's detainee memo declared—were a hard sell. In any case, Cheney et al. were more concerned with their project of restoring presidential powers that the Congress allegedly seized after Vietnam and Watergate than they were with winning a public intellectual argument. So, they chose instead to inscribe their prerogatives in secret, authoritative legal memos, in order to avoid negative public reactions or any interbranch conflicts had they been forced to defend their arguments.[13]

Bush-Cheney critics had many reasons to decry this ostensibly new approach to governance, as well as the overt and stealth efforts to change the secrecy system. Lost in the fog and frustration of the moment, however, were the critics' assumptions about the newness and radicalism of what the administration was doing. The charge that Bush-Cheney had diverged significantly from its predecessors remained unexamined.

Secret Law in the OLC before Bush-Cheney

Was the Bush-Cheney administration's decision to delay or avoid the release of OLC memos something new? We can begin to make comparisons across

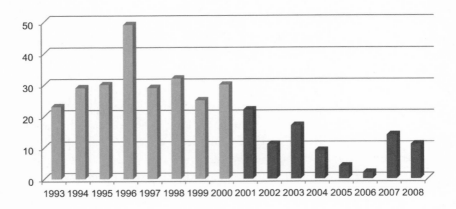

FIGURE 5.1
OLC Opinions Published within a Year of Enactment.
Source: Office of Legal Counsel, DOJ

administrations using the OLC's own publishing record. Although the OLC offers no information about currently classified opinions—a literally countless number—it does denote when known legal opinions since January 1992 were signed and, if not on the same day, when they were published and/or declassified. Figures 5.1 and 5.2 offer several points for comparing Bush-Cheney and Clinton-Gore practices. *Enactment* refers to the time when an opinion was signed and then disseminated within the executive branch.[14]

Figure 5.2 clearly shows a marked increase in the number of opinions published after a full year of enactment during the Bush-Cheney administration. Though one year is an arbitrary end point, it does reveal how many opinions were likely delayed well beyond a period for bureaucratic dissemination and review. And even if it is an arbitrary marker, it allows for clear over-time comparison. It is indeed striking that Bush-Cheney delayed for more than a year the release of *sixty-five* legal memos, whereas Clinton-Gore delayed just *two*. One of those, written a day before Bush's inauguration, probably should not count against Clinton. Short delays are typical; we should not fault his administration for failing to publish it within twenty-four hours. More interesting is how Bush-Cheney handled the January 19, 2001, memo, which contained OLC lawyers' less-than-explosive analysis of the "Applicability of the Antideficiency Act to a Violation of a Condition or Internal Cap within an Appropriation." The administration delayed its release for eight years.

The other secret Clinton-Gore memo, written May 18, 1999, involved

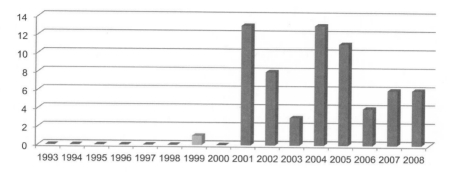

FIGURE 5.2
OLC Opinions Published >1 Year after Enactment.
Source: Office of Legal Counsel, DOJ

the confidentiality of immigrants' legal status after being recorded by census officials. The memo contained no classified information, but it might have generated political controversy during the 2000 presidential election due to its apparent sympathy for the plight of "illegal immigrants." The memo's classification and continuing secrecy, possibly done for partisan electoral purposes, was likely unjustified. Worse, Bush-Cheney officials kept it classified during their full eight-year term, leaving it up to Obama-Biden to publish it in August 2009. The example demonstrates plainly that Bush-Cheney did not invent the practice of concealing OLC opinions from the public for dubious reasons.[15]

Nonethless, Bush-Cheney officials appear to have enthusiastically embraced the practice. Figure 5.2 clearly shows an overall increase after 2001. Thirty-one of their first-term OLC opinions (34 percent of the total) were published at least four years after they were enacted; several others were concealed for nearly that long. Thirty-four Bush-Cheney OLC opinions (23 percent of the total) were published *after the 2008 election,* many not until after Obama took office. Again, these data do not account for any memos that remain hidden from view, but we can conclude with some confidence that more Bush-Cheney than Clinton-Gore OLC memos remain concealed. First, the simple fact that the Bush-Cheney administration more recently held office suggests more of its opinions remain classified. Second, the sharp criticism of Bush-Cheney practices from former Clinton-Gore OLC lawyers, such as Dawn Johnsen, also suggests the improbability of a huge, hidden trove of still-classified Clinton-era memos of a number that would subvert our analysis. Third, Bush-Cheney defenders argued that the practice of classifying entire OLC memos was especially justified after 9/11. Together with Cheney's admission that more of his administration's memos exist and Obama-Biden's embrace of most of Bush's counterterrorism, detainee, and surveillance policies, this bipartisan, post-9/11 governing posture suggests it is probable that a significant number of Bush-Cheney secret memos remain (see chapter 10). Thus, Figure 5.2 very likely *underestimates* the degree to which the Bush-Cheney administration governed in a genuinely different way compared with its immediate predecessors.[16]

Clinton-Gore Did Not Invent It: Secret Law in the Bush-Quayle and Reagan-Bush OLCs

Before the torture memos affair, the last time the "relatively unnoticed" secret OLC memos drew mainstream media attention was during the Bush-Quayle administration. The controversy related to the capture of two foreign nationals by US agents abroad. The first case involved a Mexican citizen, Dr. Humberto Álvarez Machain, whom the Bush-Quayle administration accused of being an accomplice in the 1985 kidnapping, torture, and murder of Enrique Camarena, a Drug Enforcement Administration (DEA) agent, and his pilot, Alfredo Zavala-Avelar. After Camarena's murder, the DEA remained on Álvarez's trail for five years despite strong resistance from the Mexican government, whose opposition to the US investigation resulted, in part, from the inconvenient fact of Mexican officials' involvement in the drug trade.[17]

The accusations against Álvarez were grim and conspiratorial. According to the DEA, he and a cabal of drug cartels and Mexican government officials kidnapped Camarena, whom they suspected of knowing too much about the corrupt ties between cartels and the government. Once Camarena was in the cabal's custody in Mexico, he was brutally tortured to extract information about what he knew and who else knew it. The torture was allegedly so severe that Álvarez at one point injected Camarena with lidocaine to keep the victim from suffering heart failure—only so the torture and questioning could proceed unabated. Dr. Álvarez's reputation as a brutal interrogator earned him the nickname "Dr. Mengele" by the DEA, though the comparison to the Nazi death camp doctor might have been just a tad overblown.[18]

After several unsuccessful attempts at diplomacy—Bush-Quayle officials could not persuade the Mexicans to extradite Álvarez—the United States turned to covert action. The DEA obtained a district court indictment, and after failing to locate Álvarez, it hired Mexican private agents. Without the Mexican government's awareness or approval, the US-hired bounty hunters captured Álvarez on Mexican soil in early April 1990. He was immediately taken into US custody after a short flight to El Paso, Texas. On top of demonstrating Washington's contempt for the Mexican government's decision, the rendition was a clear violation of the active extradition treaty ratified by both governments. As with most such agreements, neither signatory agreed to allow the other governmment to secretly abduct its citizens.[19]

The Mexican press, at that time under the thumb of—and probably expressing the views of—the Partido Revolucionario Institucional (PRI) government, responded to the news of the capture with justified outrage: "The intervention in Mexican territory, once again, is extremely dangerous for the sovereignty of the nation." President Carlos Salinas informed Vice President Dan Quayle of his "strong displeasure" about the operation and insisted that the countries needed "new rules of understanding" about cross-border policing. Though the extradition treaty did not expressly forbid extraterritorial abduction, US courts later said state-sponsored kidnappings violated other statutes upholding the "law of nations."[20]

Moreover, a 1980 OLC opinion stated plainly that the United States could only abduct suspects abroad "when the asylum state acquiesces to the proposed operation." Of course, the Mexican government had done no such thing. Faced with those legal restrictions, Bush-Quayle realized just how handy the OLC could be. To circumvent the extradition treaty and to avoid alerting the Mexican government of its bounty-hunting plans, the administration had its OLC lawyers secretly write a memo about "extraterritorial apprehension" in June 1989 that superseded the published one from the Carter-Mondale administration.[21]

When members of Congress learned about the secret memo—leaked before Álvarez's capture—they pressed the administration to release it, as well as any others tucked away at the DOJ. The DOJ refused, asserting in later interactions with Congress that the president had the authority to abrogate international treaties and alluding to legal reasoning in the memo it would not provide. Moreover, Bush-Quayle claimed the authority to withhold from Congress and the public *any* DOJ legal advice, even when the advice served more like law, as with OLC opinions. This was perhaps typical Bush-style unilateralism and secrecy—only it involved Bush, Sr., commonly regarded as a "kinder, gentler," and more moderate president compared with his son.[22]

The DOJ ultimately gave selected members of Congress the opportunity to see the secret memo, on the condition that they could not copy anything while reviewing it. The administration may have given in (minimally) to Congress's demands in the Álvarez case, but the interbranch conflict it generated convinced the Bush-Quayle administration it needed to institutionalize a "secret opinions policy," which would prevent Congress or the public from intruding into its secret, upside-down world (where memos tell presidents they can ignore treaties and other statutes).[23]

Administration officials announced the policy without much fanfare in a question-and-answer session during 1991 Senate Judiciary Committee hearings about a tangentially related issue, DOJ appropriations. In response to a question about DOJ memos, Attorney General Dick Thornburgh proclaimed, "There are no published or publicly available [OLC] legal opinions or analyses on this issue, and under *the Executive Branch policy on the confidentiality of Department of Justice legal advice*, we cannot disclose whether the [OLC] has provided legal advice concerning the issue." Thornburgh offered nearly identical statements in response to three additional questions. In that exchange, the Bush-Quayle administration became the first to explicitly and formally declare a "secret opinions policy," which amounted to the concealment of a secret body of law that often conflicted with unconcealed law.[24]

Álvarez's case against the US government went up to the Supreme Court, which ruled in 1992 that the United States had actually acted legally, since the extradition treaty did not *explicitly* ban extraterritorial abductions. However, later that same year, a federal district court in a separate, related case dropped the charges against Álvarez due to the apparently flimsy evidence the United States presented. Judge Edward Rafeedie told prosecutors, "You may suspect, you may have a hunch, but cases should not go to the jury based on hunches. No rational jury can make a finding that this defendant should be guilty of any of the crimes." Álvarez had maintained his innocence the entire time.[25]

The 1989 secret memo about extraterritorial abductions that was used to capture Álvarez was also used to justify the January 1990 capture of a much more famous suspect, Manuel Noriega, then the military dictator of Panama. Noriega's abduction naturally attracted more attention than Álvarez's, but unlike the Mexican government, the Panamanian government that stepped into the power vacuum after Noriega's capture did not challenge the United States or press for his release. Indeed, Panamanian officials were, by most accounts, happy to have gotten rid of him.[26]

Before Bush-Quayle

The first Bush administration's policy of secret legal opinions was only innovative in that it was formalized. Conflicts about OLC memos had erupted in the past—as happened, for example, with William Rehnquist's Nixon-era OLC papers, highlighted during his 1986 Supreme Court confirmation hearings. Although the Rehnquist memos do not appear to have been binding in any practical way (they were more advisory than authoritative), the Reagan-Bush administration publicly insisted that the president had the authority to keep *any* OLC memos secret and that the executive had done so before. A DOJ spokesman, responding to Congress's demands to see Rehnquist's OLC memos, asserted that "although some opinions from the department's [OLC] have been made public, the president can withhold opinions without giving a reason." Reagan ultimately decided not to assert executive privilege, fearing a battle with congressional Democrats and a decisive group of Republicans willing to challenge the president. The administration struck a deal with the Senate Judiciary Committee, letting selected members and staffers view the memos secretly.[27]

Unfortunately, the OLC only began publishing its legal opinions regularly in 1977—over forty-five years after its founding and the passage of the Federal Register Act. Forty-five years of binding OLC memos, forty-five years of secret law. Furthermore, only "selected" opinions after 1977 were regularly published. What percentage of the total those selected opinions represented remains unknown. Even in the supposedly more transparent Obama-Biden administration, after an election campaign in 2008 that regularly decried Bush-Cheney secrecy, the OLC remained secretive and elusive, and it embraced executive branch unilateralism on this issue. Take, as just one illustration, the following statement from the OLC website in 2013: "This web site includes [OLC] opinions that the Office has determined are appropriate for publication" (see also chapter 10).[28]

Clearly, the Bush-Cheney administration did not invent secret law in the OLC, though it used it to defy domestic and international law in new and novel ways. What the Reagan and both Bush administrations did, more than Clinton-Gore, was adopt a confrontational, uncooperative stance against the other branches of government. The latter administration was more cooperative, tending to grant Congress access to OLC opinions upon request. By contrast, during the Bush-Cheney and Bush-Quayle years and to a lesser extent during Reagan-Bush, when Congress members repeatedly asked to see secret OLC opinions they had heard existed, they were, in each case, met with strong, principled refusals, grounded on theories of inherent, unilateral presidential powers. What seemed new to critics of the Bush-Cheney administration in the 2000s was old hat to people like Thornburgh, not to mention Álvarez and Noriega.[29]

Beyond the OLC, Part 1: Secret "Controlling Interpretations" of FISA

On the morning of December 16, 2005, the American people awoke to the shocking news that their president had authorized an expansive domestic surveillance program almost immediately after the 9/11 attacks. James Risen and Eric Lichtblau's Pulitzer Prize–winning story in the *New York Times*, "Bush Lets U.S. Spy on Callers without Courts," revealed the existence of the program run by the NSA, as well as Bush-Cheney efforts to circumvent the statute governing domestic surveillance, the Foreign Intelligence Surveillance Act. Washington leaped into scandal mode, crowding out the story the White House hoped to promote—the Iraqi election from the day before. The NSA program generated rare bipartisan condemnation and surprisingly strong media criticism in the ensuing months. After refusing to comment on the story—Bush, for example, repeatedly said in a short interview on the day the program leaked that he would not discuss operational matters because of the ongoing war with "an enemy that lurks"—the president finally admitted what had happened but denied that his administration violated any laws or citizens' civil liberties.[30]

After World War II, presidents enjoyed nearly limitless authority to spy on foreign nationals abroad with a range of CIA and NSA technologies and operations. Until the late 1970s, they also could spy on citizens and foreign nationals in the United States (via the FBI), with few restrictions. It was then that Congress passed FISA, in large part a direct consequence of President Nixon's use of domestic surveillance to target political opponents, among other perceived threats. Through the 1975 Church Committee report and other investigations, Americans learned Nixon liberally used tactics developed by his predecessors, including dispatching the FBI, the CIA, and the NSA to spy on domestic antiwar protesters, suspected communists, partisan opponents, and other political enemies (among them Martin Luther King and John Lennon). Even the army deployed 1,500 plainclothes intelligence operatives across the country to monitor and infiltrate protests, disrupt protest caravans en route, create fake media channels, and introduce false rumors and propaganda blaming communists for stoking antiwar and antiracism protests.[31]

In the wake of their sunshine law victories, open government advocates in Congress passed the FISA in 1978, which severely restricted the president's authority to surveil citizens. Before FISA, that surveillance authority had rested solely on the nation's willingness to trust the government. FISA changed the equation by forcing executive branch officials to get court approval for domestic spying on suspected foreign agents and their citizen collaborators or saboteurs (the legal process for surveilling criminal suspects inside the United States is another matter altogether). In particular, FISA required warrants from the newly created Foreign Intelligence Surveillance Court (FISC). FISA also required FISC to give Congress (via the attorney general) an annual report with statistics about the number of warrants sought and approved. From the time FISA was implemented in 1979 until 2001, when Bush-Cheney took office, the executive branch approached the FISC a total of 13,087 times. *Not a single application was rejected* (though the court did occasionally ask for revisions before approving them). Perhaps reflecting the coziness of the relationship between FISC and the executive, the court operated out of the top floor of the DOJ, inaccessible from all public elevators.[32]

Because of FISC's absolute support, it was surprising Bush-Cheney found it necessary to secretly pen OLC memos allowing the NSA program to proceed outside of FISA's statutory authority, including bypassing FISC altogether. Once the news broke, senior officials attempted to persuade the nation that Bush had the inherent, constitutional right to abrogate FISA. They argued Congress implicitly authorized the warrantless surveillance program with its post-9/11 "Authorization for Use of Military Force." These arguments, like the program itself, elicited widespread condemnation. A FISC judge (James Robertson) resigned in protest. The administration needed a new plan.[33]

Senior officials were certain about one thing: they would not abandon the general surveillance strategy. New threats along with new technologies, they argued, justified a new kind of surveillance. Why not use techno-dragnet methods, employing powerful supercomputers to scan all electronic communications to more easily find the proverbial haystack needles? The computers would do the hard work, and only when machines detected threats would humans further investigate. (*And don't worry: all searches would be done with anonymizing software. Besides, no one wants to read your boring e-mails, any-*

way!) Overall, they argued, FISA was an outdated relic of the 1970s. Some supporters of the general strategy urged the administration to push for a new and improved FISA. Others, including new OLC head Jack Goldsmith, effectively pressed the White House to redesign the program on the margins and revise some of the underlying legal opinions (even before Risen and Lichtblau's story broke). Nevertheless, Vice President Cheney, his top aide David Addington, and other strong forces in the administration convinced the president to not worry about any of this and to continue the program unabated, which he largely did.[34]

Despite their resoluteness in the face of great controversy, things started to look bleak for administration officials. The ACLU, along with other organizations (such as Greenpeace and the Council of American-Islamic Relations) and individuals (James Bamford, Larry Diamond, Christopher Hitchens, Tara McKelvey, and Barnett Rubin) filed a lawsuit against the NSA in January 2006. To the surprise of many, the plaintiffs prevailed in the US District Court for Eastern Michigan in August 2006. Judge Anna Diggs Taylor's majority opinion affirmed the plaintiffs' arguments about the illegality of the NSA program, making her an overnight hero to some and a villain to others in a deeply polarized country. Immediately before the Court of Appeals for the Sixth Circuit heard the government's arguments, the administration decided to change course. Instead of reauthorizing the program, Bush-Cheney officials asked the FISA court (FISC) (that is, not the OLC) to issue a new, binding legal interpretation of FISA that would accommodate the program. The existence of FISC's "January 10th orders" became public knowledge almost immediately, once Attorney General Alberto Gonzales sent Judiciary Committee leaders Sen. Patrick Leahy (D-VT) and Sen. Arlen Specter (R-PA) a letter describing the "innovative" and "complex" new orders. The content of the January 10th orders, however, remained a mystery, although the administration used the ruling to maintain the NSA program without interruption. As the administration framed it, the program rested on even stronger legal ground because the judicial branch (FISC) had declared its support after judicial review. From the administration's perspective, things were looking up, even more so after the government scored a victory in the Court of Appeals for the Sixth Circuit, which dismissed *ACLU v. NSA* due to a lack of standing.[35]

The ACLU characteristically pressed on, appealing to the Supreme Court (the court denied *cert*) and filing a motion with the FISC for the January 10th orders, minus any legitimately classified operational details. Echoing Reagan-Bush's and Bush-Quayle's actions with the OLC, the Bush-Cheney

DOJ, *speaking for the FISC, despite the latter's location in the judicial branch,* refused to divulge any of the relevant memos, saying redactions would have been impossible: "Any legal discussion that may be contained in these materials would be inextricably intertwined with the operational details of the authorized surveillance." The DOJ also would not discuss how many secret legal memos FISC issued, suggesting there were more than one.[36]

For many citizens, including (too few) members of Congress, this shift toward secret law in the FISC was unconstitutional, contrary to FISA, and therefore unacceptable. FISA had authorized FISC narrowly, with powers only to evaluate the merits of warrant applications. FISC nevertheless created a new role for itself out of the ether, under the direct influence of the Bush-Cheney administration, in early 2007. Its new, contrastatutory mission was to produce "controlling interpretations" of FISA, which became, in Senator Feingold's words, "as much a part of this country's surveillance law as the statute itself." Secret, authoritative rules governed executive branch behavior and offered effective legal immunity to officials who followed their precepts. To the extent the debate about the OLC memos attracted media attention (aside from the initial reaction to the torture memos), the conflict about FISC memos received even less.[37]

During Senator Feingold's Judiciary Committee hearing on "Secret Law and the Threat to Democratic and Accountable Government," defenders of the FISC's new approach, such as former associate White House counsel Bradford Berenson, argued that because FISC had only helped the executive interpret FISA and because FISA only regulated the behavior of executive branch officials, any public interest benefit from disclosure of the opinions would be outweighed by the considerable national security risks and the need to maintain confidentiality in the executive. Critics of the newly asserted powers, including J. William Leonard, former head of the government's Information Security Oversight Office, found that argument untenable, noting how the FISC opinions did not solely affect government officials, as Berenson argued, because Bush's new surveillance approach potentially affected any or every citizen. Individuals who were surveilled had legal standing to sue the government on the basis that the binding secret law—by all accounts distinct from the actual statute on which it was based—had violated their constitutional rights, as well as FISA. However, because of the unyielding secrecy (the program itself, its legal foundation, and its targets all remained classified and immune from FOIA requests), surveilled citizens could not learn if they had been targeted.[38]

The fate of the January 10th orders did not matter much in the end, for two reasons. First, FISC rescinded parts of the January 10th memos months after issuing them. In March 2007 and then May 2007, FISC judges either withdrew sections of the January 10th orders or otherwise challenged the legality of parts of the surveillance program covered by the orders. The same court that created the secret memos thus revoked them in part. If that is true—the details remain cloaked in secrecy—FISC was more independent from the executive than many believed.[39]

Second, dissatisfied with the more restrictive FISC rulings issued in March and May, the administration persuaded the Democratic Party–controlled Congress to pass the FISA Amendments Act of 2008, which gave the executive almost unfettered discretion in surveillance. Why did so many Democrats support Bush after attacking him on the surveillance issue in the 2006 congressional elections? (In the House, 105 Democrats voted for the measure, with 128 against it; in the Senate, 22 of 50 Democrats voted in support.) It was probably not a coincidence that many Democratic politicians, including then senator Barack Obama (D-IL), reversed their positions on the issue once Republicans, like Obama's presidential election opponent, Sen. John McCain (R-AZ), defined the issue as a "vital national security matter." Democrats, hungry for the White House, would not let Republicans paint them as weak on terrorism in the upcoming campaign, as they had with some success in 2004 when Bush and his backers spun and chided candidate John Kerry for just about everything he said about counterterrorism policy. Three years later, Democrats seemed to act preemptively to avoid the Bush-Cheney campaign's rhetorical coercion; the president did not even have to show his weapon. Although Democratic Party leaders explained the turnaround on surveillance by touting "compromises" reached with the administration, Democrats actually got nothing policywise in return for their support (pork is another matter). What leaders like Rep. Steny Hoyer (D-MD) were calling a compromise, independent-minded legislators like Senator Feingold called a "capitulation." Indeed, as Sen. Christopher S. Bond (R-MO) reported, "I think the White House got a better deal than even they had hoped to get." He should know: he led the Senate-House negotiations.[40]

But that kind of political pressure only explains part of the Democratic turnaround. A simple money-in-politics explanation takes us much of the way there. It was also probably not a coincidence that many Democrats who supported the FISA reform bills—which included full, retroactive immunity for telecommunications corporations that secretly wiretapped for the govern-

ment—almost immediately received bountiful sums from those same companies. Many also had enjoyed telecom beneficence in the past. On top of
campaign finance incentives, it is probable that many Democrats sincerely
supported the president and the corporations on the surveillance issue but
believed they could not honestly say so to likely Democratic voters. Their
2006 campaign appeals to civil liberties were purely electoral, and empty.[41]

No matter the legislative politics that created the bills, the Protect America
Act of 2007 and then the FISA Amendments Act of 2008 set the program
Bush and Cheney built on a sturdy legislative foundation (its constitutionality was another matter). Beyond authorizing "dragnet" surveillance of phone,
fax, and Internet messages, and beyond giving retroactive immunity to the
telecommunications companies that had helped the government spy on their
customers, the new laws restructured and, in some ways, weakened the FISC.
In addition to having the authority to grant traditional warrant applications
targeted toward individuals, the court under the amended FISA was authorized to review the executive's broad plans, such as plans for dragnet surveillance. However, FISC would also be prevented from seeing any details about
who specifically would be monitored by the NSA in the dragnet, in effect
forcing FISC judges to simply trust the executive branch that officials' suspicions were justified, based on secret evidence. An already secretive court,
closely aligned with the executive and closed to the public and Congress, was
thus forced to adopt an even more deferential position vis-à-vis the executive.
Should FISC reject the executive's vague surveillance plans, which was quite
unlikely given the court's long history of deference, the government could
continue its operations unhindered as it appealed the FISC ruling, retaining
any information it wanted during the challenge.[42]

In sum, the FISA Amendments Act institutionalized both Bush-Cheney's
radical new approach to surveillance as well as the executive branch's power
to use the FISC to write secret law—"contolling interpretations" of FISA
concealed from the public. The only oversight the new law provided was the
right of Congress's judiciary and intelligence committees to review FISC's
opinions. That was a minor victory for secret law critics like Senator Feingold,
since the January 10th orders from 2007 had been off limits to congressional scrutiny. However, the court's legal opinions would remain hidden from
public view, leaving US citizens and foreign nationals wondering not only
whether the government spied on their communications but also whether
they would be able to challenge the government's implementation of FISA if
they were targeted.

Beyond the OLC, Part 2: National Security Directives

An additional form of secret law, involving presidential directives, raises legal and political conflicts similar in nature to the OLC and FISC memos. Presidential directives take many forms, from executive orders and proclamations to letters on tariffs and international trade, and most of those are published soon after they are signed. Directives issued from the White House's National Security Council, however, are typically classified at the highest levels, sometimes for decades. For the first twenty years of the sunshine era, citizens could submit FOIA requests for anything that was not "properly classified" under Exemption 1 (national security information). But after a long battle over secret NSC e-mails that spanned three administrations, Clinton-Gore in 1994 unilaterally declared that the NSC was no longer an "agency" but officially part of the Executive Office of the President (EOP) and thus immune to FOIA (see chapter 9). Federal courts backed the Democrats' discursive gambit, leaving the secrecy of national security directives—classified or not—especially deep and enduring.[43]

For most of the NSC's history, the directives were merely advisory, whether they outlined the president's policy goals with alternative courses of action, considered how existing policy would be affected by new or pending congressional statutes, or consolidated agencies' knowledge and opinions about ongoing problems. However, as the influence and secrecy of the NSC expanded, along with the national security state more generally, civil libertarians and government secrecy experts with high-level connections grew increasingly concerned that the directives were quietly persuading presidents to circumvent Congress, "commit[ting] the Nation and its resources as if they were the law of the land" in a continuing, systematic manner. If the directives were doing *that*, what would stop NSC officials (and their boss) from assuming other unconstitutional legislative powers or issuing directives that told presidents they could and should disregard existing congressional statutes in the name of national security? And few would ever know, given the directives' deep secrecy.[44]

The Bush-Cheney administration's NSC directives (the National Security Presidential Directives [NSPDs])—along with the related Homeland Security Presidential Directives issued by the White House's new Homeland Security Council—were cloaked in secrecy like those of their predecessors. Many of the sunshine-era directives and their titles remain classified, which makes it difficult to assess whether the administration used the memos in an unprecedented way. We can only analyze the few cases when memos were leaked or declassified. The known *number* of secret Bush-Cheney directives does not appear atypical compared with earlier administrations, but that tells us little about their content—specifically about whether they flouted congressional statutes, the Constitution, or common laws.

The deep secrecy of NSC memos has typically eluded researchers, before and after the institutional change in 1994. One attempt by the government's General Accounting Office in 1991 to systematically study the directives was ultimately unsuccessful (in obtaining and reviewing them), although the GAO saw fit to conclude that the directives "do not have the force and effect of law" because they "do not appear to be issued under statutory authority conferred by Congress." Though that might be true based on traditional governing norms and a faithful reading of the Constitution, the available evidence shows the memos were used just as critics like Congressional Research Service scholar Harold Relyea feared in 1988 when he wrote about "The Coming of Secret Law." Through the NSC, he observed, the executive branch "assume[d] responsibility for matters specifically entrusted to Congress" without Congress's knowledge or consent, "including either of its intelligence committees." Indeed, one of the authorities that sunshine-era executives and their NSCs unilaterally adopted involved secretly contravening laws Congress did pass.[45]

Defying Congress to Support the South African Apartheid Government

Though it may have been, to put it mildly, a long time coming, the Congress in 1986 passed the Comprehensive Anti-Apartheid Act with overwhelming majorities in the House and Senate. In a move widely seen as callous and unprincipled, President Reagan vetoed the popular bill, claiming his opposition was motivated by his deep concern for the "plight of the people of South Africa": the bill's strong sanctions would "hurt the very people they are intended to help." Nevertheless, both houses of Congress overrode the veto, making the bill public law and giving the transnational antiapartheid movement a major victory against the racist government in South Africa. The president appeared to concede defeat, issuing a run-of-the-mill executive order clarifying how the new law should be implemented. Section 4 of Executive Order 12571, for instance, instructed that the "Secretary of Commerce shall be responsible for implementing Sections 304, 321, and 502(b) of the Act."[46]

Upon closer inspection, the order betrayed some subtle resistance. Section 11, "Coordination and Policy Guidance," noted, "The Secretary of State is responsible for *ensuring that implementation of the Act is effectively integrated with and is supportive of the foreign policy of the United States*" (emphasis added). Did that mean the State Department should enforce only the sections of the law that did not conflict with the administration's wider foreign policy? Did it suggest that the *entire* law was contrary to US foreign policy and that Congress had no business articulating it (that is, foreign policy)? In any case, Section 11 did seem to suggest that somewhere, somehow, the law would not be as aggressively enforced as Congress intended. Puzzling glitches in the law's enforcement did suggest something was amiss. For example, although the law ordered an end to air travel between the United States and South Africa within ten days of passage (October 2, 1986), over a month later (on November 6) South African Airways was still booking reservations for the popular New York City–Johannesburg line. The airline had not yet been ordered by the government to stop. So it "[kept] on scheduling additional flights, a week or so at a time," said a reservations clerk.[47]

It was not until Reagan's National Security Decision Directive (NSDD) on "U.S. Policy toward South Africa" (NSC-NSDD-273) was declassified in May 1991 that the administration's reluctant approach to implementing the sanctions became clear. Although the executive branch indisputably executed major sections of the law (for instance, imposing restrictions on investment, trade, travel, and military cooperation), the NSC urged a "good-faith but *non-vindictive* implementation" and "oppos[ed] new legislative and mandatory UN sanctions." NSDD-273, combined with Section 11 of the executive order, pushed executive agencies to work against the new statute and the clear intent of Congress.[48]

The tentative introduction of the air-travel ban was an early indication that the administration would use kid gloves whenever possible with the South African government and its supporters and business partners (the "non-vindictive implementation"). Although the law stipulated the travel ban was to take effect within ten days, the government justified its delay tactics by pointing to another statute giving the president a sixty-day period to review new aviation rules and stop their implementation if they posed serious national security risks. The flight ban ultimately was approved, but the administration's invocation of the sixty-day review period reflected its willingness to flout Congress and the new statute.[49]

Sanctions from the US government (and some from Europe) are often credited with contributing to the collapse of the apartheid regime, but the extent to which the Reagan-Bush administration worked against Congress's intent—thus limiting the sanctions' impact—is currently unknown and requires additional investigation. All of the defiant moves were pulled off quietly, without notice. Administration officials simply pretended they did nothing wrong and hoped no one would challenge them. What we do know is that on several other occasions, the Reagan-Bush administration used NSC directives to contravene congressional statutes, which demonstrates their willingness, and experience, in doing so.

Using National Security Directives to Violate Domestic Propaganda Laws

In January 1983, President Reagan signed a classified NSDD memo with the inoffensive title "Management of Public Diplomacy Relative to National Security." NSDD-77's vague, bureaucratic language does not evoke what it unleashed into American society. Neither do quick descriptions of the agencies it produced: the Office of Public Diplomacy for Latin America and the Caribbean in the State Department (S/LPD), headed by Otto Reich, and the NSC Special Planning Group to coordinate with S/LPD and other State, Defense, and White House officials, directed by Oliver North and Walter Raymond, Jr. There is nothing unusual about "public diplomacy" per se, as the State Department described it (in 2013, as in earlier years)—that is, "informing and influencing foreign publics and . . . expanding and strengthening the relationship between the people and Government of the United States and citizens of the rest of the world." But what S/LPD did in reality went far beyond that, by serving as a covert propaganda program to sway the *domestic* population toward the administration's Central American policy.[50]

One of Reagan's main objectives was to increase US public support for the Contras, the US-backed, right-wing, human rights–violating militia that was attempting to overthrow the revolutionary Sandinista government in Nicaragua (which also violated human rights but less so than the Contras). Reagan had already made and would continue to make ample use of the bully pulpit to paint the Contras as "the moral equivalent of the Founding Fathers" and Nicaragua under the Sandinistas as a "totalitarian dungeon," with the "unwanted presence of thousands of Cuban, Soviet bloc and radical Arab helpers." But to maximize its "persuasive communications" (to use Otto Reich's term), the administration, through NSDD-77, employed a variety of tactics to produce domestic propaganda without government fingerprints.[51]

The program focused on: (1) shaping mass media coverage of Central American politics, including elite commentary about it, and (2) lobbying members of Congress to support Reagan's goals, especially his aim to repeal the Boland Amendments, which had prevented the administration from directly supporting the Contras because of their human rights record. The mass media track used the expertise of trained propaganda and psychological warfare specialists from intelligence agencies and the miltiary to plant articles, run ads, and influence journalists and academics. One tactic involved hiring sympathetic and/or well-compensated outsiders to write op-eds touting Reagan's view and criticizing his opponents. For example, John Guilmartin, Jr., then a professor of history at Rice University, highlighted the dangers of Sandinista military spending in a *Wall Street Journal* op-ed on March 11, 1985. Guilmartin's connection with the propaganda office is not in question. According to a memo—"'White Propaganda' Operation"—written by the S/LPD's Johnathan S. Miller to Patrick Buchanan, then director of communications for the White House, "Professor Guilmartin has been a consultant to our office and collaborated with our staff in the writing of this piece. It is devastating in its analysis of the Nicaraguan arms build-up. Officially [that is, if ever asked], this office had no role in its preparation."[52]

The same memo identified another product of the S/LPD: a "positive piece" about the Contras by Fred Francis on *NBC News with Tom Brokaw*, which purported to show the "true flavor of what the freedom fighters [Contras] are doing, i.e., not baby killing." The S/LPD also planted ghostwritten op-eds in major US newspapers. For instance, the "White Propaganda" memo identified "two op-ed pieces, one for *The Washington Post* and one for *The New York Times*" that were "being prepared for the signatures of opposition [Contra] leaders" in a response to "the outrageous op-ed piece by [Nicaraguan president] Daniel Ortega in today's *New York Times*." When they could not plant their own stories in the media, S/LPD officials used other tools to shape media coverage, including granting privileges to prominent journalists (such as early access to internal documents); persuading editors to hold (not print) stories that officials declared "erroneous," and continuously complaining of antigovernment or left-wing bias to editors and reporters when stories featured, for instance, Contra abuses (in other words, "working the refs").[53]

The S/LPD dispatched secret agents to spread the government's message in 1,570 lectures, talk show appearances, editorial board interviews, and broadcast interviews. It also sent propaganda to 1,600 college and university libraries; 520 political science faculties; 122 editorial writers; 107 religious organizations; and unknown numbers of journalists, although high-profile reporters and pundits received extra attention (including those appearing on *The McLaughlin Group* and *This Week with David Brinkley*). And that was just in its first year of operations. In one memo, the NSC outlined seventy-nine "events" S/LPD agents either organized or planned—from secretly sponsored mass media events to public rallies for the Contras (and other right-wing militias) to Sunday sermons about the Christian morality of sending aid to the Contras. In general, according to Reich, S/LPD took "a very aggressive posture vis-à-vis a sometimes hostile press," "did not give the critics of the policy any quarter in the debate," and shaped the incentives in the marketplace of ideas such that "attacking the President was no longer cost free."[54]

S/LPD's second mission, as outlined in NSDD-77, was to lobby members of Congress. To evade legal restrictions on congressional lobbying by the executive branch, the administration developed links with ostensibly independent, private outside groups and individuals, including: (1) Republican-friendly advertising and public relations (PR) firms; (2) established, politically oriented nongovernmental organizations (NGOs) such as Accuracy in Media and Freedom House; (3) ad hoc "front groups" like the American Anti-terrorism Committee and the National Endowment for the Preservation of Liberty; and (4) groups somewhere in between, like Citizens for America.[55]

The content of the propaganda and lobbying was diverse, transcending a simple anticommunist message. For example, though never tiring of calling the Sandinistas "Reds," S/LPD agents also highlighted (or fabricated) the Sandinistas' racism, anti-Semitism, terrorism, human rights abuses, and attacks on religious groups, as well as their connections with drug traffickers, Libyan leader Muammar Gaddafi, the Palestinian Liberation Organization, and Iranian leader Ayatallah Khomeini (to whom, of course, the Reagan-Bush administration was actually selling arms, in order to fund the Contras). The Contras, by contrast, were consistently presented as "freedom fighters," "good guys," "underdogs," "religious," and "poor." The complexity of the actual conflict in Nicaragua should have made any unblemished, uncritical portrayal of either side historically suspect. Both the Contras and the Sandinistas committed human rights abuses, for instance. But it is worth noting that in 1989, Human Rights Watch reported that "the *contras* were major and systematic violators of the most basic standards of the laws of armed conflict, including by launching indiscriminate attacks on civilians, selectively murdering non-combatants, and mistreating prisoners." Though the Sandinistas were also violent, independent historians and human rights organizations have generally concluded the Contras were much worse.[56]

Similarly, S/LPD agents' depictions of the Sandinistas' totalitarian dungeon (as Reagan described it) were more than a little overblown. Even claims about Sandinista authoritarianism (that is, nondemocracy) were questionable following the 1984 election, which kept Daniel Ortega and his comrades in power until 1990. S/LPD officials spearheaded a campaign to frame the election as a "sham," successfully pushing "U.S. embassies, politicians, labor organizations, non-government experts," and journalists to publicly cast doubt on the election's legitimacy. Meanwhile, independent international observers monitoring the elections, including a Latin American Studies Association (LASA) delegation, certified the process as free and fair, which was a remarkable feat given the ongoing civil war and declared state of emergency because of the war. The Sandinistas enjoyed an advantage, but according to the LASA report, "generally speaking, in this campaign the FSLN [Frente Sandinista de Liberación Nacional] did little more to take advantage of its incumbency than incumbent parties everywhere routinely do, and considerably less than ruling parties in other Latin American countries traditionally do." The ideologically diverse group of six opposition parties even received government funds and free broadcasting time, and as an editor of one of several opposition newspapers (which were still up and running) admitted to the *Washington Post,* he could have published "almost anything about politics" during the campaign, even though his *La Prensa* joined others in boycotting the election. There were some documented disruptions of antigovernment rallies, but LASA and other independent observer groups uniformly validated the election's legitimacy.[57]

The illegality of the domestic propaganda program was obvious to most who learned about it, when details emerged near the end of Reagan-Bush's second term via the Iran-Contra scandal (see the later discussion). Despite the program's fundamental illegality, administration officials did make some effort to somehow operate within the law by building the program outside of the CIA. By avoiding the CIA, they seemed to recognize the letter, but not the spirit, of 1947's National Security Act, which prohibited the CIA from engaging in domestic operations (including psyops). The evasive maneuver also brought S/LPD in line with Reagan's Executive Order 12333, which prohibited intelligence agencies from "influenc[ing] United States political processes, public opinion, policies, or media." That is why Walter Raymond, Jr., had to resign from the CIA—after thirty years of experience running propaganda operations abroad—before leading the NSC team coordinating with S/LPD. Somehow, it seemed more legal or appropriate for covert domestic propaganda operations to be run out of the White House.[58]

Despite the prudent moves, the administration broke the law. As the GAO's comptroller general outlined in his 1987 report to former representative Jack Brooks (D-TX), "S/LPD engaged in prohibited, covert propaganda activities designed to influence the media and the public to support the Administration's Latin American policies. The use of appropriated funds for these activities constitutes a violation of a restriction on the State Department annual appropriations prohibiting the use of federal funds for publicity or propaganda purposes not authorized by the Congress." As the GAO documented in an earlier report, this was not the first time the Reagan-Bush administration violated domestic propaganda laws. It proved more difficult for the GAO to conclusively demonstrate that the administration violated antilobbying laws, despite S/LPD's close relationship with groups like Citizens for America. Overall, regardless of the secret program's illegality, the authoritative, immunizing force of NSDD-77 reassured hundreds of officials that their criminal acts would never come back to haunt them. If Oliver North et al. hadn't been caught running the Iran-Contra operation, which triggered the scandal, the directive would likely have remained classified for at least twelve years (as a presidential record). And the charade—officials pretending they had done nothing wrong and hoping no one noticed or challenged them while at the same time running out the clock (of the administration and possibly of senior officials' lifetimes)—would likely have succeeded. As it turned out, even with NSDD-77's declassification and overt evidence of wrongdoing, nothing of much consequence happened to any of them.[59]

Propaganda and Secret Law in the Bush-Cheney Years: Back to the OLC

The ceremonious toppling of Saddam Hussein's giant statue in Baghdad's Firdos Square on April 9, 2003, seemed to symbolize a major turning point in the new war in Iraq. Though Hussein was still alive somewhere, the US military's stage-managed lassoing of the statue vividly illustrated that his brutal regime had finally come to an end. Back in the United States, the seemingly quick defeat of Hussein's army garnered wall-to-wall media coverage. In addition to images of the toppled statue, several stories focused on how Iraqi

Americans were responding to the dramatic events in Baghdad. One report
was in some ways typical of the media's reporting, featuring euphoric celebra-
tions in Dearborn, Denver, Kansas City, and San Jose:

> NARRATOR: The televised images from Baghdad prompted celebrations
> from Iraqi Americans all across the United States. They seemed to revel
> in the collapse of Saddam Hussein's regime, as much as they did in
> Baghdad. In suburban Detroit, hundreds of Iraqi Americans marched
> triumphantly through the streets. The community of Dearborn is
> home to America's largest Arab community. On Warren Avenue people
> chanted, "No more Saddam," as they honked horns and waved Iraqi
> and American flags.
>
> IRAQI AMERICAN 1: We love the United States! We love America! They help
> us!
>
> IRAQI AMERICAN 2: Yes!
>
> NARRATOR: In this Kansas City cafe, Iraqi Americans watch the historic
> events on TV.
>
> IRAQI AMERICAN 3: I'm very, very happy. I said, thank you, Bush. Thank
> you, U.S.A. I love Bush, I love U.S.A., because they do that for Iraqi
> people's freedom.
>
> NARRATOR: At the Arab American Center in San Jose, California:
>
> IRAQI AMERICAN 4: To see him toppled and destroyed, it's very gratifying.
> It's very gratifying to all of the Iraqis.
>
> NARRATOR: At this Mid-Eastern market in Denver, Colorado:
>
> IRAQI AMERICAN 5: I never heard anybody who said he wants to see Saddam
> stay, so they all want Saddam to go.
>
> NARRATOR: For Iraqis living in the U.S., the nearly quarter century–long
> nightmare in their homeland is now drawing closer to the end.

For Americans who caught the story, the Bush-Cheney administration appeared to have the enthusiastic support of Iraqi Americans and potentially
other American Muslims, as well as Iraqis themselves. The story, like others
with similar themes, probably dispelled lingering concerns many had about
how the war might generate dangerous anti-Americanism, not to mention
concerns about the ethical and legal problems with the aggressive, preventive
war.[60]

There was just one catch: the video was scripted, staged, and paid for by
the US State Department, and viewers were not informed that it was a wholly

government production. It is possible that the featured Iraqi Americans were authentically celebrating and praising the president, but the video's failure to disclose its source prevented viewers from independently evaluating its authenticity in light of that information. The revelation by David Barstow and Robin Stein in the *New York Times* in March 2005 that the government had produced the video came with news that it had also disseminated a wide range of "video news releases" (VNRs), including those about Medicare reform, education reform, Afghanistan, aviation security, forest and wetland preservation, computer viruses, childhood bullying, obesity, foreign agriculture markets, and holiday drunken driving. VNRs had been used by resource-poor or lazy journalists at private media organizations long before the Bush-Cheney administration, but as far as we know, those earlier videos had been produced by private corporations and nongovernmental organizations. By the time the *New York Times* broke the news, over twenty federal agencies had placed hundreds of VNRs on mainly local broadcast news shows, including in large markets like Atlanta, Chicago, Dallas, Los Angeles, and New York. The scope was immense. One VNR produced by the Office of National Drug Control Policy was broadcast on 300 television stations, reaching 22 million households.[61]

A few weeks before the *Times* story broke, David Walker, the comptroller general of the GAO, who had earlier lost a court battle against the administration involving Cheney's secretive energy task force (see chapter 4), reminded Bush-Cheney officials that what they were doing amounted to nothing less than illegal "covert propaganda." His office had made similar points in a July 2004 memo, but the White House had failed to cease and desist. Walker's February 2005 memo noted that even though government-funded information dissemination was of course legal (such as presidential speeches and agency press releases), covert "publicity or propaganda" was clearly not, as was specified in Congress's annual propaganda ban in the major appropriations bill, among other places.[62]

The OLC once again put forth an inventive alternative legal interpretation. Acting OLC head Steven G. Bradbury acknowledged that "'covert attempts to mold opinion through the undisclosed use of third parties' would run afoul of restrictions on using appropriated funds for 'propaganda,'" citing an OLC memo from 1988. Nevertheless, echoing his July 2004 opinion, which was written in response to the first GAO memo, he argued that though the VNRs may have been "covert," the OLC disagreed with the GAO's perspective because the government's videos contained "no advocacy of a particular viewpoint." The VNRs, he contended, were of a "purely informational nature," distinct from the "undisclosed advocacy that OLC had discouraged in our 1988 opinion." Therefore, agencies should feel free to produce and disseminate VNRs with appropriated funds, Bradbury asserted, even if they "conceal or do not clearly identify for the television viewing audience that the agency was the source of those materials." It apparently did not matter that some of the VNRs plainly had a "viewpoint" and that they constituted "advocacy." For example, one touted the administration's signature education policy, No Child Left Behind (NCLB), and featured a "journalist" (actually a PR professional) who editorialized that NCLB "gets an A-plus" for its tutoring and remedial education provisions. Bush's supporters and even the OLC probably would have concluded that the video did in fact contain a viewpoint if, by contrast, the correspondent had said the NCLB "gets a D-minus."[63]

Of course, Bradbury was likely insincere about his conception of viewpoints. His main goal was helping the administration circumvent inconvenient propaganda laws using legalistic word games. Perhaps to reassure anyone in the executive branch who contributed to the propaganda efforts, he reminded readers of the memo that the OLC "provides *authoritative* interpretations of law for the Executive Branch" (emphasis added)—not merely lawyerly advice. Moreover, he stated, "because GAO is part of the Legislative Branch, Executive Branch agencies are not bound by GAO's legal advice." The White House's Office of Management and Budget reaffirmed Bradbury's argument, writing in a March 11, 2005, memo, "Heads of Executive departments and agencies are reminded that it is OLC (subject to the authority of the Attorney General and the President), and not the GAO, that provides the controlling interpretations of law for the Executive Branch." The binding OLC legal opinion—the (then) secret but partially leaked "law"—would protect anyone in the executive branch and would encourage more covert propaganda.[64]

For GAO comptroller general Walker, the propaganda program, its effects, and the government's intransigence was "more than a legal issue. It's also an ethical issue and involves important good government principles. . . . We should not just be seeking to do what's arguably legal. We should be doing what's right." Bradbury said little about ethics in his opinions, but he did write in the OLC memo, in a seemingly exasperated tone, that what the government had done—merely "informing the public of the facts," in his view—was "not the type of evil" Congress had envisioned. It was unclear if he was implying they were involved in a different type of evil.[65]

Conclusion

Presidential administrations since at least Reagan-Bush have used secret legal opinions in the OLC and the NSC to support domestic covert propaganda operations. The scope of these operations was by no means comprehensively illustrated in the preceding sections. Other examples have surfaced, though any internal legal justifications remain classified. The Bush-Cheney administration, for instance, paid journalists, through public relations firms, large sums of money to tout the president's policies in print and in broadcast media. The most prominent case involved Armstrong Williams, who received $241,000 from the Department of Education through Ketchum, Inc., to promote Bush's NCLB education policy in newspaper columns and radio and television broadcasts. Maggie Gallagher, another conservative journalist, received $21,500 from Bush's Department of Health and Human Services (HHS) and then $20,000 from the DOJ to promote the administration's policies in support of traditional marriage (that is, opposing gay marriage rights). A third journalist, the conservative syndicated columnist Michael McManus, personally received about $10,000 from HHS through the Lewin Group plus $49,500 for his Marriage Savers Foundation. The administration also admitted commissioning other stories about domestic policies, to be published without dislosing the government's role. Furthermore, the Bush-Cheney Department of Defense more than once explored ways to influence US public opinion covertly, including planting information in foreign news sources that would (perhaps) echo back into US news sources.[66]

Given the administration's carefulness about its other legally dubious programs, it is likely there remain undisclosed OLC or NSC memos that provided legal justification and cover. Nevertheless, after details about some of these programs were exposed, Congress clarified, once again, that covert domestic propaganda was against the law. Months after news of the VNR propaganda program broke, on May 11, 2005, Congress passed the Emergency Supplemental Appropriations Act for Defense, the Global War on Terror, and Tsunami Relief, 2005, which stipulated:

> Unless otherwise authorized by existing law, none of the funds provided in this Act or any other Act, may be used by an executive branch agency to produce any prepackaged news story intended for broadcast or distribution in the United States unless the story includes a clear notification within the text or audio of the prepackaged news story that

the prepackaged news story was prepared or funded by that executive
branch agency.

The provision was targeted directly at the VNRs, leaving the practice of paying journalists (such as Armstrong Williams) to propagandize legally ambiguous. President Bush did appear to order a halt to the practice, saying in
January 2005 that "all our Cabinet Secretaries must realize that we will not be
paying commentators to advance our agenda. Our agenda ought to be able to
stand on its own two feet." However, it is entirely possible that the administration carried on some of its propaganda programs under new guises, backed
by new, secret legal opinions.[67]

That is precisely why federal judges, senators, and academic legal scholars have betrayed their typically restrained style to declare secret law "repugnant" and an "abomination" to the rule of law and US democracy. As Aftergood so crisply puts it, secret law "excludes the public from deliberative
process, promotes arbitrary and deviant government behavior, and shields
official malefactors from accountability." This is true on the issue of covert
domestic propaganda, as well as the other examples detailed earlier: secret
"controlling interpretations" of FISA; presidential directives pushing for half-
hearted compliance or noncompliance with federal statutes (such as the 1986
Comprehensive Anti-Apartheid Act); and OLC memos justifying extraterritorial apprehension, detainee abuse, and secret prisons. All of the sunshine-era
administrations depended on secret law to achieve their objectives in the face
of institutional constraints—some (Reagan-Bush, Bush-Cheney) more than
others (Bush-Quayle, Clinton-Gore). The analysis reached back to the Reagan-Bush administration, but one might reasonably suspect President Nixon
also succumbed to the temptation at least once or twice. We might confirm
that if only the OLC memos from forty years ago were accessible.[68]

6

PRESIDENTIAL SECRECY IN THE COURTS

Secret Evidence

One week before the attack on the World Trade Center, Hany Kiareldeen, a thirty-year-old Palestinian immigrant, allegedly held a secret meeting of terrorists in his Nutley, New Jersey, home. Among Kiareldeen's guests was none other than Nidal Ayyad, who would later be convicted and handed a life sentence for helping to plot the attack. After Ayyad's conviction, Kiareldeen reportedly told a close associate he planned to assassinate the attorney general in revenge.[1]

Kiareldeen's life in the United States was initially full of promise. He arrived from Gaza in 1990 on a student visa and enrolled in classes at Rutgers and Essex County Community College. In 1993, he married Amal Mohamed, an Egyptian immigrant. Together, they planned to enjoy a quiet family life with their baby daughter, Nour, in the far Jersey suburbs of New York City. But their marriage began to crumble soon after the wedding, to the point where Mohamed filed at least a dozen domestic violence complaints against her husband in a few short years. After the couple's difficult divorce, Mohamed refused to let Kiareldeen see Nour, his beloved daughter, despite his legal visitation rights. By 1997, Kiareldeen allegedly had become so angry and unhinged that he threatened to set off a bomb in his ex-wife's car. It would explode, he told her, when she least expected it. During the years-long ordeal, Kiareldeen was arrested several times. Still, it was not until well after the alleged meeting with Ayyad that the FBI began to fully investigate Kiareldeen.[2]

But the Immigration and Naturalization Service got to him first, arresting and detaining Kiareldeen for overstaying his student visa. He had imprudently filed INS paperwork to formally change his status, which brought him onto the agency's radar. In a hearing before an immigration court, Kiareldeen learned he would be indefinitely detained because he was a threat to the national security of the United States.

He asked to hear the incriminating evidence, so that he could at least begin to prepare to answer the charges against him in an informed manner.

Immigration judge Daniel Meisner rejected his requests. Even Kiareldeen's attorney could not review the damning evidence, Judge Meisner ruled, because it was classified. A lead attorney for the government explained, "We have to maintain confidentiality when it comes to intelligence gathering on terrorist groups." Bailiffs hauled the suspect from the court and threw him into a New Jersey jail. He stayed there and in another facility for the next nineteen months, despite his repeated claims of innocence.[3]

Kiareldeen's lawyers eventually convinced Judge Meisner to grant a second hearing. After an in camera review of the secret evidence as well as new materials submitted by Kiareldeen's lawyers, Meisner decided the government's case was full of holes, with evidence that "raised formidable doubts about the veracity of the allegations." The government's case was "too meager to provide reasonable grounds to believe that [Kiareldeen] was actually involved in any terrorist activity." As a result, Meisner granted Kiareldeen's request for an immigration status adjustment. More important, the detainee—the suspected terrorist—was free to go on a $1,500 bond.[4]

Not so fast, said the INS. With support from the Board of Immigration Appeals (BIA), the INS blocked Kiareldeen's release, even though the FBI had actually dropped its criminal investigation after the immigration court's ruling. The only recourse for the Palestinian, it seemed, was to fight outside the immigration court system. With help from the Center for Constitutional Rights (CCR), Kiareldeen filed a habeas corpus petition at the district court of New Jersey and sued just about everyone responsible for his imprisonment: the attorney general, the INS commissioner, the BIA chair, local INS directors, even the warden of the Hudson County Correctional Center. He demanded to know exactly why the government detained him indefinitely, so that he could have a chance to rebut the charges. If the INS refused to disclose the evidence or at least provide a fair summary of it, the CCR argued, he should be released. The court ruled in Kiareldeen's favor: "Here, the government's reliance on secret evidence violates the due process protections that the Constitution directs must be extended to all persons within the United States, citizens and resident aliens alike. . . . And the court finds this failure to be sufficient basis to grant the petitioner's writ of habeas corpus and direct his release from custody." The INS tried but failed to prevent his release. Despite being linked to the World Trade Center attack and the associated terrorist groups, Kiareldeen left the Hudson County Correctional Center and headed onto the streets of New Jersey.[5]

It must have been a difficult decision for the court to make. The government's secret evidence painted a damning picture of Kiareldeen. During his time in the United States, he had allegedly: (1) conspired with terrorists to blow up the World Trade Center at a meeting at his home, (2) maintained active "membership" in terrorist groups, (3) boasted of his plan to assassinate the attorney general, (4) beaten his wife repeatedly, and (5) threatened to blow her up with a bomb in her car. Kiareldeen had a shady past, officials insisted, but the details of his life as a terrorist were much too sensitive to reveal in open court. And the allegations might have been easy to believe. Kiareldeen was a Palestinian from the turbulent Gaza Strip—home base of intifada violence against the US-backed Israeli government.

Yet a closer look at the facts of the case revealed too many intolerable inconsistencies and other flaws. For one, Kiareldeen had already moved from his Nutley house before the time of the alleged conspirators' meeting there. Furthermore, during the long legal ordeal, numerous witnesses testified that he was actually a moderate, secular Muslim who rarely spoke about politics. According to those who knew him well, he did not come close to the picture the government painted of an Islamic extremist bent on mass political violence. Indeed, after his divorce and before his arrest, Kiareldeen had married a Catholic woman—not a typical move for a religiously motivated Islamic terrorist—and was living a life largely free of politics and religion in suburban New Jersey.[6]

Perhaps most important, the government's source—possibly its only one—was Kiareldeen's first wife (Amal Mohamed), who had waged a bitter custodial conflict for their daughter, Nour (she pushed for sole custody without visitation rights). She clearly had incentives to demonize him. Yet her portrait of Kiareldeen as a terrorist wife beater was pure fiction. Every domestic abuse complaint had been dismissed. Each allegation came when he tried to see Nour, which he had done strictly in accordance with divorce court instructions. New Jersey courts had also dismissed Mohamed's claim that Kiareldeen threatened to bomb her in her car. Moreover, the accusation that he had ties with the convicted terrorist Nidal Ayyad and "Islamic groups" had no basis in fact; it was another fiction she sold to the FBI. Although some in the government clung to the fictions, it became increasingly clear that the entire package of secret evidence that kept him in jail for over nineteen months came solely from an embittered ex-wife seeking to exact revenge and to keep a father away from his daughter. The government's evidence was flimsy at best.[7]

Another surprise: although the case sounds like something straight out of the post-9/11 Bush-Cheney years, Kiareldeen's ordeal came courtesy of Clinton-Gore. It was in March 1998 that Kiareldeen was arrested, and then he was freed in October 1999. It was Clinton's attorney general, Janet Reno, who was the target of Kiareldeen's mythical assassination threat. The World Trade Center attack he allegedly helped plan was the one from 1993, not 2001. And it was in 2003 that Kiareldeen got his daughter back, retaining custody of Nour after her mother failed to return from Egypt as promised.[8]

Hany Kiareldeen's story illustrates two important points about the use of secret evidence. First, classified information as evidence can be deeply unreliable, perhaps especially so with uncorroborated, uncontested human intelligence from informants. This is true whether or not witnesses and informants have conflicts of interest, as Mohamed did, or when officials express confidence in the evidence's veracity. Second, it clearly shows the executive branch had insisted on using (flawed) secret evidence in the courts before Bush-Cheney. That administration's aggressive post-9/11 policies sparked boisterous popular debates about suspected terrorists' due process rights, and those discussions probably led many people to think using secret evidence was an altogether new tactic after 9/11. But it was the Clinton-Gore administration—viewed by many during the Bush-Cheney years as a saner, Constitution-upholding model from the past—that detained nearly fifty foreign nationals after the 1993 attacks, mostly after 1996. The vast majority had Muslim and/or Arab backgrounds, a reminder that that kind of racial/religious profiling existed long before 9/11 and Bush-Cheney. Almost all of the detainees were held on the basis of secret evidence.[9]

Clinton-Gore also led a bipartisan effort in 1996 to significantly expand the government's authority to use secret evidence in immigration cases. The 1996 Antiterrorism and Effective Death Penalty Act, along with the 1996 Illegal Immigration Reform and Immigrant Responsibility Act, empowered the executive branch to detain immigrants, deny them bond, and reject their asylum requests using secret evidence. The new laws also established the separate Alien Terrorist Removal Court (ATRC) and specific Alien Terrorist Removal Procedures, which together would facilitate the deportation of accused foreign nationals—not only suspected terrorists—with secret evidence and secret evidence alone. Despite the usefulness of ATRC, Clinton-Gore, like Bush-Cheney and Obama-Biden, never used it, probably because of DOJ concerns that the Supreme Court would declare its legal basis unconstitutional. Clinton-Gore and its successors also likely objected to the statutes' clear, albeit limited, Fifth Amendment protections for defendants (see the later discussion). Instead, the administrations made ample use of the status quo option—administrative deportation hearings—which sidestepped those problems. Indeed, the executive branch increased the use of secret evidence in those hearings after the 1996 laws passed. And the practice started long before Clinton-Gore.[10]

Secret Evidence and the Power of Jilted Ex-Lovers: Another Example

Consider the case of Ellen Knauff. A German by birth, Knauff (née Boxhornova) left her country in the 1930s to live and work in Czechoslovakia. When Adolf Hitler's army invaded her new home country, she fled just before the Wehrmacht arrived in Prague. Despite her German background, Knauff managed to obtain refugee status and a visa in the United Kingdom, working as a Red Cross nurse and then as a flight sergeant who served the women's branch of the Royal Air Force (RAF). The RAF said she had served "efficiently and honorably" and "with distinction." Following the Nazis' defeat, Knauff returned to Germany and landed a job with the US War Department, working in the Civil Censorship and Signal Divisions, which gave her performance ratings of "excellent" and "very good." While working in Germany, she met Kurt W. Knauff, a naturalized American citizen and World War II veteran with an honorable discharge who had a civilian job with the army. With the army's permission, the couple married in February 1948. The Knauffs planned a future together in the United States, and the War Brides Act (of 1945) promised a relatively uncomplicated path for Mrs. Knauff's naturalization and then citizenship.[11]

Minutes after her arrival at Ellis Island in August 1948, Knauff was approached by INS officials, who had been waiting for her. They snatched her from the newly debarked group, pulled her into an interrogation room, and slammed shut her cell block door. Her pleas and protests were ignored. Knauff was held incommunicado for months, deprived of a lawyer, and denied the right to receive visits from her husband. In October, the assistant commissioner of immigration and naturalization initiated a deportation process for permanent exclusion, with no opportunity for Knauff to plead her case in a hearing before an immigration court. For the INS, she posed such a danger to national security that her appearance in court could be damaging in itself. Moreover, even the slightest chance she would prevail was too great a risk. Unbowed, she filed a habeas corpus petition, demanding to know what the fuss was about.[12]

In a time of relative peace, three years after Germany's surrender in World

War II, the US District Court for the Southern District of New York flatly rejected Knauff's habeas corpus petition. She appealed, to no avail. The Court of Appeals for the Second Circuit affirmed the lower court's decision. A Supreme Court majority also affirmed the lower courts' rulings, giving the government the green light to remove Knauff from the country permanently.[13]

The court's majority, led by Justice Sherman Minton, argued the executive had unhindered authority to remove aliens like Knauff without hearings, as a result of the Act of June 21, 1941. The act, passed after President Roosevelt declared a "national emergency" on May 27 due to Nazi army gains in Europe, gave the attorney general the discretion to identify and summarily deport foreign nationals without a hearing if they posed a security risk. The 1941 law, Justice Minton conceded, did deprive foreign nationals of due process rights. But, echoing presidential power theories that rose to prominence decades later, Minton argued that the executive branch had "inherent . . . power to control the foreign affairs of the nation," which apparently disqualified individuals' constitutional due process rights.[14]

It did not matter that the United States no longer faced a Nazi threat and that the war was long over. The national emergency from May 1941 had "not been terminated," and thus, according to Minton, "a state of war still exist[ed]"—in January 1950! President Harry Truman had made clear, in a July 1947 Orwellian proclamation, that "the emergencies declared by the President on September 8, 1939, and May 27, 1941, and the state of war continue to exist, however, and it is not possible at this time to provide for terminating all war and emergency powers." For Minton and the court in 1950 (and Justice William O. Douglas and the court in 1948's *Woods v. Miller Co.*), Truman's declaration was enough to conclude that the war, though over, went on, and that all of the "proclamations and the regulations thereunder are still a part of the immigration laws."[15]

Prominent newspapers (such as the *New York Times* and especially the *New York Post* and *St. Louis Post-Dispatch*) strongly and repeatedly challenged the court's decision and decried more generally the broad attack on civil liberties. Members of Congress joined the chorus, pressuring the Truman administration to let Knauff defend herself. The House Judiciary Committee demanded that the DOJ disclose the secret evidence. Then, the House unanimously passed a bill in support of granting her US citizenship. Nevertheless, the government refused to say why Knauff, who had received commendations from the British for her wartime service as well as the US military for her postwar service, was a spy. The Truman administration clung to its story that it had sensational, damning evidence, so sensitive that disclosure, even to federal judges, would be "prejudicial to the interests of the United States."[16]

About a month after the court's decision, the INS restarted the deportation process. And once again, Knauff challenged the order, requesting to stay in the country with her husband. When the district and appeals courts again bowed to the executive, the Knauffs' only hope was more congressional action and possibly Supreme Court intervention. The INS, however, decided to just get the job done. The day after the appeals court decision, the INS arrested Knauff—Justice Robert Jackson had freed her on bond in 1950 before the first set of court arguments—and whisked her away to New York's LaGuardia Airport. Twenty minutes before she was scheduled to leave, Justice Jackson issued an emergency stay, which was rushed to the airport just in time. Right before boarding the plane, Knauff learned of the stay and thus avoided the trip back to Germany that could have ended her hopes once and for all. Her luggage was not so fortunate, leaving with the flight across the Atlantic.[17]

Through leaks, it eventually became clear that the government's allegation that Knauff was a Czechoslovakian spy rested on very shaky evidence. For example, during a congressional hearing in March 1950, Rep. Ed Gossett (D-TX) relayed intelligence agency "gossip" about Knauff's work with the Communist-controlled Czech government. One problem with the story was that Knauff had never actually lived in Communist Czechoslovakia. The Communists took over with Soviet help in a February 1948 coup d'état, and by that time, she was back in Germany marrying Kurt Knauff. Mrs. Knauff was actually at the congressional hearing where Representative Gossett spread the rumor, and she categorically denied its truth. Yet it was nothing she had not heard before. In late 1948, a cousin's friend had corresponded with Attorney General Tom Clark, who asserted (apparently illegally, given classification rules) that Knauff "was formerly a paid agent of the Czechoslovak Government, and reported on American Personnel assigned to the Civil Censorship Division in Germany."[18]

The other shaky evidence came from three government witnesses whose testimony was concealed from Knauff and thus immune to her rebuttals. The witnesses included: a typist from the Czech Liaison Mission in Frankfurt, who had seen Knauff in the office with people thought to be spies; a Czech military major from the same office who had heard about a valuable informant code-named "Kobyla"—allegedly Knauff—from another major; and a US counterintelligence officer who heard about Knauff's spying while both were in Frankfurt. The government's case thus relied on hearsay and a typist's recollections of Knauff being in the same room as alleged spies. The evidence against Knauff was weak, a fact the immigration court finally recognized. The judges dismissed all charges against her in November 1951, finally admitting Knauff into the United States as a free woman.[19]

Though separated by a half century and driven by different fears of existential threats (communism, Islamic extremism and terrorism), the Kiareldeen and Knauff cases are strikingly similar—even more so when we learn the government's initial confidential informant against Knauff had been one of Kurt Knauff's jilted ex-lovers. The two data points are connected by many others across time, including Ignatz Mezei, Dennis Brutus, Angel Rama, Choichiro Yatani, Fouad Rafeedie, Khader Musa Hamide, Michel Ibrahim Shehadeh, Aiad Barakat, Naim Sharif, Nuangugi Julie Mungai, Mustafa Obeid, Bashar Amer, Mazen Al-Najjar, Nasser Ahmed, Ali Khalil Termos, Imad Hamad, Yahia Meddah, and Anwar Haddam. All of those cases occurred before Bush-Cheney entered office in 2001. When officials from that administration arrested and detained foreign nationals based on secret evidence, they deployed a power they inherited from earlier presidents. In that respect, what they did was not unprecedented at all. But they did take the policy to new heights.[20]

The Bush-Cheney Administration: Turning It up to 11

> These are the sort of people who would chew through a
> hydraulics cable to bring a C-17 down. . . . They are very,
> very dangerous people.
>
> —Chairman of the Joint Chiefs of Staff, Gen. Richard
> Myers

Following the FBI and INS roundup and imprisonment of Muslim, Arab, and South Asian "persons of interest" in the immediate aftermath of 9/11 as part of the FBI's PENTTBOM investigation, the Bush-Cheney administration placed the foreign nationals' immigration hearings behind an impenetrable wall of secrecy. As described in chapter 3, the DOJ's Creppy Directive regulated the trials, forbidding the press, defendants' family members, and others in society from attending the proceedings. It also classified the lawyers' own identities (when lawyers were provided). In many cases, the government concealed the trials altogether, as if they never existed.

The sweeps themselves were ham-handed and glaringly racist. In the push to detain any foreign nationals who might have had Al Qaeda sympathies, the administration deployed a crude system of racial and religious profiling that haphazardly picked up anyone they thought looked or sounded Islamic, including dark-skinned Buddhists and Hindus. Then, the administration liberally used secret evidence for the detainees' open-ended imprisonment and for their deportation proceedings. The policy was markedly different from President Bush's stated position as a candidate in October 2000:

> There is [sic] other forms of racial profiling that goes on in America. Arab Americans are racially profiled in what's called secret evidence. People are stopped. And we've got to do something about that. My friend, Senator Spencer Abraham of Michigan, is pushing a law to make sure that, you know, Arab Americans are treated with respect. So racial profiling isn't just an issue with local Police forces. It's an issue throughout our society, and as we become a diverse society, we're going to have to deal with it more and more. I just—I believe, though—I believe, sure as I'm sitting here, that most Americans really care. They're tolerant people. They're good, tolerant people. It's the very few that create most of the crises, and we just have—have to find them and deal with them.

That 9/11 caused Bush to adopt much less "tolerant" policies in the name of security is by now an old and well-told story. Nevertheless, the abrupt volteface and its consequences remain an important part of American history.[21]

The exact number of people detained under the new policy is disputed, owing to continuing secrecy about much of what happened after 9/11. One official statement claimed more than 700 foreign nationals were picked up in the initial sweeps, of which 500 were eventually deported after secret trials with secret evidence. *Not a single one* was convicted of a terrorist offense. During the two years after 9/11, over 5,000 men were detained in the United States; none were convicted of terrorist acts or conspiracies. Add to that another 8,000 who were interviewed by the FBI and another 80,000 who were asked to meet with the government for fingerprints, photographs, and special registration. The government thus probed or detained (or worse) 93,000 individuals after 9/11, none charged with a terrorism-related offense. The practice continued for the remainder of Bush-Cheney's two terms, probably eliciting some useful intelligence (for instance, filling in holes in social network analyses) but inflicting huge costs on the individuals and families involved.[22]

Leaks forced the administration to occasionally comment on the policy. Secretary of Defense Donald Rumsfeld, for example, confidently guaranteed that the detainees were "the worst of the worst." Gen. Richard Myers, chairman of the Joint Chiefs of Staff, assured Americans: "These are the sort of people who would chew through a hydraulics cable to bring a C-17 down. . . . They are very, very dangerous people." Administration officials nevertheless kept most of the details secret, concealing their specific accusations and any accompanying evidence from the public, the accused, their families, and their lawyers.[23]

That the Bush-Cheney administration detained and deported hundreds of people over several weeks in 2001 using secret evidence made its use of the policy unprecedented in scale. When it instituted a new system of military commissions to process detainees accused of being terrorists (picked up in the United States or anywhere else), it also expanded the secret evidence policy in terms of its scope. The story has been widely told and needs only a brief retelling here.

After 9/11, senior officials grappled with the unanticipated problem of what to do with all of the suspected terrorists falling into US custody. Bush-Cheney lawyers quickly put together a military commissions system, announced to the public in a military order on November 13, 2001. The new system deprived detainees of defendants' constitutional rights, including the Sixth Amendment's confrontation clause, which gives litigants the opportunity to contest submitted evidence and question witnesses. The commission system also explicitly allowed secret evidence, hearsay, and allegations and confessions from torture, setting the tribunals apart from well-established evidentiary procedures that balance defendants' rights against national security. From the administration's perspective, the defendants were stateless "enemy combatants" and terrorists captured on the (global) battlefield, not criminals. They thus did not deserve much at all, let alone constitutional protections.[24]

Federal courts found much to dislike about the new system. Most notably, in *Rasul v. Bush* (2004), the Supreme Court granted Guantanamo Bay detainees habeas corpus rights. In *Hamdan v. Rumsfeld* (2006), the court decided the commission system violated Common Article 3 of the Geneva Convention. In response, Congress, acting in concert with Bush, passed the 2006 Military Commissions Act (MCA), which explicitly institutionalized the president's military commissions system, with all of its Constitution-busting parts, save for the bits the Supreme Court explicitly forbade. The Supreme Court then challenged parts of the 2006 MCA in *Boumediene v. Bush* (2008), focusing especially on the law's habeas restrictions but also on its restrictions on a "detainee's ability to rebut the factual basis for the Government's assertion that he is an enemy combatant." Without that ability, the court decided, the detainee "may not be aware of the most critical allegations that the Government relied upon to order his detention." For these and other reasons, including unlimited and unsubstantiated use of hearsay and torture evidence, the court found that there was "considerable risk of error in the tribunal's findings of fact. And given that the consequence of error may be detention for the duration of hostilities that may last a generation or more, the risk is too significant to ignore." Congress reponded with the 2009 MCA, which developed the tribunal system the Obama-Biden administration used against "alien unprivileged enemy belligerents."[25]

Despite the Supreme Court's interventions, foreign nationals were still subject to secret evidence in military commissions or immigration courts. The unreliability problems of the past were never corrected, and they will remain that way unless Congress passes something like the Secret Evidence Repeal Act, a bill that languished in Congress before 9/11. The obstacles toward passage of that bill grew substantially after 9/11.

"So Thin a Reed"

The administration's file on Lakhdar Boumediene was filled with tales of a shady past. One leaked classified DOD report described the Algerian Bosnian man's history with the Algerian Armed Islamic Group (GIA) and Al Qaeda. As a committed Islamic extremist and global jihadi terrorist, the report alleged, he had been "active in jihad and suspected terrorist activities" in Algeria and Bosnia with the Muslim Brigade, as well as with Al Qaeda central in Pakistan and Afghanistan. In Pakistan, he worked at a madrassa, the Islamic Hira Institute in Babi. Once captured, he confessed that terrorists had "approached [him] to participate in a terrorist plot in Jordan."[26]

At the time of his October 2001 arrest in Bosnia, the DOD report continued, Boumediene's GIA cell was actively conspiring to attack the US embassy in Sarajevo. The suspected terrorist had in his possession several potentially incriminating items: identity documents from Algeria, Bosnia, and France; documents from the Kuwait-based Lajnat al-Dawa al-Islamiah (Society of Social Reform), the Abu Dhabi Welfare Organization, and the United Arab Emirates (UAE) Red Crescent Society; a Casio watch; phone numbers of the Algerian embassy in Italy; about $183 in German and Bahraini currency; and two copies of newspaper articles, one involving a youth camp run by a UAE charity and another about an attack against a US Information Service office in Kosovo.

All of the evidence, along with Boumediene's alleged links to six other suspects arrested in the raid, made him a "probable member of al-Qaida."[27]

Algeria, for unknown reasons, declined the Bosnians' offer to extradite the "Algerian Six." The United States, by contrast, eagerly volunteered, taking custody of Boumediene and the others in January 2002. He was quickly classified as an information-rich, high-security risk, a perfect candidate for the military prison at Guantanamo Bay, Cuba.[28]

Boumediene arrived at the prison hopeless and unable to answer the charges against him, given the secret evidence and Bush-Cheney's suspension of habeas corpus and other due process rights. His captors dismissed as lies his repeated claims of innocence. ("Detainee has consistently denied involvement in terrorist organizations or plots of any kind against the US. He has denied membership in the GIA and affiliation with Bosnian mujahideen despite reports indicating the contrary.") Boumediene, however, was determined not to accept his imprisonment without a fight. He staged long hunger strikes with such determination that he had to be "strapped to an iron chair and force-fed through a tube in his nose that reached into his stomach," which prison staffers did every day at 6:00 a.m. and 1:00 p.m. He spent more than a quarter of his days at Guantanamo—about two of seven years—hunger striking and resisting force-feeding.[29]

A new legal opportunity to challenge his imprisonment finally arrived via the Supreme Court in June 2004, two and a half years after Boumediene's capture. The court annouced its decision restoring habeas corpus rights for Guantanamo detainees in the landmark case *Rasul v. Bush*. The government could still hold Shafiq Rasul, Boumediene, and the other detainees as prisoners without granting them most defendants' constitutional rights, the court ruled, but after *Rasul*, the men would be able to challenge their detentions. They still faced a jerry-rigged military tribunal system that allowed hearsay and secret evidence, but they could finally take the constitutionally protected initial step, a habeas petition. Boumediene did so right away. As his case proceeded through the court system (as well as a separate challenge in the European Court of Human Rights), a much different and more accurate narrative emerged about his life, as compared with the DOD report.[30]

Unsatisfying job prospects in Algeria, not religion and politics, led Boumediene to Pakistan in the early 1990s. In Pakistan, he found work not in a terrorist-training madrassa, as the DOD thought, but in a school (a more ordinary madrassa) for Afghan ophans, financed by the Kuwaiti government, a close US ally. Boumediene's road to hell was paved not by anything he did or said while in Pakistan but by the Algerian government's paranoid suspicion of *any* Algerians visiting Pakistan. To arouse Algeria's suspicions, Boumediene did nothing more than renew his passport at the Algerian embassy in Pakistan. Just being in Pakistan at the time was enough to place him on Algeria's terrorist watch list. Because of US-Algerian intelligence ties, Boumediene also quickly fell onto US lists. The label "potential terrorist" would follow him back to Algeria for a family visit in December 1999.[31]

In the Algiers airport in 1999, security officials pulled Boumediene aside for questioning. His interrogators demanded to know about his links with the GIA, as well as Pakistani terrorist groups. He strongly denied any associations, prompting the disbelieving officials to confiscate his passport and deny his entry into Algeria to see his family. He was baffled—it was the first time he had heard about any such suspicions. His captors then informed him of a deceptively simple way out: he could apply for an amnesty program the new president, Abdelaziz Bouteflika, had inititated to reincorporate civil war insurgents into society. Just sign the papers, they said, and then he could enter Algeria with his passport, and no one would bother him again. Though Boumediene still denied the associations with the GIA, he hastily signed the amnesty application.[32]

Following the trip to Algeria, Boumediene returned to Sarajevo, Bosnia, where he and his family had lived since 1997 (before Bosnia and after Pakistan, he lived and worked in Albania). American intelligence believed his work with GIA/Al Qaeda was his main reason for originally moving to Bosnia. According to Boumediene, his employer, the Red Crescent Society of the United Arab Emirates (formerly Abu Dhabi Welfare Organization), asked him to move his family to Sarajevo where he would become the "director of humanitarian aid for children who had lost relatives to violence during the Balkan conflicts." To smooth the transition into a new life in Bosnia as a citizen, Boumediene made another error borne of haste: he bought forged official documents for about 5,000 deutsche marks. With those, he obtained dual citizenship in 1998.[33]

On October 19, 2001, a Bosnian intelligence officer approached Boumediene for an interview at his Red Crescent Society office. It was a trap: he was promply arrested, accused of conspiracies and terrorist group connections. When police stormed Boumediene's home, they found the 1999 document he signed under duress in the Algerian airport that granted him amnesty for his (probably nonexistent) civil war crimes.[34]

The Bush-Cheney administration had pushed the Bosnians hard for the arrest, believing the Algerian Six terrorists were plotting to bomb the US and British embassies in Sarajevo. Bosnian authorities, by contrast, were quite skeptical about the allegations. But Bush-Cheney officials twisted arms to great effect. US chargé d'affaires Christopher Hoh, for instance, reportedly threatened Bosnian officials that the United States would sever all ties with their country, including the withdrawal of peacekeeping troops in the war-torn region, unless the men were arrested. "If we leave Bosnia, God save your country," Hoh allegedly said. When the Bosnians did not immediately comply, the administration apparently backed up its threat by closing the US embassy in Sarajevo in October 2001, which was quickly followed by the closing of the UK embassy and a World Bank office.[35]

Meanwhile, Boumediene sat in a Bosnian jail, trapped by fictions and misleading circumstantial evidence he could not rebut. In January 2002, hope appeared by way of the Bosnian Supreme Court, which ordered his immediate release (along with the other accused members of the Algerian Six) on January 17, after a long investigation. The Bosnian Human Rights Chamber also declared on that day that Bosnian law prevented their deportation. The men were officially freed on January 18. Still, US pressure on Bosnian officials remained overwhelming. According to Alija Behmen, Bosnia's prime minister at the time, "The only way out was to deliver them" to US officials, since he and other Bosnian officials "were not interested in introducing a new period of instability in Bosnia" courtesy of the United States and its allies. The Bosnians therefore complied, delivering Boumediene and the other men to US officials in January 2002. Their Guantanamo cells were ready and waiting.[36]

Boumediene's victory at the US Supreme Court in June 2008 paved the way to his May 2009 release. The court did not free him but further guaranteed Boumediene and the other detainees their habeas rights. In a federal district court later that year, Judge Richard Leon, a Bush appointee, freed all of the Algerian Six except for Belkacem Bensayah (see note 35), after reviewing the government's secret evidence against the accused in camera. The unreliability of that evidence was at the core of Judge Leon's decision: "To allow enemy combatancy to rest on so thin a reed would be inconsistent with this court's obligation." Although some officials probably still viewed Boumediene as a terrorist, all of the investigations and legal discovery processes indicated that his only crime had been using the forged documents in 1997 to obtain Bosnian citizenship. It was a serious crime, to be sure, but one that probably did not merit subjecting him to the horrors of Guantanamo and the destruction of his life back home. As he put it after his release, "My daughter does not recognize me. I didn't see my wife for seven years. Who will give me these years back?"[37]

Conclusion: Striking a Balance—Security, Truth, and Civil Liberties

Boumediene's case, like Kiareldeen's, Knauff's, and many others across the sunshine era, underscores secret evidence's serious unreliability problem. The Constitution's framers were well aware of the possibility that individuals could be wrongly accused. The simple point of the Constitution's Sixth Amendment, which guarantees that "in all criminal prosecutions, the accused shall enjoy the right . . . to be informed of the nature and cause of the accusation; [and] to be confronted with the witnesses against him," is that accusers are sometimes wrong and that the accused should be able to point that out in court, with logic and evidence. When allegedly incriminating evidence is kept secret, the accused obviously cannot challenge it. Litigants facing criminal prosecution in federal courts can usually rely on the Sixth Amendment's protections.

Problems arise, however, when evidence crucial to a case contains classified information. Submitting that information as evidence carries potentially large national security risks if the information is later leaked or used maliciously by a defendant or his or her associates. (If the information was not properly classified in the first place—an artifact of rampant overclassification—then the risks would be minimal.) A defendant might also exploit the situation by "graymailing" the government: that is, "threaten[ing] to reveal classified information during the course of his trial in the hope of forcing the government to drop the charge against him." Because of the real tensions between constitutional rights and minimizing national security risks, Congress passed the Classified Information Procedures Act (CIPA) in October 1980. CIPA authorizes judges to evaluate the sensitivity of classified information before sharing it with defendants or releasing it in open court. If a judge deems information too sensitive to disclose, he or she can ask the government to provide redacted documents or unclassified summaries to defendants. For CIPA to work in concert with the Sixth Amendment, the substitution must be detailed enough to let defendants fairly confront their accusers' evidence. There are problems with the system, of course, but it reduces defendants' risks of being convicted of crimes based on secret evidence.[38]

The government's opponents in *civil cases*, however, cannot claim the same protections. Although secret evidence could be used against any individual, it is most often used against foreign nationals in immigration cases, when the government tries to keep an "alien" in a detention facility. Because prosecutors can submit the evidence without sharing it with defendants, they do so whenever feasible. By contrast, in nonimmigration civil cases involving the government—such as those involving FOIA appeals, contracts, and torts—the government is often the defendant or in support of a defendant. In those cases, the government usually has fewer reasons to introduce classified information as evidence and instead focuses on getting the cases dismissed. Given the justice system's structure, foreign nationals bear the brunt of the government's use of secret evidence. Ironically, if immigration violations (such as overstaying visas) were criminalized, as many conservatives advocate, the accused foreign nationals would enjoy all of the constitutional protections available to criminal defendants, including evidentiary rights, filtered through CIPA.[39]

State Secrets Privilege

Immediately after the 9/11 attacks, Sibel Edmonds did what many Americans only dreamed about doing. She dropped everything and offered herself up as a public servant to help a shaken country. The FBI was critically understaffed in its Turkish and Farsi divisions, and it just so happened that Edmonds, a Turkish American, knew both languages. Although Al Qaeda operatives mostly used Arabic, their larger network included Turkish and Farsi speakers, making Edmonds's translation skills invaluable to counterterrorism investigators.[40]

At the FBI's Washington field office on her first day of work, Edmonds encountered one of the ugliest but typical realities of bureaucratic politics. Supervisors seemed to care more about getting a bigger slice of the budgetary pie than about catching the bad guys. Nine days after 9/11, for example, her boss reportedly told her to slack, to let the work "pile up," so he could demonstrate that the unit needed to hire more translators and "expand the department." Despite his instructions, Edmonds kept at it, going through the enormous backlog of untranslated documents that might have had direct relevance for counterterrorism investigators. These efforts were not appreciated. On several mornings, she arrived at her desk only to discover her previous day's work gone. Her boss, when confronted, allegedly responded, "Consider it a lesson and don't talk about it to anybody else and don't mention it."[41]

When Edmonds was permitted to work, she discovered what seemed an endless bounty of gross incompetence. Her top secret clearance led her to documents showing the government had actually learned before the attacks of the 9/11 hijackers' intentions, as well as some of their movements inside and outside the country. Sloppy and unfinished work in the FBI's translation department had contributed to the bureau's failure to stop the attacks.[42]

She also encountered espionage and corruption. One Sunday morning in December 2001, Edmonds and her husband got a call from an FBI coworker, Melek Can "Jan" Dickerson. Dickerson, whom Edmonds barely knew, said she was "in the area with my husband"—air force major Douglas Dickerson—"and I'd love you to meet him." Would it be all right if they stopped by? she inquired. The Dickersons soon arrived, and Edmonds invited them in for tea. After pleasantries, Major Dickerson, who had worked for the military in Turkey in weapons procurement for Central and Western Asia in the early 1990s, asked about the Edmonds's involvement in the Turkish American community in Washington, DC. They might want to consider joining two of the community's most exclusive organizations, he suggested: the American-Turkish Council (ATC) and the Assembly of Turkish American Associations (ATAA). When Mr. Edmonds pointed out it would probably be difficult for them to join due to the groups' exclusivity, Major Dickerson allegedly smiled and told him: "All you have to do is tell them where your wife works and what she does, and they will let you in like that," snapping his fingers.[43]

Edmonds sat in her kitchen chair, sweating and horrified. She knew, as Jan Dickerson must have, that the FBI counterintelligence division had been investigating the ATC for espionage. Because she was prevented from talking about classified information in the presence of the men, she redirected the conversation, and soon the Dickersons left. At work in the days that followed, Jan Dickerson turned from friendly to hostile in an instant, once it was clear the Edmondses would resist her recruitment efforts. Dickerson was undeterred. In one instance, she allegedly demanded that she alone handle FBI wiretaps of a particular Turkish government intelligence officer. When Edmonds refused to allow that, Dickerson allegedly resorted to threats, such as, "Why would you want to place your life and your family's life in danger by translating these tapes?"[44]

Edmonds later had the opportunity to review Dickerson's translations, and she found many glaring omissions. For example, Dickerson had excised parts of conversations about potential spies at the State and Defense Departments who were suspected by the FBI of conspiring with a Turkish intelligence agent to obtain state secrets. Dickerson had removed sections of wiretap transcripts that would have helped the investigation, marking the gaps "not important to be translated." She had done the same on other occasions. As Edmonds sifted through Dickerson's work, she recalled the strained Sunday tea. Major Dickerson held out the prospect of a comfortable life and retirement as a result of an association with the ATC. It was obvious that the prospect involved an implicit bargain: protect Turkish officials and you will be rewarded.[45]

When Edmonds reported the strange encounters and suspicious translations to an FBI supervisor, he promised he would contact the right people. Later, she discovered the right people never received her complaint. She pressed the issue with others, including an assistant special agent, who also reverted to threats: "Do you realize what you are saying here in your allegations? Are you telling me that our security people are not doing their jobs? Is that what you're telling me? If you insist on this investigation, I'll make sure in no time it will turn around and become an investigation about you." After being ignored and admonished repeatedly, Edmonds took her discoveries to the FBI's Office of Professional Responsibility (OPR), as well as the DOJ's inspector general (IG). Apparently, that was the last straw. Edmonds was promptly fired, just six months after she started. She received only a letter saying her contract was null and void, without explanation. She was also subjected to hostile treatment on the way out:

> I was literally thrown out of the building. They even didn't give me time to take all my family photos and personal items from my desk. I'm 5 foot 4 and 100 pounds, and you had all these big burly guys forcibly taking me out of the building. . . . One of my superiors, tried to act tough and threatened me that if I said anything to the press, the congress or even a lawyer, "the next time I see you will be in jail."[46]

The bureau continued its retaliation against Edmonds and her whistle-blowing with anonymous attacks in the media, reporting, for instance, that her "'disruptiveness' hurt her on-the-job 'performance.'" Anonymous "government officials" hinted she might even be a threat to national security. Mostly, they worked to rebut and downplay her allegations, saying that the FBI had no translation problems and that they were on top of any security breaches. Paradoxically, they later acknowledged in unclassified briefings to Congress that many of her allegations were true, which led prominent senators Charles Grassley (R-IA) and Patrick Leahy (D-VT) to vouch for her and (in June 2002) press the bureau for an internal investigation. Emboldened by the FBI's concessions and the senators' support, Edmonds sued the DOJ in July 2002, claiming she had been improperly fired. A *60 Minutes* feature in October 2002 brought her allegations of incompetence, corruption, and espionage in the FBI to the attention of millions. It was an appearance she braved despite more threats from former colleagues.[47]

A week before the *60 Minutes* episode, perhaps in response to questions CBS News staffers sent to DOJ as they prepared the show, Attorney General Ashcroft filed court papers asserting the "state secrets privilege" (SSP) in *Sibel Edmonds v. Department of Justice*, "at the request of FBI Director Robert Mueller." If the DC district court supported Ashcroft's request, most of the evidence Edmonds would need to prove her allegations would become off limits—something most defendants could only dream about. The court affirmed the assertion. And because the classified evidence was so crucial to the case, the court dismissed the suit. At the same time, the government warned Edmonds she could not discuss classified matters with anyone—the media, her family and friends, or advocacy organizations. She retreated, quietly, into her private life.[48]

The official 9/11 Commission, along with 600 9/11 victims' families, brought her back out. The families had sued a large and diverse group of alleged Al Qaeda plotters and accomplices, including Osama bin Laden, the bin Laden family business, Saudi royals, Taliban leaders, banks, charities, and the government of Sudan (*Thomas Burnett, Sr., et al. v. Al Baraka Investment and Development Corp, et al.*). They subpoenaed Edmonds for her insights about the intelligence the government could have used to stop the attacks. Although the DOJ was not a party in the case, it nevertheless blocked Edmonds from speaking, asserting the SSP once again. Her closed-door testimony before the 9/11 Commission months earlier had made it clear to the administration what she knew—and what she might say on the witness stand.[49]

Ashcroft's May 2004 SSP assertion was far more expansive than the earlier one, with new restrictions on Edmonds's speech, and it justified the clampdown by citing a new wave of classifications. In short, Edmonds was effectively placed under a gag order—even more than before—with strict limits on what she could say in public or open court, including information about herself. As she would later describe it, essentially anything Edmonds related, including her date and place of birth, the languages spoken by her parents, and her educational and occupational histories, was classified at the moment when the DC district court affirmed Ashcroft's SSP assertion. "Based on this new ruling," she recounted, "my passport would be considered a top secret document since it contains my place of birth. My Virginia driving license would be considered a top secret document, since it contains my date of birth. Heck, even my resume would be considered top secret since it contains my linguistic credentials and my degrees." The SSP assertion also covered previously published and declassified information, including what came out of Congress after her 2002 private meetings and public appearances. All of these things, according to Ashcroft, "could reasonably be expected to cause serious damage to the foreign policy and national security of the United States."[50]

At the same time, the FBI sent letters to Senators Leahy and Grassley requesting that they scrub their websites of any mentions of or details about Edmonds (they complied). Senate Judiciary Committee staffers were ordered not to speak about any facet of the case. The senators also learned their prior correspondence with the DOJ, in which they vouched for her credibility and demanded an investigation into her allegations and treatment, also became top secret documents. The same went for her committee testimony, as well as FBI briefing statements about her, covering her language skills, workplace responsibilities, colleagues' names, and the specific unit where she worked (among other things). Once the DOJ's inspector general completed his report in July 2004, it too was classified. The public justification for all of this, offered by anonymous officials, was the mosaic theory: "'The problem is that while these pieces of information may look innocuous on their own, you put them all together and it reveals a picture of sensitive intelligence collection, and that's a security problem" (see chapter 3). It was by no means a new kind of claim, but it was still puzzling, especially because much of the information was already in the public record.[51]

Although Edmonds fell under the gag order, open government and whistle-blower protection groups remained free to speak—and sue. The Project on Government Oversight (POGO), a nonprofit, nonpartisan watchdog group, filed a complaint against the DOJ, arguing its actions violated the First Amendment. To the group's surprise and delight, the administration backed down. Right before a February 2005 hearing, the DOJ declassified most of the information just as quickly as it had earlier classified it. All of this came without a peep from Ashcroft about the "serious damage" the information would inflict on "the foreign policy and national security of the United States," as he had earlier warned.[52]

Though the administration's move was unexpected and unexplained, one likely factor was the inspector general's report, which had been released just a month earlier. The full document was classified, but the Office of the Inspector General published a declassified summary that reaffirmed Edmonds's credibility and verified most of her claims. According to the OIG,

> Many of Edmonds's core allegations relating to the co-worker had some basis in fact and were supported by either documentary evidence or witnesses other than Edmonds. While the evidence did not prove that the co-worker had disclosed classified information, the OIG concluded that the FBI should have investigated Edmonds's allegations more thoroughly. The allegations, if true, had potentially damaging consequences and warranted a thorough and careful review by the FBI, which did not occur. . . . With respect to Edmonds's claim that she was terminated from the FBI in retaliation for her complaints, the OIG review concluded that her allegations were at least a contributing factor in the FBI's decision to terminate her services. . . . With regard to various other allegations made by Edmonds concerning the FBI's foreign language program, our review substantiated some but did not substantiate others . . . [such as the claim that] the FBI condoned time and attendance abuse, an intentional slow down of work to support hiring additional analysts, or travel fraud.[53]

The administration's volte-face on the sensitivity of Edmonds-related documents was a clear reminder that presidents can easily abuse the state secrets privilege. Ashcroft's warnings about the dire consequences of (re)disclosure of (re)classified information were obviously inflated. Why else would his DOJ declassify them so readily, to head off POGO's lawsuit? Unfortunately, the way the administration acted was not at all unprecedented.

Origins of the State Secrets Privilege

Like so many secrecy powers presidents enjoy, the SSP appears nowhere in the Constitution. And like many other legal traditions, it was a British import, a common law privilege derived from monarchs' Crown privilege, which developed over time into the "public interest" privilege. The first time something like a state secrets doctrine appeared in court was in *U.S. v. Burr*, President Thomas Jefferson's 1807 treason trial against his former vice president, Aaron Burr. The Jefferson administration objected to Burr introducing as evidence a letter to the president from Gen. James Wilkinson because it contained state secrets. The litigants apparently settled the matter outside of court, but the court did accept the government's argument that secrets should be excluded from some trials. Later, in *Totten v. United States* (1875), the Supreme Court ruled that some kinds of government actions, even legal misconduct like reneging on an official contract with a spy, could be shielded from judicial scrutiny if disclosure of the relevant details would spill legitimate state secrets. Courts since then have made a clear distinction between a *Totten* privilege and, later, the SSP. Nevertheless, the two are obviously related, with similar origins, and both are a part of the state secrets doctrine as it developed in the United States. Early twentieth-century legal scholars, such as John Henry Wigmore, recognized the use and legitimacy of the doctrine, although until the late twentieth century, it was rarely invoked. The legal turning point, when jurists developed a clear framework for what had previously been a hazily sketched doctrine, came with 1953's *United States v. Reynolds* at the Supreme Court.[54]

The case was sparked by the 1948 crash of an air force B-29 Superfortress plane that killed three civilian scientists working for the government on a classified guided missile program. Three others survived. The scientists' widows believed air force negligence caused the crash, and they sued for damages under the Federal Tort Claims Act. To prove the allegation, they sought the air force's accident report, which reportedly contained technical evaluations as well as official statements by the crash's three survivors. The widows and the federal district court judges ran up against a brick wall, as the Truman administration refused to share the classified report, even in a controlled court setting. According to the air force's judge advocate general, disclosure of the documents would have "seriously hamper[ed] national security, flying safety, and the development of highly technical and military equipment." The air force expressed particular concern about possible leaks of information regarding "secret electronic equipment" used in the program the scientists were working on. Overall, government officials stated, "it would not be in the public interest to furnish this report." Perhaps that was true, the district court judges acknowledged. However, they would need to review the documents to critically evaluate the government's claims. To prevent leaks, they would review the documents in camera. When the air force refused to comply, the court ruled in favor of the widows, giving them a default judgment of $225,000. The Court of Appeals for the Third Circuit upheld the lower court's ruling.[55]

The Truman administration found a more receptive audience at the Supreme Court. To address the government's claim that "executive department heads have power to withhold any documents in their custody from judicial view if they deem it to be in the public interest," Chief Justice Fred Vinson and the rest of the six-to-three majority sought a "formula of compromise." Vinson acknowledged the majority's concern that surrendering "judicial control in the evidence of a case" to the "caprice of executive officers" might not be ideal. Nevertheless, the serious threats from the new Cold War demanded judicial deference to the commander in chief executive. ("We cannot escape judicial notice that this is a time of vigorous preparation for national defense.") The "compromise" they outlined was the SSP, a formalized version of the long-standing state secrets doctrine. Department heads would need only to submit a "formal claim" to courts, "after actual personal consideration by that officer." There would have to be a "reasonable danger that compulsion of the evidence will expose military matters which, in the interest of national security, should not be divulged" (the *reasonable danger* standard). Courts would then determine if the "circumstances are appropriate for the claim of privilege," but they would have to do so without reviewing the relevant information because the government would then be "forc[ed] to disclos[e] the very thing the privilege is designed to protect." The entire process rested upon judicial trust of the executive, without any meaningful verification, a problem that "present[ed] real difficulty," Vinson recognized. The practical result was that executives would have nearly uninhibited discretion in making SSP claims. The court majority urged executive self-restraint, saying the SSP "is not to be lightly invoked." Considering there would be no oversight of the executive's use of the SSP, the order for self-restraint was nothing more than a polite request.[56]

The Reynolds Framework's Corrupt Foundation

Five decades later, one of the scientist's daughters grew curious about the incident that killed her father, Albert Palya, when she was only seven weeks old. Judith Palya Loether's curiosity led her to a website specializing in declassified military accident reports, one of the tangible consequences of President Clinton's landmark 1995 executive order (see chapter 3). Not knowing exactly what to look for, she stumbled upon the 1948 accident report, which the air force had quietly declassified. Although *Reynolds* was a very well-known case, widely studied in law schools, no one had previously noticed the accident report sitting around in the public record.[57]

Truman's air force refused to share the 1948 report with Reynolds et al. and the courts because officials said it contained ultrasensitive information about cutting-edge guided missile systems and related electronic hardware. Judith

Palya Loether discovered instead that the report focused on the air force's negligence in maintaining and flying the ill-fated B-29, just as her mother and the other plaintiffs had suspected. The report richly detailed a series of flight crew and mechanics errors, as well as evidence of outright negligence. The air force, for example, had ignored regulations requiring mechanics to install heat-detector shields to prevent engine overheating. The cause of the crash was quite evident: the overheated engine eventually burst into flames. The situation was deeply embarrassing for an administration trying to demonstrate US technological superiority over its Soviet foes during the early Cold War period. In addition, the investigators discovered that the air force had trained the three crash survivors about how to escape from a crashing plane—but the scientists had not been so fortunate.[58]

Palya Loether, shocked by what seemed like an abuse of secrecy powers, filed a complaint in 2003 against the government. The other surviving widows and children joined the suit, all hoping to revive *Reynolds*. The new information made no difference. Federal district and appeals court opinions rejected the plaintiffs' accusation of "fraud upon the court" and echoed Bush-Cheney legal arguments that the original SSP assertion was justified. However, the courts seemed to accept a shifting basis for that justification. The Truman administration's SSP assertion rested upon concerns about the nature of the mission—not the aircraft—especially the group's testing of "secret electronic equipment." The Bush administration claimed instead that what was at issue was the sensitive "workings of the B-29," including its in-flight weaknesses. One way the court tried to reconcile the conflict was to note that executive branch officials can evaluate information's suitability for judicial due process in light of the "historical context." However, because security threats never cease and because this year's threat usually appears exceptionally grave, executives can portray any historical context as needing special consideration. More important for the decision, however, was the inability of the plaintiffs to reach the "demanding standard for proof of fraud upon the court." Palya Loether and the other children and widows appealed the ruling, but the Supreme Court decided against revisiting *Reynolds*.[59]

"It Is Not to Be Lightly Invoked"

The court in *Reynolds* created basic standards that presidents needed to meet if courts were to accept their SSP assertions. Justice Vinson's reasonable danger standard aimed to place boundaries around the SSP so that it would not be "lightly invoked." However, the court entrusted department heads to make proper choices, "after actual personal consideration." Over time, courts introduced more checks and balances to prevent executive misuse of what the DC appeals court in *Ellsberg v. Mitchell* called the "expansive and malleable" privilege. In that landmark case, the court argued against deferring to the executive simply because a case involves national security information: "It has been argued that certain limitations on the capacity of the judicial branch safely and reliably to evaluate invocations of the state secrets privilege should induce the courts to renounce any role in this area, i.e., to accept without question a privilege claim made by a ranking executive officer. Such an extreme solution, however, would have grave drawbacks." In *Ellsberg* and other decisions (such as *Halkin v. Helms*), the court clarified the interbranch politics of the SSP, while remaining faithful to *Reynolds's* basic framework. In particular, officials could submit unclassified affidavits that would be available to the opposition. Or they could submit classified affidavits that judges would alone review in camera and ex parte. Although these later developments tipped the relative balance of power slightly back toward the judiciary, the executive still held most of the cards. The process still gave the executive officials the most interpretive power—they could, after all, select which pieces of information to include and exclude and summarize any excluded information as they saw fit.[60]

To What Extent Has the SSP Been "Lightly Invoked"?

When we consider the total number of lawsuits directly or indirectly involving the government filed every year, the rate of SSP use has been consistently very low. In other words, the fraction of SSP assertions (numerator) per total cases (denominator) is quite small. Of the thosands of civil cases handled by federal courts every year in the post-*Reynolds* era, the government typically invoked the privilege less than five times per year, with a high of nine in 1982 (Figure 6.1). Presidents from 1953 until 1979 especially seemed to heed Justice Vinson's call for self-restraint, invoking the SSP just once or twice per year and in most years (fourteen out of twenty-six) not invoking it at all.[61]

Then, beginning with the tail end of the Carter-Mondale administration, executives began to assert the SSP more frequently. The new trend continued through the next three decades—the sunshine era—with two or fewer invocations per year occurring only about a third of the time. To be sure, the actual number of assertions per year remained relatively low, compared with the total number of cases involving the government. Still, the sunshine era

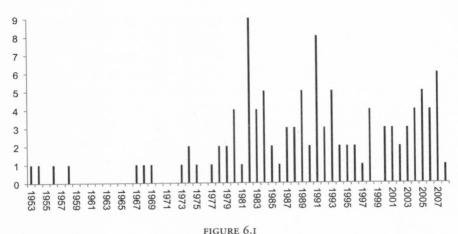

FIGURE 6.I
Annual SSP Assertions.
Source: Chesney 2007; Collaboration on Government Secrecy; Lexis-Nexis;
Westlaw

clearly stands out, with higher SSP use across Democratic and Republican administrations.

Comparing administrations is an imprecise science (if we want to call it a science at all). Counting and comparing presidents' SSP usage is even more fraught. First, lawsuits frequently begin in one administration and continue into another. A case might have started in 1999 under Clinton but continued though 2001 under Bush. Should we only count the first sdministration, even if the second continues or renews it? We could, of course, count both, but then our simple tally could be misleading. For example, the second administration might never have originated the SSP assertion in the first place, and it may have carried it forward only because reversing course was costly. Thus, giving each administration equal "credit" for the case would inflate the second's real proneness to SSP invocations. We might weight assertions, but that would require subjective assessments of an administration's taste for SSP assertions. Or we could give each administration a kind of proneness score, based on its actual record, in order to construct weights. Problems with that are discussed in the next paragraph. In any case, we would have reason to question the quantity's measurement validity.

A second reason why quantitative comparisons could be misleading is that the number of SSP-relevant cases varies over time. History does not produce an identical number of national security cases every year due to a variety of factors, including a changing social and political environment as well as randomness. Changes in the political environment, with concomitant policy changes, might provoke more cases leading to SSP assertions. Thus, a simple comparison between Bush-Cheney and Clinton-Gore neglects the quite different national security politics of the post-9/11 period, including the new policies (such as designating and detaining "enemy combatants") that plaintiffs challenged in court. Increases in SSP use during one adminstration could result from a greater taste for secrecy, but it might also result from differences in context, such as a new national security threat environment. According to this view, comparing presidents' SSP assertions is like comparing apples and oranges.[62]

It is a valid point but not so strong as to forbid conditional comparisons. After all, some of the political changes across administrations *come from* presidents' choices. Presidents do not merely react to exogenous events; they also help shape the political world from which those events emerge. Blowback factors notwithstanding, the 9/11 attacks were exogenous to the Bush-Cheney administration. Nevertheless, the president's team responded by choosing from a diverse array of policy options, none of which were self-evidently and absolutely the only choices. A Gore-Lieberman administration likely would have chosen some of those same policies, but the Democrats would surely have diverged in important ways—including on issues that generated SSP-related lawsuits under Bush-Cheney. Consequently, some of the SSP cases that emerged during Bush-Cheney might have also emerged under Gore-Lieberman, but others would not have. Plus, it is not axiomatic how administrations litigate cases. Perhaps a President Gore would have asserted the SSP exactly as Bush did, but he may have invoked it more lightly (*pace* Justice Vinson). Certainly, Gore's team would not have included advisers like Cheney, Addington, Yoo, and the other unitary executive theorists who embraced executive secrecy as central to their governing ideology (see chapter 2).

We can therefore use the data in Figure 6.1 to make conditional comparisons across administrations. Arranging the cases across years helps us avoid the observation errors that would have emerged from comparing administrations more directly (for instance, in a data table). The distinctiveness of the post-1980 period is unmistakable. Carter-Mondale started the upward trend, but Reagan-Bush clearly escalated it. And as the graph suggests, Bush-Quayle appears to have used the SSP more than any of the others (although we must remain cautious due to the overlap problem). One thing is clear: the fairly common belief that Bush-Cheney used the SSP on a unprecedented scale is not supported by the data. If anything, Bush-Quayle and Reagan-Bush deserve that distinction instead.

Expanding the Scope of the SSP During the Bush-Cheney Administration

The SSP data presented in Figure 6.1 illustrate fairly straightforwardly that Bush-Cheney did not use the privilege more frequently than all of its predecessors. Though the administration broke no records in the scale of its SSP use, it did expand the scope of the executive's SSP powers in two important ways: by extending presidents' authority to invoke the SSP after leaving office and by using the SSP to prevent judicial scrutiny of entire topics of government action (that is, not only because some specific document is classified).

By issuing Executive Order 13233 in November 2001, President Bush granted former presidents the authority to independently invoke the SSP—among other privileges—to block courts from reviewing records produced during their time in office. Bush thus gave himself and his father (as well as Presidents Clinton, Carter, and Ford) the authority to assert the privilege—and all other privileges—even against the wishes of sitting presidents:

> Former President or the incumbent President may assert any constitutionally based privileges, including those ordinarily encompassed within exemption (b)(5) of section 552. The President's constitutionally based privileges subsume privileges for records that reflect: military, diplomatic, or national security secrets (the state secrets privilege); communications of the President or his advisors (the presidential communications privilege); legal advice or legal work (the attorney-client or attorney work product privileges); and the deliberative processes of the President or his advisors (the deliberative process privilege).[63]

Bush's decree thus granted him the authority to assert the SSP for the rest of his life. And when he dies, that authority will be transferred to a designated representative or even a "series or group of alternative representatives." In a little-noticed section of the order (Section 10), Bush wrote:

> The former President may designate a representative (or series or group of alternative representatives, as the former President in his discretion may determine) to act on his behalf for purposes of the Presidential Re-

cords Act and this order. Upon the death or disability of a former President, the former President's designated representative shall act on his behalf for purposes of the Act and this order, including with respect to the assertion of constitutionally based privileges. In the absence of any designated representative after the former President's death or disability, the family of the former President may designate a representative (or series or group of alternative representatives, as they in their discretion may determine) to act on the former President's behalf for purposes of the Act and this order, including with respect to the assertion of constitutionally based privileges.

Because family members are usually the most trusted agents, the truly extraordinary policy shift likely made the SSP "hereditary, like some divine right of kings," as Aftergood has put it. However, nothing in the order makes presidents keep it in the family. Any individual or "group of alternative representatives" will do. One possibility is a president's political party, a trusted organization with an interest in protecting the reputation of its namesake former president. It all would depend on what a sick and ailing president decided when, we would hope, still mentally competent.[64]

The second major expansion of the SSP during the Bush-Cheney years involved cordoning off entire areas of government action from judicial scrutiny. Prior to Bush-Cheney, presidents had used the SSP to exclude crucial pieces of evidence from cases to force dismissal. Formal assertions pointed to the extreme sensitivity of specific documents too risky for even in camera review. The administration put a new twist on that already substantial power by claiming courts should not, for national security reasons, examine entire categories of information at the center of cases because the *subject matter* was a state secret. Bush-Cheney claimed the new power several times, when it aimed to block review of the leaked warrantless wiretapping program (*Al-Haramain Islamic Foundation, Inc. v. Bush*; *ACLU v. NSA*; *Terkel v. AT&T*; *Hepting v. AT&T*). It did the same for cases related to extraordinary rendition and torture of terrorism suspects (*El-Masri v. Tenet*; *Arar v. Ashcroft*). One consequence of the successful—and truly unprecedented—expansion of the executive's SSP authority was that those government actions (warrantless wiretapping, torture, extraordinary rendition), which many argued were unconstitutional, were also immune from judicial review. The legality of the surveillance and counterterrorism policies is obviously important and is well covered elsewhere. Here, we are focused on the nature of the administration's

SSP innovations. To better understand how the administration wielded its newly claimed power, consider *Arar v. Ashcroft*.[65]

Maher Arar's Grave Experience

About a year after 9/11, Maher Arar, a Canadian with Syrian roots, was traveling home to Ottawa after visiting family in Tunisia. During his layover at New York's JFK Airport following a long flight from Zurich, US Immigration and Naturalization Service officials asked him to step aside for questioning. Before he realized what was happening, INS badges quickly turned into FBI badges.

Agents told Arar he was a "special interest" and asked him about several Syrian Canadians from his community in Ottawa. He told them all he could remember about the men, which was not much, since they were merely acquaintances. The agents disagreed and persisted in questioning Arar for hours in the same backroom tucked in a far corner of the airport. Familiar with the basics of the US justice system, Arar asked for a lawyer. What he got instead were stern denials of his rights, followed by an eight-hour interrogation session the next morning on an empty stomach and after a sleepless night. Then, federal agents took him to New York's Metropolitan Detention Center (MDC). The agents actually presented the move as a choice between the MDC and deportation to Syria, but everyone knew Syria was not a real option for the Canadian, who had escaped his father's country years earlier for political reasons. He refused to go to Syria, so his captors dumped him in solitary confinement in an isolated cell at MDC, where he languished without many of the basic prisoner rights for twelve days, all despite his repeated claims of innocence.[66]

Arar was finally able to contact family members, who hired a lawyer. But their effort proved futile, at least in the short term. Officials periodically pulled Arar from his cell, pressuring him to voluntarily agree to go to Syria, a place he left behind in 1987 after dodging Syrian military service and escaping government repression of his family. When he reminded the INS he would likely be tortured there, the official in charge allegedly replied, without a hint of concern, that the INS itself had not signed the Geneva Conventions on Torture. Ultimately, the INS decided Arar's consent did not matter anyway. On October 8, agents took him from the prison and pushed him onto a private jet bound for Jordan. Jordanian agents blindfolded and took custody of Arar in Amman and then drove him across the border, beating him along the way.[67]

Once he was inside the Far Felestin prison, Syrian intelligence officials quickly went to work with long interrogation sessions, all along threatening him with the kinds of violence they could inflict. His dark, damp, and cold cell—"the grave"—was 3 feet wide, 6 feet long, and 7 feet high. It was (according to a later investigation) "infested with rats, which would enter the cell through a small aperture in the ceiling. Cats would urinate on Arar through the aperture, and sanitary facilities were nonexistent. Arar was allowed to bathe himself in cold water once per week. He was prohibited from exercising and was provided barely edible food. Arar lost forty pounds during his ten-month period of detention." The beatings began the morning after his arrival. The main tool was a "shredded black electrical cable . . . about two inches in diameter," which was used for eighteen hours on his palms, wrists, lower back, and hips. Captors peppered their sessions with constant threats of even worse violence, threats validated by the screams of other prisoners nearby. During one session, they stuffed his contorted body into a car tire and again threatened worse. After forcing false confessions out of him, such as the fiction that he trained with Al Qaeda in Afghanistan, Arar's US- and Canadian-supported torturers and interrogators locked him back into the grave, where he was stuck, screaming, for ten months and ten days. The beatings became less intense after October 17, but sometimes, they seemed preferable to being allowed to fester in the grave for month after month of isolation, darkness, and increasingly deep anxiety and depression.[68]

Arar's nightmare finally ended on October 5, 2003, due to a media-savvy campaign in Canada led by his wife, Dr. Monia Mazigh. Her movement pushed Canada to retrieve him from the Syrians, but the government was achingly slow. After more than ten months in captivity, Arar, broken and exhausted, returned home. The Canadian government acted as if the issue was resolved, expecting him to resume life as if nothing had happened.

The Arars and their supporters kept pushing, demanding accountability and justice, which led Canada into a national debate about his treatment, the government's complicity, and its counterterrorism policies more generally. The government in turn launched an investigation, resulting in the establishment of the official Commission of Inquiry into the Actions of Canadian Officials in Relation to Maher Arar, which concluded "categorically . . . there is no evidence to indicate that Mr. Arar has committed any offence or that his activities constitute a threat to the security of Canada." The government then took the unusual step of apologizing to Arar and his family for Canada's role in his "extraordinary rendition" and offered them over C$10 million.[69]

Unlike Canadians, most Americans had never heard about Arar, despite electing the government most responsible for his tragedy. The Bush-Cheney administration inexplicably remained suspicious of Arar, even after Ottawa's exhaustive 2006 investigation cleared his name. Arar and his supporters decided he needed to press for justice in the United States. On top of restoring his reputation and demanding accountability, he also wanted to learn what would happen if he needed to travel outside Canada, as he remained stuck on US blacklists. With help from the US-based Center for Constitutional Rights, Arar sued, arguing the government violated the Torture Victim Protection Act and the Fifth Amendment. Federal judges, from the district to Supreme Court levels, allowed *Arar v. Ashcroft et al.* to proceed but accepted the administration's claim that the judiciary had no business evaluating some of the government's policies and actions. The courts went to great lengths to avoid ruling on the state secrets claims, for fear that reviewing them and the related policies would complicate international relations.[70]

The SSP assertions came from Homeland Security's secretary, Tom Ridge, and Deputy Attorney General James B. Comey—the defendant's (Ashcroft's) deputy. (Why *wouldn't* a loyal deputy exclude evidence in a case against his boss if he could?) Because most of the details of the extraordinary rendition program were classified, the administration argued, three of Arar's complaints should not be reviewed in court. Disclosure of any of the relevant information "reasonably could be expected to cause exceptionally grave or serious damage to the national security of the United States and its foreign relations or activities." The District Court for the Eastern District of New York agreed, deciding that the court would avoid anything related to extraordinary rendition—the core of the case. Any scrutiny of the program could be disastrous for US foreign policy. Besides, Judge David G. Trager argued, it would be *embarrassing*:

> Even a ruling sustaining state-secret-based objections to a request for interrogatories, discovery demand or questioning of a witness could be compromising. Depending on the context it could be construed as the equivalent of a public admission that the alleged conduct had occurred in the manner claimed—to the detriment of our relations with foreign countries, whether friendly or not. . . . It risks "produc[ing] what the Supreme Court has called in another context 'embarrassment of our government abroad' through 'multifarious pronouncements by various departments on one question.'"

Sending Canadians off to be tortured might be wrong and unlawful, Trager argued, but we should avoid discussing the matter because it might prove embarrassing to responsible officials (that is, the administration's defendants, the Canadians, and the Jordanians). Acknowledging reality might even complicate diplomacy. As David Luban has noted, "There is no limit to the anti-embarrassment principle." Government officials' misconduct—crimes—could be aggressively shielded because disclosure might embarrass them. The nature of the crime did not matter. What seemed to matter most was whether disclosure and due process for nonofficials complicated the lives of officials, as well as the perceived legitimacy of at least two governments. The consequence was that extraordinary rendition—and other controversial policies challenged in other cases—became immune to judicial review, for all the wrong reasons. For Trager, the court's job in this bargain was near-absolute deference to the executive. To make this point, Trager quoted Justice Jackson's dissent in *Shaughnessy v. U.S.* (1953): "Close to the maximum of respect is due from the judiciary to the political departments in policies affecting security and alien exclusion."[71]

In 2008, a majority of the Court of Appeals for the Second Circuit agreed, buying the administration's claims that it had secret, though inadmissible, evidence explaining why officials linked Arar to Al Qaeda and sent him to Syria, a country the State Department condemned for torturing prisoners. The appeals court decision came *after* Canada cleared his name and *after* Secretary of State Condoleezza Rice conceded in October 2007 that her administration had mishandled Arar's case. ("We do not think this was handled particularly well . . . and we will try to do better in the future.") Still, in the courts, her administration expressed full confidence in Arar's guilt. The appeals court actually heard Arar's case twice, perhaps wanting to leave the impression it would really get to the heart of the matter. The result remained the same: federal judges sidestepped a hugely controversial issue, and associated illegal acts, because of their deference to the executive's newly claimed SSP powers. The only dissenting view from the appeals court came from Judge Robert Sack, who reminded everyone that Justice Vinson intended the SSP as "a narrow device," not be to invoked lightly. His colleagues, Judge Sack argued, instead opted for a "blunderbuss solution—to withhold categorically" Arar's opportunity to hold officials accountable due to secrecy claims, giving officials "license . . . to violate constitutional rights with virtual impunity." Sack's minority opinion failed to persuade the Supreme Court to even consider Arar's appeal. As of December 2011, he remained on the US government's terrorist list.[72]

Conclusion

Although Bush-Cheney's use of the SSP was not unprecedented in scale, the administration did expand its scope in politically consequential ways. Along with President Bush's executive order giving presidents and their designated representatives SSP authority after leaving office, the administration claimed the authority to exclude entire topics from judicial review via the SSP. In *Arar* and other cases, judges validated the new evidentiary privilege, institutionalizing it through precedent.

The continued willingness of federal judges to defer to executives, despite evidence from *Reynolds* and other cases that executives have misused the privilege, is one of the more puzzling features of SSP politics. Although judges have rejected SSP assertions, the vast majority have trusted the executive, without verification (to borrow President Reagan's phrase). One estimate from 2006 found judges approved 92 percent of SSP claims after *Reynolds*. Now that the privilege is being used to place a great deal of governmental action beyond scrutiny, that pattern of deference, if continued, has serious consequences for American democracy, especially individuals' ability to sue for civil liberties deprivations. More numerous than those abducted and sent through the extraordinary rendition program were those surveilled without warrants by the National Security Agency. Because judges accepted the government's argument that the program could not be scrutinized, perhaps millions of American citizens who had reason to believe they were illegally surveilled were unable to challenge the government, since they could not prove they had standing. Talk about "vicious circles."[73]

Presidents and their administrations might sincerely believe disclosure of something like the *Reynolds* air force accident report poses unacceptable national security risks. The problem is that the decision increasingly has been left to the president, without any monitoring or accountability from other constitutional actors. *Reynolds, Arar, Edmonds,* and the other cases offer a clear reminder that executives might not—and have not always—used the SSP in good faith, which the courts often seem content to overlook or explain away.

At the heart of the problem is the essential contestability of concepts like "national security," "reasonable danger," "acceptable risk," and "public interest." To the sincere, security-chasing executive, a botched air force mission (*Reynolds*) might give the enemy a leg up. Perhaps it demonstrates weakness or incompetence. Details about the extraordinary rendition program might have emboldened enemies or enraged citizens in the partnered countries, whose governments were promised secrecy. Presidential administrations might be quite sincere in their belief that that kind of disclosure poses too great a national security risk, even if democratic supermajorities disagree, preferring transparency and due process. Nevertheless, current SSP doctrine gives all interpretive authority to presidents, who may or may not come up with the best interpretation of the operative concepts, like "security." Since the courts have tended to show "close to the maximum of respect" for the executive in the national security realm, presidents have become in effect "interpreters-in-chief," sometimes taking full, exclusive control of the deliberative process.[74]

7

SECRET SCIENCE
FROM BUSH-CHENEY TO BUSH-QUAYLE

Secret Science

When officials are forced by circumstance to defend their secrecy decisions, they have a much easier time when they can make appeals to national security. It certainly works with judges, as we have just seen. Judges, like most Americans, tend to recognize that certain individuals and organizations want to harm the country and its interests and that those enemies could deftly use "necessary secrets" to help them inflict damage. Most also understand the folly of evaluating the risks of disclosure post hoc as a general policy. Therefore, people tend to willingly defer to officials to evaluate security risks, even if those citizens also believe the government overclassifies or is generally too risk averse. When secrecy claims can be credibly or even loosely tied to national security, officials have an automatically credulous population at their disposal.

Defending secrecy outside the security realm requires more effort. How do you justify concealing evidence of a new airborne transmission route for antibiotic-resistant bacteria emanating from giant hog farms in the Midwest, as the USDA did in 2002? What do you say to those living nearby? That citizens have no right to know about potentially major threats to public health? That too much harm would come to the pork industry if the public found out? Similarly, what led the EPA to outright lie about the very high asbestos levels its scientists found in the gray toxic dust that spread across lower Manhattan after the World Trade Center crumbled on 9/11? "White House pressure" is part of the answer, as we will see, but what motivated that? And why did several administrations work so hard to conceal evidence that may have linked Agent Orange with illnesses suffered by Vietnam War veterans? Inexplicable disbelief in toxicological science? The government's potential financial liabilities—or the dioxin industry's?

The many examples of excessive secrecy in the science realm make up an underappreciated part of the sunshine era's dark side. For most of the cases examined in this section, administrations did not have the option of citing vital security needs to justify their actions. Not having the expansive residual category called "national security" to point to made concealing science secrets more politically difficult. But that challenge did not always stop them. It only made their legitimation attempts seem feckless, as they were. It took creativity to construct even half-baked rationales once dubious secrecy decisions came to light. "We're doing this for your own safety" was harder to swallow when it came to, for example, concealing information about salmonella spreading through slaughterhouses. (The same goes for "We need to protect your privacy"—or slaughterhouse owners' trade secrets.) Perhaps the salmonella decision emerged from a well-intentioned cost-benefit analysis of the public health or macroeconomic consequences of disclosure. Or perhaps the secrecy came from everyday bureaucratic conservatism, or efforts by agency officials to avoid embarrassment. But business power is hard to rule out as an explanation—and protecting Big Pork surely doesn't fit into any credible national security narratives.

Indeed this and the next chapter lay bare the interest group politics of government secrecy more than any of the others. In case after case, we see administrations with distorted, undemocratic priorities, putting private interests above public ones, often with serious public health or environmental consequences. As a result, several of the stories in this section pack an even stronger emotional punch compared with cases from earlier chapters. They will infuriate, especially because the excuses offered are much less tenable. Few of the secrets fall anywhere close to "what you need to *not* know" (see chapter 2). And the secrecy decisions often had genuinely severe consequences, such as those related to tainted meat, radiation leaks, and dioxin contamination.

The secrecy also warped the democratic process. When citizens cannot learn about the public health risks in their communities, they cannot make informed choices about their bodies and futures, and those of their children. Underinformed citizens also cannot punish those who let toxins into their communities in the first place. Concealing scientific information thus can keep vital information about life and death from citizens, which not only stunts the deliberative process—as limited as it might normally be—but also keeps people in harm's way, placing them at risk at levels generally higher than those related to national security. Indeed, it is probably not even close: hazards like cancers and industrial accidents have annual fatality risks of 1 in 540 and 1 in 53,000, respectively, as compared to transnational terrorism, with a rate of 1 in 12,500,000. Science secrecy can be exceptionally costly to public health.[1]

To the extent the history of science secrecy has been told before, it has focused on specific administrations, such as Seth Shulman's 2008 book on Bush-Cheney. More often, we get scattered stories, disconnected episodes that offer little sense of the larger, ongoing historical problem. This neglected corner of the sunshine era's dark side is surprisingly large—encompassing dozens of cases across four administrations, on top of those discussed in chapter 10. Compared with some of the other dimensions of the secrecy system, the cross-administration variation here is large. Although Bush-Quayle and Clinton-Gore had their moments, Reagan-Bush and Bush-Cheney clearly emerge as the repeat offenders among the bunch.[2]

The history begins with Bush-Cheney and then moves in reverse chronological order (as with some of the earlier chapters). During Bush-Cheney's time in power, many accused the administration of abusing its secrecy powers in the science realm in *unprecedented* ways—both in scale and scope. Many came to believe that what the administration did was new and thus especially worrisome. Some of the conflicts became front-page news, reaching large audiences, in part because of the expanding reach of the Internet. With that kind of attention, and without a handy comparative historical analysis of earlier administrations, it certainly *seemed* new.

To evaluate the unprecedented claim, we can first establish the facts of the Bush-Cheney administration and then make comparisons with earlier ones. The comparative historical analysis evaluates every allegation, with an attempt to get to the heart of the matter. Some don't quite pan out, although most do. In those transgressive cases, the government clearly suppressed proprietary scientific information—about microbes, toxins, public lands, and so forth—without good reason (that is, they were not necessary secrets). Much of the time, administrations simply kept quiet and hoped no one noticed. Sometimes, things spiraled out of control and officials reverted to other tactics, such as word games and running out the clock. We begin, again, in the aftermath of the 9/11 attacks.

The Bush-Cheney Administration

Some of the most indelible images from September 11 involve the building-sized puffs of gray smoke that rose as the Twin Towers crumbled to the ground—steel beams, windows, computers, elevators, passenger jets, and all. The smoke after rising seemed to chase the unfortunate through lower Manhattan's streets. Everything in the surrounding area, from cars and subway stops to apartments and delis, wound up blanketed with light gray ash.

Many immediately recognized the health dangers of so much smoke and ash circulating through the city. Scientists from the Environmental Protection Agency were out collecting air and dust samples to determine their toxicity levels well before most people stopped weeping in front of their televisions. The EPA initially focused on lead and asbestos but quickly expanded the analysis to look for benzene, cadmium, chromium, dioxin, manganese, mercury, particulate matter, polychlorinated biphenals (PCBs), and polycyclic aromatic hydrocarbons (PAHs). It was hard to imagine how the toxins would *not* be there, in the refuse of incinerated building materials, fluorescent lights, window glass, lead solder joints, and jet fuel residue.[3]

The results of those early tests were not encouraging. Twenty-five percent of the initial "bulk dust" samples contained unsafe levels of asbestos. Forty-six percent of subsequent EPA tests from inside buildings, like Stuyvesant High School, Public School 234, Manhattan Borough Community College, and Jacob Javits Convention Center, found toxins well above safe levels. Later tests showed asbestos consistently above the EPA's working threshold level (70 s/mm^2), including one sample containing nearly five times the threshold (336 s/mm^2) near Stuyvesant more than six months after the attacks.[4]

Research in the ensuing years documented symptoms appearing and persisting in a large part (more than 50 percent) of the affected population, including coughing, wheezing, nosebleeds, headaches, and chest pain. Other research predicted long-term dangers for the exposed, including fetuses in utero when the smoke and ash spread. A 2011 study in the prominent medical journal *Lancet* found the cancer risk for male firefighters who worked at Ground Zero was 19 percent higher than for those who did not work there. Toxin-related deaths also came quickly. One coroner linked the 2006 lung disease death of James Zadroga, a thirty-four-year-old police detective, to his exposure. Many other families of deceased emergency workers believed the victims' deaths were caused by their Ground Zero experiences.[5]

Despite the EPA's knowledge, soon after the attacks, of the real and potential (that is, still uncertain) risks from toxic exposure, officials instead chose secrecy and deception. On September 13, the EPA announced that "monitoring and sampling . . . have been very reassuring" and that "there appear to be no significant levels of asbestos dust in the air in New York City." Three days later, it reported: "Our tests show that it is safe for New Yorkers to go back to work in New York's financial district." The EPA had actually planned to warn financial

district workers on Water Street to *not* go back to work, but Samuel Thern-
strom, the associate director of communications for the White House Council
on Environmental Quality (CEQ), ordered the agency to say the opposite,
recommending workers return when the district reopened on September 17.[6]

Indeed, the White House took complete control of EPA public communications immediately after the attacks, demanding that all public statements
had to be approved by the National Security Council. The CEQ would coordinate all "health and safety communications," which included altering EPA
press releases, to eliminate statements expressing risk. The White House had
EPA head Christie Todd Whitman announce on September 18, "I am glad
to reassure the people of New York . . . that their air is safe to breathe." Three
days later, she added that "a host of potential contaminants are either not
detectable" or not at unsafe levels. An October 3 EPA press release declared,
"Data Confirms No Significant Public Health Risks," even though internal
documents showed EPA scientists were far from making such a grand conclusion. Had officials actually announced the scientists' results, some showing
dangers and others showing uncertainties, rescue workers and everyone else
near Ground Zero would have probably taken greater safety precautions, preventing at least some of the illnesses and deaths that followed.[7]

One explanation for the disjuncture between the internal test results and
the agency's reassuring public statements involves crisis management communications. In the wake of the attacks, the American public was deeply
fearful and uncertain, and this was especially so for New Yorkers. The Bush-
Cheney administration misled the public in part because it wanted to tamp
down fears and restore order, to minimize the disaster's economic costs, and
to demonstrate strength to allies and adversaries. As the Court of Appeals for
the Second Circuit put it in a case brought by emergency medics, "Everyone
knows . . . that one essential government function in the wake of disaster is
to put the affected community on a normal footing, i.e., to avoid panic, keep
order, restore services, repair infrastructure, and preserve the economy." As a
result, the judges concluded, the government's secrecy and deception should
not have "shock[ed] the conscience" and did not amount to "deliberate indif-
ference" or intent to cause harm. The government, they argued, used textbook
crisis communications tactics with the best of intentions.[8]

Another explanation for the administration's actions highlights scientific
uncertainty about the actual health dangers from the toxins. The EPA definitely found toxins, but as every good environmental toxicologist knows,
"the dose makes the poison." And even though scientists found higher-than-

threshold doses, the actual health impacts were unknown. Even a decade after 9/11, once researchers had reduced many of the uncertainties, some scientists continued to discount the impact of Ground Zero exposure. After the Obama-Biden administration publicly listed fifty cancers linked to Ground Zero toxins, one University of Texas biostatistician proclaimed: "To imagine that there is strong evidence about any cancer resulting from 9/11 is naive in the extreme." In any case, the confident reassurances government officials gave to emergency workers and the public in the weeks after 9/11 contained few uncertainties. They said everything was fine.[9]

Another explanation for the secrecy and deception does not assume the administration acted in good faith. This more provocative explanation sees senior officials favoring partisan allies and private sector supporters over the public interest—a completely ordinary kind of politics, alarming only because Bush-Cheney's early response to the national emergency seemed untainted by such things. Some of the Republicans' top financiers, after all, came from the energy, chemical, and manufacturing industries—all actively fighting numerous, protracted, and very expensive asbestos lawsuits. Halliburton was only one of several that faced enormous real and potential asbestos liabilities. The company's legal conflicts attracted disproportionate media attention because of Cheney's prior stint as its CEO. But Halliburton's conflicts and liabilities illustrate what was as stake in the science conducted near Ground Zero (especially but not only involving asbestos). By December 2001, Halliburton had settled 194,000 asbestos claims, and it estimated its total gross liability to be $704 million. One jury in late 2001 ordered the company to pay $30 million to five plaintiffs. Many other cases—against Halliburton and other companies—were proceeding through the system in September 2001. It is no wonder tort reform, pushed by many of the same interests, was a centerpiece of Bush-Cheney's 2000 campaign. Policy proposals aimed to limit consumer and worker damages in individual and class action lawsuits (about medical malpractice, toxic exposure, and other harms).[10]

Overall, interests supporting Bush-Cheney had much riding on government pronouncements about safe levels of asbestos and other chemicals. Although the administration was intensely and, in many ways, sincerely focused on counterterrorism and public safety after 9/11, it is hard to believe that this focus completely crowded out other agenda issues and ended politics as usual. Political favoritism, which manifested in concealing scientific information from the public, is at least as reasonable an explanation as clumsy public relations or cautious scientific interpretation.

"National Security" Justifications Only Go So Far

This combination of ideas and interests likely motivated most of the Bush-Cheney administration's frequent and wide-ranging efforts to conceal proprietary scientific information. We only know about the leaked and botched efforts, but there were many of those, including episodes involving environmental health, climate science, nuclear energy, agricultural science, species protection, reproductive and women's health, sexual education, infectious diseases, and consumer and workplace safety. Although the administration also propagated misleading and distorted messages about scientific issues being debated nationally, this chapter looks only at Bush-Cheney efforts to conceal exclusive information (that is, keep secrets).[11]

Some of the secrecy seemed to grow out of the administration's extreme risk aversion in the name of public safety after 9/11. But as with the Ground Zero toxins example, everything was not as it seemed. For instance, White House officials asked the National Academy of Sciences (NAS) in 2002 to withhold from publication a scientific report on agricultural bioterrorism that concluded the nation's food system and the Department of Agriculture were vulnerable to terrorist attacks. The scientists who wrote the report deliberately withheld classified and sensitive but unclassified security information, identified vulnerabilities only in broad terms, and sent drafts to army, FBI, and Homeland Security officials for approval (they all approved), but senior officials nonetheless blocked its publication.[12]

Perhaps the decision was strictly motivated by the administration's concern that terrorists could use details in the paper for malicious purposes. Mosaic theory had already risen to newfound prominence at the highest levels of government after 9/11 (see chapter 3). According to this theory, even seemingly innocuous information could become dangerous if crafty enemies knew how to piece things together, like a mosaic. Thus, though scientists and security information officers who wrote and proofed the paper scrubbed it of anything obviously useful to terrorists, who knew what enemies might do with what remained?

But ignoring the influence of interests only yields incomplete explanations. In this case, given the continuing secrecy about the matter, we can only speculate about which interests could have influenced the decision to ax the NAS report. Agribusinesses certainly had a lot at stake, since they could have incurred costs from new laws once the information was published. The report also likely did not sit well with officials in the USDA, which funded the report but wound up being identified as having a variety of weaknesses. Although that fact might have offered the USDA new budgetary opportunities in the unending bureaucratic scramble for resources, it also potentially tarnished the reputations of officials responsible for the identified weaknesses (at least the ones that should have been handled earlier). Ideas, interests, and institutions jointly influence elite decision making, and the political choice to suppress the NAS report was probably no exception.[13]

Nevertheless, given the clear link with counterterrorism, the administration's suppression of the report could be credibly rationalized on national security grounds without much difficulty. Indeed, it was probably a main reason for the secrecy, explaining why so few outside of the NAS challenged the suppression decision and pressed for disclosure. Without that outside pressure, the administration did not need to bother with any of the tactics often deployed to evade sunshine laws. In other cases, such national security rationalizations did not come so easily, as we will see. One can attempt to make *everything* national security related, as Bush-Cheney's redefinitions of "critical infrastruture" arguably did (see chapter 3), but fewer people take the bait when it comes to, say, protecting endangered species or regulating greenhouse gases. That is why the suppression of scientific information can lay bare the interest-based politics of secrecy much more clearly than in the national security realm. Take, for example, the EPA's decision in 2006 to reduce industries' pollution-reporting requirements.[14]

Toxins and Tainted Meat: "Necessary Secrets"?

The EPA's Toxic Release Inventory (TRI) was created in 1986 as a part of the Emergency Planning and Community Right to Know Act, a law sparked by the massive chemical leak at the facilities of Union Carbide (now Dow Chemical) in Bhopal, India, in 1984, which killed at least 10,000 and maimed over 555,000 survivors. The TRI was crafted as a publicly accessible database where citizens could learn about the nature and local prevalence of more than 650 toxic chemicals spread by industry polluters. Businesses that released or disposed of more than 500 pounds of one of the toxins had to fill out a detailed EPA report (Form R) that would be incorporated in the database. Pollution of less than 500 pounds required a less detailed short form (Form A). There was one exception: the 500-pound rule did not apply to twenty particularly dangerous chemicals—persistent bioaccumulative toxins (PBTs) like mercury, lead, and dioxins. Industries releasing or disposing PBTs needed to complete the detailed report, regardless of the scale of pollution.[15]

In 2005, the Bush-Cheney EPA proposed a rule change that promised to radically alter TRI's reporting framework. First, it allowed industries to use the short form for pollution under 5,000 pounds, increasing the minumum threshold tenfold. The only exception was dioxin pollution. Second, it eliminated the exception for nineteen of the twenty most dangerous PBTs (only dioxins would remain). Third, the proposed rule allowed businesses to submit reports half as frequently as before (every other year rather than yearly).[16]

During the public comment period after the EPA published its proposal, 122,420 individuals and groups filed comments expressing positions on the changes. Of that number, 122,386 argued against and 34 argued in favor of the relaxed standards. Despite the enormous amount of opposition to the proposal, the administration adopted two of the three provisions. Somehow, the last one (about frequency of reporting) attracted enough negative media attention that the EPA dropped it. Overall, by adopting the two rules, the Bush-Cheney administration sided with 0.0278 percent of the commenting public (34 of 122,420), instead of the 99.9722 percent who announced their opposition. As OMB Watch put it, the 122,386 commenters who objected could have filled two Yankee Stadiums, with 7,296 still waiting in line, whereas the proposal's supporters might have filled a corporate boardroom—an environment those commenters probably knew well. Although most citizens did not weigh in on the matter, it is doubtful the victorious 0.0278 percent were more representative of public opinion than the 99.9722 percent wanting more transparency. Regardless, the victors celebrated their new right to discharge more toxins without letting local residents know the details. In this case, the turn from transpanency to secrecy did not produce more government secrets. However, the administration's unpopular re-regulatory efforts removed otherwise unavailable scientific information from the public sphere and weakened a lesser known but still important sunshine law, 1986's Emergency Planning and Community Right to Know Act.[17]

A clearer example of hard-to-defend, interest-based *government* secrecy stemmed from 2002, when the Bush-Cheney administration developed a system to prevent state governments from publishing the names and locations of businesses that sold contaminated meat. The USDA's initiative came in the wake of a meat recall in July of that year, which caused widespread consumer concern. USDA officials traveled the country, pushing fourteen state governments to sign "memorandums of understanding" in which the federal government promised to give states timely alerts of meat recalls (for instance, due to mad cow disease). In exchange, states had to promise to withhold details from their citizens, including the names of the places—grocery stores, restaurants, ballparks—where contaminated meat had been sold. For one mad cow outbreak that prompted a recall in 2004, the USDA and Pacific Northwest state governments withheld the names of 582 groceries, restaurants, and food processors that had purchased and distributed 19 tons of potentially tainted beef. The USDA issued only a general press release, with very few details.[18]

The de facto gag order probably resulted in part from a shared desire by the government and the industry to get tainted meat episodes out of the news as quickly as possible. Ongoing consumer uncertainty about the safety of the meat supply did not help the cause of the industry, which suffers from reduced demand during such crises and which donates generously to both political parties. Another, more commonly heard justification rested on the fact that recalls sometimes sequester more meat than is necessary, due to incomplete information about the geographic spread of the pathogens. Therefore, during a recall, some businesses identified as purveyors of tainted meat might not have actually sold it and thus unjustly suffer, financially and reputationally. Once "Jason's Diner" is remembered as the place that sold mad cow burgers, customers might hesitate before going there again. Why not prevent unnecessary harms for "clean" businesses?

Besides, the USDA argued, "if you are concerned whether you may have purchased the product, you can call your retail store. They would know." Though retailers and restaurants had every right to tell customers whether they had ever stocked the tainted meat (state governments, not private businesses, signed the memorandums of understanding), we can imagine why they would not. First, why would they? A smart but not completely honest business owner would quickly and quietly get rid of the tainted stuff, while denying he or she ever had it, for the same reputational reasons. In the case of mad cow outbreaks after the USDA order, some businesses probably just sold the meat anyway. They may have heard scientists talking about the very low health risks involved in eating beef from a mad cow. Research plainly demonstrated the disease only destroys the animal's brain, spinal cord, and digestive tract. Thus (in the unlikely event that processing is done perfectly), no pathogens should wind up in the meat supply.[19]

That businesses would know if they had once stocked tainted meat was also a naively hopeful assumption, given the enormity and complexity of the food distribution system. Would a corner gas station really know if it ever sold beef jerky packages tainted with mad cow? Would all restaurants know if they once purchased a few pounds of contaminated steak? Not all businesses keep perfect records. By contrast, federal and state government officials did have the information, but they opted to keep it hidden. Some list sitting on someone's desk stayed there, despite the value it would have had for consumers and businesses. Ultimately, the USDA claimed the recall successfully recaptured 21,000 out of 38,000 pounds (55 percent) from the market—slightly higher than the recall average. That means at least 17,000 pounds were consumed or discarded.[20]

Overall, the secrecy benefited the few at the expense of the many, and it did not rise to the level of a so-called necessary secret. Suppressing the unclassified information could not be justified by citing national security needs, so the USDA opted for something almost equally unconvincing. In response to FOIA requests by *Spokesman-Review* reporters, the USDA declared it could not disclose the information because to do so would reveal the "trade secrets of private enterprise." According to the DOJ, FOIA officers are supposed to follow the "'common law' definition of the term 'trade secret' that differs from the broad definition used in the Restatement of Torts." In particular, officers should follow the DC circuit appeals court definition, seeing a trade secret as "a secret, commercially valuable plan, formula, process, or device that is used for the making, preparing, compounding, or processing of trade commodities and that can be said to be the end product of either innovation or substantial effort." One has to strain to place a gas station's beef jerky sale within that definition. It was yet another example of the administration playing word games with the law to keep secrets—and not an especially clever attempt at that.[21]

Antibiotic-Resistant Bacteria and Other "Politically Sensitive" Subjects

Another of the USDA's many achievements during the Bush-Cheney administration involved suppressing information about the potential public health effects of factory farming. The expansion of "concentrated animal feeding operations" (CAFOs) in the 1990s gave the world cheaper meat, but the industrialization of the countryside inflicted many new social costs on neighboring communities. People living near CAFOs found themselves suddenly living next to gigantic urine-and-feces factories belching noxious fumes day and night. The awful stench was only one of several negative externalities the

CAFOs produced. Other social costs inflicted on CAFO neighbors included illness, property devaluation, and a reduced quality of life.

The USDA was on the case, with its Swine Odor and Manure Management Research Unit (SOMMRU) in the Agricultural Research Service (ARS). When microbiologist Dr. James Zahn's bosses at the ARS asked him to analyze the "chemical constituency of volatiles from swine manure and ways to abate odors," he agreed. (In all other contexts, that kind of request would have been taken as a crude insult.) How might the government help solve this growing problem of hog farm pollution, if only to reduce the pungent odors?[22]

Zahn and a colleague, Dr. Alan Dispirito of Iowa State University, ventured out to analyze dust particles from CAFOs. While inspecting the samples, they discovered something quite surprising: about 90 percent of the bacteria on dust particles had developed antibiotic resistance. Previous research had shown CAFOs as a source of resistant organisms but had not identified an airborne route for the germs to spread. It was an alarming discovery. Because dust travels easily in the air, the bacteria had very likely moved into the respiratory systems of local residents and their livestock. Armed with important new data, Zahn wanted to present his findings. He went to the 2001 meetings of the American Society of Animal Science and the National Pork Board Symposium. He also published related work on "volatiles and odors from swine manure" with colleagues. All of it passed muster with his ARS/USDA bosses. Then, in early 2002, they abruptly changed their minds.[23]

As Zahn prepared in February to present his work to the Adair County (Iowa) Board of Health, he received word that ARS officials had reversed their earlier decision to permit him to speak. Set aside, for now, the questionable general policy of scientists requiring permission to speak. In Zahn's case, the rationale for censoring his research presentation rested on his alleged lack of expertise: it was not about protecting classified or even sensitive "critical infrastructure information." According to Dr. John H. Marburger III, who directed the White House's Office of Science and Technology Policy (OSTP), the ARS censored Zahn because he wanted to speak on subjects outside his "primary area of scientific expertise and government work, management of odors from hog operations." An ARS spokesman agreed with Marburger that Zahn "wasn't qualified to talk about the bacteria." It was a strange argument, considering that Zahn, who completed a Ph.D. in microbiology, had published peer reviewed work with titles like "Monitoring Antibiotic Resistance in Biological Waste Treatment Systems" and "Evidence for Transfer of Tylosin and Tylosin-Resistant Bacteria in Air from Swine Production Facilities Using Sub-therapeutic Concentrations of Tylan in Feed." ARS's research director, Brian Kerr, had a slightly different take on why he stopped Zahn from speaking in Adair: "The main reason we elected not to speak at those meetings was we refocused on the mission of our unit. That mission did not include antibiotics or antibiotic resistance. Another reason is that the meetings would include speaking on human-health impacts. We do not do that." This was another strange argument, given that the ARS's Swine Odor and Manure Management Research Unit boasts on its website that "the mission of the [SOMMRU] is to solve critical problems in the swine production industry that impact production efficiency, environmental quality, and *human health*" (emphasis added). One of SOMMRU's specific goals was finding ways to prevent the "release of pathogens into the environment," such as antibiotic-resistant bacteria.[24]

Altogether, Zahn's bosses stopped him from presenting his findings on at least five and possibly up to eleven additional occasions (the administration admitted to only five). Many talks, such as the one at the International Commission of Agricultural and Biosystems Engineering and American Society for Agricultural Engineering joint conference in 2002, would have drawn primarily academics. Others, like the one in Adair County, would have attracted a broader audience. Especially worrisome for ARS officials was the conference organized by celebrity activist Robert F. Kennedy, Jr., for "family farm advocates and environmental and civic leaders in Clear Lake, Iowa," a town literally encircled by CAFOs.[25]

Two questions remain unanswered. What really happened in Zahn's case? And does information about antibiotic-resistant bacteria from CAFOs fall into the category of "necessary" government secrets? The administration's statements about Zahn, as we have seen, rested on very weak ground. What, then, prompted the ARS's abrupt shift in early 2002? The only other detail in the public record that might explain the ARS decision is a "fax trail" about the Adair talk that Zahn found before resigning in May 2002. An environmental group in Iowa had sent a notice of his upcoming talk to a Des Moines television station. Someone there apparently shared the fax with people at the Iowa Pork Producers Association, who forwarded the announcement to the National Pork Producers Council, which happened to share a building with the ARS's local office. The message then volleyed to Kerr, Zahn's boss, who called his own boss in the ARS's Peoria, Illinois, office—who promptly gave the suppression order for the Iowa talk. Usually, the direct influence of interest groups is hard to pin down. In this case, Big Pork's influence was easy to detect, and it was probably a significant factor in the ARS's decision.[26]

Even if Big Pork had not directly intervened, the ARS might still have silenced Zahn or any other scientist who wanted to talk about airborne pathogens from CAFOs. Indeed, the USDA kept a "List of Sensitive Issues for ARS Manuscript Review and Approval by National Program Staff," which it used to prevent dangerous ideas from reaching the public. The list of twenty-eight items included noted national security threats like "boll weevil eradication" and "glassy-winged sharpshooter/Pierce's disease," as well as "megadoses of nutrients that may be beneficial to human health/nutrition" and "research findings and recommendations that are contrary to current dietary guidelines or may be used in food labeling." Some items probably deserved the special attention, such as "bioterrorism/attacks on agriculture" and "biological items that may affect trade and export negotiations." Others probably did not, among them "animal well-being" and "agricultural practices with negative health and environmental consequences, e.g., global climate change; contamination of water by hazardous materials (nutrients, pesticides, and pathogens); animal feeding operations or crop production practices that negatively impact soil, water, or air quality." Indeed, taxpayer-funded scientific information related to most of the topics on the list should arguably have been automatically disseminated into the marketplace of ideas. Instead, the ARS had a policy of putting politically controversial science through a filter. And the list was infinitely elastic. If a USDA scientist's work covered an unanticipated "sensitive" subject, administrators simply expanded the list, as they did in Zahn's case ("antibiotic/antimicrobial resistance"). It is unknown how many times the ARS under Bush-Cheney silenced scientists with the list or how many researchers decided not to study something sensitive for fear of the censorship and career risks.[27]

We don't know who was ultimately to blame for Zahn's ordeal. Marbuger, the White House's OSTP director, discounted the weight of the "sensitive issue" policy in 2004, and he denied the ARS had ever censored scientists, saying, "ARS headquarters review [sic], when required, do not censor, or otherwise deny publication of, the research findings, but may aid in the interpretation and communication of the results, including providing advance alert to others." At the same time, he did confirm the ARS stopped Zahn from speaking on five occasions because "he was not authorized to discuss the public health ramifications of his observations." Zahn and his colleagues maintained he never did plan to discuss health consequences—only the discovery of the dangerous bacteria from CAFOs and the fact that health scientists would probably find it interesting.[28]

Maybe these really were necessary secrets. However, no one even tried to justify the secrecy and censorship on the basis of national security, personal privacy, diplomacy, or any of the usual rationales. Even if the censorship was really about Zahn's expertise (which seems unlikely but possible) or heightened public concerns about antibiotic resistance from industrial farming, the secrecy could hardly be justified by any of the reasonable exceptions to transparency cited in presidential speeches and decrees. The case history suggests CAFO interests were prioritized over everyone else's. Zahn was even explicitly told to be mindful of the agribusinesses that would be affected by his research. That was perhaps a reasonable request and not a surprising one, given what we know about the bounds of business interests' "structural power." But the "don't make big business mad" secrecy justification has thus far failed to attain anything close to democratic validation.[29]

Climate Science: "Making the President Look Good"[30]

The Bush-Cheney administration's efforts to suppress proprietary scientific information were probably most aggressive on the subject of climate science. Throughout its eight years in office, the administration promoted "skepticism" about climate change, blocked policies regulating greenhouse gases, and pushed prodrilling and proexploration initiatives. Whether or not senior Bush-Cheney officials sincerely believed scientists had not conclusively shown the human causes of global warming, powerful factions in their electoral coalition counted on their strong opposition. If that opposition required suppressing scientific information, however, they faced some serious difficulties.

Compared with other issues in which the government had a monopoly on information (for example, Ground Zero toxins), climate science thrived inside and outside government labs. Scientists in the EPA, National Aeronautics and Space Administration (NASA), National Oceanic and Atmospheric Administration (NOAA), and several other agencies were discovering patterns mirroring those from the broader scientific community. Climate change skeptics, by contrast, were few and far between. Skepticism is an inherent part of science, to be sure, but by the early 2000s climate scientists had converged around something like a consensus, with a vast majority from around the world agreeing with the nature of the problem and the critical role of human civilization as a causal factor. Inconveniently for Bush-Cheney, a major turning point came in the month of its inauguration, with the publication of the Intergovernmental Panel on Climate Change's

(IPCC's) *Climate Change 2001: IPCC Third Assessment Report*—a cogent statement of that near-consensus.

HOW TO TALK ABOUT POLAR BEARS

Four days after Bush's 2001 inauguration, Jana Goldman, a public affairs officer at the NOAA, sent an e-mail to Ronald Stouffer, a scientist in its Geophysical Fluid Dynamics Laboratory (GFDL). Goldman wrote, "If you get *any* press requests for IPCC please bump them to public affairs before you agree to an interview." The IPCC had just issued its seminal report documenting anthropogenic climate change, and though the president claimed he took the issue "very seriously" the White House was privately preparing to derail policy efforts to combat it, including Bush's March 2001 withdrawal from the Kyoto Protocol. Over time, the administration developed a policy mandating (climate and other) scientists to: (1) obtain preapproval for any interactions with journalists; (2) predict interview questions and submit their likely responses, to ensure the answers would be consistent with the president's preferences; (3) allow supervisors to monitor media communications; and (4) give up their right to state their personal opinions during interviews, even after assuring journalists they were not speaking on behalf of their agency. Jana Goldman was just a messenger and enforcer of that policy, but she was a consistent one nonetheless.[31]

Many topics were automatically considered sensitive, in large part because whatever scientists had to say about them conflicted with what the president and his party were saying. The NOAA's "media tracking logs," for instance, specifically urged caution with the following subjects: "hurricanes and climate change," "percentage of CO2 in greenhouse effect," "sea level rise," "global surface and satellite temperature measurements," "unusually warm lake temperatures," "amount of $$ [*sic*] spent on climate change," "climate change," and "arctic info." To ensure scientists spoke with caution, public affairs officers monitored (or claimed to monitor) all communications between NOAA scientists and the media, Congress, and the public.[32]

Inside and outside the NOAA, government monitoring of scientists' speech grew more elaborate and intensive over time. Eventually, some officials realized that monitoring did not go far enough in supporting the president's policy preferences. What good was it to only listen and record what scientists had to say, if what they had to say failed to "make the president look good" (as one NASA press officer, George Deutsch, described his job)? To better accomplish their objectives, information gatekeepers moved more extensively into the spaces where scientists interacted with the rest of the world, such as at professional meetings and in academic journals. Part of the problem, it seemed for Bush-Cheney officials, was that journalists increasingly went to climate science conferences, due to the growing importance and political prominence of climate change. Some agencies simply ordered their scientists not to speak about sensitive issues or required them to rehearse roughly scripted Q&A sessions before leaving headquarters. Thus, a new Fish and Wildlife Service policy ordered scientists from its Alaska bureau to refrain from having discussions about their work on "climate change, sea ice, and/or polar bears" during professional trips. Only "official spokesmen," either public affairs officers or screened scientists who "underst[ood] the administration's position," would be allowed to discuss agency work about the banned topics or otherwise interact with anyone asking questions about those issues, "particularly polar bears." Even though the Bush-Cheney administration was not the first to suppress scientific information, or push public affairs officers in front of scientists when journalists came calling, never before had an administration developed a policy regulating speech about polar bears, as far as we know.[33]

The White House sent gatekeepers across the government, implementing the climate science secrecy widely. The number of instances where information was blocked or filtered to fit the White House's political agenda is unknown, since we only have statements by scientists and public affairs officers who chose to speak out. We also have leaked or released (by FOIA) documents showing the development of the general gatekeeping policy, within and across agencies. What is clear from the scattered data is that the impositions and restrictions touched numerous scientists, preventing many from sharing unclassified, important, and otherwise unavailable information with the public (see Table 7.1). Many were likely intimidated and engaged in self-censorship of one form or another. Several others, among them NASA's Dr. James Hansen, decided the stakes were too high to comply—given the risks to the earth's biosphere and to American democracy.

JAMES HANSEN VERSUS THE GATEKEEPERS

Of all the scientists who spoke out against the administration's information policies, Hansen drew the most public attention, probably because of his long-standing prominence in climate science, including his role as director of NASA's Goddard Institute for Space Studies. Hansen had faced meddle-

some government gatekeepers in the past, and he did not hesitate to let the
world know about it. During the Bush-Cheney years, however, he grew more
determined than ever to tell citizens about the speech restrictions he and his
colleagues faced. Although many of the policies were implemented right after
Bush's inauguration, Hansen waited to take a public stand until 2004, when
he and most Americans were deciding on whether to reelect Bush-Cheney.

One week before the election, Hansen returned to the University of Iowa,
his alma mater, to "speak as a private citizen" on "Dangerous Anthropogenic
Interference: A Discussion of Humanity's Faustian Climate Bargain and the
Payments Coming Due." His opening sentence helped explain the title and
generated a whole lot of buzz: "I have been told by a high government official
[NASA administrator Sean O'Keefe in 2003] that I should not talk about
'dangerous anthropogenic interference' with climate, because we do not know
how much humans are changing the Earth's climate or how much change is
'dangerous.'" He continued, "In my more than three decades in the government, I have never seen anything approaching the degree to which information flow from scientists to the public has been screened and controlled as it
is now." The information suppression—targeting the unpublished results of
government studies—occurred in two basic ways:

> First, there is a selection of what results will be reported publicly. Results
> that yield evidence of natural climate variations, or which cast doubt on
> interpretations of anthropogenic climate effects, receive favorable treat-
> ment and are promptly disseminated. Results that would raise concerns
> about climate change are slowed and in some cases dismissed as not of
> sufficient interest for public dissemination. Second, there is commonly
> a massaging of the text of the scientific messages that are presented.
> Wording is altered to make the message about climate change to ap-
> pear to be less serious, or, among the various results in a paper, the ones
> highlighted are those that do not raise concern about climate change.

In other words, public affairs workers, many of them politically appointed,
sifted through papers, lectures, interview responses, and website postings to ensure messages about otherwise unavailable scientific results reflected the president's stated views. Science the president did not like or would find politically
inconvenient needed to wait. Hansen was not the only one crying foul, even
within NASA. Earlier in October of the election year, "three NASA scientists
and several officials at NASA headquarters and at two agency research centers"

TABLE 7.1
Government Climate Scientists (%)
Who "Perceived or Personally Experienced . . . "

46%	. . . pressure to eliminate the words *climate change, global warming,* or other similar terms from a variety of communications.
46%	. . . new or unusual administrative requirements that impair climate-related work.
43%	. . . changes or edits during review that changed the meaning of scientific findings.
38%	. . . the disappearance or unusual delay of websites, reports, or other science-based materials relating to climate.
37%	. . . statements by officials at their agencies that misrepresented scientists' findings.
25%	. . . situations in which scientists have actively objected to, resigned from, or removed themselves from a project because of pressure to change scientific findings.
58%	. . . one or more incidents of political interference (experienced personally) within the past five years.

Source: Donaghy et al. 2007.

had come forward, complaining about the clampdown. Hansen's prominence and personal responsibility for his allegations, however, brought the news to national headlines and editorials two days before the 2004 election.[34]

Sometimes, agency officials just rewrote scientists' reports. Even the White House got directly involved. Philip Cooney, chief of staff of the White House CEQ, who declared in 2007 that "my sole loyalty was to the president and advancing the policies of his administration," decided to take matters in his own hands. His loyalty to Bush apparently led him to fundamentally alter scientific reports on climate change in 2002 and 2003—excising whole sections, deleting parts of others, and inserting conditioning language to make conclusions more doubtful about climate change than scientists intended. In place of deleted sections and academic references, he included citations to the few, generally discredited papers that questioned the widespread scientific consensus. Although a person's professional background does not always shape all of his or her actions once in power, it is worth noting that Cooney was not a climate scientist (or anything close) but a former lobbyist with the American Petroleum Institute, a fossil fuel industry lobbying group promoting climate change denial and blocking carbon emission regulations. It is possible but doubtful that his "editing" happened without the knowledge of his White House colleagues, since he coordinated with them frequently about all of the reports coming from the thirteen-agency US Climate Change Science Program (CCSP).[35]

Cooney was not the only official who partook. According to a joint Union of Concerned Scientists–Government Accountability Project survey of hundreds of government scientists, 43 percent "perceived or personally experienced changes or edits during review that changed the meaning of scientific findings" (Table 7.1). The results demonstrate the problem was "beyond the anecdotal" and indicate a consistent, aggressive campaign by the White House, through its political appointees, to conceal climate science information, much of which was otherwise unavailable to the public.[36]

Conclusion: The Bush-Cheney Administration

A full history of all known examples of Bush-Cheney suppression of scientific information would continue for hundreds of pages. We would need to include cases involving endangered species, the health risks of pharmaceuticals, safety flaws wih all-terrain vehicles (ATVs) and other automotive products, reproductive and women's health, HIV/AIDS, and many more—none about national security. The Union of Concerned Scientists (UCS) kept a running tally of the Bush-Cheney "abuses of science," most of which involved censorship or other kinds of information suppression but not necessarily secrecy. In the administration's eight years, the UCS counted over 100 examples—and those were only the cases in the public record.[37]

Although there is no evidence Bush-Cheney officials directly interfered in the scientific process (as in, *You'll need to revise that model, Dr. Smith*), we have unambiguous evidence that high-level officials doctored reports, blocked scientists from publicly speaking, or otherwise concealed proprietary information that would have been in the public interest. Dr. Richard Carmona, Bush's surgeon general from 2002 until 2006, described the administration's record this way: "Anything that [didn't] fit into the political appointee's ideological, theological or political agenda [was] often ignored, marginalized or *simply buried.*" Overall, he "was astounded" by the "partisanship and political manipulation" he witnessed inside the government. However, since Carmona was new to Washington, he realized he "had no reference point. I asked myself whether this was just happening to me as a new Surgeon General, or whether this was a norm for all Surgeons General." Whether the Bush-Cheney administration resorted to secret science more than its predecessors is the subject to which we now turn.[38]

"An Unprecedented Pattern of Behavior"?

In February 2004, the Union of Concerned Scientists circulated a statement accusing "high-ranking Bush administration political appointees across numerous federal agencies" of suppressing and distorting scientific information. Scores of prominent scientists, including 52 Nobel laureates, 63 National Medal of Science recipients, and 195 members of the National Academies, had signed the declaration by the time Bush-Cheney left office. By 2008, over 15,000 scientists had signed it, all agreeing with its claim that "other administrations have, on occasion, engaged in such practices, but not so systematically nor on so wide a front." A UCS report published at the same time highlighted the "unprecedented pattern of behavior" in the administration. Like the petition, it conceded that "no administration has been above inserting politics into science from time to time." However, "a number of authoritative sources" from "Republican and Democratic administrations" have "asserted that the Bush administration is, to an unprecedented degree, distorting and manipulating the science meant to assist the formation and implementation of policy."[39]

That the administration distorted and manipulated science—and, in particular, suppressed unclassified proprietary information—on numerous occasions is beyond question, as the last section demonstrated. However, we still lack the kind of systematic comparative historical analysis that would help evaluate the scientists' "unprecedented" argument. Bush-Cheney defenders certainly seemed to think nothing was terribly unusual. For example, Kent Laborde, a NOAA public affairs officer, claimed his agency's restrictive information policies predated Bush-Cheney but had never been as vigorously enforced. White House OSTP director, Marburger, by contrast, argued previous administrations had acted just like Bush-Cheney, just as systematically. For instance, Marburger responded to critics' claims about the USDA's "List of Sensitive Issues," noting that "USDA-ARS headquarters has had a long-standing, routine practice (at least 20 years) that has spanned several Administrations to require review of research reports of high visibility topics." The fact that *Clinton-Gore's USDA had an almost identical list* was never mentioned during public debates—either because it was not known at the time or because it was disregarded for partisan purposes. Table 7.2 shows how Bush-Cheney's list from 2002 was adapted, with a few changes, from Clinton-Gore's list from 2000.

Even though no Clinton-Gore USDA scientists publicly cried foul, we

TABLE 7.2
Comparing 2000 and 2002 USDA "Sensitive" Lists*

2000 Clinton Administration	2002 Bush Administration
Creation of transgenic food or feed organisms by genetic engineering (human-directed splicing, altering, deletion, antisense reassembly, or other asexual recombining of DNA or RNA, including subsequent activities to regenerate whole transgenic organisms from cells or tissues or to transfer genetically engineered DNA from one organism to another to enhance its potential utility)	Creation of transgenic food or feed organisms by genetic engineering
Studies of genetically engineered organisms in the field, especially studies of the potential for gene escape, effects of transgenic organisms on nontarget species, or development of resistance of pests or pathogens to genetically engineered plant pesticides	Studies of genetically engineered organisms in the field
Cloning of animals by somatic cell nuclear transfer	Cloning of animals by somatic cell nuclear transfer
Somatic cell fusion to recombine DNA in ways that cannot be achieved through sexual crossing	Somatic cell fusion to recombine DNA in ways that cannot be achieved through sexual crossing
Mutagenic/carcinogenic materials and detection methods	
	Dioxin research
Plant, microbial, and animal patent policy	Plant, microbial, and animal patent policy
Agricultural practices with negative health and environmental consequences, e.g., global climate change; contamination of water by hazardous materials (nutrients, pesticides, and pathogens) exceeding health advisory or maximum contamination limits; animal feeding operations or crop production practices that negatively impact soil, water, or air quality in terms of public health/ environmental policy, etc.	Agricultural practices with negative health and environmental consequences, e.g., global climate change; contamination of water by hazardous materials (nutrients, pesticides, and pathogens); animal feeding operations or crop production practices that negatively impact soil, water, or air quality
Boll weevil eradication program	Boll weevil eradication program
International plant germplasm policies	International plant germplasm policies

(continued on next page)

TABLE 7.2
Continued

2000 Clinton Administration	2002 Bush Administration
Research findings and recommendations that would be contrary to current dietary guidelines or may be used in food labeling	Research findings and recommendations that are contrary to current dietary guidelines or may be used in food labeling
Megadoses of nutrients that may be beneficial to human health/nutrition	Megadoses of nutrients that may be beneficial to human health/nutrition
Radiolytic products in food	Radiolytic products in food
Harmful microorganisms and their products (e.g., aflatoxin, mycotoxin, fumonisin, salmonella, E. coli) in agricultural commodities (crops and animals) or in food with significant public health/policy implications (NPS will clear also with FSIS)	Harmful microorganisms and their products (e.g., aflatoxin, mycotoxin, fumonisin, salmonella, E. coli) in agricultural commodities
Pesticides or animal drugs in foods above approved tolerance levels	Pesticides or animal drugs in foods above approved tolerance levels
All transmissible encephalopathy (TSE) research	All transmissible encephalopathy (TSE) research including BSE research
Herbicide-resistant crop plant research	Herbicide-resistant crop plant research
Animal well-being/animal use	Animal well-being/animal use
Biological items that may affect trade and export negotiations, e.g., fire blight in apples, TCK smut, insect infestations in export products, etc.	Biological items that may affect trade and export negotiations, e.g., fire blight in apples, TCK smut, karnal bunt, insect infestations in export products, etc.
Narcotic plant control	Narcotic plant control
Methyl bromide topics that relate to policy and/or regulatory actions	Methyl bromide topics that relate to policy and/or regulatory actions
Medfly/Malathion replacements	Medfly/Malathion replacements
Any technical issue that is likely to affect policy and regulatory matters in other agencies/departments, the health/well-being of the public at large, and/or invoke intense public perceptions and concerns	
Antibiotic/antimicrobial resistance	Antibiotic/antimicrobial resistance
Bioterrorism/attacks on agriculture	Bioterrorism/attacks on agriculture
	Glassy-winged sharpshooter/Pierce's disease
	Sudden oak death
	Citrus stem canker
	Anthrax

(continued)

TABLE 7.2
Continued

2000 Clinton Administration	2002 Bush Administration
	Emerging diseases or pest research that relates to policy and/or regulatory actions

*After 2003, the ARS changed the name and continued making updates to the "List of High Profile Topics."
Source: USDA ARS.

cannot conclude that none were affected by the list. And that brings us back to the scientists who signed the UCS report. Did they fall victim to the recency bias—or other, political biases? Did they simply get caught up in the passions of the moment? Were their memories correct?[40]

The Clinton-Gore Administration

Compared with Bush-Cheney, the Clinton-Gore administration left office with far fewer science-secrecy conflicts under its belt. One might have gotten a different impression from the Democrats' critics, who frequently attacked what they saw as the administration's routine "politicization" of science, including its "secret science." Much of the criticism pointed directly at Gore, due to his alleged efforts to stifle evidence contradicting his progressive environmental policy preferences. Before Gore became the vice president, his environmental advocacy made him a reliable Bush-Quayle stump speech joke in the 1992 election: he was the "ozone man"—"kooky," "crazy," and "far out." Others delivered the darker, underlying message: he would be dangerous in power because of his Stalinist tendencies. Gore's suggestion that Americans turn to environmentalism as a "central organizing principle" in the political economy allegedly reflected his secret preference for a command-and-control economy managed by a liberty-squelching government (Cold War red baiting survived the end of the Cold War). After the election, somewhat more incisive critics lambasted the vice president's "unprecedented . . . interference" in government scientists' work and claimed he appointed "antiscience, antitechnology ideologues," "yes-men," and "untalented nonentit[ies]" to important agency posts. Overall, there were many noisy, insinuating attacks, but few critics offered credible arguments and evidence documenting extensive "intimidation" and interference (that is, a high noise-to-signal ratio). And though Gore's critics sometimes loosely threw accusations of "secret science" into the mix, the public record shows very few cases that can be described that way. One accusation that withstands scrutiny involves a secret CIA program called Measurements of Earth Data for Environmental Analysis (MEDEA).[41]

Gore, MEDEA, and Secret Science in the CIA

By the 1970s, the US intelligence community had at its disposal a wide assortment of powerful aerospace, sonar, and ship-based technologies to capture virtually everything on the surface of the earth or inside its oceans. The government's machines had far greater sophistication than any private sector counterparts, and they had a singular purpose: to increase the government's intelligence capacity during the Cold War. Intelligence analysts may have also used the world's best satellites to satisfy personal intellectual curiosities, but their bosses valued them narrowly for their spying capabilities. Senior officials wanted to know about nuclear bomb tests and missile launches, not desertification and Arctic ice melts.[42]

Senator Gore (D-TN) considered that a huge missed opportunity. In 1990, he pressed for change in a bill cosponsored with Sen. Sam Nunn (D-GA) that directed the military and intelligence agencies to use their unparalleled resources—satellites, supercomputers, reconnaissance aircraft, ships, and sonar arrays—to monitor global environmental changes. After the bill passed, Bush-Quayle CIA officials met secretly with carefully chosen academic scientists to discuss the Strategic Environmental Research Program's potential uses, as well as its feasibility, given the classified status of the technologies and their data. The planning group apparently came up short. The program quietly drifted off the political agenda (or it was pushed). But with Gore's urging, CIA director Robert Gates in 1992 revived the process, creating the Environmental Task Force, which first met in October 1992 after its participants acquired the requisite security clearances.[43]

After Clinton-Gore took control of the government in 1993, the CIA under R. James Woolsey, Jr., institutionalized the program and renamed it MEDEA, after the woman in the Greek myth who promised to help Jason and the Argonauts capture the Golden Fleece if Jason promised to marry her. (The CIA's Linda Zall, who named the program, worked closely with the military and intelligence agencies' long-running secret JASON group of nongovernment science advisers.) By 1994, the CIA had given high-level security clearances to seventy government and nongovernment scientists who worked across eleven thematic panels, analyzing scientific data all other citizens could not see. Although other organizations (such as NASA and private companies) operated satellite programs and shared data with nongovernment scientists, MEDEA's classified technologies delivered image resolutions "15 to 30 times sharper" than any other systems, with clarity down to the 1-meter level. Everyone cleared into MEDEA thus had exclusive knowledge—information unavailable to everyone else, scientist or not.[44]

About a year after Gore's MEDEA was up and running, administration officials appeared to recognize the shaky national security basis for keeping the satellite images secret. At the very least, they decided the benefits of disclosure outweighed the security risks. Clinton's February 1995 Executive Order 12951, "Release of Imagery Acquired by Space-Based National Intelligence Reconnaissance Systems," promised the declassification of over 800,000 satellite images from the *Argon, Corona,* and *Lanyard* systems (Keyhole [KH]-1 through KH-6), giving agencies eighteen months for evaluation and transition. Only the images would be released—not information about the systems themselves. In a separate February 1995 announcement, Gore touted his commitment to transparency and "common-sense" environmental and security policy: "The Cold War is over. Communism has collapsed. We no longer face the threat of a large-scale war with the former Soviet Union. Selectively declassifying information we already have gathered during this period is a common-sense way to address new threats to global and regional security, including depletion of food and water supplies and the ozone layer, large-scale destruction of forests and global warming linked to pollution." Like the administration's other declassification programs (see chapter 3), this one helped reduce the amount of excessive secrecy. Likewise, the program had important limitations. First, the declassification plan excluded data gathered by other satellite systems probably used by MEDEA, including *Gambit* (KH-7, KH-8) and *Hexagon* (KH-9, "Big Bird"). The administration never explained why. Second, the disclosures would only include images captured between 1960 and 1972. The historical data—old pictures of forests, rivers, deserts, coastlines, glaciers, and so forth—offered environmental scientists and advocates in the late 1990s a very limited bounty. How useful were climate change data with a 1972 end point? Given the exclusions and MEDEA's continuing work, the secret science thus continued mostly uninterrupted.[45]

Underscoring the irony of the continuing secrecy after Clinton's order, only one of more than twelve MEDEA reports completed from 1994 to 1998 was declassified. Moreover, MEDEA-affiliated scientists faced large obstacles when trying to publish academic articles based on the secret data. For example, William H. Schlesinger and Nicholas Gramenopoulos submitted their provocative paper documenting "no climate-induced changes in woody vegetation in the Sudan, 1943–1994." But because their analaysis used classified data, the flagship journal *Science* refused to publish the study. The anonymous peer reviewers would not overlook the fact they could not inspect the data. *Science*'s editor pointed out what should have been obvious to the authors: "If reviewers can't judge what is presented, we're not going to publish." When the study did appear in *Global Change Biology*, the editors of that journal attached a disclaimer:

> Many of the data for this paper are in classified intelligence archives. As a consequence, the options for evaluating the paper and for ensuring that other scientists can reproduce the analysis are constrained. Publication of this paper in *Global Change Biology* is intended to illustrate the potential use of, and stimulate discussion on the role of, classified data in the open scientific literature. Limitations on access to the data make it impossible for the journal's usual review process to assess all aspects of data quality, selection or interpretation.

The disclaimer probably undermined the credibility of the work for many scientists, perhaps especially because the study pushed against the growing consensus on climate change, however localized the results were ("woody vegetation in the Sudan"). Why trust scientific conclusions about such a controversial issue reached with secret data? Climate change skeptics probably saw conspiracies galore. (*I bet there are scores of studies just like this showing climate change to be a farce! That's why there's so much secrecy!*) Such are the hazards of excessive secrecy.[46]

That images of changes in woody vegetation in the Sudan were considered state secrets in 1996 demonstrates the limits of the declassification initiative. Probably tens of millions of other images—of desertification in Paraguay, mangrove loss on Caribbean islands, and so on—were overclassified during and after the MEDEA program (Bush-Cheney killed it in 2002; Obama-Biden resurrected it in 2011). The potential scientific—and electoral—value of that secret information cannot be quantified. However, we can probably agree that the national security basis for the secrecy was unjustified or at least quite weak. We are, after all, talking about images of forests and deserts—the fruits of the technologies, not the machines themselves. And we have not even discussed the clear FACA violation. Public officials met secretly with private citizens on an environmental task force, with secret transcripts and reports. Add another one to the Clinton-Gore tally from chapter 4. Overall, this is a clear instance of secret science in the Clinton-Gore administration. Give Gore's critics at least some credit.[47]

Soot, "Secret Science," and the EPA

Another accusation of secret science in the Clinton-Gore administration, involving confidential data the EPA used to help justify new pollution regulations, does not hold up as well. There is no question the administration blocked public access to raw, individual-level survey data tracing the medical histories of more than 550,000 participants in a prospective cohort study of US adults. Clinton-Gore also refused to fully disclose agency memos about the regulatory process. And the administration fought against a bill to expand FOIA, proposed by congressional Republicans, that promised to let citizens access "all data produced" by studies supported by the federal government. Although the Clinton-Gore administration clearly kept unnecessary secrets in this case, some of its critics' accusations fell flat. Plus, the story ends with protransparency organizations joining the administration in opposing the proposed FOIA amendment, for reasons that will become clear.

In 1994, after ignoring a Clean Air Act requirement (42 U.S.C. 7409(d)) for two years, the Clinton-Gore EPA began a long-delayed reevaluation of federal air quality regulations (Bush-Quayle earlier ignored it for one year, in 1992). Dozens of agency scientists, drawing from their own and outside research, ultimately recommended stricter national air pollution standards for ground-level ozone (smog) and new ones for particulate matter (soot), previously unregulated. The proposed soot rules were motivated by a growing body of research demonstrating the pollutant's health hazards, including an added heart disease risk for adults and added mortality risk for asthmatic children.[48]

Of the many studies the EPA cited, there was one, by C. Arden Pope and colleagues (then at Harvard and the American Cancer Society), that established a statistically significant link between soot and fatal lung and heart disease, after controlling for major risk factors like cigarette smoking. To ensure that study's validity (that is, to independently verify the authors' conclusions), EPA scientists obtained the research group's proprietary data. When antiregulation interests sought the same data, the EPA, as well as Pope et al., refused to provide them on privacy grounds. The data contained personal and medical data linked to hundreds of thousands of Americans, the scientists argued. Why disclose such sensitive information to apparently hostile interest groups? Those groups dismissed the privacy explanation, arguing that the scientists wanted to hide the "junk science" underlying their "extremist" environmental policy agenda. Others simply saw a clear window of opportunity, since a constructed controversy about secret science might just scuttle the regulations. In any case, the opposition stepped up its fight, using lobbying, congressional action, and a media strategy to accuse the administration of secret science, hinting at a cover-up. It certainly did not help the administration that someone inside the Treasury Department leaked an e-mail written by Secretary Robert Rubin that indicated the EPA had limited interagency deliberations, possibly intentionally, to hasten the process: "There is no forum. EPA held one briefing—albeit a long one—on 10/16 for interested agencies. Next step will be a cursory review by [the OMB]. Then the rules will be proposed. That's it. (How do you spell S-L-A-M D-U-N-K?)." Whether or not history followed Rubin's plans, Clinton approved the EPA's recommendations in June 1997, over the objections of the antiregulation interests.[49]

Once the new regulations were in place, opponents kept up the fight, with Pope et al.'s soot data as a focal point. Anything less than full public access was depicted as a sign of the new rule's flimsy foundations and of something shady going on at the EPA. The administration countered with a compromise. The EPA, administrator Carol Browner said, would still refuse to give congressional Republicans everything they wanted—full public access—because of privacy concerns and because Harvard University, not the government, actually owned the data. However, Harvard and Pope et al. would share the data with the nonprofit, nonpartisan Health Effects Institute, whose analysts would privately evaluate the data and associated statistical models. Funding for the exercise would come from the EPA and auto companies (the institute's fifty-fifty sponsors). Because General Motors (GM), Ford, and Chrysler strongly opposed the regulations, they would not have backed the plan (as they did) if they thought the deck was stacked against them. Even so, congressional Republicans rejected the administration's offer as insufficient.[50]

In the House of Representatives, Commerce Committee chairman Tom Bliley (R-VA) threatened subpoenas. He smelled a rat in the OMB's unusually quick review of the EPA's report and recommendations—three weeks for very technical documents that dwarfed *War and Peace* many times over (the first of three volumes on soot alone filled 1,076 pages). Representative Bliley also saw the regulations as potentially tyrannical. Who would stop the EPA from forcing local communities to "ban barbecues and fireplaces"? he asked the EPA's Browner when she testified before his committee. Before the subpoena threat, Bliley successfully pushed the OMB to give him its independent cost-benefit analysis, but it came larded with redactions, courtesy of the EPA. After hearing rumors that the EPA had forced the OMB into the fast review and the OMB had advised other agencies not to speak publicly about the new regulations, he used his authority as Commerce Committee chair to find out. His approach worked, up to a point. Clinton-Gore handed over internal documents, including some critical of the new rules, but drew the line at those published after December 13, 1996, when the EPA published its proposals in the *Federal Register*. The Department of Transportation also refused to release several documents because they "involved the White House."[51]

Sen. Richard Shelby (R-AL) encountered the same set of difficulties and pretended executive branch secrecy was something Clinton-Gore invented ("What the heck? Can you imagine the arrogance?"). His solution was a proposed bill that aimed to expand FOIA so all citizens could access "all data produced" by studies supported by the federal government. Who could possibly oppose more transparency? his supporters asked.[52]

Suddenly, the fight over what Republicans called the EPA's secret science transformed into a larger one with enormous consequences for FOIA, government transparency, and the policy-making process more generally. That last possibility was not lost on business interests hostile to environmental regulation. "If implemented properly, this rule will do more for regulatory reform than all the legislation passed in the last 10 years!" gushed the US Chamber of Commerce. The Associated Equipment Distributors, the international trade association, echoed the chamber: "We consider the Shelby amendment to be the most important regulatory reform enacted into law in recent memory." Several other conservative interests, such as the Competitive Enterprise Institute, Citizens for a Sound Economy, and the Gun Owners of America, embraced Senator Shelby's proposal, seeing its far-reaching potential. Its reach "is virtually limitless and can be extended into areas other than health and safety," concluded the Chamber of Commerce. The reason they were all so excited was that the law would let them inspect government and nongovernment scientists' work down to the smallest detail, giving them myriad new opportunities to discredit studies' assumptions, methods of analysis, and conclusions, fairly or not.[53]

Notably absent from Senator Shelby's cheering section were open government groups, typically at the forefront of protransparency laws. One, OMB

Watch, argued the law would unfairly exclude business corporations from the same kinds of disclosure requirements placed on universities and other nonprofit organizations. If the bill passed, corporations supported by federal funds through subsidies, contracts, or other means would not be subject to FOIA requests for data related to their government-funded scientific research. As OMB Watch's Gary Bass put it, the law "applies to a Y.M.C.A. that receives a Federal grant, but not to Boeing that is doing a range of research through contracts." Scientists and university administrators also tended to oppose Senator Shelby's bill. For one, many were understandably reluctant to give everyone access to all of their work, including first drafts, notebook scribblings, e-mails with collaborators, and other parts of the research process the law targeted ("all data"). Hostile, deep-pocketed interests might use the amended FOIA to distort scientists' work. "We are very concerned that [the FOIA amendment] could involve actions designed to discredit scientists and discourage researchers from addressing controversial topics," the president of the Association of American Universities warned.[54]

Scientists and administrators also argued anyone seeking raw data could access research subjects' confidential, sensitive information. To that criticism, Senator Shelby and his supporters offered the assurance that FOIA's Exemption 6 would still protect personal privacy. But as statisticians noted, there are ways to decipher individual identities using group-level variables (for example, gender, city, hospital, disease, and treatment)—though the ability to do that should not be exaggerated. If identified by interests with a stake in a study's outcome, subjects might face pressure to respond to researchers' questions in certain ways (that is, by being more favorable toward those interests). Moreover, some potential research subjects, knowing about the potential loss of privacy, might refuse to participate. One sociologist whose research involved interviewing rape victims expected few of her subjects would participate in her studies if they thought their personal information could be accessible via FOIA. Overall, critics—including transparency groups—expressed concerns that Shelby's proposed FOIA amendment would stifle research on a range of controversial topics.[55]

Although their opponents' objections sounded far-fetched to Shelby's supporters, there was actually some precedent for the scientists' concerns. Many still had Paul Fischer on their minds. The Medical College of Georgia professor had recently published, with colleagues, a landmark study in the *Journal of the American Medical Association* (*JAMA*) about the effects of cigarette advertising on children. The study documented a disturbing trend: young children (three to six years old) were quite familiar with cigarette company cartoon mascots like Joe Camel. Moreover, the images were as familiar to them as Mickey Mouse and the Disney Channel logo. Many children also demonstrated surprising knowledge about the differences between cigarette brands. Other work in the same *JAMA* issue showed underaged teenagers were more likely than adults to favor Camels.[56]

R. J. Reynolds Tobacco, manufacturer of Camel cigarettes, launched a two-front war—in the media and in courtrooms—against Fischer's study and others like it. Corporate spokespeople moved through newsrooms, insisting to writers, editors, and news anchors that Joe Camel was marketed to twenty-somethings, not children. And even if they did try to target children, one R. J. Reynolds spokesperson said, the government in response would "step in and restrict our ability to communicate with the adult smoking market"—a claim seemingly ignorant of the fact that tobacco company lobbyists had an enviable record on K Street.[57]

To raise doubt about the new studies, R. J. Reynolds officials needed ammunition. First, they subpoenaed Fischer's records, including the names and addresses of the young children interviewed for his study, ostensibly to verify their participation. Fischer resisted, as most researchers protecting sensitive data would. His employer, the Medical College of Georgia, however, did not resist and advised Fischer to comply or get his own lawyer to fight the subpoena. He did just that and won, but the battle was not yet over. After Fischer's court victory, an attorney for the medical school inexplicably reminded the tobacco company in a newspaper interview of Georgia's strong Open Records Act (ORA), saying something like (from Fischer's memory), "We would have turned over all these data" if R. J. Reynolds had filed an ORA request. A week later, Fischer received the company's ORA request for "everything in my office," including the childrens' names and addresses. He reluctantly gathered his materials but submitted them to a judge in a last-ditch effort to forestall disclosure. After keeping them for a year, Fischer said, the court, "under very mysterious circumstances," gave all of his materials to R. J. Reynolds. All along the way, the company pressured the college and filed multiple legal motions. Company officials got everything and assured the affected families they would respect their confidentiality.[58]

It is not clear how far R. J. Reynolds got with its "reinterviewing" process, although the company denied having any contact with families. However, the company admitted it had every intention of doing so, if not for the public criticism. Its deputy general counsel conceded that "as soon as the objection was raised, everybody recognized that we didn't need and didn't want to bother the parents of these 3- and 6-year-old children." Apparently, before the objection arose, they needed and wanted to bother them.[59]

Fischer's story resonated with critics of Senator Shelby's bill because it provided a good example of what a large corporation might do with access to scientists' records. R. J. Reynolds might have resisted the temptation to press forward as aggressively as it initially intended, but not all companies or private interests would do the same. As Congress debated the proposal, other researchers reported they had been targeted in similar ways. For example, Dr. Bruce Psaty, whose work demonstrated risks of blood pressure medication, claimed pharmaceutical companies harassed him with his state's FOIA laws. Senator Shelby and his staff acknowledged the potential for misconduct but offered the weak assurance that even if abuses occurred, "we can address those. We will be alert to those." Another potential problem was FOIA requesters' use of the courts to appeal FOIA denials based on the personal privacy exemption. Surely, *some* judges could be convinced there were good reasons for releasing sensitive information, such as survey respondent names. In general, critics of Senator Shelby's proposal saw it as a powerful new tool for corporate interests, including its use as a deterrent, suppressing research and related government regulations perceived to be disastrous to corporate bottom lines.[60]

Despite these criticisms, the amendment passed as a two-sentence rider in the 1999 budget bill, which directed the OMB to administer the new rule. Because the word *data* was left undefined, the OMB circulated a proposal and solicited public comments, receiving 8,350 responses within sixty days (and 800 more after the deadline). Fifty-five percent supported the OMB's proposal, which excluded from FOIA requests most of the controversial information categories (such as early drafts, preliminary analyses, and communications with colleagues). Whether personal privacy would still be protected was less certain, since the new rule excluded disclosure when that "would constitute a clearly unwarranted invasion of personal privacy, such as information that could be used to identify a particular person in a research study." It was up to FOIA officers, lawyers, and judges to interpret what *clearly unwarranted invasion* meant. Was invasion of personal privacy sometimes warranted? Would statisticians still have access to demographic or other group-level variables, or was that "information that could be used to identify" individuals? Despite some reservations about the final version, Senator Shelby welcomed his victory. Whether Shelby's victory beat back excessive government secrecy is another matter altogether.[61]

Conclusion and Another Example

The FOIA amendment that emerged from the soot and smog conflict was a strange victory for transparency advocates. On the one hand, it promised to shine light on some information citizens had a right to know. On the other, it opened up the possibility of giving potentially hostile private interests access to confidential information, as had happened in the past (for example, with Dr. Fischer versus R. J. Reynolds). The FOIA amendment also carved out exceptions for corporations supported by federal funds, whose data would remain protected when the related research did not directly influence public policy making. The so-called EPA study at the heart of the debate was, in fact, a study done by academic researchers working at a private institution (Harvard). Their analysis, which laid bare their hypotheses, assumptions, methodology, and statistical reasoning, was published after a rigorous double-blinded peer review process, which went a long way in correcting small and large errors (the reviewers presumably had access to the data). What was secret about their nongovernment study was their raw microlevel dataset, complete with their subjects' personal information, which the nongovernmental researchers had earlier guaranteed would remain confidential. Even if that was secrecy, it was not *government* secrecy. However, the puzzlingly redacted and fully secret memos about the regulatory process indicate the administration was not blameless.

Overall, Clinton-Gore critics' secret science accusations were usually unsubstantiated. Another one, however, sullies their record further, especially because the secrecy had such serious consequences. In short: Clinton-Gore's Federal Aviation Administration (FAA) failed to disseminate critical safety warnings about Boeing 757s, which probably caused four crashes, killing thirteen people. The government had known for years the jets produced a dangerous "wake turbulence" (or "wake vortex") behind its engines, putting trailing planes in jeopardy, even 2 to 3 miles out. But the FAA failed to adequately warn air traffic controllers about the problem. It instead waited until it was too late, after a fatal December 1993 crash, which led the *Los Angeles Times* to investigate a string of accidents and close calls involving 757s. In particular, the *Times* found the 757s implicated in four separate crashes in 1993, killing at least thirteen individuals, and forty-six close calls from 1983 to 1993. Scientists inside the government, including the FAA's chief scientist, others at NASA and NOAA, and partner agencies from other countries (for instance, the UK's Civil Aviation Authority), had pressed the issue for years, but FAA officials dismissed the warnings, in part due to their concerns about how disclosure would affect Boeing as well as US airlines.[62]

The FAA's failure to act was the result of active, knowing negligence; it was not just mismanagement or bureaucratic incompetence. The agency's secrecy about the matter was actively enforced. *Times* journalists were repeatedly rebuffed when trying to obtain FAA documents via FOIA. The agency only relented after the newspaper appealed the rejections in court. Once they were released, the documents plainly revealed officials' awareness of the deadly game they were playing. One memo written by Chief Scientist Robert Machol warned FAA administrators of impending disaster (a "major crash"). In response, an official wrote, "Bob: A note of caution—please watch your wording—I don't want 'smoking guns' in our files."[63]

The Clinton-Gore administration obviously deserves blame for this one, for the FAA's secrecy in 1993 was a direct cause of the crashes. And Bush-Quayle deserves blame as well: it was a Bush-Quayle FAA official in 1989, after all, who requested that Machol avoid the smoking guns. However ignoble their eventual turnaround, the FAA wound up releasing the documents and ordering new landing rules at airports.[64]

The Bush-Quayle Administration

James Hansen prepared for his May 1989 congressional testimony in the usual way. After putting together a brief summary about the science community's best understanding of the worrisome new global warming trend, he submitted his report to the OMB for review. The OMB's role as the White House's executive branch information coordinator was well established (see chapter 8). It reviewed and, if all went well, approved and released any intra-government communications about anything construed to have policy statements. From personal experience, Hansen knew the Reagan-Bush administration had been unusually restrictive in regard to scientific information, but he expected few problems with the new Bush-Quayle administration. After all, George H. W. Bush had just won a major election following a campaign promising he would "combat the greenhouse effect with the White House effect."[65]

Hansen received his report back from the OMB just before the scheduled testimony. It had been rendered into a completely different set of scientific arguments, with expectations and observations Hansen had never made in the original. In place of sentences describing scientific models linking greenhouse gases, climate change, and weather events (such as droughts and storms), the OMB inserted other sentences that emphasized—and increased—the amount of uncertainty surrounding the models. Instead of Hansen's clear statement linking human activities with climate change, the OMB added unjustified uncertainty, and it claimed the relative weight of anthropocentric versus nonhuman effects "remains scientifically unknown," despite the evidence pointing to the former.[66]

When Hansen testified before the Senate Commerce Subcommittee on Science, Technology and Space, he acknowledged what had happened, risking White House reprisals for his defiance. Senator Gore got the ball rolling, asking about a section of Hansen's submitted testimony.

HANSEN: "The last paragraph in that section which seems to be in contradiction to [another section] was not a paragraph which I wrote. It was added to my testimony in the process of review by OMB, and I did object to the addition of that paragraph because in essence it says that I believe that all scientific conclusions that I just discussed are not reliable, and I certainly do not agree with that."

GORE: "The statements which were changed by OMB were not statements about policy. They were statements about the scientific data, correct?"

HANSEN: "I do not believe that the science aspects of the testimony should be altered."

In the same hearing, the director of NOAA's Geophysical Fluid Dynamics Laboratory, Dr. Jerry Mahlman, revealed that his testimony had also been altered by the OMB, in "objectionable and unscientific" ways. The White House denied wrongdoing, saying Hansen's and Mahlman's statements were changed because they reflected policy preferences, not government scientists' work or the science community's consensus.[67]

What took Bush-Cheney a least a year to do after inauguration in 2001 had happened in less than four months after Bush-Quayle took office in 1989. Had Hansen and Mahlman not been as courageous as they were, we probably would never have known about the OMB's interventions early in 1989. And that the White House strongly defended its actions was a loud signal to scientists across the government that Bush-Quayle officials would probably do it again. Even though the Hansen and Mahlman incident did not involve proprietary scientific information—they summarized the contemporary understanding of climate science inside and outside government—other episodes did. One place where such suppression occurred so frequently as to suggest it was institutionalized was in the USDA's Forest Service.

Forest Service Managers versus the "Ologists"

During the four years of the Bush-Quayle administration, at least five scientists and one wilderness ranger risked their careers and reputations to report ongoing and extensive efforts by the Forest Service to suppress, alter, and even destroy their work. Hundreds of other FS workers—100 in 1992 alone—privately complained about their experiences to the whistle-blower organization Governmental Accountability Project. FS officials acted secretly and unilaterally in some cases; in others, they directly pressured scientists to alter their reports. In all cases, the objectives were the same: to suppress proprietary scientific information in order to make FS reports more favorable to the timber industry. Researchers who refused to do so faced ceaseless workplace intimidation and real or threatened demotions.[68]

Some had their work suppressed or blocked several times. For example, Marynell Oechsner, a wildlife biologist, found her contributions to environmental impact statements (EISs) ignored or altered beyond recognition, several times over. One EIS detailed the probable harms to a grizzly bear habitat from a timber sale in Idaho's Kootenai National Forest. If the sale went forward as proposed, Oechsner concluded in her analysis, it would put local bear populations at risk. Because grizzlies were listed as a threatened species in 1975 in the lower forty-eight states, under the Endangered Species Act the sale should have been denied or its details revised. But instead of breaking that sad news to the timber companies as they were sharpening their saws, Oechsner's supervisors took the easier path of eliminating her findings from the final report. They then issued a formal notice of the timber sale, which claimed no harm would come to threatened, endangered, or other protected sensitive species.[69]

In a different EIS, Oechsner determined that a proposed road-building plan in an Idaho old-growth forest theatened a federally protected wildlife habitat (not to mention the trees). Once again, her research was excised without explanation. Only after she and several colleagues complained to regional managers was her work restored, which left the habitat protected. All along the way, she faced reprisals, including workplace intimidation as well as poor performance evaluations. "For me," she explained, "'dissension,' in the form of speaking up for the resources, taking a stand for wildlife, precipitated a threat of removal, reassignment or demotion." She eventually requested and got a transfer to another site.[70]

Oechsner's experiences were not unique. FS officials pressured another biologist, Francis Mangels, to eliminate a section of his timber sale EIS demonstrating how the project would harm a protected bald eagle population. When Mangels refused, he faced harsh workplace intimidation and, ultimately, demotion. Jeff DeBonis, a FS timber sales planner in Oregon, faced harassment after circulating a report identifying clear negative effects from national forest road building.[71]

Conflicts between FS scientists and supervisors had grown so widespread during Bush-Quayle—continuing an earlier trend from Reagan-Bush—that the opposing sides coalesced under nicknames. Managers and their industry partners called the disobedient biologists "ologists." The scientists called themselves "combat biologists." After Clinton-Gore took over in 1993, the dynamic apparently continued, although no FS scientists came forward to accuse the Clinton-Gore FS of outright suppression or manipulation of their work or speech.[72]

Gulf War Illness

The 1991 invasion of Iraq accomplished nearly all of the White House's objectives, most notably forcing Saddam Hussein's army to retreat from Kuwait. At least as important was what the president's son would fail to accomplish twelve years later: finding and disposing of Iraqi weapons of mass destruction, including biological and chemical weapons, long-range missiles, and an incipient uranium enrichment program. Following Hussein's surrender in March 1991, the UN Special Commission (UNSCOM) and the International Atomic Energy Agency (IAEA) spent more than a decade locating, monitoring, and destroying Iraq's weapons caches and labs. Several sites were already well known to the United States and its allies in early 1991. With the war's end, they immediately went to work.[73]

The army's order to incinerate Khamisiyah came days after Hussein's surrender. US inspectors had earlier verified that storage facilities at the southern Iraqi site contained copious amounts of sarin, cyclosarin, and mustard gases. On March 4, 1991, the Thirty-Seventh Engineer Battalion began its demolitions, destroying 37 of Khamisiyah's 100-some bunkers. Explosions rocked the desert through March 20. Troops and explosive ordnance disposal technicians at the site took precautions, knowing full well the nerve agents would swirl around with every blast, but they did not have all of the relevant information to maximize safety (for example, that nerve agents were loaded into 122-mm rockets). Worse, at least 100,000 soldiers in the vicinity were left completely unprotected, as were unknown numbers of local Iraqis. Engineers, technicians, and other officials had miscalculated the downwind trajectory of the nerve agents, which caused the limited safety zone that put the 100,000-plus individuals in harm's way. People in the vicinity without knowledge of the mission at Khamisiyah had no idea what hit them.[74]

Soldiers who had fought the Iraqi army weeks earlier had a much better idea. On numerous occasions, coalition forces reported Iraqi chemical attacks. Veterans of one group stationed in Jubail in northern Saudi Arabia (the Twenty-Fourth Naval Mobile Construction Battalion) reported feeling ill immediately after an incoming Iraqi bomb exploded on January 19, 1991, which apparently spread a cloud of poisonous mustard gas. "I put my gas mask on right away, but by the time I got to the bunker, my hands and face were burning, and I couldn't breathe," one recalled. Another said, "Right after I got into the bunker, my lips started turning numb, and the numbness lasted for several days. We washed down and that seemed to help, but people started coming up with blisters." Well before the reported attacks, soldiers had prepared for chemical warfare, all having received at least minimal training. Hussein had used chemical weapons against Iraqi Kurds in Halabja a few years earlier, after all, and he had threatened to do the same if coalition forces invaded. The fear of chemical attacks probably led to some false alarms. However, the battalion in Jubail had real reasons for worry, beyond all of the blistering and burning. Two of three M-256 mustard gas detection kits tested positive, and chemical alarms activated as the cloud descended. Another unit, the 644th Ordnance Company, had reported a similar experience two days earlier.[75]

In the years that followed, thousands of veterans who suffered Iraqi chemical attacks or worked near Khamisiyah on those fateful demolition days trickled into veterans' hospitals. They reported almost identical symptoms, including fatigue, headaches, joint pain, nausea, memory loss, dizziness, rashes, and gastrointestinal illness. As information about their common experiences spread, veterans' groups, medical professionals, and politicians began to talk about a "Gulf War syndrome" or "Gulf War illness." The official government response was a firm and consistent denial: veterans had not been exposed to chemical agents—at Khamisiyah or on the battlefield—and they would not be entitled to special damages, disability payments, or care. The response mimicked how the government had responded to Vietnam War veterans reporting illnesses from Agent Orange exposure (see chapter 8), although the newer version was arguably more challenging for veterans because officials flatly denied the fact of Gulf War exposure (Vietnam veterans were told not to worry about their Agent Orange exposure).[76]

To pull it off, officials would need to refute evidence like the Twenty-Fourth Naval Mobile Construction Battalion's positive detection kit readings and the chemical alarms. DOD officials first (in 1991) continued with a strategy of denial, saying, for instance, that the extremely loud explosion the soldiers heard was not actually from a bomb but from a sonic boom caused by nearby aircraft. Five years later, they changed the explanation, admitting the noise "probably" resulted from an intercepted Iraqi Scud missile but absolutely not one loaded with nerve gas. The burns and other symptoms, the DOD said, were likely caused by "rocket propellent" and were not "consistent with a chemical attack." It was rather inconvenient for the DOD's narrative when combat logs written by an aide to Gen. H. Norman Schwartzkopf were declassified in 1996, for they described a "chemical attack at Jubail" on January 19 as well as the "mustard positive" tests soliders had reported. ("It's damn hard to mess up those tests," a Twenty-Fourth Battalion soldier said.) The DOD claimed the tests done at the site were false positives, perhaps caused by the rocket propellent. The more reliable test, they claimed, was the negative one from several miles away. It also did not help the government's argument that the army's own Chemical School in 1996 countered the DOD's official story, saying, "The school knew of no research suggesting that the rocket propellent, red fuming nitric acid, would cause a false positive on an M-256 kit."[77]

As more unambiguous evidence moved into the public sphere, the DOD adjusted its position. In November 1993 (during Clinton-Gore), the DOD finally acknowledged that troops might have been exposed to nerve agents during postcombat demolitions (as in Khamisiyah) but never on the battlefield. Then in 1997, without an official change in position, the department contacted about 15,000 veterans just to tell them they might have been exposed to toxic chemicals during the war. Still, for many years, the government dismissed any likely health effects, saying levels of exposure were probably too small to be medically significant. In effect, the message was something like: *Yes, you probably encountered some nerve agents, but don't worry too much about it.* It took a long time before the DOD acknowledged the seriousness of the nerve agent exposures, which scientists linked to brain damage and cancer.

Eventually, the DOD offered limited compensation and treatment to those who qualified.[78]

The DOD and CIA for years ruled out the possibility that Iraq used chemical weapons on Coalition forces. In 1997, six years after Hussein's surrender, the CIA continued to argue that "Iraq did not use chemical weapons during Desert Storm." Later, the government had to backtrack a bit about that as well. For example, the Advisory Committee on Gulf War Veterans concluded in a 2008 unclassified report that even if there was no evidence that soldiers endured "large scale, high dosage" chemical attacks, "military personnel were exposed to low-level chemical agents in theater," although "questions remain[ed] about the extent" of exposure. In addition, Khamisiyah might not have been an isolated incident: "Additional chemical exposures might have occurred during and after the Gulf War, in locations other than . . . Khamisiyah."[79]

The government's turnaround and greater transparency came as a relief to hundreds of thousands of veterans. However, all of the denials and secrecy from prior years remained deeply puzzling. Why did both administrations so strongly deny exposure despite having General Schwarzkopf's aide's classified combat logs detailing the "mustard positive . . . chemical attack at Jubail"? What was the story behind other, "lost or destroyed" entries from the Schwarzkopf logs that veterans' groups learned about through a FOIA denial? Why did DOD officials in 1991 ignore or dismiss loud and credible warnings from their Czech allies that Iraqis were using chemical weapons against American soldiers, something veterans only learned about in 1996? The Czechs, with a reputation for excellent mobile chemical detection, reported timely positive nerve agents tests when further safety precautions could have helped. On several occasions, Czech soldiers donned protective gear while their American allies were left vulnerable.[80]

Veterans wondered what drove all of the secrecy. Was there some hidden national security justification? Was it just to conceal incompetence and avoid embarrassment? The truth would certainly damage the emerging collective memory of the Gulf War as a "perfect victory," one that swept away the old "Vietnam syndrome." Or were commanders and their supporters mostly protecting their reputations and averting a public relations nightmare, to stifle news that DOD officials knowingly failed to protect troops from chemical agents? And imagine the public relations headache when the media reminded citizens—as the veterans were still suffering—that US, UK, and German companies, with government approval, supplied Hussein's government with equipment and precusors for Iraqi WMD programs during the 1980s Iran-Iraq War.[81]

A key reason for the secrecy involves the potential financial liabilities entailed in compensating the exposed. More than 250,000 veterans "suffer from persistant, unexplained symptoms," according to a 2009 National Research Council report. Treating their illnesses is one—very expensive—thing. Compensating 250,000-some veterans, through legal payouts or disability payments across lifetimes, is in another league altogether.[82]

This case history, though squarely in our Bush-Quayle section, clearly spills over into Clinton-Gore territory. And obviously, the latter administration deserves much of the blame for the puzzling secrecy. Clinton's government in 1995 did launch the Presidential Advisory Committee on Gulf War Veterans' Illnesses to investigate and ultimately reveal some of the details about what happened in Iraq. Moreover, the administration declassified many relevant documents, such as (some of) Schwarzkopf's aide's combat logs, as part of its broader declassification program initiated in 1995. But questions remained after the commission terminated in 1997 and after more documents reached the public sphere. Indeed, the conflict only arrived at something close to a resolution nearly twenty years after it began.

Meat Secrecy: "Fecal Soup" and Streamlined Inspections

It sounded straight out of Upton Sinclair's *The Jungle*, except it was 1989, not 1906: "To start with, the plants are filthy. The floors regularly are covered with grease, fat, sand and roaches. Bugs are up and down the sides of the walls. . . . Chickens regularly fall off the line and into all the muck on the floor. The supervisors have workers put them back on the line." Not only that, former Perdue Chicken factory worker Donna Bazemore told members of Congress, supervisors at her plant routinely forced employees to remove tags marking diseased birds and return them to the line. If any pieces fell onto the blood-and-guts-slicked floor, workers had to retrieve them and place them back onto the conveyor belt. Moreover, employees sometimes had to urinate and vomit as they worked the line because managers severely restricted bathroom breaks. "As a result," she warned, "consumers get chicken that we wouldn't feed to our dogs."[83]

Bazemore's testimony was shocking for its vivid detail but also because many Americans believed the government when it said the country's meat supply was the safest in the world, despite occasional lapses, all quickly corrected. Two years earlier, *60 Minutes* had broadcast an exposé of horrifying conditions at a Simmons Processing Plant in Southwest City, Missouri. As happened at the Perdue plant, supervisors told workers to remove tags from "chickens infected with salmonella, riddled with cancer, oozing with pus, and smeared with feces." Hobart Bartley, a whistle-blowing USDA inspector who worked there, spoke about birds routinely being tossed into a "chilling bath," where they would float in a water pool filled with feces, dried blood, and hair—all done to "clean" them and have them absorb liquid for a heavier selling weight. The bath instead spread salmonella from dirty to clean birds, infecting much of the plant's inventory. CBS News found a 58 percent rate of salmonella in Simmons chickens, compared with 35 percent, then the national average. Later investigations found even worse rates. A lawsuit filed by the Government Accountability Project (GAP) in 1989 revealed salmonella contamination in one major plant had reached 76 percent. Moreover, one inspector told CBS that "as much as 50 per cent of the birds that go by us are contaminated by a generous amount of fecal and feed contamination." A former USDA microbiologist later remarked, "It's no different than sticking that bird in your toilet before you eat it." Many Americans were horrified by Bartley's tales of "fecal soup" and salmonella in a major processing plant, but at least some were convinced by the USDA's director of inspection, who assured everyone that the USDA had fixed the problems. The Simmons chickens, he said, were an isolated problem. The USDA then demoted and reassigned whistle-blower Bartley to another plant.[84]

At the root of these production and inspection failures was a new regulatory regime the USDA initiated in 1984. A combination of forces—including rapidly growing consumer demand for meat and the ascendance of neoliberal ideology favoring deregulation and smaller government—had chipped away at the USDA's historically strong meat inspection regime, developed after *The Jungle* and improved in the 1950s and 1960s. Increasingly starved of resources, the USDA moved to "streamlined" inspection services starting in 1984. In the beef market, it unrolled a "streamlined inspection system," a pilot program that soon encompassed about a fifth of the market. Poultry inspection processes were also streamlined, which meant that the USDA pulled one out of every three inspectors, leaving those who remained responsible for seventy birds per minute on average—more than doubling the thirty birds per minute standard of a decade earlier. The USDA let "good" plants self-regulate, concentrating its dwindling cadre of inspectors to the "bad" sites.[85]

As the growing army of whistle-blowers with vivid stories attested, the so-called streamlining had disastrous consequences. Though USDA spokespeople responded to each revelation with assurances that they were surprising aberrations, another whistle-blower in 1989 reported the agency was well aware of the more widespread problem of filth and contamination in meat plants that resulted from the streamlining. This whistle-blower, former USDA microbiologist Gerald Kuester, also completed a study documenting the alarmingly high salmonella rates (such as 76 percent at the end of the process in one Puerto Rican plant, with about 24 percent due to cross-contamination). To maintain the fiction of a top-notch inspection regime, the USDA suppressed his findings.[86]

Although pressure for change, such as the GAP lawsuit, started in 1989, policy makers were pushed into action only after children started dying. In January 1993, right around the time of Clinton-Gore's inauguration, hundreds of people grew ill and four children died of hemolytic-uremic syndrome in an outbreak of *E. coli O157:H7* from hamburgers served at Jack in the Box restaurants in Washington State. It is not clear whether Clinton-Gore would have forced a change at USDA without the outbreak, but the president announced in February 1993 that the administration intended to hire 160 additional meat inspectors. The USDA's secret reports about the streamlined system, however, were never released.[87]

Summary: The Bush-Quayle Administration

The Bush-Quayle and Clinton-Gore administrations each left office with what seems a better track record than Bush-Cheney's. Reaching precise conclusions about who was worse is probably unwarranted. First, episodes of science secrecy are not equal. Does one censored and harassed Bush-Quayle Forest Service biologist equal one instance of Clinton-Gore refusal to release data from the EPA soot report? Probably not. Second, we can only evalute cases in the public record. We can (and did) dive deeply into that record for examples, but many other case histories probably remain hidden somewhere at the USDA, the FS, the EPA, and so on. It is, however, noteworthy that many more scientists and other whistle-blowers complained publicly or anonymously about suppression during the Bush-Quayle administration. It is also worth noting that the episodes that carried over into the new administration, such as the FS conflicts and the Gulf War exposure, were brought closer to resolution by Clinton's team. Yet the evidence is clear that both administrations kept alive science secrecy tools, several created by Reagan-Bush (for instance, the "sensitive issues" list and similar gatekeeping tools), that were later used, frequently and aggressively, by Bush-Cheney. We now turn to the innovators of those tools, another administration that took science secrecy to unprecedented levels.

8

SECRET SCIENCE
THE REAGAN-BUSH ADMINISTRATION

A "Dense Fog of Concealment" about Agent Orange: Secret Data, a Bungled Study, and the Impact on Vietnam Veterans

During the Vietnam War, the US military sprayed 72,918,928 liters of weaponized herbicides across Vietnam. Approximately 65 percent contained 2,4,5-trichlorophenoxyacetic acid (2,4,5-T) and 2,3,7,8-tetrachlorodibenzo-p-dioxin (TCDD), two of the most toxic substances on the planet. Most people, soldiers included, knew the related compounds by their sanitized common names—Agent Orange, Agent Pink, Agent Purple, Agent White, and Agent Blue. (They were given those nicknames because of the colored identification bands on the storage containers.) The military purposes were manifold, as a *Nature* paper summarized: "to defoliate forests and mangroves, to clear perimeters of military installations and to destroy 'unfriendly' crops as a tactic for decreasing enemy food supplies." Beyond the devastation they wrought on vegetation, the toxins also worked as chemical weapons, terrorizing civilian and military Vietnamese alike. Whether use of these toxins constituted state "terrorism" remains a matter of debate, although officials must have anticipated some of the effects of spraying over 47 million liters of TCDD over human-inhabited farms and forests and around buildings. For the Vietnamese, the effects included skin burns; starvation; birth defects, miscarriages, and stillbirths; and environmental destruction and biodiversity loss. The long-term health and environmental effects were more numerous, for the Vietnamese population and environment as well as for American war veterans.[1]

After US soldiers returned home from Vietnam, many of them started showing up at doctors' offices and VA hospitals with strange symptoms: "They complained of cancer and deformed children or children born dead. They complained of miscarriages, loss of sex drive, and low sperm counts. They complained of strange aches and weaknesses all over the body, weird

245

lumps in their flesh that would appear, festering sores that would not heal, ugly things that doctors would tell them were precancerous, but with no explanation of where they came from." Because the veterans' complaints seemed unconnected and inexplicable, the first wave of patients did not raise alarm bells at VA headquarters or anywhere else. VA doctors treated the patients, but they were not considered part of a diagnostic cohort. It was not until the late 1970s that the recurrent complaints grew familiar enough to suggest a pattern, a syndrome. One of the first frontline VA workers to piece it together and raise questions was Maude deVictor, a veterans benefit counselor in Chicago. Others at the VA soon joined deVictor in alerting supervisors, who then passed the news upward.[2]

The VA's public response, which would foretell its behavior across administrations, was a bitter mix of denial about TCDD's toxicity for humans and accusations saying veterans were trying to scam Uncle Sam. Indeed, many VA officials accused the "wounded warriors" of being dishonest, money-grubbing moochers who made up or exaggerated their symptoms for selfish reasons. Others responded with more compassion, still not believing the veterans but seeing them as ignorant dupes who were misled and vulnerable to emotional appeals by swindlers seeking fortunes from the government and chemical companies like Dow and Monsanto. Some of the skeptical VA officials were probably sincere in their denial of the chemicals' toxicity, taking cues from a prominent 1974 National Academies of Sciences study of "The Effects of Herbicides in South Vietnam," which showed inconclusive results. Other officials, as we will see, seemed to run on willful ignorance or pure cynicism. All were worried about the government's decades-long financial liabilities if veterans had to be compensated.[3]

Whatever their motivations, senior VA officials worked hard to deflate and deflect concerns raised by employees like deVictor, as well as claims by journalists, environmentalists, attorneys, and veterans groups that argued Agent Orange caused the veterans' medical problems. Other government departments joined the VA in its strong rejectionism. Most of the time, officials based their public statements on a professed fidelity to science. In reality, when pressed by members of Congress and other veterans' advocates to systematically analyze Agent Orange's health effects, the executive branch seemed to fear what scientists would actually say. For instance, in 1979, the deputy assistant secretary of defense responded to a veteran's mother who pleaded for more science with an absurd statement: "We do not believe that a study of the health of our Vietnam veterans would add to the knowledge of the long-term health

effects" of Agent Orange. The Defense Department lobbied Congress to sty-
mie proposed investigations, at one point saying it was "extremely doubtful
that a retrospective epidemiological study" would offer much knowledge. The
VA, for its part, ordered doctors and administrators at its medical facilities
to refuse new patient requests to examine Agent Orange–related complaints.
Meanwhile, thousands of boxes of DOD records, filled with troop exposure
data, sat in government warehouses, ready to be analyzed. The government's
rejectionist, antiscience stance was ultimately repudiated by members of Congress—led by Sen. Alan Cranston (D-CA) and Rep. Tom Daschle (D-SD)—
who commissioned a $100 million study for the VA to probe the connection
between Agent Orange and the symptoms veterans and their families were
exhibiting.[4]

The VA did not rise to the occasion. Although it was forced to follow
Congress's order, the VA had a lot of leeway to design the study to achieve the
outcome it desired. The agency could not guarantee an exonerating scientific
conclusion, but officials recognized they could stack the deck to improve the
odds. The strategy was simple: enlist scientists who were clearly already on the
rejectionist team, including those closely connected to the dioxin-producing
chemical industry. Thus, the VA chose the chemist Dr. Alvin Young to design
the study, probably because he seemed deeply convinced that herbicides were
safe for humans. Indeed, his enthusiasm for herbicides like Agent Orange
sometimes reached eccentric levels. Although there were pockets of scientists
defending the chemical at the time, few were saying things like Young did,
such as that he found "great comfort" in having been "significantly exposed"
to the toxins. In testimony before the Environmental Protection Agency in
1980, Young further demonstrated his hardened, reflexive, proherbicide position:

When I first got into the herbicide business, which was in 1960, we
weren't concerned about toxicity. . . . My heavens, we didn't consider the
phenoxy herbicides toxic. We sprayed each other. We used to play it as a
game, and we would go to our supervisor and say, are these things toxic
and the answer was always, oh, no, no, no. Herbicides are not toxic. And
as you read the old manuals . . . indeed you find exactly that.

He was the right man for the job as far as the VA was concerned.[5]

Joining Young to design the research protocol was Dr. Gary Spivey, then
a professor of public health at the University of California–Los Angeles

(UCLA). As an eminent, tenured UCLA epidemiologist, Spivey had impeccable credentials. However, on the Agent Orange issue, his public statements suggested he would find common cause with Young. In testimony before the California Assembly for a proposed veterans bill, Spivey made clear his skepticism about Agent Orange's toxicity: "The fear which is generated by the current publicity is very likely to be the most serious consequence of the use of Agent Orange." Though Spivey's use of probabilistic language ("very likely") demonstrated his commitment to science and indicated he might keep an open mind, many veterans noticed that the VA went out of its way to hire individuals who clearly supported its biases. Veterans groups pleaded with the new administration to replace Spivey and Young with less partial scientists, pointing to the Reagan-Bush campaign promises to better care for veterans. The new administration's VA rebuffed them and pressed on with its plan.[6]

Two years after Congress ordered the study, the VA finally approved its protocol, sending it out for peer review in August 1981. The reviews came back loaded with biting criticisms and accusations of fraud. The anonymous reviewers were unified in their critique of the design's vagueness. Some noted it seemed cooked up specifically to reach some desired outcome—not to get to the bottom of the issue. One wondered whether the design had been drafted in a "conspiratorial atmosphere." Another wrote, "Only the barest traces of substance are permitted by the author to leak out beneath a dense fog of concealment." One pointed out that "the document here submitted is superficial and cannot in itself be the basis for a definitive study." Spivey had anticipated some of these criticisms, but his responses and justifications failed to convince the reviewers. For instance, he defended the design's evasiveness about which ailments would be tracked by saying that if veterans knew those details, they would report the related symptoms (for, say, psychosomatic or financial reasons), and any causal inferences would thus be suspect. That argument, however, was undercut by the fact the design was not available to the public. Indeed, it was the protocol's secrecy that prompted congressional hearings about Spivey's design. The "dense fog of concealment" grew thicker when Spivey declined to attend Senate Veterans Affairs Committee hearings, sending his university dean in his stead. Veterans groups again announced their skepticism that the VA would conduct an unbiased, transparent study. The distrust worked in both directions, as the VA increasingly viewed its patients with deep suspicion and assumed they were generally after undeserved damages.[7]

Because of veterans' credible accusations about the VA's bias and because the VA surely seemed to be using delaying tactics, a bipartisan group in Congress asked the Reagan-Bush administration to transfer the study from the VA to the Centers for Disease Control (CDC), an agency with a reputation for honest, capable scientific inquiry. In 1982, the administration acceded to the request. By 1987, the White House Agent Orange Task Force—headed by Alvin Young, the proherbicide chemist—ordered the CDC to immediately stop its work, saying a "scientifically valid Agent Orange Exposure Study was not possible." What Young did not mention was that the barriers to a valid study were primarily erected by Reagan-Bush officials.[8]

CDC scientists working on the project spoke about officials' recurring interference in their work. The meddling was so unusual and severe that several scientists believed there was political pressure to deliberately bungle the study. According to one statistician, CDC officials "changed the design of [the study] so often and switched variables so frequently that the results were meaningless. Researchers sometimes made up data to fill in gaps in the records. . . . At one point people lost track of what was true and what was false." Against the strong objections of statisticians, administrators also insisted the military's spraying and exposure records were incomplete, making statistical inferences impossible. "That was just baloney," a statistician recalled. "That was completely false." In particular, CDC administrators worked to discredit Richard Christian, the director of the Environmental Support Group in the DOD who had worked meticulously to recover, organize, and prepare tens of thousands of boxes of records—the government's proprietary exposure data—for the Agent Orange analysis. CDC scientists expressed full confidence in Christian and in his record management skills. Meanwhile, the relatively less skilled administrators leading the charge against Christian had once confused Viet Cong records with US troop records. Despite the scientists' expressions of support for Christian, CDC officials accused him of mismanaging and possibly withholding records, although independent analysis of that claim was impossible given the tight data secrecy. The White House began an investigation. Young and his Agent Orange Task Force told Christian his work would be scrutinized in a peer review process, although it was obvious that process would not follow typical scientific procedures. Meanwhile, the DOD's proprietary data—which if analyzed properly would have cleared everything up—sat in boxes, with big bureaucratic obstacles in the way. All of the interference stymied the efforts of the CDC working group. "We were doing bad science at the CDC" as a result, one scientist confessed. "We knew we were doing bad science . . . a number of us were saying so."[9]

After years of agency-hopping, foot-dragging, data secrecy, and political interference, the government finally published its study of Agent Orange's health effects on veterans. Given all it had been through, the report arrived stillborn and deeply blemished. Many veterans and public health advocates believed that was the point: if the government could not believably demonstrate Agent Orange's safety, at least it could sustain an aura of scientific uncertainty. During a congressional investigation two years later, Rep. Ted Weiss (D-NY) suggested that "either [the study] was a politically rigged operation, or it was a monumentally bungled operation." The CDC did little to clear things up. Dr. Vernon N. Houk, a CDC administrator in charge of the Agent Orange study, rejected both of Representative Weiss's allegations: "I'm sorry you think it was bungled. We think it was good science." Houk's defense of the study of course contradicted what his scientists were saying. Perhaps that was why he felt compelled to add that if one had to choose between incompetence or political manipulation, then some form of ineptitude would be closer to the truth of what happened with the study. The contradictions were numerous. Another involved the White House Agent Orange Task Force's order to halt the study in 1987. Houk said *he* was the one who convinced Young and the White House to stop the study because of validity concerns. At the same time, he proudly defended it as "good science." Why would he try to halt good science?[10]

Conclusion

Although Vietnam veterans had many reasons to heap scorn on the Carter-Mondale and Bush-Quayle administrations, Reagan-Bush officials worked the hardest to keep the truth about Agent Orange from coming out. After Congress forced them to launch a comprehensive study using the DOD's secret, proprietary data, senior officials made it impossible for government scientists to complete their work, and nongovernmental scientists could get nowhere near the information. Sick veterans had to wait until 1990 for the tide to turn.

Epilogue

Despite all of the forces arrayed against them, many veterans and their supporters continued the fight in elections, in the halls of Congress, and in the courts. One of the loudest proveteran voices to emerge happened to be from a man responsible for much of the spraying. As late as 1986, Adm. Elmo R. Zumwalt, Jr., maintained that his order to spray Agent Orange over the Mekong Delta was the right choice, despite how it might have affected his family: "Knowing what I now know, I still would have ordered the defoliation to achieve the objectives it did, of reducing casualties. But that does not ease the sorrow I feel for [my son] Elmo, or the anguish his illness, and Russell's disability, give me." Elmo III, who fought with his father in Vietnam, was diagnosed with lymphoma in 1983 and then Hodgkin's disease in 1985. The admiral's grandson, Elmo Russell Zumwalt IV, was born with a brain disorder that caused serious learning disabilities. Nevertheless, in 1986, when the CDC was botching the study, Admiral Zumwalt seemed to believe the VA's reassurances. His son was more doubtful:

> I am a lawyer and I don't think I could prove in court, by the weight of the existing scientific evidence, that Agent Orange is the cause of all the medical problems—nervous disorders, cancer and skin problems—reported by Vietnam veterans, or of their children's serious birth defects. But I am convinced that it is. . . . I realize that what I am saying may imply that my father is responsible for my illness and Russell's disability.

The men nevertheless remained close, writing a book together in 1986 that they later transformed into a television movie.[11]

After his son's death in 1988 at age forty-two and after some of the revelations from congressional hearings and elsewhere about the collapse of the CDC study emerged, Admiral Zumwalt began to openly and vigorously criticize the government he had previously trusted. In a classified report to the VA and in congressional testimony, he accused the government and the chemical industry of excessive secrecy and of manipulating the VA/CDC study's progress to prevent the truth from coming out. Before he dived into the scientific literature, Zumwalt recalled, he believed, like many others, that "there was insufficient scientific evidence to support a linkage between his illness and Agent Orange exposure. That was, of course, the conventional propaganda. The sad truth which emerges from my work is not only is there credible evidence linking certain cancers and other illnesses with Agent Orange, but that government and industry officials credited with examining such linkage intentionally *manipulated or withheld* compelling information of the adverse health effects." He was especially harsh on the CDC's Houk, who, according to Zumwalt, "made it his mission to manipulate and prevent the true facts from being determined." Once Zumwalt acquired critically important information, he changed his perspective—as many of his fellow citizens would have done if they had had unrestricted access to the secret data or at least an honest analysis of it.[12]

Whether Houk, Young, other CDC and VA officials, or top Reagan-Bush administration officials purposely rigged or simply bungled the Agent Orange study, they got what they probably wanted, at least in the short term. Thousands of afflicted veterans were prevented from claiming expensive benefits because the government was able to keep a cloud of uncertainty hanging over the human health effects of 2,4,5-T and TCDD. Once that effort collapsed in the 1990s and 2000s, veterans had more success pressing the issue in the court system, especially against the chemical companies. Almost immediately after Zumwalt's open attack on the government's secrecy and dishonesty in 1990, the government under Bush-Quayle finally acknowledged Agent Orange's health effects. The government eventually helped some of the remaining victims. Others could not wait that long.[13]

The Wider War to Protect Dioxins and Their Manufacturers

Several major chemical accidents in the 1970s and 1980s underscored the dangers of dioxin. A runaway chemical reaction in a small factory in Seveso, Italy, in 1976 led to the worst known industrial release of TCDD in history. It polluted an 18-square-kilometer area, about 20 kilometers north of Milan, and left immense human destruction in its wake, from cancers to in utero effects. Only 35 percent of children born to significantly exposed parents were boys, and *no boys* came from the most exposed parents. In the United States, the slowly unfolding disaster at Love Canal put dioxin on the front pages before Agent Orange did. The large-scale contamination of the land and population in Niagara Falls, New York, started in the 1940s but only came into full view in the late 1970s. In 1982, another dioxin nightmare befell the small town of Times Beach, Missouri—although, as with Love Canal, the story began years earlier.[14]

Though it was less than 20 miles from St. Louis, Times Beach was a world away from the big city. The residents of this small town (never more than 1,240) mostly lived in cottages, mobile homes, and modest houses on stilts, and the local government never had enough money to pave its dusty dirt roads. The only booming industry was booze—residents apparently drank enough to support thirteen saloons. Dust from the 16 miles of unpaved roads made farming during some summers very cumbersome. Farm owners and town planners were thus always on the lookout for relatively inexpensive remedies. Russell Martin Bliss, a nearby horse farmer, found a seemingly perfect solution to the dust problem. Bliss also ran a business hauling and disposing "waste oil," and he discovered that spraying his oil around the farm worked beautifully for keeping the dust down. Moreover, it had the added benefit of killing most of the flies bugging his horses in their stables. He soon marketed a waste oil spray service around the area, attracting local horse farmers and other businesses and organizations.[15]

One family quickly came to regret their decision to hire Bliss. A day after he sprayed her Shenandoah Stables in nearby Moscow Mills, Judy Piatt found her horses had become very sick. Many of them soon lost much of their hair and body weight, and they developed festering sores. After a debilitating illness, they died, as would countless wild birds that fell lifeless from their nests onto the contaminated soil below. Piatt's family also got sick, especially her two young daughters. One was hospitalized for weeks due to bleeding and severe gastrointestinal (GI) and kidney problems. Another of Bliss's waste oil customers, the owner of a local arena, discovered dead horses, birds, dogs, and cats. Two more children fell ill, including one who developed severe kidney disease. As the spraying continued, a wave of patients began appearing at local hospitals, complaining of puzzling new symptoms and illnesses, including arthritis, nosebleeds, nausea, GI problems, and brain and immune system defects in newborns.[16]

Following the spate of human illnesses and animal deaths, officials from the Missouri Division of Health quietly asked the CDC to help them figure out what was happening, even though some state officials already had their suspicions. CDC scientists arrived in August 1971 but soon claimed they could not conclusively determine which dangers lurked within the waste oil. As a result, Bliss continued spraying.[17]

Judy Piatt's family, however, filed a lawsuit and demanded more information from Bliss. Given the devastation his product wrought, it was hard to believe his claim that he had only used repurposed motor oil, just as he did at his own farm, allegedly without ill effects. It took another CDC field study, this one in 1974, to reconfirm what the agency had discovered the prior year: alarming amounts of dioxin (TCDD) and polychlorinated biphenyls (PCBs) in soil samples. Dioxin levels were at 30,000 parts per billion (ppb), far surpassing levels considered safe (such as the EPA's 2011 maximum contaminant level of 30 parts per *quadrillion* in water). Not only that, the CDC confirmed Bliss's waste oil was the source of the contamination at multiple sites. It turned out Bliss had not simply used old motor oil, as he claimed, but had sprayed waste oil mixed with a dioxin-laced toxic soup he (possibly inadvertently) picked up at the Northeastern Pharmaceutical and Chemical Company, Inc. (NEPACCO), one of his clients. In the land around NEPACCO, things were even worse: enough dioxin at such high concentrations (343,000 ppb) to kill every US citizen. Therefore, by 1974, the CDC, the EPA, and Missouri state officials already knew about the area's pockets of extreme toxicity and their sources. By 1975, the CDC had told the EPA that the nearby town of Imperial, Missouri, was so toxic it needed immediate evacuation. But the EPA did nothing with that news. The CDC, by contrast, at least tried to do something, albeit late. But it still concealed the urgent news about Imperial for two years.[18]

All of the secrecy and delays caused government inaction and thus accumulating misery through most of 1980. Meanwhile, Bliss continued to spray, hitting thirty sites around the state, including all of Times Beach. Unaware of the potential problems, municipal officials and private landowners there had hired Bliss's waste oil company to tame the still unpaved roads. It was cheap, effective, and seemingly safe for the community.[19]

At the end of 1980, the Carter-Mondale administration finally began remedial action. The Environmental Enforcement Section (EES) of the DOJ sued NEPACCO and Syntex Agribusiness, Inc., claiming both stored and disposed of dioxin illegally. The one-two punch of *US v. NEPACCO* and the new "Superfund" law in 1980 left affected Times Beachers who knew about the problem hopeful for justice and environmental restoration. It may have taken Carter-Mondale officials far too long, but they had finally set things on the right track.[20]

Hopes were dashed, however, once the Reagan-Bush administration took power in 1981. Compared with some of his predecessors, Reagan was a new kind of Republican president. Whereas President Nixon created the EPA in the early 1970s, Reagan worked hard to weaken that agency and the laws it administered. The influence of polluting industries was part of the equation, but in addition, Reagan was a true believer in supply-side economics. As a result, he preached the gospel of environmental deregulation, which he believed would maximize economic growth and liberty (environmental protection and related public health issues were not a priority). In practice, this meant filling the EPA with like-minded officials, many from industries the EPA regulated.

It also meant slashing the EPA's budget, especially in its enforcement division. Ongoing or planned projects, including Superfund cleanups, were delayed or halted.[21]

Reagan's newly appointed EPA officials went on the offensive, parroting chemical industry statements about the safety of dioxin and other toxins. Rita Lavelle, the new hazardous waste section director, declared the toxicological science on dioxin was still inconclusive, mirroring what Agent Orange enthusiast Alvin Young and others at the VA were saying. Dioxin producers were even bolder in their public reassurances—despite knowing better. Dow's president, Paul F. Oreffice, for instance, claimed on a March 1983 NBC *Today* show that "there is absolutely no evidence of dioxin doing any damage to humans except for something called chloracne. It's a rash . . . and there is no evidence of any damage other than this rash which went away soon after." As *US v. NEPACCO* slowly progressed, Dow and the other producers continued pumping dioxins into the environment with few limitations. And Bliss continued spraying around Missouri.[22]

Despite the animal die-offs and human illnesses from the 1970s, which were tragic but scattered, most Times Beachers, including the mayor, were unaware of the severity of the problem they faced. Then, in November 1982, a local journalist told municipal officials he had heard Times Beach was on some EPA "toxic towns" list. The news spread, and residents began to share stories and piece things together: the animal deaths, the human illnesses, the treated roads that turned purple and smelled awful, and the baseball field built on land Bliss used to dump extra oil. They pleaded for government action, but the Reagan-Bush administration did nothing. Lavelle's response was particularly offensive: she recommended that Times Beach residents avoid eating contaminated dirt. When local parents asked the EPA to erect fences around contaminated sites to keep their children safe, Lavelle refused the request, saying fences would probably just attract curious kids, luring them to climb over into the sites. Anxious residents had to wait nine months because EPA administrator Anne M. Gorsuch (later Anne Gorsuch Burford) kept her cleanup crews and scientists in Washington for no clear reason. Only after an EPA insider leaked an embarrassing document to the Environmental Defense Fund and after residents generated national publicity by passing a collection jar around town to fund their own chemical tests did EPA scientists finally return.[23]

Scientists in hazmat suits descended upon Times Beach, confirming residents' worst fears and invalidating what officials like Lavelle and industry executives like Oreffice had been arguing for years. And then came the flood. Just as soil samples were ferried off to the EPA's labs, nature intervened, making the problem worse but also quickly bringing the situation to its conclusion. An exceptionally bad winter rainstorm flooded the Meramec River, transforming Times Beach into a strange archipelago of rooftops and submerged pickup trucks and sedans. The floodwaters spread dioxin across town—onto front lawns and porches and into living rooms and basements. Residents were evacuated until the waters receded.[24]

Despite this turn of events and despite more alarming lab results, Lavelle continued to downplay the situation in Times Beach, saying it did not rise to the level of an emergency. The CDC, by contrast, recommended that everyone leave the area immediately and that no one should *ever* return. In other words, Times Beach should be—and would be—evacuated forever. Local police got the message, erecting roadblocks and escorting residents to the edge of town. The new facts on the ground discredited Lavelle and, for many in Congress, also her boss, EPA administrator Gorsuch. After it was already too late, the White House stripped Lavelle of the Times Beach portfolio in January 1983 and then fired her a few weeks later, after she committed perjury at a congressional hearing. Nine more political appointees soon followed her out the door.[25]

The evening news programs were awash in images of the besieged ghost town, as former residents described what had happened there. Times Beachers spoke disbelievingly about the government's secrecy and gross incompetence. It took the dramatic, publicized evacuation to force Congress to remember its oversight duties. To be sure, Rep. John Dingell (D-MI) and Rep. Elliot Levitas (D-GA) had already launched an investigation of the EPA months earlier for Superfund-related inaction and allegations of corruption. But it took the evacuation to provoke wider legislative interest and action, by Democrats and Republicans alike.

Two subcommittees investigating the matter quickly ran up against a brick wall. The administration refused to provide requested documents related to Times Beach and other contaminated sites. Subpoenas were no more successful, as lawyers in the White House and the DOJ responded with an unusual claim of executive privilege—unusual because the privilege was asserted relatively infrequently but also because of the reasons given for their claim. The rationale had nothing to do with national security or foreign policy; instead, the argument was that the relevant sites were Superfund sites—or might be one day—and therefore counted as open and active enforcement cases. Thus,

Reagan-Bush officials contended, the Superfund files needed secrecy just like sensitive information from ongoing criminal investigations. White House lawyers also argued they had to protect the sanctity of "internal deliberations" and "prosecutorial strategy" within the executive branch—arguments frequently made later by Bush-Cheney lawyers, as we have seen. Perhaps Reagan-Bush really believed in their principled, though contestable, argument. Perhaps they instead threw a handful of arguments into the mix in the hope one might stick. Few were persuaded, even among Republicans in Congress.[26]

When EPA administrator Gorsuch arrived on Capitol Hill empty-handed for a hearing in early December 1982, Representative Levitas's subcommittee voted to hold her in contempt. A week later—just a few days after the Times Beach flood—the House Public Works Committee followed suit. The escalating interbranch conflict about Reagan's executive privilege claims had frustrated so many in Congress that the full House took the unusual step of voting Gorsuch in contempt (295 to 105, with about 50 Republicans voting with the Democrats). The White House did not budge, despite its weakened position. Indeed, the situation motivated the administration to take an even bolder action: it sued Congress. The DC district court dismissed the lawsuit in early February 1983, pushing the two branches to reach an accommodation, which they ultimately did. The White House agreed to release Times Beach and other Superfund-related documents.[27]

Reagan-Bush effectively voided the compromise almost as soon as it was signed, plainly demonstrating that any White House concession would be illusory. Days before the EPA was scheduled to provide Congress with the promised documents, officials announced many of them had somehow gone missing, including a large number of the Times Beach files. Congressional investigators found evidence that Gorsuch and Lavelle aides might have shredded or otherwise removed them, but EPA officials' strong denials left the matter unresolved, having reached a he said/she said impasse. The administration's delaying, document mishandling and/or shredding, and privilege-claiming tactics seemed to be working. And to deflect some of the blame away from the White House, another fall guy fell. Gorsuch continued to face intense pressure from legislators, appearing before six congressional committees. Despite keeping mum as members of Congress grilled her, she soon followed Lavelle out of the administration.[28]

In 1984, the administration finally sued Bliss, the waste oil sprayer who started the mess (along with companies like NEPACCO). The discovery process showed he had repeatedly lied, including about what happened on his own horse farm. His story had always been that nobody should worry about his service because he had first tested it on his personal property—and it worked great! It turned out Bliss had, in fact, used the waste oil and experienced many of the ill effects that others encountered. Instead of his animals miraculously resisting dioxin contamination, seventy chickens and a dog succumbed to the toxin's deadly power. He kept that secret for over a decade.[29]

Protecting Paper and Pulp Mills: The EPA's Secret Dioxin Studies

Although dioxin contamination can come from a variety of sources—including natural processes (such as volcanic eruptions and forest fires) and political processes (such as chemical warfare with Agent Orange or the poisoning of politicians, as happened to former Ukrainian president Viktor Yushchenko)—the primary source is industrial pollution, whether from manufacturers or inefficient and ill-designed waste incinerators. Dioxin is almost always a manufacturing by-product, resulting from the burning of chlorinated compounds. Producers of herbicides and pesticides, animal feed, wood preservatives, metals, and paper all indirectly make and release dioxins as a part of their routine business. The paper industry, however, deserves a special prize—or punishment—for being a market leader in dioxin pollution.[30]

Pulp and paper mills produce dioxin when they use chlorine to bleach office paper, coffee filters, toilet paper, diapers, and other goods. Mills had chlorinated their products for decades, but mill town residents in the 1980s grew increasingly concerned about dioxin after hearing about Times Beach, Love Canal, Seveso, and the Agent Orange controversy. The EPA launched a study of mill town pollution in 1980, but three years later Congress ordered the agency to more comprehensively analyze the scope and effects of dioxin pollution in the United States in the National Dioxin Study (NDS). To its credit—given what happened during Reagan-Bush's first term—the EPA began to publish important new research that shed light on the dioxin problem. In one report from 1985, scientists concluded TCDD and HxCDD were "probable human carcinogens," easily absorbed into human tissues, and overall extremely toxic. A 1986 report concluded dioxins were "prevalent in the general U.S. population"—that is, not only in mill towns or places like Times Beach. The studies were informative, but the EPA missed Congress's December 1985 deadline for releasing the full NDS. At issue were several EPA studies administrators refused to publish.[31]

One 1983 study of Wisconsin mill towns showed alarmingly high levels of dioxin in downstream fish and effluent samples. Other studies from 1985 and 1986 also demonstrated high dioxin concentrations in fish samples from Maine, Minnesota, and Oregon. Note that the administrators who blocked the studies' release were those who took over *after* Gorsuch and Lavelle left the scene. Although dioxin victims and other interested citizens did not know about the EPA's secret dioxin studies, they did begin to wonder about the NDS's delay. Carol Van Strum, a freelance writer, and her husband, Paul Merrell, decided to investigate.[32]

Van Strum found the EPA completely unwilling to cooperate. The agency effectively rejected her FOIA request for the NDS and related documents—citing the "deliberative process privilege" (Exemption 5)—and released very little information amid large black chunks of redacted text. It was not clear why scientific studies of dioxin in mill towns were considered protected "inter-agency or intra-agency memorandums or letters which would not be available by law to a party other than an agency in litigation with the agency." (Dominant court interpretations have done little to help clarify that rather "opaque" [DOJ] bit of legalese.) Faced with what still seemed like unjustified secrecy, Van Strum and Merrell pushed for an administrative appeal. When the EPA rejected that as well, the couple set out to create a kind of alternative NDS, using all available public information as well as interviews with an anonymous EPA scientist. In 1987, they published *No Margin for Safety: A Preliminary Report on Dioxin Pollution and the Need for Emergency Action in the Pulp and Paper Industry*. The book's argument about business's power over the EPA was not completely shocking, given what scholars of interest group politics, along with anyone else paying attention to politics, already knew. Still, the alleged secret deals between agency and industry officials to conceal evidence of dioxin pollution reeked of improper influence, verging on corruption. And for *No Margin* readers previously unaware of the controversy, the EPA's secrecy seemed obviously unjustified. Perhaps the book's main influence was in inspiring a whistle-blower. *No Margin* caught the eye of a sympathetic insider at the American Paper Institute (API), the industry's trade association and lobbying arm that had pushed hard against dioxin regulations. Whether the API employee was settling scores or was genuinely disgusted by his or her employer's prodioxin lobbying, he or she sent Greenpeace a trove of internal API documents supporting the book's allegations.[33]

The documents revealed in stark language the API's collaborative/antagonistic relationship with the EPA, along with the API's aggressive public relations efforts to hide or distort information about dioxin's many dangers. One document, for instance, noted that "the industry has been able to forestall major regulatory and public relations difficulties by, among other things, agreeing to cooperate in a joint study with EPA." Another told of successful API efforts to force the EPA to "rethink" its evolving risk assessment and even to publicly state at one point that dioxin causes "no harm to [the] environment or public health." After a private meeting with EPA administrator Lee M. Thomas, in which the API pressed the case that the only problem with dioxin was its faulty "public perception," the API representative reported that "Administrator Thomas indicated a willingness to cooperate with the industry to ensure that the public would not be unduly alarmed about this issue." At the same time, EPA scientists were discovering more and more reasons to be alarmed, although their agency bosses concealed their findings.[34]

The documents also showed the API helped shape the EPA's response plan for Van Strum's FOIA requests, as well as the agency's broader dioxin PR strategy. API vice resident Carol Raulston, for instance, wrote, "EPA has agreed to the following: to characterize the information (about dioxin contamination) as meaningless, used only to establish testing procedures; to respond with a letter to Ms. Van Strum today, but to ship the material on April 1; to meet with us to discuss the public affairs strategy on this and how subsequent requests for information will be handled." Even though the API clearly had some influence within the agency—including knowledge about Van Strum's FOIA letter and the EPA's planned response—the industry group also plotted to "improve intelligence gathering within EPA," identifying "adversaries" and developing and using "allies" to help its cause. For the public at large, the API developed a PR campaign to "keep all allegations of health risks out of the public arena—or minimize them; avoid confrontations with government agencies, which might trigger concerns about health risks or raise visibility of issue generally; maintain customer confidence in integrity of product; achieve an appropriate regulatory climate." On the front lines of the PR war were industry-funded and industry-directed "dioxin response teams," whose mission was to allay public fears when they arose, just in case API's ongoing efforts to cleanse the marketplace of ideas of dioxin-related information were not 100 percent successful.[35]

Armed with the API documents, Van Strum sued the EPA in late January 1987, alleging the agency illegally denied her FOIA requests. Judge Owen Panner of the US District Court for the District of Oregon allowed Van Strum to take depositions from EPA officials to confirm the truthfulness of their affadivits. On the basis of those statements and the API documents, Judge Panner agreed with Van Strum's collusion argument, saying the documents "appear to support the existence of an agreement between the EPA and the industry to suppress, modify, or delay the results of the joint EPA-industry study, or the manner in which they are publicly presented." He also recognized that "the existence of pending issues regarding the good-faith of EPA's affidavits, the adequacy of EPA's search pursuant to the FOIA request, and the possible waiver of EPA's exemption claim for a group of the identified documents" strongly suggested the need for a longer discovery period, which Van Strum sought. It did not matter in the end, as the district and appeals courts ultimately ruled with the Reagan-Bush administration, saying officials had acted appropriately, despite the secret science and the secret EPA/API collaboration. Van Strum's appeals in 1990 and 1992 were unsuccessful, although the Court of Appeals for the Ninth Circuit asked the EPA to better justify its puzzling decision to withhold dioxin-related information. Since the court's request carried no negative consequences if ignored, the agency did not comply.[36]

Concealing and Fudging Mortality Rates at the VA

> New book-burners have crept in silently on cats' feet, stealing access to information from our people.
>
> —Rep. Major R. Owens (D-NY)[37]

Well before the Reagan-Bush administration took office, Veterans Administration hospitals in some parts of the country had developed a reputation for providing a lower-than-average quality of care compared to non-VA hospitals, with higher risks of preventable and consequential errors. In October 1980, for instance, the VA ordered its Miami hospital to stop all heart surgeries for one year after reports emerged showing its cardiac unit was responsible for significantly higher rates of surgical deaths, compared with other VA units and the national average. Over four years later (in December 1984), top VA officials ordered the same hospital to halt heart surgeries after a report in the *Fort Lauderdale Sun-Sentinel* revealed still higher-than-average mortality rates. In November 1984 alone, six out of seventy-five Miami cardiac patients (8 percent) died on the operating table, a much higher rate than the VA's national average for heart surgeries (5.2 percent). Those and other revelations led many Americans to wonder whether the VA health system was fundamentally flawed or if, instead, the worrisome reports revealed outlier problems within a generally effective system. As a result of increasing pressure by veterans groups, public interest groups, and veteran-friendly politicians, the VA appointed an independent panel to investigate the scale and scope of the problem. After reversing an earlier decision to keep the report secret, the VA released it publicly in April 1985. The results were shocking.[38]

The panel found that the VA's hospital in Washington, DC, had cardiac surgery mortality rates three times greater than the overall national average. At other VA hospitals, rates reached six times the average. Some of the poor performance was explained by surgeons' relative inexperience at sites that had fewer cardiac patients annually (as in less populated rural areas). But the significant differences could not be blamed on inexperience alone or on differences in patient backgrounds and characteristics. Something else was amiss. Indeed, over half of the audited facilities had preventable, fatal medical errors, which meant dozens of veterans had needlessly died. To stem the tide and further study the problems, the VA announced it would shutter cardiac units at fifteen of forty-seven VA hospitals.[39]

As the worrisome numbers splashed across the front pages, House subcommittees called hearings to investigate the issue. Members of Congress were also interested in other lingering problems, including an unusually high number of VA medical malpractice cases, a spate of doctors working with lapsed or revoked medical licenses, and the questionable and possibly corrupt practice of doctors accepting "gratuities" from pharmaceutical companies. With the prominent news reports and congressional committees gearing up, there was a sense within Washington and within the VA that the department would finally be held accountable.[40]

Five days before a hearing at the House Government Operations Subcommittee on Intergovernmental Relations and Human Resources, the VA's chief medical director, Dr. John W. Ditzler, unexpectedly resigned. Perhaps it is more accurate to say he demoted himself, moving from his position as chief medical director at 172 VA hospitals and 227 outpatient clinics to a single VA hospital in San Francisco. Lest anyone think that was strange, to say nothing of the timing, a VA spokeswoman reassured Americans that Ditzler's resignation and transfer was "not connected in any way with the hearing. It's just a coincidence." Ditzler also chose not to—or was ordered not to—appear before Congress. He "had some medical meetings to attend and could not be there," the spokeswoman vaguely said. VA officials asked Dr. John A. Gronvall to appear in Ditzler's place and to become the department's new medical director.[41]

Gronvall clearly inherited a mess, not necessarily of Ditzler's making. He immediately set out to clean it up and to salvage the VA's tarnished reputation. He and VA administrator Thomas K. Turnagem, for instance, closed several cadiac units, improved internal monitoring systems, and sent reassuring messages to the public. (One message read: "In the last year our cardiac surgery has been thoroughly reviewed, and we think we are on target." A less reassuring and persuasive message stated: "Mortality is not a sufficient measure of quality, all by itself.") Meanwhile, grim details continued to emerge about the still-bruised VA system, including unusual numbers of critical medical mistakes outside cardiac units as well as a rash of patient suicides in psychiatric wards (for example, there were 134 suicides in 1984 and overall 1,224 "incidents" that could have ended that way). Realizing the VA needed to learn more about the scope of the problem, Gronvall commissioned a panel to survey the system and establish benchmarks to measure progress over time.[42]

Preliminary results—shared only with top VA officials—confirmed that the problem was system-wide. Nearly 12 percent of VA hospitals had high mortality rates, compared with 2.5 percent of private sector hospitals. And patients treated at VA hospitals were more than four times more likely to die than if they had chosen non-VA hospitals. For Gronvall, these were unacceptable statistics, so much so that he ordered researchers to keep the results secret and quietly make adjustments to their statistical models to yield more palatable results. Gronvall apparently thought the VA could not withstand the public's reaction to the truth, although he might have genuinely found the numbers to be implausibly high and thus produced in error. Either way, he ordered his subordinates to tweak their statistical models for a better outcome—an unethical and possibly fraudulent move in the world of quantitative research. Keeping the results secret required almost no effort by Gronvall—a simple diktat did the trick. The consequences of the secrecy, however, were potentially deadly. If the original results (the high rates) were accurate, veterans would have unknowingly walked into medical facilities that were much more likely to kill them. Rep. Major Owens (D-NY), speaking a few years earlier on a related matter, saw a parallel with how the Communists governed the Soviet Union: "Russia was concerned about its infant mortality rate, so it stopped publishing statistics."[43]

If not for one of his researchers, Gronvall's secrecy and statistical manipulations probably would never have surfaced publicly. Dr. Francis E. Conrad, then the VA's director of quality assurance, challenged Gronvall's order, although he tried to keep the matter an internal one. Conrad confronted Gronvall in agency meetings. He wrote memos criticizing the order, one of which rejected Gronvall's concern that the agency could not withstand any more public criticism. But Conrad's efforts had little influence within the agency or on Gronvall himself. So Conrad went public, describing the order to hide the results and change the statistical model and alleging Gronvall was motivated more by bureaucratic politics (that is, rebuilding the VA's reputation, no matter the facts) than by science and the public interest.[44]

After an investigation, the government's General Accounting Office declared it found no evidence Gronvall acted inappropriately. It was a surprising conclusion, given Gronvall's admission that he ordered subordinates to manipulate their statistical analysis to avert the "inevitable" negative criticism. The GAO's report also relied mostly on information the VA provided, which at the very least limited the breadth of the report and made any conclusions tenative. A more complete, credible analysis would have gathered information independently.[45]

But for the VA, it was just what the doctor ordered. The GAO's report largely put the matter to rest in Washington. Follow-up investigations would have yielded little fruit anyway, since both of the story's main protagonists soon died, suddenly and unexpectedly. The turn of events had all the trappings of a sensationalist political thriller, even though what happened was probably just coincidental. Conrad's violent end was the more dramatic of the two. In early April 1988, just after he went public with his allegations, he traveled to Chicago to help his daughter find a new apartment. After inspecting one unit, he and his daughter went downstairs to discuss details with the building manager. Out of nowhere, a man burst into the rental office and quickly starting stabbing the manager. Conrad tried to stop the assault, which prompted the attacker to brutalize him, along with another office manager. The attacker was reportedly an enraged tenant, upset about his eviction notice. Chief Medical Director Gronvall also died unexpectedly, at a young age. He suffered a heart attack while vacationing with his family at Nags Head, North Carolina, two years later.[46]

The OMB's New Filter

Most of the new consumer technologies introduced in the 1980s—videocassette recorders, video games, microwave ovens, answering machines, fax machines, personal computers—came with few known health risks. Yes, some Americans feared microwave oven radiation, but most scientists who studied the matter concluded microwaves were safe. Studies of early 1980s "video display terminals" (VDTs) (that is, desktop computer monitors), however, suggested higher risks, including serious illness to women.

From 1980 until 1986, managers from more than a dozen businesses across the country called the government about what seemed abnormally high rates of miscarriages, stillbirths, and other pregnancy complications among women workers who regularly used radiation-emitting VDTs. Women's groups discovered a wider problem, finding unusually high rates of pregnancy complications in at least twenty-three companies. In a United Airlines office in San Francisco, for instance, 48 of 300 women worked while pregnant in the early 1980s. Half of those pregnancies ended with miscarriages, stillborns, or birth defects—a rate much higher than average. Women from across the country who called into a hotline set up by the group 9 to 5, National Association of Working Women (9to5) reported alarmingly high complication rates: 68 percent of callers who regularly used VDTs described abnormal pregnancies. That number was no doubt inflated by self-selection bias, but the connection between VDTs and women's health at the very least presented a scientific puzzle, given the many reported cases and the unclear causal mechanisms.[47]

The CDC's National Institute for Occupational Safety and Health (NIOSH) decided enough suggestive evidence had emerged to merit a systematic analysis of the hypothesized link between VDTs and female reproductive health. Nongovernmental studies were already under way in the early 1980s, but all had important limitations, such as small sample sizes. NIOSH therefore designed a large, systematic study of women VDT users, who by the early 1980s numbered about 7 million. In 1983, NIOSH announced partnerships with major telecommunications companies, including BellSouth and AT&T, to interview 3,000 telephone operators, half of whom used VDTs regularly. Although company executives believed the study would unfairly tarnish the industry's reputation, they had little choice but to comply (or appear compliant). AT&T, though reluctant, was the more cooperative of the two, at least initially. BellSouth worked hard to stop the study before it could begin.[48]

Although NIOSH was technically in charge of the study, BellSouth insisted that the protocol needed independent peer review, to "ensure that the results would be valid"—which probably really meant something like "to ensure the results would not harm our reputation and profitability and make us vulnerable to lawsuits." The company expressed a particular concern about the survey's stress and infertility questions. Although NIOSH's protocol had already gone through an internal review process by agency scientists, the government tolerated BellSouth's decision to conduct its own review, for which it hired two academic epidemiologists. Once completed, BellSouth sent the reviewers' criticisms to NIOSH—as well as the White House's Office of Management and Budget. NIOSH, to its credit, acknowledged some flaws and adjusted the research design accordingly. Not content with the now higher-quality study, both companies set out to further complicate NIOSH's plans by abruptly transferring scores of long-distance operators to VDT workstations, thereby depleting the study's control group. Perhaps the move resulted only from business needs, but the unexpected transfers were certainly puzzling, especially because the companies were well aware of the research design. NIOSH scientists in response mobilized to start the surveys right away. But they again ran up against obstacles, this time from the OMB.[49]

The OMB ordered NIOSH to halt its VDT research in December 1985, challenging the study's scientific merits and pointing to unspecified "flawed statistical techniques." Never before had OMB stopped a NIOSH study for methodological reasons. What made the OMB's intervention even more puzzling was that NIOSH had taken its design through two separate peer review processes—the usual one plus BellSouth's review by Harvard and Brown University epidemiologists. The OMB's intervention occurred at a time when more and more women around the country were using potentially dangerous VDT workstations, as "microcomputers" grew less expensive and increasingly common.[50]

Six months later, OMB officials announced they would consider giving NIOSH another shot, but the protocol would need some changes. This time around, their concerns had little to do with flawed statistical techniques. The real problems were the survey questions about stress and infertility—the same questions that had rankled BellSouth. For NIOSH scientists, eliminating the infertility questions was an odd choice, considering reproductive health complaints had sparked NIOSH's interest in the first place. Getting rid of the workplace stress questions was also odd, especially because stress was increasingly seen as an independent cause of work-related illness, in government and nongovernment studies. In fact, another NIOSH study of BellSouth workers had just found both stress and VDT use to be associated with chest pain. Leaving stress questions out of the survey would therefore undermine the analysis, since researchers would not be able to control for its effects.[51]

BellSouth and AT&T, worried about potential liabilities and tarnished reputations, had an interest in ensuring the VDT study would never be taken seriously. Toward that goal, company executives won the OMB's help in guaranteeing the analysis had spurious correlations. OMB officials of course denied BellSouth's influence and expressed confidence in the new, denuded survey, saying, for instance, "We believe we've got a balanced questionnaire which will enable us to get the information we need." It was not clear what they meant by "balanced"—were they balancing interests, good and bad survey research methodologies, or something else? What kind of information did they "need"? Information clouded by uncertainty? Meanwhile, BellSouth cynically told reporters it "would have no problem" if the OMB ultimately included the stress and infertility questions, despite having lobbied hard against them a few weeks earlier.[52]

The OMB's interventions were extraordinary for several reasons. First, as noted, the office had rarely interfered with government scientists' choices in the past. Second, OMB's legal authority to review government science was rooted in its statutory responsibility to reduce bureaucratic red tape and unnecessary government spending (for example, on paperwork costs). The Paperwork Reduction Act (PRA) of 1980, signed by President Carter, was motivated by Congress's growing concern about reducing waste and increasing efficiency in government. The PRA established, among other things, a unit in the OMB called the Office of Information and Regulatory Affairs (OIRA), whose mission was, among other things, to streamline information collection processes in the executive branch, eliminating waste and duplication and "maximiz[ing] the utility of information created, collected, maintained, used, shared and disseminated by or for the Federal Government." Those are broad mandates, but only a willfully strained interpretation of PRA would see OIRA as a scientific peer review panel, especially one that could unilaterally stop and manipulate research designs. PRA's congressional supporters explicitly argued that politically appointed OMB officials in the White House should not have veto authority on scientific ideas, even if they were trained experts. Granted, the text of the PRA does give the OMB some discretion in determining whether information collected by agencies will have "practical utility" and whether the information agencies collect "is necessary for the proper performance of [its] functions." However, a plain reading of the "practical utility" and "proper performance" sections envisions an OIRA that challenges, say, a NASA study of football injuries—something clearly outside of NASA's orbit. Rejecting NIOSH's analysis of the health risks of workplace stress and VDT radiation for pregnant women was entirely consistent with the occupational health agency's mission and responsibilities.[53]

Overall, the OMB's decision to strike selected questions from NIOSH's survey defied the PRA in at least two ways. First, the demanded revisions to the survey had nothing to do with cutting costs or increasing bureaucratic efficiency. Second, the elimination of those questions ensured the study would have *less* "practical utility." As noted earlier, one of the major unresolved questions in the scientific literature was whether the radiation effect was spurious, given other independent variables, such as stress. Striking those variables from the analysis almost guaranteed other scientists would note the study's validity and reliability problems. The unresolved questions would remain, demanding further inquiry—probably by another costly, incomplete government study. Unless we count the data *almost* collected by NIOSH, the case of the deliberately botched VDT study is not fundamentally about suppressing proprietary scientific information. However, because of the relatively abundant paper trail surrounding the case, it usefully illustrates the mechanisms Reagan-Bush OIRA officials used to control scientific information, deployed elsewhere for secrecy purposes, without as many traces.

Liberally Using the New Authority

Along with the VDT study, the OIRA used its new filter in the 1980s to suppress a range of scientific endeavors with "practical utility." Scientists working on occupational, reproductive, pharmaceutical, and environmental health risks as well as infectious disease and racial and ethnic discrimination all found their proposals axed by an increasingly assertive and disapproving OIRA. Those scientists had experiences much like their colleagues at NIOSH: OIRA's political appointees manipulated designs and inhibited data collection.[54]

The OMB also prevented the disclosure of scientific information from research already completed, and it blocked regulations that would have disseminated proprietary public health information. For example, the OMB in 1982 suspended an FDA rule that would have ordered aspirin manufacturers to warn consumers of the risks of a relatively rare but sometimes fatal disease called Reye's syndrome, which strikes a proportion of aspirin-taking children under certain conditions (such as those with chicken pox or the flu). Against all of the available evidence, including the FDA's extensive internal (that is, exclusive) scientific review process, the OMB shelved the rule after meetings with Aspirin Foundation of America representatives, who insisted the risks from aspirin were still unproven. The decision had little to do with the PRA's mandate of reducing costs and increasing bureaucratic efficiency. In December 1985, after about 200 more children died from Reye's syndrome (in addition to hundreds more who got it but survived), the OMB finally allowed the FDA's labeling requirement to proceed, effective late May 1986. Later studies reconfirmed aspirin's risks, including one showing some groups taking aspirin were thirty-five times more likely to get Reye's syndrome, compared with similar groups not taking it.[55]

The OMB used its new secrecy power liberally. In another case, OMB officials weakened a regulation proposed by Occupational Safety and Health Administration (OSHA) scientists that would have protected about 70,000 hospital workers from a highly toxic chemical, ethylene oxide, used to sterilize medical equipment when other cleaning methods were ineffective. Although the science about ethylene oxide's health risks was relatively new in the early 1980s, the literature had already demonstrated strong links with cancer, miscarriage, and chromosomal damage for the chronically exposed (such as hospital workers using it daily). Few scientists disputed the dangers. In a case brought by Public Citizen, federal district judge Barrington D. Parker agreed that the plaintiffs had "presented a solid and certain foundation showing that workers are subjected to grave health dangers from exposure to ethylene oxide." The OMB, however, decided to toss aside OSHA's new rule, concluding without evidence that workers would probably be fine, since they used the chemical for short periods at a time. Then, when OSHA scientists began to study the risks of chronic short-term exposure, the politically appointed OSHA administrator, R. Leonard Vance, unilaterally shut down the research over the scientists' strong objections, leaving the data inaccessible to all but senior officials and well-connected corporate executives. Vance's decision came immediately after a meeting with officials from Union Carbide, a top manufacturer of the chemical. It is not hard to guess what the scientists likely discovered and thus what OSHA concealed.[56]

Expanding and Institutionalizing the OMB's New Authority

Just before his second inauguration, President Reagan signed Executive Order 12498, explicitly institutionalizing the OMB's new centralized regulatory and scientific vetting authority. The order was ostensibly about creating "coordinated processes" with more presidential oversight, new mechanisms of interagency accountability, and other reasonable-sounding ideas. However, the order's main effect was to require all agencies to submit proposed regulations to the OIRA to ensure they were consistent "with the Administration's policies and priorities." The OMB's new filter was one of the cheapest and most subtle instruments of political power that Reagan-Bush officials developed for domestic policy. It was also endlessly pliable.[57]

The OMB used it, for instance, to edit government scientists' congressional testimony. As we saw previously, Bush-Cheney and Bush-Quayle officials did the same thing, but it was Reagan-Bush's OMB that set the precedent. And as in the later episodes, James Hansen, the climate scientist, experienced the White House's interference firsthand. In 1985 or 1986, Hansen's NASA supervisors sent his written congressional testimony for OMB approval, as was newly required. OMB officials—none of them climate scientists—disagreed with Hansen's arguments about the nature and causes of climate change, and they suggested he alter his scientific statements. And as we have seen, Hansen was probably hardwired to resist those kinds of encroachments. In this case, he decided to testify as a private citizen, in order to offer his undiluted insights. Others were not so brave. The OMB censored or altered scientific speech about government studies with proprietary data and results on several other occasions—how many times, we can only guess. Some scientists probably self-censored in the new information environment.[58]

Conclusion

Whether they were motivated by interests (such as BellSouth and Union Carbide) or neoliberal ideas, officials in the Reagan-Bush administration constructed a new role for the OMB that suppressed scientific information across a range of issues important to the public. Although they did not invent OIRA itself, Reagan's White House officials quickly transformed it into something that transcended its statutory function. Economists and statisticians in the OMB assumed the role as the government's primary judge of what constituted good and necessary science. If anyone had wondered before 1985 whether political bias would taint that role, Executive Order 12498 only made it explicit, by requiring agency output to be consistent "with the Administration's policies and priorities." How many times OIRA used the power to conceal proprietary scientific information for political purposes remains unknown.

Safeguarding Nuclear Secrets

Every one of America's Cold War presidents justifiably used strict security measures to prevent military secrets from falling into the hands of Soviet spies. To be sure, some individuals, including J. Edgar Hoover and Sen. Joseph McCarthy, entertained fantasies of Communist agents permeating and controlling all centers of social power. But in truth, Soviet spies indeed worked hard to steal American secrets, just as American spies did in the Eastern bloc. Of utmost concern for both sides was information about nuclear science and technology. Although excessive secrecy was clearly a problem during the Cold War, transparency advocates tended to accept the legitimacy of nuclear secrecy because of the high stakes.[59]

All administrations held on tightly to US nuclear secrets, but Reagan-Bush efforts were remarkably aggressive. For example, in the immediate aftermath of the Chernobyl nuclear accident in the Ukrainian Soviet Socialist Republic, the White House issued a gag order on scientists in the Departments of Energy and Agriculture, the Nuclear Regulatory Commission (NRC), and the Lawrence Livermore and Brookhaven Laboratories. Apparently fearing that nuclear scientists might scare Americans with predictions of potential Chernobyl-like accidents on US soil, the White House forbade all but a few senior officials to speak with journalists about anything nuclear related. From the White House's perspective, this was no gag order at all; they merely "encouraged [scientists] to avoid speculation" about the causes and consequences of Chernobyl. "Of course . . . [scientists could] respond to questions of fact," officials insisted, unless, it seemed, those questions of fact involved the government's secret estimates of accident scenarios in the United States. And the gag order was even more restrictive than that. A senior public affairs officer from Lawrence Livermore later admitted, "I was told in no uncertain terms to stop talking to reporters and to stop my people from talking to reporters."[60]

Clampdowns of that nature were fortunately rare during the Reagan-Bush administration, as far as we know. More common were aggressive efforts to suppress *unclassified* nuclear information. To cite one example, soon after taking office Reagan asked Congress to amend the Atomic Energy Act of 1946 to better protect sensitive nuclear information. The proposed changes sounded quite reasonable, prohibiting:

the unauthorized dissemination of unclassified information pertaining to: (A) the design of production facilities or utilization facilities; (B) security measures (including security plans, procedures, and equipment) for the physical protection of (i) production or utilization facilities, (ii) nuclear material contained in such facilities, or (iii) nuclear material in transit; or (C) the design, manufacture, or utilization of any atomic weapon or component if the design, manufacture, or utilization of such weapon or component was contained in any information declassified or removed from the Restricted Data category by the Secretary.

The amended law also authorized the secretary of the Department of Energy to propose more specific administrative rules for handling unclassified controlled nuclear information (UCNI), followed by a public comment period. When the DOE published its proposal in 1983, administrators got an earful.[61]

Nongovernment and government scientists, environmental groups, labor unions, universities, and state governments all argued the new rules would harm public safety, deprive democratic citizens of unclassified information, and otherwise unfairly impose costs on individuals and organizations. Labor unions argued the proposed regulations would allow the government to keep health-related information from nuclear workers, forcing them to blindly accept the government's claims about potential health risks. State governments hosting federal nuclear facilities argued the rules would unnecessarily conceal information about radiation from exposed or concerned citizens. University administrators and librarians found the proposed regulations overly burdensome, since the new rules required them to sift through countless documents to determine whether they contained UCNI. Then, too, UCNI collections would need constant monitoring and special attention. In light of the public comments, the DOE actually made some concessions and attached a new list of exceptions to the final draft of regulations, published in 1985. Still, as some of the same critics pointed out, the new UCNI rules imposed sweeping new restrictions on unclassified information dissemination in the public and private sectors, including a new b(3) exemption to the FOIA.[62]

With the new authority to legally conceal UNCI, the administration found yet another way to selectively disclose proprietary scientific information that validated its policy arguments, while suppressing information that refuted them. Thus, when nuclear plant workers and their unions demanded stricter safety rules, due to their concerns about chronic exposure to low levels of radiation (as well as nuclear accidents), the administration pointed to DOE science that suggested low-level radiation from nuclear plants did not pose a great risk to workers and nearby communities. Reagan-Bush officials did not mention the secret science that contradicted that view. For instance, the DOE knew but failed to mention that radiation exposure has cumulative effects and that the type of radiation from nuclear plants (ionizing) is more dangerous than low-frequency nonionizing radiation, with higher risks of leukemia, lymphoma, and lung and pancreatic cancers. In this case, the secrecy did not end the debate, as scientists, environmentalists, antinuclear activists, and the workers themselves already knew at least some of the conflicting findings from nongovernment scientists working in the relatively young field of low-level radiation exposure.[63]

At least as puzzling was the DOE's refusal to open its huge medical database of nuclear workers. When independent scientists learned the DOE had invested $46 million since 1964 to maintain secret medical records of over 300,000 nuclear plant workers, they eagerly sought—and were denied—the data for independent analysis. For example, the Three Mile Island Public Health Fund filed a FOIA request in May 1987, which the DOE rejected on personal privacy grounds (Exemption 6)—even though all of the workers' personal identifying variables (names, genders, ethnicities, residential and occupation locations, and the like) could have been eliminated. In any case, officials argued, anyone interested could read what DOE scientists had already published. They would even throw in the tailored datasets produced for those projects. And since they were such good sports, they would allow selected "qualified researchers" to access the database once it was completed—in 1996. The new UCNI rules prevented scientists and nuclear workers from pressing the matter. Moreover, the secrecy had nothing to do with the original impetus of the UCNI rule: safeguarding nuclear secrets from Soviet spies. And given the government's history of violating citizens' basic freedoms by subjecting them, unknowingly, to radiation experiments, there were other reasons to be skeptical of the administration's claims.[64]

Radiation Experiments on Americans and Increasing Nuclear Secrecy

As if the Cold War's "mutually assured destruction" nuclear arms race was not concerning enough, Americans in the 1970s and 1980s learned about the major nuclear reactor accidents (meltdowns) at Chernobyl and Three Mile Island in Pennsylvania, as well as long-secret, less-detectable accidents at the Savannah River, South Carolina, site. And then there were the experiments.

First came news the government conducted radiation experiments on citizens starting in the mid-1940s, beginning with an unsuspecting car crash victim injected with plutonium. Then Americans learned scientists at the Hanford, Washington, nuclear site deliberately leaked radiation just to see what would happen in neighboring communities.[65]

The Hanford site was a product of the secret Manhattan Project, the government's fast-track mission to develop a nuclear bomb in the midst of World War II. Once that war transitioned into the Cold War, US officials wanted to predict what would happen after a nuclear accident, especially around less sophisticated Soviet reactors. For that task, they needed information—as scientifically valid as possible. Because nuclear war would be the price of using Soviet citizens as guinea pigs, US officials instead chose to use Washingtonians. If anyone wanted to compile a list of the most spectacular assaults on public health by the US government, the Green Run experiment would probably top the list. Three Mile Island is rightly considered the worst nuclear *accident* on US soil in history, but Green Run remains the worst nuclear *attack*, despite the sad irony of it being launched by the federal government.

On December 3, 1949, Hanford scientists—following orders and without public warning—deliberately leaked clouds of highly radioactive substances (such as iodine-131 and xenon-133) through the plant's smokestacks. Their job was to study the effects on communities up to 60 miles away, including Washington's Tri-City area of Richland, Pasco, and Kennewick. What happened should not have been a big surprise, as scientists already knew how dangerous those chemicals were, although they had never been tested on humans at such high doses. Three Mile Island was horrifying enough, but northwest Washington suffered a fate far worse: the radioactive clouds were nearly *1,000 times as toxic*. The release of iodine-131 alone surpassed legal limits 11,000 times over, and those legal limits were alarmingly high by contemporary standards. The radioactive wind blew all the way to California, through Oregon. The exact biological toll from the experiment remains unknown, but the region suffered very high rates of cancers and other illnesses, not to mention the damage to nonhuman forms of life. Much of that damage came courtesy of Green Run, although other Hanford experiments, illegal dumping, and radioactive spills due to mismanagement also caused untold harms. Altogether, in its first decade Hanford spewed "470,000 curies of radioactive iodine" into the region, whereas Three Mile Island "only" spilled 15 curies. Residents began to refer to especially afflicted areas as "death miles"—enter at your own risk. After about a decade of delay, Hanford scientists resumed regional-scale experimentation in 1962, in a yearlong program that pumped radioactive iodine into the air and tracked its effects on humans, animals, soils, and vegetation.[66]

Researchers who had heard about the area's rumored death miles, cancer clusters, and toxic gardens began in the 1980s to poke around libraries and conduct interviews with Tri-City residents. Investigative journalists also increasingly reported on damages to people in the areas around Savannah River (in South Carolina) and Rocky Flats (in Colorado), as well as Ohio's Fernald Nuclear Materials plant (or "Fernald Feed Materials Production Center"), where the government gave nearby residents $73 million because the plant leaked uranium dust for years. Bit by bit, information leaked out, creating a mosaic of the US nuclear secrecy regime.[67]

The Reagan-Bush administration clearly was not solely responsible for the government's nuclear accidents and experiments or the associated secrecy. A full accounting would include all presidents from Truman on. However, in the midst of the public's increasing awareness of what the government did to citizens on US soil throughout the Cold War, the Reagan-Bush administration responded to the news with silence and even greater secrecy. Rep. Edward Markey (D-MA) accused the White House of having a "bunker mentality."[68]

As the public wanted to know more, doors to nuclear agencies were slammed without warning or explanation, shutting off already constricted points of access. For example, the Nuclear Regulatory Commission, whose mission centered around public health and safety, announced without warning or hearings that it would sharply reduce access to its activities. A close NRC vote of three to two in April 1985—the same month that the DOE's new UCNI rules were finalized—determined that interested citizens could no longer attend or record NRC meetings and that the NRC would no longer provide meeting transcripts and recordings. Citizens lost access to one of the only places they had to learn about nuclear safety. For NRC chair Nunzio Palladino, the new information controls did not go far enough.[69]

Fearing the new UNCI rules would fail to protect sensitive unclassified information, Palladino lobbied hard for new statutory exemptions in the sunshine laws (FOIA and FACA/GITSA). Moreover, to prevent the public from seeing the NRC's meeting minutes, Palladino argued the body should redefine the term *meetings*—as only those gatherings where the NRC took an official position. Finally, faced with a panel whose members did not unanimously support him, he argued the NRC should once and for all scrap the five-person panel and instead appoint one administrator (guess who!). The other panelists unsurprisingly objected, choosing to remain onboard and depriving Palladino of his fantasy of turning the NRC into his own personal fiefdom. But Palladino got everything else he wanted, consequently walling off the one source of nuclear safety information the public had.[70]

As once-secret information about nuclear accidents and attacks on US citizens began to spill, Reagan-Bush officials' main response was to clam up as much as possible. With a bunker mentality, they created new UCNI controls, played word games (the NRC's *meetings*), and pushed for new sunshine law exemptions to prevent further leakage. Other administrations also aggressively kept nuclear secrets; Reagan-Bush distinguished itself by creating new secrecy tools and setting several new precedents.

Other Ways to Keep Unclassified Information from Scientists

Before the sunshine era, presidential administrations barely had to think about controlling sensitive but unclassified scientific information. They essentially held on to whatever they wanted. Once information flowed more freely in the new legal environment, officials did whatever they could to conceal what they considered sensitive, whether or not the information in question even merited a FOIA exemption. For example, the FBI's Library Awareness Program from 1973 until the late 1980s surveilled foreign nationals—especially those who looked Eastern European—if they seemed interested in SBU information in public libraries. Some might have been spies; most were probably scholars. The FBI recruited a corps of librarian informers to do most of the dirty work. Those who refused or seemed insufficiently cooperative were investigated (this was probably a large number, given librarians' general commitment to transparency and open access). Everyone who learned about the program, whether they participated or not, had to sign legal documents swearing to secrecy (they faced gag orders). Fortunately for the unhappily gagged, the FBI dismantled the program once members of Congress disclosed it in a 1987 congressional hearing. The government's next attempt to monitor library patrons—as far as we know—was initiated fifteen years later with the USA PATRIOT Act.[71]

A major step to systematize what had been a scattered array of secrecy initiatives came with Reagan's National Security Decision Directive 145 (NSDD 145), entitled "National Policy on Telecommunications and Automated Information Systems Security." Among other things, the September 1984 order gave the military the authority to control all unclassified sensitive security information. At the core of NSDD 145 was the White House's concern that clever enemies could masterfully combine bits of seemingly innocuous un-classified information to build a mosaic that might, when put together, reveal the government's most sensitive classified secrets (see chapters 2 and 3). Specifically, NSDD 145's authors argued that "information, even if unclassified in isolation, often can reveal highly classified and other sensitive information when taken in aggregate."[72]

Due to some administrative confusion about what specifically qualified as SBU information and what constituted "national security," the White House issued a second directive in October 1986, the second in its National Tele-communications and Information Systems Security Policy series (NTISSP 2). But the memo, signed by Reagan's national security adviser, John Poindexter, did little to narrow the definition of *national security interests*. Quite the con-trary. NTISSP 2 vested the military with the authority to control SBU infor-mation relevant to national security "or other Federal Government interests." And Poindexter's vision of "government interests" and the range of potentially sensitive information was boundless:

> [SBU] information is information the disclosure, loss, misuse, alter-ation, or destruction of which could adversely affect national security or other Federal Government interests. National security interests are those unclassified matters that relate to the national defense or the for-eign relations of the U.S. Government. Other Government interests are those related, but *not limited to the wide range of Government or Government-derived economic, human, financial, industrial, agricultural, technological, and law enforcement information*, as well as the privacy or confidentiality of personal or commercial proprietary information pro-vided to the U.S. Government by its citizens.

Sensitive information thus included any "government-derived" informa-tion related to "human information"—a rather convenient way of making anything up for grabs. Just in case, the addition of "not limited to" kept all options available. Poindexter's memo effectively claimed executive authority to reach into and "protect" information produced by industries, universi-ties, mass media, nonprofits, or any other sources. Anything the government owned, or would or could own, fell within this new orbit.[73]

The government had already started to move in this direction before NSDD

145 and NTISSP 2. For instance, members of the Society of Photo-Optical Instrumentation Engineers (SPIE) learned in August 1982 that the DOD had ordered at least 100 scientific papers removed from the group's conference proceedings. Then again, in April 1985, the DOD demanded that SPIE stop 25 scheduled conference presentations, ostensibly because the papers in question might have given the Soviets strategically valuable secret information about laser technologies and satellite communications. Engineers could attend the other presentations—but only if SPIE officials barred noncitizens from entering, with a few exceptions (the DOD provided a list of approved foreign nationals). Before NSDD 145 and NTISSP 2, justifying such actions took some legalistic creativity. In the case of the optical engineers, the administration based its interventions on a liberal reading of the Export Control Act (ECA), which had previously been used to restrict exports of military-related technologies and scarce commodities during wartime. The White House reasoned it could stretch the ECA to include exports of sensitive *information,* including arcane engineering conference papers. The national security justification, as usual, discouraged criticism, as did the muted threats about cutting off public research funding. Although some engineers still complained, the SPIE complied.[74]

With NTISSP 2, NSDD 145, and the new interpretation of ECA, the administration pioneered and then institutionalized quite effective new ways of clamping down on the flow of proprietary scientific information—broad enough to include ideas written on a page, recorded on computer equipment, and discussed at scientific meetings and university seminars. In addition to the examples cited here, Reagan-Bush used the new secrecy tools to conceal otherwise unavailable information about superconductivity, as well as obviously national security–centric topics like milk production and labor statistics. It did not matter if the information came from government or nongovernment scientists. Entire fields, such as cryptography, were marked as inherently sensitive. Others, like semiconductor physics, contained subfields that required blanket censorship. Concerns about superconductivity research became so pronounced that the White House proposed a separate FOIA exemption. As a result of the genuinely unprecedented intervention in nongovernment science, scientists and librarians across a range of disciplines were warned by their supervisors to tightly control "sensitive" information from anyone suspicious, especially foreign nationals. Scientific and professional groups took it upon themselves to exclude foreign nationals from their meetings and discussion groups. Scientists confessed to self-censorship. Professional and personal reputations were at stake, not to mention research funding.[75]

Once Reagan-Bush's scientific information control policies became more widely known, from media reports and congressional hearings, the administration appeared to relent. It became deeply inconvenient for the White House that NTISSP 2 had been written by Poindexter, who was knee deep in the Iran-Contra scandal. The relatively obscure document became a focal point for administration critics. As a result, Poindexter's successor, Frank Carlucci, rescinded it. Nevertheless, the White House quietly argued that with NSDD 145 still on the books, the policy would essentially continue uninterrupted. In any case, the policy was further institutionalized, with a few twists, with the Computer Security Act (CSA) of 1987. One difference was that the CSA vested some control into a new civilian-led National Institute for Standards and Technology. Still, the continuing presence of NSDD 145 gave the National Security Agency the justification it needed to continue to oversee all government computer systems and scoop up and guard any information deemed SBU. And much of the rest of the bureaucracy by that point had internalized the logic of mosaic theory and had adjusted risk perceptions accordingly.[76]

The administration's stated national security concerns, as always, were prima facie reasonable, especially in the context of great power politics. The Soviets of course were interested in stealing any informational advantage enjoyed by the United States and vice versa. Nevertheless, the administration reached deep into government and nongovernment science with a brazenness that seemed strongly at odds with its steady beat of political rhetoric about small government.

Conclusion

By the time Reagan left office, the administration had become embroiled in multiple secret science controversies—about Agent Orange, Times Beach, Hanford, VA mortality data, and the many other cases analyzed here. We could have easily spent another chapter learning about Reagan-Bush secrecy involving formaldehyde, forestry, wildlife poisonings, acid rain, workplace carcinogens, AIDS, and beyond. And those are just the examples in the public record, probably representing only a portion of the total.

The institutional legacies were also significant. Reagan-Bush officials pioneered and then institutionalized several new secrecy tools. They armed the OMB's OIRA with the authority to monitor and censor government science, part of an explicit attempt to bring scientific information in line with "the Administration's policies and priorities." They used administrative orders and creative new interpretations of statutes to create and keep scientific secrets, whether they came from government or nongovernment scientists. They experimented with word games to dodge sunshine laws, such as the NRC's redefinition of *meetings*. Overall, in terms of scale and scope, the Reagan-Bush administration developed a record that was in many ways truly unprecedented.

9

WHEN ALL ELSE FAILS
SHREDDING, BURNING, DELETING, OR WHATEVER IT TAKES

> But when you talk about destruction, don't you know you can
> count me out (*in!*)
>
> —The Beatles, "Revolution"

Nixon's Advice

Nineteen eighty-six was a big year for Richard Nixon. Twelve years had passed since he had resigned from the presidency, and the country in many ways was still polarized around the issues that forced him out, especially the Watergate scandal and his handling of the Vietnam War. But by 1986, the disgraced former president had somehow managed to rebuild his reputation to such an extent that *Rolling Stone* magazine named Nixon to their "Who's Hot: The New Stars in Your Future" list, next to celebrities like *Family Ties* sitcom star Michael J. Fox and heavyweight boxing champion Mike Tyson. Then, almost incredibly, he reemerged in the Gallup organization's annual poll that asked Americans who they most admired. "People see me and they think, 'He's risen from the dead,'" Nixon remarked at the time with no small amount of self-grandeur. It was only eight years earlier, during a small gathering of politicians before Vice President Hubert Humphrey's funeral, when Nixon looked "like he was four feet tall, all shrunk up in himself and gray as a ghost," according to Howard Baker, the former Republican senator. "Nobody would get near him. Nobody would talk to him. Everybody was afraid of him."[1]

Nixon's resurrection and inexplicable popularity in the mid-1980s made the typically awkward, self-serious man comfortable enough to openly joke about his criminal misdeeds (also easier to do when backed by another president's immunizing pardon). At a 1986 Associated Press (AP) luncheon at the American Newspaper Publisher Association's conference in San Francisco, Nixon stepped to the podium and proceeded to give what publishers and editors took as a statesmanesque speech, lauding Reagan's undying support for the brutal Contra militia in Nicaragua and the decision to bomb Libya in Operation El Dorado Canyon. His remarks drew a standing ovation from the crowd, filled with some of the same people who contributed to his downfall and attended the AP luncheon thirteen years earlier where he famously declared, "I'm not a crook." Feeling loose and confident after the 1986 speech, Nixon turned to the audience for questions, something he avoided in his later White House years. Naturally, people wanted to talk about Watergate. One member of the audience stood up and asked the former president what he had learned from the debacle. What advice might he give future presidents or, better yet, the current president, who was in the early days of his own debacle, the Iran-Contra affair? Nixon did not skip a beat: *"Just destroy all the tapes,"* he said with a mischievous grin, to a roar of laughter. He was probably only half joking.[2]

Before the sunshine era, destroying government documents was of course illegal, especially, as in Nixon's case, when it obstructed a criminal investigation. The Federal Records Act of 1950 clearly stated that "no federal records may be destroyed" unless an agency obtained prior approval from the National Archives. Even so, executive branch officials after 1950 had little reason to fear prosecution, and mostly, they acted with impunity. In the thick of the Watergate investigation, for example, White House counsel John Dean admitted to destroying cables connecting President John F. Kennedy to South Vietnamese president Ngô Đình Diệm's coup and assasination. During the Kennedy and Johnson administrations, shredding Vietnam-related documents was customary in the Defense Department. Daniel Ellsberg, then working at DOD, recalled warming up to his very own "burn bag," something everyone seemed to have, the contents of which no one questioned:

> On the other side of the desk was what I was informed was a burn bag, a huge paper sack that came up to my waist, heavy brown paper stiff enough to stand up by itself, top edges folded back, to take classified trash paper, anything I discarded. . . . For the first half hour I was diffident about discarding secret documents, but before long I was throwing them into the bag with abandon. The bag had been filled by midday, was taken away to be burned somewhere in the basement and replaced by two more.

Although it was probably filled with copies of already existing documents, the temptations of the burn bag were difficult to resist.[3]

Nixon and his team burned with abandon, but it was the shredding that did them in. Nixon aide G. Gordon Liddy, one of the main Watergate "plumbers" (to stop leaks), recalled "shredding stuff left and right." John Ehrlichman, Nixon's assistant for domestic affairs and the head of the plumbers unit, asked White House counsel John Dean to shred documents related to the break-in, as well as forged government cables and files stolen from whistle-blower Ellsberg's psychiatrist's office. Although Dean balked, L. Patrick Gray, the acting director of the FBI, complied. Nixon himself, of course, got into trouble when investigators discovered the president had asked his secretary to erase sections of his (now infamous) tapes. When Nixon in 1986 said, "Just destroy the tapes!," he was probably thinking about how foolish he had been in not asking her to destroy all of them.[4]

The new sunshine laws likely reined in some of the illegal behaviors by making document preservation rules and their associated penalties even more explicit. The laws—and the political conflicts out of which they grew—also raised public awareness about transparency and secrecy. Although the changes increased the real and perceived costs of illegally destroying government information, we cannot accurately estimate the breadth of sunshine-era destruction or systematically compare the administrations. Government secrecy is already inherently difficult to study. Secrecy about shredding is even trickier, as shredders take great care to hide their tracks and to minimize accomplices and witnesses. As Nixon said in 1986, "You can't be too careful" when going this route. However, by assembling leaks, confessions, and substantiated accusations, a mosaic of America's post-Nixon shredding history begins to emerge.

The Shredding Party

Coincidentally, a few months after Nixon's "just destroy all the tapes" joke, senior Reagan-Bush officials found themselves hunched over a shredder in an office corridor in the Old Executive Office Building, desperately destroying incriminating documents. Inside the office door, DOJ lawyers pored over files related to the Iran-Contra affair, the illegal arms-trading operation made public after the Nicaraguan government intercepted a spy plane carrying weapons to the right-wing Contra guerrillas in October 1986. Lt. Col. Oliver North, who coordinated the operation out of the White House, later told Congress about what happened that day in Washington: "They [the lawyers] were sitting in my office, and the shredder was right outside, and I walked out and shredded documents . . . they were sitting in my office reading, and I'd finish a document and . . . I'd walk up and I'd go out and shred it. They could hear it. The shredder was right outside the door." Although North, his secretary Fawn Hall, and National Security Adviser John Poindexter had planned their "shredding party" in advance, the intensifying scrutiny pushed it forward. The group moved at such a furious pace that, at one point, they jammed the machine, trying to shred eighteen pages at the same time. Their desperation, along with some arrogance, convinced them it was appropriate to call the government's Crisis Management Center, which quickly sent a technician to fix the machine.[5]

When the lawyers reading the files took breaks, the "party" moved from shredder to computer. Thousands of startlingly frank e-mails needed to be deleted—750 from North, 5,012 from Poindexter. In their day-to-day work on Iran-Contra and other matters, the men came to believe the White House's e-mail system was largely a back-channel method of communication, immune to records laws. They called the network their "Private Blank Check." As a result, the e-mails contained much juicier details than their more carefully crafted but still incriminating memos. Poindexter, North, and Hall worked feverishly to delete everything they could.[6]

After news broke about the operation (that is, the administration's illegal support of the Contras, along with its illegal arms trading with the Iranians), Reagan fired the shredding party and pretended he was out of the loop. North and Poindexter were later convicted as felons, although the DC appeals court vacated the convictions on Fifth Amendment grounds (self-implication). All along the way, they maintained their innocence. "I don't believe I ever did anything that was criminal," North (non)confessed to Congress, where he was offered limited immunity in exchange for honest testimony. In former National Security Adviser Robert McFarlane's view, North acted as a patriot, shredding documents only to protect his boss: "I took it [the shredding] not as an act of malice, but just a statement to me that he [North] was going to make sure that I [McFarlane] wasn't hurt. And I took it as a statement of a subordinate trying to be loyal." For McFarlane, only North's intentions mattered, not that he acted criminally. Well-intentioned officials, by that logic, should be given some slack under the law.[7]

During the trials, prosecutors obtained thousands of memos and cables the defendants had tried to push down the memory hole. One, marked "for your eyes only," asked its recipient in no uncertain terms to "destroy this memo" after reading it. Another, an intelligence "finding" signed by Reagan, implicated Israel as a conduit for the delivery of eighteen Hawk antiaircraft missiles to Iran, in exchange for hostages and cash for the Contras. When the Iran-Contra scandal erupted, Poindexter tossed it into his burn bag, right after a meeting with Reagan and Attorney General Edwin Meese, in which the president ordered Meese to develop the most forgiving historical narrative possible. The surviving copy of the document proved to be rather inconvenient for that narrative's credibility. On the same day, North showed Poindexter a notebook further linking the president to the illegal covert operations. As Poindexter later recalled, "I had the impression that he was going to destroy that notebook. . . . I didn't tell him not to." About a month earlier, after the Nicaraguan government shot down the Contra supply plane, another National Security Council staffer had shown Poindexter incriminating memos. The staffer later remembered that he left the meeting with Poindexter with the "clear implication [that] we would probably be better off without those memos." Poindexter later admitted all of the shredding was an effort to save Reagan from political embarrassment.[8]

Shredding Secrets: When Blocking Access Is Not Enough

Although North and his backers denied the shredding party had acted criminally or even inappropriately, federal law clearly stated otherwise. The fact that North and Poindexter were convicted as felons shows that the justice system had the potential to hold even senior officials accountable. However, the special legal privileges they enjoyed also highlighted the limits of that accountability system. They avoided prison largely because of their ability to win far-reaching immunity in exchange for honest congressional testimony— something most felons cannot do. A few years later, former defense secretary Caspar Weinberger and five others accused in the Iran-Contra scandal also enjoyed special accountability-defying privileges: presidential pardons, just like Nixon's.[9]

The pardons and the immunity privileges reminded many Americans, including Iran-Contra prosecutor Lawrence E. Walsh, that "powerful people with powerful allies can commit serious crimes in high office—deliberately abusing the public trust without consequence." None saw the inside of a jail cell or suffered serious consequences, beyond a few more dings to their already dinged reputations. Still, they came closer to real justice than any law-breaking officials would ever want. The shredding party's brush with the law underscored the high stakes involved in illegal document destruction. Nixon's more consequential episode—the metastasizing scandal, the looming impeachment, and his ultimate resignation—cast an even larger shadow. Getting caught destroying state secrets was serious business. Senior officials like North and McFarlane may have sincerely believed they acted out of patriotic impulses, but they knew they had to go to extraordinary lengths to hide their illegitimate secrets, destroy them when disclosure became a possibility, and finally cover their tracks. Whatever good intentions they thought they had, they could not let incriminating or politically embarrassing information into the public sphere. When the existing set of secrecy tools were too weak, when the information seemed too vulnerable to scrutiny, Nixon, North, and Poindexter turned to desperate measures, just like many others across the sunshine era.[10]

National Security Archive versus Reagan, Bush, and Clinton

As Washington, DC, prepared for President-Elect George H. W. Bush's inauguration in January 1989, federal workers readied boxes of computer hard drives and backup tapes for their looming destruction. The boxes contained the handpicked exceptions to a seemingly rule-bound Reagan-Bush administration, then working with National Archives and Records Administration officials to preserve and archive documents in accordance with relevant federal records laws (for example, the Presidential Records Act). Somewhere within the pile lay backups of e-mails the Iran-Contra shredding party believed they had permanently deleted on that desperate late November Thursday in 1986.[11]

Oliver North and his coconspirators knew the White House kept backup tapes of all official e-mails, but they felt confident knowing technicians erased the tapes every two weeks. They did not expect someone like Lt. Col. Patrick M. McGovern to ditch the usual routine. With haste and foresight, McGovern, a military commander in charge of information security, made at least two copies of the tapes right around the time of North's and Poindexter's departures. At some point in 1987, FBI investigators rummaged through the tapes, gathering copies of incriminating e-mails that later appeared in the official Tower Commission's Iran-Contra report and the ongoing legal disputes.[12]

But investigators must have missed some important e-mails because Reagan-Bush officials later blocked further access to the historical treasure trove McGovern had saved. However, probably because of the intense scrutiny of the Iran-Contra scandal, the administration chose not to destroy the tapes, instead letting them sit for another year in some remote executive branch office. Once the political heat subsided, they would have more chances to destroy the evidence. Soon before Bush's 1989 inauguration, Reagan's last national security adviser, then Lt. Gen. Colin Powell, gave the final orders for the tapes' destruction. White House officials, possibly including Powell, had somehow convinced the NARA Office of Presidential Libraries director, John Fawcett, that the e-mails should not be considered protected federal and presidential records, notwithstanding all of the historically significant ones released earlier. When confronted about his office's decision to dispose of the tapes, Fawcett actually likened federal e-mails to "telephone message slips," as in "While you were out. . . . " NARA and the White House quietly proceeded with the plan to destroy the tapes during the transfer of power.[13]

If not for the curiosity and initiative of Eddie Becker, a researcher from the National Security Archive, the plan would likely have succeeded. Becker called a NARA contact and asked about the e-mails' fate. To their credit, NARA staffers responded with the truth, saying the tapes were scheduled for destruction two days later. After Fawcett refused to reconsider, National Security Archive director Scott Armstrong and his team hurriedly filed a restraining order request at the DC district court. As a kind of insurance policy for the e-mails, the National Security Archive also submitted FOIA requests, assuming federal judges would object to NARA destoying documents identified by FOIA requesters.[14]

At 5:15 p.m. on inauguration eve, the court opened up the proceedings in *Scott Armstrong et al. v. Ronald Reagan et al.* As a reflection of how seriously Reagan-Bush officials viewed the conflict, they sent John Bolton, the acting attorney general. Bolton strongly defended the administration's plan to destroy the tapes, comparing it to taking pictures off a wall before an office move:

BOLTON: "Your Honor, the outgoing staff members of the White House, who will be leaving tomorrow, are doing what anyone does when they leave one job to go to another. They are taking the pictures off their walls. They are cleaning out their desks and they are eliminating . . . "

THE COURT: "They [the plaintiffs] are not seeking a restraining order against taking pictures off the wall."

BOLTON: "I understand that, Your Honor, but what is going on here is not some sinister conspiracy. What is going on here is the normal termination of one staff to give room for the other staff to come in . . . "

THE COURT: "That may be true, but what is happening to the material that's the subject of this litigation?"

BOLTON: "It is being prepared for deletion."

THE COURT: "What?" [that is, "Still?!"]

Bolton continued by saying Reagan-Bush wanted nothing more than to ensure an "orderly transfer of power": "It would be as if the halls of the White House were filled with furniture from the outgoing adminstration." Thus, it was "nothing more than normal housecleaning." Finding Bolton's arguments unpersuasive, senior district court judge Barrington Parker issued a restraining order against Reagan, Bush, and the NSC, giving the plaintiffs exactly what they sought. Though Bolton confessed in court that "some deletions have [already] been made over the course of the last several days," he pledged that the White House would honor the ruling. Judge Parker did not penalize the administration for the fait accompli deletions.[15]

Because the National Security Archive and coplaintiffs only won a temporary restraining order, the case dragged on through the Bush-Quayle years. The tapes survived the entire presidential term, but the administration blocked access to them as the case proceeded. Once Bush-Quayle lost its reelection bid in 1992, senior officials began to view the tapes' existence with great alarm, for Clinton, Gore, and other Democrats would soon have access to thousands of potentially scandalous Iran-Contra e-mails—or anything else lurking in the cache of documents Reagan-Bush almost destroyed in 1989. Worse (for the Republicans), Judge Charley R. Richey on January 6, 1993, granted the National Security Archive's request to widen the lawsuit to include backup tapes from the Bush-Quayle administration. DOJ lawyers offered little more than rehashed arguments from 1989. E-mails were fundamentally different, they argued, nothing like printed memos or other protected records. Thus, there was no reason to protect them. The judges were again unpersuaded and ruled against the defendants, keeping the plaintiffs' hopes alive. The defendants found that an intolerable decision.[16]

On the night before Clinton's inauguration, senior Bush-Quayle officials ordered NARA employees to pack up 4,852 tapes so they could be ferried out of Washington the next morning. Government workers at the Old Executive Office Building carted the boxes into rented vans, the contents of each box hurriedly scribbled onto scraps of paper. The illegal act—seizing sequestered evidence at the center of a pending lawsuit—was given some legal cover, however weak, the next morning. On Clinton's Inauguration Day, Bush negotiated what he hoped was a conclusive deal with the government's head archivist, NARA's Donald Wilson. The deal the two struck did what the courts would not do: it affirmed the exceptionalism of electronic messages and gave Bush "exclusive legal control" of the tapes. Wilson, who had supported Reagan-Bush's plan to destroy the e-mails, seemed to care little about directly interfering with an ongoing federal lawsuit. "These are just some computer backup tapes," he later proclaimed, pretending not to see what the fuss was all about. Around three weeks later, Wilson announced his resignation from the NARA, stating only that he had seized an exciting new opportunity far from Washington. In April 1993, he started his new job: executive director of the George Bush Presidential Library (and Foundation), then under construction at Texas A&M University, with a salary of $129,000 a year (equal to about $205,000 in 2012 dollars).[17]

About a month later, the court rejected the deal, making Wilson the only lasting beneficiary. The deal violated the Federal Records Act, the court ruled, and it interfered with an active lawsuit. Despite the setback, Reagan, Bush, and their supporters found what seemed an unlikely ally, the new administration. Not only would Clinton-Gore keep *Armstrong v. Executive Office of the President* alive by picking up where Bush-Quayle left off, the new administration also would publicly back the questionable deal between Bush and Wilson. In addition, it failed to properly preserve the tapes as outlined by law. By May 1993, many of the tapes were deteriorating or inexplicably damaged, and the administration did nothing to arrest their decline. For that, the court charged the White House with civil contempt.[18]

Despite the new energies Clinton-Gore put into the case, the DC appeals court in August 1993 unanimously affirmed the district court's ruling that the tapes fell under the purview of the FRA. Perhaps anticipating the same result from the Supreme Court, administration officials chose not to appeal. But they were hardly ready to give up. They may have lost the battle in the courts for this set of NSC records, but they would win the war with executive power.[19]

In March 1994, the administration announced NSC records were no longer subject to FOIA requests. Since 1947, the NSC—officially an "agency"—had advised presidents and agencies across the government on foreign policy matters. Clinton's 1994 decree unilaterally redefined the NSC, declaring it no longer an agency but part of the Executive Office of the President and thus under the purview of the Presidential Records Act. That meant unclassified NSC records would be immune from FOIA requests for five years after Clinton left office, and classified records could not be sought (with or without redactions) until January 2013. Clinton, perhaps trying to distinguish himself as more transparent than his Republican predecessors, argued that he only made the change reluctantly, saying the administration had to do it because the appeals court forced its hands. Besides, officials argued, they would allow the NSC to "voluntarily" disclose information they deemed appropriate for public consumption.[20]

New FOIA exceptions typically spring from congressional or court action, a fact not lost on Judge Richey. Clinton's move to insulate the NSC, he ruled, was "arbitrary and capricious" and "contrary to history, past practice, and the law." Richey gave the administration less than two weeks to develop a new plan. Instead, Clinton-Gore appealed—and won.[21]

The DC court of appeals heard the final set of arguments in *Armstrong v. Executive Office* in September 1995. A year later, a divided (two-to-one) court ruled to overturn Richey's decision, giving Clinton-Gore a major and rare victory in the legal fight that had lasted seven and a half years. (The Supreme Court denied *cert* to the National Security Archive's appeal.) Judge Douglas Ginsburg argued, "Because the NSC operates in close proximity to the President, who chairs it, and because the NSC does not exercise substantial independent authority, we conclude that the NSC is not an agency within the meaning of the FOIA." For the first time since 1947, when President Harry S. Truman created the NSC, the organization's records would enjoy the same kind of protections granted to the Offices of the President and Vice President (and later, the Council of Economic Advisers and the Office of Administration). President Clinton, reluctant or not, discursively constructed another layer to the secrecy regime.[22]

Judicial Watch versus (Clinton-Gore) Department of Commerce

A year and a half into Clinton-Gore's first term, rumors swirled around Washington about shady political fund-raising practices in the Department of Commerce. One story had senior DOC officials offering corporations coveted spots on international trade missions in exchange for donations to the

Democratic National Committee and Clinton-Gore's reelection campaign. It was a simple quid pro quo: Democrats got the money, and businesses could tap into new markets, build networks, and enjoy government sponsorship. Not exactly the kind of news conservative Republicans would take passively. Judicial Watch, a conservative legal and education foundation, filed a FOIA request for records related to the trade missions. After months of waiting, followed by testy conversations with uncooperative DOC officials, JW sued in January 1995. Four months later, Judge Royce C. Lamberth of the DC court of appeals ordered the DOC to comply, dismissing officials' claims that they were already working hard to answer the FOIA request. What happened next was a case either of regrettable bureaucratic negligence, as the government claimed, or of frantic officials obstructing justice.[23]

As part of her work as senior aide to DOC secretary Ronald H. Brown, Melinda Yee took detailed notes during the trade missions. If anyone had documents to satisfy JW's FOIA request, it was Yee. Nevertheless, DOC FOIA officials working on the case appeared to strain themselves to avoid Yee, even to the point where they pretended not to see her sitting at her desk when they visited her officemate (this happened several times). During all of the coming and going in July 1995, Yee threw the notes away. She later claimed she was unaware of the federal lawsuit and court order.[24]

Around the same time, Yee retained the counsel of John R. Tisdale, a former Arkansas law partner of White House deputy counsel Bruce R. Lindsey. Her decision to lawyer up—or, more likely, her supervisors' decision—probably had something to do with the fact that, along with her notes, she grabbed a batch of fund-raising documents on the way to the burn bag. The White House connection was probably no coincidence, and having an attorney of Tisdale's caliber likely helped a lot. Tisdale successfully persuaded Judge Lamberth to believe the government's argument. "I don't think we've seen evidence beyond mere negligence so far," Lamberth concluded in December 1996.[25]

Two years later, he changed his mind. He had long nursed serious doubts about Yee's testimony. On top of that, later depositions revealed a "flurry of document shredding" at the DOC after Secretary Brown died in an airplane crash in Croatia in April 1996. Brown's scheduler, Dalia Traynham, testified that Brown's senior assistants, Barbara Schmitz and Melanie Long, asked her to shred documents after the crash. Former deputy undersecretary of commerce David Rothkopf also admitted he took sensitive documents when he left the DOC for another job, probably because the files "would be beyond the reach of [JW] or other curious parties," as an increasingly skeptical Judge

Lamberth put it. Additionally, the DOC sent a trove of trade mission documents to Howard University for a commemorative "Ron Brown, Jr., collection" established after Brown's untimely death. According to officials, the transfer of photographs, audio recordings, and videotapes put those materials out of FOIA's reach for many months. But Howard University refused to confirm the DOC's narrative, even a year later. Indeed, the university *never had a Ron Brown collection*. Finally, Brown's former business partner, Nolanda B. Hill, told the court that White House officials ordered the secretary to "slow-pedal" the DOC's search for trade mission documents and that Brown himself confided in her that seats on the trips were, in fact, being sold for $50,000 to deep-pocketed campaign contributors. For Judge Lamberth, the evidence "strongly substantiate[d] the claim that the agency was deliberately destroying and jettisoning documents."[26]

Faced with the growing pile of incriminating evidence and hoping to stop the bleeding, the DOC took the very unusual step of asking for a snap guilty "judgment against itself." By contrast, JW proclaimed its "vehement opposition" to the DOC's request to be judged guilty, hoping for more secrets to surface. Ultimately, the federal court did find the DOC guilty, concluding officials had "illegally destroyed and removed from its custody responsive documents, apparently in an attempt to circumvent the disclosure requirements of the FOIA and the orders of this Court." Yet despite all of the incriminating evidence, involving multiple DOC officials, Judge Lamberth punished just one DOC attorney.[27]

The Bush-Cheney Administration

As this book has extensively demonstrated, officials in the Bush-Cheney administration used a variety of methods—some they invented, others they borrowed—to circumvent open government laws they believed unduly constrained executive power. When that proved difficult, top officials developed other means to uphold secrecy. Sometimes, the methods they used were not at all illegal but plainly defiant. For instance, Cheney boasted to Bob Woodward in 2004: "I don't keep a diary" or use e-mail, "and I don't write letters." He also suggested, with a tinge of regret, that others in the government probably did the same, to the detriment of the historical record: "The investigations that have occurred over the years, the role of the special prosecutors and so forth have dried up a major source for history." Cheney also admitted off-the-record verbal communications were used for evasive reasons. One way of circumventing the rules thus involved changing communication practices so as not to leave a paper trail. At other times, Bush-Cheney officials' methods were plainly illegal. Though they were not the first to destroy documents, the available evidence suggests they did take the practice to new heights.[28]

The Ethics Department's "Missing" E-mails

Amid all of the fanfare surrounding the November 25, 2001, capture of John Walker Lindh—the so-called American Taliban—the Bush-Cheney administration made its first foray into illegal e-mail deletion (as far as we know). Lindh's capture in Afghanistan was hugely exciting for administration officials. As detainee number 001, he was the first feather in their cap in the war on terror. Moreover, Lindh's US citizenship made him an especially loathesome public enemy. Photographs of the CIA's trophy went viral, showing the scrawny, bearded, dirty, and dazed twenty-year-old strapped naked to a stretcher with duct tape, with a "Shit Head" sign over his blindfold. Instead of feeling revulsion about citizen Lindh's treatment, most Americans wanted more: 71 percent approved of stripping him of his constitutional due process rights, allowing, for instance, the use of self-incriminating statements he made before being allowed a lawyer.[29]

A few details of Lindh's capture and treatment are central to the story. After a brief encounter with Afghan warlord Abdul Rashid Dostum's troops and then CIA agents, who beat and threatened to kill him unless he divulged information, an injured Lindh languished for a week in a frozen, flooded, feces-laden prison basement as Taliban fought off Northern Alliance soldiers. One of the CIA agents, Johnny "Mike" Spann, died in the battle, which began after Taliban detainees, who had been double-crossed by Dostum, staged an unsuccessful prison revolt. Lindh, along with about 100 others, surrendered to US forces on December 1. He asked for but was denied a lawyer. Lindh's parents in California, however, independently hired one on December 3, even though they had not spoken with their son.[30]

James Brosnahan immediately notified the government of his role as Lindh's lawyer. He contacted the offices of John Ashcroft (Justice), Donald Rumsfeld (Defense), Colin Powell (State), and George Tenet (CIA) and requested a meeting with his detained client. For backup, he asked the Red Cross to inform Lindh that his parents had hired a lawyer. The administration, however, blocked all communications. Senior officials were actively debating treason

and terrorism charges, as well as the broader issue of treating terrorism suspects as part of a separate criminal class. Ultimately, they chose to deprive
Lindh of his due process rights and all conventional prisoner-of-war protections. This was an unconventional war. His lawyer would have to wait.[31]

Meanwhile, Lindh endured brutal conditions—officials kept him blindfolded, malnourished, and sleep deprived inside a freezing, windowless steel
shipping container. His only respite came when comparatively more lawful
FBI agents arrived to interrogate him. On December 9, one of those agents
finally read Lindh his Miranda rights, although the agent did add, "Of course,
there are no lawyers here" to the words about a prisoner's right to an attorney. He also never mentioned that Lindh actually had an attorney who was
actively trying to see him. During the lawyerless December 9 interview, the
FBI elicited a confession from Lindh. Some agents immediately recognized
the problem: any lawyer, let alone a highly skilled one like Brosnahan, could
easily attack the credibility of that kind of confession. In fact, two days earlier, FBI agent John De Pue had contacted the DOJ from Afghanistan about
the very same issues. Were lawyer-free interrogations legally appropriate?, he
asked. Would the confession survive?[32]

Jesselyn Radack, a 1995 Yale Law graduate recruited into the DOJ's Professional Responsibility Advisory Office (PRAO), took De Pue's call. After
consulting with her colleagues, Radack sent De Pue an e-mail on Friday, December 7, informing him that "Walker's [Lindh's] father retained counsel for
him" and that she had "consulted with a Senior Legal Advisor here at PRAO
and we don't think you can have the FBI agent question Walker [Lindh]. It
would be a pre-indictment, custodial overt interview, which is not authorized
by law." De Pue's response suggested the FBI got the message: "Thanks much.
I have passed you [sic] assessment along and will keep you posted on this."
When Radack returned to work on Monday, December 10, she learned from
De Pue that the FBI disregarded Radack's advice. They continued their e-mail
correspondence:

> RADACK: "You just advised that the Deputy Legal Advisor of the FBI stated
> that an agent went and interviewed Walker over the weekend, not
> knowing that Walker was a represented person. . . . The interview may
> have to be sealed or only used for national security purposes; however,
> I don't have enough information yet to make that recommendation."
> DE PUE: "Ugh. We are trying to figure out what actually transpired and
> what, if anything, Walker said. It may well be that the questioning was

for intelligence purposes and that he was questioned as any other prisoner of war would be."

DE PUE: "If what you are telling us is true—and I am sure that it is—the FBI needs to b [sic] alerted at once."

De Pue alerted the FBI, and the message traveled at least as high as Michael Chertoff, who was the DOJ's assistant attorney general for the Criminal Division (and later the second secretary for Homeland Security). Despite the questionable legal methods, the DOJ decided to proceed, building a case against Lindh based largely on the dubious confession. To handle the lawyer issue, Bush-Cheney officials chose to brazenly dissemble. Aschroft stepped up to the microphone at a Janaury 15, 2002, press conference and said, "The subject here is entitled to choose his own lawyer, and to our knowledge has not chosen a lawyer at this time." Three weeks later, Ashcroft insisted Lindh's rights were being "carefully, scrupulously honored." Lindh ultimately waited fifty-four days for the DOJ to honor his constitutional right to a lawyer, despite having asked for one right away and despite Brosnahan's insistent efforts to meet with him.[33]

Because the e-mail trail so clearly contradicted Ashcroft's statements, Radack tactfully pressed the matter within the DOJ. When that went nowhere and subtle signs from supervisors told her to back off, she relented and moved on to other cases. Weeks later, she learned the supervisors filed an unscheduled work performance evaluation on her. Months earlier, they had praised her work and recommended a raise. The new evaluation was harsh but vague in its criticisms, questioning her judgment and fitness to work at PRAO. It was also unsigned, indicating her supervisors anticipated she might sue. One of her bosses personally advised her to quit in light of the new review. She wouldn't want the review to become official and forever follow her around, telling future employers she was a rabble-rouser, would she?[34]

The evaluation completely took Radack by surprise. She had not touched the Lindh case for weeks. Besides, it was not as if she leaked the e-mails to the press or loudly or aggressively pressed the matter at work. So she decided to stay, confident and committed to her role as a legal ethics adviser. An interaction with the lead prosecutor on the Lindh case a few weeks later helped explain the abrupt turn of events. Randy Bellows, the prosecutor, e-mailed Radack on March 7 to fulfill the court's order to gather all DOJ communications related to the case. Her PRAO supervisors had submitted two e-mails, he wrote. Did she remember writing more, including any giving legal advice to the FBI? Yes, she replied, adding that the PRAO should have submitted all documents in hard copy, as the law required. She searched around the office.[35]

Everything was gone, including her e-mails and forms she had filed several weeks earlier. With help from tech support, she recovered the e-mails, and with those, she prepared a memo with hard copy attachments. When she delivered the file to Claudia Flynn, a supervisor, Radack asked if she should send the file to prosecutor Bellows or directly to the court. Flynn said to do neither: "No, *I'll* handle it." Radack had reason to doubt her boss's sincerity, for Flynn previously had insisted she "sent everything that was in the file." Once Radack reconstructed and delivered the file, Flynn grumbled to her, "Now I have to explain why [PRAO] shouldn't look bad."[36]

Disgusted, Radack resigned, and she was soon offered a position at the law firm Hawkins, Delafield, and Wood. But the administration was not through with her just yet. After Michael Isikoff published the e-mails in *Newsweek*—she has admitted to leaking them—the government attacked her reputation and forced her out of her new job. They told the law firm Radack was under investigation for vaguely defined "criminal" activity. And it was not enough to push her out of her DOJ ethics job for being too ethical or her new job after leaving the government. The Bush-Cheney administration also placed her on the no-fly list—a list developed for suspected terrorists but increasingly used for whistle-blowing lawyers and political dissidents.[37]

The OLC's Missing E-mails

The 2004 leak of secret legal memos from the DOJ's Office of Legal Counsel authorizing torture generated torrents of criticism from legal scholars and human rights activists around the world. As described in chapter 5, the Bush-Cheney White House brushed off the attacks by downplaying the memos' importance, despite the fact executive branch officials could use them to claim immunity, including from criminal prosecution. White House counsel Alberto Gonzales argued the memos merely explored "broad legal theories"; they were "irrelevant and unnecessary to support any action taken by the President." Deputy Attorney General James B. Comey offered similar arguments, saying, for instance, that Jay Bybee's infamous memo narrowly defining torture was just "abstract academic theory"; besides, he added, "we're scrubbing the whole thing." By contrast, Bybee's former OLC colleague John Yoo continued to defend the memos' ideas, as well as their legal power. Thus, in December 2005, he argued no treaty and, in some cases, no law could stop the president, as commander in chief during wartime, from doing what he believed was necessary—including "crushing the testicles of a person's [a detainee's] child." "I think it depends on why the President thinks he needs to do that," Yoo concluded.[38]

Republican Party control of both houses of Congress in 2004 severely limited the potential for serious investigations into the memos, as well as actual abuse and torture of detainees by Bush-Cheney officials. There were, however, a few Republicans, like Rep. Frank Wolf (R-VA), who were troubled enough by the so-called torture memos that they challenged their own party's administration in a climate of heightened political fear, risking being labeled "soft on terrorism." Almost immediately after the legal memos story broke, Wolf sent a letter to the DOJ's inspector general and its Office of Professional Responsibility to demand an investigation. One of the OPR's first steps when opening the inquiry in July 2004 was to ask the new OLC head, Assistant Attorney General Jack Goldsmith, to turn over all records related to Bybee's memo, including the still-classified document itself. Goldsmith sent Steven Bradbury, then the principal deputy assistant attorney general, to meet with the head of the OPR, H. Marshall Jarrett. Bradbury arrived, Bybee's memo in hand, but delivered an unusual request. According to the OPR, Bradbury "asked us not to pursue our request for additional material," akin to how a commanding officer would order a subordinate to "stand down." The OPR said it would "consider the issues raised by Bradbury" but again asked the OLC for all relevant documents.[39]

The cat-and-mouse game continued, as the OLC delayed and then offered a "relatively small number of emails, files, and draft documents" and, after another OPR request, a little bit more. The OLC's reticence slowed the OPR's investigation in more ways than one: "We were told that most of Yoo's email records had been deleted and were not recoverable. Philbin's email records from July 2002 through August 5, 2002—the time period in which the Bybee Memo was completed and the Classified Bybee Memo . . . was created—had also been deleted and were reportedly not recoverable." Perhaps trying to soften perceptions about the OLC's suspicious acts, Goldsmith's office backtracked but just a little: "Although we were initially advised that Goldsmith's records had been deleted, we were later told that they had been recovered and we were given access to them." There might have been a legitimate technical mishap, but the revelations certainly suggested the possibility the OLC deleted e-mails to obstruct the investigation. Remarkably, the OPR barely seemed to care, reporting the news of the missing e-mails in a footnote.[40]

And then there was the puzzling delay in the report's publication. The OPR held the report for over five years, waiting until 2009 to share it with Congress and another six months before publishing it (in a late Friday afternoon "document dump"). By that time, the OPR's recommendation that the DOJ charge Yoo and Bybee with "intentional professional misconduct" had little purchase in an Obama-Biden administration intent on "look[ing] forward and not backwards" on any alleged crimes and improprieties of the Bush-Cheney administration. The five-year delay also limited any opportunities to hold Bush-Cheney or the Republican Party responsible in the 2004, 2006, and 2008 elections.[41]

Once the report was finally published, scholars and journalists who had waited for years to read it pored over its contents. It was hard not to notice that remarkable footnote on page 5. Although the OPR downplayed the missing e-mails, NARA director Paul M. Wester was concerned enough to send a letter to the DOJ asking for more details, reminding Justice that his agency was obligated to investigate "allegations of unlawful or accidental removal, defacing, alteration, or destruction," under the Code of Federal Regulations. As Georgetown Law professor David Luban reported around the same time, government lawyers' e-mails are *always* stored and are *always* recoverable because of the DOJ's e-mail system. Citizens for Responsibility and Ethics in Washington (CREW) urged the DOJ to consider a criminal investigation, arguing the e-mail deletions violated the Federal Records Act. As CREW noted in a letter to Wester, OLC lawyers have "an unambiguous obligation to retain," as outlined in the OLC manual, "all notes, documents, and e-mails that are important to understanding a decision in the office."[42]

Pressure on the DOJ grew after Sen. Patrick Leahy held a Judiciary Committee hearing on the OPR report, in which he challenged the report's credibility. How could the inquiry be complete when "investigators were denied access to key witnesses and documents"? "In fact," he stated, "my first question to the Justice Department witness today is going to be, 'Where are Mr. Yoo's e-mails, which, by law'—by law—'are required by law to be maintained'?" During his questioning of Acting Deputy Attorney General Gary G. Grindler—Obama's appointee—Leahy insisted the OPR's footnote was a serious matter indeed:

> The U.S. Code is very, very clear about these records [having] to be retained. In fact, it has penalties provided by law [18 U.S.C. Section 641

and 18 U.S.C. Section 2071] for the removal or destruction of these records. . . . The American people have a right to know, but we also have a right to know why these critical records were deleted. Why were they kept from the Federal investigators? Has the Department opened an investigation into the circumstances surrounding the destruction of the e-mails?

Grindler promised the senator and the committee he would direct the DOJ's technology staff to try to retrieve the missing e-mails.[43]

The DOJ's official response to Leahy's and NARA's request for more information finally arrived on March 25, 2010. The letter essentially restated Grindler's claim that the DOJ's tech experts would look into the matter. Ten months later, the DOJ reported back to NARA, saying it had "satisfied its obligations under the Federal Records Act" because it "determined that OLC has retained 'adequate and proper documentation' of the conclusions in the memoranda." The DOJ also found "backup tapes" that allowed officials to recover "additional emails," although it was vague about what percentage of the deleted ones were found. Why were OLC lawyers (or their supervisors) allowed to delete them in the first place? We don't know, and we won't investigate, said the DOJ: "We have not, and cannot, especially given the passage of time, determine whether an unauthorized destruction of records occurred." For unknown reasons, Wester and the NARA expressed their satisfaction with the government's efforts. The DOJ, despite the problematic "passage of time" that follows all crimes, continued thousands of other criminal investigations and prosecutions.[44]

Post 9/11 Detainee Videotapes, Part 1

As described in earlier chapters, the Bush-Cheney administration arrested and detained 762 Muslim, Arab, and South Asian foreign nationals after 9/11 (the PENTTBOM investigation), most of them picked up around New York City on minor charges, such as traffic offenses, various misdemeanors, and identification fraud. Allegations proved false but still gave authorities the pretext to dump hundreds of suspected terrorists into jail without evidence of any wrongdoing. In one case, police officers stopped three men in Manhattan for a traffic violation on September 15, 2001. The officers found "plans to a public school" inside their car—*clearly they must be plotting an attack!* On that suspicion alone, the police arrested the three and treated them as likely Al Qaeda operatives, even after their employer confirmed their story that they were construction workers building the school.[45]

Authorities forced eighty-four "high interest" men—ostensibly the most dangerous—into Brooklyn's Metropolitan Detention Center, a high-security facility run by the US Bureau of Prisons (BOP). Contrary to typical practice, the DOJ implemented a "no bond" policy, as well as a "communication blackout," preventing the detainees from contacting lawyers and family members to post bail or for any other reason. Foreign nationals picked up for similar offenses (for instance, traffic violations) before 9/11 typically could post bond or otherwise avoid imprisonment. Relatively few had to endure Immigration and Naturalization Service facilities while awaiting hearings, surely not a desirable option but decidedly better than a place like MDC.[46]

The suspected terrorists needed to be monitored day and night, BOP assistant director Michael Cooksey told BOP regional directors on September 13 and 20. The BOP's northeast region director, David Rardin, passed the order down to his wardens, including the one running MDC, who outfitted all detainee cells with video cameras by mid-October. The new policy was apparently intended to prevent Al Qaeda members from falsely accusing prison guards and interrogators of physical abuse. British officials had recently shared with their US counterparts a prized discovery—Al Qaeda's "training manual"—from a Manchester, England, counterterrorism raid in May 2000. The 180-page document, "Military Studies in the Jihad against the Tyrants," covered everything from explosives to Islamic jihadist ethics (such as no drinking or fornicating allowed, even for would-be suicide bombers). The chapter on handling capture and detention advised students to distract officials by complaining of unlawful abuse, which would gum up the justice system and slow prosecutions. The cameras wound up making prison life better for some of the detainees; the monitoring system seemed to curb abuse and mistreatment by prison officials. One detainee remembered a prison guard saying, "If the camera wasn't on, I would have bashed your face. The camera is your best friend."[47]

Yet even with the cameras rolling, some twenty MDC guards could not help themselves. They twisted arms, hands, and fingers. They physically restrained the men for very long periods, pulling and stepping on their leg chains along the way just for painful effect. They kept prisoners awake at all hours of the day and night with bright lights, making many sick from sleep deprivation. Guards slammed detainees against walls, in and out of cells. The guards even adopted a favorite spot for wall slamming: against an American flag T-shirt hanging on a concrete wall (on the shirt: "These colors don't run"). All of this treatment was captured on tape.[48]

The tapes also illegally captured conversations between detainees and their attorneys. Some MDC employees warned prisoners their meetings would be recorded, decreasing the value of those discussions. Attorney General Ashcroft in October 2001 did authorize an exception to the law preventing such monitoring and recording: the DOJ could determine that the surveillance would likely reduce direct threats to national security. The DOJ never invoked the exception for detainee-attorney meetings at MDC.[49]

As the tapes documenting abuses and illegalities piled up, prison officials had to grapple with Regional Director Rardin's inconvenient October announcement ordering wardens to preserve all tapes "indefinitely." Fortunately for the implicated, the BOP replaced Rardin just in time, and the new director revoked his tapes policy right away. The new regional director, Mickey Ray, concluded thirty days' preservation would be enough, except for tapes documenting abuses, because detainees could eventually sue. As directed, MDC officials began to reuse many of the older tapes, exercising a great deal of discretion about the meaning of "abuse." They also took the liberty of destroying selected tapes—a necessary step, they said, to "free up storage space" at the sprawling prison. Director Ray's new rule gave prison officials a possibly fleeting opportunity to destroy the evidence. Who knew if Washington would reverse its policy again?[50]

Once cleared of wrongdoing and released, detainees shared stories of the widespread abuse they experienced and witnessed at MDC. The DOJ's inspector general looked into the matter and confirmed there was "a pattern of physical and verbal abuse"—it was not a matter of a few "bad apples." BOP officials categorically rejected the charges, declaring none of the foreign nationals were mistreated. What a shame, they acknowledged, that there were no videos to prove it. That might have been the end of the story, leaving everyone to speculate whether the BOP told the truth. But DOJ investigators in August 2003 found several hundred tapes that had escaped destruction, in an MDC storage room officials had earlier neglected to mention.[51]

What the tapes documented immediately discredited prison officials' claims and corroborated the detainees' tales of abuse: the wall slammings, the arm and finger twistings, the prolonged ankle shackling. There were also "unexplained gaps" in some of the tapes, indicating the worst parts had been erased. Moreover, MDC officials had failed to report the tapes on inventory forms. Had investigators not stumbled upon the storage room, most people would probably have dismissed the detainees' abuse allegations as terrorist propaganda or dishonest efforts to win financial damages.[52]

The Missing Abu Ghraib Pages

News of the rediscovered MDC tapes appeared and then quickly disappeared from major media sources. Six months later, the leaked photos of abused detainees at the US-run Abu Ghraib prison in Iraq inflamed passions, grabbing headlines for years. The images instantly became iconic and, for critics of Bush-Cheney's war in Iraq and on terror, emblematic: naked, soiled prisoners dragged around by leashes; guards smiling with thumbs up next to piles of naked, bleeding, bent-over, humiliated men; and, most iconic of all, the black-cloaked, hooded figure standing arms outstreched atop a small cardboard box with electric cables hanging from his arms. White House and DOD officials insisted the perpetrators were just a few "bad apples." All of the evidence suggested otherwise.[53]

The military first took Abu Ghraib abuse allegations seriously in January 2004—months before the images were leaked—when Lt. Gen. Ricardo S. Sanchez ordered an internal investigation into the responsible unit, the 800th Military Police Brigade. Sanchez assigned Maj. Gen. Antonio M. Taguba to head the inquiry on January 31. In March 2004, Taguba distributed his secret report, "Article 15-6 Investigation of the 800th Military Police Brigade" ("The Taguba Report"), to a select group at DOD.[54]

Once the photos leaked, members of Congress and human rights organizations demanded that the White House declassify and release Taguba's report. The DOD refused to go that far, but Secretary Rumsfeld did offer the Senate Armed Services Committee (SASC) a copy, with selections from the document's extensive annexes, after he and the chairman of the Joint Chiefs of Staff, Richard Myers, testified at the "Mistreatment of Iraqi Prisoners" hearing on May 7. Public demands for its release already had subsided a bit after it leaked two days earlier, even though what appeared online was a small sample of the full report. Whereas the Taguba Report totaled 6,000 pages, the online versions contained about 50.[55]

As SASC staffers began to sort through what the DOD dropped off, they grew increasingly skeptical. Something just did not look right. There were surely lots of pages in the DOD's binders, but some staffers wondered if they really totaled 6,000 as promised. So they placed the DOD's stack next to 6,000 blank pieces of paper. The difference was obvious. The blank pages towered over the DOD report; at least a third of Taguba's document had never arrived. A little digging revealed the missing pages included memos from senior military officials who investigated the abuse allegations, as well as statements from prison guards, intelligence officials, and witnesses—information crucial to determining the scope of the problem and the proper allocation of blame.[56]

SASC staffers on May 20 contacted the DOD about the missing pages. Lawrence Di Rita, deputy assistant secretary of defense for public affairs, described the conversation: "The committee staff said, hey, we've reviewed this thing and some pages are missing, some pages are out of order, there's some mislabeling." Di Rita cheerfully downplayed the page gap, insisting the DOD would never deliberately withhold crucial documents from the SASC: "What was submitted was what we had. The perception that was left was unfortunate, which is that we were somehow trying to withhold something from the committee. That was certainly not the case." But, for the sake of interbranch comity, the DOD promised to send SASC a CD-ROM with the full report. Plus, the DOD's assistant secretary for legislative affairs, Powell Moore, on May 25 vowed to personally contact General Taguba in Kuwait to ensure the SASC received a "complete and certified copy."[57]

Two weeks later, the SASC chair, Sen. John Warner (R-VA), announced the DOD still had not fulfilled its promise, but he gave the department the benefit of the doubt: "I continue to believe that the Department is complying in good faith with this request, and will continue to monitor its cooperation on these and other matters connected to our oversight of the prisoner abuse situation." Missing still were crucial source documents, including Red Cross reports about Abu Ghraib, as well as a memo from Maj. Gen. Geoffrey Miller, head of the Guantanamo Bay prison, detailing his recommended interrogation methods for Abu Ghraib prisoners. Congressional pressure yielded only a few more crumbs. Whenever forced to explain the secrecy, Bush-Cheney officials recycled disproven arguments. For example, on the issue of the Red Cross papers, officials pointed to the organization's confidentiality rules, even as the Red Cross repeatedly urged the administration to give Congress the full set, beginning with an official declaration of consent on May 8. On June 24, DOD officials met with the SASC in a closed-door session, which was supposed to resolve the matter. Instead of Abu Ghraib–related reports, however, they brought documents about Guantanamo. By the end of June, two months after the scandal erupted, the SASC still was waiting for most of the missing pages, as well as other promised documents.[58]

Not once did the administration officials assert executive privilege, which, even if legally questionable in this case, would have provided a formal justification for their actions. Instead, they resorted to foot-dragging, evasiveness, and lies. Finally, after months of obstructing the investigation, the DOD released a redacted version of the Taguba Report—minus 7 of 106 annexes— to the ACLU in October 2004, a year after it filed a FOIA request. By that time, just before the 2004 election in which Republicans and Democrats tried to outhawk each other, the mass media had almost completely dropped the story. Although the scandal significantly and negatively affected voters' perceptions of Bush's performance, the issue had largely receded from the headlines. Major media organizations had by then turned to other issues, such as whether Democratic presidential candidate John Kerry faked his Vietnam War injuries.[59]

Post-9/11 Detainee Videotapes, Part 2

The CIA caught its first big fish in the war on terror in early 2002, when agents in Pakistan "smoked out" Abu Zubaydah from an apartment in a Faisalabad suburb. He had escaped the aerial bombardament of Al Qaeda bases by traveling through Afghanistan and Pakistan dressed as a burka-clad woman. The CIA, with help from a taxi driver and Pakistani agents, tracked Zubaydah down in late March 2002. The capture was the stuff of Hollywood thrillers. According to the official narrative, Zubaydah and his associates huddled in their dark apartment, putting the finishing touches on a bomb. Swarms of black-clad US and Pakistani agents burst in, finding a "still hot" soldering iron among other tools and supplies. Zubaydah fled, climbed to the building's roof, and jumped from rooftop to rooftop, even as shots rang from below. Hit three times by gunfire (in the thigh, stomach, and groin), he fell 25 feet to the street. Agents scooped him up and tossed him into a pickup truck next to his shackled colleagues. Only when an observant agent climbed aboard and shined a light on Zubaydah's face did everyone realize they had indeed caught such a big fish.[60]

Zubaydah was barely alive—falling in and out of consciousness, oozing pints of blood. The CIA needed him alive and awake, given all of the intel stuffed into his brain. A symbolic scalping would not do. Things got so dire that the CIA escorted a "world-class medical expert" from Johns Hopkins Medical School to Pakistan in order to save the terrorist's life. CIA director George Tenet felt it necessary in his autobiography to assure readers that it was "not that we had any sympathy for Zubaydah; we just didn't want him dying before we could learn." Three days after capture, the CIA transferred the recovering Al Qaeda detainee to one of its "black sites," this one in Thailand near the Udon Thani Thai Royal Air Force Base. The White House gave the FBI first crack at Zubaydah, most likely due to the bureau's longer history of running interrogations. The move seemed to pay off: agents developed a good rapport with him, at least to the point where they got him talking. But Bush and his team quickly grew impatient. They wanted actionable information *now*. So they handed the reins over to less experienced CIA interrogators, who, standing by at the black site, barged in and took control (a perfect twist in our clichéd Hollywood thriller). Rejecting the FBI's "good cop" approach, the CIA opted for a "bad cop" strategy. When Zubaydah clammed up, just as the FBI warned he would, CIA agents "took the gloves off," following White House instructions. They proceeded with what the administration called "enhanced interrogation methods" (EIMs) or what most of the world called "torture."[61]

The CIA agents kept Zubaydah naked and sleep deprived in a floodlit, freezing-cold cell. They blasted hard rock music for hours on end; they beat him near his gunshot wounds; and according to Zubaydah, they locked him in a "tiny coffin" so small he could not stand or stretch, his body so contorted that his gunshot wounds kept reopening. Anonymous CIA sources adamantly rejected the coffin claim, saying the enclosure they used was more like a small, steel-caged dog crate covered with towels (to restrict vision and airflow). Overall, in the first few months of Zubaydah's detention, the approved list of EIMs included "body slaps, face slaps, hooding, stress positions, walling, immersion in water, stripping, isolation, and sleep deprivation, among others." Waterboarding came later, after the OLC circulated a secret legal memo in late July/early August 2002 authorizing the technique. CIA agents waterboarded him eighty-three times in August, plus an unknown number of times after that.[62]

That the CIA videotaped these sessions in graphic detail is at first puzzling, especially because the EIMs appear to violate domestic and international laws. Were the tapers—and tape-watchers in the White house—sadists? The tapes reportedly showed Zubaydah in great distress, "vomiting and screaming" and beaten to a pulp. Why else would agents create material evidence of possibly criminal abuse? There are several more likely reasons. First, senior White

House and CIA officials believed their new interrogation protocol fell clearly within the law, through official legal interpretations of the relevant statutes (see chapter 5). Second, officials grew anxious that they might kill or seriously injure Zubaydah or that he would die from wounds suffered during his capture, so they wanted a full record of his experience to defend themselves if necessary. They expected the CIA would be accused "by Congress, by prosecutors, by the American public and by Muslims worldwide" of murdering Zubaydah if he died in their custody. Taping everything from interrogations to "having his bandages changed" would "ensure a record of Abu Zubaydah's medical condition and treatment should he succumb to his wounds and questions arise about the medical care provided to him by the CIA." Third, CIA officials thought the tapes would "assist in the preparation of the debriefing reports, although . . . they rarely, if ever, were used for that purpose." Finally, the agency was testing out new EIMs and therefore "had intense interest in keeping abreast of all aspects of Abu Zubaydah's interrogation." In other words, what worked and what did not? Furthermore, the use of EIMs was still shrouded in secrecy at that time, and as a result, Bush-Cheney torture policies had not yet emerged as a controversial political issue.[63]

As the tapes began to pile up, some officials started to wonder if keeping such detailed records was a good idea. A few months after taping began, agents pressed the stop button and dismantled the cameras that captured Zubaydah's ordeal. As former CIA official A. B. Krongard later explained, "By that time, paranoia was setting in."[64]

There had been splits within the CIA and the rest of the government about the risks and benefits of taping—not to mention EIMs—from the beginning. But the CIA only seriously began to question the practice as the interrogation sessions became increasingly aggressive and as the possibility of having a taped record of Zubaydah's death in captivity became a conceivable result. Senior officials had just learned (in August 2002) that army Special Forces had killed a detainee, Mohammed Sayari, in Lwara, Afghanistan. Photographs taken at the scene became evidence in an internal criminal investigation; a sergeant with military intelligence even consulted with investigators about a "possible war crime." These and other incidents apparently brought the risks of what the CIA was doing to Zubaydah and other "highest value" detainees more sharply into focus. Plus, officials wondered, what if someone leaked the tapes?[65]

CIA clandestine service officers dispatched a cable to Washington in August 2002. By most accounts, it emphasized the serious "security risks" posed by the tapes and concluded that the best option was to destroy them. About two weeks later, senior CIA officials decided the tapes were a security risk for current and future agents and emphasized "the danger to all Americans should the tapes be compromised." Although the CIA locked the tapes in safes at maximum-security black sites, officials worried about field officers sending copies to media or human rights organizations. Because of those risks and because the "continued retention of these tapes . . . is not/not [*sic*] required by law," the officials also decided the best remedy would be to destroy them. For officers in the field, the first policy change arrived on October 25, 2002. Everyone should continue taping, headquarters announced, but agents could record over the previous day's tapes. Meanwhile, CIA attorneys conducted a "random independent review" of existing tapes and analyzed months' worth of cables. From this analysis, senior officials concluded the record outside the tapes (that is, in the cables) "was full and exacting," which "remov[ed] any need for tapes." The plan to destroy was thus finalized. Senior attorneys in the CIA's Office of General Counsel (OGC), with the exception of Scott W. Muller, concluded that preserving the tapes as federal records was "not required by law."[66]

Although a final decision had been made, CIA officials remained deeply divided about the EIMs, the tapes, and their pending destruction. Some, including Director Tenet, agreed the tapes needed to go but apparently voiced some skepticism about the OGC's convenient conclusion. The controversy spilled over into Congress, when the OGC notified Rep. Porter J. Goss (R-FL) and Rep. Jane Harman (D-CA) about the issue. Both likewise contested the OGC's assessment that the tapes were not "official records." The White House also came to disagree with the OGC's assessment. Senior White House lawyers, including Gonzales, Addington, Harriet E. Miers, and National Security Council senior counsel John B. Bellinger III, met with Muller, the OGC lawyer, on several occasions to discuss what to do with the tapes. By May 11, 2004, Addington and Gonzales ordered the CIA to preserve them. The next year, the director of national intelligence, John D. Negroponte, agreed with Goss, the new CIA director, to save the tapes. The OGC's earlier recommendation to destroy was dead in the water.[67]

The tide would turn in late 2005 and very quickly. On November 2, Dana Priest exposed the CIA's black site secret prison program in the *Washington Post*, alerting Americans to a years-long Bush-Cheney policy. As soon as they heard Priest's story would be published, despite the CIA's and White House's best efforts to persuade senior editors to hold it, officials immediately began shutting down the black sites and moving detainees elsewhere. The next day, Judge Leonie Brinkema, who was presiding over the case against Al Qaeda operative Zacarias Moussaoui, demanded that the administration either "confirm or deny that it has video or audiotapes" of its interrogations. Brinkema had repeatedly requested tapes of Moussaoui's interrogations since 2003. And each time, the CIA claimed to a clearly skeptical judge that no such tapes existed, which was true only because by then they had been destroyed. After Priest's story broke, the CIA provided Brinkema only with "intelligence summaries" of the interrogations. Congress also began to pressure the CIA about the tapes. One (unidentified) legislator sent a letter to the CIA's inspector general on November 4 demanding an investigation.[68]

That same day, senior CIA officials drafted an order approving the other tapes' destruction, based on the OGC's legal opinion, which stood in stark contrast to the White House's position from 2004. Senior CIA officials, especially Jose A. Rodriguez, Jr., who was then head of the clandestine branch, decided the agency had to move decisively despite all of the legal uncertainty. Field officers were actively shutting down the black sites in Africa, Asia, and Europe, starting bonfires to "destroy papers and other evidence of the agency's presence," as Rodriguez put it. One base chief, in the orange glow of the bonfires, asked Rodriguez if she should toss the tapes in with the other "evidence." Just as Rodriguez was about to say yes, a cable from Langley executives arrived, ordering all agents to "hold up on the tapes. We think they should be retained for a little while longer."[69]

After all that dithering, Rodriguez gave the final order on November 8, 2005: there was "no legal or OIG requirement to continue to retain the tapes." CIA lawyers had provided Rodriguez with additional "legal guidance," noting that the tapes posed a "grave risk" to the "personal safety" of the CIA officers who employed the EIMs. Rodriguez and his supporters also believed the "propaganda damage to the image of America would be immense" if the tapes ever leaked. Thus, destroying them was justified by "grave national security reasons." To ensure they would never resurface, the tapes needed an "industrial strength" shredder. By 12:30 p.m. on the next day, November 9, CIA officials had shredded ninety-two videotapes. Five days later, the CIA finally got back to Judge Brinkema, telling her it did not have any tapes.[70]

Top CIA officials were acutely aware of the potential consequences. In a November 10 e-mail from an unknown author to Dusty Foggo (the CIA official later convicted of bribery), Rodriguez indicated he had told Goss and other colleagues he was ready to "take the heat." Goss apparently laughed, saying it was he who would take the heat, but nevertheless, he agreed with the decision to destroy. Goss also agreed with Rodriguez that "the heat from destroying is nothing compared to what would be if the tapes ever got into public domain." Senior CIA attorney John Rizzo, by contrast, was reportedly "upset" about the destruction, though his colleagues could not determine if he simply felt "left out," if he had "substantive" concerns, or if "he was on the hook to notify [White House counsel] Harriet Miers of the status of the tapes." In another November 10 e-mail, a CIA senior official inquired about the extent to which there had been an "improper" destruction, pointing in Rodriguez's direction. Who in the CIA had "lied" or "misstated the facts"? The e-mail's author argued it all stank of self-interested abuse of power: "It is not without relevance that [*redacted*] figured prominently in the tapes, as [*redacted*] was in charge of [*redacted*] at the time and clearly would want the tapes destroyed." That mysterious figure—perhaps Rodriguez, perhaps not— did not have to worry about "this latest 'wrinkle'" again.[71]

After the tape destruction became public in late 2007, Paul M. Wester, Jr., the National Archives director, sent a letter to the CIA's director of information management services, in which he reminded the agency that "no Federal records may be destroyed except under the authorization of a records disposition schedule approved by the Archivist of the United States." Agency officials responded with a wave of the hand: "The bottom line is that these videotapes were not federal records as defined by the Federal Records Act." Ultimately, destroying the tapes drew no negative consequences. A federal prosecutor in November 2010 decided against going after Rodriguez or any other CIA officials. A federal judge agreed; holding those who were responsible accountable "would serve no beneficial purpose." Rodriguez went on to tell his story in *Hard Measures: How Aggressive CIA Actions after 9/11 Saved American Lives*, boosting sales with appearances on *60 Minutes* and Fox News. He insisted he did nothing wrong: "I was not depriving anyone of information about what was done or what was said. I was just getting rid of some ugly visuals that could put the lives of my people at risk." He recalled that in the moment just before he ordered the tapes' destruction, "I took a deep breath of weary satisfaction and hit Send."[72]

The lack of accountability—for federal records destruction, for obstruction of justice—was a pattern, not a fluke. As the two former chairs of the official 9/11 Commission, former Republican governor Thomas Kean and Democratic congressman Lee Hamilton, put it bluntly in a 2008 op-ed: "Those who knew about those videotapes—and did not tell us about them—

obstructed our investigation. . . . Government officials decided not to inform a lawfully constituted body, created by Congress and the president, to investigate one the greatest tragedies to confront this country. We call that obstruction." There were other examples. For instance, the CIA admitted destroying interrogation tapes of Abd al-Rahim al-Nashiri, the alleged Saudi mastermind of the 2000 USS *Cole* bombing in Yemen. After his arrest in November 2002, al-Nashiri was subjected to a variety of EIMs, including waterboarding but also threats of impalement with a revved-up power drill and shots from a loaded handgun. And then there were the tapes of US citizen Jose Padilla's interrogations.[73]

Post-9/11 Detainee Videotapes, Part 3: The Last Interrogation of a US Citizen

Brooklyn-born Jose Padilla was arrested on May 8, 2002, for conspiring with Al Qaeda to blow up high-rises with a radiological dirty bomb. Although Padilla had been tracked by the CIA and FBI while overseas in Pakistan and other places, the administration decided to wait until his return to the United States to avoid extradition problems and to monitor his communications and interactions along the way. The FBI arrested him in Chicago on a material witness warrant related to 9/11, issued by the chief judge of a grand jury meeting in the southern district of New York. Once detained, Padilla was sent to New York's Metropolitan Correctional Center, where he met with a court-appointed lawyer, who filed motions for his release. As is customary, the district court scheduled a hearing for Padilla, set for June 11, about a month later.[74]

Two days before the hearing, President Bush issued an order, in the form of a memo to Defense Secretary Rumsfeld, declaring Padilla an "enemy combatant," despite his US citizenship. Bush defended his action as being "in accordance with the Constitution and consistent with the laws of the United States, including the Authorization for Use of Military Force Joint Resolution (Public Law 107-40)." He also asserted, "based on the information available to me from all sources," that Padilla was a "grave danger" and therefore that "it is in the interest of the United States" to "detain him as an enemy combatant"—effectively stripping him of a wide range of rights, from habeas corpus to access to counsel to freedom from extralegal indefinite detention. Then, without informing Padilla's attorney, Donna Newman, the administration pushed the court to vacate the material witness warrant and moved Padilla from the federal prison to a military brig in Charleston, South Carolina. It was there that he was subjected to a full menu of EIMs, recorded onto eighty-eight DVDs.[75]

As soon as Newman heard about Padilla's new status and transfer to military custody, she filed a habeas corpus petition and sued the government to contest Bush's unilateral action. That suit moved quickly through the system, ending at the Supreme Court in June 2004, which decided against Padilla on a technicality in a five-to-four decision. Padilla's defense team corrected the error but lost again at the Court of Appeals for the Fourth Circuit, which issued a strong opinion upholding the constitutionality of the administration's actions. Bush, the appellate judges decided, had the authority to hold Padilla indefinitely and declare him an enemy combatant under the Non-detention Act, on the basis of Congress's 2001 Authorization for Use of Military Force.[76]

Legal experts, apparently including many in the White House, came to believe the appeals court's decision was too sweeping. Padilla's appeal of the decision risked letting a divided Supreme Court declare the administration's detention policies unconstitutional. To prevent that outcome, the administration ordered that Padilla be moved back into civilian custody, effectively redefining him as a citizen and vacating the case. Ironically, because Padilla's lawyers wanted the Supreme Court to hear their appeal, they opposed the administration's move. That is, the government plucked Padilla back up from subcitizen status even as his lawyers tried to stop them. Whether out of legal convenience or because they believed Padilla had been thoroughly damaged by his interrogations and detention (or both reasons), government authorities dropped their earlier argument about the grave dangers of letting him into the civilian court system.[77]

The administration's case against Padilla then became much less grandiose. The charges were still serious: "material support to terrorists, and conspiring to murder individuals who are overseas." However, the administration officials completely dropped the justification they had used for years to persuade judges, legislators, and the public of the need for Padilla's exceptional treatment—that Padilla was part of an Al Qaeda cell planning to set off a radioactive dirty bomb in an American city.[78]

Padilla's case would run on for several more months before a jury in Florida's southern district court convicted him on conspiracy charges. During the court's investigation into his mental capacity to stand trial, Judge Marcia Cooke demanded all of the interrogation tapes from the Defense Intelligence Agency (DIA). In a response that a Human Rights Watch attorney said was "the kind of thing you hear when you're litigating cases in Egypt or Morocco or Karachi," the DIA claimed it had unfortunately "lost" one of the DVDs. Padilla's last major interrogation session, which likely involved government agents pulling out all the stops to solicit information from him, had *somehow* gone missing. If the tape indeed documented abuse, Judge Cooke might have changed her evaluation of Padilla's mental state. Evidence of torture would also have verified Padilla's allegations in the criminal case, as well as in a civil case against former OLC lawyer John Yoo.[79]

Faced with yet another case of document destruction, National Archives director Paul Wester sent the DIA a letter asking for details. DIA officials had already searched for the video after the request from Judge Cooke—who supposedly "made no adverse comment"—yet they again "diligently search[ed] all files . . . to no avail." But they would change their internal preservation and maintenance procedures, "to avoid accidental record disposal or destruction in the future." Although they again destroyed evidence—in this case, an official federal record—the Bush-Cheney administration officials once more got off scot free with an "oops" and a pledge to be more careful next time.[80]

"And then we found 22 million emails . . . "

The e-mail archiving system the Clinton-Gore administration implemented in 1994 had some serious problems. The design flaws in the Automated Record Management System (ARMS) led to a range of bizarre glitches, such as the system's failure to preserve e-mails sent by officials whose name began with the letter "D." When he learned about the issues, Rep. Dan Burton (R-IN) was angry—and it had little to do with his first name. Burton accused the administration of exploiting the glitch, deliberately "losing" or withholding e-mails from congressional overseers. To investigate, he convened hearings before his House Committee on Oversight and Government Reform in 2000. Congress's nonpartisan General Accounting Office looked into the matter, but its investigators concluded the missing e-mails resulted primarily from technical flaws (such as the "D" problem), although they criticized the White House for poor records management practices. As a result of Burton's prodding and the GAO's report, the administration spent $11.7 million to successfully recover 200,000 e-mails and fix the system.[81]

The new and improved ARMS, however, had another set of unforeseen flaws. When Bush-Cheney officials switched the White House's e-mail client-server system from Lotus Notes to Microsoft Exchange in 2002, they discovered ARMS did not seem to work well with Exchange. Because of the costs of switching back, they kept ARMS/Exchange running and started to look for a new archiving system.[82]

By January 2003, the problem had become serious enough that the White House chief information officer (CIO) sent a memo to all Office of Administration (OA) staffers, warning that the administration might face "legal proceeding[s]" if nothing changed. The CIO may or may not have known at that point that ARMS failed to preserve *all* e-mails for a period, starting as early as January 3, 2003. The exact moment the CIO learned about that problem is unknown. However, by March, senior Bush-Cheney officials clearly knew about another problem: the system's failure to archive "bcc" e-mail addresses (for individuals who were copied, or "cc-ed," on a message secretly). Despite the accumulating problems, the White House's search for a replacement moved at a snail's pace. Officials filled out forms, but the contracting process had barely begun. Finally, in mid-October, the administration chose Booz Allen Hamilton to start developing the Electronic Communications Records Management System (ECRMS). But months later, nothing had changed. E-mails by the thousands were falling into a digital black hole. In January 2004, a year after the CIO sounded the alarm, the White House was still "operating at risk by not capturing and storing messages outside the e-mail system," as NARA officials put it after a meeting with OA and Booz Allen.[83]

Around the same time, the ostensibly technical problem grew into a legal and political one, by intersecting with one of the most legally consequential scandals of the Bush-Cheney administration. "Plamegate" erupted once it became clear someone in the administration had deliberately leaked the identity of a covert CIA officer, Valerie Plame, to avenge her husband's July 2003 *New York Times* op-ed disputing Bush-Cheney claims about Iraq's pursuit of weapons of mass destruction. By the end of January 2004, DOJ special counsel Patrick Fitzgerald had persuaded a grand jury of the DC district court to issue three subpoenas for e-mails related to the investigation—e-mails that likely had gone down that digital black hole.[84]

White House officials responded to the subpoenas in two ways. First, they hired Microsoft Premier Support to analyze why the Executive Office of the President had such difficulty giving Fitzgerald the e-mails. Of course, the EOP had known about the archiving problems for over a year. Microsoft's tech experts thus discovered what the White House already knew: "There is no current mechanism to transfer Exchange e-mail into ARMS" (other problems, including frequent server crashes, probably did not escape the CIO's notice before the inquiry). The decision to hire Microsoft was very likely an

attempt to create a data point in a legal paper trail documenting official ignorance about the problem. The internal CIO memos, then still secret, plainly
showed otherwise.[85]

Second, David Addington, the vice president's counsel, sent Fitzgerald's office a memo claiming that the Office of the Vice President (OVP)—the focus
of the investigation—was making every effort to comply with the subpoena.
In particular, Addington said the OVP searched for e-mails related to Plame
and her husband, former ambassador Joe Wilson, as well as the twenty-six
reporters who were under investigation for the leak, including Matthew Cooper, John Dickerson, Judith Miller, and Robert Novak. We have no record of
Fitzgerald's initial reaction, but it is clear he was ultimately dissatisfied with
the OVP's response. Fitzgerald's office had reason to believe the OVP was not
completely forthcoming, including the possibility that Addington deliberately limited the search parameters.[86]

For some of the reporters under investigation, Addington searched the archive widely and deeply. For example, for Robert Novak, he searched for "Novak," which would have turned up e-mails referencing his full or last name.
Slate's John Dickerson received a similar treatment. By contrast, Addington
searched only for "Matthew Cooper" e-mails, thus potentially overlooking
messages with the shorter name "Matt"—which happened to be part of Cooper's e-mail address (matt_cooper@timemagazine.com). He searched for Judith Miller's e-mails in much the same way (that is, using "Judith Miller" but
not "Judy," and so forth). Addington's possibly deceptive research, along with
the ongoing, unaddressed archiving problems, produced an attenuated batch
of e-mails, delivered to Fitzgerald's office without explanation.[87]

After years of reminders and warnings from OA, NARA, Microsoft, and
Booz Allen Hamilton, the new archiving system, ECRMS, was finally tested
in January 2005. Meanwhile, ARMS remained in place, with senior officials
probably knowing exactly what that meant. Almost a year later, in October
2005, the OA launched an internal study to determine the scope of the problem. By then, more than five million e-mails were "missing."[88]

OA analysts counted 473 days ("red days") of missing e-mails from the
most senior offices, including the president's White House office and the
OVP (see Table 9.1). They also identified 229 days ("yellow days") when
the archives contained too few e-mails, compared to what was statistically
predicted. Although the red days might have occurred randomly, there do
seem to be some interesting coincidences, at least with regard to the OVP.

TABLE 9.1
Red Days, Yellow Days: Missing E-mails from
the Executive Office of the President

	Red Days	Yellow Days
White House Office [President]	12	28
Office of the Vice President (OVP)	16	30
Office of Public Diplomacy	11	7
National Security Council	47	9
President's Foreign Intelligence Advisory Board	20	14
Council of Economic Advisers	103	29
Council on Environmental Quality	81	5
Office of Management and Budget	59	10
Office of National Drug Control Policy	20	24
Office of Science and Technology Policy	15	39
Office of the US Trade Representative	73	10
Office of Administration (OA)	16	24
Total	473	229

Source: National Security Aarchive 2008.

For example, one string of red days in 2003 (October 1–3 and 5) happened immediately after two key turning points during the Plamegate investigation. On September 30, the DOJ announced the beginning of its investigation. On that same day, President Bush announced, "If the person [who leaked Plame's identity] has violated law [*sic*], the person will be taken care of. And so I welcome the investigation." Not all coincidences have meaning, but the timing does suggest the possibility that the OVP—the source of the leak—took advantage of the fog surrounding the archival problems to remove potentially incriminating e-mails from the system. That possibility is buttressed by two other facts. First, someone removed e-mails from White House backup tapes during that October stretch (along with other critical red day periods). Second, investigators detected highly ususual and unexplained OVP e-mail file transfers during the same period. Moreover, the defective system sometimes crashed e-mail boxes, and restoration efforts *somehow* neglected key officials' mailboxes, including that of the OVP's I. Lewis "Scooter" Libby—the man at the center of Fitzgerald's investigation.[89]

The OA sent a detailed summary of its study to White House counsel Harriet Miers in October 2005. The memo also contained specific recommendations for recovering the nearly 6 million missing e-mails. Even as more senior officials joined the OA in sounding alarms about legal problems, nothing changed. When the OA staffers sent Special Counsel Fitzgerald a similar briefing, they elicited a stronger reaction.[90]

Fitzgerald was characteristically professional and empirical. At the end of one of his many letters to Libby's lawyers, he wrote: "We are aware of no evidence pertinent to the charges against defendant Libby which has been destroyed. In an abundance of caution, we advise you that we have learned that not all email of the [OVP] and the [EOP] for certain time periods in 2003 was preserved through the normal archiving process on the White House computer system." To the White House's dismay, Fitzgerald filed his letter in court—a routine practice during a criminal trial but rather inconvenient for people wanting to keep secrets. The AP's February 2, 2006, story on Fitzgerald's letter finally punctured the White House's years-long silence about the ongoing archiving problems. NARA officials immediately asked the White House for an explanation. No worries, said the OA attorney. Though the millions of e-mails were not archived, the White House "believed [they] existed and could be accounted for." Meanwhile, the White House made no effort to recover them, and the same, problematic system remained in place.[91]

In August 2006—three and a half years after the administration first detected (or formally recorded) problems with the Microsoft/ARMS pairing—the new system, ECRMS, was finally ready for full implementation. In a private e-mail, someone in the CIO's office highlighted the significance: "ECRMS is the most important system that we have implemented in a long time. . . . This is our number 1 priority." All that remained were two signatures: one from the head of the OA, another from the new White House CIO, Theresa Payton. She refused.[92]

Payton offered a technical explanation, which included concerns about how millions of old e-mails would clog up the new system and how ECRMS did not effectively separate official and personal e-mail records. She also argued the multimillion dollar archiving system, created and fine-tuned over several years, would prevent the White House from fully complying with statutory requirements. For those reasons, Payton dumped ECRMS, leaving millions of federal records unsecured—soon gone forever. It was probably not her decision alone.[93]

When NARA officials checked in with the OA six months later about the new system, they were very surprised to hear that Payton had rejected ECRMS and that "emails [were] no longer being preserved in a formal electronic recordkeeping system." Once again, the OA dismissed concerns about missing e-mails. But that position quickly dissolved once CREW published a report citing the OA's (outdated) 5 million estimate and Fitzgerald's Plamegate court filing. Senior Bush-Cheney officials finally stopped dismissing the problem, but their new position—essentially, "Oops!"—suggested the issue was news to them. "We screwed up, and we're trying to fix it," White House spokesperson Dana Perino reassured everyone in April 2007. However, Perino did acknowledge the possibility that "up to five million" e-mails were indeed "missing."[94]

The White House's new position prompted a call from NARA officials, who asked for the secret OA study and pushed for the restoration process to finally begin. Pressure also came from other directions. The Senate Judiciary Committee, now dominated by a Democratic majority (after the 2006 election), issued a subpoena for any e-mails related to the apparently politically-motivated firing of seven district attorneys in late 2006. CREW, which had issued the game-changing report in April, filed suit against the OA to compel the White House to respond to a FOIA request. In addition to any "missing emails," CREW sought records related to: the existing system's (ARMA's) problems, the ECRMS debacle, White House predictions of public opinion effects once the problem was revealed, and lists containing the specific dates of missing e-mails.[95]

The White House responded with a whopper of an announcement: the OA was no longer covered by FOIA. The administration's position—"OA is not an 'agency' as defined by FOIA"—took inspiration from Clinton-Gore's winning argument in *Armstrong v. Executive Office of the President*. Bush-Cheney's declaration came as a bit of a shock to OA's active FOIA staff, which had processed sixty-five FOIA requests in 2006. The administration officials acknowledged the tension between their declaration and the on-the-ground reality. But they asserted it was not a problem: "To be sure, OA currently has regulations implementing FOIA and has not taken the position in prior litigation that it is not subject to FOIA. However, the D.C. Circuit has held that this is not probative on the question of whether an EOP unit does, in fact, satisfy FOIA's definition of 'agency.'" Thus, even though the OA was actually an agency at the moment of the announcement, a court might someday redefine it. White House officials also stressed the OA's unique relationship with the president. Like the NSC in *Armstrong*, they argued, the OA "wields no authority, let alone substantial authority, independent of the President," and therefore, like the President, it was immune to FOIA requests.[96]

Not swayed by this logic and unwilling to surrender to the administration's word-gamesmanship, CREW filed a second lawsuit in September. The National Security Archive filed a separate suit, leading the DC circuit court to consolidate them. Within the government, NARA increased its pressure. Archivist Allen Weinstein contacted White House counsel Fred Fielding, urging "utmost dispatch" in dealing with the problem. As we have seen, the administration, like its predecessors, had not cared much about NARA's concerns, and this time was no exception. All that NARA's general counsel could do was write a summary memo of the situation: "We still have made almost zero progress in actually moving ahead with the important and necessary work that is required for a successful transition [from ARMS]. . . . [O]ur repeated requests . . . have gone unheeded. . . . Of most importance, we still know virtually nothing about the status of the alleged missing White House emails." The White House had by that point actually started installing a new system, but every indication suggested it did not expect the system to work until the end of Bush-Cheney's second term. Moreover, during the transition from ARMS, officials discovered more missing e-mails, including some that had been manually deleted from the user interface. An organization with a functioning archive system could solve that problem without much difficulty.[97]

Payton, the White House CIO who blocked the new archive system upon her arrival, turned her sights toward the 2005 OA study. The analysis, she told House Oversight Committee staffers, seemed unreliable and therefore not credible. Despite her confident assertions, she denied NARA's request for a copy of the study, although a selected group of individuals were allowed to look at it with their hands tied behind their backs (that is, they could not copy it). The from-out-of-nowhere attack on the OA study then percolated upward, into scripted White House press briefings. The White House also insisted, contrary to the OA report's claims of several hundred red days (Table 9.1), that "we have no reason to believe that any e-mail at all are missing."[98]

Meanwhile, the CREW/National Security Archive lawsuit began to yield fruit. DC circuit judge Henry Kennedy in November 2007 issued a restraining order and demanded that the White House preserve all backup tapes or other archival materials, since the existing system was so pockmarked. DC circuit magistrate Judge John M. Facciola then demanded in early January 2008 that the administration act immediately because anything already stored was "increasingly likely to be deleted or overridden with the passage of time." However encouraging those developments were, the plaintiffs' hopes would soon be dashed. In June, DC circuit court judge Colleen Kollar-Kotelly issued a historic ruling. Finding the administration's August 2007 argument about

OA persuasive, she wrote, "the Court concludes that OA is not an agency subject to the FOIA because it . . . lacks substantial independent authority." Therefore, "the Court shall dismiss this case in its entirety." The plaintiffs appealed, but about a year later, they faced the same verdict from the DC appeals court. By then, Bush-Cheney's reign had ended, and it was the Obama-Biden administration celebrating victory. Despite their promises of greater transparency, Obama-Biden officials rejected pleas from open government groups to keep OA accessible to FOIA requests. They openly welcomed the new secrecy category as a necessary tool for good governance.[99]

Summary

Whether the delays, denials, sudden policy shifts, and seeming incompetence were all part of a concerted effort to conceal Bush-Cheney e-mails for as long as possible is probably unknowable. Any documents confirming that suspicion would not likely have made it past the nearest burn bag. The outcome of the bizarre six-year effort to implement a new e-mail archiving system, however, clearly redounded to the administration's benefit. Officials sustained a plausible causal story about their inability to comply with federal open records laws as a result of technological problems. Crucial communications related to the Plame investigation, the fired district attorney investigation, and torture and surveillance policies were "lost," potentially forever or at least until the new administration took control in January 2009. The Obama-Biden administration made an early commitment to let past transgressions slide and then embraced Bush-Cheney's argument about OA, with all its material consequences.[100]

After losing in the DC appeals court, CREW and the National Security Archive reached a settlement with the government, which prevented the plaintiffs from appealing the case to the Supreme Court. Though the 2009 settlement came after the transfer of power to Obama-Biden, the 2008–2009 negotiations unearthed—and possibly caused—the recovery of millions of e-mails previously considered lost. In fact, technicians found *22 million* e-mails, more than four times the OA's estimate from 2005. Nevertheless, a large portion of the e-mails were now FOIA-proof, as a result of the White House's legal victory. Plus, according to a letter from NARA director Paul Wester, many of the e-mails were still "not recoverable" or "had been [improperly] deleted." It is an interesting coincidence that the unrecoverable ones happened to be from John Yoo and Jay Bybee, the OLC lawyers who wrote the most controversial legal opinions about torture, detention of terrorist suspects, and domestic surveillance (see chapter 5).[101]

Another Wrinkle in the E-Mail Saga

Despite the incapacitated archival system, some in the Bush-Cheney White House still bristled whenever they sent e-mails. Every time, a message box popped up with a reminder saying the message would be archived. The system was broken, but there still was a possibility of later recovery. That possibility is probably what led several officials to use nongovernmental e-mail accounts for some of their most delicate official communications. "We knew E-mails could be subpoenaed," an anonymous aide told a reporter. However, they reasoned, Clinton-Gore officials got away with it before, so it must be okay: "We saw that with the Clintons but I don't think anybody saw that we were doing anything wrong." Though that was potentially true, no one had ever provided evidence of official business on the private Clinton-Gore accounts held by the president and vice president, as well as the first and second ladies.[102]

The news that senior Bush-Cheney officials used e-mail addresses from gwb43.com and georgewbush.com (2004 Bush-Cheney reelection websites), RNC.com (Republican National Committee), and AOL.com for official government business broke in late March 2007, just before the White House admitted it might have lost millions of e-mails. Those with accounts included Karl Rove, deputy chief of staff and senior adviser to the president; Rove's executive assistant Susan Ralston; Rove's aide Barry Jackson; and Deputy Director for Political Affairs Scott Jennings. In total, "roughly 50" White House officials used RNC e-mail accounts, although not all individuals were identified. The officials' extralegal communications might never have surfaced if not for separate congressional investigations of the US attorneys' firings, the lobbyist Jack Abramoff's corruption and contacts with the White House, and the "politicization of the General Services Administration."[103]

In late March 2007, Rep. Henry Waxman (D-CA), chairman of the House Committee on Oversight and Government Reform, sent letters to the RNC and the Bush-Cheney reelection campaign to inquire about the e-mails and to demand that they preserve them. Waxman also sent a letter to White House counsel Fred Fielding, citing unambiguous evidence of official wrongdoing. In one e-mail, Ralston instructed two of Abramoff's aides to communicate with her through her RNC account because of "security issues" in the White

House. Abramoff, who was convicted in 2006 of fraud and conspiracy, once mistakenly sent a message to Ralston on her RNC pager, but it somehow was redirected into the White House system. Responding to his colleague Kevin Ring's February 7, 2003, message describing that Ralston "said it is better to not put this stuff in writing in their e-mail system because it might actually limit what they can do to help us, especially since there could be lawsuits, etc.," Abramoff had stated: "Dammit. It was sent to Susan on her rnc [*sic*] pager and was not supposed to go into the [White House] system." The other officials—Jennings, Jackson, and Rove—used their nongovernmental accounts to discuss a range of issues, from partisan electoral strategy to replacements for the fired district attorneys to getting an Abramoff client an official Medal of Freedom.[104]

RNC and Bush-Cheney campaign executives, along with White House officials, responded by saying what had happened was a "mistake." The administration then pledged it would "aggressively work[] to correct" that mistake, probably with the same spirit of due diligence that it demonstrated with the larger e-mail scandal. Unfortunately, they confessed, many of the e-mails were likely "lost" forever because the RNC maintained a policy until 2004 of deleting its entire e-mail server every thirty days. Sometime in 2004, the RNC changed course and started preserving all e-mails.[105]

Moreover, RNC officials, including Chairman Mike Duncan, ignored House Oversight Committee requests/demands for more information, including: the names of all "roughly 50" administration officials with RNC accounts, the total number of e-mails used in potentially inappropriate ways, and the e-mail messages themselves. What the RNC did instead was send lawyers to meet with Oversight Committee staff and propose a compromise: they would search for all relevant information using no more than eight search terms, including "political briefing" and "Hatch Act"—as if most individuals violating the Hatch Act would have written "Hatch Act Violation" in the subject line of their e-mails. Moreover, as Waxman noted in a letter to Duncan,

> the search terms proposed by the RNC would not have located a January 19, 2007, e-mail from an official in Karl Rove's office to an official at the General Services Administration transmitting a copy of Powerpoint slides prepared by the White House that list the top 20 Democratic targets in 2008. That e-mail read: "Please do not email this out or let people see it. It is a close hold and we're not supposed to be emailing it around."

For these and other reasons, the extremely limited search term method pro-posed by RNC lawyers—reminiscent of Addington's approach to Fitzgerald's subpoena—"risk[ed] overlooking potentially responsive documents." Ulti-mately, the administration and the RNC used the tried-and-true method of just running out the clock.[106]

Conclusion

By focusing on the well-documented cases of shredding and deleting that exist in the public record, this chapter may well have massively underrepresented the amount of document destruction that actually occurred. The National Security Archive's Kate Doyle estimated in 1999 that just 3 percent of federal records escape the burn bag or the delete button. We cannot know whether that estimate, which sounds shockingly low, is accurate. However, we can say records are frequently destroyed, and repercussions are rare. Just to take one example: when I asked the USDA for pre-2000 versions of the ARS's "sensitive issues" list (see chapter 7), officials claimed the agency occasionally revised its Word document and never kept hard copies. Hard copies of the widely circulated document once existed, but no one had to keep them. What was I to do? Threaten a lawsuit? Write an academic paper? If nothing hap-pened to Bush-Cheney officials after "losing" millions of official e-mails, what could I expect to gain from pressuring officials in some small USDA office who probably didn't have the documents anymore, anyway?[107]

Then there are all of the official communications that go unrecorded. Al-though it is probably too much to ask officials to write down every orally communicated message, we still might consider it problematic that they de-liberately communicate that way to conceal information. Some, like Vice President Cheney, had a firm policy of not writing anything down, with cer-tain exceptions. On top of that, Cheney prevented others from recording his comments and the details of his meetings. The US military's Joint Special Operations Command (JSOC) similarly "instructs its members not to write down important information," for fear of FOIA—even though JSOC infor-mation qualifies for classification or FOIA exemptions by default.[108]

The episodes this chapter recounted—the missing e-mails, the shredded documents, the destroyed videos—were cases where officials were somehow caught red-handed when the pressure was on. Other episodes popped up in earlier chapters (such as shredding during the Clinton-Gore health care task force conflict). Many, many others probably came and went "without a trace"; a long line of criminal officials successfully covered their tracks. What we have here is only a fragmentary history of official, illegal destruction—a mosaic of the secrecy system's underbelly.[109]

10

"THE MOST OPEN AND TRANSPARENT ADMINISTRATION IN HISTORY"?

It seemed like a headline straight out of the Bush-Cheney years—but worse: US APPROVES TARGETED KILLING OF AMERICAN CLERIC. The April 2010 story in the *New York Times* reported on the Obama-Biden administration's decision to kill Anwar al-Aulaqi, a US citizen, at some later date, without a trial or any other features of the due process system. Later leaks revealed the White House maintained a secret "kill list" of terrorist suspects, reportedly including at least a few other US citizens. The administration did not typically discuss the extrajudicial assassinations program in public. However, two months before Obama-Biden killed Aulaqi, Director of National Intelligence Dennis C. Blair disclosed that intelligence agencies claimed the authority to target Americans. But he was vague about the specifics, including the knotty question of how the administration approached the issue legally: "If we think that direct action will involve killing an American, we get specific permission to do that." Further leaks revealed that the "special permission" came straight from the White House, which gave CIA and JSOC agents the authority to kill citizens.[1]

Al-Aulaqi, a purveyor of Islamist anti-American propaganda, no doubt learned about his presidential death sentence right away, despite living in the far reaches of Yemen. He had an active online presence, with a popular blog, a Facebook page, and a YouTube channel. The news of his impending death predictably elicited more denunciations of the US government and its depravities. Being geographically and ideologically far from the United States, he was in no position to hire a lawyer. However, his father, Nasser al-Aulaqi, did just that, enlisting the ACLU, which partnered with the Center for Constitutional Rights.

The ACLU's case against the government raised serious constitutional issues, especially regarding violations of the Fourth and Fifth Amendments and the bill of attainder clause. It also sparked a (mostly elite-level) political debate about the legality of extrajudicial killings of US citizens—an amazing historical turn in its own right, happening during the presidency of a liberal

Democratic Party leader and Nobel Peace Prize winner. Only later—in early 2013 with the leak of a related DOJ white paper—would the issue garner wider national attention. No one contested the fact that Anwar al-Aulaqi preached the indiscriminate killing of US civilians. The evidence was online for all to see. But the Obama-Biden administration insisted Al-Aulaqi was no mere propagandist but an operational member of Al Qaeda who actively recruited and coached terrorists and planned attacks on US citizens, including the failed plot by the "underwear bomber," Umar Farouk Abdulmutallab. Al-Aulaqi acknowledged meeting Abdulmutallab but denied operational involvement. When the ACLU asked to see the evidence, the government refused, asserted the state secrets privilege, and asked the DC district court to dismiss the case. The court complied, emphasizing Nasser Al-Aulaqi's lack of standing. Al-Aulaqi was left impotent in staving off the assassination of his son. And the ACLU and its supporters were left with few ways to legally challenge the extraordinary new expression of executive power.[2]

About ten months later, JSOC agents killed Al-Aulaqi by firing Hellfire missiles from a Predator drone hovering over Yemen's Al Jawf region. The drone attack killed four, including another US citizen, Samir Khan, who may or may not have been on Obama's "kill list." Khan was likely a target, however, because of his work as editor of Al Qaeda's *Inspire* magazine. Two weeks later, US drones struck another American in Yemen, Abdulrahman al-Aulaqi, the cleric's sixteen-year-old son, at a restaurant with his seventeen-year-old Yemeni cousin. The boy apparently had nothing to do with his father's work. Officials said they regretted the error; they allegedly tried to kill someone else. Remarkably, the administration was not held accountable for mistakenly killing a citizen—a sixteen-year-old accused of (and convicted of) no crimes—save for some harsh words on the media periphery. Another US citizen, Jude Kenan Mohammad, met his fate—death by Predator drone—in November 2011 in South Waziristan, Pakistan, where he allegedly worked as a recruiter for Al Qaeda.[3]

Through leaks, it eventually became clear Obama-Biden's policy of extrajudicial killings rested upon a classified Office of Legal Counsel memo, which provided the legal justification for depriving citizens of constitutional due process guarantees. It seemed like Bush-Cheney-style "secret law" all over again, something many thought Obama-Biden had rejected. The policies and processes remained shrouded in secrecy, but Attorney General Eric Holder spoke obliquely about them in a May 2012 speech. He offered hints about how the memo allowed the president to twist around the Fifth Amendment's due process clause: "'Due process' and 'judicial process' are not one and the same, particularly when it comes to national security. The Constitution guarantees due process, not judicial process." After unilaterally reinterpreting the meaning of *due process,* the administration apparently created a kind of star chamber in the executive branch to make critical life-and-death decisions. The unitary executive theorists from the Bush-Cheney administration must have been proud (see chapter 2).[4]

The Al-Aulaqi case, with its secret presidential kill list, secret OLC legal memo justifying the extrajudicial killing of citizens, and expansive SSP assertion, placed candidate Obama's inspiring rhetoric about hope and change in stark contrast to what was, at a minimum, Bush-Cheney business as usual. The case not only incorporated what open government and civil liberties advocates considered some of the worst parts of the Bush-Cheney years but also upped the ante. Though Bush-Cheney tortured US citizens (such as Jose Padilla) and maintained what Seymour Hersh called an "executive assassination ring" targeting foreign nationals, the Republicans never claimed the authority to kill citizens outside the criminal justice system (as far as we know). Yet despite Obama's turnaround, Democratic partisans lined up behind the president. At the very least, many could quietly admit, with Sen. Ron Wyden (D-OR), that they "expected better" (although Wyden's criticism went deeper than that, as we will see). Perhaps the transgressions were not as bad as they seemed. After all, the administration frequently touted its "unprecedented" commitment to and record of transparency.[5]

The Promise

After the deeply secretive Bush-Cheney administration, Obama-Biden supporters expected more. Candidate Obama in 2008 (vaguely) promised major changes from the Bush-Cheney status quo, including a restoration of the rule of law and an unwavering commitment to open government. At first, it seemed like he would deliver.

One minute after Obama's inauguration, on the first blog post on a revamped WhiteHouse.gov website, the administration reminded Americans that the president was "committed to making his administration the most open and transparent in history." The next day, the president issued memos directing his subordinates to ensure "an unprecedented level of openness in Government." In a separate swearing-in ceremony, he lamented that "for a

long time now there's been too much secrecy in this city," pledging "the beginning of a new era of openness":

> This administration stands on the side not of those who seek to with-
> hold information, but those who seek to make it known. . . . I will also
> hold myself, as president, to a new standard of openness. Going for-
> ward, any time the American people want to know something that I or
> a former president wants to withhold, we will have to consult with the
> attorney general and the White House counsel, whose business it is to
> ensure compliance with the rule of law. . . . Let me say it as simply as
> I can. Transparency and the rule of law will be the touchstones of this
> presidency.

These were promises the president could keep, since he was not dependent on
the other branches of government to succeed in doing so. They required his
leadership and control of the bureaucracy, as well as a solid commitment to
principles he claimed to uphold. Reforming bureaucratic practice, especially
in the change-resistant secrecy system, was no easy task. Previous presidents,
however, had managed to use decrees and other means to move the system
marginally closer to our "acceptable world" (see chapter 2).[6]

Through the end of Obama-Biden's first term, after the Al-Aulaqi affair
and dozens of other controversies, the administration insisted it had kept
its promise. Chief of Staff Jacob Lew claimed, without hesitation or caveats,
that "this administration has been the most transparent ever." Press Secretary
Jay Carney, a year earlier, said: "This president has demonstrated a commitment to transparency and openness that is greater than any administration
has shown in the past, and he's been committed to that since he ran for President and he's taken a significant number of measures to demonstrate that."
Reflecting on his first term in February 2013, Obama proclaimed, "This is
the most transparent administration in history." Senior officials across all four
years never stopped beating that drum.[7]

A "Glass Half Full"?[8]

There is no question the Obama-Biden administration took steps to increase
transparency and openness. On his second day in office, President Obama revoked Bush's 2001 changes to the Presidential Records Act, which had erected

new barriers around former presidents' papers (Obama did, however, keep Bush's inclusion of vice presidential papers). On the same day, he ordered all "appropriate executive departments and agencies" to contribute specific, actionable recommendations to an "open government directive" (OGD), which would push the executive branch toward more transparent, participatory, and collaborative governance. In December 2009, the White House's OMB finally issued a corresponding directive to all relevant government agencies outlining the specific steps they needed to take to: "publish government information online," "improve the quality of government information," "create and institutionalize a culture of open government," and "create an enabling policy framework for open government." The requirements were unambiguous, such as publishing "at least three high-value data sets" on the new Data. gov site, and creating open government web pages with specific public feedback features. Agencies and departments were given latitude in implementing the OGD, but the White House did institute "agency-wide internal control assessments" and interagency coordination groups to ensure the "high-level senior officials" would indeed be held accountable "for the quality and objectivity" of their initiatives. In practice, this meant citizen access to unclassified but undisseminated information like "hospital report cards, dangerous workplaces, airport delays, wildfires and even calories in foods," as Gary Bass, OMB Watch director, pointed out. None of Obama-Biden's predecessors did anything remotely as progressive on this dimension of transparency, what scholars call "proactive transparency" or "affirmative disclosure." It was a major advance, and not the only one.[9]

In September 2009, the administration announced it would disclose the names and details from the White House visitors logs on a monthly basis—a truly unprecedented step toward open government. Interested citizens could, for the first time, browse the logs, posted online (with important exceptions, discussed later). They could also scrutinize logs for the vice president's residence as well as two executive office buildings. Obama's 2013 boast about his administration's record notably focused on these changes: "This is the most transparent administration in history. And I can document how that is the case. Everything from every visitor that comes into the White House is now part of the public record. That's something that we changed. Just about every law that we pass, every rule that we implement, we put on line for everybody."[10]

Classification Rates

Perhaps more significant were Obama-Biden's efforts on classification. Executive Order 13526 explicitly affirmed Obama's commitment to open government and transparency. Specifically, it reinstitutionalized, with a few tweaks, Clinton's major declassification program. Obama's decree created the Systematic Declassification Review (SDR) program through the new National Declassification Center (NDC), and it roused Clinton's automatic, mandatory, and discretionary declassification review programs, all killed by Bush in 2003.[11]

As Figure 10.1 shows, the program failed to take off during Obama-Biden's first term, when declassification rates trailed behind Bush-Cheney's. Indeed, Bush maintained relatively higher rates, even after he gutted Clinton's program in 2003, declassifying on average 32.7 million pages per year from 2004 to 2008. By contrast, Obama-Biden declassified an average of 26.1 million pages per year between 2009 and 2012. To be sure, comparing quantities of declassified pages only goes so far. For instance, earlier declassification efforts might have genuinely succeeded in clearing out agencies' secret libraries. But it is remarkable how little had changed during Obama-Biden, even after the ambitious launch of SDR and the NDC. By early 2012, the administration was far behind its own declassification goals. It estimated in December 2009 "more than 400 million pages" were ripe for declassification. Two and a half years later, the NDC had cleared just 41.8 million pages (10.5 percent).[12]

Some of the blame could be directed at bureaucratic impediments, such

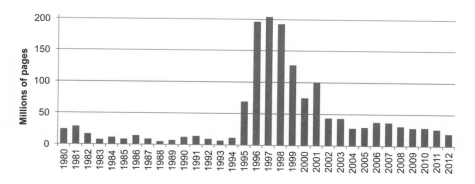

FIGURE 10.1
Declassification, 1980–2012.
Source: 1997, 2011, and 2012 ISOO Reports to the President

as the still-active Kyl-Lott Amendment of the 2000 Defense Authorization Act, which required information officers to guarantee each potentially declassified page was "highly unlikely to contain Restricted Data or Formerly Restricted Data" about US nuclear programs. One way agencies complied with the statute was through multiple referrals—sending documents around the government to ensure they posed low risks. Despite Obama's insistence in 2009 that "further referrals of these records [open to declassification] are not required" unless they "clearly and demonstrably reveal" the identities of human intelligence sources or information about weapons of mass destruction, information workers apparently could not drop the old habit of sending cleared documents around the government for multiple reviews. It slowed the process considerably. One 1983 document about a Soviet-directed military exercise, for example, cleared fourteen different agencies but still awaited a final declassification decision at the end of 2012.[13]

Although his government barely made a dent in the 400-million-page backlog, Obama's record on reducing *over*classification—another major goal from 2009—appears relatively stronger. To be sure, Obama-Biden added to our ever-expanding catalog of absurdist overclassification tales. To cite one example, we learned in July 2013 that 9/11 mastermind Khalid Sheikh Mohammed had taken up vacuum cleaner design, with the CIA's permission, while imprisoned in one of the agency's black sites in Romania in the early 2000s (he had training as a mechanical engineer). That Mohammed's tinkering stayed secret for a decade is questionable enough. That the government effectively placed a vacuum cleaner gag order on his lawyer is what makes the story so memorable. "It sounds ridiculous," Jason Wright said, "but answering this question [about the tinkering], or confirming or denying the very existence of a vacuum cleaner design, a Swiffer design, or even a design for a better hand towel would apparently expose the U.S. government and its citizens to exceptionally grave danger."[14]

Nevertheless, the administration took some important steps. The president's January 2009 Executive Order 13526 demanded yearly training of original classification authorities (OCAs) in "proper classification (including the avoidance of over-classification)." Derivative classifiers were required to train "at least once every two years." The decree also established a two-year Fundamental Classification Guidance Review (FCGR) program, which required departments and agencies to "comprehensively review" their policies to ensure they met the order's standards (Section 1.9). Obama also had help from Congress's Reducing Over-Classification Act of 2010, which promised

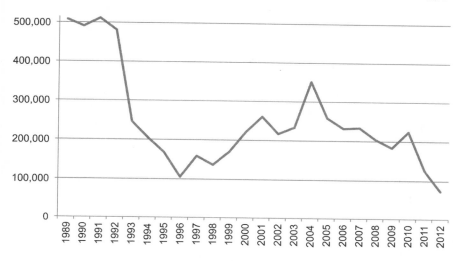

FIGURE 10.2
Original Classification Decisions, 1989–2012.
Source: Annual ISOO Reports

to facilitate interagency information sharing and further tighten the rules to prevent overclassification. All of the efforts appeared to stem the overclassification tide by 2012 (see Figure 10.2).[15]

Original classification decisions dropped 43 percent from 2010 to 2011, followed by another steep drop of 43 percent in 2012, to a record low of 73,477. Granted, those reductions followed a substantial increase in classification decisions from 2009 to 2010, and there was no guarantee that the trend would continue through Obama-Biden's second term. Nevertheless, the ISOO did find evidence that the observed decrease was due to a "greater adherence to executive order guidance on the incorporation of original decisions into classification guides" by OCAs, whose agencies updated the guides as a result of Obama's FCGR process. If OCAs continued to follow the new rules, then the decrease likely continued or at least did not reverse back to Bush-Cheney levels. See chapter 3 for caveats about reliability problems with ISOO data.[16]

At the same time, however, the number of derivative classification decisions skyrocketed, from the already very high 23.2 million during Bush-Cheney's last year in office to 54.7 million in 2009, 76.6 million in 2010, 92.1 million in 2011, and 95.2 million in 2012 (Figure 10.3). The numbers are startling. Although the ISOO pointed out that the record-breaking num-

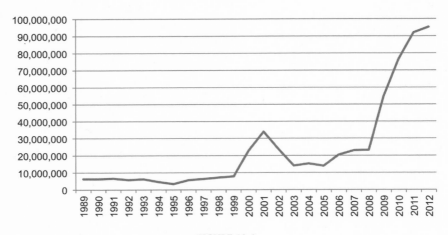

FIGURE 10.3
Derivative Classification Decisions, 1989–2012.
Source: Annual ISOO Reports

bers were largely due to new measurement rules that, for the first time, fully counted "classified web pages, blogs, wikis, bulletin boards, instant messaging, etc.," the daily realities of the less controlled *process* of derivative classification should keep us from being too sanguine (see chapter 3). Obama did issue new classification training standards for those with derivative classification authority. However, given the huge number of people involved—millions scattered around the country in the public and private sectors, who may or may not have been trained properly—there are reasons to be skeptical. Plus, derivative classifiers very likely make new secrets, despite government promises to the contrary (see chapter 3).[17]

FOIA Administration

The administration's record was also mixed on unclassified information and FOIA requests. President-Elect Obama made improving FOIA administration a top priority, leading to another promising January 2009 directive, in which he in effect restored the Reno Memo's standard of "maximum responsible disclosure" (see chapter 3). Obama urged his FOIA officers to follow a "presumption in favor of disclosure. . . . In the face of doubt, openness prevails." The directive also complemented the OGD's proactive transparency initiative, noting that "the presumption of disclosure also means that agencies should take affirmative steps to make information public."[18]

The extent to which the new rules pushed agencies into action remained unclear, but FOIA administration under Obama-Biden moved in a positive direction, albeit very slowly. In the year following the January 2009 memo, less than 15 percent of government agencies demonstrated "any concrete changes in their FOI practices," according to the National Security Archive's Knight Open Government Survey. In March 2010, White House chief of staff Rahm Emanuel and White House counsel Bob Bauer distributed a memo urging agencies to "improve implementation" of the January 2009 memo. That push from the top seemed to do the trick. The next Knight Survey found more than half of the agencies were well on their way toward compliance. Although there was still quite a lot of variation across agencies, the study concluded, "a gradual move toward better discretionary release practices appears to be underway." Other open government groups, including OpenTheGovernment.org and OMB Watch, reached similar conclusions.[19]

Conclusion

For this slow but steady progress, the most prominent open government groups in the United States took the unprecedented step of giving President Obama, in early 2011, an award for his "deep commitment to transparency." All of those groups—the National Security Archive, OMB Watch, OpenThe-Government.org, Project on Government Oversight, and Reporters Committee for Freedom of the Press—acknowledged the administration had fallen short in a number of ways. Still, they said there were reasons for cautious optimism. Progressive change in American politics rarely happens instantaneously. Veto points, entrenched interests, and other obstacles always stand in the way. As OMB Watch's Gary Bass noted,

> At the midpoint of President Obama's term, we can say that his commitment to open government is truly extraordinary. That's not to say we're happy with every action taken under the Obama administration; we're not. We've got a long way to go to reach the point where government is consistently delivering the openness that the American people deserve. However, it's important to remember how far we've come in a little more than two years—and to acknowledge it.[20]

These Are Not Reflections of a "Most Transparent Administration"

That the administration chose to accept the open government award behind closed doors struck many as a sign the groups had badly miscalculated. The irony was not lost on the award-givers themselves. OMB Watch's Bass, for instance, was baffled by the administration's decision: "It's almost a theater of the absurd to have an award on transparency that isn't transparent." Nevertheless, the groups stuck with their assessments, seeing Obama as a proven ally with a lot of potential. "The irony is that everything the president said [in secret] was spot-on," Bass recalled. The secret meeting was probably just a "victory lapse," as the comedian Jon Stewart put it.[21]

Another set of open government activists vehemently disagreed. In an open letter to the award presenters, Sibel Edmonds, Daniel Ellsberg, Coleen Rowley, and a host of other individuals and organizations demanded the presenters "Rescind President Obama's 'Transparency Award' Now." Far from making slow but steady progress, "the Obama administration's record on secrecy and surveillance is a disgrace and should not be sanitized by unearned prizes." Accepting the award in private was not the main issue; it was only emblematic of Obama-Biden's lamentable record.[22]

At issue were a range of complaints, including the administration's liberal use of the state secrets privilege, its aggressive attacks on government whistle-blowers, and its secret assassination program that killed at least three citizens (the fourth, Jude Kenan Mohammad, was still alive at that time). The signatories, along with other critics, also offered harsher assessments of the Obama-Biden administration's ostensible successes, from its progress on the OGD to the visitors logs to the effort to reduce overclassification. Take, for instance, the curious development of the OGD.

President Obama's January 2009 memo introducing the OGD promised a sea change in government transparency, and it called for more citizen participation in and collaboration with government decision making. The memo asked agencies to submit specific recommendations. The OMB's December 2009 directive incorporated and synthesized those proposals. Further developments, however, remained a mystery, for the administration concealed them. The AP, for example, filed a FOIA request for information about the development of the OGD directive. The administration responded with hundreds of heavily redacted pages—including an e-mail discussing the AP's FOIA request and others discussing OGD rules that didn't make the cut—all justified by FOIA's deliberative process exemption. The AP reported on the sad irony of those dark blots in its 2011 "Sunshine Week" progress report. If the OGD had ultimately produced dazzling results, then we might reasonably overlook the secrecy. But Obama-Biden's slow progress in the first term was hardly dazzling.[23]

Consider also the unveiling of the White House visitors logs, Obama's celebrated effort to reduce lobbyists' influence in his administration. That anyone with an Internet connection could monitor the guest list was no doubt a step forward. But the ease with which officials flouted the letter and spirit of the new policy undermined its credibility. For one, the new rules contained several vaguely defined exceptions: "purely personal guests," guests whose visits "would threaten national security interests," and guests involved in "particularly sensitive meetings," such as potential Supreme Court nominees. As we have seen throughout the book, all administrations exploit ambiguously worded secrecy rules, some more than others. Though Obama-Biden officials might not have abused their interpretive powers, their successors easily could. The framework invites it. Plus, citizens, legislators, and judges have no way of verifying whether executive branch officials use the exceptions judiciously. In the colorful language of political science, the process contains no horizontal or vertical accountability mechanisms.

We do not know how frequently Obama-Biden abused the visitor log exceptions, but we do know officials defied the policy—easily and without consequence. The Center for Public Integrity discovered huge gaps in the public database, with hundreds of thousands of names and visit details missing. Moreover, administration officials used evasive tactics to ensure their meetings would escape the logs. Thus, instead of meeting lobbyists at the White House or other executive office buildings, officials often met them across the street at Caribou Coffee and other locations. The off-the-books meetings occurred so frequently that they became common knowledge in Washington. It was just how officials did their jobs in the new institutional environment. One lobbyist who met with White House staffers several times over cappuccinos at Caribou said that the administration at some level wanted to comply with its own rules but that officials simply "[had] to do their job[s]." When confronted with the seeming hypocrisy, top White House officials denied any wrongdoing and merely restated that the administration was taking "unprecedented steps to increase the openness and transparency," apparently on other dimensions.[24]

Only under pressure from Judge Beryl A. Howell of the US District Court for the District of Columbia, in response to a Judicial Watch FOIA lawsuit, did Obama-Biden release more—but far from all—of the names and details (overall, "very thin gruel," assessed Steven Aftergood). Each round of selective visitor log disclosures came with heaps of self-congratulations, such as one September 2012 White House announcement hailing "Obama's commitment to government transparency." Away from the spotlight, officials aggressively fought Judicial Watch in court, claiming the logs were immune to FOIA. Building on precedents set by Clinton-Gore (National Security Council records) and Bush-Cheney (Office of Administration records), Obama-Biden officials argued the Secret Service–managed records "are not agency records subject to the FOIA." Instead, they asserted, "these records are records governed by the Presidential Records Act, 44 U.S.C. §2201 et seq., and remain under the exclusive legal custody and control of the White House Office and the Office of the Vice President." This time, the tried-and-true word game tactic of claiming "Agency X is not an agency" failed.[25]

Unclassified Information

Upon taking office, President Obama was unequivocal about FOIA's importance, saying it was "the most prominent expression of a profound national commitment to ensuring an open Government." His reinstitutionalization of Clinton-Gore's "presumption of disclosure" standard, after being pushed aside by Bush-Cheney, signaled he and his administration would take that national commitment seriously. The Obama-Biden record on FOIA and unclassified information disclosure more generally, however, was mixed at best.

For example, the percentage of fully granted FOIA applications—when applicants got everything they wanted—remained lower in Obama-Biden's first term than in all but one of the Bush-Cheney years (47.5 percent in 2008, as in 2010) (Figure 10.4; see chapter 3 for a note on methods). Worse, the Bush-Cheney average for full grants across eight years was 61.7 percent, whereas Obama-Biden could only manage 43.5 percent. A relative increase of partial grants made up most of the difference, but the Democrats did fully deny FOIA requests in record numbers (Bush-Cheney's eight-year average was 4.2 percent; Obama-Biden's first term average was 5.4 percent). Though the amount of secrets protected in the partial grants remains unknown—that is, the ratio of redacted to unredacted information in the disclosures—partial grants necessarily involve more secrecy than full grants. There might not have been an epidemic of outright denials, but there was an outbreak of re-

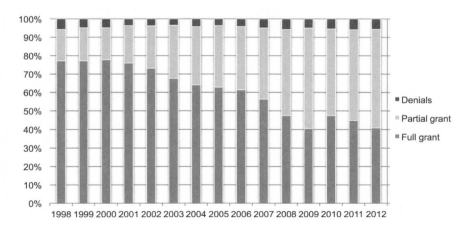

FIGURE 10.4
FOIA Grant Rates, 1998–2012.
Source: Coalition of Journalists for Open Government; FOIA.gov; government
agency annual FOIA reports

dactions. Recall also the failure of the administration to make a dent in the FOIA backlog.

Also consider the Obama-Biden administration's problematic record on controlled unclassified information (CUI)—what Bush-Cheney called sensitive but unclassified information (see chapter 3). The administration, once again, promised progressive change. In November 2010, the president published Executive Order 13556 on CUI, in which he openly criticized the "ad hoc, agency-specific policies, procedures, and markings to safeguard and control this [unclassified] information, such as information that involves privacy, security, proprietary business interests, and law enforcement investigations." At issue were "improvised access controls"—markings like "For Official Use Only," "Sensitive Security Information," and "Not for Public Dissemination" —that agencies tended to use haphazardly and, arguably, excessively. "This inefficient, confusing patchwork," Obama continued, "has resulted in inconsistent marking and safeguarding of documents, led to unclear or unnecessarily restrictive dissemination policies, and created impediments to authorized information sharing. The fact that these agency-specific policies are often hidden from public view has only aggravated these issues." As Obama recognized, the problem collided with his stated open government commitments, and therefore, he outlined a new system that would "emphasize the openness and uniformity of Government-wide practice."[26]

Two years later, there were still "more than 100 different policies for such information across the Executive branch," according to the ISOO. The "ad hoc, agency-specific approach" was still creating "inefficiency and confusion, leading to a patchwork system that fail[ed] to adequately safeguard information requiring protection, and unnecessarily restrict[ed] information sharing by creating needless impediments." This was despite the fact that the CUI office in the ISOO issued an "implementation guidance" memo to agencies after "robust interagency processes" with "working groups" and much discussion of "categories and subcategories." In short, there seemed to be a lot of bureaucratic energy put into the process with seemingly little to show for it, at least by the end of the first term.[27]

Worse, some of the government's largest departments were moving in the opposite direction, which could not have escaped the White House's attention. DOD, for example, proposed a regressive CUI rule at the same time (in July 2011) the ISOO offered progressive guidance. DOD officials sought to safeguard any CUI protected by the DOD's prior ad hoc markings, thereby "grandfathering" the secrets despite Obama's new system and without any regard for whether they deserved continued protection. Moreover, the DOD proposed it would turn Obama's presumption of disclosure (and OGD) on its head, implementing its own presumption of secrecy standard. DOD officials announced that "unclassified Government information shall not be posted on websites that are publicly available or have access limited only by domain/ Internet Protocol restriction"—in essence, all unclassified information should be presumed protected until proven otherwise. The final rule—or at least the parts published in the DOD's June 2012 instruction manual "Security of Unclassified DoD Information on Non-DoD Information Systems"—abandoned the grandfathering proposal but kept the latter one (the presumption of secrecy in Section 2(i)).[28]

Another of the government's largest and most important departments, the DOJ, moved decidedly away from the letter and spirit of Obama's 2009 FOIA memo. The DOJ proposed new FOIA guidelines that would have let its information officers *lie* to applicants about the existence of records sought by FOIA applicants. To pull that one off, DOJ officials utilized a strained interpretation of a 1986 FOIA amendment that authorized agencies, under specific conditions, to "treat [requested] records as not subject to the requirements of" FOIA (5 U.S.C. Section 552(c)). In practice, that meant issuing FOIA denials without the need to cite specific exemptions (in essence: *No, you can't have the documents you requested. Why? Because I said so.*). The conditions were limited to instances when a FOIA applicant: (1) was the unknowing subject of an ongoing criminal investigation, (2) sought information about an undisclosed government informant, and (3) sought FBI records involving intelligence or terrorism when the existence of those records was already classified.[29]

Evidence that Obama-Biden DOJ officials already had lied to FOIA applicants emerged in *Islamic Shura Council of Southern California et al. v. FBI*, a FOIA case involving the FBI's covert surveillance and investigation of Muslims and mosques in the United States. As the case proceeded, the District Court for the Central District of California discovered the FBI had deceived the plaintiffs and the court about the existence of relevant records. Judge Cormac J. Carney lambasted the FBI for its actions, stating plainly that "the Government lied to the court." It is hard to reconcile Obama-Biden's claims to be the most transparent administration in history with Judge Carney's scathing criticism:

> The Government asserts that it had to mislead the Court regarding the Government's response to Plaintiffs' FOIA request to avoid compromising national security. The Government's argument is untenable. The Government cannot, under any circumstance, affirmatively mislead the Court. The United States Constitution entrusts the Judiciary with the power to determine compliance with the law. It is impossible for the Court to determine compliance with the law and to protect the public from Government misconduct if the Government misleads the Court.

A response by an administration seeking the "most transparent" crown might have included expressions of embarrassment and contrition or at least an abandonment of official FOIA lying (which may or may not have started with *Islamic Shura Council v. FBI*). Instead, the DOJ upped the ante, proposing to institutionalize FOIA lying.[30]

Differences between FOIA-evading techniques might at first seem small. Information officers already had the authority to deny FOIA requests without citing specific exemptions (for instance, "what has been requested is not a record subject to the FOIA")—the "*no because I said so*" response. A more evasive response is the so-called Glomar denial, by which agencies can "neither confirm nor deny" the existence of records for specific national security and personal privacy reasons (*We cannot tell you whether your requested documents even exist.*). The DOJ wanted to go one step further by letting FOIA officers across the government outright lie and pretend that specific "records did not exist" (Section 16.6(f)(2)), even if they really did (*We are rejecting your FOIA request because nothing of the kind exists* [but actually it does].). FOIA officers were supposed to use the deception tool under the three conditions noted earlier (undisclosed government informants, ongoing investigations of applicants, or FBI terrorism and intelligence information). However, as we have seen, secrecy powers have a tendency to expand in scale and scope beyond their initial legal purpose. In the end, a bipartisan group of senators, judges, and open government advocates sounded the alarm, arguing the proposed rule would clearly have interfered with judicial review in FOIA cases and further eroded public confidence in government integrity. The political resistance worked: Obama-Biden's DOJ abandoned the proposed change in November 2011.[31]

Other cases of a less than stellar record on unclassified information abound. For example, the Department of Homeland Security, following the Bush-Cheney playbook, routinely referred FOIA applications by specific media and activist groups to senior political appointees in the White House for special scrutiny. In particular, FOIA requests sent by the ACLU, the Electronic Frontier Foundation (EFF), the Electronic Privacy Information Center (EPIC), Human Rights Watch, the Identity Project, and the Associated Press all were singled out for an "extra layer of review." Thus, Obama-Biden, widely viewed as politically liberal, maintained a policy of politically filtering FOIA activities of some of the country's most prominent human rights, civil liberties, and open government groups—not to mention the AP, a mainstream media organization.[32]

Also consider Obama-Biden's case against Thomas Drake, the National Security Agency whistle-blower. In addition to taking the unusual step of trying to prosecute Drake with the Espionage Act (see the later discussion), the administration sought to exclude from the trial *unclassified* information, a legal action without precedent. The secrecy action clearly riffed off of the SSP, which had developed after *Reynolds* as an evidentiary tool to exclude classified information from trials. In *USA v. Drake*, Obama-Biden prosecutors cited the *Classified* Information Procedures Act, as well as the National Security Agency Act of 1959, as the basis for excluding the *unclassified* information.[33]

These examples, among others, were reminders that Obama-Biden abandoned its open government commitments whenever convenient. The examples do not discredit the administration's more positive steps on FOIA and unclassified information. Still, the record hardly tilts toward "the most transparent ever" designation, as senior officials so frequently boasted. The remainder of this chapter expands the analysis to include the areas investigated elsewhere in the book, such as FACA, secret law, secret evidence, suppressing and concealing science, and shredding. The broader comparative analysis brings us to the same conclusion.

Secret Law

In early January 2009, President-Elect Obama announced several nominees for top DOJ positions, including Dawn Johnsen to head the Office of Legal Counsel. It seemed a clear sign the incoming administration would repudiate the use of secret law (see chapter 5), as Johnsen had been a prominent critic of the practice during the Bush-Cheney years. Despite Johnsen's experience as an OLC lawyer under Clinton-Gore and as a tenured law professor at Indiana University, unyielding Republican Party opposition in the Senate forced her to withdraw her nomination.[34]

Once in power, the administration made additional moves suggesting it would abandon the controversial practice of using secret executive branch legal memos to justify seemingly illegal official actions. In early March 2009, Obama-Biden released nine secret OLC memos (and more later), covering some of the most contentious Bush-Cheney policies, including warrantless domestic wiretapping, enhanced interrogations and other detainee treatment issues, and unilateral presidential rejection and withdrawal from international treaties. Bush-Cheney supporters and former officials lambasted the administration for releasing the memos. One anonymous "former top official" said it was an "unbelievable" decision that caused "grave damage to our national security." "We have laid it all out for our enemies," one critic declared. A few weeks later, the administration quieted some of that criticism, plus dissent emanating from the intelligence community, by explicitly granting legal immunity to CIA interrogators who relied on the memos as they waterboarded terrorism suspects. Though the immunity deal blocked opportunities to hold the CIA accountable—which was unlikely to happen in the first place given OLC memos' binding, immunizing authority—the release of the memos clearly demonstrated another tilt toward transparency.[35]

Killing Aulaqi et al.

Months went by before the issue of secret law arose again. When it did, Obama-Biden officials revealed they had reversed their earlier position and aligned themselves with most of their sunshine-era predecessors. (The other possibility: they were never really opposed to secret law, only its use for interrogations and so forth.) The turning point came when news leaked that Obama-Biden's OLC had issued a secret memo justifying and legally authorizing the extrajudicial assassination of US citizen Anwar al-Aulaqi. The administration did not publicly comment on the memo, but anonymous officials leaked key details, including its June 2010 origins and its apparent requirement that killing could only follow frustrated attempts to capture and prosecute citizens. FOIA lawsuits filed by the *New York Times* and the ACLU (among others), as well as strong public criticism by some of the president's copartisans in the Senate, failed to convince the administration to disclose the memo or even acknowledge its existence. Attorney General Holder, for instance, dismissed Sen. Ron Wyden's concerns, expressed in public correspondence. But Holder did offer hints about how the administration approached the question of extrajudicially killing citizens in a speech a few weeks later.[36]

Although Holder sidestepped questions about the memo in his March 2012 speech at Northwestern University School of Law, he did speak in broad terms about the "legal principles that guide . . . and strengthen" the administration's national security policies, including its rather unique conception of constitutional due process. One of the strongest legal arguments against the killing of Anwar al-Aulaqi, his teenaged son Abdulrahman, Jude Kenan Mohammad, and Samir Khan—not to mention all of the other drone attack victims in Pakistan, Somalia, and Yemen—was the Fifth Amendment's simple but powerful guarantee of due process: "No person shall be . . . deprived of life, liberty, or property, without due process of law." Traditionally, that process involved the judiciary, which makes determinations about crimes and their punishments. Holder rejected that widely accepted view, saying, "'Due process' and 'judicial process' are not one and the same, particularly when it comes to national security." He did not elaborate much but argued the administration's position was backed by unnamed Supreme Court decisions recognizing the flexibility of the due process clause and the balance between victims' "private interests" and the government's interest. He also pleaded for empathy, especially about the "burdens the government would face in providing additional process" in a national security context. Of course, no one—including legislators, judges, and Northwestern Law professors—could independently evaluate those and related quite consequential legal arguments because of the memo's continuing deep secrecy.[37]

The Willingness to Nullify Laws

Another problem with the memo's secrecy involved the very real possibility it authorized executive branch officials to ignore statutes, as had happened many times before (see chapter 5). Indeed, the OLC under Obama-Biden had already indicated its comfort in issuing statute-defying memos. For example, in a published memo about the "Unconstitutional Restrictions on Activities of the Office of Science and Technology Policy [OSTP]" by a congressional budget bill, the OLC concluded the legislature's interference in executive branch activities (the White House OSTP) "constitutionally interfere[s] with the President's foreign affairs power *and may be disregarded by Executive Branch agencies*" (emphasis added). That memo and at least one more ("Constitutionality of Section 7054 of the Fiscal Year 2009 Foreign Appropriations Act") clearly demonstrated the Obama-Biden OLC's willingness to authorize executive branch officials to "disregard" the law. The administration's classified interpretation of sections of the PATRIOT Act probably also creates irreconcilable tensions with existing (published) law, although the act's secrecy prevents us from including it as another verifiable example here.[38]

Wyden's Warning: The PATRIOT Act's "Secret Interpretation"

The first hint that Obama-Biden had a secret interpretation of the PATRIOT Act came during remarks Sen. Russell Feingold made at a 2009 Senate hearing. Although Feingold was judicious in his language and did not explicitly speak about it—probably to keep his Intelligence Committee information privileges—he did point attentive observers in the right direction. First, he confirmed the government had "information about the use of Section 215 orders"—the "business records" provision, involving FBI domestic surveillance powers—that "Congress and the American people deserve to know." Then, he subtly connected the dots: "Since the Patriot Act was first passed in 2001, we have learned important lessons, and perhaps the most important of all is that Congress cannot grant the government overly broad authorities and just keep its fingers crossed that they won't be misused, or interpreted by aggressive executive branch lawyers in as broad a way as possible." Senator Feingold and his congressional allies then pushed for PATRIOT Act reforms to increase transparency and protect civil liberties, despite the overwhelming bipartisan opposition that supported the status quo.[39]

During one of several congressional debates about renewing sections of the PATRIOT Act in May 2011, Wyden stepped onto the Senate floor with a more direct message, carried live on C-SPAN:

> I want to deliver a warning this afternoon: When the American people find out how their government has secretly interpreted the Patriot Act, they will be stunned and they will be angry. And they will be asking senators, "Did you know what this law actually permits?" "Why didn't you know before you voted on it?" The fact is that anyone can read the plain text of the Patriot Act, and yet many members of Congress have no idea how the law is being secretly interpreted by the executive branch, because that interpretation is classified. It's almost as if there are two Patriot Acts, and many members of Congress haven't even read the one that matters. Our constituents, of course, are totally in the dark. Members of the public have no access to the executive branch's secret legal interpretations, so they have no idea what their government thinks this law means.

Wyden's cosponsor of PATRIOT Act reforms, Sen. Mark Udall (D-CO), also alerted Americans about the administration's secret interpretation in a floor speech, pointing specifically to Section 215, along with Section 206 (Roving Wiretaps) and the so-called lone wolf provision. In a media interview, Udall confirmed that Section 215 was the main issue and that at least one secret memo had been written by the attorney general, not by OLC lawyers, as is usually the case. ("There is a specific opinion by the attorney general on that. The justice department does not do this that often.") The administration responded to the senators' challenge with vague statements about how the Foreign Intelligence Surveillance Court and members of Congress "were aware of how the executive branch was interpreting and using surveillance laws." By "members of Congress," officials meant a very small number of selected legislators on the Intelligence Committee, and it was not clear if "surveillance laws" in the statement included the PATRIOT Act. Still, the senators pressed on. They proposed an amendment to the law that would have induced more transparency. They launched a volley of public letters back and forth with the DOJ, making news every time with warnings about a shadow PATRIOT Act.[40]

Finally, in March 2012, after still more letters from Wyden and Udall and stepped-up citizen activism, including a much publicized FOIA request from the ACLU, the DOJ officials acknowledged the secret legal memos' existence. That was about all they said, although they did also claim that FOIA's Exemption 5 (the deliberative process privilege) justified the secrecy, indicating the memos were actually not classified. Around the same time, the EFF received a FOIA denial telling a similar story: the memos existed, but Exemption 5 protected them. The EFF, along with the ACLU and the *New York Times*, once again sued the DOJ. And once again, the organizations encountered a federal judiciary that seemed reflexively deferential to executive secrecy claims.[41]

Secret Law beyond the DOJ

As chapter 5 demonstrated, presidents have for decades used secret law, inside and outside the OLC. Most of the non-OLC examples come from the National Security Council, but Bush-Cheney invented a novel way of directing the FISC—officially part of the judicial branch—with secret "controlling interpretations." Through Obama-Biden's first term, no evidence surfaced showing the administration secretly interfering with FISC proceedings. However, the administration's NSC did continue the sunshine-era tradition of issuing secret memos, which in the past had authorized executive branch officials to disregard statutes (such as Reagan-Bush's NSDD-77, which authorized illegal domestic propaganda).

The evidence about secret Obama-Biden NSC memos is clear enough. Of fourteen presidential policy directives (PPDs), only four were released by the end of Obama's first term. Seven of the remaining ten had secret names, although the NSC released "fact sheets" summarizing two of them. In addition to the PPDs, the NSC produced eleven presidential study directives (PSDs) but only published two. The name of one PSD (#5) remained classified; the NSC issued a fact sheet and report for another. Through the end of the first term, the NSC managed to prevent leaks for all of its secret memos as well as comments about the memos, making further analysis here impossible.[42]

The second way Obama-Biden dabbled in secret law outside the OLC involved the State Department. One known case concerned Doli Syarief Pulungan, an arms exporter with a history of working at the margins of the law and sometimes beyond (such as shipping arms to embargoed countries). The administration arrested and jailed Pulungan for exporting 100 Leupold Mark 4 CQ/T rifle scopes to Indonesia, a violation of State Department rules because they were "manufactured to military specifications." The catch: Pulungan violated regulations he could not have known about. Only officials with proper security clearances had access to the State Department "munitions list" and related details at the Directorate of Defense Trade Controls. Yes, Judge Frank H. Easterbrook acknowledged, Pulungan knowingly shipped weapons to what he believed was an embargoed country. However, he could not have knowingly or "willfully" acted contrary to the specific rules because of their secrecy. Judge Easterbrook then took the usual step of criticizing the administration for using "the sort of secret law" the Supreme Court condemned in *Panama Refining Co. v. Ryan*, which involved an unpublished regulation that remained "in the hip pocket" of an executive branch official (see chapter 5). For a democracy to work, Judge Easterbrook continued, "a regulation is published for all to see. People can adjust their conduct to avoid liability. A designation by an unnamed official, using unspecified criteria, that is put in a desk drawer, taken out only for use at a criminal trial, and immune from any evaluation by the judiciary, is the sort of tactic usually associated with totalitarian régimes. Government must operate through public laws and regulations." Easterbrook's words and ruling clearly had little impact on Obama-Biden officials, as they continued using secret law after the 2009 case. In the absence of leaks and additional public court cases, we can only speculate about whether secret law in the State Department was a general or rare phenomenon.[43]

Conclusion

The cases covered in this section have established two facts about Obama-Biden. First, the administration demonstrated a willingness to keep and use secret legal memos, inside and outside the OLC. The very existence of some, let alone their content, was kept secret from Congress and the public. Second, Obama-Biden demonstrated a willingness to use secret legal memos to effectively nullify laws. How many times the administration did so remains a mystery.

Obama-Biden's record on secret law appears quite at odds with the administration's early protransparency efforts and rhetoric. The March 2009 declassification and release of Bush-Cheney's secret OLC memos on torture and related subjects suggested officials might take a different approach. Either they reversed their initial position or they never really objected to secret law in the first place. If it was the latter, the early declassifications might have had much more to do with the memos' specific content (such as torture) rather than their secrecy.[44]

Secrecy and the Courts

State Secrets Privilege

On the issue of excessive secrecy, candidate Obama in 2008 tended to criticize the incumbent in very general terms, as when he promised on his website he would reverse "President Bush's policy of secrecy." Abuse of the state secrets privilege was one exception. On the same campaign website, under "ethics," the Democrats lamented that "secrecy dominate[d] government actions" under Bush-Cheney. Along with "ignor[ing] public disclosure rules," the incumbents had "invoked a legal tool known as the 'state secrets' privilege more than any other previous administration to get cases thrown out of civil court." Obama-Biden's promises on this issue were implicit, but any reasonably attentive voter might have concluded that an Obama administration would cut back on SSP assertions, or at least limit the practice of invoking the SSP to force dismissals.[45]

Eight months after inauguration, it seemed Obama would deliver on the campaign promise. Attorney General Holder announced new SSP guidelines and promised the privilege would be "invoked only when necessary and in the narrowest way possible." The DOJ instituted new rules and new review committees to guarantee that any SSP assertion would have "strong evidentiary support for it," based on a "more rigorous standard"—the "significant harm standard." The administration also pledged to refrain from using the SSP to shut down cases, whenever possible. Specifically, Holder promised to "narrowly tailor the use of the [SSP] whenever possible to allow cases to move forward in the event that the sensitive information at issue is not critical to the case." The extent to which the administration adhered to the new system with a measurable impact on SSP assertions is unknown—the DOJ never followed up with a policy evaluation report for the public to scrutinize. It did, however, circulate a very brief report to Congress in April 2011 in which it claimed to scrupulously follow the 2009 guidelines. But the report was vague and short on details, instead citing previously published case documents. And despite Holder's pledge to "provide periodic reports on all cases in which the privilege is asserted to the appropriate oversight Committees in Congress," the DOJ completed only that one April 2011 report during the entire 2009–2013 presidential term. Obama-Biden's "most transparent" boasts were not helped by refusing to comment on or release the report for another fifteen months.[46]

We can, however, examine all known SSP cases to assess the frequency with which Obama-Biden officials invoked the SSP, as well as the way they did so. As chapter 6 demonstrated, tallying up the number of SSP cases per administration offers interesting comparisons, but it can be misleading, given the nonconstant number of cases brought over time as a result of the changing political environment. Another problem with quantitative comparisons is that some cases overlap administrations; a case might, say, start under Clinton-Gore and continue under Bush-Cheney. But if we are to evaluate the administration's pledge to adopt a "more rigorous standard" in invoking the SSP, we should at least begin by comparing usage patterns—keeping the caveats at the top of our heads.

The data in Figure 10.5 suggest slight but visible differences between early Bush-Cheney and early Obama-Biden practices. Indeed, 2009–2011 looks a lot like 2001–2003, although the drop in 2012 does not match 2004's upturn. Likewise, half of the 2009–2011 cases originated before Obama-Biden took office, and five of Bush-Cheney's early cases originated under Clinton-Gore (three in 2001, one in 2002, and one in 2005). Although we will need to wait until 2017 to properly compare the Obama-Biden administrations with its predecessors, the data again show Reagan-Bush as the reigning champion. Bush-Quayle clearly litigated quite a few SSP cases, although many of those originated under Reagan-Bush.[47]

Perhaps a more useful assessment of the Obama-Biden record would focus on whether the administration stopped using the SSP to dismiss cases. After all, this was the part of Bush-Cheney SSP jurisprudence candidate Obama criticized most strongly. The 2009 DOJ guidelines also promised the administration would use the SSP "in the narrowest way possible," suggesting the department might limit motions for dismissal on SSP premises.

The record indicates the administration did no such thing. Of the nine SSP cases Obama-Biden authorities litigated, they sought dismissals in five or six (or seven), depending on how one counts older cases with complex histories and how one interprets the approach in *Nasser al-Aulaqi v. Obama et al.* (in which al-Aulaqi's father tried to save his son's life). In that case, three senior officials submitted unclassified, public SSP assertions. CIA director Leon Panetta explicitly sought dismissal. In their separate SSP assertions, the director of national intelligence, James R. Clapper, and DOD secretary Rob-

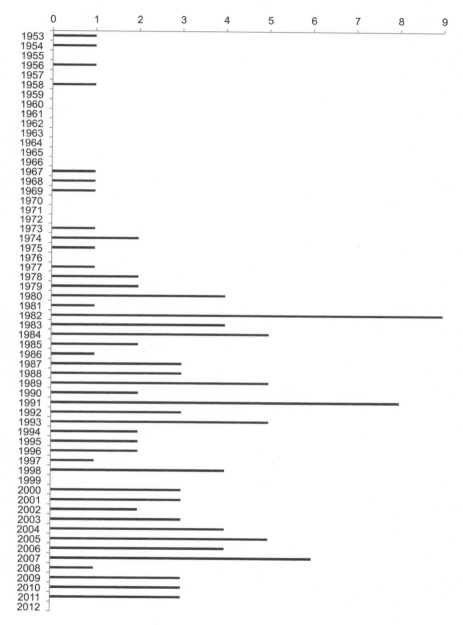

FIGURE 10.5
Annual SSP Assertions, 1953–2012.
Source: Chesney 2007; COGS State Secrets Cases; WestLaw; Lexis-Nexis

ert Gates did not go that far. The administration was obviously divided on the issue. Nevertheless, DOJ lawyers did push to dismiss the case, listing the SSP among other factors meriting dismissal (another was Nasser al-Aulaqi's lack of standing). In the event those reasons were unpersuasive, the DOJ argued, the SSP assertion offered sufficient grounds for dismissal. Thus, if we had to determine whether Obama-Biden sought to dismiss the case, we would need to answer "yes, sort of."[48]

Categorizing the other cases comes more easily. In *Mohamed v. Jeppeson Dataplan*, which originated in 2007, Obama-Biden reasserted Bush-Cheney's earlier SSP in February 2009 and essentially argued that "the entire subject matter [that is, extraordinary rendition of terrorist suspects] of the case is a state secret" (ACLU) (Jeppeson Dataplan, Inc., provided rendition services; Obama the candidate opposed extraordinary rendition). When the Ninth Circuit Appeals Court disagreed, reversing a lower court's decision to dismiss, the administration asked for a rehearing of the case before an en banc panel of judges. Even as it pleaded for another shot, the administration continued to grumble about the need for dismissal.[49]

In *Jewel v. NSA*, Obama-Biden officials followed Bush-Cheney in pushing for dismissal based on the SSP. They did the same in *Shubert et al. v. Obama*, as well as part of *Fazaga v. FBI*. In the latter case, the administration actually referred back to the DOJ's reform pledge, saying it had "narrowly invoke[d] the privilege" after following the "thorough, multi-stage review process" outlined in 2009. The consequence was indeed a narrower SSP invocation, as the DOJ sought to dismiss only some of the plaintiffs' complaints. Still, *Fazaga* involved a SSP-based motion to dismiss, in a case involving FBI agents spying on Muslim Americans in California, in their mosques, and in their larger communities.

The two SSP cases in which Obama-Biden did *not* seek dismissals were *Horn v. Huddle*, a case that originated in 1994, and *General Dynamics Corps. v. United States,* also from the early 1990s (the first SSP in 1993). With another, *Al-Haramain Islamic Foundation v. Obama et al.,* the administration inherited a case where courts under Bush-Cheney had already rejected SSP-based motions to dismiss. We can only speculate about whether Obama-Biden would have done the same (that is, assert the SSP like Bush-Cheney had), all else equal.[50]

It might be true that the particular cases arising during Obama-Biden's first term uniquely merited SSP-based motions to dismiss. Moreover, administration officials did inherit about half of the cases from Bush-Cheney. Drastically changing their predecessors' litigation approach would have had potentially significant political and legal costs. Still, there was little evidence—aside from the narrower SSP invocation in *Fazaga*—that Obama-Biden pursued a different course than the one the candidates, and then the new administration, criticized in 2008 and 2009.

Secret Evidence

As indicated in chapter 6, the difference between secret evidence and the SSP is not always clear, as both involve executives' evidentiary strategies in federal trials. Administrations claim the SSP to exclude evidence because litigants' access to it would allegedly threaten national security. By contrast, they sometimes seek to include but conceal from defendants evidence that affects judicial verdicts and punishments. Secret evidence tends to attract less political attention, in large part because the tactic disproportionately affects foreign nationals. Politicians have fewer incentives to care about noncitizens, and citizens tend to mistakenly believe foreigners do not enjoy constitutional due process protections.

When the secret evidence issue emerged in the 2008 presidential campaign, during broader discussions of Bush-Cheney's military commissions system, Obama expressed reservations about its efficacy (rather than, say, its constitutionality). Because the system allowed secret, hearsay, and coerced evidence (that is, evidence obtained through torture), Obama argued the process could not "sort out the suspected terrorists from the accidentally accused." He generally took a firm position against the commissions system, saying terrorism cases were "too important to be held in a flawed military commission system that has failed to convict anyone of a terrorist act since the 9/11 attacks and that has been embroiled in legal challenges." Once in office, the president placed a 120-day moratorium on military tribunals, and he announced his administration would prosecute terrorist suspects in federal courts, including Al Qaeda's 9/11 "mastermind" Khalid Sheikh Mohammed. Obama also signed the Military Commissions Act of 2009, which eliminated some of the thornier parts of 2006's MCA, including its very permissive section on secret evidence (the new one, however, again backed the principle of a separate justice system and promised its continuation). Furthermore, the administration resisted congressional Republican pressure to resume the tribunals and to file new charges against Guantanamo detainees. Obama's resilience on the issue endured even after fearful events like the failed 2009 bombing attempt on Christmas Day (by "underwear bomber" Umar Farouk Abdulmutallab).[51]

Then, again, came the reversal. In March 2011, Obama announced he would reinstate the military commissions. The president, officials claimed, made his decision only reluctantly. Attorney General Holder blamed congressional Republicans, who blocked every effort to try Guantanamo detainees in the criminal justice system. Blaming obstructionist Republicans in 2011 may have helped reassure Obama's voters, but the charge was a half-truth at best. Senior administration officials had flirted with the idea of resuming the trials early on in the first term. In May 2009, as the first moratorium was about to conclude, an anonymous official confided to the *New York Times* that Obama's top aides were already softening on the issue: "The more they look at it, the more commissions don't look as bad as they did on Jan. 20." In any case, with the revival of military commissions came the reintroduction of secret evidence, which the MCA of 2009 still permitted. Compared with 2006's MCA, the new law offered defendants a greater chance to see and challenge evidence used against them, such as in redacted or summarized forms. But all was left up to the discretion of the military judge, who could decide whether defendants could have even that restricted kind of access. The tribunals finally resumed about a year later.[52]

Before the military commissions of 2012, Obama-Biden officials had already used secret evidence at least once. In fact, they did so at the same time they publicly criticized its use during the tribunal moratorium, in a case against Rajwinder Kaur, an Indian political asylum seeker. Kaur and her husband, Harpal Singh Cheema, fled their Punjab, India, home for California in 1993 as a result of being targeted by the Indian government for Singh's involvement with the Sikh separatist movement. Immigration officials in California arrested and detained Singh soon after the couple arrived in the United States. In prison, he often had to suffer through solitary confinement for twenty-three hours a day, until he "chose" to be deported in 2006. He told an immigration judge in 2006 that he would rather "die in a real jail in front of his people" than remain imprisoned in the United States without due process. Kaur, however, stayed in the United States, partly because she feared imprisonment and torture in India, but also because she sought permanent residency status so she could work legally and help family members immigrate.[53]

The DOJ fought against Kaur's asylum request. Department officials alleged she tried to smuggle her daughter and nephew into the country, an unlawful act that they said barred any asylum considerations. To support the smuggling story, DOJ lawyers claimed they had damning evidence—but because it was classified, Kaur and her lawyers could not review or challenge it. The DOJ would not even give the defendant a "proper summary" of the evidence, as the Classified Information Procedures Act required. The DOJ insisted the evidence came from "reliable confidential sources," apparently thinking that assertion could void CIPA. Judge Margaret McKeown and the Ninth Circuit Appeals Court disagreed, claiming Obama-Biden's actions were "fundamentally unfair and violated her due process rights." Kaur could resume her quest for asylum, the court ruled, without the hindrance of secret evidence.[54]

Conclusion

Governments have many reasons—sometimes good ones—for entering evidence in a trial while keeping it concealed from the defendant (see chapter 6). Preventing the defendant from challenging the veracity of the evidence or the credibility of the witness or source, however, violates the civil liberties upon which the entire justice system rests. The fact that secret evidence, when eventually disclosed, has often been unreliable makes the problem even more serious. CIPA offers a reasonable, if imperfect, trade-off. That Obama-Biden sought to clearly defy CIPA and to use secret evidence at all in the case against Kaur indicates a less than stellar record—although the administration followed a well-established sunshine-era tradition.

The flip-flop on military tribunals also shows Obama-Biden embracing secret evidence, despite early rhetoric criticizing it. Although Obama might not have initiated a new system of military commissions if he had presided in 2001, he did choose to follow Bush's lead in sustaining a system based on hearsay and secret and coerced evidence. Perhaps Obama surrendered to Republican pressure, as the conventional wisdom suggests, rather than invest much "political capital" in trying to persuade legislators and the public about the rightness of his position. Or perhaps he again got what he wanted.

The Federal Advisory Committee Act

The Obama-Biden administration approached the Federal Advisory Committee Act in a much different way than its two immediate predecessors had. Both Clinton-Gore and Bush-Cheney spent their first years in office ducking FACA in order to design health care and energy policies with the help of outside interests but without the hindrance of citizen monitoring. Both administrations used word games with challengers and the courts to get away with their circumventions legally. Along with Bush-Quayle and especially Reagan-Bush, the sunshine-era administrations developed quite a repertoire of FACA-defying tactics, all of which landed in President Obama's lap when he took over in 2009.

Instead of following the contentious path charted in 1993 and 2001, Obama-Biden officials in 2009 pushed to restore the battered sunshine law, part of their early, wider commitment to transparency. The first move came in September, when the administration announced lobbyists would no longer be allowed to serve on federal advisory committees, following FACA's explicit demand that officials avoid "inappropriately influence" from "special interest[s]." The policy change also followed Obama's campaign pledge to reduce the influence of lobbyists in his administration. Earlier efforts, such as the publication of the White House visitors logs, might have fallen short (see the earlier discussion). And though officials circumvented the White House lobbyist ban by meeting at nearby cafés, the new restrictions raised lobbying costs sufficiently to push K Street to petition for a return to the past.[55]

The administration also created new tools to help citizens monitor task forces. The interactive online FACA database, open to anyone visiting the Federal Interagency Databases Online, fully detailed the goings-on in hundreds of advisory committees. It provided task force members' names, meeting details, committee reports and recommendations, and a range of other relevant data. The proactive transparency tool suggested Obama-Biden officials had no interest in battling FACA as their predecessors had. Instead, they ignored FACA and its procedures altogether when it came to policy making and advisory bodies they deemed particularly important.[56]

Obamacare and Bowles/Simpson

In December 2009, Freedom Watch, an offshoot of the conservative Judicial Watch legal advocacy group, sued the administration for flagrantly violating FACA with the secretive "Obama Health Reform De Facto Advisory Committee" (OHRDFAC). The problem for Freedom Watch head Larry Klayman—who earlier led the charge against Clinton's health care task force—was in establishing that OHRDFAC actually existed in reality. And reality made life difficult for Klayman: the administration had established no such committee while developing the Patient Protection and Affordable Care Act ("Obamacare"). Despite that fact, Klayman complained in court that the

"Committee was subject to and failed to comply with" FACA. Remarkably, the District Court for the District of Columbia agreed. Although OHRD-FAC was a construct in Klayman's mind, something like it had existed. Nevertheless, following precedent, Judge Richard W. Roberts said Klayman could not force the president to abide by FACA's openness requirements unless the "de facto advisory committee" was actually still meeting.[57]

The administration's response to the court was short and evasive. White House deputy counsel Kimberley Harris pointed to the "President's commitment to engage a broad range of stakeholders in the national debate on health care reform." As evidence, Harris cited the participation of Planned Parenthood, the US Chamber of Commerce, and "many other individuals and entities" (not named) who "attended meetings at the White House, at times in groups." She produced a link to a White House blog entry from July 29, 2009, entitled "Full Videos: The Health Care Stakeholder Discussions," that proudly touted "the President's dedication to transparency in the health reform process." The blog post presented eight YouTube videos of meetings from the previous four months. Although Harris did not note it, interested citizens like Klayman could have also reviewed the White House's "Regional Forums" on a separate website, which featured videos and photographic slideshows from most but not all of the forums. Citizens could also have examined the White House Health Care Stakeholder Discussions web page, also with selective audiovisual documentation from forums about particular issues (for example, "Health Reform and Small Business"). Despite all of these (selectively documented) meetings of executive branch officials and private interests discussing what would become Obamacare, Deputy Counsel Harris flatly denied the existence of a health care task force. After identifying some of the "meetings at the White House," she asserted that "the entity that plaintiff describes in the complaints as the 'Obama Health Reform De Facto Advisory Committee' . . . does not exist and has never existed."[58]

The argument, though technically true, was disingenuous. Worse, it was defiant, given Judge Roberts's recognition that *something* like OHRDFAC existed. Nevertheless, Judge Roberts changed course and accepted the government's claim that the meetings did not collectively constitute an ongoing formal advisory committee, arguing, "Freedom Watch further has not rebutted the government's evidence, in the form of the Harris Declaration made under penalty of perjury, that no formal advisory committee on health care reform exists." As a result, the court dismissed most of Klayman's complaints. First, Judge Roberts argued, the quasi-task force no longer met, making advance notice of committee meetings and the opportunity to participate infeasible. Second, the health care meetings "were in the nature of 'an unstructured arrangement in which the government seeks advice from what is only a collection of individuals who do not significantly interact with each other,' a 'model [that] does not trigger FACA'" (incorporating a quote from *AAPS v. Clinton*, the earlier health care task force case). However, precedent (that is, *Judicial Watch v.* [Cheney's] *NEPDG*) and Judge Roberts's earlier acknowledgment that something OHRDFAC-like existed led the court to press Obama-Biden to comply with FACA more thoroughly and directly than it had on its websites. Judge Roberts did not demand meeting minutes, transcripts, and member names. Instead, he politely asked Obama-Biden for a better explanation for why it had not provided that information. The administration failed to respond by the end of its first term.[59]

Perhaps emboldened by their successful circumvention strategy, Obama-Biden officials moved to place the prominent Bowles/Simpson debt commission outside of FACA's purview, despite its clear identity as a task force. When Obama established the National Commission on Fiscal Responsibility and Reform (NCFRR) with an executive order, he neglected to mention FACA or anything related to "transparency," "open records," "public," and so forth. Indeed, it was as if FACA did not exist. This time, however, Speaker of the House John Boehner (R-OH) pointed out the obvious, sending a letter on March 3, 2010, to NCFRR chairmen Erskine Bowles and Alan Simpson that stated:

> President Obama committed that his Administration would create an unprecedented level of openness in government. Assuming this level of openness extends to the critical proceedings of the Commission, does that mean [FACA] will fully apply to the Commission and any subcommittees created by the Commission? In creating other commissions, President Obama has explicitly referenced FACA, yet reference to the Act was omitted in the Executive Order creating the Commission. If it is your intent to have all proceedings of the Commission adhere to FACA, will the Commission notice all meetings in the Federal Register 15 days in advance, open all meetings to the public, and make all meeting minutes available for public inspection?

Almost two months later—a day after NCFRR first met—fifteen congressional Democrats urged Obama to open the proceedings, although they stopped short of demanding full FACA compliance. The administration abruptly changed course, filing a FACA charter that unambiguously acknowledged the law's authority over the commission. Meeting minutes, videos, and the like ensued, available to all interested Internet users at their discretion. Without the bipartisan pressure—and, perhaps, without weak knees—the administration probably would have continued to flout FACA.[60]

A final instance of the "what FACA?" strategy occurred at the very end of Obama-Biden's first term. Following the tragic school shooting in Newtown, Connecticut, in December 2012, Obama announced the creation of a gun control task force led by Vice President Joseph Biden. The task force began meeting the next day. The administration never filed a charter, never announced public participation, and never released full transcripts or other records of the task force's work. Freedom Watch again sued the administration for violating FACA, but its efforts to force the administration to comply with the law failed.[61]

FACA and the Czars

One of several recurring criticisms of Obama-Biden during its first term involved the proliferation of so-called czars, individuals the president put in charge of different policy areas. Much of the criticism came from Obama's partisan opponents, including those caught in the grips of a conspiracy theory or two. As a result, complaints about czars tended to induce a lot of eye rolling, especially among Democrats and other political elites. However, many sober individuals had serious legal concerns about the czarification of the White House, including the fact that approximately forty-two unelected officials secretly shaped policy in collaboration with outside interests, without any public or congressional approval or oversight. Earlier administrations had appointed at least as many.[62]

When the czars are examined for what they often were—senior officials consulting secretly with private interests about specific policy questions—they and their actions do seem at odds with FACA. For example, Obama appointed Carol Browner, the former Clinton-Gore EPA director, as the director of the White House Office of Energy and Climate Change Policy; her job entailed coordinating all relevant policy efforts. No one in the administration referred to her as a czar, and she certainly did not call herself that. It was a title conferred by major media organizations and Washington elites. Still, Browner and her associates did often meet privately with industry representatives, and they did not disclose details about those discussions. On at least one occasion (a meeting about fuel efficiency standards), Browner insisted on secrecy, allegedly ordering all participants to "put nothing in writing, ever." Although reports of that demand caused a bit of a stir around Washington, nothing came of it. No one filed legal complaints, and no one demanded FACA compliance. Indeed, Browner's top colleague during the meeting, Mary Nichols, director of California's Air Resources Board, bragged about the lack of transparency: "That was one of the ways we made sure that everyone's ability to talk freely was protected." One could easily mistake the speaker for Cheney or Addington circa 2001–2002.[63]

Browner's meetings could probably have been defended in court, as in *AAPS v. Clinton*, as "unstructured arrangement[s] in which the government seeks advice from what is only a collection of individuals who do not significantly interact with each other." That sort of "model does not trigger FACA." However, it is not something we would expect to find in an administration touting its commitment to open government. We have no evidence showing the tactic was pervasive in the work of Browner or the other czars. But given the White House's apparent comfort with evading FACA on major policies, it is not unreasonable to hypothesize that it followed such practices on more than one occasion.

Conclusion

Unlike their predecessors, Obama-Biden officials advanced the cause of open government by making efforts to restore, rather than only batter, FACA. First, they banned lobbyists from serving on task forces, in keeping with the law's insistence that officials should not be "inappropriately influenced" by "special interests." Second, they developed interactive web tools for citizens to monitor the many hundreds of task force meetings held across the government. Databases had been available previously, but they had never been so easily accessible.

Obama-Biden's first term also stands out for having comparatively few "fire alarms" raised by Congress and the public about attempts to subvert FACA's open records and participation rules. True, Congress complained about how Bowles/Simpson *almost* went FACA free. Once those complaints surfaced, however, the administration took the unusual step (given the history) of complying with the law. Efforts to circumvent FACA for the Obamacare quasi task force, Biden's gun control task force, and the czar meetings were obviously

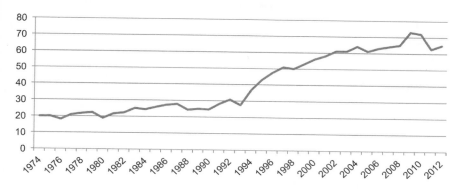

FIGURE 10.6
FACA Meetings (%) Closed to the Public, 1974–2012.
Source: FIDO.GOV database; OpenTheGovernment.org annual
Secrecy Report Cards

more problematic. Beyond betraying the open government cause with each individual evasion, the administration established new FACA-defying precedents for later administrations to use and build upon. Perhaps that is a more important part of its record than the comparatively few public conflicts.[64]

The administration also continued—and ramped up—the little-noticed trend of officially closing task force meetings to the public (Figure 10.6). Following earlier increases by Bush-Cheney and Clinton-Gore, Obama-Biden broke new records in 2009 and 2010, closing 73 percent and 72 percent of task force meetings, respectively. That nearly three-quarters of its task force meetings were closed to the public in those years was hardly something befitting a "most transparent" administration. Only time will tell if the tick downward in 2011 will continue beyond 2012. That downturn, it is worth noting, only brought Obama-Biden back near Bush-Cheney's highpoint (or, given what the numbers mean, low point).[65]

Secret Science

The Memos

The Obama-Biden administration entered office with a pledge to "guarantee scientific integrity throughout the executive branch." In a March 2009 memo, Obama summarized the problem, alluding only indirectly to his predecessor's record (see chapter 7):

The public must be able to trust the science and scientific process informing public policy decisions. Political officials should not suppress or alter scientific or technological findings and conclusions. If scientific and technological information is developed and used by the Federal Government, it should ordinarily be made available to the public. To the extent permitted by law, there should be transparency in the preparation, identification, and use of scientific and technological information in policymaking. The selection of scientists and technology professionals for positions in the executive branch should be based on their scientific and technological knowledge, credentials, experience, and integrity.

The politicization of science—of which suppressing proprietary scientific information was a part—was not a new problem that emerged during the Bush-Cheney years. However, government scientists in those years struggled with repressive, intrusive officials to a degree not seen since Reagan-Bush. In his memo, Obama asked his director of the White House Office of Science and Technology Policy, John Holdren, to "develop recommendations for Presidential action designed to guarantee scientific integrity throughout the executive branch," based on the Open Government Directive, within 120 days; 648 days later, Holdren issued his memorandum. It took a lawsuit to force him to do so.[66]

Holdren's guidelines were not very specific, leaving the details up to agencies, guaranteeing further delay. Given Obama's emphasis on integrity and transparency, Holdren sprinkled his recommendations with the expected paeans to the virtues of open government. A closer reading, however, showed Holdren and the White House wanted to further institutionalize some of the most criticized parts of Bush-Cheney governance—indeed, some of the very practices that had made critics question the agencies' integrity in the first place. For example, Bush-Cheney political appointees regularly pushed aside agency scientists when journalists came calling. Holdren's late 2010 memo instructed agency heads to "offer articulate and knowledgeable spokespersons," not the scientists themselves, to accept interviews with journalists "about the scientific and technological dimensions" of studies. During the Bush years, political appointees were caught on several occasions actually preventing federal scientists from speaking to the public. Scientists in some agencies were allowed to speak—but only in consultation with a nonscientist boss. Holdren similarly put scientists on a leash: "Scientists may speak to the media and the

public" but only "with appropriate coordination with their immediate supervisor and their public affairs office." He justified the overarching free speech
restrictions on the widely accepted need to protect classified information. But
as we have seen, very few secrecy conflicts about scientific information even
involve classified information.[67]

It was not an auspicious start—never mind that the administration was
already about halfway through its first term when Holdren circulated his instructions. To underscore the paradoxical nature of it all, a few days later
the OSTP also released to a FOIA applicant, Public Employees for Environmental Responsibility, a trove of documents from meetings and reports
produced in the run-up to Holdren's memo. However, they were heavily redacted. Deliberations about Obama's new rules on integrity and transparency
were blacked out.[68]

By November 2011—two and a half years after Obama's memo—many of
the relevant agencies still had not developed and published their more specific
rules. Holdren then urged agencies to comply, in a post on the White House's
blog. He did the same in February 2012. Anything would do, he pleaded,
even if the new rules were "still in draft form." Most agencies finally complied
by the last deadline, aside from three rather large units—the Department of
Homeland Security, the Department of Defense, and the Department of Labor.[69]

The Record

Six months after Bush-Cheney left office, science journalists still grumbled
about the public affairs "minders" they had to deal with instead of actual
government scientists. When scientists were allowed to speak, minders ines-
capably joined the conversations. Although Bush-Cheney did not invent the
practice, journalists grew to loathe it once the Republicans increased its use.
But Obama-Biden promised change and begged for patience. Top EPA officials, for instance, reassured journalists, "We're not the Bush administration.
Those days are left behind."[70]

A year later, the problems had still not gone away. One-third of those
surveyed in a random sample of approximately 400 science journalists concluded Obama-Biden had by then done a "poor job," due to the minders, the
FOIA response delays, and other obstacles to open government. By July 2010,
one of the main associations for government scientists, Public Employees for
Environmental Responsibility (PEER), reported that it was "getting com-

plaints from government scientists now at the same rate we were during the Bush administration" and that the conflicts rarely involved classified national security information. Examples included: Pacific Northwest biologists who were pressed to "downplay the impact of dams on wild salmon" populations after observing (that is, collecting data on) real problems; biologists in the West forced to suppress data showing negative environmental effects from cattle grazing on publicly owned land; and Florida water-quality experts who were prevented from analyzing the impact of economic development on the complex Everglades ecology. The Union of Concerned Scientists similarly reported that levels of political meddling through July 2010 rivaled those from the Bush-Cheney years.[71]

Probably the most egregious case of suppressing proprietary scientific information involved the British Petroleum/Deepwater Horizon oil spill, caused by an oil rig explosion in the Gulf of Mexico on April 20, 2010. One of the ongoing criticisms of the administration's public communications during the months-long crisis was the seemingly deliberate underestimation of the severity of the spill. The National Oceanic and Atmospheric Administration announced—and clung to—an estimate of 5,000 barrels per day despite widespread dissent from engineers and scientists outside the government (the generally accepted final estimate was 50,000 barrels of oil a day). When NOAA was asked to defend its methodology as the oil gushed relentlessly, the agency refused to disclose its assumptions and analysis in detail, and it declined to address expert critics' specific complaints. The OMB also refused to allow NOAA scientists to speak publicly about their spill estimates.[72]

About a month after the explosion, NOAA officials also tried to muzzle nongovernmental marine scientists who discovered "undersea oil plumes," a fact that undermined the official narrative that the spill was only a surface-level event. Due to government pressure, science consultants from public universities who discovered the plumes waited until August 2010 to publicly report the finding—and reveal Obama-Biden's free speech restrictions. The oceanographers and marine biologists also reported that senior coast guard and NOAA officials (including Director Jane Lubchenco) threatened or tried to discredit them in order to force their silence. The message seemed clear: do not dare speak about this publicly. It felt like being "beat[en] up" by a puzzlingly aggressive administration. When NOAA finally accepted the fact of gigantic undersea plumes, it still refused to disclose the relevant data. Officials would not even give the data back to the outside scientists who collected it. When pressed by a journalist, a senior NOAA scientist in charge of oil spills said he was "sure we will release the data" at some unspecified later date. As for the scientists' test tubes and petri dishes? "I'm not sure where they are," he admitted.[73]

Finally, when photojournalists attempted to independently document the geographic spread of the oil spill, they found the government had implemented airspace restrictions that kept them from flying over the Gulf of Mexico. Only administration officials had access to that information. Although some of the other acts of information suppression were possibly caused by honest errors or strong scientific disagreements, imposing a journalistic no-fly zone over the Gulf of Mexico was not.[74]

Once crews finally capped the well, Obama-Biden implemented a controversial six-month moratorium on offshore oil drilling. During the drilling freeze, the Department of the Interior hired a group of independent engineers and scientists to review industry standards and extant regulations. The group of outside experts then submitted their recommendations to the DOI, which issued a report suggesting the group favored the moratorium.[75]

According to the DOI's inspector general, however, senior officials in the White House actually edited the DOI's report to make it appear that all members of the group uniformly backed the moratorium (they did not). Not willing to let their views be manipulated, several scientists and engineers complained publicly about the White House's substantive edits. DOI officials insisted that there was no effort to "mislead the public" and that the problem was really a misunderstanding between the expert panel and the DOI. It was a simple mistake, they said, not a suppression of the scientists' actual beliefs. Whether that was true remains unknown, although the assertion looks suspicious in light of all the other oil spill obfuscations.[76]

The EPA's Fracking Studies

On two separate occasions, the Obama-Biden EPA suppressed proprietary information from scientific reports that documented significant amounts of well water contamination resulting from natural gas drilling via hydraulic fracturing ("fracking"). In each case, the EPA dutifully responded to citizens' complaints, sending scientists to investigate. In Parker County, Texas, they went to Steve Lipsky's house after he reported his water had easily combusted and bubbled like champagne. (A local environmentalist who saw the water thought Alka-Seltzer was the better comparison.) Finding signs of methane pollution there and around the county, the EPA launched a wider study of the region to determine as conclusively as possible whether the pollution was linked to fracking, which the Range Resources Corporation (RRC) strongly denied.[77]

Armed with evidence, the scientists disputed the RRC's claims. Indeed, the EPA was so convinced of RRC's blame that it ordered the company to immediately fix the mess it created and help protect Texans from toxic, flammable well water methane and carcinogenic benzene. The EPA's December 7, 2010, order—authorized by the Safe Drinking Water Act (SDWA)—demanded that RRC supply alternative water sources to affected families, "install explosivity meters" in their homes, and repair the tainted aquifer. At first, RRC complied with the order, but it abandoned its remedial work once Texas state regulators came to the company's rescue by clearing it of blame.[78]

The EPA dug in for a fight, suing RRC in January 2011 for violations of the SDWA (§ 1431(b)), claiming it had ultimate authority on national environmental laws, including the SDWA (§ 1431(a)). To corroborate and expand on the earlier analyses in order to bolster the lawsuit, the agency hired Dr. Geoffrey Thyne, an independent geochemist. Like his EPA peers, Thyne traced the methane to RRC's drilling, using isotopic analysis—essentially comparing the "chemical fingerprint" of methane found in the water with methane from the natural gas trapped in the Barnett Shale. Thyne's work comported with similar analyses in nearby areas, giving the EPA an even stronger body of evidence that RRC and its fracking competitors were unleashing high levels of toxins—and negative externalities—into Parker County's water supply and the marketplace more generally. But as the evidence accumulated to support its case, the EPA abruptly and inexplicably gave up. On March 29, 2012, it withdrew its emergency order and dropped its lawsuit. The move was probably easier to justify in public, given that agency officials had kept Thyne's study secret.[79]

Eventually, the EPA's motivation for the reversal became clear: it needed RRC's cooperation for a national fracking study. But in light of the EPA's moves against RRC, the company refused to comply. Its attorney did not bother to spin RRC's terms for cooperation: "So long as the agency continued to pursue a 'scientifically baseless' action against the company in Weatherford, it would not take part in the study and would not allow government scientists onto its drilling sites." Ten months later, news about the EPA's suppression of Thyne's data and analysis came to light. Six months after that, the EPA again stood accused of suppressing proprietary scientific information.[80]

The residents of Dimock, Pennsylvania, like so many other Americans who live near fracking sites, began to feel that their complaints about flaming water and recurring physical ailments would never be taken seriously. And then, in late 2011, the EPA came to the rescue, much like it did in Parker County, Texas. The prospects for remedial action initially looked good: the agency reported it "surveyed residents regarding their private wells and reviewed hundreds of pages of drinking water data supplied to the agency by Dimock residents, the Pennsylvania Department of Environmental Protection and Cabot [Oil and Gas Corporation]." In light of that evidence, the EPA decided "to take further action," sampling water from sixty-four wells and even "delivering water supplies as a precautionary step." To the surprise of local residents who could still light up their water, the EPA then announced in July 2012 that residents had nothing to worry about: local fracking had not contaminated their wells. ("There are not levels of contaminants present that would require additional action by the Agency.") EPA officials conceded that one well had too much manganese, an easily treatable problem. Otherwise, they said, toxin levels did not surpass EPA standards.[81]

Unbeknown to Pennsylvanians, scientists in the EPA were telling their bosses in reports and PowerPoint presentations that many wells actually contained methane and arsenic, as well as manganese. A year after the "everything's OK" announcement, someone within the agency leaked a report documenting the pollution and connecting it to Cabot's drilling. Some of the toxins lingered in the water six to eight months after drilling. Some lingered longer. When pressed, the EPA brushed away the disjuncture between the leaked science and the July 2012 announcement. It "was not shared with the public," EPA officials stated, because "it was a preliminary evaluation," the work of one scientist. The question that remained, said Duke University's Dr. Robert B. Jackson, was why the EPA had all of the historical and proprietary data, as well as reports from his own research team, and then "walk[ed] away from Dimock."[82]

Why they did so in Dimock—and in Pavilion, Wyoming, in June 2013 in a separate case—and why the EPA kept secret the otherwise unavailable information from local residents and the wider public remains a mystery. In the Parker County case, EPA authorities surely seemed to make a crude cost-benefit judgment, sacrificing the Lipskys and other Texans for what seemed the greater good of a comprehensive national study, which they believed required RRC's cooperation. It was probably not what citizens would support if asked, but an understandable move nonetheless, one untainted by corruption or other kinds of crude interest-based politics. Not exactly a Faustian bargain, but in the ballpark. However, if EPA officials acted with what many would argue was undue secrecy and disregard for the public health in order to protect private fossil fuel corporations, many more Americans would likely have objected.[83]

Conclusion

On several occasions—only some recounted here—the Obama-Biden administration demonstrated a business-as-usual approach to its scientists and proprietary scientific information. Despite the administration's apparent good intentions to restore scientific integrity and transparency, Obama-Biden political appointees, including White House officials, often acted like their much criticized predecessors. A couple of transgressions might be understandable in such a large government, even one committed to open government. After all, there is only so much a president can do. Yet even though Obama-Biden might not have suppressed scientific information as frequently as Bush-Cheney and Reagan-Bush did, the administration's violations of "scientific integrity" were too numerous and deliberate to be brushed off as mere outliers.[84]

Conclusion

With remarkable consistency across the secrecy dimensions, the Obama-Biden administration took important steps forward, in the direction of our more "acceptable world" (see chapter 2), followed by at least as many steps backward. In numerous cases, the efforts transcended mere memos and inspiring speeches. Rule changes on FACA and FOIA administration and classification activity had (mixed) material consequences. New procedures in the DOJ for SSP assertions established a framework that still might (someday) reduce its use. Guidelines to promote transparency across agencies controlling proprietary scientific information were finally coming online by the end of the first term. And compared with its predecessors, Obama-Biden appeared to more strongly resist the temptation to shred, delete, and burn. There were, however, a few notable exceptions.

In December 2012, the EPA's Office of Inspector General announced it would begin an "audit of certain EPA electronic records management practices," as a result of investigative reporting and a subsequent investigation by House Science, Space and Technology Committee leaders. The targeted accounts included those of EPA head Lisa Jackson, who used "private and alias email accounts to conduct official business" under the alias "Richard Windsor." The inspector general's audit did not begin until after Obama's second inauguration, but the administration began releasing the e-mails in response to FOIA requests soon after Jackson announced her resignation on December 27, 2012. The administration claimed she told Obama about her wishes right after his reelection—before the audit announcement but right around the first news reports. Later, investigative journalists discovered other senior officials—including Health and Human Services secretary Kathleen Sibelius—also used private e-mail accounts for their government work.[85]

Another case of federal document destruction involved a Secret Service sex scandal that erupted during the president's April 2012 trip to Cartagena, Colombia, for a Summit of the Americas meeting. In Cartagena, Drug Enforcement Administration officials arranged for a prostitute to visit Secret Service agents' hotel rooms. Once the scandal broke, three DEA agents deleted incriminating data from their government-issued smart phones. Two of the agents did so *after* learning about a DOJ inspector general investigation of the matter. The likelihood of criminal obstruction charges, however, was reduced after the IG compelled the agents to submit to interviews. Neither the IG nor DOJ prosecutors identified criminal charges. Overall, the absence of shredding stories in the public record indicates either a more scrupulous administration—or a more successfully cunning one.[86]

Epilogue: Snowden's Revelations

Before Edward Snowden's 2013 whistle-blowing,[87] we already knew quite a bit about how far the National Security Agency had taken its domestic surveillance operations. In 2005, the *New York Times* reported (after a thirteen-month delay) that the NSA had undergone a sea change following 9/11, turning its vast snooping powers inward on US citizens, monitoring calls and e-mails with potential Al Qaeda links. The NSA and other intelligence agencies had spied on citizens before, but the Bush-Cheney administration secretly circumvented the warrant-based wiretap system established by the Foreign Intelligence Surveillance Act, relying on a secret interpretation of the PATRIOT Act's Section 215 to surveil Americans without target-specific court orders. Whistle-blowers William Binney (NSA), Thomas Drake (NSA), Mark Klein (AT&T), Thomas Tamm (DOJ), and others later offered more details about the agency's wiretapping program, including its costs, origins, glitches, intrusiveness, and support from major telecommunications corporations. They also shared insights about the NSA's bulk data collection and data mining programs (such as "Stellar Wind") that scooped up information on an even grander scale, gathering intelligence on *everyone*, not just alleged terrorists—just in case the data would later prove useful. Thus, before Snowden, Americans had an increasingly clear picture of what the secretive NSA had become: to many, a giant, insatiable, deep-pocketed spy agency rummaging through the world's e-mails, texts, phone calls, video calls, Internet searches, and social media activities. Maybe NSA analysts had to jump through a few more hoops to examine US citizens' digital footprints, but the agency with an allegedly overseas mission had collected an enormous database of Americans' conversations, behaviors, and Internet curiosities—ostensibly only to track terrorists.[88]

The official story after 2005 followed the politically useful "9/11 changed everything" narrative. As former NSA director Gen. Michael Hayden framed it in 2008: "I had an agency that . . . for decades—well, since the mid-1970's—had, frankly, played a bit back from the line so as not to get close to anything that got the agency's fingers burned in the Church-Pike era." That was when the Church Committee in 1975 paved the way toward FISA after alerting Americans about government spying on nonviolent civil rights and antiwar activists (including Martin Luther King, Jr.), members of Congress and their staffs (among them Sen. Adlai Stevenson and Rep. Abner Mikva), a Supreme Court justice (William O. Douglas), and "journalists . . . teachers, writers, and publications." FISA reined in the errant NSA by requiring federal Foreign Intelligence Surveillance Court warrants for domestic surveillance. It also introduced stronger congressional oversight. In the ensuing years, the FISC may have justifiably earned a reputation for being deferential to the NSA (see chapter 5), but the added scrutiny probably helped to keep the agency much closer to the line separating the legal and illegal. After "9/11 changed everything," Bush-Cheney unleashed the NSA, allowing it to operate outside FISA, especially through the President's Surveillance Program (2001–2007). Policy makers from the White House down to the NSA worried less about burning the "agency's fingers." They had a war to wage.[89]

Though the "gloves came off" after 9/11, Hayden and other senior officials insisted they scrupulously followed the law. To the extent they actually did, the law's ambiguity helped a great deal. For example, "foreign intelligence information" in FISA included "information with respect to a foreign power . . . that relates to . . . the conduct of the foreign affairs of the United States"—

making anything with even a faint trace of the international fair game. Other loopholes expanded the possibilities toward infinity, such as the PATRIOT Act's Section 215, which amended FISA to authorize the collection of a broad spectrum of "tangible things" as "business records." When exploiting the ambiguities in public proved too politically costly, compliance with the law rested upon secret memos with wily legal interpretations. Secretly revised regulations also did the trick. Obama-Biden, for instance, secretly updated the NSA's "minimization procedures" (to de-identify targets in whole or part) in October 2011 in order to authorize direct, warrantless surveillance of US citizens under Section 702 of the FISA Amendments Act of 2008 (FAA), which explicitly forbade that kind of thing. The section's title gave it away: "Procedures for Targeting Certain Persons outside the United States Other Than United States Persons." After the FAA, the NSA by most accounts worked more closely with the FISC than it had between 2001 and 2007. However, some of Snowden's leaks revealed the NSA had spurned the court's (generally permissive) rulings without consequence. The leaks also showed the NSA had developed ways to circuitously spy on large numbers of Americans. Examples include the "three-hop" query method and the MUSCULAR program (for instance, "Google Cloud Exploitation").[90]

Snowden's whistle-blowing—through the reporting of Laura Poitras, Glenn Greenwald, and Barton Gellman et al.—has offered the most comprehensive public profile of the NSA's post-9/11 activities to date. The leaks also have allowed Americans to compare officials' public claims about the programs' scale, scope, and legality with classified information that often betrayed those statements. For instance, it was hard to square oft-repeated claims that the *National Security* Agency only tapped phones and hacked computer networks to protect national security with evidence suggesting the NSA spied on Brazil's Petrobras oil company, France's Ministry of Foreign and European Affairs, and "Google infrastructure." What generated even more anger at home and abroad were leaked NSA documents showing spying on leaders of allied democratic countries, including Brazilian president Dilma Rousseff, German chancellor Angela Merkel, and others who weren't terrorists or even adversaries. As late as August 2013, President Obama insisted the NSA focused strictly on counterterrorism: "I don't have an interest and the people at the NSA don't have an interest in doing anything other than making sure that where we can prevent a terrorist attack, where we can get information ahead of time, that we're able to carry out that critical task. We do not have an interest in doing anything other than that." The White House subsequently amended Obama's description, adding cybersecurity and counterproliferation of weapons of mass destruction to the NSA's declared portfolio. Even if we utilize the NSA's broader, more forgiving mission statement—"Our mission is to answer questions about threatening activities that others mean to keep hidden"—the leaks suggested an agency out of control. Either that or it had adopted a cynical, expansive, and even irrational interpretation of "threatening activities," to include (among other examples): spying on Rousseff, Merkel, and others; surveilling climate change negotiators during the 2007 conference in Bali; monitoring the internal communications of Amnesty International, Human Rights Watch, and other rights groups; and hacking into UN secretary general Ban Ki-moon's office network to obtain his talking points before an April 2013 White House meeting with Obama. By November 2013, the best that Obama-Biden's dwindling band of defenders could muster was "everybody does it"—all countries spy on each other, and everyone works to gain an "information advantage" (the NSA's broadest, boundless mission statement). Though that might be true, few countries have US-level capabilities. More important, "everybody does it" avoids the credible allegation that senior NSA and White House officials from Bush-Cheney through Obama-Biden flouted the law, lied to citizens, ignored FISC rulings, laughed at the NSA's mission statement, and violated the Constitution (especially the Fourth Amendment).[91]

The debate about the NSA thus involved concerns about the agency's lack of restraint, its lawlessness, and its role in building an unconstitutional, undemocratic "surveillance state." The debate about Snowden's *actions* fundamentally came down to whether he spilled secrets worth keeping (on top of the nature of his crimes, if any). To his critics, Snowden betrayed the NSA's "sources and methods"—to many, necessary secrets by default—by distributing details about specific surveillance programs and the agency's corporate and foreign government collaborators. The consequences would be ruinous, they warned. Bad guys who learned about the tech firms' close cooperation with the NSA looked for alternatives. Terrorists and child pornographers changed tack once they learned the agency sabotaged the Internet's main encryption tools with bugs and backdoor entry points. And then Congress, because of the foolish public uproar, wanted to pass reforms that would hinder the NSA's good work. Snowden's actions were therefore criminal and damaging to US national security, now and in the future—*that* is why he should be criminally charged, they argued.[92]

Snowden's defenders (and critics of the NSA's secrecy more broadly) first reminded everyone that Al Qaeda had known about NSA surveillance since the 1990s. Did anyone seriously think terrorists didn't already operate with that in mind? To this charge, Snowden's critics answered: "Yes, but the terrorists didn't know all the details, such as which companies participated in PRISM, and with that ignorance Al Qaeda made a lot of helpful 'mistakes.'" These arguments revolved around assumptions and evaluations of the programs' *effectiveness*. The NSA's defenders essentially argued that we can trust the executive branch to determine whether its own programs work well. Besides, the interbranch oversight mechanisms worked just fine, thank you very much. NSA critics generally agreed about the need for signals intelligence (SIGINT) systems to track actual terrorists and others who planned violent acts. However, excessive secrecy prevented smart people outside the NSA—including executive branch officials, legislators, and judges—from independently assessing the programs' effectiveness, taking into account the costs, benefits, and possible alternatives. The secretive, insulated NSA approached SIGINT with a "cloistered expert approach" (see chapter 2), at the risk of building and managing relatively ineffective programs.[93]

The NSA's secrecy also prevented independent evaluation of the programs' *legality*. Until Snowden's leaks, the government fought to dismiss lawsuits filed by citizens who believed they were surveilled in violation of the Fourth Amendment. Judges sided with the government time and again, agreeing that plaintiffs lacked standing—all because the secrecy blocked them from proving it as in *Amnesty et al. v. Clapper*. The leaks offered evidence that made lawsuits challenging the programs' constitutionality harder to dismiss. Days after the *Guardian* revealed that the NSA had collected metadata from all Verizon Business customers, including the ACLU, the organization filed suit, claiming it could prove it had standing (*ACLU v. Clapper*). At the same time as Obama-Biden and Bush-Cheney officials urged judges to dismiss lawsuits based on standing issues or the state secrets privilege, they argued the existing interbranch oversight mechanisms effectively scrutinized NSA programs to ensure their legality. But those checks and balances had serious limitations.[94]

First, even though FISC may have indeed acted as a robust, independent oversight authority, the court's reputation for rubber-stamping executive branch requests suggested otherwise (consider the 100 percent approval of warrant requests from 1979 until 2001). Plus, the court's rulings remained classified until the leaks occurred (which so far have released only some rulings), preventing independent verification of their soundness. Second, although Congress played an important oversight role, legislators often encountered what they considered extreme secrecy, which kept them from fulfilling their responsibilities. Sometimes, officials failed to adequately respond to legislative inquiries. They even failed to mention the existence of certain programs, including to Intelligence Committee leaders. For instance, Obama-Biden officials apparently did not brief the relevant committees about MUSCULAR because it operated under the authority of Executive Order 12333, instead of statutes like FISA and FAA. Before Snowden, citizens had to rely on the vague but chilling warnings about the agency's post-9/11 operations from a small handful of legislators, especially Sen. Ron Wyden and Sen. Mark Udall. Given their Intelligence Committee commitments, as well as their incomplete information due to the NSA's extreme secrecy, the senators could only offer the tiniest fragments—not enough to construct an intelligible mosaic.[95]

One could write a book examining all of the specific revelations and another volume—a political thriller—tracing Snowden's dramatic escapades. Here, I can add only a few concluding thoughts. First, to the extent the leaked classified documents revealed excessive secrecy, Obama-Biden obviously deserved much of the blame. But so should Bush-Cheney officials, since they initiated many of the programs their successors continued and expanded (such as PRISM). This point is relevant to the book's comparative historical analysis of administrations. Second, the (unfortunately too brief) analysis given here inclines us toward the conclusion that much of the information was indeed overclassified (that is, there was excessive secrecy) because of the real potential that some of the domestic surveillance was unconstitutional. Just because something falls into the usual protected secrecy categories, such as "sources and methods," does not automatically make its concealment justified (see chapter 2). In this case, we have surveillance programs that, at the very least, had disputable legality (a systematic legal analysis this is not). Given the inadequacy of the existing checks-and-balances system surrounding the NSA, many of the programs escaped oversight and did not effectively receive an independent assessment of their legality and constitutionality. Some members of Congress had relatively extensive knowledge of the programs, but many faced excessive secrecy and did not have access to the administrations' secret interpretations of the relevant laws. Rep. James Sensenbrenner (R-WI), who, as Judiciary Committee chair in 2001, helped lead the House to pass the PATRIOT Act, expressed seemingly genuine shock at the administration's apparent reading of the measure's Section 215, once he learned about it through Snowden's leaks: "The administration's interpretation to allow for bulk collection is at odds with Congressional intent." FISC's permissive judges generally knew more, but even they encountered a less than forthcoming executive branch, as the leaks revealed (see, for example, Judge Reggie Walton's complaints in the March 2009 order).[96]

Third, none of these criticisms imply that the responsible officials acted with bad intentions. Most probably sought to defend US national security and protect citizens from harm (that kind of public-spirited motivation can coincide with officials' more self-interested ambitions, due to the NSA's incentive structure). But the US Constitution is not rendered moot once someone believes he or she is operating in good faith. Americans never amended the document to offer well-intentioned elites—or anyone else—legal immunity. And history shows that citizens should not trust officials' good intentions when it comes to secret surveillance systems, especially with weak interbranch oversight mechanisms. The Church Committee's revelations about decades of government spying on nonviolent activists ("subversives") comprise one important reminder of how unchecked surveillance programs might expand beyond their original mission. NSA defenders in 2013 liked to point out that the Church Committee's revelations involved actions from decades back; therefore, concerns about an overly intrusive NSA were not relevant to the post-FISA era. The men and women at the helm were single-mindedly focused on stopping "threatening activities," they reassured us; give them the benefit of the doubt. For instance, former NSA general counsel and Homeland Security official Steward Baker responded to the revelation that the agency was "gathering records of online sexual activity and evidence of visits to pornographic websites as part of a proposed plan to harm the reputations of those whom the agency believes are radicalizing others through incendiary speeches" with this argument: "At some point you have to say we're counting on our officials to know the difference" between using spying tools against foreign enemies and using them against "domestic political opponents" (note, however, that one of the targets in the leaked documents was a "U.S. person").[97]

But that leaves us with what amounts to a "trust us" doctrine: trust us that "there are good people running these programs"; that those people will define *radicalizing* in a way most democratic citizens would support; and that officials would not abuse their considerable powers to use the private, legal online behaviors of "radicals" against them. This is an awfully risky and politically naive approach for a democratic society, especially one with such a checkered past. And it's a clear reminder why the debate about surveillance policy is as much about "security," "liberty," and "privacy" as it is about "power."

11

CONCLUSION

On a randomly chosen day in December 2012, the power of America's sunshine laws was on full display. The FBI chose December 21, the Friday before Christmas, to finally release FOIA-ed documents showing the bureau's secret surveillance of the Occupy Wall Street movement. The documents, though heavily redacted, revealed the FBI's close cooperation with large corporations, especially banks, in monitoring and gathering intelligence on Occupy protesters in New York and across the country. Despite acknowledging the nonviolent mission and behavior of the movement's protesters, the government deployed counterterrorist resources in the operation, treating Occupiers as potential terrorists. The decision to surveil might have been wrong or unconstitutional, but FOIA at least gave citizens the opportunity to learn about those possible misdeeds—even if the postelection release reduced the likelihood that voters would hold representatives accountable.[1]

On December 21, the State Department (DOS) also revealed it had known in 1997 about the Colombian army's complicity in a bloody paramilitary attack on peasants in Miraflores, a small coca-growing town about 110 miles outside Bogotá. The National Security Archive, an open government group, obtained freshly declassified DOS documents showing the assault by the right-wing United Self-Defense Forces of Colombia's (AUC) left twelve peasants dead and displaced many more. According to DOS sources, the Colombian government "had been fully aware in advance of [AUC commander Víctor Carranza Niño's] plans and activities in Miraflores and had facilitated the operation from beginning to end." It was another piece of evidence showing that Clinton-Gore knew about AUC-army collaboration but left its close relationship with the Colombian government unaffected.[2]

Americans also learned on December 21 that about two-thirds of the country's air traffic control facilities were seriously overstaffed, an inefficiency costing taxpayers millions. Bloomberg News obtained the details via FOIA requests sent to the Federal Aviation Administration. As a result of Bloomberg's reporting, members of Congress persuaded the FAA's assistant inspector general to launch an audit, a first step toward a solution to the problem.[3]

Declassified and FOIA-ed documents published on that one day alone thus produced fodder for citizens with diverse concerns and ideologies about subjects ranging from recent domestic surveillance of nonviolent activists to contemporary public sector waste and inefficiency to questionable alliances with human rights–violating governments. The other sunshine laws were also working for the cause of government transparency on December 21, 2012.

For example, the Interior Department announced the names of industry and civil society members of the Extractive Industries Transparency Initiative (EITI) Committee, a task force created to help the government implement the EITI, part of the international Open Government Partnership. Before FACA, it would have been unusual for citizens to know which (and how many) panel members from fossil fuel and mining companies like Exxon, Chevron, and Rio Tinto were designing regulations with government officials and civil society group representatives. The participation of the latter—in this case, people from Project on Government Oversight, Earthworks, and United Steelworkers (among others)—might have also been unusual, not to mention the existence of a "transparency initiative" and an "open government partnership" in the first place. Finally, on the same December day, anyone who cared to look could have learned of several upcoming public task force meetings, including the Safety and Occupational Health Study Section of the National Institute for Occupational Safety and Health, the Twin Falls (Idaho) District Resource Advisory Council, the Environmental Management Site-Specific Advisory Board of Nevada, the Arts Advisory Panel Meeting, the Center for Scientific Review, and the National Cancer Institute.[4]

These examples and many others like them illustrate how the sunshine laws of the 1970s substantially revised the way information flowed through the American political system. They forced presidents and their administrations to disclose secrets that had no business being hidden, and citizens therefore had more knowledge about government action. Because information disclosure and dissemination is a social activity, it was not as if individual citizens only benefited when they personally filed FOIA requests or scoured through FACA filings. Anyone who wanted to could spread the word through websites, books, magazines, newspapers, radio stations, protest signs, word of mouth, and so forth. Whether major media outlets actually did spread the word and whether citizens engaged in civil discussions about the issues are important concerns for other books.

One reason the system worked as well as it did involves the active participation of the other branches of government. As we have repeatedly seen,

administrations were not always compliant with their open government requirements (to put it mildly). The new legal framework created by the sunshine laws and other statutes around the same time (such as the Classified
Information Procedures Act of 1980) produced new sources of leverage with
which federal judges and members of Congress could hold executives accountable. When presidents failed to meet their obligations, power holders
from the other branches (sometimes) called them out. Congressional incentives to monitor and criticize executives for their secrecy existed prior to the
sunshine laws. However, the new system gave representatives new tools because the laws made specific kinds of secrecy illegitimate and even illegal. For
instance, before FACA, executive branch officials met secretly with private
sector representatives to draft new regulations or pieces of legislation. Members of Congress complained, but they had no recourse. After FACA, legislators could denounce the secrecy as a violation of the law, inflicting political
and sometimes legal costs on an administration.

The courts were at least as important on FOIA and FACA issues and in
their adjudication of the executive's evidentiary claims. One of the most potent parts of FOIA gives citizens the right to appeal in court agencies' refusal and redaction decisions. Without that option, administrations could
withhold information without consequence—without a second opinion from
judges, who usually do not share executive officials' political and professional
incentives. The judiciary's involvement in FACA decisions, as we have seen,
has proved less fruitful than FOIA appeals, in large part due to the timing of
court challenges in the context of relatively short-run task forces. Administrations throughout the sunshine era have exploited this timing issue, a version
of the tactical move called running out the clock throughout this book.

Judges have also frequently taken a deferential position vis-à-vis the executive on state secrets privilege and secret evidence claims. Still, the fact that
judges have *sometimes* challenged the executive has probably led to a relatively
more restrained use of the evidentiary privileges than would otherwise have
occurred. Although courts tend to defer to presidents on national security
issues, they have developed a credible threat as a result of the occasional snub.

It is hard to deny that the new legal framework placed serious constraints
on executive branch officials. As we saw in the introduction, Kissinger's joke
from 1975 reflected how quickly the new rules took hold: "Before the [FOIA],
I used to say at meetings, 'The illegal we do immediately; the unconstitutional
takes a little longer.' But since the [FOIA], I'm afraid to say things like that."
However, as Kissinger's joke so perfectly illustrates, the arrival of the sun-

shine laws did not extinguish excessive government secrecy once and for all. In many ways, the new system just pushed secrets into darker corners. We have seen numerous Kissinger-esque evasions of the law throughout the book, with the most desperate examples described in chapter 9. Dick Cheney was a master of the game, habitually keeping official information out of the public record. In a March 2000 interview about his time as secretary of defense for Bush-Quayle, he proudly spoke about his "leer[iness] about putting anything down on paper," as a result of the tumultuous experience of working in the imploding Nixon-Ford White House. The only reason "Don [Rumsfeld] and I survived and prospered in that environment [was] because we didn't leave a lot of paper laying around." There were several reports that Cheney continued this practice upon becoming vice president and preached the gospel of its wisdom to all senior officials who would listen. Estimating the amount of that kind of resulting secrecy and how it varied across administrations is a fool's errand. However, the book demonstrated that we can create a mosaic of the sunshine-era secrecy system and compare administrations using the bits of paper that *were* left lying around, disclosed through official and unofficial channels.[5]

One thing is clear: despite all the power of the sunshine laws and any positive spillover effects they—or the underlying movement that brought them—may have had, excessive secrecy still reigned in the sunshine era. It occurred in the widely criticized Bush-Cheney administration, whose secrecy was indeed "unprecedented" in some of the categories we have investigated here. Yet Bush-Cheney officials generally followed trails blazed by their predecessors, who developed the tools and tricks used to circumvent or poke holes in the sunshine laws. Reagan-Bush set many of the precedents. But all administrations' officials have overclassified and wrongly withheld unclassified information using circumvention strategies, usually deploying a mix of tactics, including running out the clock; playing word games; and simply pretending they did nothing wrong, hoping no one challenged the farce. Clinton-Gore officials defied FACA by (among other things) calling their health care task force members "consultants"; Bush-Cheney officials called their energy task force members "guests" and "visitors." Bush-Quayle used a variety of tactics to conceal proprietary information about the health effects of Agent Orange and other dioxins; Reagan-Bush did the same, as did Carter-Mondale. All administrations did what they could, for a variety of reasons (ideology, interest groups, and so on), to twist around the statutes when they deemed it necessary. All diverged from their own protransparency rhetoric and rules.

Excessive secrecy was a constant, although some administrations performed relatively worse than others along the different dimensions.

The problem becomes even more severe when we consider how the secrecy system seems to resist change. To be sure, positive change did sometimes occur. Clinton's ambitious declassification program released over 860 million pages of secrets in the last half of his presidency. The vast majority of the information shed light on historical matters—things not directly relevant to voters judging politicians of the late 1990s. But if anything made secrecy relatively less excessive during the sunshine era, it was Clinton's program. Yet even that rare example of change ran up against powerful forces inside the bureaucracy. Six major intelligence agencies put the brakes on the program, plugging up what they considered unwise leaks. Perhaps Clinton changed his mind as well and quietly coordinated with those agencies. In any case, President Bush in 2003 killed the program for good and even implemented a governmentwide *re*classification program (recall the effort to reconceal General Pinochet's cocktail preference). Other open government initiatives faced internal resistance. The declassification program was merely one of the most administratively effective.

By arguing that the "system" resists change or exists as an autonomous entity, we miss fuller, more precise explanations for repeated failures to reform it. In particular, we ignore agency at our peril. Clinton implemented the declassification program; Bush killed it. Both presidents had particular information policy preferences, shaped by their ideologies and other political commitments, as well as the "nature of the times" (for example, settled versus unsettled times). The men and women who worked as intelligence officials also had distinctive priorities, competencies, and personalities, as well as their own political commitments. Some had the temerity and resources to resist presidential prerogatives, openly or subtly.[6]

However crucial agency is to understanding government secrecy, there are reasons to save the concept of a partially autonomous, change-resistant secrecy system. On the one hand, all of the endogenously caused historical variation we observed in this book—changes due to officials making choices—shows a dynamic, adaptable system. On the other hand, we are unlikely ever to purge the more or less constant prosecrecy forces, such as bureaucratic conservatism/risk aversion, Weber's "sure power instinct," interest group appeasement, and the temptation to use power to avoid public embarrassments. The personal and organizational incentives that guide decision makers are embedded deep within the system and will endure. Officials can make efforts to modify the incentive structures—compare the Reno and Ashcroft Memos—but we are probably stuck with an unshakable core that tilts the government toward excessive secrecy, unless someone discovers a way to rid human civilization of the prosecrecy forces (another option, adopting anarchy, or "cooperation without hierarchy or state rule," is just as unlikely). For these and the other reasons outlined in chapter 2, efforts to fix the excessive secrecy problem rarely went far or lasted very long—no matter the party or personality in the White House.[7]

What Can Be Done?

If the system is resistant to change, can anything rein in excessive secrecy, bringing us closer to an "acceptable world" (see chapter 2)? Executive leadership definitely helps. Both Clinton-Gore and Obama-Biden made open government a priority. Although we can criticize the limited scope and success of their efforts—especially Obama-Biden's—both administrations stood out from their sunshine-era counterparts by pushing initiatives and hiring pro-transparency agents to implement them. Nevertheless, the efforts barely made a dent; they certainly did not bring about permanent change. Plus, as is often the case, focusing on presidential leadership can quickly devolve into waiting for the proverbial knight on a white horse. Putting sustained, postelection pressure on presidents is at least as important as nominating and voting for them when they were candidates promising change.

Selecting and pressuring better leaders also applies to the legislature. A legislative majority can pressure presidents like no other, forcing them to sign or veto bills and to reorder their policy agendas. A veto of a popular open government bill might produce considerable political costs for a president and his or her party, especially if the veto cannot be credibly justified on national security grounds. That was a primary reason why Nixon and Ford signed most of the sunshine era's open government bills into law. Both personally opposed the changes or dealt with intense internal opposition from senior advisers (including Cheney in both administrations). After the sunshine laws, several other protransparency bills passed, such as 2012's Whistleblower Protection Enhancement Act, an important but flawed law. More frequently, bills get stuck at the committee level, as happened with the perennial State Secrets Protection Act. Other much-needed bills, among them one targeting FACA violations, have not made it even that far.[8]

Some members of Congress have emerged as leaders in the fight against excessive secrecy, including most recently (and to varying degrees): former senator Russell Feingold (D-WI), Sen. Ron Wyden (D-OR), Sen. Mark Udall (D-CO), Sen. Patrick Leahy (D-VT), Sen. Sheldon Whitehouse (D-RI), Rep. Henry Waxman (D-CA), Rep. Christopher Shays (R-CT), and Rep. Frank Wolf (R-VA). Leading lights from earlier eras, such as Sen. Daniel Patrick Moynihan (D-NY), Rep. Robert T. Matsui (D-CA), and Rep. Major Owens (D-NY), can be found fighting the hard fight in various parts of the book. One cannot help noticing the partisan bias of that list. Reading the book's comprehensive, comparative historical analysis indeed makes clear that Democrats have more often been at the forefront of the open government cause, including in the political coalition that brought the sunshine laws through Congress. The preponderance of Democrats might have been partly a function of Republican Party dominance of the White House for most of the period; we would expect the partisan opposition to more vigorously criticize presidential administrations. Indeed, many Democrats did seem to abandon the cause once Obama-Biden arrived in Washington, and many Republicans found some protransparency religion once Democrats took the White House. Real, institutional change does not permit cutting copartisans slack. However, many Democrats stuck with it, Senators Wyden and Udall most prominently. This study did not systematically investigate the partisan question, but we can leave with the tentative conclusion—ripe for future research—that Democrats seem more likely to steer the system closer to our acceptable reality. But that by no means excuses the many transgressions of Obama-Biden and Clinton-Gore.

Selecting good representatives and then holding them accountable cannot be the only solution to our excessive secrecy problem. Even the best leaders, waving righteous new laws, run up against powerful forces in the vast government bureaucracy. If "powerful forces" sounds a bit conspiratorial, recall we are simply referring to strong, albeit mundane and universal, tendencies stitched into agencies' DNA. These include individual bureaucrats' risk aversion incentives and agencies' information-hoarding impulses, which result from intragovernment battles for budgets and governing influence. The extent to which leaders can restructure the underlying incentives remains unclear. Chapter 3 presented evidence that the Ashcroft Memo on FOIA administration seemed to change many information officers' behaviors, but that memo encouraged *more* risk aversion, a much easier bureaucratic nudge. The Clinton-era Reno Memo it replaced pushed bureaucrats in the opposite direction and probably caused relatively more disclosures, but we have no direct evidence that it significantly changed behaviors at the individual level. Perhaps there is little senior officials can do, as former Information Security Oversight Office director Steven Garfinkel argued: "You know what? The Janet Reno memorandum is all but meaningless. The John Ashcroft memorandum is all but meaningless. What you do every day on the job is what is truly meaningful in the area of access to government information." Information workers have strong incentives to be risk averse; they know that if they screw up, by disclosing necessary secrets, their country could suffer, not to mention their careers. Dismissing the potential power of new protransparency guidelines, however, is fatalistic, and it too easily gives up on realistic solutions that can have marginal effects. Bureaucratic conservatism will endure, but better training of information officers, on top of more determined and consistent monitoring and evaluation programs—by supervisors, inspectors general, and agencies like the ISOO—would likely make a real difference in those officers' discretionary judgments. It wouldn't take much to design and implement new systems. For example, many agencies randomly select and inspect the work of classification authorities to verify that they have properly protected classified information. It would require little more than a presidential memo to launch a similar random inspection program to limit overclassification or overly restrictive FOIA responses. The directive would need to explicitly link the evaluations to bureaucrats' overall job performance reviews, which affect salary and promotion opportunities. Random inspections with material consequences are powerful; they concentrate minds wonderfully (as a Samuel Johnson–quoting quality control officer or tax auditor might say).[9]

What about tamping down on agencies' information-hoarding impulses? The obstacles are at least as high, given their foundation in the bureaucracy's sure power instinct (Weber) and its quest for survival. Although agency restructuring can help to facilitate information sharing across agencies, there are upper limits on how far it can go. For example, the government's post-9/11 information-sharing programs in many ways succeeded, but after a decade, big problems remained. Former senator Joseph Lieberman (I-CT), a leader on this issue after the attacks, boasted at a 2011 Senate hearing that "barriers to information sharing have been taken down, significantly improving the quality and quantity of information." But as two leaders of the Markle Task Force on National Security in the Information Age, Zoë Baird Budinger and Jeffrey H. Smith, testified, even though "information sharing has become more widespread and the government has made real changes that are necessary to respond to new threats . . . progress has been too slow in some places and has lacked adequate guidance or oversight in others." That slow progress was likely caused in no small part by the agencies' deeply rooted hoarding incentives. "Knowledge is power" remains just as relevant today as it was during Weber's era—and before him, Francis Bacon's (*"ipsa scientia potestas est,"* 1597). And though policy entrepreneurs could probably more aggressively push information sharing within the government to reduce its presence at the interagency level, the sure power instinct would survive, taking new forms (for example, more centralized forms) or aligning against other actors and organizations (such as those in the international system). The prospects for reform here are far more limited.[10]

Business power over government agencies is another problem with few solutions—unless, somehow, we can forge a system with more bureaucratic autonomy. So many of the cases explored in this book ultimately came down to decisions taken on behalf of for-profit businesses against the public interest, including: the weakening of the TREAD Act's disclosure requirements to protect tire companies (chapter 3); the scores of FOIA (b)(3) exemptions to benefit private interests ranging from avocado importers to watermelon growers (chapter 3); all of the conflicts to protect dioxin and asbestos manufacturers (among other toxins) (chapters 4, 7, and 8); and efforts to keep secrets on behalf of factory farmers and others in the meat industry (chapters 7 and 8), as well as energy, forestry, paper, and telecommunications corporations (chapters 4, 7, and 8). In some of those cases, the government also clearly had its own interests in mind. Take, for instance, the years of foot-dragging, secrecy, and deception to avoid all of the potential financial liabilities resulting from Vietnam War soldiers' exposure to Agent Orange (chapter 8). From Carter-Mondale to Clinton-Gore, senior officials fought for secrecy to avoid those costs. Many of them also seemed to drink the industry's Kool-Aid about the chemical's safety or otherwise felt compelled to fight on behalf of implicated corporations, which faced huge financial and reputational liabilities of their own.

Checks and Balances

The sunshine laws were supposed to push the country in the opposite direction. Only the politically naive should have expected the executive branch to rise to the occasion and unfailingly follow the letter and spirit of the laws. But Madison's system of interbranch checks and balances can be marshaled to do much of the heavy lifting by producing strong incentives for Congress and the judiciary to promote "horizontal accountability" and, as a consequence, the public interest. (As Madison put it: "The constant aim is to divide and arrange the several offices in such a manner as that each may be a check on the other that the private interest of every individual may be a sentinel over the public rights.") But as we have seen, the other branches seemed to have a limited appetite for reining in all the evasive maneuvers and serial dishonesty.[11]

Federal judges understandably defer to the executive on national security matters—given the separation of powers and the judiciary's relatively limited capabilities and expertise to evaluate intelligence and threats. However, the post–World War II era is littered with cases of executive branch officials making tenuous appeals to national security, cloaked in secrecy. Several judges featured in the book clearly brought the appropriate amount of skepticism and wielded the judiciary's countervailing authorities to evaluate the executive's national security appeals, reject legalistic word games and other evasive maneuvers, and otherwise push back. That some judges sometimes push back keeps officials at least *somewhat* uncertain about whether they can "get away with it." But many judges seem perfectly content with an unleashed executive, despite all of the historical evidence reminding them of the wisdom—and constitutional duty—of interbranch skepticism. The more judges heeding the call, the more powerful the constraint on executive branch officials to reduce overclassification and comply with the sunshine laws. It is perhaps an obvious point, but that does not diminish its importance.

Overall, Congress has displayed a stronger appetite for holding the executive accountable, often for purely electoral and partisan reasons, with notable exceptions. Representatives hold testy hearings, they write letters, and they make accusations in the media. But they rarely threaten subpoenas or budget cuts due to excessive executive branch secrecy. And far too many push for and get passed new statutory exemptions to the sunshine laws to satisfy their backers (as with the FOIA (b)(3) exemptions). Although those are often bizarrely specific, such as the one protecting watermelon growers, transparency laws more generally are written in ways that invite word games—leaving it up to administrations to define phrases like *national security, critical infrastructure information,* and *task force members.* Unless representatives prefer to unilaterally grant the executive those interpretive powers, they should write laws with more detailed definitions, with very specific parameters. The same goes for provisions inviting running-out-the-clock tactics. FACA and the corresponding case law, for instance, has allowed administrations to complete

FACA-defying task force activities despite serious lawsuits challenging them in real time. The law could be rewritten to specifically authorize judges to order injunctions to halt task force work until a court order or settlement is reached, with rare, clearly specified exceptions (see the last section of chapter 4). Simply put, transparency laws must have teeth, and they must not make circumventing them easy.

The Role of Whistle-Blowers and Other Citizens

Whistle-blowing, when done right (not directly endangering innocent people, violating their privacy, and so forth), can help offset the secrecy system's excesses. However, it is limited as a mechanism for triggering large-scale institutional change. It is not that whistle-blowing cannot have huge effects. Daniel Ellsberg's leak of the Pentagon Papers to national newspapers, Chelsea (née Bradley) Manning's leak of the Iraq and Afghan war logs and the State Department "cables," and Edward Snowden's leak of top secret National Security Agency documents about domestic surveillance all shook domestic and international politics in profound ways (such as driving Nixon toward criminal acts and ultimately to his resignation, helping spark the "Arab Spring" and providing greater clarity about the nature and consequences of the wars in Afghanistan and Iraq, and prompting a domestic and international debate about the scope and scale of NSA surveillance). Many other whistle-blowers, including those described in this book, have exposed wrongdoing and made powerful people extremely nervous, for all the right reasons. But whistle-blowing works at the margins of the system, sporadically releasing bits of information, usually at a great cost to the protagonist. It is not a systemic fix. This is true even in the post-Wikileaks era, when cryptological tools like Tor can help guarantee anonymity through encryption and large chunks of raw information can be disseminated without large mass media organizations as intermediaries. Leaks work, but they will not by themselves stem the tide of overclassification or compel the OLC to disclose secret legal memos.

Most of all, change requires a loud, sustained roar from civil society demanding it, during and after elections. In the meantime, incremental improvements in the balance between acceptable and excessive secrecy will have to do. So will whistle-blowing done right. Potential whistle-blowers will likely find new obstacles after Manning famously—and so easily—downloaded a torrent of secrets onto a disguised Lady Gaga CD. Technological fixes no doubt proliferated after that, although Snowden managed to download thousands of files from the ultrasecretive NSA while working for Dell and Booz Allen Hamilton. And whistle-blowers have discovered a surprisingly hostile Obama-Biden administration. It may have been hard to believe given their 2008 campaign promises, but the Democrats used the Espionage Act against whistle-blowers in unprecedented ways. They also subjected Manning to prolonged, severe treatment that major human rights organizations have harshly criticized.[12]

This book began with Henry Kissinger laughing about his ability to break the law without consequence. It is fitting to conclude with Daniel Ellsberg, Kissinger's close acquaintance, who demonstrated the countervailing power of whistle-blowing. Before Wikileaks, before Manning, before Snowden, Ellsberg had this to say about spilling illegitimate secrets:

> I have come to feel that the most widespread form of complicity with evil is in keeping silence about it. And a great deal of this silence reflects a sense of obligation to keep promises, to keep secrets. In other words, the moral obligation to prevent or expose wrongdoing or to avert a disastrous course of action often confronts the fact that you have made a promise to keep the information in question secret. To break that promise will usually be very costly to your career and in addition will be seen by many people as a wrong thing to do and a mark of bad character. Yet very often the consequences of keeping that promise may be to allow a policy to go forward that harms a vast number of people. To the extent that this is a moral dilemma, it can't be resolved in general terms. But what I learned from my own experience was that a single individual who is ready to reveal the truth about a dangerous situation at whatever cost to his own career may possess the power to save a great many lives.[13]

NOTES

Preface and Acknowledgments

1. Meg Greenfield, *Washington* (New York: PublicAffairs, 2001), p. 94.

Chapter 1: Introduction

1. State Department, Memorandum and Conversation, #01525, March 10, 1975, http://nsarchive.files.wordpress.com/2010/11/kiss-foia.pdf; White House Report to the President, "Kissinger Trip to the Middle East, March 7–22, 1975," Trip Book, Vol. 2(1), Kissinger Reports on USSR, China, and Middle East Discussions, Box 3, 1975, http://www.fordlibrarymuseum.gov/library/document/0331/1553959.pdf; Chaim Kaufmann, "An Assessment of the Partition of Cyprus," *International Studies Perspectives* 8, no. 2 (2007): 206–223.

2. State Department, Memorandum and Conversation.

3. On the institutional causes of policy stability in the United States ("incremental at best"), see Ellen Immergut, "Institutions, Veto Points, and Policy Results: A Comparative Analysis of Health Care," *Journal of Public Policy* 10, no. 4 (1990): 391–416; George Tsebelis, "Decision Making in Political Systems: Veto Players in Presidentialism, Parliamentarism, Multicameralism and Multipartyism," *British Journal of Political Science* 25 (1995): 289–325; Jacob Hacker, "The Historical Logic of National Health Insurance," *Studies in American Political Development* 12 (1998): 57–130. See also James Mahoney, "Conceptualizing and Explaining Punctuated versus Incremental Change" (paper presented at the Lansing B. Lee/Bankard Seminar in Global Politics, University of Virginia, Charlottesville, May 4, 2012); Paul Pierson, *Politics in Time* (Princeton, NJ: Princeton University Press, 2004). On the social movement for more open government and executive branch accountability, see Katherine A. Scott, *Reining in the State: Civil Society and Congress in the Vietnam and Watergate Eras* (Lawrence: University Press of Kansas, 2013). The first version of FOIA, signed in 1966, was mostly greeted by shrugs across the bureaucracy. The amendment passed in 1974 ordered agencies to: give explicit reasons for keeping requested documents secret (i.e., citing the exemptions); publish information about what they did release; establish deadlines for FOIA responses to combat delays; create an appeals process for requesters who were denied information; and grant fee waivers or reductions for requesters seeking information in the public interest (e.g., journalists and academics hoping to publish the information, compared with corporations wanting

the information for a competitive business advantage). See, e.g., Angus Mackenzie, *Secrets: The CIA's War at Home* (Berkeley: University of California Press, 1997), pp. 60–61.

4. Athan G. Theoharis, ed., *A Culture of Secrecy: The Government and the People's Right to Know* (Lawrence: University Press of Kansas, 1999); David J. Samuels and Matthew Soberg Shugart, "Presidentialism, Elections, and Representation," *Journal of Theoretical Politics* 15, no. 1 (2003): 33–60.

5. On the floodlit society, see Edward Alden and Franz Schurmann, *Why We Need Ideologies in US Foreign Policy* (Berkeley, CA: Institute of International Studies, 1990), p. 66; David N. Gibbs, "Secrecy and International Relations," *Journal of Peace Research* 32 (1995): 213–228, at 225.

6. See chapter 2's discussion of the governing ideology of Vice President Dick Cheney et al., which includes a principled defense of government secrecy and an argument for retrenchment in information policy. See also Gabriel Schoenfeld, *Necessary Secrets: National Security, the Media, and the Rule of Law* (New York: W. W. Norton, 2010); Peter Singer, "In a World with Terrorism, Too Much Transparency Is Utopian," *Daily Star* (Lebanon), August 21, 2010. Other arguments emphasize how lobbyists and interest groups use government transparency to maximize their influence against the public interest. See, e.g., the discussion of the lobbyists' response to the opening of 1986 Tax Reform Act hearings before the Senate Finance Committee in Douglas Arnold, *The Logic of Congressional Action* (New Haven, CT: Yale University Press, 1992), p. 121. See also Archon Fung, Mary Graham, and David Weil, *Full Disclosure: The Perils and Promise of Transparency* (Cambridge: Cambridge University Press, 2007); Lawrence Lessig, "Against Transparency: The Perils of Openness in Government," *New Republic* 9 (2009): 37–44.

7. Dana Priest and William M. Arkin, "A Hidden World, Growing beyond Control," *Washington Post*, July 19, 2010, p. A1, http://projects.washingtonpost.com/top-secret -america/articles/a-hidden-world-growing-beyond-control/.

8. Joint Security Commission, "Redefining Security: A Report to the Secretary of Defense and the Director of Central Intelligence," February 28, 1994, http://www.fas.org/ sgp/library/jsc/index.html; Thomas S. Blanton, Testimony for the Hearing on "Emerging Threats: Overclassification and Pseudo-classification," U.S. House Subcommittee on National Security, Emerging Threats, and International Relations, Committee on Government Reform, Serial No. 109-18, March 5, 2005, http://www.gwu.edu/~nsarchiv/ news/20050302/index.htm; Donald H. Rumsfeld, Secretary Rumsfeld Press Conference in Phoenix, August 26, 2004, http://www.defense.gov/transcripts/transcript.aspx? transcriptid=2714; Steven Aftergood, "Reducing Government Secrecy: Finding What Works," *Yale Law and Policy Review* 27 (2009): 399–416, at 403; Erwin N. Griswold, "Secrets Not Worth Keeping: The Courts and Classified Information," *Washington Post*, February 15, 1989, p. A25.

9. *CNSS et al. v. DOJ*, Civil Complaint filed with U.S. District Court for the District of Columbia, p. 3, December 5, 2001, http://epic.org/open_gov/foia/detainee_complaint .pdf; William Fisher, "Untangling a Twisted Web to Search for U.S. Secrets," *Inter Press*

Services, [Aftergood quote], November 29, 2004; John Dean, *Worse Than Watergate: The Secret Presidency of George W. Bush* (New York: Little, Brown, 2004), p. ix; David E. Sanger, "The Washington Secret Often Isn't," *New York Times,* October 23, 2005, p. D1; "Fixation with Secrecy," *New York Times,* August 28, 2006, p. A14; OpenTheGovernment .org, *Secrecy Report Card* (Washington, DC: OpenTheGovernment.org, 2006); Senator Russ Feingold, "Secret Law and the Threat to Democratic and Accountable Government," Testimony before the U.S. Senate Committee on the Judiciary Subcommittee on the Constitution, Senate Hearing 110-604, Serial No. J-110-89, April 30, 2008, p. 1; Jennifer LaFleur, "Talking with the Former FOIA Czar," *ProPublica,* March 12, 2009, http://www.propublica.org/article/talking-with-the-former-foia-czar.

10. Scott Wheeler, "Obama, Most Secretive President Ever," Newsmax.com, January 26, 2009, http://www.newsmax.com/Politics/obama-secrets/2009/01/26/id/340057; Leonard Downie, Jr., and Sara Rafsky, *The Obama Administration and the Press: Leak Investigations and Surveillance in Post-9/11 America* (New York: Committee to Protect Journalists, 2013), p. 2. The bill of particulars against Bush-Cheney is long and familiar, including: soaring rates of document classification and FOIA application rejections; increased use of the state secrets privilege; secret legal memos in the executive branch justifying torture and who knows what else; secret trials with secret evidence; scientists gagged for speaking about global warming and other subjects; secret warrantless surveillance; and CIA "black site" prisons. During the Bush-Cheney years, it seemed something new would leak to the press every week, causing another uproar until the next one. Investigative journalists, policy analysts, and open government advocates released reports detailing new and old outrages. It was hard not to come to the conclusion that something exceptional, something *unprecedented*, was afoot. Even before the 9/11 critical juncture, the administration found itself in major secrecy-related scuffles with members of Congress and other government officials, including the aforementioned energy task force fight and a prolonged, passive-aggressive conflict with the National Archives and Records Administration (NARA) over the PRA and the scheduled release of George H. W. Bush's presidential papers.

11. Patrice McDermott, *Who Needs to Know? The State of Public Access to Federal Government* (Lanham, MD: Bernan Press, 2007); Seth Shulman, *Undermining Science* (Berkeley: University of California Press, 2008); Mark Rozell, *Executive Privilege: Presidential Power, Secrecy, and Accountability* (Lawrence: University Press of Kansas, 2010); Louis Fisher, *In the Name of National Security: Unchecked Presidential Power and the Reynolds Case* (Lawrence: University Press of Kansas, 2006); Ted Gup, *Nation of Secrets: The Threat to Democracy and the American Way of Life* (New York: Doubleday, 2007); Robert M. Pallitto and William G. Weaver, *Presidential Secrecy and the Law* (Baltimore, MD: Johns Hopkins University Press, 2007); Alasdair Roberts, *Blacked Out: Government Secrecy in the Information Age* (New York: Cambridge University Press, 2006); Schoenfeld, *Necessary Secrets*; Geoffrey R. Stone, *Top Secret: When Our Government Keeps Us in the Dark* (Lanham, MD: Rowman & Littlefield, 2007). Also see Daniel Patrick Moynihan, *Secrecy: The American Experience* (New Haven, CT: Yale University Press, 1998).

12. James Mahoney and Kathleen Thelen, "A Theory of Gradual Institutional Change," in *Explaining Institutional Change: Ambiguity, Agency, and Power,* ed. Mahoney and Thelen (Cambridge: Cambridge University Press, 2010), pp. 1–37; Vivien A. Schmidt, "Discursive Institutionalism: The Explanatory Power of Ideas and Discourse," *Annual Review of Political Science* 11 (2008): 303–326; Stephen Bell, "Do We Really Need a New 'Constructivist Institutionalism' to Explain Institutional Change?" *British Journal of Political Science* 41, no. 4 (2011): 883–906.

13. Ira Katznelson, "Periodization and Preferences: Reflections on Purposive Action in Comparative-Historical Social Science," in *Comparative Historical Analysis in the Social Sciences,* ed. James Mahoney and Dietrich Rueschemeyer (Cambridge: Cambridge University Press, 2003), pp. 270–301; David E. Pozen, "The Mosaic Theory, National Security, and the Freedom of Information Act," *Yale Law Journal* 115 (2005): 628–679; Jameel Jaffer, "The Mosaic Theory," *Social Research* 77, no. 3 (2010): 873–882.

14. Rozell, *Executive Privilege.* See also Morton Rosenberg, "Presidential Claims of Executive Privilege: History, Law, Practice, and Recent Developments," Congressional Research Service, CRS Report RL30319, August 21, 2008. Rosenberg helpfully lists every executive privilege claim from Kennedy to Bush, Jr., in an appendix (pp. 37–41), clearly showing an uptick in use during the Clinton-Gore and Bush-Cheney administrations. However, the list does not comport with Rozell's cases. As Rozell notes elsewhere, "It is not easy to make direct comparisons—but clearly there are cases of presidents who have exercised this authority properly, and cases of others who have overreached." Mark J. Rozell, "Executive Privilege" (transcript of live Q&A event), *Washington Post,* July 20, 2007, http://www.washingtonpost.com/wp-dyn/content/discussion/2007/07/20/DI2007072000830.html.

Chapter 2: Excessive Secrecy and Institutional Change

1. President John F. Kennedy, "The President and the Press," Address before the American Newspaper Publishers Association, New York City, April 27, 1961, http://www.jfklibrary.org/Research/Ready-Reference/JFK-Speeches/The-President-and-the-Press-Address-before-the-American-Newspaper-Publishers-Association.aspx. President Kennedy was clearly not an open government radical. In the same speech, he tempered his call for greater openness with a plea for more secrecy: "I refer, first, to the need for a far greater public information; and, second, to the need for far greater official secrecy."

2. For example, the US government closely tracked the Soviet military with the *Corona* reconnaissance satellite from 1960 until 1972. The system worked well, as former senator Daniel Patrick Moynihan recalled: "If the Soviets had ever decided to launch an invasion through the celebrated Fulda Gap, we would have known about it weeks in advance, and it would not have succeeded." Had detailed information about the *Corona* fallen into Soviet hands, Communist Party leaders would have adjusted their strategy and tactics to evade the satellite's camera, rendering it useless. Moynihan, *Secrecy,* p.

80. Interestingly, the Soviets probably knew about the *Corona* project, although not by name. A capsule from a failed 1959 launch landed on the Arctic island of Spitzbergen, which was formally under Norwegian control but had numerous Soviet mining interests. The novelist Alistair MacLean then published *Ice Station Zebra*, which drew from reports about the fallen capsule. The novel later became the basis of a Hollywood movie starring Rock Hudson and Ernest Borgnine, with a former CIA agent who worked with *Corona* as a technical adviser. See Philip Taubman, *Secret Empire: Eisenhower, the CIA, and the Hidden Story of America's Space Espionage* (New York: Simon & Schuster, 2003), pp. 286–287.

3. David Carr, "A Nation at War: Coverage; Pentagon Says Geraldo Rivera Will Be Removed from Iraq," *New York Times,* April 1, 2003, p. B14; Alessandra Stanley, "A Nation at War: The TV Watch; Two Correspondents, One Predictable Outcome," *New York Times,* April 1, 2003, p. B14; Tim Weiner, "1917 Paper on Troop Movements Still Classified," *Baltimore Sun,* December 17, 1991, http://articles.baltimoresun.com/1991-12-17/news/1991351019_1_secrecy-classified-confidential-documents; Elaine Sciolino, "Panel from C.I.A. Urges Curtailing of Agency Secrecy," *New York Times*, January 12, 1992, p. A1; Craig Nelson, "Perspective; Secrecy," *St. Petersburg (FL) Times,* July 11, 1993, p. 1D; Katherine Pfleger, "Your Government Is Hiding Something from You," *St. Petersburg (FL) Times,* June 23, 1999, p. 1D; Kate Doyle, "The End of Secrecy," *World Policy Journal* 16, no. 1 (1999): 34–51.

4. David Kocieniewski, "I.R.S. Sits on Data Pointing to Missing Children," *New York Times,* November 13, 2010, p. A1. According to the 9/11 Commission, Moussaoui's arrest would have prompted US allies to quickly begin investigations. His arrest would also have helped agents questioning Ahmed Ressam, another detainee and Al Qaeda member. Both consequences of a fuller Moussaoui investigation "would have broken the logjam." National Commission on Terrorist Attacks upon the United States, *The 9/11 Commission Report: Final Report of the National Commission on Terrorist Attacks upon the United States* (New York: W. W. Norton, 2004), pp. 276, 541; National Security Archive, "Declassification, Reclassification, and Redeclassification," PowerPoint presentation, n.d., p. 13, http://www.gwu.edu/~nsarchiv/nsa/foia.html, accessed May 24, 2011; Scott Shane, "Since 2001, Sharp Increase in the Number of Documents Classified by the Government," *New York Times,* July 3, 2005, p. A14.

5. Wikileaks, "Collateral Murder," April 5, 2010, http://wikileaks.org/wiki/Collateral_Murder,_5_Apr_2010, accessed January 23, 2011; Agence France Press, "Reuters Employees Killed during Iraq Battle: US Military," *Agence France Press,* July 13, 2007; Chris Lefkow, "Video Posted of Apache Strike Which Killed Reuters Employees," *Agence France Press,* April 5, 2010.

6. In its case against Manning, the government tried to prove that the video's leak aided enemies. See, e.g., Tom Ramstack, "Air Attack Video Given to Wikileaks Could Help Enemy: Witness," *Reuters,* June 12, 2013, http://www.reuters.com/article/2013/06/12/us-usa-wikileaks-manning-idUSBRE95B14020130612.

7. Associated Press, "Method behind AP-Ipsos Poll on Iraq," *USA Today*, February 24, 2007, http://www.usatoday.com/news/nation/2007-02-24-iraqi-deaths-results_x.htm.

8. Senate Select Committee to Study Governmental Operations with Respect to Intelligence Activities [Church Committee], *Book 1: Foreign and Military Intelligence: Final Report* (Washington, DC: Government Printing Office, 1976), Senate Report 94-755, 1976, p. 12, cited in Doyle, "End of Secrecy," p. 40.

9. "You" in both questions refers to citizens in a functioning democracy, a democracy that upholds core democratic processes, such as representation and accountability, and supports core democratic values and commitments, such as equal rights in citizenship, equal opportunity, and equal and irrevocable civil liberties. The term *necessary secrets* comes from Schoenfeld, *Necessary Secrets*. Also, we might add to the list other generally accepted categories, such as attorney-client privilege. See also Dave Eggers, *The Circle* (New York: Alfred A. Knopf, 2013), for a chilling fictional treatment of the tension between transparency and privacy.

10. In the first question, *need* is arguably too strong a word, since it implies citizens *require* every available bit of information to fulfill their democratic roles. However, *need* works perfectly in the second question. We might loosely define *need* in the first instance as what you could learn if you wanted to, without much difficulty.

11. Defense Department Committee on Classified Information, *Report to the Secretary of Defense by the Committee on Classified Information* (Washington, DC: Department of Defense, November 8, 1956), p. 6; Public Interest Declassification Board, "Selected Recommendations on Classification and Declassification from Major Reviews of Secrecy," June 22, 2007, http://www.archives.gov/pidb/meetings/06-22-07-hofius.pdf, accessed May 24, 2011; Task Force on Secrecy, *Report of the Defense Science Board, Task Force on Secrecy* (Washington, DC: Office of the Director of Defense Research and Engineering, July 1, 1970), http://www.fas.org/sgp/othergov/dsbrep.pdf, accessed March 31, 2014; Commission to Review DOD Security Policy and Practices, "Keeping the Nation's Secrets: A Report to the Secretary of Defense," 1985, http://www.fas.org/sgp/library/stilwell.html, accessed March 31, 2014; Griswold, "Secrets Not Worth Keeping"; Joint Security Commission, "Redefining Security"; Commission on Protecting and Reducing Government Secrecy, "Report of the Commission on Protecting and Reducing Government Secrecy," Senate Document 105-2, 1997, http://www.fas.org/sgp/library/moynihan/sum.html, accessed March 31, 2014; Rumsfeld, Secretary Rumsfeld Press Conference in Phoenix; Aftergood, "Reducing Government Secrecy," p. 403; Steven Aftergood, "Telling Secrets," *ForeignPolicy.com*, 2010, http://www.foreignpolicy.com/articles/2010/10/15/telling_secrets; Blanton, Testimony for the Hearing on "Emerging Threats."

12. Kean, Commissioner Richard Ben-Veniste, and the commission in general agreed overclassification and interagency information prevented the government from stopping the attacks. Richard Ben-Veniste, Prepared Statement before the Subcommittee on National Security, Emerging Threats, and International Relations, House Committee on Government Reform, March 5, 2005, http://www.gwu.edu/~nsarchiv/news/20050302/

stmt_ben-veniste.pdf; Commission on Protecting and Reducing Government Secrecy, "Report," chap. 2, p. 36; Blanton, Testimony for the Hearing on "Emerging Threats"; "Credible Classifications" editorial, *Washington Post,* July 13, 2004, p. A14; Aftergood, "Telling Secrets"; President Obama, "Classified Information and Controlled Unclassified Information," Memorandum for the Heads of Executive Departments and Agencies, May 27, 2009, http://www.whitehouse.gov/the_press_office/Presidential-Memorandum -Classified-Information-and-Controlled-Unclassified-Information/.

13. President Richard M. Nixon, "Remarks at a Reception for Returned Prisoners of War," May 24, 1973, transcript and film available at American Presidency Project, University of California–Santa Barbara, http://www.presidency.ucsb.edu/ws/index .php?pid=3856#ixzz1wSrUQYOB; Daniel Ellsberg, *Secrets: A Memoir of Vietnam and the Pentagon Papers* (New York: Penguin, 2003); Commission on Protecting and Reducing Government Secrecy, "Report," p. 36; Inspector General, Department of Defense, "White Paper: Classification and Declassification within the Department of Defense," 1975, letter of transmittal and page i, cited in Commission on Protecting and Reducing Government Secrecy, "Report." A recent defense of government secrecy is Schoenfeld, *Necessary Secrets,* 2010.

14. The ISOO's main categories include personnel security; physical security; information security; professional education, training, and awareness; security management, oversight, and planning; and unique items. ISOO, *2010 Cost Report,* National Archives and Records Administration, 2010, pp. 1, 2, 5, http://www.fas.org/sgp/isoo/2010costs .pdf; Lee H. Hamilton, "The Costs of Too Much Secrecy" op-ed, *Washington Post,* April 13, 1992, p. A21; Doyle, "End of Secrecy," p. 55 ("salaries, safes").

15. Sunshine-era presidents have defined the classification categories this way: "(1) 'Top Secret' shall be applied to information, the unauthorized disclosure of which reasonably could be expected to cause exceptionally grave damage to the national security that the original classification authority is able to identify or describe. (2) 'Secret' shall be applied to information, the unauthorized disclosure of which reasonably could be expected to cause serious damage to the national security that the original classification authority is able to identify or describe. (3) 'Confidential' shall be applied to information, the unauthorized disclosure of which reasonably could be expected to cause damage to the national security that the original classification authority is able to identify or describe." See, e.g., President Barack Obama, Executive Order 13526: Classified National Security Information Memorandum, December 29, 2009, Section 1.2, http://www.gpo.gov/fdsys/pkg/ FR-2010-01-05/pdf/E9-31418.pdf. See also Priest and Arkin, "Hidden World"; Dana Priest and William M. Arkin, *Top Secret America: The Rise of the New American Security State* (New York: Little, Brown, 2011); Richard Reeves, *President Nixon: Alone in the White House* (New York: Simon & Schuster, 2001), p. 331; Frank Rich, "Kiss This War Goodbye," op-ed, *New York Times,* July 31, 2010, p. 8; Greg Miller, "How Many Security Clearances Have Been Issued? Nearly Enough for Everyone in the Washington Area," *CheckPoint Washington,* September 20, 2011, http://www.washingtonpost.com/blogs/

checkpoint-washington/post/how-many-security-clearances-has-the-government-issued-nearly-enough-for-everyone-in-the-washington-area/2011/09/20/gIQAMW3OiK_blog .html. Those approved for top secret clearances range from senior officials to "packers/craters"—that is, movers. See Max Fisher, "Top Secret Clearance Holders So Numerous They Include 'Packers/Craters,'" *Worldviews/Washington Post,* June 12, 2013, http://www. washingtonpost.com/blogs/worldviews/wp/2013/06/12/top-secret-clearance-holders-so -numerous-they-include-packerscraters.

16. G. W. Schulz, "Government Secrecy Orders on Patents Have Stifled More Than 5,000 Inventions," *Threat Level,* April 16, 2013, http://www.wired.com/threatlevel/2013/ 04/gov-secrecy-orders-on-patents/.

17. David E. Pozen, "The Mosaic Theory, National Security, and the Freedom of Information Act," *Yale Law Journal* 115 (2005): 628–679; Jameel Jaffer, "The Mosaic Theory," *Social Research* 77, no. 3 (2010): 873–882; Peter Grier, "Washington Post Series: How Many Secrets Did It Spill?" *Christian Science Monitor,* July 21, 2010.

18. Although the United States is in some ways decentralized, as a result of federalism and presidentialism the national security state and the associated secrecy system are governed almost exclusively by the executive branch.

19. Josiah Ober, *Democracy and Knowledge: Innovation and Learning in Classical Athens* (Princeton, NJ: Princeton University Press, 2010). See also Elizabeth Anderson, "The Epistemology of Democracy," *Episteme* 3, no. 1-2 (2006): 8–22; Friedrich A. Hayek, "The Use of Knowledge in Society," *American Economic Review* 35 (1945): 519–530.

20. Ober, *Democracy and Knowledge*; Anderson, "Epistemology of Democracy"; James C. Scott, *Seeing Like a State: How Certain Schemes to Improve the Human Condition Have Failed* (New Haven, CT: Yale University Press, 1998); Scott E. Page, *The Difference: How the Power of Diversity Creates Better Groups, Firms, Schools, and Societies* (Princeton, NJ: Princeton University Press, 2007). See also Aftergood, "Telling Secrets."

21. David Halberstam, *The Best and the Brightest* (New York: Random House, 1972), p. 655; Victor S. Navasky, "How We Got into the Messiest War in Our History," *New York Times,* November 12, 1972, http://www.nytimes.com/books/98/03/15/home/halberstam -best.html; James C. Thomson, "How Could Vietnam Happen? An Autopsy," *Atlantic,* April 1968, http://www.theatlantic.com/magazine/archive/1968/04/how-could-vietnam -happen-an-autopsy/306462/, accessed March 31, 2014; Alasdair Roberts, "National Security and Open Government," *Georgetown Public Policy Review* 9, no. 2 (2004): 69–85; Yuen Foong Khong, *Analogies at War: Korea, Munich, Dien Bien Phu, and the Vietnam Decisions of 1965* (Princeton, NJ: Princeton University Press, 1992); James Fallows, *Blind into Baghdad: America's War in Iraq* (New York: Vintage, 2006).

22. Page, *Difference*.

23. Ober, *Democracy and Knowledge*; Anderson, "Epistemology of Democracy"; Hayek, "Use of Knowledge."

24. Moynihan, *Secrecy,* pp. 79–80, emphasis in original; Aftergood, "Reducing Government Secrecy," pp. 398–399. See also Elizabeth Goitein and David M. Shapiro, *Reduc-*

ing Overclassification through Accountability (New York: Brennan Center for Justice, New York University School of Law, 2011); Charles F. Parker and Eric K. Stern, "Blindsided? September 11 and the Origins of Strategic Surprise," *Political Psychology* 23, no. 3 (2002): 601–630.

25. Jack L. Goldsmith, Testimony before Senate Committee on the Judiciary Hearing on "Preserving the Rule of Law in the Fight against Terrorism," 110th Congress, 2007, p. 9, http://www.gpo.gov/fdsys/pkg/CHRG-110shrg39358/pdf/CHRG-110shrg39358 .pdf; Rep. Chris Shays, Statement before the Subcommittee on National Security, Emerging Threats, and International Relations, House Committee on Government Reform, March 5, 2005; Heather Brooke, "Overclassification—A Direct Threat to National Security," *HeatherBrooke.org*, August 1, 2005, http://heatherbrooke.org/2005/overclassification/; Hamilton, "Costs of Too Much Secrecy."

26. On pundits' poor predictive abilities, see Philip Tetlock, *Expert Political Judgment: How Good Is It? How Can We Know?* (Princeton, NJ: Princeton University Press, 2005). Anderson, "Epistemology of Democracy."

27. James Bamford, "The NSA Is Building the Country's Biggest Spy Center (Watch What You Say)," *Threat Level*, March 15, 2012, http://www.wired.com/threat-level/2012/03/ff_nsadatacenter/all/1. On the argument about how excessive secrecy makes it difficult to protect truly necessary secrets, see Steven Garfinkel [former ISOO director], Testimony before the House Committee on Government Operations Hearings on Executive Order on Security Classification, March 10 and May 5, 1982, p. 146; Mackenzie, *Secrets,* p. 96.

28. The difference between the country's founders and contemporary Supreme Court majorities on this issue is rather stark: "The right to access public information . . . is not a 'fundamental' privilege or immunity of citizenship." *McBurney et al. v. Young*, April 29, 2013, 133 S. Ct. 1709, at 2. James Madison, 1798, *Virginia Resolutions*; John Adams, "A Dissertation on the Canon and Feudal Law," *The Works of John Adams*, vol. 3 (1765); Thomas Paine, *The Rights of Man* (London: J. S. Jordan, 1792).

29. Moynihan, *Secrecy*, p. 168; Sam Archibald, "The Early Years of the Freedom of Information Act, 1955 to 1974," *PS: Political Science and Politics* 26, no. 4 (1993): 726–731; House Committee on Government Operations, "Availability of Information from Federal Departments and Agencies," 86th Congress, House Report 86-2084 (Washington, DC: Government Printing Office, 1960), p. 36. (COINTELPRO is the acronym for a series of FBI programs together known as the Counter Intelligence Program.) The House committee report also displayed an understanding of the problems with the CEA approach introduced previously: "Those elected or appointed to positions of executive authority must recognize that government, in a democracy, cannot be wider than the people." See also Stephen Kinzer, *Overthrow: America's Century of Regime Change from Hawaii to Iraq* (New York: Times Books, 2007); Athan G. Theoharis, *Spying on Americans: Political Surveillance from Hoover to the Huston Plan* (Philadelphia: Temple University Press, 1978).

30. On the cue-taking model, see Samuel L. Popkin, *The Reasoning Voter: Communi-*

cation and Persuasion in Presidential Campaigns (Chicago: University of Chicago Press, 1991); Arthur Lupia and Mathew McCubbins, *The Democratic Dilemma: Can Citizens Learn What They Need To Know?* (Cambridge: Cambridge University Press, 1998); cf. Larry M. Bartels, "Uninformed Votes: Information Effects in Presidential Elections," *American Journal of Political Science* 40 (1996): 194–230; Scott L. Althaus, "Information Effects in Collective Preferences," *American Political Science Review* 92 (1998): 545–558; Richard R. Lau and David P. Redlawsk, "Advantages and Disadvantages of Cognitive Heuristics in Political Decision Making," *American Journal of Political Science* 45 (2001): 951–971; James Kuklinski and Paul Quirk, "Reconsidering the Rational Public: Cognition, Heuristics, and Mass Opinion," in *Elements of Reason,* ed. Arthur Lupia, Mathew McCubbins, and Samuel Popkin (New York: Cambridge University Press, 2000), pp. 153–182; Jason Ross Arnold, "The Electoral Consequences of Voter Ignorance," *Electoral Studies* 31, no. 4 (2012): 796–815.

31. Dawn E. Johnsen, Testimony before the U.S. Senate Committee on the Judiciary Subcommittee on the Constitution, Hearing on "Secret Law and the Threat to Democratic and Accountable Government," April 30, 2008; Aftergood, "Telling Secrets."

32. Most democratic theorists tend to worry about low levels of trust in government. However, some have seen certain kinds and levels of distrust as potentially healthy and in the liberal and Madisonian traditions. See Richard J. Hofstadter, "The Paranoid Style in American Politics," *Harper's*, November 1964, pp. 77–86; cf. Russell Hardin, "Do We Want Trust in Government?" in *Democracy and Trust,* ed. Mark E. Warren (Cambridge: Cambridge University Press, 1999), pp. 22–41. See also Thomas C. Ellington, "Won't Get Fooled Again: The Paranoid Style in the National Security State," *Government and Opposition* 38, no. 4 (2003): 436–455.

33. Mark Memmott, "Survey Finds More Information Kept from Public," *USA Today,* March 12, 2006; Thomas Hargrove, "Scripps Poll—Government Secrecy Is as Strong as Ever," *Scripps Howard News Service*, March 14, 2010, http://www.sunshineweek.org/ManageArticles/ArticleView/tabid/68/ArticleId/71/Scripps-Poll-Government-Secrecy-is-as-Strong-as-Ever-71.aspx. The literature on trust and perceptions of excessive secrecy is in its infancy. See, e.g., Suzanne J. Piotrowski and Gregg G. Van Ryzin, "Citizen Attitudes toward Transparency in Local Government," *American Review of Public Administration* 37, no. 3 (2007): 306–323. The specific public opinion data are as follows. When asked if the government should maintain a high level of secrecy surrounding military operations, 59.8 percent said it "definitely should" in 1996 and 55.9 percent agreed in 1998 (for domestic terrorism, it was 60 percent in 1996 and 53.3 percent in 1998). On diplomatic initiatives (37.4 percent in 1996, 32.4 percent in 1998) and the intelligence budget (27.9 percent in 1996, 24.8 percent in 1998), far fewer Americans believed the government as a general rule should maintain high levels of secrecy. Others thought the government *probably* should maintain secrecy, increasing the majority seemingly in favor of the status quo. A seminal piece on the problematic survey response is John Zaller and Stanley Feldman, "A Simple Theory of Survey Response," *American Journal of Political Science* 36 (1992): 579–616.

34. Ellsberg, *Secrets*, pp. 237–239, emphases in original. In 2013, I described Ellsberg's remarks to a former senior official from the Obama-Biden administration. Is the disconnect still so large? I asked. He argued that the information revolution significantly decentralized information flows and contributed (with other unidentified causes) to more open, trusting, back-and-forth relationships between insiders and outsiders without clearances (e.g., "experts"). Insiders may know more details about the world, he said, but well-informed outsiders are not "180 degrees" off base.

35. On the question of bureaucratic redundancy, including the distinction between "good and bad redundancies," see James Q. Wilson, *Bureaucracy: What Government Agencies Do and Why They Do It*, 2nd ed. (New York: Basic Books, 2000), p. 274; Martin Landau, "Redundancy, Rationality, and the Problem of Duplication and Overlap," *Public Administration Review* 29, no. 4 (1969): 346–358.

36. Jacques Derrida took it a few steps further: "There is no political power without control of the archive, if not of memory." Derrida, *Archive Fever: A Freudian Impression* (Chicago: University of Chicago Press, 1995), p. 4n1. (He continued: "Effective democratization can always be measured by this essential criterion: the participation in and the access to the archive, its constitution, and its interpretation.") Max Weber, *Essays in Sociology*, trans. and ed. H. H. Gerth and C. Wright Mills (New York: Oxford University Press, 1946), 233–234; Commission on Protecting and Reducing Government Secrecy, "Report," Appendix A: Loyalty; Sibel Edmonds, "Biography," *JustACitizen.com*, n.d., http://justacitizen.com/articles_documents/SibelEdmonds-Long%20BIO-.htm, accessed June 24, 2013; David Kohn, "Lost in Translation," *60 Minutes*, September 10, 2009, http://www.cbsnews.com/stories/2002/10/25/60minutes/main526954.shtml; P. K. Rose, "Two Strategic Intelligence Mistakes in Korea, 1950: Perceptions and Reality," *Studies in Intelligence* 11 (Fall–Winter 2001): 57–65, https://www.cia.gov/library/center-for-the-study-of-intelligence/csi-publications/csi-studies/studies/fall_winter_2001/article06.html; Matthew W. Aid, "Declassification in Reverse: The U.S. Intelligence Community's Secret Historical Document Reclassification Program," National Security Archive, February 21, 2006, http://www.gwu.edu/~nsarchiv/NSAEBB/NSAEBB179; Griswold, "Secrets Not Worth Keeping." See also the "internal threat" justification in David N. Gibbs, "Secrecy and International Relations," *Journal of Peace Research* 32, no. 2 (1995): 213–228.

37. James Clapper, "Nomination of Lieutenant General James Clapper to Be Director of National Intelligence," Hearing of the Senate (Select) Intelligence Committee, July 20, 2010; Commission on Protecting and Reducing Government Secrecy, "Report," Appendix G: Major Reviews of the U.S. Secrecy System; Public Interest Declassification Board, "Selected Recommendations," p. 4; Commission to Review DOD Security Policy and Practices, "Keeping the Nation's Secrets"; Weber, *Essays in Sociology*; Wilson, *Bureaucracy*; Herbert A. Simon, *Administrative Behavior* (New York: Macmillan, 1947); Avinash Dixit, "Power of Incentives in Private versus Public Organizations," *American Economic Review* 87, no. 2 (1997): 378–382.

38. On bureaucratic autonomy, see, e.g., Daniel Carpenter, *The Forging of Bureaucratic*

Autonomy: Reputations, Networks, and Policy Innovation in Executive Agencies, 1862–1928 (Princeton, NJ: Princeton University Press, 2001); Chalmers Johnson, *MITI and the Japanese Miracle: The Growth of Industrial Policy, 1925–1975* (Stanford, CA: Stanford University Press, 1982).

39. Steven Aftergood, "National Security Secrecy: How the Limits Change," *Social Research: An International Quarterly* 77, no. 3 (2010): 839–852, at 841.

40. This sort of ideological rhetoric often points to the Constitution. But it is worth noting that Article II said nothing about executive branch secrecy, although in Article I, the Constitution did authorize Congress to "keep a Journal of its Proceedings, and from time to time publish the same, excepting such Parts as may in their Judgment require Secrecy." "What government should do" involves a state's responsibilities and priorities vis-à-vis society, the economy, and the international system.

41. President Clinton, "Executive Order 12958: Classified National Security Information," April 17, 1995, http://www.gpo.gov/fdsys/pkg/FR-1995-04-20/pdf/95-9941 .pdf; President Bush, "Executive Order 13292: Further Amendment to Executive Order 12958, as Amended, Classified National Security Information," March 25, 2003, http:// www.gpo.gov/fdsys/pkg/FR-2003-03-28/pdf/03-7736.pdf. Even President Nixon joined *that* chorus. ("The interests of the United States and its citizens are best served by making information regarding the affairs of Government readily available to the public. This concept of an informed citizenry is reflected in the Freedom of Information Act and in the current public information policies of the executive branch.") See President Richard M. Nixon, "Executive Order 11652: Classification and Declassification of National Security Information and Material," June 8, 1972, http://www.fas.org/irp/offdocs/eo/eo-11652 .htm, accessed March 31, 2014.

42. Gordon Silverstein, "Bush, Cheney, and the Separation of Powers: A Lasting Legal Legacy?" *Presidential Studies Quarterly* 39, no. 4 (2009): 878–895; Heidi Kitrosser, "The Accountable Executive," *Minnesota Law Review* 93 (2009): 1741–1777. For a defense of the theory, with a reminder that Bush-Cheney's application of it sometimes violated its core, see Steven G. Calabresi and Christopher S. Yoo, *The Unitary Executive: Presidential Power from Washington to Bush* (New Haven, CT:: Yale University Press, 2008). See also Charlie Savage, *Takeover: The Return of the Imperial Presidency and the Subversion of American Democracy* (New York: Little, Brown, 2007); Barton Gellman, *Angler: The Cheney Vice Presidency* (New York: Penguin, 2008).

43. Gellman, *Angler*; Alexander Hamilton, "Federalist Paper #70," *The Federalist Papers* (1788; repr., New York: Signet Classics, 2003). John Yoo, the famous (or infamous) Bush-Cheney Justice Department lawyer, sUET adherent, and University of California–Berkeley law professor, has demonstrated particularly grievous historical inconsistencies. In 2000, during the last days of the Clinton-Gore administration, Yoo lamented the Democratic president's unilateral approach to foreign affairs, specifically regarding the Anti-ballistic Missile Treaty and the Kosovo air war: "In order to achieve their foreign policy goals, the Clinton administration has undermined the balance of powers that exist

in foreign affairs, and [they] have undermined principles of democratic accountability that executive branches have agreed upon well to the Nixon Administration." Soon after Bush-Cheney took office, Yoo began to assert that the president should unilaterally control foreign policy. Then, once Obama-Biden took office, he once again began to criticize presidential unilateralism. See, e.g., Yoo, "The Imperial President Abroad," Presentation at The Rule of Law in the Wake of Clinton Conference at the Cato Institute, 2000, http://www.cato.org/events/000712con.html (video at http://www.cato.org/realaudio/con-07-12-00p4.ram) (no text or transcript available).

44. Gellman, *Angler*, p. 96; Laurence McQuillan, "For Bush, Secrecy Is a Matter of Loyalty," *USA Today*, March 14, 2002, p. 1A; PBS Frontline, "Cheney in His Own Words," online appendix to *The Dark Side* documentary, n.d., http://www.pbs.org/wgbh/pages/frontline/darkside/themes/ownwords.html#1.

45. Graham Allison, "Conceptual Models and the Cuban Missile Crisis," *American Political Science Review* 63, no. 3 (1969): 689–718; Gellman, *Angler*.

46. Savage, *Takeover*, pp. 9, 51–52; "Dick Cheney Recalls the Ford Presidency," *National Journal* 17, no. 2 (January 12, 1985): 71; Vice President Cheney, "Vice President's Remarks at the Gerald R. Ford Journalism Prize Luncheon Followed by Q&A," National Press Club, June 19, 2006, http://georgewbush-whitehouse.archives.gov/news/releases/2006/06/20060619-10.html; Sean Wilenz, "Mr. Cheney's Minority Report," *New York Times*, July 9, 2007, p. A17; PBS Frontline, "Cheney in His Own Words." Administration officials did push the notion that "9/11 changed everything," which was less a reflection of their changed thinking than of their interest in taking advantage of the opportunity to push for policy changes. See the later discussion for the full quote.

47. Gellman, *Angler*, p. 101; McQuillan, "For Bush"; Savage, *Takeover*, pp. 75–76, 84, 159, emphasis added; White House, "The Vice President Appears on ABC's This Week," January 27, 2002, http://georgewbush-whitehouse.archives.gov/vicepresident/news-speeches/speeches/vp20020127.html. On interelite persuasion, see Mark Blyth, "Powering, Puzzling, or Persuading? The Mechanisms of Building Institutional Orders," *International Studies Quarterly* 51, no. 4 (2007): 761–777. See also Samuel Kernell, *Going Public: New Strategies of Presidential Leadership*, 3rd ed. (Washington, DC: CQ Press, 1997).

48. Alexander L. George and Andrew Bennett, *Case Studies and Theory Development in the Social Sciences* (Cambridge, MA: MIT Press, 2005), p. 10. It is possible—but not very likely—that 9/11 would have substantially changed Gore's governing ideology into something resembling Bush's.

49. David R. Mayhew, *Divided We Govern: Party Control, Lawmaking, and Investigations, 1946–2002*, 2nd ed. (New Haven, CT: Yale University Press, 2005). Mayhew shows how divided government makes a president's life more difficult, although not as much as is commonly believed. Intraparty unity and party discipline are also important factors.

50. Critical junctures allow for big, rapid change, giving *agents* rare opportunities to push aside some of the constraining *structures* to reach those agents' preferred outcomes.

They expand the range of feasible political possibilities. Though change can be bidirectional, some directions (e.g., expansion of the secrecy system) are more likely. See Ira Katznelson, "Periodization and Preferences: Reflections on Purposive Action in Comparative-Historical Social Science," in *Comparative Historical Analysis in the Social Sciences,* ed. James Mahoney and Dietrich Rueschemeyer (Cambridge: Cambridge University Press, 2003), pp. 270–301; Ellen Immergut, "Institutions, Veto Points, and Policy Results: A Comparative Analysis of Health Care," *Journal of Public Policy* 10, no. 4 (1990): 391–416; George Tsebelis, *Veto Players: How Political Institutions Work* (Princeton, NJ: Princeton University Press, 2002).

51. On rally effects, see John Mueller, "Presidential Popularity from Truman to Johnson," *American Political Science Review* 64, no. 1 (1970): 18–34. On windows of opportunity, see John W. Kingdon, *Agendas, Alternatives, and Public Policies,* 2nd ed. (New York: Longman, 2010). See also Doyle, "End of Secrecy," p. 34. Also note that shifts in public preferences about value priorities can happen outside of national security emergencies. New technologies, for example, might increase citizens' sensitivity to their personal privacy (e.g., concerns about identity theft), prompting congressional action to push corporations and government agencies to safeguard that information; in the process, security and secrecy would be privileged over liberty and transparency.

52. On the question of 9/11 as a critical juncture in academic work, I searched Google Scholar in June 2011, April 2012, and June 2012, and each time, I found very little (search terms were "'critical juncture,' September 11" and "'critical juncture,' 9/11"). On critical junctures, see, e.g., Katznelson, "Periodization and Preferences"; Paul Pierson, "Increasing Returns, Path Dependence, and the Study of Politics," *American Political Science Review* 94 (2000): 251–267; Ruth Berins Collier and David Collier, *Shaping the Political Arena: Critical Junctures, the Labor Movement, and Regime Dynamics in Latin America* (Princeton, NJ: Princeton University Press, 1991); James Mahoney, "Path Dependence in Historical Sociology," *Theory and Society* 29 (2000): 507–548; Mahoney, "Path Dependent Explanations of Regime Change," *Studies in Comparative and International Development* 36, no. 1 (2001): 111–141; B. Guy Peters, Jon Pierre, and Desmond S. King, "The Politics of Path Dependency: Political Conflict in Historical Institutionalism," *Journal of Politics* 67 (2005): 1275–1300; Giovanni Capoccia and R. Daniel Kelemen, "The Study of Critical Junctures Theory, Narrative, and Counterfactuals in Historical Institutionalism," *World Politics* 59 (2007): 341–369. Despite being hyperbolic, "9/11 changed everything" was a common piece of rhetoric in the years after the attacks. In 2003, Cheney said: "In a sense, 9/11 changed everything for us. 9/11 forced us to think in new ways about threats to the United States, about our vulnerabilities, about who our enemies were, about what kind of military strategy we needed in order to defend ourselves." See Cheney, "Remarks by the Vice President," Tacoma, WA, December 22, 2003, http://georgewbush-whitehouse.archives.gov/news/releases/2003/12/20031223-1.html. He made an almost identical statement on *Meet the Press* on September 14, 2003, http://www.msnbc.msn.com/id/3080244/ns/meet_the_press/t/transcript-sept/#.T9eudBdrPZU. Another major

Bush-Cheney figure, Deputy Secretary of State Richard Armitage, rejected Pakistani intelligence officials' claims to put the attack in historical perspective, informing them instead on 9/11 that "history begins today." See PBS Frontline, Interview with Richard Armitage, *Return of the Taliban,* July 20, 2006, http://www.pbs.org/wgbh/pages/frontline/taliban/interviews/armitage.html.

53. It is of course true that Bush-Cheney created the Department of Homeland Security (DHS), which was a major institutional change—but that did not alter the sunshine-era secrecy system. James Mahoney and Kathleen Thelen, "A Theory of Gradual Institutional Change," in *Explaining Institutional Change: Ambiguity, Agency, and Power,* ed. Mahoney and Thelen (Cambridge: Cambridge University Press, 2010), pp. 16–17. As a general rule, critical junctures do not always produce "radical change"—"sudden bends in the path of history"—disrupting the "lock-in" effects seen during "equilibrium" periods, as pioneering theorists were arguing in the 1990s. Recent developments in historical institutionalist theory have themselves displaced some of those earlier ideas. Along with Mahoney and Thelen, "Theory of Gradual Institutional Change," see Peters, Pierre, and King, "Politics of Path Dependency"; T. J. Pempel, *Regime Shift: Comparative Dynamics of the Japanese Political Economy* (Ithaca, NY: Cornell University Press, 1998), cited in Wolfgang Streeck and Kathleen Thelen, "Introduction: Institutional Change in Advanced Political Economies," in *Beyond Continuity,* ed. Streeck and Thelen (Oxford: Oxford University Press, 2005), p. 3. Although we can define *institutions* as rules (and their enforcement mechanisms), as is common, we can also widen the definition a bit. Mahoney and Thelen, in "Theory of Gradual Institutional Change," pp. 7–8, for example, argue they are "distributional instruments laden with power implications." In this book, it is the distribution of information in a democracy that is most important, where excessive government secrecy is associated with an unjust distribution of information.

54. Collier and Collier, *Shaping the Political Arena,* p. 27; Mahoney, "Path Dependence"; James Mahoney, *The Legacies of Liberalism: Path Dependence and Political Regimes in Central America* (Baltimore, MD: Johns Hopkins University Press, 2002); Capoccia and Kelemen, "Study of Critical Junctures Theory"; Jack Goldsmith, *The Terror Presidency: Law and Judgment inside the Bush Administration* (New York: W. W. Norton, 2009), p. 181; Savage, *Takeover,* p. 51. Cheney (and Donald Rumsfeld) had at least *considered* more radical actions to boost executive power during critical junctures in the past. In the 1980s, Cheney was chosen to help draft a plan the federal government would use if the Soviets attacked the capital. According to one of the group's planners, the plan envisioned an emergency government without Congress, since "it would be easier to operate without them," and a new constitutional line of succession that bypassed the Congress. James Mann, *Rise of the Vulcans: The History of Bush's War Cabinet* (New York: Viking, 2004), pp. 138–145; Mann, "The Armageddon Plan," *Atlantic Monthly,* March 2004, http://www.theatlantic.com/past/docs/issues/2004/03/mann.htm.

55. *McBryde v. Committee to Review Circuit Court Council Conduct,* 264 F.3d 52 (DC Appeals Court, 2001).

56. Stephen Bell, "Do We Really Need a New 'Constructivist Institutionalism' to Explain Institutional Change?" *British Journal of Political Science* 41, no. 4 (2011): 883–906.

57. Ronald R. Krebs and Jennifer K. Lobasz, "Fixing the Meaning of 9/11: Hegemony, Coercion, and the Road to War in Iraq," *Security Studies* 16, no. 3 (2007): 409–451, at 412. See also Jason M. K. Lyall, "Pocket Protests: Rhetorical Coercion and the Micropolitics of Collective Action in Semiauthoritarian Regimes," *World Politics* 58, no. 3 (2006): 378–412. Although they are obviously related concepts, there are important differences between rhetorical coercion and Tulis's "rhetorical powers." The latter concept focuses on president-public interactions, rather than interbranch or other interelite interactions. See Jeffrey K. Tulis, *The Rhetorical Presidency* (Princeton, NJ: Princeton University Press, 1988).

58. President George W. Bush, "Address to a Joint Session of Congress and the American People," September 20, 2001, http://georgewbush-whitehouse.archives.gov/news/releases/2001/09/20010920-8.html.

59. "Ashcroft: Critics of New Terror Measures Undermine Effort," CNN, December 6, 2001, http://articles.cnn.com/2001-12-06/us/inv.ashcroft.hearing_1_military-tribunals-terrorism-probe-attorney-general-john-ashcroft?_s=PM:US; Capoccia and Kelemen, "Study of Critical Junctures Theory"; Krebs and Lobasz, "Fixing the Meaning of 9/11." Brenadan Nyhan maintains a tremendously valuable list of episodes since 9/11 when prominent Republicans attacked Democrats in this manner. Nyhan, "Republican Attacks on Dissent since 9/11," n.d., http://www.brendan-nyhan.com/blog/gop-dissent-attacks.html, accessed March 6, 2014; see also Nyhan, "Attacks on Dissent against President Obama," n.d., http://www.brendan-nyhan.com/blog/attacks-on-dissent-against-president-obama.html, accessed March 6, 2014. The full and formal name of the USA PATRIOT Act is the Uniting and Strengthening America by Providing Appropriate Tools Required to Intercept and Obstruct Terrorism Act.

60. Art. III, Sec. 3 of the Constitution describes treason this way: "Treason against the United States, shall consist only in levying War against them, or in adhering to their Enemies, giving them Aid and Comfort." See also Nyhan, "Republican Attacks on Dissent," emphasis added; Helen Dewar, "Lott Calls Daschle Divisive; GOP Attacks Prompted by Remarks on Direction of War," *Washington Post,* March 1, 2002, p. A5; Steven Thomma, "In Congress, a Partisan Spat over Terror Fight," *Philadelphia Inquirer,* March 1, 2001, articles.philly.com/2002-03-01/news/25342544_1_senator-daschle-terror-fight-tough-questions, accessed March 31, 2014.

61. Wesley W. Widmaier, "Constructing Foreign Policy Crises: Interpretive Leadership in the Cold War and War on Terrorism," *International Studies Quarterly* 51 (2007): 779–794, at 780 ("material conditions"); Jane K. Cramer and A. Trevor Thrall, "Introduction: Understanding Threat Inflation," in *American Foreign Policy and the Politics of Fear: Threat Inflation since 9/11,* ed. Thrall and Cramer (New York: Routledge, 2009), pp. 1–15, at 1 ("disinterested analysis").

62. Collier and Collier, *Shaping the Political Arena;* Katznelson, "Periodization and Preferences."

Chapter 3: Keeping Secrets, during Settled and Unsettled Times

1. Laura Donnelly, "9/11 Survivor Tells How He 'Surfed' 15 Floors down the Collapsing Tower," *Telegraph* (London), September 8, 2012, http://www.telegraph.co.uk/news/worldnews/september-11-attacks/9530013/911-survivor-tells-how-he-surfed-15-floors-down-the-collapsing-tower.html, accessed March 10, 2014; Jim Ritter, Chief, Vehicle Performance Division, National Transportation Safety Board, "Flight Path Study—United Airlines Flight 93," February 19, 2002, p. 2, http://www.ntsb.gov/doclib/foia/9_11/Flight_Path_Study_UA93.pdf.

2. Lance Morrow, "The Case for Rage and Retribution," *Time,* September 12, 2001, p. 48; Dan Balz and Bob Woodward, "America's Chaotic Road to War," *Washington Post,* January 27, 2002, p. A1.

3. President George W. Bush, "Statement by the President in His Address to the Nation," September 11, 2001, http://georgewbush-whitehouse.archives.gov/news/releases/2001/09/20010911-16.html. By September 25, the name of the mission was changed to Operation Enduring Freedom, after the administration learned that "infinite justice" was a way many Muslims perceived the final judgment of Allah. See "Infinite Justice, Out—Enduring Freedom, In," *BBC News,* September 25, 2001, http://news.bbc.co.uk/2/hi/americas/1563722.stm, accessed June 2, 2011. By 2008, the Bush-Cheney administration still spoke about the "long war" and the probably unending "global war on terrorism." See, e.g., US Army, "Army Posture Statement; Strategic Context," 2008, http://www.army.mil/aps/08/strategic_context/strategic_context.html ("We are in an era of persistent conflict").

4. Project for the New American Century (PNAC), *Rebuilding America's Defenses: Strategy, Forces, and Resources for a New Century* (Washington, DC: PNAC, 2000), p. 51. Gallup, "Presidential Approval Ratings—George W. Bush," http://www.gallup.com/poll/116500/presidential-approval-ratings-george-bush.aspx, accessed June 2, 2011; Virginia A. Chanley, "Trust in Government in the Aftermath of 9/11: Determinants and Consequences," *Political Psychology* 23, no. 3 (2002): 469–483. On settled and unsettled times, see Katznelson, "Periodization and Preferences."

5. Krebs and Lobasz, "Fixing the Meaning of 9/11." Among 9/11-themed songs were Alan Jackson's "Where Were You (When the World Stopped Turning)?"; Toby Keith's "Courtesy of the Red, White & Blue (The Angry American)"; and Neil Young's "Let's Roll." See Brian Mansfield, "Country Music, in 9/11 Time," *USA Today,* September 6, 2002, p. 9D.

6. President Bush, "Remarks by the President in Photo Opportunity with the National Security Team," September 12, 2001, http://georgewbush-whitehouse.archives.gov/news/releases/2001/09/20010912-4.html; "'New War' to Be Fought with Unprecedented Secrecy," CNN.com, September 17, 2001, http://articles.cnn.com/2001-09-17/us/ret.us.secret.war_1_pentagon-war-plans-world-trade-center?_s=PM:US.

7. President Harry S. Truman, "Executive Order 10290: Prescribing Regulations Es-

tablishing Minimum Standards for the Classification, Transmission, and Handling, by Departments and Agencies of the Executive Branch, of Official Information Which Requires Safeguarding in the Interest of the Security of the United States," § 26(d), September 24, 1951, http://www.trumanlibrary.org/executiveorders/index.php?pid=262; President Reagan, "Executive Order 12356: National Security Information," § 1.3(b), April 2, 1982, http://www.archives.gov/federal-register/codification/executive-order/12356.html, emphasis added; President Clinton, "Executive Order 12958: Classified National Security Information," § 1.8(e), April 17, 1995, http://www.fas.org/sgp/clinton/eo12958.html; David E. Pozen, "The Mosaic Theory, National Security, and the Freedom of Information Act," *Yale Law Journal* 115 (2005): 628–679; Jameel Jaffer, "The Mosaic Theory," *Social Research* 77, no. 3 (2010): 873–882. See also *Halperin v. CIA*, 629 F.2d (DC District Court, 1980), 144, 150): "Each individual piece of intelligence information, much like a piece of jigsaw puzzle, may aid in piecing together other bits of information even when the individual piece is not of obvious importance in itself"; also see *US v. Marchetti*, 466 F.2d (Fourth Circuit Appeals Court, 1972), 1309, 1318; *Halkin v. Helms*, 598 F.2d (DC Appeals Court, 1978), 1, 8; *CIA v. Sims*, 471 U.S. 159 (Supreme Court, 1985); *J. Roderick MacArthur Found. v. F.B.I.*, 102 F.3d 600 (DC Appeals Court, 1996)—all cited in *Detroit Free Press v. Ashcroft*, 303 F.3d 681 (Sixth Circuit Appeals Court, 2002).

8. Howard Morland, "The H-Bomb Secret: To Know How Is to Ask Why," *Progressive*, November 1979, p. 5; *US v. Progressive, Inc.*, 467 F. Supp. 990 (Western Wisconsin District Court, 1979); James Barron, "Erwin Kroll, 63, Crusading Editor of *The Progressive*," *New York Times*, November 3, 1994, p. B15.

9. Robin Toner, "A Nation Challenged: Flow of Information; Reconsidering Security, U.S. Clamps down on Agency Web Sites," *New York Times*, October 28, 2001, p. B4; Richard Dahl, "Does Secrecy Equal Security? Limiting Access to Environmental Information," *Environmental Health Perspectives* 112, no. 2 (2004): 104–107; "'New War' to Be Fought." Lots of other dual-use information vanished right after 9/11, covering water sources and facilities, electric plants, and transportation and computer networks, among other subjects.

10. President Bush was of course not the first to use a mass preventive detention policy. President Roosevelt's administration also employed one against 110,000 Japanese Americans after the Pearl Harbor attack. Amy Goldstein, "A Deliberate Strategy of Disruption; Massive, Secretive Detention Effort Aimed Mainly at Preventing Terror," *Washington Post*, November 4, 2001, p. A1; Joseph Marguiles, *Guantanamo and the Abuse of Presidential Power* (New York: Simon & Schuster, 2006). There were three categories of detainess: (1) INS detainess ("individuals who were questioned in the course of the investigation and detained by the INS for violation of the immigration laws"); (2) criminal detainees; and (3) material witness detainees ("persons detained after a judge issued a material witness warrant to secure their testimony before a grand jury"). *CNSS v. DOJ*, No. 02-5254 and No. 02–5300 (June 17, 2003), pp. 3–4; *CNSS v. DOJ* (Civil Action 01-2500); Neil A. Lewis, "A Nation Challenged: The Detainees; Detentions after Attacks Pass 1,000, U.S. Says," *New York Times*, October 30, 2001, p. B1; Declaration of Michael E. Rolince [Sec-

tion Chief, FBI Counterterrorism Division], In Bond Proceedings re: Ali Abubakr Ali Al-Maqtari, U.S. DOJ, Executive Office for Immigration Review, Immigration Court, October 11, 2011, pp. 5–6, reproduced as appendix B to Human Rights Watch, *Presumption of Guilt: Human Rights Abuses of Post–September 11 Detainees,* 2002, http://www.hrw.org/reports/2002/us911/USA0802.pdf. The "inverted" mosaic theory noted earlier is often the rationale that underlies government surveillance operations.

11. Goldstein, "Deliberate Strategy"; Marguiles, *Guantanamo*; Amy E. Hooper, "Investigating Terrorism: The Role of the First Amendment," *Duke Law and Technology Review* 2 (2004): 2; David E. Pozen, "Deep Secrecy," *Stanford Law Review* 62, no. 2 (2010): 257–340.

12. Lewis, "Nation Challenged." The plaintiffs included: Center for National Security Studies; American Civil Liberties Union; Electronic Privacy Information Center; American-Arab Anti-discrimination Committee; American Immigration Law Foundation; American Immigration Lawyers Association; Amnesty International USA; Arab-American Institute; Asian-American Legal Defense and Education Fund; Center for Constitutional Rights; Center for Democracy and Technology; Council on American Islamic Relations; First Amendment Foundation; Human Rights Watch; Multiracial Activist; Nation Magazine; National Association of Criminal Defense Lawyers; National Black Police Association, Inc.; Partnership for Civil Justice, Inc.; People for the American Way Foundation; Reporters Committee for Freedom of the Press; and the World Organization against Torture USA.

13. *CNSS v. DOJ* (Civil Action 01-2500 (GK)).

14. *CNSS v. DOJ,* DC Appeals Court, esp. pp. 18–19. Judge Karen L. Henderson also sat on the three-judge panel, and Judge David S. Tatel filed a dissenting opinion. Also see *Manna v. DOJ,* 51 F.3d 1158 (Third Circuit Appeals Court, 1995), 1158, 1165. The court's decision joined others in a growing list of appellate-level cases "holding that the courts must defer to the executive on decisions of national security" and, more generally, bowing toward Bush-Cheney visions of executive authority: "In undertaking a deferential review we simply recognize the different roles underlying the constitutional separation of powers. It is within the role of the executive to acquire and exercise the expertise of protecting national security. It is not within the role of the courts to second guess executive judgments made in furtherance of that branch's proper role." The courts' deference, it was argued, included a general trust in the executive to make appropriate decisions about mass detentions and sweeping secrecy. It did not matter that none of the foreign nationals picked up in the post-9/11 sweep were charged with terrorist crimes. *CNSS v. DOJ,* DC Appeals Court, p. 23. Judge Sentelle's argument for deference pointed to the third, fourth, and seventh circuit courts' similarly stated positions. See also Jaffer, "Mosaic Theory."

15. *North Jersey Media Group, Inc. v. Ashcroft,* 308 F.3d 198 (Third Circuit Appeals Court, 2002); *North Jersey Media Group, Inc. v. Ashcroft,* F. Supp. 2d 288 (New Jersey District Court, 2002), 205. The two-part test originated in *Richmond Newspapers, Inc. v. Virginia,* U.S. 555 (Supreme Court, 1980), 448.

16. *Detroit Free Press v. Ashcroft.* Judges Martha Craig Daughtrey and James G. Carr joined Judge Keith in hearing the case. See also Pozen, "Mosaic Theory," p. 663.

17. Savage, *Takeover*, p. 96. See also Pozen, "Mosaic Theory," pp. 661–663; *ACLU v. DOJ*, 321 F. Supp. 2d 24 (DC District Court, 2004). The district court rejected the ACLU's request to overturn the DOJ's FOIA denial regarding the PATRIOT Act's Section 215 (unofficially known as the "libraries provision"). The ACLU sought information only on the frequency of its use. The government argued that disclosure of the nameless, place-less, and subtanceless statistics would help terrorists identify "safe harbors" in which to plot their attacks free from surveillance. The court was sympathetic: "The significance of one piece of information may frequently depend on knowledge of many other items of information. Although the statistics to which plaintiffs seek access may appear, on their face, to be innocuous, their disclosure would be harmful to national security. This is because the information that has already been placed in the public domain (through statutorily required disclosures, media accounts, etc.), coupled with the classified information that has not been released, represent pieces of the mosaic which reveal a very significant and meaningful picture of the FBI's investigative efforts in the post–September 11, 2001 war on terror." Eventually, the government released the statistics anyway, apparently making the determination that only *sometimes* would seemingly innocuous bits of information get into the ever-vigilant terrorists' hands. See Jaffer, "Mosaic Theory," pp. 874–875.

18. Jules Lobel, "The Preventive Paradigm and the Perils of Ad Hoc Balancing," *Minnesota Law Review* 91 (2007): 1407–1450; David Cole and Jules Lobel, *Less Safe, Less Free: The Failure of Preemption in the War on Terror* (New York: New Press, 2007); Ron Suskind, *The One-Percent Doctrine: Deep inside America's Pursuit of Its Enemies since 9/11* (New York: Simon & Schuster, 2006). As Suskind documented, Cheney promoted the concept of the 1 percent doctrine after 9/11, saying, for example: "If there's a 1% chance that Pakistani scientists are helping al-Qaeda build or develop a nuclear weapon, we have to treat it as a certainty in terms of our response. It's not about our analysis. . . . It's about our response."

19. "'New War' to Be Fought"; Hendrika (Erna) Ruijer, "Proactive Transparency: The Proactive Disclosure of Information by Government Agencies in the USA and the Netherlands" (Ph.D. diss., Virginia Commonwealth University, 2013).

20. Attorney General John Ashcroft, "Memorandum for Heads of All Federal Departments and Agencies; Re: The Freedom of Information Act," October 12, 2001, http://www.gwu.edu/~nsarchiv/NSAEBB/NSAEBB84/Ashcroft%20Memorandum.pdf.

21. Attorney General Janet Reno, "Memorandum for Heads of Departments and Agencies; Subject: The Freedom of Information Act," October 4, 1993, http://www.justice.gov/oip/foia_updates/Vol_XIV_3/page3.htm; President William J. Clinton, "Memorandum for Heads of Departments and Agencies; Subject: The Freedom of Information Act," October 4, 1993, http://www.fas.org/sgp/clinton/reno.html; Attorney General William French Smith, "Attorney General's Memo on FOIA," May 4, 1981, http://www.justice.gov/oip/foia_updates/Vol_II_3/page3.htm; Committee on Government Reform—Mi-

nority Staff, Special Investigations Division, *Secrecy in the Bush Administraion,* report prepared for Rep. Henry A. Waxman, 2004, p. 5, www.democrats.reform.house.gov., accessed May 20, 2011; Government Accountability Office, "Freedom of Information Act: Agency Views on Changes Resulting from New Administration Policy," Report to the Ranking Minority Member, Committee on the Judiciary, U.S. Senate, September 2003; Amanda Fitzsimmons, "National Security or Unnecessary Secrecy? Restricting Exemption 1 to Prohibit Reclassification of Information Already in the Public Domain," *I/S: A Journal of Law and Policy for the Information Society* (2008): 1–45, at 14–16.

22. Tom Beierle and Ruth Greenspan Bell, "Don't Let 'Right to Know' Be a War Casualty," *Christian Science Monitor,* December 20, 2001, p. 9; "On the Public's Right to Know," *San Francisco Chronicle,* January 6, 2002, http://articles.sfgate.com/2002-01-06/opinion/17526910_1_public-scrutiny-public-documents-freedom.

23. Steven Garfinkel, Presentation before the American Society of Access Professionals, December 11, 2001, http://www.justice.gov/archive/oip/foiapost/2001foiapost22.htm; Reporters Committee for Freedom of the Press (RCFP), *Homefront Confidential: How the War on Terrorism Affects Access to Information and the Public's Right to Know* (Arlington, VA: RCFP, 2002), available at http://www.rcfp.org/homefrontconfidential/foi.html; Rebecca Daugherty, "Ashcroft's FOI Act Memo Prompts Concerns," *News Media & The Law* (Winter 2002): 25, http://www.rcfp.org/node/102260.

24. The General Accounting Office became the Government Accountability Office in 2004. GAO, "Freedom of Information Act: Agency Views on Changes Resulting from New Administration Policy," GAO-03-981, Report to the Ranking Minority Member, Committee on the Judiciary, U.S. Senate, September 2003. Sen. Partick Leahy (D-VT) asked the GAO to study the matter in February 2002. The survey, administered from October 2002 to April 2003, interviewed 183 out of 205 contacted FOIA officers. See also House Government Reform Committee's revised (March 12, 2002) *Citizen's Guide on Using the Freedom of Information Act and the Privacy Act of 1974 to Request Government Records,* House Report 107-37, which openly rejected Ashcroft's logic: "Contrary to the instructions issued by the Department of Justice . . . the standard should not be to allow the withholding of information whenever there is merely a 'sound legal basis' for doing so." Appealing to Reno's interpretation of the FOIA, the Government Reform Committee report argued, "Above all, the statute requires Federal agencies to provide the fullest possible disclosure of information to the public." See also RCFP, *Homefront Confidential.*

25. The government began to systematically track FOIA requests and responses starting in 1998. (Each agency publishes its own record.) The Coalition of Journalists for Open Governments periodically gathered and collated FOIA statistics until 2008, using a sample of twenty-nine agencies. Coalition of Journalists for Open Government, "Trend Charts 1998–2008," April 7, 2009, http://www.sunshineingovernment.org/index.php?cat=213, accessed February 1, 2013. Four agencies were often excluded from final analyses because a disproportionate amount of their FOIA requests involved personal privacy data. The Center for Effective Government (CEG), in its own analyses, also focused on

the twenty-five agencies. See Sean Moulton and Gavin Baker, "Freedom of Information Act Performance, 2012: Agencies Are Processing More Requests but Redacting More Often," Center for Effective Governance, Washington, DC, 2013, p. 24, http://www.for effectivegov.org/files/info/fy2012-foia-analysis.pdf. The government in 2009 made the compartmentalized statistics easier to analyze and aggregate with its FOIA.gov website. However, the data only go back to 2008. Data in Figure 3.1 from 2008 came from FOIA .gov and agency websites (FOIA.gov had many gaps).

26. It is also likely that potential FOIA applicants were cowed by the administration's prosecrecy stance, which might help explain the decline in submissions or the (unobserved here) nature and scope of requests. Similarly, FOIA officers might have adopted more guarded positions during the administration—partially due to agency memos but also due to the administration's more general prosecrecy approach.

27. Andrew H. Card, Jr., "Memorandum for Heads of Executive Departments and Agencies: Action to Safeguard Information Regarding Weapons of Mass Destruction and Other Sensitive Documents Related to Homeland Security," March 21, 2002, http:// www.justice.gov/archive/oip/foiapost/2002foiapost10.htm; GAO, "Transportation Security Administration: Clear Policies and Oversight Needed for Designation of Sensitive Security Information," GAO-05-677, June 2005.

28. Laura L. S. Kimberly, Richard L. Huff, and Daniel J. Metcalfe, "Memorandum for Departments and Agencies: Safeguarding Information Regarding Weapons of Mass Destruction and Other Sensitive Records Related to Homeland Security," March 21, 2002, http://www.justice.gov/archive/oip/foiapost/2002foiapost10.htm. On ambiguous rules in the context of institutional change, see Mahoney and Thelen, "Theory of Gradual Institutional Change." See also James Q. Wilson, *Bureaucracy: What Government Agencies Do and Why They Do It* (New York: Basic Books, 1991).

29. Bill Sammon, "White House Tells Web Sites to Delete Data; Anything Useful to Terrorists," *Washington Times*, March 21, 2002, p. A1; Congressional Research Service (CRS), "'Sensitive but Unclassified' and Other Federal Security Controls on Scientific and Technical Information: History and Current Controversy," CRS Report for Congress, #RL31845, July 2, 2003.

30. CRS, "'Sensitive but Unclassified'"; President Carter, Presidential Directive NSC-24, "Telecommunications Protection Policy," November 16, 1977, http://www.jimmy carterlibrary.gov/documents/pddirectives/pd24.pdf, accessed March 10, 2014.

31. CRS, "'Sensitive but Unclassified'"; Savage, *Takeover,* p. 102.

32. See chapter 2 on "layering." See also CRS, "'Sensitive but Unclassified' Information and Other Controls: Policy and Options for Scientific and Technical Information," CRS Report for Congress, #RL33303, December 29, 2006, pp. 11–12; National Institute of Standards and Technology, "Advising Users on Computer System Technology," *CSL Bulletin* (November 1992).

33. Robert Block, "U.S. Law Shields Company Data Tied to Security," *Wall Street Journal*, February 18, 2004, p. B1.

34. Homeland Security Act, § 212(3)(A)–(C), Public Law 107-296; DOJ, "Homeland Security Law Contains New Exemption 3 Statute," *FOIA Post,* January 27, 2003, http://www.justice.gov/oip/foiapost/2003foiapost4.htm; Gellman, *Angler,* p. 63; Joint Security Commission, "Redefining Security," chap. 2 ("Classification Management").

35. Rena Steinzor, "'Democracies Die behind Closed Doors': The Homeland Security Act and Corporate Accountability," *Kansas Journal of Law and Public Policy* 12 (2003): 641–670.

36. President Clinton, Executive Order 13010: "Critical Infrastructure Protection," July 15, 1996, available at http://www.fas.org/irp/offdocs/eo13010.htm; President Bush, Executive Order 13228: "Establishing the Office of Homeland Security and the Homeland Security Council," October 8, 2001, available at http://www.fas.org/irp/offdocs/eo/eo-13228.htm.

37. CIIA, § 212(5)(c). Before the bill passed, the government invited public comment on several sections, including the indirect submission route. The public sided fifteen to five against the procedure. Nevertheless, the government decided to retain it. See *Federal Register* 71, no. 170 (September 1, 2006): Rules and Regulations, pp. 52, 263.

38. The law (§ 214(b)) also offered new protections (from FACA) for communications between private sector representatives (e.g., lobbyists) and DHS officials. For example, as a 2004 House Committee of Government Reform investigation noted, "A corporate lobbyist may now meet secretly with DHS officials to urge changes to federal immigration or customs regulations if the lobbyist asserts that the changes are related to the effort to protect the nation's infrastructure." Committee on Government Reform, *Secrecy in the Bush Administration,* p. 9; Steinzor, "Democracies Die," pp. 643–644, 650; LaFleur, "Talking with the Former FOIA Czar"; OMB Watch, "DHS Fails to Protect Critical Infrastructure," September 12, 2006, http://www.ombwatch.org/node/3047. When the CIIA passed in 2002, private interests owned approximately 70 to 85 percent of the country's critical infrastructure. On rent seeking, see, e.g., Anne Krueger, "The Political Economy of the Rent-Seeking Society," *American Economic Review* 64, no. 3 (1974): 291–303; Joseph E. Stiglitz, *The Price of Inequality: How Today's Divided Society Endangers Our Future* (New York: W. W. Norton, 2012); Gordon Tullock, *The Economics of Special Privilege and Rent Seeking* (New York: Springer, 1989). Though criticisms of the CIIA tended to come from civil liberties and transparency groups, others stationed elsewhere on the ideological spectrum recognized the law's many potential dangers. For instance, Mark Tapscott of the conservative Heritage Foundation wrote, "One need not be a Harvard law graduate to see that, without clarification of what constitutes such vulnerabilities, this loophole could be manipulated by clever corporate and government operators to hide endless varieties of potentially embarrassing and/or criminal information from public view." See Tapscott, "Too Many Secrets," *Washington Post,* November 20, 2002, p. A25.

39. New protections for CII also ironically increased risks to public safety. For example, the Federal Energy Regulatory Commission's (FERC's) "critical energy infrastructure information" (CEII) protects information about the electric (including nuclear), gas, oil,

and hydropower industries and their facilities. Some CEII probably deserves protection. But protection does not come without risk. Take, for instance, a gas pipeline accident in 2000 that killed twelve citizens. Reporters using FERC information discovered that government inspectors had not checked the pipeline for corrosion since 1950. The 2000 accident was unfortunately not an isolated event. The Reporters Committee for the Freedom of the Press concluded over 200 people had been killed and over 1,000 injured due to preventable pipeline accidents between 1985 and 1994. FERC information also led researchers to identify potential dangers—accidents waiting to happen. However, if the FERC's new category of CEII had been in effect in 2000, journalists, researchers, and citizens would probably have never learned about the many pipeline problems. As a result, it is unlikely the Congress would have been pressured to pass the Pipeline Safety Improvement Act of 2002. The final CEII rules were implemented in 2003. Federal Energy Regulatory Commission, Critical Energy InfrastructureInformation, 68 Fed. Reg. 48386, August 10, 2003; Ellen Nakashima, "FERC Seeks to Limit Critical Energy Data," *Washington Post,* March 6, 2002, p. A17; Committee on Government Reform, *Secrecy in the Bush Administration,* pp. 14–15; CRS, "Critical Infrastructure Information Disclosure and Homeland Security," Report for Congress #RL31547, January 29, 2003, p. 15; Rena Steinzor (on behalf of the Natural Resources Defense Council), Testimony before the Committee on Governmental Affairs, U.S. Senate, Regarding Critical Infrastructure Information, May 8, 2002; Scott, *Seeing Like a State,* 1998; "Overkill in the Name of Security," *St. Petersburg (FL) Times,* July 14, 2002, p. 2D. Also see Steinzor, "Democracies Die"; Jennifer LaFleur, *The Lost Stories,* Reporters Committee for Freedom of the Press White Paper (Arlington, VA: RCFP, 2003), p. 3. Sen. Patrick Leahy, *Congressional Record,* November 19, 2002, pp. S11405–S11455, http://www.fas.org/sgp/congress/2002/s111902.html. See also Leahy's comments about the law's reference to "information" rather than "records," which has potentially significant legal consequences. The CIIA was written to allow for easy use of the FOIA's Exemption 3, which covers information exempted by statutes. Other exemptions also apply, such as Exemption 1 (national security) and Exemption 4 (trade secrets and commercial or financial information obtained from a person [that is] privileged or confidential). See CRS, "'Sensitive but Unclassified.'"

40. The exact number of b(3)'s remains contested. A Collaboration on Government Secrecy (COGS) analysis from American University, for instance, found only 156 statutes "truly qualify" as b(3)'s, which contrasts sharply with the more than 300 that federal agencies claimed to have recently used, as well as the 172 cited in the ProPublica study. See COGS, "Exemption 3 Statutes," n.d., http://www.wcl.american.edu/lawandgov/cgs/about.cfm#exemption3 and http://www.wcl.american.edu/lawandgov/cgs/existing_exemption_3_statutes.cfm, accessed July 20, 2013; Jennifer LaFleur, "FOIA Eyes Only: How Buried Statutes Are Keeping Information Secret," ProPublica.org, March 14, 2011, http://www.propublica.org/article/foia-exemptions-sunshine-law; Intelligence Authorization Act for Fiscal Year 2003, Public Law 107-30, § 312; Defense Authorization Act for Fiscal Year 2005, § 1034; U.S. Code, § 50 USC 403g (Intelligence Sources and Methods); U.S. Code, Title 7, Chap-

ter 80 (Watermelon Research and Promotion); Committee on Government Reform, *Secrecy in the Bush Administration*. Some new restrictions are debatable but not quite as controversial. For instance, Bush signed a law in 2005 placing new restrictions on information related to "products of commercial satellite operations," such as "land remote sensing." Though that might have been good counterterrorism policy, it also blocked researchers from using satellite data to monitor wars, natural disasters, deforestation, desertification, refugee flows, etc. National Defense Authorization Act for Fiscal Year 2005, http://www .fas.org/sgp/congress/2004/s2400-imagery.html. Another one prohibited agencies from disclosing information to foreign governments. A rare exception to the pattern of weakening was the OPEN Government Act of 2007, which mitigated problems related to monitoring and reporting, response delays, and application fees. It also created an "ombuds-type office," the Office of Government Information Services at the National Archives, "to mediate conflicts between agencies and requesters and review agency FOIA performance." See Thomas Blanton, Meredith Fuchs, and Kristin Adair, "President Signs FOIA Amendment; First FOIA Reform Bill in More Than a Decade Becomes Law," National Security Archive, January 2, 2008, http://www.gwu.edu/~nsarchiv/news/20071218/index.htm. Finally, after several years of attempts, Congress finally passed the OPEN FOIA Act of 2009, which promised to help citizens monitor new b(3) provisions. See, e.g., Angela Canterbury [Director of Public Policy, Project on Government Oversight], Testimony before the House Committee on Oversight and Government Reform on "The Freedom of Information Act: Crowd-Sourcing Government Oversight," March 17, 2011, http:// www.pogo.org/pogo-files/testimony/government-secrecy/gs-foia-20110317.html.

41. The TREAD Act is Public Law 106-414, passed on November 1, 2000. The advocacy group Public Citizen alleged there was a cover-up running "over a decade." See http://www.citizen.org/autosafety/suvsafety/ford_frstone.

42. NHTSA, "Confidential Business Information," A Rule by the National Highway Traffic Safety Administration, July 28, 2003, http://www.federalregister.gov/ articles/2003/07/28/03-19069/confidential-business-information; Gup, *Nation of Secrets*, p. 12; Committee on Government Reform, *Secrecy in the Bush Administration*, pp. 12–14.

43. Nate Jones, "The Next FOIA Fight: The B(5) 'Withhold It Because You Want To' Exemption," *Unredacted* [National Security Archive], http://nsarchive.wordpress.com/ 2014/03/27/the-next-foia-fight-the-b5-withold-it-because-you-want-to-exemption/; Mahoney and Thelen, "Theory of Gradual Institutional Change." See also National Security Archive, "The FOIA and President Ronald Reagan," http://www2.gwu.edu/~nsarchiv/ nsa/foia/reagan.html, accessed April 12, 2014 ("Reagan made no attempt at a major legislative overhaul of the FOIA"). The other presidents, as noted, also did not try to fundamentally change the FOIA.

44. "'Sunshine Week' Poll: Majority Say Washington Is 'Secretive,'" *Editor & Publisher*, March 12, 2006, http://www.editorandpublisher.com/Archive/-Sunshine-Week-Poll-Majority-Say-Washington-is-Secretive-; George Mauzy, "Scripps Survey Says Govern-

ment Too Secretive," *Outlook* [Ohio University, home of Scripps Survey Research Center], March 15, 2006, http://www.ohio.edu/outlook/05-06/March/353n-056.cfm.

45. There was one exception in the procession. See chapter 2. Weiner, "1917 Paper"; Sciolino, "Panel from C.I.A."; Nelson, "Perspective." See also Steven Aftergood, "Is the Secrecy System an Autonomous Entity?" *Secrecy News,* March 21, 2011, http://www.fas.org/blog/secrecy/2011/03/autonomous.html.

46. Clinton, "Executive Order 12958."

47. Ibid. See, especially, the order's sections on "systematic declassification review" and "mandatory declassification review." Clinton's order also created an automatic declassification protocol for documents over twenty-five years old, but this did not go into effect until 2006. See David Banisar, *Government Secrecy: Decisions without Democracy* (Washington, DC: People for the American Way, 2007), p. 15. More than 4 million Kennedy-related pages were declassified, and over 8 million war crimes–related documents (with multiple pages) were released. Clinton also noted, "Our democratic principles require that the American people be informed of the activities of their Government. Also, our Nation's progress depends on the free flow of information." In isolation, the text might suggest Clinton was motivated by his governing ideology. However, Reagan ("it is essential that the public be informed concerning the activities of its Government," in Executive Order 12356) and Bush, Jr. (Clinton words verbatim) used the same language. See Reagan, "Executive Order 12356"; President George W. Bush, "Executive Order 13292: Further Amendment to Executive Order 12958, as Amended, Classified National Security Information," March 25, 2003.

48. Of course, as psychologists would remind us, many people exaggerate the historical significance of present-day problems. Thus, the view from 1995 might have seemed equally bleak.

49. Scott Shane, "U.S. Reclassifies Many Documents in Secret Review," *New York Times,* February 21, 2006, p. A1; E-mail from J. William Leonard [former ISOO director and DOD deputy assistant secretary of defense for security and information operations], to the author, July 10, 2013. Leonard indicated DOD also objected to Clinton's executive order, but those concerns "were more budgetary-based rather than policy-based."

50. Shane, "U.S. Reclassifies"; Matthew W. Aid, "Declassification in Reverse: The U.S. Intelligence Community's Secret Historical Document Reclassification Program," National Security Archive, February 21, 2006, http://www.gwu.edu/~nsarchiv/NSAEBB/NSAEBB179, accessed June 16, 2011; Paul Farhi, "U.S., Media Settle with Wen Ho Lee," *Washington Post,* June 3, 2006, A01; *USA v. Wen Ho Lee* (grand jury indictment), 99-1417, December 10, 1999, http://www.fas.org/irp/ops/ci/docs/lee_indict.html; Gup, *Nation of Secrets,* pp. 98–99. Congressional action (the Kyl-Lott Amendment in the 1999 defense bill) was another reason for Secretary Bill Richardson's decision to shut down DOE's declassification program. See http://www.fas.org/sgp/congress/hr3616am.html.

51. Gup, *Nation of Secrets,* p. 99; Shane, "U.S. Reclassifies"; Aid, "Declassification in Reverse."

52. Gup, *Nation of Secrets,* p. 99; Shane, "U.S. Reclassifies"; Aid, "Declassification in Reverse."

53. Aid, "Declassification in Reverse," emphasis added.

54. National Security Archive, "Dubious Secrets Update; 14 Million New Secrets Last Year: Here's One of Them," NSA Electronic Briefing Book No. 90, May 3, 2004, http://www.gwu.edu/~nsarchiv/NSAEBB/NSAEBB90/index2.htm. As soon as Allende took power in 1970, President Nixon ordered his CIA head, Richard Helms, to "make the economy scream." The US ambassador to Chile, Edward Korry, was polite in public with Allende but much less so behind closed doors, with jaw-dropping disdain for Chilean citizens: "Once Allende comes to power we shall do all within our power to condemn Chile and all Chileans to utmost deprivation and poverty." On whether Pinochet was a dictator (rather than simply the leader of the military junta), we can turn to his own claim that "not a leaf moves in this country if I am not moving it. *I want that to be clear!*" (emphasis added). That is only one quote, but it reflects the power dynamics within the junta, where Pinochet was clearly in charge, with few constraints. See Mary Helen Spooner, *Soldiers in a Narrow Land: The Pinochet Regime in Chile* (Berkeley: University of California Press, 1994), p. 163; Robert Barros, *Constitutionalism and Dictatorship: Pinochet, the Junta, and the 1980 Constitution* (Cambridge: Cambridge University Press, 2002). See also Reporters Committee for Freedom of the Press, *Federal Open Government Guide,* 10th ed. (Arlington, VA: Reporters Committee for Freedom of the Press, 2009), p. 16; Scott Shane, "Since 2001, Sharp Increase in the Number of Documents Classified by the Government," *New York Times,* July 3, 2005, p. A14; Peter Kornbluth, "Chile and the United States: Classified Documents Relating to the Miltiary Coup, September 11, 1973," National Security Archive Electronic Briefing Book No. 8, http://www2.gwu.edu/~nsarchiv/NSAEBB/NSAEBB8/nsaebb8i.htm; Frank Church, "Covert Action: Swampland of American Foreign Policy," *Bulletin of the Atomic Scientists* 32 (February 1976): 7–11.

55. Doyle, "End of Secrecy," 34–51, at 35; Commission on Protecting and Reducing Government Secrecy, "Report."

56. Bush, "Executive Order 13292." About the coincidental timing: Agencies opposed to Clinton's order had pushed for new guidelines soon after Bush's inauguration in 2001. However, the White House—including Cheney's office—did *nothing* to facilitate the order's progress through the bureaucracy. Without any leadership, the OMB had to obtain "complete interagency consensus" before bringing the order to the president. As former ISOO director Leonard put it, "There was no leadership out of the WH or OVP one way or the other." The order "was purely an initiative of the bureaucracy. . . . As a result, in order to move an EO through the OMB coordination process without any WH weight behind it requires complete consensus. Nothing will move forward to the President's desk unless OMB can report complete interagency consensus. It took the bureaucracy a while to achieve that. The beginning of the Iraq War was purely coincidental. In fact, I was astonished when the President took time to consider the EO revision during the same week that Iraq hostilities began." E-mail from Leonard to the author.

57. Although the opening paragraphs in the two orders are similar, the few differences are notable. Bush excised Clinton's statement about how "dramatic changes have altered" the nation's threats, changed Clinton's interest in protecting "our participation within the community of nations" to the less multilateral "our interactions with foreign nations," and added the need to protect "our homeland security" and the need to secure information related to "transnational terrorism."

58. Jennifer Loven, "Lawyer Says Bush Didn't Specify Libby as One to Leak Intelligence Data," *Associated Press,* April 8, 2006; David E. Sanger and David Johnston, "Bush Ordered Declassification, Official Says," *New York Times,* April 10, 2006, p. A14; Banisar, *Government Secrecy,* p. 15; Jonathan Chait, "Power from the People," *New Republic,* July 26, 2004, p. 15. See also Louis Fisher, "Deciding on War against Iraq: Institutional Failures," *Political Science Quarterly* 118, no. 3 (2003): 389–410. Manipulation of intelligence reports also occurred at the agency level, as Fisher documented in 2003. Fisher (p. 408) noted the puzzling discepancy between the first sentence of a pivotally important CIA report on Iraqi WMD ("Baghdad has chemical and biological weapons . . . ") and the rest of the document. Fisher demonstrated that "the detailed analytical section that follows contradicts the flat assertion, providing statements that are much more cautious and qualified," such as "Iraq has the ability to produce chemical warfare (CW) agents within its chemical industry." As Fisher noted, first sentences of CIA reports attract quite a bit more attention than the wonky, cautious details later on.

59. Reagan, Executive Order 12356, Section 1.6(c); Clinton, Executive Order 12958; Ross Gelbspan, *Break-Ins, Death Threats and the FBI: The Covert War against the Central America Movement* (Boston: South End Press, 1991), p. 17; Shane, "U.S. Reclassifies"; RCFP, *Federal Open Government Guide;* National Security Archive, "Dubious Secrets Update"; Al Kamen, "Millions of Secrets," *Washington Post,* May 3, 2004, p. A19. It is possible the DIA reclassified the Pinochet biography due to his unexpected arrest in London in 1998 and return to Chile in 2000. He faced corruption charges relating to plundered assets he laundered and kept abroad during his time as president.

60. In addition to shutting down the declassification programs, Bush reversed Clinton's order to have the archivist create a "declassification database" accessible to citizens. See Clinton, Executive Order 12958, § 3.8. Bush's mosaic theory reads as follows: "Compilations of items of information that are individually unclassified may be classified if the compiled information reveals an additional association or relationship that: (1) meets the standards for classification under this order; and (2) is not otherwise revealed in the individual items of information. As used in this order, 'compilation' means an aggregation of pre-existing unclassified items of information." See Kevin R. Kosar, Congressional Research Service Analyst, "Security Classification Policy and Procedure: E.O. 12958, as Amended," CRS Document #97-771, p. 10, http://www.fas.org/sgp/crs/secrecy/97-771 .pdf; Committee on Government Reform, *Secrecy in the Bush Administration,* p. 45; Bush, "Executive Order 13292"; Arvin S. Quist, "Classification of Compilations of Informa-

tion," Oak Ridge K-25 Site, Oak Ridge National Laboratory, Department of Energy, 1991, http://www.fas.org/sgp/library/compilations.pdf.

61. ISOO, *Report to the President* (1985); ISOO, *Report to the President* (1989), p. 4. Original classification activity is every "initial determination by an OCA [original classification authority] that information owned by, produced by or for, or under the control of the United States Government requires protection because unauthorized disclosure of that information reasonably could be expected to cause damage to national security." ISOO, *Report to the President* (2010), p. 6. See also Steven Aftergood, "Vice President Refuses to Report Classification Activity," *Secrecy News,* May 26, 2006, http://www.fas.org/blog/secrecy/2006/05/vice_president_refuses_to_repo.html; Peter Baker, "White House Defends Cheney's Refusal of Oversight," *Washington Post,* June 23, 2007, p. A2.

62. ISOO, *Report to the President* (2009), pp. 1, 3, 8. I thank Peggy Ushman, a senior program analyst at the ISOO, for her detailed explanation of SCGs in a series of e-mails.

63. ISOO, *Report to the President* (2010), pp. 8–9.

64. Ibid.; ISOO, *Report to the President* (2009), p. 7. The ISOO implemented new procedures in 2009 that standardized these procedures across the government. In particular, it instructed agencies not to count, e.g., forwarded e-mails but instead to count "only those messages containing new original or derivative classification decisions."

65. Mike German [ACLU], "ISOO Report for Fiscal Year 2009 and Derivative Classification," April 15, 2010, http://www.aclu.org/files/assets/Inerested_Persons_Memo_re_ISOO_Report_for_FY_2009_and_Derivative_Classification.pdf; Commission on Protecting and Reducing Government Secrecy, "Report"; Priest and Arkin, "Hidden World." On the problem of how privatization (and "contracting out") of government services affects the implementation of transparency policies, see Alasdair S. Roberts, "Structural Pluralism and the Right to Information," *University of Toronto Law Journal* 51, no. 2 (2001): 243–271.

66. ISOO, *Report to the President* (2008), pp. 23–24; ISOO, *Report to the President* (2009), p. 18; German, "ISOO Report." The ISOO in 2008 also found that two-thirds of official government classification guides used by agencies "had not been updated within the past five years" (three-fourths for the largest agencies).

67. ISOO, *Report to the President* (2010), p. 6; German, "ISOO Report."

68. Gellman, *Angler,* pp. 393, 470. In Bush's order (#13292), see, e.g., § 1.3(e), 1.6(c), 1.7(c)(3).

Chapter 4: Violating FACA from the Start

1. Alison Mitchell, "The 2000 Campaign: The Texas Governor; Bush Criticizes Gore for Wanting to Use Petroleum Supply," *New York Times,* September 22, 2000, p. A18; Ben Macintyre, "Why George Bush Is Praying for the Snow," *Times* (London), September 23, 2000; Gerhard Metschies, "Prime Numbers: Pain at the Pump," *Foreign Policy,* June 11,

2007, http://www.foreignpolicy.com/articles/2007/06/11/prime_numbers_pain_at_the
_pump. The Gore-Lieberman campaign's take on the so-called energy crisis de-emphasized
Bush's call for more drilling and deregulation and resurrected the Democratic Party's periodic anti–"Big Oil" populism, found usually during election years. Gore spoke surprisingly infrequently about climate change.

2. Federal Advisory Committee Act, Sec. 5(b)(2), available at http://epic.org/open_gov/
faca.html.

3. FACA charter requirements are in Sec. 9 (c)(2)(A–J). The definition of an advisory
committee is in Sec. 3(2). Details about transcripts, etc., are in Sec. 10.

4. Emphasis added. Transcript of Cheney's interview on ABC's *This Week*, January 27,
2002, http://georgewbush-whitehouse.archives.gov/vicepresident/news-speeches/speeches
/vp20020127.html. See also Gellman, *Angler.*

5. Gellman, *Angler,* pp. 91–93.

6. The "act now, deal with the consequences later" stance was an enduring feature
of the Bush-Cheney years. The infamous, anonymous quote mocking the "reality-based
community" by a "senior aide" reflected the position quite well: "We're an empire now,
and when we act, we create our own reality. And while you're studying that reality—
judiciously, as you will—we'll act again, creating other new realities, which you can study
too, and that's how things will sort out. We're history's actors . . . and you, all of you, will
be left to just study what we do." Ron Suskind, "Faith, Certainty and the Presidency of
George W. Bush," *New York Times Magazine,* October 17, 2004, http://www.nytimes
.com/2004/10/17/magazine/17BUSH.html.

7. Office of Rep. Henry A. Waxman, "White House Asked for Information on Energy
Task Force Operations," April 19, 2001, https://waxman.house.gov/white-house-asked
-information-energy-task-force-operations; Rep. Waxman and Rep. Dingell, Letter to the
Honorable David Walker, Comptroller General, GAO, April 19, 2001, https://waxman
.house.gov/sites/waxman.house.gov/files/Letter_from_Reps._Waxman_and_Dingell_to_
GAO.pdf; Gellman, *Angler,* p. 93, emphasis added.

8. David S. Addington, Letter to Reps. Tauzin and Burton, May 4, 2001, http://waxman
.house.gov/sites/waxman.house.gov/files/Letter_from_Counsel_to_Vice_President_
Cheney_to_Reps._Tauzin_and_Burton.pdf; Addington, Letter to Anthony Gamboa,
General Counsel, GAO, May 16, 2001, https://waxman.house.gov/sites/waxman.house
.gov/files/Letter_from_Counsel_to_Vice_President_Cheney_to_GAO.pdf. For a more
detailed and comprehensive analysis of the energy task force case, see Mitchel A. Sollenberger and Mark J. Rozell, "The Unitary Executive and Secrecy in the Bush Presidency:
The Case of the Energy Task Force Controversy," in *The Unitary Executive and the Modern
Presidency,* ed. Ryan Barilleaux and Christopher Kelly (College Station: Texas A&M University Press, 2010), pp. 145–162; Rozell, *Executive Privilege,* pp. 155–167; Pallitto and
Weaver, *Presidential Secrecy,* pp. 208–211.

9. *Walker v. Cheney,* 230 F. Supp. 2d 51 (DC District Court, 2002), note 11 ("Plaintiff
asserts in his brief that he also requires the information in order to determine whether

the Federal Advisory Committee Act ["FACA"], 5 U.S.C. app 2 [2002], applied to the NEPDG. But no claim under FACA [or the Administrative Procedure Act] has been asserted in the Complaint, and issues relating to FACA are, if anything, tangential to this lawsuit."). The vice president's office argued the GAO did not have the authority to investigate NEPDG because the GAO allegedly only had the authority to audit the executive's financial transactions. Besides, Cheney asserted, GAO was only authorized to review "results" of task force programs, not their proceedings, and the vice president is not listed under "agency" in the GAO's founding statute. Also, the GAO investigation allegedly interfered with executive branch activity. See GAO, "Fact Sheet on GAO's Access Case," January 31, 2002, http://www.gao.gov/accessfs.pdf; David M. Walker, Letter to Rep. Waxman, January 30, 2001, http://oversight-archive.waxman.house.gov/documents/20040830 153946-87031.pdf. Interestingly, Walker noted the he and the GAO had prepared to sue Cheney in August 2001, but the September 11 terrorist attacks caused him to wait.

10. William L. Watts, "Iraq Oil Map among U.S. Energy Task-Force Files," *CBS MarketWatch,* July 18, 2003, http://www.marketwatch.com/story/iraq-oil-map-among-us -energy-task-force-files; Simon English, "Cheney Had Iraq in Sights Two Years Ago; Newly Released Papers Could Indicate War Motive," *Telegraph* (London), July 22, 2003, p. 25; *Judicial Watch v. NEPDG,* F. Supp. 2d 16 (DC District Court, 2002), 233.

11. *Cheney v. U.S. District Court for D.C.,* 542 U.S. 367 (Supreme Court, 2004); Linda Greenhouse, "Justices' Ruling Postpones Resolution of Cheney Case," *New York Times,* June 25, 2004, p. A19; Dana Milbank and Justin Blum, "Document Says Oil Chiefs Met with Cheney Task Force," *Washington Post,* November 16, 2005, p. A1; Pallitto and Weaver, *Presidential Secrecy,* pp. 208–211; Rozell, *Executive Privilege,* pp. 155–167.

12. *In Re: Cheney,* 406 F.3d 723 (DC Appeals Court, 2005); *In Re: Cheney,* 334 F.3d 1096 (DC Appeals Court, 2003); David Stout, "Appeals Court Backs Cheney in Secrecy Case," *New York Times,* May 11, 2005, p. A1. For the "guest" list, see "Energy Task Force Meetings Participants," *Washington Post,* 2006, http://www.washingtonpost.com/wp-srv/ politics/documents/cheney_energy_task_force.html, accessed June 1, 2011. The identity of the first invitee for the first energy task force meeting on February 1, the Electric Vehicle Association of the Americas, was hardly representative of the group of invitees as a whole.

13. On political actors exploiting ambiguity on the path to institutional change, see Mahoney and Thelen, "Theory of Gradual Institutional Change."

14. Executive Order 13212, http://ceq.hss.doe.gov/nepa/regs/eos/eo13212.html; Committee on Government Reform, *Secrecy in the Bush Administration,* pp. 40–41; Minerals Management Service (MMS), "White House Task Force on Energy Project Streamlining Holds Open Houses," press release, 2002, http://www.boemre.gov/ooc/press/2001/ press1113.htm; Dustin Bleizeffer, "Groups: Public Cut from White House Task Force on Streamlining," *CasparStar-Tribune,* July 25, 2003, http://trib.com/news/state-and-regional/ groups-public-cut-from-white-house-task-force-on-streamlining/article_6ee14f2a-de5b-5e30-8495-ca97f6c3d02a.html#ixzz1mHNfQFRa, accessed February 13, 2012.

15. Committee on Government Reform, *Secrecy in the Bush Administration*; Gargi

Chakrabarty, "Drilling Council Called Off; Energy Task Force to Use Other Ways of Streamlining," *Rocky Mountain News,* March 2004; National Resources Defense Council, "Conservation Groups Accuse White House of Renewing Secret Energy Meetings," press release, July 24, 2003, http://www.nrdc.org/media/pressreleases/030724.asp, accessed February 13, 2012.

16. President Bush, Executive Order 13210: Presidents Commission to Strengthen Social Security, http://www.gpo.gov/fdsys/pkg/FR-2001-05-04/pdf/01-11505.pdf; Committee on Government Reform, *Secrecy in the Bush Administration,* pp. 39–40; Leigh Strope, "Bush's Social Security Commission to Meet in Private Subgroups Closed to the Public," *Associated Press,* August 18, 2001; Commission on Protecting and Reducing Government Secrecy, "Report"; Moynihan, *Secrecy;* Gellman, *Angler,* p. 93.

17. Eric Pianin, "Shuttle Panel Neutrality a Concern; Payroll, Secrecy, Lead to Questions about Ties to NASA," *Washington Post,* May 12, 2003, p. A8; Kathy Sawyer, "NASA Hoping Stars Align for New Quest; Consensus Slow to Emerge on Return to Space," *Washington Post,* December 17, 2003, p. A41.

18. Gary Stoller, "Official Says Air Task Force May Violate Law," *USA Today,* September 20, 2001, p. 1B. There were other conflicts not emphasized here, many of which involved environmental and pharmaceutical policy, and some were more about the "balance" of the task forces, rather than their secrecy. See, e.g., James V. Grimaldi, "EPA Official to Examine Proposed Rule on Laundries," *Washington Post,* January 14, 2005, p. A7; Michelle Bryner, "NRDC Challenges EPA's Ethylene Oxide Panel Nominees," *Chemical Week,* June 28, 2006, p. 40; "FDA Avoids Violation by Cancelling Meeting, Says Public Citizen," *Pharma Marketletter,* June 18, 2006; Neil Franz, "Animal Rights Groups File Suit over HPV Testing Program," *Chemical Week,* September 18, 2002, p. 14; "US Pharmacists and Chain Drugstores Sue Govt over Medicare Rx Plan," *Pharma Marketletter,* July 20, 2001.

19. On FACA's exclusions, see Sec. 4(b). See also the Homeland Security Act, Sec. 214(b), 232(b)(2), and 311(i).

20. Sidney A. Shapiro, Testimony before the Subcommittee on Information Policy, Census, and National Archives of the Committee on Oversight and Government Reform, U.S. House of Representatives, Hearing on the Federal Advisory Committee Act, April 2, 2008. On the FDA panel, see *Food Chemical News v. Young,* 900 F.2d 328 (DC Appeals Court, 1990), 329–330, cited in Shapiro, Testimony. On the OMB memo, see *Federal Register* 68, 54023, September 15, 2003, cited in Committee on Government Reform, *Secrecy in the Bush Administration,* p. 42. The House of Representatives in 2010 passed the Federal Advisory Committee Act Amendments of 2010 (H.R. 1310), which targeted these loopholes. However, the measure stalled in the Senate, never making it out of the 111th Congress. As of February 15, 2012, a similar bill (H.R. 3124) was languishing in a House committee.

21. Shapiro, Testimony.

22. Dick Cheney, *In My Time: A Personal and Political Memoir* (New York: Threshold Editions, 2011), pp. 317–318.

23. The commission was created with President Bush, Executive Order 13328: Commission on the Intelligence Capabilities of the United States Regarding Weapons of Mass Destruction, February 6, 2004. See also Executive Office of the President, Office of Administration, June 30, 2004, "Notice of Meeting of the Commission on the Intelligence Capabilities of the United States Regarding Weapons of Mass Destruction," *Federal Register*, 69, 39481, cited in Committee on Government Reform, *Secrecy in the Bush Administration*, p. 39. For two of the DHS conflicts, see Alice Lipowicz, "Group Seeks Disclosure Waiver for IT Protection Meetings," *Newsbytes*, October 13, 2005, and Al Kamen, "Fitness Report," *Washington Post*, December 2, 2005, p. A21.

24. FACA Annual Reports, http://fido.gov/facadatabase/PrintedAnnualReports.asp, accessed July 21, 2013; OpenTheGovernment.org, annual Secrecy Report Cards, http://www.openthegovernment.org/press_room/reports, accessed July 21, 2013. Only a few agencies' task forces—the CIA, the Federal Reserve System, and specific sections of the Department of Homeland Security (its Office of Science and Technology and any advisory groups dealing with "critical infrastructure information")—are automatically immune from FACA. The Bush-Cheney administration argued also that the law exempted task forces created within the Executive Office of the President (EOP).

25. Don Van Natta, Jr., "Enron's Many Strands: Energy Policy; White House Could Be Sued on List Access," *New York Times*, January 26, 2002, p. C1; Sara Fritz, "For Cheney, Preserving Secrecy Not a Matter of Legal Principle," *St. Petersburg (FL) Times*, January 28, 2002, p. 3A.

26. Paul Bedard, "First Lady's Task Force Broke Law on Secrecy," *Washington Times*, January 29, 1993, p. A1.

27. Ibid.

28. Ibid.; Karen Riley, "Health-Care Panel's Procedures Checked; Official to Look into 'Sunshine' Laws," *Washington Times*, January 30, 1993, p. A1.

29. Bedard, "First Lady's Task Force"; Riley, "Health-Care Panel's Procedures"; Bedard, "GOP Knocks for Hillary; Demands Open Door at Health Meetings," *Washington Times*, February 5, 1993, p. A1; Dana Priest, "GOP Congressman Questions Hillary Clinton's Closed-Door Meetings," *Washington Post*, February 10, 1993, p. A5; Bedard, "Suit Planned to Open Hillary's Meetings," *Washington Times*, February 9, 1993, p. A1; Paul Bedard and Karen Riley, "Clinton Defends Secret Meetings," *Washington Times*, March 5, 1993, p. A6; Robert Pear, "Hillary Clinton's Health Role Disputed," *New York Times*, March 6, 1993, p. A7.

30. Pear, "Hillary Clinton's Health Role."

31. Ibid.; Judi Hasson and Judy Keen, "Health Reformers Eye Red Tape, 'Sin Taxes,'" *USA Today*, March 9, 1993, p. 4A.

32. The case was filed in early February by the Association of American Physicians and Surgeons, the American Council for Health Care Reform, and the National Legal and Policy Center. See Robert Pear, "Judge Puts Limits on Secret Sessions for Health," *New York Times*, March 11, 1993, p. A1; Dana Priest, "First Lady Is a Government 'Outsider,'

Judge Rules; White House Is Told Some Meetings of Hillary Clinton's Health Panel Must Be Held in Public," *Washington Post,* March 11, 1993, p. A18; Paul Bedard, "Hillary Says She Won't List Staff Names," *Washington Times,* March 12, 1993, p. A1; Priest, "Health Task Force Ruling Appealed," *Washington Post,* March 23, 1993, p. A8.

33. Robert Pear, "Ending Its Secrecy, White House Lists Health-Care Panel," *New York Times,* March 27, 1993, p. A1.

34. *Association of American Physicians and Surgeons v. Hillary Rodham Clinton,* 997 F.2d 898 (DC Appeals Court, 1993); Bedard, "Hillary Says She Won't"; Robert Pear, "Court Rules That First Lady Is 'De Facto' Federal Official," *New York Times,* June 23, 1993, p. A1; Pear, "Judge Says Health Panel Erred by Withholding Data," *New York Times,* November 10, 1993, p. B18; "Where, Please, Are the Health Task Force Records?," *Washington Times,* October 29, 1993, p. A22; Bedard, "Judge Demands Health Panel's Papers from White House," *Washington Times,* November 19, 1993, p. A1. Several of the task force members also did not submit required conflict-of-interest and financial disclosure forms. See Bedard, "Health Panel's Ethics Questioned; Disclosure Forms Not Completed," *Washington Times,* October 1, 1993, p. A1.

35. David S. Broder, "Physicians Allege Conflicts on Health Care Task Force," *Washington Post,* March 24, 1994, p. A26; Robert Pear, "The Health Care Debate: Litigation; Justice Dept. Defends Setup of Care Panel," *New York Times,* July 26, 1994, p. A16; Paul Bedard, "Tales of Shredding Prompt Probe of Hillary's Task Force," *Washington Times,* September 1, 1994, p. A4; Neil A. Lewis, "Court Clears Clinton Aide in Lying Case," *New York Times,* August 25, 1999, p. A16.

36. Robert Pear, "Misconduct Found on Clinton Health Plan," *New York Times,* December 2, 1994, p. A22; Toni Locy, "Justice Department to Release Health Panel Documents," *Washington Post,* December 2, 1994, p. A6.

37. Lewis, "Court Clears Clinton Aide"; Toni Locy, "Government Ordered to Pay Sanctions for Dishonesty about Health Care Task Force," *Washington Post,* December 19, 1997, p. A21; Al Kamen, "Sunday in the Loop," *Washington Post Magazine,* September 19, 1999, p. W04.

38. For all of his political gifts, President Clinton was perhaps least skilled in the arts of interpretive games. Probably the best example of his weakness was his infamous discursion on what "'is' is." In his grand jury testimony, he tried to reconcile his earlier comments that "there's nothing going on between us" (himself and Monica Lewinsky) with clear evidence the two did have a sexual relationship. When pressed in court, he said: "It depends upon what the meaning of the word 'is' is. If the—if he—if 'is' means is and never has been, that is not—that is one thing. If it means there is none, that was a completely true statement."

39. "Panel Seeks to Meet in Secret; Security Policy Group Studies Law's Loopholes," *Washington Times,* September 19, 1995, p. A4. The first meeting of the SPB was on September 7, 1994. By August 1996, four more meetings had occurred. During the same period, the SPF met twelve times. "Minutes[,] First Meeting of the Security Policy Ad-

visory Board," August 19, 1996, Institute for Defense Analysis, http://www.fas.org/sgp/advisory/spab2.html.

40. DOJ, Memorandum to Peter Saderholm, n.d., cited in "Panel Seeks to Meet."

41. *Northwest Forest Resource Council v. Espy*, 846 F. Supp. 1009 (DC District Court, 1994); Scott Sonner, "Judge Refuses to Block Clinton Forest Plan," *Seattle Times*, March 4, 1994; Tom Kenworthy, "Judge Refuses to Block Federal Forestry Plan," *Washington Post*, March 22, 1994, p. A3.

42. Kenworthy, "Judge Refuses to Block"; Scott Sonner, "Judge Throws Clinton Forest Plan into Doubt," *Spokesman-Review* (Spokane, WA), March 5, 1994, p. B5; Associated Press, "Forest Plan Team Acted Illegally, Judge Says," *Register-Guard* (Eugene, OR), March 22, 1994, p. 4C. Even though FEMAT was apparently stacked with environmentalists, the Native Forest Council wanted a forestry policy that would decrease logging well beyond what FEMAT was suggesting.

43. Sonner, "Judge Throws Clinton"; Associated Press, "Forest Plan Team"; Scott Sonner, "Timber Interests May Take Judge's Comments as Cue to Sue," *Associated Press*, March 29, 1994. FEMAT's plan continued without interruption toward Dwyer's desk. After delaying implementation for a few months, the plan "quietly went into effect," except for timber sales, which were introduced later. Dwyer ultimately overturned his 1991 injunction and said the administration had adequately addressed his earlier concerns. See Rob Taylor, "Judge Will Wait to Lift Timber Ban; Environmental and Industry Challenges Will Be Considered First," *Seattle Post-Intelligencer*, May 21, 1994, p. B1; Mercury News Wire Services, "Timber Industry to Sue Clinton Plan," *San Jose Mercury News*, April 13, 1994, p. 3F; Sonner, "Suit Filed to Block Clinton Plan," *Associated Press*, May 2, 1994.

44. For example, both courts noted that "a court's review of an agency decision under this standard is 'narrow and deferential.'" Both cited judicial deference repeatedly. *Wyoming Sawmills, Inc. v. US Forest Service et al.*, 179 F. Supp. 2d 1279 (Wyoming District Court, 2001); *Wyoming Sawmills, Inc. v. US Forest Service et al.*, 383 F.3d 1241 (Tenth Circuit Appeals Court, 2004); 2 U.S.C. § 1534: "State, Local, and Tribal Government Input," http://www.law.cornell.edu/uscode/text/2/1534. See also Associated Press, "Enzi: Forest Service Violated Federal Law in Developing Roadless Ban," *Associated Press*, July 15, 2000; Audrey Hudson, "GOP Awaits Ruling on Whether Environmental Plan Violated Law," *Washington Times*, July 17, 2000, p. A4; Associated Press, "Wyoming Sues to Block Roadless Initiative," *Associated Press*, May 18, 2001.

45. Associated Press, "Enzi" ("We're really confident about the legal underpinnings of our proposal. . . . [W]e didn't have any illegal communications with environmentalists or anyone else"). Another example where the administration firmly denied a potential FACA violation involved a series of education reform meetings at the Department of Education. See, e.g., Lamar Alexander, "Where Bold Education Reform Is Found," *Christian Science Monitor*, October 17, 1997, p. 19; David Frank [Department of Education communications director], Letter to editor, *Christian Science Monitor*, October 28, 1997, p. 20. On the SEC's meetings with Wall Street executives, see Ianthe Jeanne Dugan, "SEC Prepares

for Cyber-age Trading; Levitt Draws Fire for Meetings in Private with Wall St. Leaders," *Washington Post,* February 18, 2000, p. E1. On the Dietary Guidelines Advisory Committee, in which the administration concealed information about a task force member's conflict of interest and about individuals considered but not selected for the committee, see Sally Squires, "USDA Loses a Battle in War on Diet Guides; Judge: Agency Violated Information Act," *Washington Post,* October 4, 2000, p. A31. On the Department of Energy task forces—the National Ignition Facility and the Rebaseline Validation Review—see Curt Suplee, "DOE Faces Suit on Nuclear Project; Review Panel Broke Law, Group Alleged," *Washington Post,* September 26, 2000, p. A25. On the technology advisory committee, see John F. Harris, "White House Advisory Panel Meeting in Secrecy," *Washington Post,* January 17, 1998, p. A8 ("A senior official at the health care agency [Health Care Financing Administration], in a letter to the GAO, acknowledged the panel was in an apparent violation of open-meeting laws and pledged that it would be revamped to include only government employees, who are allowed to meet privately."). Finally, the court of appeals in Atlanta ruled that the administration violated FACA when it held closed-door meetings with scientists to discuss listing sturgeon as an endangered species. See Associated Press, "Court Upholds Ban on Sturgeon Report," *Tuscaloosa (AL) News,* July 28, 1994, p.6B; "The Secrecy of the Clinton Crowd," *Arkansas Democrat-Gazette,* March 31, 1994, p. 8B.

46. Some of the additional charges of FACA violations did not hold up. See, for example, the conflict about access to records and meetings of the Clintons' legal fund. Toni Locy, "Group Sues for Access to Clinton Legal Fund," *Washington Post,* August 5, 1994, p. A18; Locy, "Judge Dismisses Challenge to Clinton Defense Fund," *Washington Post,* February 22, 1995, p. A12; Michael Hedges, "Judge Rejects Clinton Fund Probe," *Washington Times,* April 18, 1995, p. A3.

47. Philip J. Hilts, "Conflict-of-Interest Issue Arises in Debate on Alar; EPA Advisers Became Consultants to Maker," *Washington Post,* May 26, 1989, p. A21.

48. Although President Reagan might have been the first to welcome the social conservatives into the party with an enthusiastic, warm embrace, it was President Nixon and Sen. Barry Goldwater who really got the ball rolling. See Paul Pierson and Theda Skocpol, eds., *The Transformation of American Politics: Activist Government and the Rise of Conservatism* (Princeton, NJ: Princeton University Press, 2007). See also Rick Perlstein, *Nixonland: The Rise of a President and the Fracturing of America* (New York: Scribner, 2008), and Perlstein, *Before the Storm: Barry Goldwater and the Unmaking of the American Consensus* (New York: Hill and Wang, 2001).

49. On the Comstock era (and related issues), see Daniel Carpenter, *The Forging of Bureaucratic Autonomy: Reputations, Networks, and Policy Innovation in Executive Agencies, 1862–1928* (Princeton, NJ: Princeton University Press, 2001). On the puritanical and "social gospel" traditions in American history, see James Morone, *Hellfire Nation: The Politics of Sin in American History* (New Haven, CT: Yale University Press, 2004).

50. *Washington Post v. National Council on the Arts, NEA,* Civil Action No. 92-0955

(DC District Court, 1991); Kim M. Shipley, "The Politicization of Art: The National Endowment for the Arts; The First Amendment, and Senator Helms," *Emory Law Journal* 40 (1991): 241–301; Kim Masters, "Arts Panel Urges End to Grant 'Pledge': Breaks with NEA on Anti-obscenity Restriction," *Washington Post,* August 4, 1990, p. G1; Eric Brace, "Suit Seeks Open NEA Meetings," *New York Times,* April 22, 1992, p. B7; Associated Press, "Judge Says Arts Agency May Keep Meetings Closed," *New York Times,* April 30, 1992, p. C15. As an "independent agency" of the executive branch, the NEA enjoys more autonomy than other units. For instance, board members (i.e., the National Council on the Arts) are "appointed by the President and approved by the Senate for six-year, staggered terms," leaving some without direct links to incumbents. When Congress creates independent agencies by statute, it usually makes it difficult for presidents to fire the agency heads. The NEA also does not answer to any of the cabinet secretaries. See "National Council on the Arts: History and Purpose," [nd], National Endowment for the Arts, http://www.nea.gov/about/NCA/About_NCA.html, accessed July 9, 2013.

51. The formaldehyde meetings occurred on June 19, July 28, and August 14, and the DEHP meetings occurred on August 20, September 1, and September 29. "Those EPA-CMA Meetings," *Chemical Week,* November 4, 1981, p. 13; Philip Shabecoff, "Environment Aide's Industry Talks Criticized," *New York Times,* October 22, 1981, p. A22. It is not clear why the industry thought a comment about smoking rats' blood served its public relations interests.

52. Shabecoff, "Environment Aide's Industry Talks"; "Those EPA-CMA Meetings."

53. Shabecoff, "Environment Aide's Industry Talks"; "Those EPA-CMA Meetings."

54. Cass Peterson, "EPA Pesticide Standard-Setting Challenged in Suit," *Washington Post,* May 27, 1983, p. A19; Felicity Barringer, "Industry's Influence Chronicled; Liberal Group Lists Access to Regulators," *Washington Post,* October 12, 1983, p. A21; Philip Shabecoff, "E.P.A. Will Re-investigate 13 Disputed Pesticides," *New York Times,* September 21, 1984, p. A17; Peterson, "EPA Agrees to Reexamine Pesticide Actions; Secret Sessions with Industry Cited," *Washington Post,* September 21, 1984, p. A19.

55. Cass Peterson, "Watt Gets Public-Lands Advice in Private," *Washington Post,* February 11, 1982, p. A21.

56. Cass Peterson, "Overseers of the Uncle's Acreage," *Washington Post,* January 11, 1982, p. A11; "Business Interests Ride Federal Range," *Washington Post,* February 11, 1982, p. A21; John Stanley, "Ben Avery Trail, Southwestern Arizona," *Arizona Republic,* June 12, 2006, http://www.azcentral.com/travel/hiking/articles/2006/06/12/20060612benavery02.html.

57. Peterson, "Watt Get Public-Lands Advice."

58. Herbert H. Denton and Charles R. Babcock, "Reagan Denies Gift Givers Seek 'Benefit,'" *Washington Post,* May 16, 1982, p. A1.

59. "Public Lands," *Washington Post,* May 4, 1982, p. A21; 1982 to 2012 dollar conversion performed with an inflation calculation at http://www.dollartimes.com/calculators/inflation.htm, accessed May 15, 2012.

60. Special to the *Christian Science Monitor*, "Watt Using Sportsmen as Advisers?" *Christian Science Monitor*, June 15, 1982, p. 5.

61. Cass Peterson, "Still Keeping His Powder Dry," *Washington Post*, November 8, 1982, p. A17. Watt's reputation as a conservative "ideologue"—or perhaps a "free-market environmentalist" ideologue—was broadly accepted during the 1980s and beyond. Indeed, he did little to challenge the characterization. Moreover, it is not intended here as an insult. See also Joseph C. Harsch, "The Decline of the Ideologues" [op-ed], *Christian Science Monitor*, March 19, 1986, p. 15; Gil Troy, *The Reagan Revolution: A Very Short Introduction* (Oxford: Oxford University Press, 2009), p. 83.

62. Peterson, "Still Keeping His Powder Dry"; Cass Peterson, "Feud Continues over a Group Linked to Watt," *Washington Post*, January 17, 1983, p. A11; Peterson, "Panel Throws a Damper on Watt Wetlands Plan," *Washington Post*, January 26, 1983, p. A19; Peterson, "Sinkholes in Wetlands Bill," *Washington Post*, March 15, 1983, p. A21. Watt's resignation from his post as interior secretary came later in 1983, yet it had nothing to do with his law breaking, although that certainly was one source of controversy. His ouster had more to do with his confrontational style and his inability to rein it in. Speaking before US Chamber of Commerce lobbyists—a warm, welcoming crowd for Watt and Reagan Republicans—he "joked" about the composition of an independent commission created by Congress to investigate suspicious federal coal leases sold by the DOI to private interests. When asked to describe the commissioners, he said, "We have every kind of mix you can have . . . a black . . . a woman, two Jews and a cripple. And we have talent." See Melinda Beck, "James Watt's Last Gaffe?," *Newsweek*, October 3, 1983, p. 45; "Comments Are Mixed on Watt's Resignation," *New York Times*, October 10, 1983, p. D10. Watt's hatred of environmentalists continued well after he left office. In 1991, he half joked to a "cattlemen's association" in Wyoming: "If the troubles from environmentalists cannot be solved in the jury box or at the ballot box, perhaps the cartridge box should be used." See David Helvarg, *The War against the Greens* (Boulder, CO: Big Earth, 2004), p. 237.

63. The conservative Washington Legal Foundation joined Public Citizen on the ABA case. *Public Citizen v. DOJ et al.*, 491 U.S. 440 (Supreme Court, 1989); *Public Citizen v. Commission on the Bicentennial of the US Constitution*, 622 F. Supp. 753 (DC District Court, 1985), 759; David Burnham, "Panel Headed by Chief Justice Is Sued over Closed Meetings," *New York Times*, October 11, 1985, p. B7; Cheryl Frank, "Panel's Nadir? Closed Meetings Spark Suit," *ABA Journal* 72 (January 1986): 20; Linda Greenhouse, "Court Vacancy Renews Debate on A.B.A. Role," *New York Times*, December 27, 1987, p. A24; Sen. Charles E. Grassley, "Judging the Judges: A Memo to the A.B.A.," *Christian Science Monitor*, February 11, 1988, p. 15; Greenhouse, "U.S. Court Upholds Bar Association's Screening of Federal Judges," *New York Times*, August 18, 1988, p. A18; Frank J. Murray, "ABA's Role on Judges Ruled Out; Liberals Assail, Conservatives Hail," *Washington Times*, March 23, 2001, p. A1.

64. Cass Peterson, "The Federal Report; Executive Notes," *Washington Post*, September 30, 1982, p. A21; Pres. Reagan, Executive Order 12332: Establishment of the National

Productivity Advisory Committee, November 10, 1981; Wayne King and Irvin Molotsky, "Washington Talk: Briefing; What Is a Meeting?," *New York Times,* February 2, 1987, p. B6. One Iran-Contra participant threatened later to sue the group because of FACA and other issues. See "Washington Talk: Briefing; Litigation over a Chart," *New York Times,* March 10, 1987, p. A24.

65. George C. Wilson, "Precise Non-nuclear Arms Urged; Reagan to Receive Commission Report," *Washington Post,* January 10, 1988, p. A1; Cass Peterson, "Outdoors Report Won't See Light of Day; Not Even Panel Members Can View National Recreation Study," *Washington Post,* February 6, 1987, p. A21; Peterson, "U.S. to Release Report's Summary; Interior Department Still Withholding Full Recreation Document," *Washington Post,* February 7, 1987, p. A5.

66. Robert Pear, "Reagan Aide Disputes Poverty Rate," *New York Times,* November 4, 1983, p. D16; Howard Kurtz, "Stockman Says Aid to Poor Has Risen," *Washington Post,* November 4, 1983, p. A2.

67. Robert Pear, "US Weighing Change in Poverty Programs," *New York Times,* April 23, 1984, p. A1.

68. "Poverty Parley Is Termed Illegal," *Washington Post,* April 26, 1984, p. A21; Robert Pear, "Disputed Meeting on U.S. Benefits Is Canceled by the Census Bureau," *New York Times,* May 4, 1984, p. A19; "Poverty Meeting Canceled," *Washington Post,* May 4, 1984, p. A19; Representative Matsui, Statement before the Subcommittee on Census and Population of the Committee on Post Office and Civil Service and the Subcommittee on Oversight of the Committee on Ways and Means, U.S. House of Representatives, Joint Hearing on the Census and Designation of Poverty and Income, May 15, 1984, p. 4. Despite e-mails and phone conversations with DOC and specifically CB officials, a FOIA request to the CB, repeated forays into legal databases (e.g., LexisNexis), and the dogged efforts by several extremely helpful academic and (VA) government librarians, I was unable to find more details about Representative Matsui's lawsuit. The government said it had no records on file about it; the databases told a similar story. News stories about the episode never identified the case number or Matsui's colitigants.

69. *Public Citizen [et al.] v. National Economic Commission,* 703 F. Supp. 113 (DC District Court, 1989), 114, 121–122; Omnibus Budget Reconciliation Act of 1987, Public Law 100-203, Title 2, Sec. 2101; Daniel B. Moskowitz, "Journalists Fight Closed Meetings," *Washington Post,* December 5, 1988, p. F20; Richard K. Berg, Stephen H. Klitzman, and Gary J. Edles, *An Interpretive Guide to the Government in the Sunshine Act,* 2nd ed. (Chicago: American Bar Association, 2005), p. 352.

70. *Public Citizen v. National Economic Commission;* Thomas N. Bethell, "Roosevelt Redux: Robert M. Ball and the Battle for Social Security," *American Scholar* (2005): 60–73. Controversial also were the underlying assumptions themselves, the basis for the group's forecasting models. Though economists, citing Milton Friedman, frequently embrace their models' simplifying assumptions, such assumptions are often seen elsewhere as unrealistic, verging on ludicrous, and dangerously misleading in policy making (for

instance, assumptions about perfect market competition; perfect prices; rational, om-
niscient market actors; and here, given that it was the 1980s, any variety of supply-side
tenets). Milton Friedman, "The Methodology of Positive Economics," in his *Essays in
Positive Economics* (Chicago: University of Chicago Press, 1953), pp. 3–43.

71. *Public Citizen v. National Economic Commission*, at 199, 122, 126–127; Nathaniel
C. Nash, "Panel Barred from Meeting in Private," *New York Times,* December 10, 1988,
p. A11; Robert D. Hershey, Jr., "Judge Rules Economic Panel Can't Hold Meetings in
Secret," *New York Times,* January 6, 1989, p. A13.

72. President Ronald Reagan, "President's Private Sector Survey on Cost Control
in the Federal Government," June 30, 1982, http://www.reagan.utexas.edu/archives/
speeches/1982/63082d.htm; David Burnham, "House Unit Starts Inquiry on Reagan
Panel's Work," *New York Times*, September 16, 1982, p. B11; Burnham, "Questions Rising over U.S. Study and Role of Company Executives," *New York Times*, September 28,
1982, p. A1.

73. Burnham, "Questions Rising."

74. Ibid.; Cass Peterson, "Administration Said to Skirt Conflict Law," *Washington Post,*
October 6, 1982, p. A23; David Burnham, "Study on U.S. Personnel Costs Called Sham
by Congressman," *New York Times,* April 15, 1983, p. B10.

75. William H. Miller, "Peter Grace: Moonlighting Cost-Cutter," *Industry Week,* June
11, 1984, p. 51; Peter Grier, "Saving Grace, or How Not to Waste the Taxpayers' Money,"
Christian Science Monitor, July 5, 1983, p. 3; Grier, "Survey Lists Ways to Trim $60 Billion
from US Agencies," *Christian Science Monitor,* April 6, 1983, p. 1; Robert M. Cohen,
"Reagan's Cost Control 'Bloodhounds' Are Hounded by Charges of Conflicts," *National
Journal* 15, no. 3 (January 15, 1983): 122; Cass Peterson, "Tycoon Preaches Savings to
the U.S.," *Washington Post,* September 26, 1983, p. A11.

76. Cass Peterson, "Rep. Ford Threatens Subpoena; Justice Dept. Files on Panel With-
held," *Washington Post,* November 9, 1982, p. A19; Peterson, "Hill Committee Issues
Subpoena for Justice Files," *Washington Post,* November 25, 1982, p. A17; Peterson and
Karlyn Barker, "Advocacy Groups File Food Suit," *Washington Post,* January 6, 1983, p.
A21; *National Anti-hunger Coalition v. Executive Committee of the President's Private Sector
Survey on Cost Control,* 557 F. Supp. 524 (DC District Court, 1983); "Mum's the Word,"
National Journal 15, no. 11 (March 12, 1983): 543; Robert Pear, "Reagan Hunger Call,"
Washington Post, August 5, 1983, p. A8; [Washington News (news brief)], October 31,
1983, *United Press International*; Peterson, "Food Stamp Plan Attacked," *Washington Post,*
April 12, 1983, p. A15; "Hunger Suit Dismissed," *Washington Post,* March 1, 1983, p.
A15.

77. President Reagan, "Remarks at Los Angeles County Board of Supervisors' Town
Meeting, March 3, 1982," 18 Weekly Comp. Pres. Doc. 264, http://www.presidency.ucsb
.edu/ws/index.php?pid=42230.

78. President Reagan, Memorandum from the President to Edwin Meese III on the
"Task Force on Food Assistance," August 2, 1983, 19 Weekly Comp. Pres. Doc. 1086,

http://www.reagan.utexas.edu/archives/speeches/1983/80283c.htm; Robert Pear, "Hunger Panel Cancels Final Meeting," *New York Times*, December 13, 1983, p. B10; Mary McGrory, "Choking on Hunger; Muzzled," *Washington Post,* January 15, 1984, p. D1.

Chapter 5: Secret Law

1. Quote in chapter heading is from Sen. Russ Feingold, Testimony before the U.S. Senate Committee on the Judiciary Subcommittee on the Constitution, Senate Hearing on "Secret Law and the Threat to Democratic and Accountable Government," Hearing 110-604, Serial No. J-110-89, April 30, 2008, p. 1.

2. Dana Priest and R. Jeffery Smith, "Memo Offered Justification for Use of Torture; Justice Dept. Gave Advice in 2002," *Washington Post*, June 8, 2004, p. A1.

3. Ibid.; Susan Schmidt, "Ashcroft Refuses to Release '02 Memo; Document Details Suffering Allowed in Interrogations," *Washington Post,* June 9, 2004, p. A1; John P. Elwood, Testimony before the U.S. Senate Committee on the Judiciary Subcommittee on the Constitution, Senate Hearing on "Secret Law and the Threat to Democratic and Accountable Government," Hearing 110-604, Serial No. J-110-89, April 30, 2008. Note that they stopped short of invoking executive privilege, but they did pay homage to attorney-client privilege. See Rozell, *Executive Privilege*.

4. John C. Yoo, "Memorandum for William J. Haynes II, General Counsel of the Department of Defense," Office of Legal Counsel, DOJ, March 14, 2003, https://www.aclu.org/pdfs/safefree/yoo_army_torture_memo.pdf; Karen J. Greenberg and Joshua L. Dratel, eds., *The Torture Papers: The Road to Abu Ghraib* (New York: Cambridge University Press, 2004); David Cole, ed., *The Torture Memos: Rationalizing the Unthinkable* (New York: New Press, 2009).

5. Walter E. Dellinger et al., "Guidelines for the President's Legal Advisors," *Indiana Law Journal* 81, no. 4 (2006): 1349. The guidelines were written and endorsed by nineteen former OLC attorneys. See also the US Constitution, Art. II, Sec. 3. As a result of this interpretive power, critics have suggested the OLC acts almost like a supreme court within the executive branch that makes final determinations on legal questions. See, e.g., Savage, *Takeover*. This view, however compelling, fails to incorporate a president's authority to reject OLC opinions he or she disagrees with. As such, the point about a supreme court within the executive still holds, but it is the president, not the OLC, that assumes the power of the supreme court. See, e.g., Sandy Levinson, "Professional Competence," *Balkinization* (blog), May 20, 2007, http://balkin.blogspot.com/2007/05/professional-competence.html; Jack Balkin, "Is the Office of Legal Counsel Constitutional? Some Notes on the American Conseil Constitutionnel," *Balkinization* (blog), February 18, 2009, http://balkin.blogspot.com/2009/02/is-office-of-legal-counsel.html.

6. Public Acts of the First Congress, Chap. 14, Sec. 2 (1 Stat. 68, September 15, 1789); Steven Aftergood, Statement before the U.S. Senate Committee on the Judiciary Subcommittee on the Constitution, Senate Hearing on "Secret Law and the Threat to Democratic

and Accountable Government," April 30, 2008, Hearing 110-604, Serial No. J-110-89, pp. 77–87; Harold C. Relyea, "The Coming of Secret Law," *Government Information Quarterly* 5, no. 2 (1988): 97–116. The Supreme Court case was *Panama Refining Co. v. Ryan*, 293 U.S. 388 (Supreme Court, 1935). See Rick McKinney, "A Research Guide to the Federal Register and the Code of Federal Regulations," *Law Library Lights* 46, no. 1 (2002): 10; Jeff Shesol, *Supreme Power: Franklin Roosevelt vs. the Supreme Court* (New York: W. W. Norton, 2011), pp. 89–94.

7. The OLC emerged in 1934 right at the onset of this expansion of the presidency. Frances McDonald, "At the Federal Register, Tending to the Details of Democracy," *Prologue Magazine* [National Archives and Records Administration] 36, no. 3 (2004): 48–53. See also FOIA's text: 5 U.S.C. § 552 (a)(2)(a–c).

8. See Feingold, Testimony, p. 2; Dawn E. Johnsen, Testimony before the U.S. Senate Committee on the Judiciary Subcommittee on the Constitution, Senate Hearing on "Secret Law and the Threat to Democratic and Accountable Government," Hearing 110-604, Serial No. J-110-89, April 30, 2008, p. 125.

9. The sixty-four are just the ones that have been declassified, leaked, or referred to indirectly in other documents. See ProPublica's invaluable dataset: http://www.propublica.org/special/missing-memos. The actual number, of course, remains unknown to all but those with the relevant security clearances. Also note that Yoo's sentence ("Congress may no more regulate . . . ") appeared in several of the memos.

10. E.g., Elwood, Testimony, p. 6; Sen. Sam Brownback, Bradford A. Berenson, and David B. Rivkin, Testimony before the U.S. Senate Committee on the Judiciary Subcommittee on the Constitution, Senate Hearing on "Secret Law and the Threat to Democratic and Accountable Government," Hearing 110-604, Serial No. J-110-89, April 30, 2008, pp. 4, 10, and 13, respectively.

11. Feingold, Testimony, p. 18; Aftergood, Statement; Sen. Whitehouse, Remarks on the Foreign Intelligence Surveillance Act, Senate floor, December 7, 2007, U.S. Senate, http://www.fas.org/irp/congress/2007_cr/fisa120707.html.

12. For example, former attorney general William Rogers in 1958 argued that executive privilege applies to a range of executive branch communications, including "advisory opinions." Rogers, "Constitutional Law: The Papers of the Executive Branch," *American Bar Association Journal* 44 (1958): 941–942; Matthew Cooper Weiner, "In the Wake of Whitewater: Executive Privilege and the Institutionalized Conflict Element of Separation of Powers," *Journal of Law and Politics* 12 (1996): 806–810.

13. Savage, *Takeover*; Andrew Rudalevige, *The New Imperial Presidency: Renewing Presidential Power after Watergate* (Ann Arbor: University of Michigan Press, 2005); Gellman, *Angler*.

14. "Opinions by Date and Title," OLC, DOJ, http://www.justice.gov/olc/memoranda-opinions.html, accessed September 19, 2011. The 2008 data include Bush-Cheney opinions published in January 2009, right before Obama took office. The 2001 data include one memo that was originally enacted under Clinton. Note that pre-1993 memo publica-

tion dates were unavailable (i.e., we only have enactment dates). It is also worth noting the multiple reasons why the OLC may delay publication. The first involves classification, and the second involves delayed approval from client agencies (e.g., if an opinion is written for NASA, the OLC waits for NASA's approval before publication). The latter reason explains many of the short-term delays, such as those of one to two months. Phone conversation with Bette Farris, supervisory paralegal, OLC, January 2, 2013. Also keep in mind that Cheney in 2009 confirmed the existence of others and argued for their release. Of course, this was after he left office, which suggests the limits of an ideological explanation for Cheney's penchant for secrecy (i.e., if he was a pure ideologue, he would have insisted upon Obama-Biden's secrecy authority). See David Kaye, "Bush Memos: What Do They Reveal?" *Los Angeles Times*, April 29, 2009, http://www.latimes.com/news/opinion/opinionla/la-oew-kaye-carafano29-2009apr29,0,6696340.story#axzz2pev5qlZj.

15. Randolph D. Moss, Acting Assistant Attorney General, Office of Legal Counsel, "Relationship between Illegal Immigration Reform and Immigrant Responsibility Act of 1996 and Statutory Requirement for Confidentiality of Census Information," Memorandum for the General Counsel, Department of Commerce, May 18, 1999.

16. Johnsen, Testimony; Rivkin, Testimony; Kaye, "Bush Memos." It is true that Obama declassified and released some of the controversial OLC memos from the Bush-Cheney administration. However, the action was limited to a small number (four). See Associated Press, "CIA Employees Won't Be Tried for Waterboarding," MSNBC, April 17, 2009, http://www.msnbc.msn.com/id/30249847/#.TwNiJTVrPZU.

17. Elaine Shannon, "Snatching Dr. Mengele," *Time*, April 23, 1990. On the PRI's involvement with the drug trade, see, e.g., Sam Dillon and Christine Biederman, "Secretary to Mexican Patriarch Discloses Links to Drug Barons," *New York Times*, February 26, 1997, p. A1, and Tracy Wilkinson, "Former Mexico PRI Governor Pleads Guilty in Drug-Trafficking Case," *Los Angeles Times*, August 3, 2012, http://latimesblogs.latimes.com/world_now/2012/08/former-state-governor-from-mexicos-pri-pleads-guilty-in-drug-trafficking-case.html.

18. Shannon, "Snatching Dr. Mengele."

19. *U.S. v. Alvarez-Machain*, No. 91-712 (Supreme Court, 1992). Another wrinkle that complicated diplomacy was the fact that one of Camarena's narco-torturers was the brother-in-law of former Mexican president Luis Echeverría (r. 1970–1976). Enrique Krauze, "Mexico at War," trans. Hank Heifetz, *New York Review of Books*, September 27, 2012, http://www.nybooks.com/articles/archives/2012/sep/27/mexico-war/.

20. Harold Hongju Koh, "Protecting the Office of Legal Counsel from Itself," *Cardozo Law Review* 15 (1993): 513–523; Shannon, "Snatching Dr. Mengele"; Linda Hossie, "Abduction of Physician to Face Drug-Torture Case Puts U.S., Mexico at Odds," *Globe and Mail* (Canada), April 28, 1990; Chappell Lawson, *Building the Fourth Estate: Democratization and the Rise of a Free Press in Mexico* (Berkeley: University of California Press, 2002), pp. 13–58; Linda Greenhouse, "Justices Hear Case about Foreigners' Use of Federal Courts," *New York Times*, March 31, 2004, A16. The Bush-Cheney administration

maintained as late as December 2007 that it had the authority to kidnap foreign nationals, including citizens of close ally Great Britain. See, e.g., David Leppard, "US Says It Has Right to Kidnap British Citizens," *Sunday Times* (London), December 2, 2007, p. 1. Mexico at that time was a competitive authoritarian state with a dominant party system. See, e.g., Steven Levitsky and Lucan Way, *Competitive Authoritarianism: Hybrid Regimes after the Cold War* (Cambridge: Cambridge University Press, 2010).

21. OLC, 1980, "Extraterritorial Apprehension by the Federal Bureau of Investigation," cited in Koh, "Protecting the Office," p. 518.

22. Koh, "Protecting the Office," p. 519.

23. Mark Rozell, "Executive Privilege and the Modern Presidents: In Nixon's Shadow" [symposium], *Minnesota Law Review* 83 (1999): 1115.

24. Senate Judiciary Committee, "Department of Justice Authorization for Appropriations, Fiscal Year 1992" (Part 2—Appendix), Serial No. 12, July 11 and 18, 1991, pp. 25 (emphasis added), 37, 143, 185; Ryan J. Barrilleaux and Mark J. Rozell, *Power and Prudence: The Presidency of George H. W. Bush* (College Station: Texas A&M University Press, 2004).

25. *U.S. v. Alvarez-Machain*; Murray Campbell, "Mexican MD Free in Death of Drug Agent," *Globe and Mail* (Canada), December 15, 1992. Foreign governments and their citizens expressed outrage at the Supreme Court's decision. See, e.g., Phillip McCarthy, "Abduction Can Be Legal," *Sydney Morning Herald* (Australia), August 24, 1992, p. 14.

26. Rozell, *Executive Privilege,* p. 119.

27. Rozell, "Executive Privilege"; Rozell, *Executive Privilege,* pp. 103–104; Al Kamen and Ruth Marcus, "Reagan Uses Executive Privilege to Keep Rehnquist Memos Secret," *Washington Post,* August 1, 1986, p. A1; Howard Kurtz, "Rehnquist Memos Described," *Washington Post,* August 7, 1986, p. A15. The Reagan-Bush administration had earlier rejected requests to publish OLC memos during a conflict about the President's Private Sector Survey on Cost Control (see chapter 4). The memo justified keeping the task force members' names concealed, which was a clear violation of FACA. See Cass Peterson, "Rep. Ford Threatens Subpoena; Justice Dept. Files on Panel Withheld," *Washington Post,* November 9, 1982, p. A19.

28. Kamen and Marcus, "Reagan Uses Executive Privilege"; DOJ OLC, http://www .justice.gov/olc/opinions.htm, accessed March 20, 2013.

29. Rozell, "Executive Privilege," p. 1114.

30. James Risen and Eric Lichtblau, "Bush Lets U.S. Spy on Callers without Courts," *New York Times,* December 16, 2005, p. A1; Lichtblau and Risen, "Justice Deputy Resisted Parts of Spy Program," *New York Times,* January 1, 2006; Edward Alden and Holly Yeager, "Bush Faces Republican Revolt over Spying," *Financial Times,* February 9, 2006, http://www.ft.com/cms/s/0/c879f464-98fe-11da-aa99-0000779e2340.html; "NSA Has Your Phone Records: 'Trust Us' Isn't Good Enough," *USA Today,* May 11, 2006, http:// usatoday30.usatoday.com/news/opinion/editorials/2006-05-11-phone-records_x.htm. See American Civil Liberties Union, "Motion of the American Civil Liberties Union

for Release of Court Records," August 8, 2007, filed with the FISC, pp. 3–4. On the issue of strong media criticism being "surprising," see, e.g., W. Lance Bennett, Regina G. Lawrence, and Steven Livingston, *When the Press Fails: Political Power and the News Media from Iraq to Katrina* (Chicago: University of Chicago Press, 2007). For Bush's statements, see *NewsHour with Jim Lehrer* interview with President Bush, December 16, 2005, http://www.pbs.org/newshour/bb/white_house/july-dec05/bush_12-16-05.html; President's Radio Address, December 17, 2005, 41 Weekly Comp. Pres. Doc., http://georgewbush-whitehouse.archives.gov/news/releases/2005/12/20051217.html.

31. Christopher H. Pyle, "Domestic Spying—Again?", *Hartford (CT) Courant,* November 20, 2002, https://www.mtholyoke.edu/media/pyle-hartford-courant-domestic-spying-again, accessed April 11, 2014.

32. Eric Lichtblau, *Bush's Law: The Remaking of American Justice* (New York: Pantheon Books, 2008), pp. 188–189. The FISC is also unique for "hear[ing] arguments only from the Justice Department without adversarial lawyers to raise opposing views, and because Chief Justice John G. Roberts Jr. has unilateral power to select its members." See David E. Sanger and Charlie Savage, "Obama Is Urged to Sharply Curb N.S.A. Data Mining," *New York Times,* December 19, 2013, p. A1. The FISC statistics came from "Foreign Intelligence Surveillance Act Court Orders 1979–2012," Electronic Privacy Information Center (EPIC), http://epic.org/privacy/wiretap/stats/fisa_stats.html, accessed April 13, 2014. EPIC used data from the DOJ's annual reports, which are archived at the Federation of American Scientists' Intelligence Resource Program website, http://www.fas.org/irp/agency/doj/fisa/, accessed April 13, 2014. EPIC's data show that the court finally began rejecting applications starting in 2003. It rejected 11 from 2003 to 2009. Thus, FISC rejected 11 applications out of 33,949 total from 1979 to 2012. FISC also began to disclose in 2000 how many "pen register" applications it reviewed. The government submitted 1,981 of those to the court from 2000 to 2012. FISC approved all of them. According to EPIC, "Pen registers and [the related] trap and trace ("PR/TT") devices collect metadata from calls coming in to and going out of specific phone lines, respectively." See "EPIC v. DOJ—Pen Register Reports," EPIC, http://epic.org/foia/doj/pen-reg-trap-trace/#background, accessed April 13, 2013. In addition, as the Federal Judiciary Center (FJC) points out, FISA "established a Foreign Intelligence Surveillance Court of Review [FISC-Review], presided over by three district or appeals court judges designated by the Chief Justice, to review, at the government's request, the decisions" of the FISC. However, FISC-Review never actually met before 2002 "because of the almost perfect record of the [DOJ] in obtaining the surveillance warrants and other powers it requested" from FISC. FJC, "Foreign Intelligence Surveillance Court," *History of the Federal Judiciary,* http://www.fjc.gov/history/home.nsf/page/courts_special_fisc.html, accessed March 20, 2013.

33. Carol D. Leonnig and Dafna Linzer, "Spy Court Judge Quits in Protest: Jurist Concerned Bush Order Tainted Work of Secret Panel," *Washington Post,* December 21, 2005, p. A01. See also ACLU, "Motion of the American Civil Liberties Union for Release of Court Records," August 8, 2007, filed with the FISC (esp. note 5).

34. Jack Goldsmith, *The Terror Presidency: Law and Judgment inside the Bush Administration* (New York: W. W. Norton, 2007); ACLU, "ACLU v. NSA: The Challenge to Illegal Spying," n.d., http://www.aclu.org/national-security/aclu-v-nsa-challenge-illegal-spying, accessed March 20, 2013.

35. ACLU, "Motion"; ACLU, "ACLU v. NSA"; Attorney General Gonzales, Letter to Senators Leahy and Specter, January 17, 2007, available at http://graphics8.nytimes.com/packages/pdf/politics/20060117gonzales_Letter.pdf, accessed April 11, 2014. On polarization, see Nolan McCarty, Keith T. Poole, and Howard Rosenthal, *Polarized America: The Dance of Ideology and Unequal Riches* (Cambridge, MA: MIT Press, 2006); Marc Hetherington and Jonathan Weiler, *Authoritarianism and Polarization in American Politics* (New York: Cambridge University Press, 2009).

36. ACLU, "Motion"; Matthew G. Olsen, John C. Demers, Nicholas J. Patterson, and Mathhew A. Anzaldi [DOJ attorneys], "Opposition to the American Civil Liberties Union's Motion for Release of Court Records," August 31, 2007, p. 14, http://www.fas.org/irp/agency/doj/fisa/aclu-doj-resp083107.pdf, accessed April 11, 2014, cited in Aftergood, Statement.

37. Feingold, Testimony, p. 2.

38. Berenson, Testimony; J. William Leonard, Testimony before the U.S. Senate Committee on the Judiciary Subcommittee on the Constitution, Senate Hearing on "Secret Law and the Threat to Democratic and Accountable Government," Hearing 110-604, Serial No. J-110-89, pp. 11–13.

39. Carol D. Leonnig and Ellen Nakashima, "Ruling Limited Spying Efforts: Move to Amend FISA Sparked by Judge's Decision," *Washington Post,* August 3, 2007, p. A1; Joby Warrick and Walter Pincus, "How the Fight for Vast New Spying Powers Was Won," *Washington Post,* August 12, 2007, p. A1.

40. President Bush said this in March 2004: "Some are skeptical that the war on terror is really a war at all. My opponent said, and I quote, 'The war on terror is less of a military operation, and far more of an intelligence-gathering law enforcement operation.' I disagree—strongly disagree. . . . After the chaos and carnage of September the 11th, it is not enough to serve our enemies with legal papers. With those attacks, the terrorists and their supporters declared war on the United States of America, and war is what they got." President Bush, Remarks at a Bush-Cheney Reception in Boston, Massachusetts, March 25, 2004, in *Public Papers of the Presidents of the United States: George W. Bush, 2004,* bk. 1, *January 1 to June 30, 2004,* ed. Office of the Federal Register (Washington, DC: National Archives and Records Administration, 2004), p. 458; Jonathan Chait, "Kerry's Other War Record: How Bush Distorts His Opponent's Views on Terrorism," *Slate,* April 13, 2004, http://www.slate.com/articles/news_and_politics/politics/2004/04/kerrys_other_war_record.html; "Bush Campaign to Base Ad on Kerry Terror Quote," CNN, October 11, 2004, http://www.cnn.com/2004/ALLPOLITICS/10/10/bush.kerry.terror/. See also Eric Lichtblau, "Deal Is Struck to Overhaul Wiretap Law," *New York Times,* June 20, 2008, p. A1; Paul Kane, "Obama Supports FISA Legislation, Angering Left," *Washington*

Post, June 20, 2008, http://voices.washingtonpost.com/44/2008/06/obama-supports-fisa
-legislatio.html; Daniel W. Reilly, "Top Dems Are Cool to FISA Deal," *Politico,* June
19, 2008, http://www.politico.com/blogs/thecrypt/0608/Top_Dem_Senators_Cool_to_
FISA_deal.html.

41. Chris Frates, "Dems Who Flipped on FISA Immunity See More Telecom Cash," *Politico,* June 24, 2008, http://www.politico.com/blogs/thecrypt/0608/Dems_who_flipped
_on_FISA_immunity_see_more_telecom_cash.html; Lindsay Renick Mayer, "FISA Flip-
floppers Got $8,000 from Telecom," *Open Secrets* (blog), June 26, 2008, http://www
.opensecrets.org/news/2008/06/fisa-flipfloppers-got-8000-fro.html; Ryan Singel, "Democratic Lawmaker Pushing Immunity Is Newly Flush with Telco Cash," *Threat Level,*
October 18, 2007, http://www.wired.com/threatlevel/2007/10/dem-pushing-spy/.

42. Another important consequence of the new rules was that the court was less able
to protect against "unreasonable searches" as outlined in the Fourth Amendment to the
Constitution. ACLU, "Senate Passes Unconstitutional Spying Bill and Grants Sweeping
Immunity to Phone Companies," July 9, 2008, http://www.aclu.org/national-security/
senate-passes-unconstitutional-spying-bill-and-grants-sweeping-immunity-phone-comp.

43. As a result of Clinton-Gore's efforts, NSC directives fell under the (shifting) rules
of the Presidential Records Act. Harold C. Relyea, "Presidential Directives: Background
and Overview," *CRS Report for Congress,* 2008, Congressional Research Service, Order
Code 98-611 GOV, http://www.fas.org/sgp/crs/misc/98-611.pdf, accessed January 15,
2014. Some types of directives, such as export control regulations and transportation security directives (TSPs), do not appear to raise the same kinds of legal conflicts as the types
covered here. On TSPs, see Steven Aftergood, "The Secrets of Flight: Why Transportation Security Administration Guards Don't Have to Tell You What They Won't Tell You,"
Slate, November 18, 2004, http://www.slate.com/id/2109922/. On export controls, see
Aftergood, "Court Rebukes Government over 'Secret Law,'" *Secrecy News,* 2009, http://
www.fas.org/blog/secrecy/2009/07/secret_law-3.html. Courts have continued to uphold
NSC's post-1994 official location in the White House and its immunity to FOIA requests.
See, e.g., *Main Street Legal Services, Inc., v. National Security Council,* Memorandum and
Order 13-CV-00948 (Eastern New York District Court, 2013); Josh Gerstein, "Judge
Rejects Bid to FOIA National Security Council," *Politico,* August 7, 2013, http://www
.politico.com/blogs/under-the-radar/2013/08/judge-rejects-bid-to-foia-national-security-
council-170147.html.

44. Relyea, "Coming of Secret Law," p. 108. Among declassified NSC memos, one
interesting example is Memo from Henry Kissinger to Secretary of State, Secretary of Defense, and Director of the CIA, "Situation in Vietnam," National Security Study Memorandum 1 (NSSM-1), January 21, 1969, http://www.fas.org/irp/offdocs/nssm-nixon/
nssm_001.pdf, accessed July 21, 2013. What is particularly fascinating about this memo is
that it was, in fact, written largely by Pentagon Papers leaker and Nixon/Kissinger enemy
Daniel Ellsberg. See Ellsberg, *Secrets,* chap. 15.

45. Aftergood, Statement; Relyea, "Coming of Secret Law," p. 108. The FAS keeps

a running list at: http://www.fas.org/irp/offdocs/nspd/index.html. See also GAO, "National Security: The Use of Presidential Directives to Make and Implement U.S. Policy," Report # GAO/NSIAD-92-72, 1992, https://www.fas.org/irp/offdocs/gao-nsiad-92-72 .pdf, accessed July 11, 2011.

46. President Reagan's remarks came after Congress overrode his veto. See "Statement on the Comprehensive Anti-Apartheid Act of 1986," October 2, 1986, archived at the Ronald Reagan Presidential Library, accessible at http://www.reagan.utexas.edu/ archives/speeches/1986/100286d.htm. See also President Reagan, "Implementation of the Comprehensive Anti-Apartheid Act," Executive Order 12571, October 27, 1986, archived at the Ronald Reagan Presidential Library, accessible at http://www.reagan.utexas .edu/archives/speeches/1986/102786d.htm. An organized antiapartheid movement in the United States began pressuring the government to confront South Africa around 1969, when President Nixon adopted a conciliatory stance toward the racist South African government (although the US government had offered covert support, including intelligence leading to Nelson Mandela's arrest, for many years before that). Members of Congress had been pushing for an antiapartheid bill for over fifteen years. See Donald R. Culverson, "The Politics of the Anti-Apartheid Movement in the United States, 1969–1986," *Political Science Quarterly* 111, no. 1 (1997): 127–149; David Johnston, "C.I.A. Tie Reported in Mandela Arrest," *New York Times*, June 10, 1990, p. A15.

47. Reuters, "Review May Postpone U.S. Air-Service Ban against South Africa," *Globe and Mail* (Canada), November 6, 1986, p. A12.

48. NSC, "U.S. Policy toward South Africa," NSC-NSDD-273, May 7, 1987, http:// www.fas.org/irp/offdocs/nsdd/nsdd-273.htm, accessed June 5, 2011. The directive was declassified years later, on May 17, 1991, after Nelson Mandela was released from the Robben Island prison and his African National Congress movement/party was legalized. See also Barilleaux and Rozell, *Power and Prudence*, p. 105, emphasis added.

49. Reuters, "Review May Postpone."

50. NSC (and President Reagan), "Management of Public Diplomacy Relative to National Security," NSDD-77, January 14, 1983 [declassified in 1996], http://www.fas.org/ irp/offdocs/nsdd/nsdd-077.htm, accessed June 12, 2011.

51. E.g., Jim Lobe, "Reagan Asks Again for Nicaraguan Rebel Support," *IPS-Inter Press Service*, July 18, 1984; Peter Kornbluh, "Bush's Contra Buddies," *Nation*, May 7, 2001, pp. 6–9.

52. John Guilmartin, Jr., "Nicaragua Is Armed for Trouble," *Wall Street Journal*, March 11, 1985. The military spending was in large part a reaction to the US government's secret, continuing armament of the Contras, despite the Boland Amendment (see also chapter 9). This was the reason for the so-called Iran-Contra scandal that would later embroil the administration. Memorandum from Johnathan S. Miller (S/LPD) to Pat Buchanan, "'White Propaganda' Operation," March 13, 1985, http://www.gwu.edu/~nsarchiv/ NSAEBB/NSAEBB40/00940.pdf, accessed June 4, 2011. The memo was declassified during the congressional investigations into the Iran-Contra affair.

53. Memorandum from Miller to Buchanan, "'White Propaganda' Operation." The op-eds were apparently never published. Robert Parry and Peter Kornbluh, "Iran-Contra's Untold Story," *Foreign Policy* 72 (Autumn 1988): 3–30.

54. Parry and Kornbluh, "Iran-Contra's Untold Story," p. 17; Christian Smith, *The U.S. Central America Peace Movement* (Chicago: University of Chicago Press, 1996), pp. 268–269; National Security Council, "Chronological Event Checklist," March 20, 1985, cited in Greg Grandin, *Empire's Workshop: Latin America, the United States, and the Rise of the New Imperialism* (New York: Owl Books, 2006), pp. 126–128; Rep. Lee H. Hamilton and Rep. Daniel K. Inouye, *Report of the Congressional Committees Investigating the Iran/Contra Affair* (Darby, PA: Diane Publishing, 1987), pp. 34, 48; Reich memo to Raymond, S9460, March 1, 1986, cited in Hamilton and Inouye, *Report of the Congressional Committees,* p. 52n45.

55. Grandin, *Empire's Workshop,* p. 124; GAO, Response to Rep. Jack Brooks, B-229069, 66 Comptroller General 707, September 30, 1987, http://redbook.gao.gov/13/fl0061375.php, accessed July 2, 2011.

56. Office of Public Diplomacy for Latin America and the Caribbean (S/LPD), "Public Diplomacy Action Plan: Support for the White House Educational Campaign," March 12, 1985, http://www2.gwu.edu/~nsarchiv/NSAEBB/NSAEBB40/00934.pdf, accessed July 1, 2011; S/LPD, "Ninety-Day Plan," December 17, 1985, cited in Grandin, *Empire's Workshop,* pp. 125–126, 261; S/LPD, "Public Diplomacy Plan Explaining U.S. Central American Policy to the U.S. Religious Community," September 18, 1986, cited in Grandin, *Empire's Workshop,* pp. 125–126, 261; Human Rights Watch [AmericasWatch], "Nicaragua," in *Human Rights Watch World Report,* 1989, accessible at http://www.hrw.org/legacy/reports/1989/WR89/Nicaragu.htm, accessed July 7, 2011.

57. Wayne A. Cornelius et al., "The Electoral Process in Nicaragua: Domestic and International Influences: The Report of the LASA Delegation to Observe the Nicaraguan General Election of November 4, 1984," November 19, 1984; Robert J. McCartney, "Sandinistas' Foes Always Intended to Boycott Vote," *Washington Post,* July 30, 1984, A1. The boycott did show significant domestic opposition to Ortega and the Sandinistas. However, 75 percent of registered voters did turn out to vote that November. Alma Guillermoprieto and David Hoffman, "Document Describes How U.S. 'Blocked' a Contadora Treaty," *Washington Post,* November 6, 1984, A1.

58. Parry and Kornbluh, "Iran-Contra's Untold Story"; President Reagan, Executive Order 12333: United States Intelligence Activities, http://www.archives.gov/federal-register/codification/executive-order/12333.html, accessed July 12, 2011; Grandin, *Empire's Workshop,* p. 124.

59. GAO, "Comments on Lobbying and Propaganda Activities of the Office for Public Diplomacy for Latin America and the Caribbean," B-229069, September 30, 1987, http://www.gao.gov/assets/200/193596.pdf, accessed July 12, 2011. The report cited Sec. 501 of the Departments of Commerce, Justice and State, the Judiciary, and Related Agencies Appropriations Act, 1985, Pub.L. No. 98-411, August 30, 1984, 98 Stat. 1545.

See also GAO, "Examination of Recent Public Information Activities of the Small Business Administration," B-223098, B-223098.2, October 10, 1986, http://www.gao.gov/assets/380/373407.pdf, accessed July 14, 2011.

60. The events in Firdos Square, presented in the media at the time as crowded, spontaneous, and Iraqi led, were actually directed by the US government. The major US media organizations made reporting choices that exaggerated the size of the Iraqi crowd and suggested the events were grassroots and spontaneous occurrences. See David Zucchino, "Army Stage-Managed Fall of Hussein Statue," *Los Angeles Times,* July 3, 2004; "FCC Commissioner Says Broadcasting VNRs without Disclosure May Violate Federal Law," *Democracy Now!* April 6, 2006, http://www.democracynow.org/2006/4/6/fcc_commissioner_says_broadcasting_vnrs_without.

61. One set of VNRs was broadcast in forty of the largest markets. David Barstow and Robin Stein, "Under Bush, a New Age of Prepackaged News," *New York Times*, March 13, 2005, p. 1.

62. See David M. Walker [comptroller general of the United States], "Prepackaged News Stories," GAO report B-304272, February 17, 2005, http://www.gao.gov/decisions/appro/304272.htm, accessed June 23, 2011. Though Walker appeared to dance around that specific accusation in much of the memo, he did explicitly refer to the government's program as "covert propaganda" in note 3 on page 2. An earlier memo written by Anthony H. Gamboa, the GAO's general counsel, was also explicit about covert propaganda. See Gamboa, "Matter of: Department of Health and Human Services, Centers for Medicare & Medicaid Services—Video News Releases," GAO report B-302710, May 19, 2004, http://www.gao.gov/decisions/appro/302710.htm, accessed June 23, 2011.

63. OLC, "Whether Appropriations May Be Used for Informational Video News Releases," March 1, 2005. The 2005 memo, strangely enough, was not available on the OLC website (accessed July 12, 2011). It was, however, attached to an Office of Management and Budget memo published on the (Obama) White House website. See http://www.whitehouse.gov/sites/default/files/omb/assets/omb/memoranda/fy2005/m05-10.pdf, accessed June 11, 2012. Bradbury cited OLC, "Legal Constraints on Lobbying Effort in Support of Contra Aid and Ratification of the INF Treaty," 12 Op. O.L.C. 30, 40, February 1, 1988. OLC, "Expenditure of Appropriated Funds for Informational Video News Releases," July 30, 2004, http://www.justice.gov/olc/opfinal.htm, accessed April 21, 2014; Robert Pear, "Buying of News by Bush's Aides Is Ruled Illegal," *New York Times,* October 1, 2005, p. A1.

64. Joshua B. Bolton, "Use of Government Funds for Video News Releases," OMB Memorandum for Heads of Departments and Agencies, M-05-10, March 11, 2005, http://georgewbush-whitehouse.archives.gov/omb/memoranda/fy2005/m05-10.pdf, accessed May 26, 2011.

65. Christopher Lee, "Administration Rejects Ruling on PR Videos; GAO Called Tapes Illegal Propaganda," *Washington Post*, March 15, 2005, A21.

66. Pear, "Buying of News"; Howard Kurtz, "Writer Backing Bush Plan Had Gotten

Federal Contract," *Washington Post*, January 26, 2005, p. C1; Suzanne Goldenberg, "Bush Payola Scandal Deepens as Third Columnist Admits Being Paid," *Guardian* (London), January 29, 2005, p. 17; James Dao and Eric Schmitt, "A Nation Challenged: Hearts and Minds; Pentagon Readies Efforts to Sway Sentiment Abroad," *New York Times*, February 19, 2002, A1; National Security Archive, "Rumsfeld's Roadmap to Propaganda," National Security Archive Electronic Briefing Book No. 177, January 26, 2006, http://www.gwu .edu/~nsarchiv/NSAEBB/NSAEBB177/. See also James Bamford, "The Man Who Sold the War: Meet John Rendon, Bush's General in the Propaganda War," *Rolling Stone*, November 17, 2005, available at http://www.commondreams.org/headlines05/1118-10.htm, accessed April 12, 2014.

67. Public Law 109-13, § 6076, 110 Stat. 231, 301; Bush, Press Conference, January 26, 2005, http://georgewbush-whitehouse.archives.gov/news/releases/2005/01/20050126-3 .html.

68. Kenneth Culp Davis, "The Information Act: A Preliminary Analysis," *University of Chicago Law Review* 34 (1967): 761–816, at 779; *Torres v. I.N.S.*, 144 F.3d 472 (Seventh Circuit Appeals Court, 1998), 474, cited in Aftergood, Statement; Feingold, Testimony, p. 1.

Chapter 6: Presidential Secrecy in the Courts

1. *Hany Mahmoud Kiareldeen v. John Ashcroft et al.*, 273 F.3d 542 (Third Circuit Court of Appeals, 2001); Eyal Press, "The Strange Case of Hany K," *American Prospect*, December 19, 2001, http://prospect.org/article/strange-case-hany-k; John Kifner, "F.B.I. Says Man Is Terrorist, but Family Sees Plot by Ex-Wife," *New York Times*, June 27, 1998, p. B1; Ronald Smothers, "Man's Release Leads to Hope in I.N.S. Cases," *New York Times*, October 27, 1999, p. B1; David Cole, "Secret Trials," *Human Rights Magazine* (ABA), 28 (Winter 2001): 8; Cole, "Enemy Aliens," *Stanford Law Review* 54 (May 2002): 953–1004; David Cole and James X. Dempsey, *Terrorism and the Constitution*, rev. ed. (New York: New Press, 2006), pp. 157–158; Hany Kiareldeen, Testimony before the House Judiciary Committee on the Use of Secret Evidence, May 23, 2000, http://www.fas.org/ sgp/congress/2000/kiareldeen.html, accessed July 19, 2011; Anthony Lewis, "Abroad at Home: The Story of K," *New York Times*, October 26, 1999, p. A27.

2. After the divorce, Kiareldeen managed an electronics store in Passaic, New Jersey, and lived with a new wife in nearby Bloomsfield. Press, "Strange Case"; Kifner, "F.B.I. Says"; Smothers, "Man's Release"; Cole, "Secret Trials"; Cole, "Enemy Aliens"; Cole and Dempsey, *Terrorism and the Constitution*; Kiareldeen, Testimony; Lewis, "Abroad at Home."

3. Press, "Strange Case"; Kifner, "F.B.I. Says"; Smothers, "Man's Release"; Cole, "Secret Trials"; Cole, "Enemy Aliens"; Cole and Dempsey, *Terrorism and the Constitution*; Kiareldeen, Testimony; Lewis, "Abroad at Home"; *Kiareldeen v. Reno*, 71 F. Supp. 2d (New Jersey District Court, 1999), 402.

4. Press, "Strange Case"; Kifner, "F.B.I. Says"; Smothers, "Man's Release"; Cole, "Secret Trials"; Cole, "Enemy Aliens"; Cole and Dempsey, *Terrorism and the Constitution*; Kiareldeen, Testimony; Lewis, "Abroad at Home"; David Cole, "Secrecy, Guilt by Association, and the Terrorist Profile," *Journal of Law and Religion* 15 (2001): 267–288, at 272. Cole, a Georgetown Law professor, was one of Kiareldeen's attorneys.

5. *Kiareldeen v. Ashcroft*; *Kiareldeen v. Reno*.

6. Kifner, "F.B.I. Says"; Press, "Strange Case."

7. Matthew Purdy, "Our Towns; Custody Fight Disguised as Terror Case," *New York Times*, January 29, 2003, p. B1; Press, "Strange Case"; *Kiareldeen v. Ashcroft*, at 548.

8. Mohamed dropped Nour off with a friend, who tracked Kiareldeen down when Mohamed did not return from Egypt as promised. After seeing his daughter, Kiareldeen reported signs of neglect, including multiple cavities and evidence of persistent truancy (from the second grade). Purdy, "Our Towns."

9. Estimates for the number of post–1993 WTC detentions range from twenty-four to over fifty. The attorney general of the United States was empowered by the 1996 laws to determine which foreign nationals were ATRC worthy. Press, "Strange Case"; ACLU, "Support the Secret Evidence Repeal Act," July 14, 1999, http://www.aclu.org/immigrants -rights/support-secret-evidence-repeal-act, accessed August 5, 2011; Beth Lyon, "Secret Evidence," *Writ*, June 21, 2000, http://writ.news.findlaw.com/commentary/20000621_ lyon.html, accessed June 24, 2011; John Dorsett Niles, "Assessing the Constitutionality of the Alien Terrorist Removal Court," *Duke Law Journal* 57 (2007): 1833–1964.

10. See 8 U.S.C. § 1532 ("Establishment of removal court"); Niles, "Assessing the Constitutionality"; Carl Tobias, "The Process Due Indefinitely Detained Citizens," *North Carolina Law Review* 85 (2007): 1687, at 1723; Stephanie Cooper Blum, "Use It and Lose It: An Exploration of Unused Counterterrorism Laws and Implications for Future Counterterrorism Policies," *Lewis and Clark Law Review* 16, no. 2 (2012): 677–739, at 703–714.

11. Ellen Raphael Knauff, *The Ellen Knauff Story* (New York: W. W. Norton, 1952); "Reprieve," *Time*, May 29, 1950, http://content.time.com/time/magazine/article /0,9171 ,888783,00.html, accessed July 28, 2011; Louis Fisher, "To Have and to Hold," *Legal Times* 32, no. 11 (March 16, 2009): 38–39; Charles D. Weisselberg, "The Exclusion and Detention of Aliens: Lessons from the Lives of Ellen Knauff and Ignatz Mezei," *University of Pennsylvania Law Review* 143 (1995): 933–1034; *Knauff v. Shaughnessy*, 338 U.S. 537 (Supreme Court, 1950); *Knauff v. Watkins*, 173 F.2d. 599 (Second Circuit Appeals Court, 1949).

12. Knauff, *Ellen Knauff Story*; Weisselberg, "Exclusion and Detention"; Fisher, "To Have and to Hold"; *Knauff v. Shaughnessy*.

13. *Knauff v. Shaughnessy*; Knauff, *Ellen Knauff Story*; Weisselberg, "Exclusion and Detention."

14. Act of June 21, 1941 (55 Stat. 252, 22 U.S.C. § 223); *Knauff v. Shaughnessy*, at 542, 544; David Cole, "Are Foreign Nationals Entitled to the Same Constitutional Rights

as Citizens?," *Thomas Jefferson Law Review* 25 (2003): 367–388, at 375n36; Steve Vogel, "How the Pentagon Got Its Shape," *Washington Post Magazine*, May 27, 2007, p. W16. In *Knauff v. Shaughnessy*, Minton argued, "An alien who seeks admission to this country may not do so under any claim of right. Admission of aliens to the United States is a privilege granted by the sovereign United States Government." This was reasonable enough, but then Minton continued: "Whatever the procedure authorized by Congress is, it is due process as far as an alien denied entry is concerned." Congressional acts defined the bounds of constitutional rights, perhaps even precluding judicial review. And then, with not a small amount of logical inconstency, he stated, "The exclusion of aliens is a fundamental act of sovereignty. The right to do so stems not alone from legislative power but is inherent in the executive power to control the foreign affairs of the nation. When Congress prescribes a procedure concerning the admissibility of aliens, it is not dealing alone with a legislative power. It is implementing an inherent executive power."

15. President Harry S. Truman, "Statement by the President upon Signing Resolution Terminating Additional Emergency Powers," July 25, 1947, http://trumanlibrary.org/publicpapers/viewpapers.php?pid=1931; Public Law 239, 80th Congress (61 Stat. 449); George Orwell, *1984* (London: Secker and Warburg, 1949); *Knauff v. Shaughnessy*, at 544 and 546, citing *Woods v. Miller Co.*, 333 U.S. 138 (Supreme Court, 1948), note 3; Weisselberg, "Exclusion and Detention," pp. 955–957.

16. *Knauff v. Shaughnessy*, at 539; "Reprieve"; Knauff, *Ellen Knauff Story*, pp. 82–83n124, cited in Weisselberg, "Exclusion and Detention," pp. 958–959n127; Fisher, "To Have and to Hold."

17. "Reprieve"; Knauff, *Ellen Knauff Story*; Weisselberg, "Exclusion and Detention"; Fisher, "To Have and to Hold."

18. Weisselberg, "Exclusion and Detention," p. 960, including note 132, and p. 964n164; Ellen Knauff and Rep. Gossett, "Exclusion of Ellen Knauff," Hearings before House Subcommittee No. 1 of the House Committee on the Judiciary, on H.R. 7614, 81st Congress, 2nd Session, March 27, 1950; Knauff, *Ellen Knauff Story*, p. 54. "Reprieve." The importance of the Red Scare context was emphasized in David N. Atkinson, "Justice Sherman Minton and the Balance of Liberty," *Indiana Law Journal* 50, no. 1 (1974): 34–59, at 48.

19. Even so, the government over the years relentlessly fought her attempts to become a citizen, leading her to finally give up her quest, accepting permanent residency status. Weisselberg, "Exclusion and Detention," pp. 961–962, 964n163; Glendon Schubert, *Dispassionate Justice: A Synthesis of the Judicial Opinions of Robert H. Jackson* (Indianapolis, IN: Bobbs-Merrill, 1969), p. 206.

20. Anthony Lewis, "Abroad at Home; Case for Asylum," *New York Times*, August 26, 1983, p. A23; Lewis, "Abroad at Home; Requiem for a Victim," *New York Times*, December 1, 1983, p. A27; "Headliners; On Second Thought," *New York Times*, August 24, 1986, p. D9; Bruce Fein, "Giving Secrecy a Bad Name," *Washington Times*, June 9, 1992, p. F1; Lewis, "Abroad at Home; Without Any Right?," *New York Times*, April 14,

1988, p. A35; Ernest McCarus, ed., *The Development of Arab-American Identity* (Ann Arbor: University of Michigan Press, 1994), p. 203; Nat Hentoff, "Injustice at the Justice Department," *Washington Post,* December 9, 1995, p. A25; Susan Aschoff, "USF Instructor Linked to Jihad Denied Bail," *St. Petersburg (FL) Times,* June 7, 1997, p. 3B; Aschoff, "Pray, Read, Eat, Then Repeat," *St. Petersburg (FL) Times,* July 14, 1997, p. 1B; Benjamin Weiser, "In Lawsuit, I.N.S. Is Accused of Illegally Detaining Man," *New York Times,* September 16, 1997, p. B2; William Branigin, "Secret U.S. Evidence Entangles Immigrants; Rarely Used Law Now Falls Most Heavily on Arabs," *Washington Post,* October 19, 1997, p. A3; Aschoff, "Some of the Secret Evidence Cases," *St. Petersburg (FL) Times,* December 21, 1997, p. 1B; David Cole, "If All Don't Have Rights, None of Us Do," *Los Angeles Times,* March 19, 1998; Susan Taylor Martin, "Saved from Saddam, in Limbo in Lincoln," *St. Petersburg (FL) Times,* December 8, 2002, p. 1A; Committee on Immigration and Nationality Law and Committee on Communications and Media Law, "Dangerous Doctrine: The Attorney General's Unfounded Claim of Unlimited Authority to Arrest and Deport Aliens in Secret," *Record* (New York Bar Association) 59, no. 1 (2004): 5–40; Richard A. Serrano, "Detained, without Details," *Los Angeles Times,* November 1, 2003, p. A1. See also Cole and Dempsey, *Terrorism and the Constitution;* Susan M. Akram, "Scheherezade Meets Kafka: Two Dozen Sordid Tales of Ideological Exclusion," *Georgetown Immigration Law Journal* 14 (1999): 51.

21. *Turkmen v. Ashcroft,* 02 CV 23-7 [Fourth Amended Complaint] (Eastern New York District Court, September 13, 2010), http://ccrjustice.org/files/726%20Fourth%20 Amended%20Complaint.pdf; Transcript of "The 2nd Presidential Debate," *PBS,* October 11, 2000, http://www.pbs.org/newshour/bb/election/2000debates/2ndebate3.html, accessed May 28, 2011. Spencer Abraham was an Arab American Republican senator from Michigan.

22. Lily Fu Swenson, Deputy Associate Attorney General, Prepared statement delivered to the Hearing on Border Security and Claims, Concerning Immigration Removal Procedures Implemented in the Aftermath of the September 11th Attacks, House Judiciary Subcommittee on Immigration, June 30, 2005; Banisar, *Government Secrecy,* p. 25; David Cole and Jules Lobel, *Less Safe, Less Free: Why America Is Losing the War on Terror* (New York: New Press, 2007). Anticipating some of the administrative problems in dealing with the large number of foreign nationals, President Bush on November 13, 2001, released a military order, "Detention, Treatment, and Trial of Certain Non-citizens in the War against Terrorism." The president defined a "certain non-citizen" as "any individual who is not a United States citizen with respect to whom I determine from time to time in writing that . . . (i) is or was a member of . . . al Qaida; (ii) has engaged in, aided or abetted, or conspired to commit, acts of international terrorism, or acts in preparation therefor, that have caused, threaten to cause, or have as their aim to cause, injury to or adverse effects on the United States, its citizens, national security, foreign policy, or economy; or (iii) has knowingly harbored one or more individuals described [above]." The president alone claimed sole authority in determining anyone a terrorist,

even anyone with the "aim to cause . . . adverse effects on the U.S . . . economy," which in a broad reading of the order could include just about anyone challenging the authority of the US government or its international corporations. By most accounts, the administration restricted itself to individuals suspected to be Al Qaeda members or affiliates. Full text of the order can be accessed at http://georgewbush-whitehouse.archives.gov/news/ releases/2001/11/20011113-27.html, accessed July 15, 2011. We should also include individuals like Yassin Aref, convicted with secret evidence in a 2007 FBI-instigated terror plot that many viewed as entrapment.

23. Ben Fenton, "Taliban Prisoners Are 'Unlawful Combatants,'" *Telegraph* (London), January 12, 2002, http://www.telegraph.co.uk/news/worldnews/asia/afghanistan/1381248 /Taliban-prisoners-are-unlawful-combatants.html; Brigitte L. Nacos, Yaeli Bloch-Elkon, and Robert Y. Shapiro, *Selling Fear: Counterterrorism, the Media, and Public Opinion* (Chicago: University of Chicago Press, 2011); Thrall and Cramer, *American Foreign Policy.*

24. Jane Mayer, *The Dark Side: The Inside Story of How the War on Terror Turned into a War on American Ideals* (New York: Doubleday, 2008); President Bush, "Detention, Treatment, and Trial of Certain Non-citizens in the War against Terrorism" (Military Order), November 13, 2001, 66 *Federal Register* 57833, http://georgewbush-whitehouse.archives .gov/news/releases/2001/11/20011113-27.html, accessed September 14, 2011.

25. *Boumediene v. Bush,* 553 U.S. 723 (Supreme Court, 2008); *Rasul v. Bush,* 542 U.S. 466 (Supreme Court, 2004); *Hamdan v. Rumsfeld,* 548 U.S. 557 (Supreme Court, 2006). In the case against Boumediene, the court found "the hearsay evidence is lacking corroboration," putting the executive branch on notice that it had to provide more information backing its sources' "credibility and reliability."

26. Department of Defense, "Memorandum for Commander, United States Southern Command; SUBJECT: Recommendation for Continued Detention under DoD Control for (CD) for Guantanamo Detainee, ISN US4AG-010005DP (S)," April 1, 2008, http:// wikileaks.org/gitmo/prisoner/10005.html, accessed August 4, 2011.

27. Ibid.

28. Ibid.

29. Ibid.; Edward Cody, "Ex-Detainee Describes Struggle for Exoneration," *Washington Post,* May 26, 2009, p. A1. When Boumediene heard that candidate Obama had won the presidential election, he apparently celebrated—assuming Obama would soon close Guantanamo—by eating a slice of pizza. Since he had not eaten solid food for two years (he had been fed the liquid food Ensure through tubes), the pizza made him sick. Kate Pickert, "Q&A: Defending the Detainees," *Time,* November 26, 2008.

30. Center for Constitutional Rights, "Boumediene v. Bush / Al Odah v. United States," n.d., http://ccrjustice.org/ourcases/current-cases/al-odah-v.-united-states, accessed August 3, 2011; *Boumediene v. Bosnia and Herzegovina,* European Court of Human Rights (Fourth Section), Council of Europe, November 18, 2008, http://www.unhcr.org/refworld/pdfid/ 4a54bbb90.pdf.

31. Cody, "Ex-Detainee Describes Struggle." Algeria in the 1990s had annulled the

country's first postindependence democratic elections because the pro-Sharia Islamic Salvation Front (political party) had won a supermajority in the parliament, which would have given it the authority to change the constitution. As a result of the annulment, a civil war broke out and lasted until 2002, when the Islamic Salvation Army was forced to surrender.

32. *Boumediene v. Bosnia and Herzegovina.*

33. DOD, "Memorandum for Commander"; *Boumediene v. Bosnia and Herzegovina*; Lakhdar Boumediene, "My Guantanamo Nightmare," *New York Times,* January 8, 2012, p. SR9. It remains unclear whether he obtained his Bosnian citizenship credential illegally. In his 2012 op-ed, he merely stated, "In 1998, I became a Bosnian citizen." Thus, he chose not to publicly challenge the charges—but that does not necessarily affirm the validity of the accusations.

34. Boumediene, "My Guantanamo Nightmare"; Cody, "Ex-Detainee Describes Struggle"; Seema Jilani, MD, "Algerians, Freed from Guantanamo, Still Paying the Price," *McClatchy Newspapers,* September 9, 2009; BBC Worldwide Monitoring, "Bosnian Foreign Minister Confirms Embassy Closures for Security Reasons," *BH Radio 1,* October 17, 2001; BBC Worldwide Monitoring, "Bosnia: World Bank Closes Offices in Sarajevo for Security Reasons," October 19, 2001; Craig Whitlock, "At Guantanamo, Caught in a Legal Trap; 6 Algerians Languish Despite Foreign Ruling, Dropped Charges," *Washington Post,* August 21, 2006, p. A1. The State Department (in the *Post* article) adamantly denied it did anything to "threaten or intimidate" the Bosnian authorities.

35. Although Boumediene eventually attracted the most attention among the Algerian Six because of the Supreme Court case, the Bush-Cheney administration considered Belkacem Bensayah the group's leader. In fact, the public case against Bensayah appeared to have more evidentiary support, although a European Court of Human Rights investigation found reasons to be skeptical. Though the Algerian Six was presented as a cohesive unit, a terrorist cell, Boumediene's link to Bensayah was probably weak, entirely based on Red Crescent business. Bensayah had been to the office for social services before his arrest. After his early October arrest, his wife went to the Red Crescent seeking additional assistance. Boumediene was there and helped Mrs. Bensayah find a suitable lawyer for her husband. It was on that day that the rest of the "group" was arrested. See Cody, "Ex-Detainee Describes Struggle." *Boumediene v. Bosnia and Herzegovina*, pp. 4 including note 1, 9. At Guantanamo, Boumediene saw no reason to deny the fact that he helped Bensayah find a lawyer. ("Detainee admitted knowing, providing aid to, and obtaining a lawyer for AG-10001 [probably Bensayah]. Detainee claimed he hired a lawyer without knowing the charges against AG-10001.") Cody, "Ex-Detainee Describes Struggle"; *Boumediene v. Bosnia and Herzegovina*; DOD, "Memorandum for Commander," p. 7.

36. Cody, "Ex-Detainee Describes Struggle"; *Boumediene v. Bosnia and Herzegovina*; DOD, "Memorandum for Commander."

37. Jilani, "Algerians: Freed from Guantanamo"; William Glaberson, "Judge Orders 5 Algerians Freed from Guantanamo Detention," *New York Times,* October 21, 2008;

Boumediene v. Bosnia and Herzegovina, p. 2; Whitlock, "At Guantanamo." Approximately 600 Guantanamo detainees have been released, in most cases due to the flimsiness of the evidence supporting their imprisonment. Other Guantanamo detainees remain trapped in Cuba in part because of secret evidence. Of the 600 released, the government alleges that 16 percent have associated with "terrorist" groups (that is, not necessarily Al Qaeda or related groups accused of plotting directly against the United States), and 12 percent are being surveilled. Kimberly Dozier, "Officials: Fewer Gitmo Detainees Re-offended," *Associated Press,* March 5, 2012.

38. Edward C. Liu and Todd Garvey, "Protecting Classified Information and the Rights of Criminal Defendants: The Classified Information Procedures Act," Congressional Research Service Report #R41742, April 2, 2012, http://www.fas.org/sgp/crs/secrecy/R41742.pdf, accessed August 4, 2012; David Cole, Testimony before House Committee on the Judiciary, Hearing on the "Secret Evidence Repeat Act of 1999, Part I," H.R. 2121, 106th Congress, Serial No. 97, February 10, 2000; Cole and Dempsey, *Terrorism and the Constitution,* p. 152; *US v. Sterling*, 1:10CR485 [Defendant's Response to Government's Motion for In Camera Hearings] (Eastern Virginia District Court, [August 19,] 2011), 6, http://www.fas.org/sgp/jud/sterling/081911-oppose158.pdf, accessed June 4, 2013. For a more critical perspective, see Wen Ho Lee's arguments described in *US v. Lee,* 90 F. Supp. 2d 1324 (New Mexico District Court, 2000).

39. In Boumediene's case, the appeals court reviewed the secret evidence in camera. Nevertheless, the judge's comments about the evidence, as well as all of the information released through outside investigations, indicated the unreliability of the secret evidence. On foreign nationals' equal rights in criminal cases, see *Mazen Al Najjar v. Janet Reno*, 97 F. Supp. 2d 1329 (Southern Florida District Court, 2000); *Kwong Hai Chew v. Colding*, 344 U.S. 590 (Supreme Court, 1953); Lewis, "Abroad at Home; Without Any Rights?," p. A35; Robert Timothy Reagan, *National Security Case Management: An Annotated Guide* (Washington, DC: Federal Judicial Center, 2011), p. 21, http://www.fjc.gov/public/pdf.nsf/lookup/TSGuid01.pdf/$file/TSGuid01.pdf.

40. ACLU, "Sibel Edmonds: A Patriot Silenced, Unjustly Fired but Fighting Back to Help Keep America Safe," January 26, 2005, http://www.aclu.org/national-security/sibel-edmonds-patriot-silenced-unjustly-fired-fighting-back-help-keep-america-safe; Sibel Edmonds and Philip Giraldi, "Who's Afraid of Sibel Edmonds?" (interview), *American Conservative,* November 1, 2009, http://www.theamericanconservative.com/articles/whos-afraid-of-sibel-edmonds/.

41. Sibel Edmonds, "Biography," JustACitizen.com (her personal website), http://justacitizen.com/articles_documents/SibelEdmonds-Long%20BIO-.htm, accessed August 25, 2013; David Kohn, "Lost in Translation," *60 Minutes* (CBS News), September 10, 2009, http://www.cbsnews.com/stories/2002/10/25/60minutes/main526954.shtml.

42. ACLU, "Sibel Edmonds"; Kohn, "Lost in Translation."

43. Kohn, "Lost in Translation"; Christopher Deliso, "An Interview with Sibel Edmonds," Antiwar.com July 1, 2004, http://www.antiwar.com/deliso/?articleid=2917; Da-

vid Rose, "An Inconvenient Patriot," *Vanity Fair,* August 15, 2005, http://www.vanityfair
.com/politics/features/2005/09/edmonds200509; Mathieu Verboud and Jean-Robert Vi-
allet, *Une Femme à Abattre* (Kill the Messenger) (film), Zadig Productions, 2006.

44. Kohn, "Lost in Translation"; Deliso, "Interview with Sibel Edmonds"; Rose, "Inconvenient Patriot."

45. Kohn, "Lost in Translation"; Deliso, "Interview with Sibel Edmonds"; Rose, "Inconvenient Patriot."

46. ACLU, "Sibel Edmonds"; Kohn, "Lost in Translation"; National Commission on
Terrorist Attacks, *The 9/11 Commission Report: Final Report of the National Commission
on Terrorist Attacks upon the United States* (New York: W.W. Norton, 2004); Deliso, "Interview with Sibel Edmonds."

47. ACLU, "Sibel Edmonds"; Kohn, "Lost in Translation"; James V. Gramaldi, "FBI
Whistle-Blowers Allege Lax Security, Possible Espionage," *Washington Post,* June 19,
2002, p. A10; *Sibel Edmonds v. DOJ,* 04-5286 [Reply Brief of the Plaintiff-Appellant]
(DC Appeals Court, 2005), 14.

48. Kohn, "Lost in Translation"; Barbara Comstock, DOJ Director of Public Affairs,
"Regarding Today's Filing in *Sibel Edmonds v. Department of Justice*" (press release), October
18, 2002, http://www.fas.org/irp/news/2002/10/doj101802.html; Eric Lichtblau, "Material Given to Congress in 2002 Is Now Classified," *New York Times,* May 20, 2004, p. A18.

49. *Burnett v. Al Baraka Investment,* MSC 04-203 (RBW) [Declaration of Attorney
General John Ashcroft] (DC District Court, [May 13,] 2004), http://www.fas.org/sgp/
jud/edmonds051404.pdf.

50. Ibid. The published declaration of course did not provide details about what was
classified (such as her date of birth), but she later was able to talk about it. The details,
however, were available to the judges, who examined the classified version (in camera,
ex parte). See also Lichtblau, "Material Given to Congress"; Sibel Edmonds, "Gagged,
but Still Going Strong," Antiwar.com, 2005, http://www.antiwar.com/edmonds/?article
id=5954; Kohn, "Lost in Translation"; CNN, "$116 Trillion Lawsuit Filed by 9/11 Fam-
ilies," CNN.com, August 15, 2002, http://articles.cnn.com/2002-08-15/justice/attacks
.suit_1_bin-three-saudi-princes-trillion-lawsuit?_s=PM:LAW; "Fmr. FBI Translator: White
House Had Intel on Possible Airplane Attack Pre-9/11" (interview with Sibel Edmonds),
Democracy Now!, March 31, 2004, http://www.democracynow.org/2004/3/31/fmr_
fbi_translator_white_house_had.

51. Edmonds, "Gagged"; Lichtblau, "Material Given to Congress"; ACLU, "Sibel Edmonds." The FBI sent the Senate Judiciary Committee an e-mail on May 13, 2004, saying, "The FBI would like to put all Judiciary Committee staffers on notice that it now
considers some of the information contained in two Judiciary Committee briefings to be
classified." After details about those briefings and the court case in which the state secrets
privilege was asserted, the e-mail continued, "Any staffer who attended those briefings,
or who learns about those briefings, should be aware that the FBI now considers the
information classfied and should therefore avoid further dissemination." See *Project on*

Government Oversight (POGO) *v. Ashcroft*, [no case number] [Complaint for Declaratory and Injunctive Relief] (DC District Court, 2004), 4.

52. *POGO v. Ashcroft*, 2004; POGO, "Justice Department Caves In: Allows Publication of Retroactively Classified Information; Lawsuit Challenged Classification of Public Information," February 22, 2005, http://www.pogo.org/pogo-files/alerts/government-secrecy/gs-oc-20050222.html.

53. OIG, DOJ, "A Review of the FBI's Actions in Connection with Allegations Raised by Contract Linguist Sibel Edmonds," January 2005, http://www.justice.gov/oig/special/0501/index.htm; OIG, DOJ, "Update on the July 2004 Report, 'A Review of the FBI's Actions in Connection with Allegations Raised by Contract Linguist Sibel Edmonds,'" Audit Report 05-33, Appendix 7, July 2005, http://www.justice.gov/oig/reports/FBI/a0533/app7.htm. The FBI also acknowledged Dickinson once had a relationship with a Turkish intelligence agent and worked for the ATC. In addition, it acknowledged the bureau had cut corners for many new employees after 9/11, sidestepping full background checks for new translators with security clearances.

54. The Crown privilege gave kings and queens the discretionary authority to withhold information from the Parliament, the court system, and the public. William G. Weaver and Robert M. Pallitto, "State Secrets and Executive Power," *Political Science Quarterly* 120, no. 1 (2005): 85–112; Liu and Garvey, "Protecting Classified Information"; Carrie Newton Lyone, "The State Secrets Privilege: Expanding Its Scope through Government Misuse," *Lewis and Clark Law Review* 11, no. 1 (2007): 99–132; Bruce Fein, (Prepared) Statement of Bruce Fein before the House Judiciary Committee Regarding the State Secrets Privilege, Hearing on H.R. 5607, "State Secrets Protection Act of 2008," Serial No. 110-155, July 31, 2008, http://judiciary.house.gov/hearings/printers/110th/43832.PDF; Louis Fisher, "The State Secrets Privilege Is Too Easy to Abuse," Nieman Watchdog Project, November 17, 2006, http://www.niemanwatchdog.org/index.cfm?background id=142&fuseaction=Background.view; Fisher, *The Constitution and 9/11: Recurring Threats to America's Freedoms* (Lawrence: University Press of Kansas, 2008), pp. 248–285.

55. *Reynolds v. US*, 192 F.2d 987 (Third Circuit Appeals Court, 1951); *Brauner v. US*, 10 F.R.D. 468 (Eastern Pennsylvania District Court, 1950); *US v. Reynolds*, 345 U.S. 1 (Supreme Court, 1953); Weaver and Pallitto, "State Secrets"; Robert M. Chesney, "State Secrets and the Limits of National Security Litigation," *George Washington Law Review* 75, no. 5-6 (2007): 1249–1332; Amanda Frost, "The State Secrets Privilege and Separation of Powers," *Fordham Law Review* 75, no. 4 (2007): 1931–1964; Amanda Frost and Justin Florence, "Reforming the State Secrets Privilege," *Advance: The Journal of ACS Issue Briefs* (Spring 2009): 111–130; Warren Richey, "Security or Coverup? How a Murky Case Became Precedent," *Christian Science Monitor,* June 8, 2006, p. 1; Louis Fisher, *In the Name of National Security: Unchecked Presidential Power and the Reynolds Case* (Lawrence: University Press of Kansas, 2006); Barry Siegel, *Claim of Privilege: A Mysterious Plane Crash, a Landmark Supreme Court Case, and the Rise of State Secrets* (New York: Harper, 2009).

56. *US v. Reynolds*; Weaver and Pallitto, "State Secrets"; Chesney, "State Secrets"; Louis

Fisher, "Congressional Access to National Security Information," *Harvard Journal on Legislation* 45 (2008): 219–235. The government, after winning the case, offered the widows and their families a $170,000 settlement, which the families accepted. Richey, "Security or Coverup?"

57. Richey, "Security or Coverup?"

58. Ibid.; Savage, *Takeover,* pp. 170–171. The government had offered Reynolds et al. the chance to call the three survivors to testify (in lieu of the report). However, the survivors probably would have been prevented from discussing internal air force training procedures. As Justice Vinson described the proposed deal, "The witnesses would be allowed to refresh their memories from any statement made by them to the Air Force, and authorized to testify as to all matters except those of a 'classified nature.'" *US v. Reynolds,* p. 5.

59. *Herring, Loether et al. v. US,* 424 F.3d 384 (Third Circuit Appeals Court, 2005); Richey, "Security or Coverup?"

60. *Ellsberg v. Mitchell,* 709 F.2d 51 (DC Appeals Court, 1983), 57–58; *Halkin v. Helms* [Halkin II], 690 F.2d 977 (DC Appeals Court, 1982); Lyone, "State Secrets Privilege."

61. As indicated, the figure used data from Chesney, "State Secrets," and an archive maintained at American University's Collaboration on Government Secrecy (COGS), http://www.wcl.american.edu/lawandgov/cgs/ssp_cases.cfm, accessed April 6, 2012. Cases were confirmed against case records in the Lexis-Nexis and Westlaw legal databases, which helped identify cases absent from the sources (note that any omissions in Chesney probably resulted from his focus on whether courts adjudicated claims). The legal databases also helped correct citation errors. Another resource for SSP data can be found at Laura K. Donohue's State Secrets Archive at Georgetown University Law Center, http://apps.law.georgetown.edu/state-secrets-archive/about.cfm, accessed September 27, 2012. Also see Frost and Florence, "Reforming," pp. 113–115, for an earlier comparison of 2001–2006 and 1991–2000. That analysis, done before the end of Bush-Cheney's second term, already showed Bush-Cheney using SSP more frequently than Clinton. Compare Chesney, "State Secrets," p. 1301, who argued that "the available data do suggest that the privilege has continued to play an important role during the Bush administration, but it does not support the conclusion that the Bush administration chooses to resort to the privilege with greater frequency than prior administrations or in unprecedented substantive contexts."

62. Chesney, "State Secrets," pp. 1301–1302, similarly noted caution with these kinds of quantitative comparisons, especially given the war-filled Bush years. He expanded on the argument in an e-mail to the author from October 2012.

63. President George W. Bush, "Executive Order 13233—Further Implementation of the Presidential Records Act," November 1, 2001, http://www.archives.gov/about/laws/appendix/13233.html; Steven Aftergood, "Govt Denies Fraud in 1953 State Secrets Ruling," *Secrecy News* 8 (January 26, 2004), http://www.fas.org/sgp/news/secrecy/2004/01/012604.html. Bush's executive order cited arguments in *Nixon v. Administrator of General*

Services: "The Court ruled that constitutionally based privileges available to a President 'survive[?] the individual President's tenure. . . . The Court also held that a former President, although no longer . . . a Government official, may assert constitutionally based privileges with respect to his Administration's Presidential records, and expressly rejected the argument that 'only an incumbent President can assert the privilege of the Presidency.'"

64. Aftergood, "Govt Denies Fraud."

65. Frost, "State Secrets Privilege"; Glenn Greenwald, "The 180-Degree Reversal of Obama's State Secrets Position," Salon.com, February 10, 2009, http://www.salon.com/2009/02/10/obama_88/; Weaver and Pallitto, "State Secrets," p. 111. ("The impulse of the Bush administration [was] to expand the use of the privilege to prevent scrutiny and information.") Surveillance disputes were neutralized by the SSP during at least eight cases in the 1970s and 1980s.

66. Maher Arar, "Maher's Story," http://maherarar.net/mahers%20story.php, accessed August 14, 2013; Arar, "Maher Arar Speaks about His Rendition and Torture" (video), Center for Constitutional Rights, http://ccrjustice.org/arar, accessed August 14, 2013; Darius Rejali, "The Dirty Secret about 'Clean' Torture," *Human Rights Now Blog*, June 14, 2011, http://blog.amnestyusa.org/waronterror/the-dirty-secret-about-clean-torture/.

67. Arar, "Maher's Story"; Arar, "Maher Arar Speaks"; Rejali, "The Dirty Secret."

68. Arar, "Maher's Story"; Arar, "Maher Arar Speaks"; Rejali, "The Dirty Secret"; Mayer, *Dark Side,* pp. 129–134; *Arar v. Ashcroft,* 414 F. Supp. 2d 250 (Eastern New York District Court, 2006), 254.

69. Arar, "Maher's Story"; Arar, "Maher Arar Speaks"; Rejali, "The Dirty Secret"; *Arar v. Ashcroft,* 414 F. Supp. 2d 250; Commission of Inquiry into the Actions of Canadian Officials in Relation to Maher Arar, *Report of the Events Related to Maher Ahar: Analysis and Recommendations* (Government of Canada report), p. 59, http://www.pch.gc.ca/cs-kc/arar/Arar_e.pdf, accessed August 16, 2012. *Time* magazine in Canada had earlier named him 2004's "Newsmaker of the Year."

70. Frost, "State Secrets Privilege"; *Arar v. Ashcroft,* 414 F. Supp. 2d 250; *Arar v. Ashcroft,* 532 F.3d 157 (Second Circuit Court of Appeals, 2008); *Arar v. Ashcroft,* 585 F.3d 559 (Second Circuit Court of Appeals, 2009). False confessions from other detainees and weak links to a couple of Canadian suspects prompted his initial appearance on terrorist watch lists.

71. *Arar v. Ashcroft,* 414 F. Supp. 2d 250; *Arar v. Ashcroft,* 532 F.3d 157; *Arar v. Ashcroft,* 585 F.3d 559; David Luban, "An Embarrassment of Riches," Balkinization, March 4, 2006, http://balkin.blogspot.com/2006/03/embarrassment-of-riches.html.

72. *Arar v. Ashcroft,* 414 F. Supp. 2d 250; *Arar v. Ashcroft,* 532 F.3d 157; *Arar v. Ashcroft,* 585 F.3d 559; *Arar v. Ashcroft,* 130 S.Ct. 3409 (Supreme Court, 2010); "U.S. Handling of Arar Case 'By No Means Perfect': Rice," *CBC News,* October 24, 2007, http://www.cbc.ca/news/world/story/2007/10/24/rice-arar.html. Rice's admission came before the House Foreign Affairs Committee on October 24. Ronald Crelinsten, "On the Border

with a Frightened Giant," *Toronto Star,* December 12, 2011, www.thestar.com/opinion/
editorialopinion/2011/12/12/on_the_border_with_a_frightened_giant.html.

73. Richey, "Security or Coverup?"; Fisher, "State Secrets Privilege."

74. Luban, "Embarrassment of Riches"; Greenwald, *With Liberty and Justice*; Alasdair
MacIntyre, "The Essential Contestability of Some Social Concepts," *Ethics* 84, no. 1
(1973): 1–9. Worse, David Luban (in 2008) argued that SSP doctrine has evolved to allow presidents to override laws in the name of security, leading to an "interpreter-in-chief
override," akin to the "commander-in-chief override." Supporters want to stop legislators
and lawyers from "backseat driv[ing] on the battlefield." Luban, "On the Commander in
Chief Power," *Southern California Law Review* 81 (2008): 477–571.

Chapter 7: Secret Science

1. John Mueller and Mark G. Stewart, "Hardly Existential: Thinking Rationally about
Terrorism," *Foreign Affairs,* April 2, 2010, http://www.foreignaffairs.com/articles/66186/
john-mueller-and-mark-g-stewart/hardly-existential. Obviously, not all cancers are caused
by environmental harms.

2. See also Chris Mooney, *The Republican War on Science* (New York: Basic Books,
2006); John Holbo, ed., *Looking for a Fight: Is There a Republican War on Science?* (West
Lafayette, IN: Parlor Press, 2006).

3. Office of Inspector General, Environmental Protection Agency, "EPA's Response to
the World Trade Center Collapse: Challenges, Successes, and Areas for Improvement,"
Report #2003-P-00012, August 21, 2003, p. 11; Michelle Shepard and Scott Simmie, "A
Breath of Dust-Filled Air," *Toronto Star*, September 11, 2002, p. B7. One team of investigative journalists who produced the documentary *Dust to Dust: The Health Effects of 9/11*
concluded that the attacks spread 400 tons of asbestos; 90,000 tons of jet fuel with benzene; 200,000 pounds of lead and cadmium from computers; up to 2 million pounds of
PAHs from diesel fires; and 420,000 tons of crystalline silica from concrete, plasterboard,
and glass. See Anita Gates, "Buildings Rise from Rubble While Health Crumbles," *New
York Times*, September 11, 2006, p. E6.

4. Office of Inspector General, "EPA's Response," p. 14; s/mm² stands for structures
per millimeter squared.

5. Anthony DePalma, "Officials Slow to Hear Claims of 9/11 Illnesses," *New York
Times*, September 5, 2006, p. A1; Rachel Zeig Owens et al., "Early Assessment of Cancer
Outcomes in New York City Firefighters after the 9/11 Attacks: An Observational Cohort
Study," *Lancet* 378, no. 9794 (2011): 898–905; Sydney Ember, "Study Suggests Higher
Cancer Risk for 9/11 Firefighters," *New York Times,* September 2, 2011, p. A17; Phillip
J. Landrigan et al., "Health and Environmental Consequences of the World Trade Center
Disaster," *Environmental Health Perspectives* 112, no. 6 (2004): 731–739; Robin Herbert
et al., "The World Trade Center Disaster and the Health of Workers: Five-Year Assessment

of a Unique Medical Screening Program," *Environmental Health Perspectives* 114, no. 12 (2006): 1853–1858.

6. *Lombardi v. Whitman*, 485 F.3d 73 (Second Circuit Appeals Court, 2007); Office of Inspector General, "EPA's Response," pp. 9, 15–17, 131; Anthony DePalma, "New Docs Detail How Feds Downplayed Ground Zero Health Risks," ProPublica.org, September 8, 2011, http://www.propublica.org/article/new-docs-detail-how-feds-downplayed-ground -zero-health-risks. The FOIA documents ProPublica.org obtained from the CEQ can be found at https://www.propublica.org/documents/item/229887-ceq-foia-7-12-08-sec1. Several months after the attack, President Bush signed a secret order giving the EPA head the authority to classify information. Corky Siemaszko, "EPA's 9-11 'Secret' '02 Exec Order Let Agency Bury Info on Air Hazards," *New York Daily News,* July 28, 2006, p. 4.

7. On September 12, the EPA's chief of staff e-mailed all senior agency officials, instructing them that "all statements to the media should be cleared through the NSC [National Security Council] before they are released." *Lombardi v. Whitman*; Office of Inspector General, "EPA's Response"; DePalma, "New Docs"; Siemaszko, "EPA's 9-11 'Secret.'"

8. *Lombardi v. Whitman*, at 75.

9. DePalma, "New Docs"; Mike Stobbe, "Experts Say Science Lacking on 9/11 and Cancer," *CBS News,* June 20, 2012, http://www.cbsnews.com/8301-505245_162-57456943/ experts-say-science-lacking-on-9-11-and-cancer/. The evidence of negative health effects was apparently strong enough to prompt Congress in 2010 to pass a bill giving victims $4.3 billion for treatment and damages.

10. As CEO, Cheney led the company's acquisition of Dresser Industries in 1998. Following the purchase, Halliburton officials realized Dresser's asbestos liabilities were greater than they initially knew. See Neela Banerjee, "Haliburton Battered as Asbestos Verdict Stirs Deep Anxieties," *New York Times,* December 8, 2001, p. C1; Dana Milbank, "For Cheney, Tarnish from Halliburton; Firm's Fall Raises Questions about Vice President's Leadership There," *Washington Post*, July 16, 2002, p. A1. See also Lorraine Woellert, "Tort Reform: Is the Road Clear at Last?," *Business Week*, November 15, 2004, http://www .businessweek.com/magazine/content/04_46/b3908408.htm.

11. President Bush's August 2001 announcement about his stem cell research policy is one example of the administration distorting but not concealing science. In a televised speech, Bush presented what seemed like a reasonable compromise for the contentious debate, which pitted religious conservatives against scientists and other citizens who saw great potential in embryonic stem cell research for treating a slew of stubborn diseases. Bush authorized continued research on "60 genetically diverse stem cell lines" that "already exist" and "have the ability to regenerate themselves indefinitely." The benefit, he argued, was that the "life and death decision has already been made," which in theory would have pleased the conservatives (it did not). The problem with his statement, as scientists and journalists quickly and loudly proclaimed, was that the real number was far lower; probably under a dozen lines were up and running, and they had limited po-

tential for continuing research. As the critics' loud objections demonstrated, Bush was not *concealing* otherwise unavailable scientific information—the facts were in the public domain—but he chose to mislead many Americans by using information only a few scientists accepted. Bush, "President Discusses Stem Cell Research," President Bush's White House web archive, August 9, 2001, http://georgewbush-whitehouse.archives.gov/news/releases/2001/08/20010809-2.html. Chris Mooney, *The Republican War on Science* (New York: Basic Books, 2005); John Holbo, ed., *Looking for a Fight: Is There a Republican War on Science?* (West Lafayette, IN: Parlor Press, 2006).

12. Richard Monastersky, "Publish and Perish?," *Chronicle of Higher Education* A 16 (October 11, 2002).

13. The USDA and Homeland Security were jointly responsible for asking NAS to pull the report, which calls into question the bureaucratic reputation argument. However, it is plausible that USDA officials persuaded Homeland Security officials to withhold publication, using mosaic theory or related ideas to emphasize risks. See Blyth, "Powering," on the phenomenon of interelite persuasion. Monastersky, "Publish or Perish?," reports that the department funded the study, but it is not clear whether others also contributed financially. On bureaucratic interests and motivations, see Wilson, *Bureaucracy*; Carpenter, *Forging*; Daniel Carpenter, *Reputation and Power: Organizational Image and Pharmaceutical Regulation at the FDA* (Princeton, NJ: Princeton University Press, 2010).

14. The NAP report was eventually published as a book on April 30, 2003, although it is not clear whether it was revised after redactions. See Committee on Biological Threats to Agricultural Plants and Animals, National Research Council, *Countering Agricultural Bioterrorism* (Washington, DC: National Academies Press, 2003).

15. Banisar, *Government Secrecy*; OMB Watch, *Against the Public Will: Summary of Responses to the Environmental Protection Agency's Plans to Cut Toxic Reporting* (Washington, DC: OMB Watch, December 2006).

16. OMB Watch, *Against the Public Will*; OMB Watch, "EPA Finalizes Rules for Toxics Release Inventory," January 9, 2007, http://www.ombwatch.org/node/3126.

17. OMB Watch, *Against the Public Will*, p. 2.

18. Gup, *Nation of Secrets,* pp. 11–12; Sabin Russell and Nanette Asimov, "State Can't Say Who Sold Beef: Rules Bar Telling Which Stores, Restaurants Had Tainted Meat," *San Francisco Chronicle,* January 3, 2004, http://www.sfgate.com/health/article/State-can-t-say-who-sold-beef-Rules-bar-telling-2832619.php; Carla K. Johnson, "USDA Keeps Tainted Meat's Destination Secret," *Spokesman-Review* (Spokane, WA), June 27, 2004, http://www.spokesman.com/stories/2004/jun/27/usda-keeps-tainted-meats-destination-secret/.

19. Given all of the deficiencies in the USDA's regulatory and enforcement system, as well as the shortcuts taken by processors at slaughterhouses and packaging plants despite the potential social costs, reasonable people might be loathe to trust the system. Tainted ground beef alone sickens tens of thousands a year, stemming from a failure to control *E. coli*. Much of the ground beef in stores and restaurants is "made from a mix of slaughterhouse trimmings and a mash-like product derived from scraps that were ground together."

See, e.g., Michael Moss, "The Burger That Shattered Her Life," *New York Times*, October 4, 2009, p. A1.

20. Russell and Asimov, "State Can't Say"; Johnson, "USDA Keeps"; Gup, *Nation of Secrets*. Some of the stores and restaurants were identified in newspapers, but the number fell far short of the total. *Anderson v. Department of Health and Human Services*, 907 F.2d 936 (Tenth Circuit Appeals Court, 1990); *Public Citizen Health Research Group v. FDA*, 704 F.2d 1280 (DC District Court, 1983).

21. Johnson, "USDA Keeps." Office of Information and Privacy (DOJ), "Exemption 4," *Justice Department Guide to the Freedom of Information Act*, 2004, http://www.justice.gov/oip/exemption4.htm, accessed March 23, 2012.

22. Union of Concerned Scientists (UCS), "Analysis of Airborne Bacteria Suppressed," n.d., http://www.ucsusa.org/scientific_integrity/abuses_of_science/airborne-bacteria.html, accessed April 7, 2012; Honorable John H. Marburger III, "Statement on Scientific Integrity in the Bush Administration," Office for Science and Technology Policy, April 2, 2004, available at http://stephenschneider.stanford.edu/Publications/PDF_Papers/Responseto CongressonUCSDocumentApril2004.pdf, accessed April 13, 2014; Cory Hatch, "Another Something Foul in the Air above Hog Farms," *Triplepoint Magazine,* 2005, http://www.bu.edu/sjmag/scimag2005/features/hogfarm.htm.

23. Marburger, "Statement on Scientific Integrity"; Hatch, "Another Something Foul"; Ben Harder, "Suspended Drugs," *Science News* 164, no. 1 (July 5, 2003): 5–6; Jose R. Bicudo et al., "Odor and VOC Emissions from Swine Manure Storages," *Proceedings of the Water Environment Federation* 5 (2002): 123–135.

24. Zahn later said, with unnecessary modesty, "I never purported to be an authority on microbial transfer. But it was an important finding and it needed to be reported." Geoff Brumfiel, "Bush Administration Dismisses Allegations of Scientific Bias," *Nature*, April 8, 2004, p. 589. See also Perry Beeman, "Ag Scientists Feel the Heat," *Des Moines Register,* December 1, 2002, p. 1A; Marburger, "Statement on Scientific Integrity"; Hatch, "Another Something Foul"; UCS, "Analysis"; Shulman, *Undermining Science,* pp. 38–39; Robert F. Kennedy, Jr., "The Junk Science of George W. Bush," *Nation,* February 19, 2004, pp. 11–18; James A. Zahn, J. Anhalt, and E. Boyd, "Evidence for Transfer of Tylosin and Tylosin-Resistant Bacteria in Air from Swine Production Facilities Using Sub-therapeutic Concentrations of Tylan in Feed," *Journal of Animal Science* 79 (2001): 189; Langus T. Angenent, Margit Mau, Archana Jindal, Usha George, James A. Zahn, and Lutgarde Raskin, "Monitoring Antibiotic Resistance in Biological Waste Treatment Systems," *Proceedings of the Water Environment Federation*, no. 15 (2001): 740–754.

25. Shulman, *Undermining Science*; Harder, "Suspending Drugs"; Kennedy, "Junk Science"; UCS, "Analysis"; Department of Natural Resources, State of Iowa, "Animal Confinements in Iowa," http://www.iowadnr.gov/Portals/idnr/uploads/afo/maps/confinement_au.pdf, accessed August 4, 2011. Clear Lake is in the county in the second row from the top, seventh from the left.

26. Beeman, "Scientists Feel the Heat."

27. Ibid.; UCS, "Analysis"; Shulman, *Undermining Science*; Adrianne Appel, "Top Scientists Want Research Free from Politics," *Inter-Press Service News Agency,* February 14, 2008, http://ipsnews.net/news.asp?idnews=41205. The 2002 list can be found here: http://www.mwa.ars.usda.gov/mwa/b&f/files/senlist.pdf, accessed July 27, 2011.

28. Marburger, "Statement on Scientific Integrity." Fortunately, it did not take long for other scientists to publish on the subject, offering corroborating evidence. See examples in Brumfiel, "Bush Administration," and Hatch, "Another Something Foul."

29. On business power, see, for starters, Jacob Hacker and Paul Pierson, "Business Power and Social Policy: Employers and the Formation of the American Welfare State," *Politics & Society* 30, no. 2 (2002): 277–325; Charles E. Lindblom, *Politics and Markets: The World's Political-Economic Systems* (New York: Basic Books, 1977); Lindblom, "The Market as Prison," *Journal of Politics* 44, no. 2 (1982): 324–336.

30. Shulman, *Undermining Science,* p. 26.

31. E-mail from Jana Goldman to Ronald Stauffer, January 24, 2001, cited in Tarek Maassarani, *Redacting the Science of Climate Change: An Investigative and Synthesis Report* (Washington, DC: Government Accountability Project, 2007), p. 8. Goldman confided to a scientist on June 3, 2002, "I'm still not even sure about certain things and I've been here for three years! I think we are OK on this one as it's not a sensitive subject—like climate change" (p. 27).

32. Maassarani, *Redacting the Science,* pp. 14–15; Juliet Eilperin, "Censorship Is Alleged at NOAA," *Washington Post,* February 11, 2006, p. A7; Eilperin, "Climate Researchers Feeling Heat from White House," *Washington Post,* April 6, 2006, p. A27; Larisa Alexandrovna, "Commerce Department Tells National Weather Service Media Contacts Must Be Pre-approved," *The Raw Story,* October 4, 2005, http://rawstory.com/news/2005/Commerce_Department_tells_Nationa_1004.html.

33. Andrew C. Revkin, "Memos Tell Officials How to Discuss Climate," *New York Times,* March 8, 2007, p. A17; Union of Concerned Scientists, "Designated Spokesperson Required for Polar Bear Travels," www.ucsusa.org/scientific_integrity/abuses_of_science/designated-spokesperson.html, accessed August 4, 2011; Savage, *Takeover,* p. 107. The fixation on polar bears was due in part to a lawsuit seeking to force the administration to list the bears as a threatened species. In addition, Al Gore's prominent film, *An Inconvenient Truth,* melodramatically highlighted the plight of polar bears. On the Reagan-Bush administration's use of public affairs officers in communications with journalists, see Mackenzie, *Secrets,* pp. 98–99.

34. James E. Hansen, "Dangerous Anthropogenic Interference: A Discussion of Humanity's Faustian Climate Bargain and the Payments Coming Due," presentation in the Distinguished Public Lecture Series at the Department of Physics and Astronomy, University of Iowa, Iowa City, October 26, 2004, pp. 1, 15; Andrew C. Revkin, "The War over U.S. Science," *International Herald Tribune,* October 21, 2004, p. A10; Revkin, "NASA Expert Criticizes Bush on Climate; President Has Ignored the Dangers, He Says," *New York Times,* October 27, 2004, p. A6; "Subverting Science," *New York Times,* October 31,

2004, p. D10; Mark Bowen, *Censoring Science: Dr. James Hansen and the Truth of Global Warming* (New York: Penguin, 2008).

35. It was Rick S. Piltz, a whistle-blower who was a senior associate at CCSP, who first brought Cooney's acts to light. Suzanne Goldenberg and James Randerson, "Bush Appointees 'Watered Down Greenhouse Science,'" *Guardian* (London), March 20, 2007, p. 18. U.S. House of Representatives, Committee on Oversight and Government Reform, "Political Interference with Climate Change Science under the Bush Administration," Investigative Report, December 2007, http://permanent.access.gpo.gov/lps94771/20071210101633.pdf; U.S. House of Representatives, Committee on Oversight and Government Reform, "Allegations of Political Interference with the Work of Government Climate Change Scientists," Public Hearing, Serial No. 110-1, January 30, 2007; Andrew C. Revkin, "Bush Aide Softened Greenhouse Gas Links to Global Warming," *New York Times,* June 8, 2005; Stephen Leahy, "When Science Inconveniences Bush," *Inter-press Service News Agency,* April 27, 2006. Shulman, *Undermining Science*; Maassarani, *Redacting the Science*; Revkin, "Climate Expert Says NASA Tried to Silence Him," *New York Times*, Jauary 29, 2006, p. C1.

36. Francesca T. Grifo, Ph.D., Written testimony for the hearing on "Allegations of Political Interference with the Work of Government Climate Change Scientists," House Committee on Oversight and Government Reform, Serial No. 110-1, January 30, 2007, p. 58. See also Timothy Donaghy, Jennifer Freeman, Francesca Grifo, Karly Kaufman, Tarek Maassarani, and Lexi Shultz, *Atmosphere of Pressure: Political Interference in Federal Climate Science* (Cambridge, MA: UCS/GAP, 2007); Peter N. Spotts, "Has the White House Interfered on Global Waming Reports?," *Christian Science Monitor*, Jauary 31, 2007, p. 1.

37. The listing for "Tabernaemontana rotensis (a plant)," for instance, involves the FWS's decision not to list the plant as a species, in order to circumvent the Endangered Species Act. See also, e.g., Dana Milbank, "White House Web Scrubbing; Offending Comments on Iraq Disappear from Site," *Washington Post*, December 18, 2003, p. A5. ("The federal Centers for Disease Control and Prevention and USAID have removed or revised fact sheets on condoms, excising information about their effectiveness in disease prevention, and promoting abstinence instead. The National Cancer Institute, meanwhile, scrapped claims on its Web site that there was no association between abortion and breast cancer.")

38. National Council for Research on Women, *MISSING: Information about Women's Lives,* a report from the National Council for Research on Women, 2004, http://www.ncrw.org/sites/ncrw.org/files/report.pdf; Richard Carmona, Testimony before the Committee on Oversight and Government Reform, U.S. House of Representatives, Hearing on "The Surgeon General's Vital Mission: Challenges for the Future," Serial #110-38, pp. 34–35, emphasis added; Savage, *Takeover,* p. 106. For a comprehensive list of "abuses of science," see Union of Concerned Scientists, "Timeline of Abuses of Science," http://www.ucsusa.org/scientific_integrity/abuses_of_science/a-to-z-guide-timeline.html, accessed July 31,

2012. The list contains instances "when individual cases of political interference in science were exposed and reported in the mainstream press." Of course, many Bush-Cheney officials denied any wrongdoing. For example, a NASA spokesman declared, "There are no plans in place to intimidate or stifle science." Another administrator, a twenty-four-year-old who was forced to resign because he had lied on his résumé, maintained, "There is no pressure or mandate, from the Bush administration or elsewhere, to alter or water down scientific data at NASA, period." See Eilperin, "Censorship Is Alleged." By contrast, John H. Marburger III, President Bush's top science adviser, conceded the administration encouraged a kind of information coherence, which might ruffle some feathers: "This administration . . . tries to be consistent in its messages. It's an inevitable consequence [i.e., complaints about suppression] that you're going to get this kind of tuning up of language [about climate science]." See Andrew C. Revkin, "Bush vs. the Laureates: How Science Became a Partisan Issue," *New York Times*, October 19, 2004, p. F1. Additionally, in response to James Hansen's claims of the administration's censorship and intimidation, the deputy assistant for public affairs at NASA similarly argued that the information controls Hansen and all other NASA scientists felt were solely "about coordination" of the information coming from the executive branch. See Revkin, "Climate Expert." An administration supporter, Myron Ebell, the director of energy and global warming policy at the Competitive Enterprise Institute, similarly argued that message discipline, even as far as editing scientists' reports, was necessary for "consistency" in aligning agency activities with the president's objectives. See Revkin, "Bush Aide."

39. All emphases added. Union of Concerned Scientists (UCS), "2004 Scientist Statement on Restoring Scientific Integrity to Federal Policy Making," http://www.ucsusa.org/scientific_integrity/abuses_of_science/scientists-sign-on-statement.html, accessed July 14, 2012; UCS, *Scientific Integrity in Policymaking: An Investigation into the Bush Administration's Misuse of Science* (Cambridge, MA: UCS, 2004); UCS, "Prominent Statement Signatories," http://www.ucsusa.org/scientific_integrity/solutions/big_picture_solutions/prominent-statement-signatories.html, accessed July 14, 2012.

40. I submitted a FOIA request for earlier USDA lists. The USDA responded (on July 19, 2012) by saying: "As the electronic version of the list was periodically updated, the content of the previous version was replaced and a hard copy was not maintained." Later, a USDA official claimed the sensitive lists were only used to filter scientific reports—never for FOIA applications: "The purpose of the 'List of High Profile Topics' and the 'Sensitive Issues' was to provide an additional line of approval for publications of a high profile nature so that higher level management was made aware of these topics and/or publications. The FOIA Office did not consult these lists in processing FOIA requests, as they were not applicable to the FOIA process." E-mail from Stasia Hutchinson (FOIA/PA Office, Research, Education, and Economics, USDA) to author, July 11, 2013. See also Eilperin, "Climate Researchers" ("We've always had the policy, it just hasn't been enforced."); Marburger, "Statement on Scientific Integrity," p. 9.

41. Jay Branegan, "Is Al Gore a Hero or a Traitor?," *CNN*, April 19, 1999, http://www

.cnn.com/ALLPOLITICS/time/1999/04/19/gore.html; Albert Gore, Jr., *Earth in the Balance: Ecology and the Human Spirit* (New York: Houghton Mifflin Harcourt, 1992), pp. 7, 269 ("I have come to believe that we must take bold and unequivocal action: we must make the rescue of the environment the central organizing principle for civilization"); Dan Rather and Richard Threlkeld, "A Look at the Presidential Campaigns," *CBS Evening News* (Transcript), October 29, 1992 (Bush: "If you listen to Governor Clinton and ozone man, if you listen to them—you know why I call him ozone man? This guy is so far off in the environmental extreme, we'll be up to our necks in owls and out of work for every American. This guy's crazy. He is way out! Far out, man!"); Henry I. Miller, "The Corrosive Effects of Politicized Regulation of Science and Technology," in *Politicizing Science: The Alchemy of Policymaking,* ed. Michael Gough (Stanford, CA:Hoover Institution Press, 2003), pp. 50–53; Revkin, "Bush vs. the Laureates," p. F1. James Hansen conceded that Gore's advocacy and personality might have occasionally intimidated government scientists, even to the point where they sometimes "got a little fed up with him." Still, the restrictive environment inside the government under Clinton-Gore came nowhere close to what scientists experienced under Bush-Cheney. As Hansen put it, "It was not institutionalized the way it is now [in 2004]." For Gore's critics, the ouster of Princeton scientist William Happer from a Department of Energy Bush-Quayle political appointment was particularly loathsome. Happer believed his contrary views about climate change prompted his firing ("I lost a federal position because of citing scientific research findings that undermined a politician's rhetoric"). Though the conflict was unpleasant, Happer's experience was a fairly typical one for political appointees who stayed on during a transfer of power from one administration to another. It also does not quite qualify as an example of suppressing proprietary scientific information, unless we incorporate the potential climate science under Happer that might have challenged the emerging consensus. If that lost science counts, then we would need to also count lost work in all analogous situations. See Alan Shaw, *University Research Centers of Excellence for Homeland Security: A Summary of a Workshop* (Washington, DC: National Research Council, National Academies Press, 2004), p. 18; William Happer, Jr., Testimony before the U.S. House Subcommittee on Energy and Water Development Appropriations, House Energy and Water Development Appropriations Committee for 1994, Part 5: Department of Energy, CIS-NO 93-H181-37, April 26, 1993, pp. 613, 615; Happer, "Harmful Politicization of Science," in *Politicizing Science: The Alchemy of Policymaking,* ed. Michael Gough (Stanford, CA: Hoover Institution Press, 2003), pp. 28, 45–46; Miller, "Corrosive Effects." See also "Political Cleansing at the Energy Department," *Washington Times,* May 14, 1993, p. F2; Holman Jenkins, Jr., "Al Gore Leads a Purge," *Wall Street Journal,* May 25, 1993, p. A14; A. Berry, "Top Climate Scientist Axed," *Herald Sun* (Melbourne, Australia), May 17, 1993; Ronald Bailey, "Political Science: When Science Is Made to Fit Policy Requirements of Politicians," *Reason* 25, no. 7 (December 1993); Richard S. Lindzen, "Is There a Basis for Global Warming Alarm?," Independent Institute, http://www.independent.org/publications/article.asp?id=1714; Jay Ambrose, "What about the Left-Wingers Who Put

Politics over Science?," *Manchester Union Leader,* April 3, 2006, available at http://www
.freerepublic.com/focus/f-news/1608157/posts, accessed April 13, 2014; Gerald E. Marsh,
"Goracle Gushings on Faith-Based Science," *USA Today Magazine,* January 2008, pp.
10–13; Interior Department, "Transition Information for Incoming Presidential Appointees," http://www.doi.gov/hrm/primer3.htm#A, accessed July 3, 2012.

42. Jeffrey T. Richelson, "Scientists in Black," *Scientific American,* February 1998, pp.
48–55. A few satellites, like the KH1 through KH8 systems (KH = keyhole), were functional by the early 1960s.

43. Ibid.; Office of the Vice President, The White House, "Vice President Joins CIA
Director to Declassify Satellite Imagery," February 24, 1995, available at https://www.fas
.org/irp/news/1995/95i0224.htm; Philip Shabecoff, "Senator Urges Military Resources
Be Turned to Environmental Battle," *New York Times,* June 29, 1990, p. A1; Patrick E.
Tyler, "Senators Propose Shift of Defense Funds to Study Environment," *Washington Post,*
June 29, 1990, p. A7; Osha Gray Davidson, "The CIA and the Pentagon Declare War
on Climate Change," *OnEarth* (Natural Resources Defense Council), January 6, 2010,
http://www.onearth.org/blog/the-cia-and-the-pentagon-declare-war-on-climate-change;
Will Rogers and Jay Gulledge, *Lost in Translation: Closing the Gap between Climate Sci-
ence and National Security Policy* (Washington, DC: Center for a New American Security
[CNAS], 2010), pp. 23, 38.

44. Richelson, "Scientists in Black"; Office of the Vice President, "Vice President Joins
CIA Director"; Shabecoff, "Senator Urges Military Resources"; Tyler, "Senators Propose
Shift"; Davidson, "CIA and the Pentagon"; Rogers and Gulledge, *Lost in Translation.*

45. President Clinton, "Executive Order 12951: Release of Imagery Acquired by
Space-Based National Intelligence Reconnaissance Systems," *Federal Register* 60, no. 3
(February 22, 1995): 10789–10790; Office of the Vice President, "Vice President Joins
CIA Director"; Robert L. Perry, *A History of Satellite Reconnaissance: The Perry Gambit
and Hexagon Histories,* Center for the Study of National Reconnaissance, National Reconnaissance Office (Washington, DC: Government Printing Office, 2012), http://www.nro
.gov/history/csnr/programs/docs/prog-hist-05.pdf, accessed October 7, 2013. Clinton
did not specify the date restrictions in his order; Gore did in the press release. Also, they
may have made the decision to selectively declassify earlier, but the announcement came
with an executive order, which often requires months of bureaucratic development.

46. Richelson, "Scientists in Black"; William H. Schlesinger and Nicholas Gramenopoulos, "Archival Photographs Show No Climate-Induced Changes in Woody Vegetation in
the Sudan, 1943–1994," *Global Change Biology* 2, no. 2 (1996): 137–141.

47. Rogers and Gulledge, *Lost in Translation*; Andrew Moseman, "Spying for Science:
Military Satellites Aid Civilian Research," *Popular Mechanics,* March 3, 2010, http://www
.popularmechanics.com/science/space/4326977, accessed October 4, 2013; Deborah Za-
barenko, "U.S. Releases Unclassified Spy Images of Arctic Ice," *Reuters,* July 17, 2009, http://
www.reuters.com/article/2009/07/17/us-climate-arctic-images-idUSTRE56F6N22009
0717; William J. Broad, "C.I.A. Revives Sharing Data with Climate Scientists," *New York*

Times, January 4, 2010, p. A1. The Obama-Biden administration declassified information about Gambit and Hexagon in September 2011—though only "more than 90 historical records" were released. See National Reconnaissance Office (NRO), "Declassified Records," Gambit and Hexagon Programs, n.d., http://www.nro.gov/foia/declass/gambhex .html, accessed October 7, 2013; Center for the Study of National Reconnaissance, NRO, "The Gambit and Hexagon Programs," http://www.nro.gov/history/csnr/gambhex/index .html, accessed October 7, 2013.

48. It took a lawsuit by the Environmental Defense Fund and the American Lung Association to force the regulatory process via court order. *American Lung Association et al. v. Browner*, 884 F. Supp. 345 (Arizona District Court, 1994); *American Lung Association v. Browner*, Civil Action No. 92-5316 (Eastern New York District Court, 1992); *Environmental Defense Fund v. Thomas*, 870 F.2d 892 (Second Circuit Appeals Court, 1989); *American Lung Association et al. v. EPA*, 134 F.3d 388 (DC Appeals Court, 1998), 390. See also US EPA, "Air Quality Criteria for Particulate Matter," Final Report, Washington, DC, EPA 600/P-95/001, April 1996, http://cfpub.epa.gov/ncea/cfm/recordisplay .cfm?deid=2832, accessed July 5, 2012; Bill Nichols, "Clean-Air Proposal Is Kicking Up Dust; White House Quietly Seeks Common Ground," *USA Today*, June 5, 1997, p. A4; H. Sterling Burnett, "Secrets at the EPA," *Washington Times*, August 29, 1997, p. A21. Interest groups coalesced around the report in predictable ways. The recommendations elicited strong support from environmental groups and nongovernmental health organizations like the American Cancer Society. Industry groups, such as the National Association of Manufacturers and others representing the fossil fuel industry, lobbied against the proposed regulations, warning of the high costs to businesses, which would ultimately hurt consumers. Using an argument seldom heard anymore, they also warned of the unintended health consequences of the pollution regulations, including increased vulnerability to ultraviolet radiation and thus skin cancer, because there would be less protective ozone in the air. Partisans generally lined up in predictable ways too, with the exception of some New England Republicans who supported the proposal and some Democrats from manufacturing districts (e.g., Rep. John Dingell of Michigan) who opposed it.

49. C. Arden Pope III et al., "Particulate Air Pollution as a Predictor of Mortality in a Prospective Study of U.S. Adults," *American Journal of Respiratory and Critical Care Medicine* 3, no. 3 (1995): 669–674; "A Regulatory Steamroller," *Washington Times*, May 16, 1997, p. A20; "Secret Science," *Washington Times*, February 11, 1999, p. A20; Kenneth Smith, "EPA Has a Secret," *Washington Times*, May 13, 1999, p. A21; Joyce Howard Price, "Group Tries to Force EPA to Release Data; Shelby Unable to Get Pollution Figures," *Washington Times*, May 16, 1999, p. C3; Steven Milloy, "More 'Secret Science' at EPA," *Environment and Climate News* (Heartland Institute), July 1999, http://news.heartland.org/ newspaper-article/1999/07/01/more-%E2%80%98secret-science%E2%80%99-epa; Milloy, "The EPA's Secret Science," *FoxNews*, February 2, 2001, http://www.foxnews.com/ story/0,2933,833,00.html.

50. John Schwartz, "Research Law Fight: Right to Know, or to Squelch?," *Washington*

Post, April 5, 1999, p. A7; Philip J. Hilts, "A Law Opening Research Data Sets Off Debate," *New York Times,* July 31, 1999, p. A1; Platt's Inside Energy, "Congress Grills EPA's Browner Again over Proposed 'Soot and Smog' Rules," *Energy Report* 25, no. 20 (May 19, 1997).

51. "Regulatory Steamroller"; Rep. Tom Bliley, "Bliley Hints at Subpoenas against White House, Treasury, and DOT," *Congressional Press Releases,* May 9, 1997; Platt's Inside Energy, "Congress Grills."

52. "Regulatory Steamroller"; Price, "Group Tries to Force EPA"; Hilts, "Law Opening Research Data"; Cindy Skrzycki, "The Regulators; Data Disclosure; Business Wants to Breach a Stonewall," *Washington Post,* June 11, 1999, p. E1.

53. Hilts, "Law Opening Research Data"; Anthony J. Obadal, Counsel to the Associated Equipment Distributors, Testimony before the House Government Management, Information, and Technology Subcommittee of the Government Reform Committee, Hearing on "H.R. 88, Regarding Data Available under the Freedom of Information Act," 106th Congress, Serial No. 106-107, June 15, 1999. See also Naomi Oreskes and Erik M. Conway, *Merchants of Doubt: How a Handful of Scientists Obscured the Truth on Issues from Tobacco Smoke to Global Warming* (New York: Bloomsbury, 2010); David Michaels, *Doubt Is Their Product: How Industry's Assault on Science Threatens Your Health* (New York: Oxford University Press, 2008).

54. Hilts, "Law Opening Research Data"; Gary D. Bass, Testimony before the U.S. House Government Management, Information, and Technology Subcommittee of the Government Reform Committee, Hearing on "H.R. 88, Regarding Data Available under the Freedom of Information Act," 106th Congress, Serial No. 106-107, July 15, 1999.

55. Schwartz, "Research Law Fight"; Skrzycki, "Regulators."

56. Schwartz, "Research Law Fight"; Hilts, "Law Opening Research Data"; "RJ Reynolds Wants Data on 'Old Joe' Ads," *Morning Edition,* National Public Radio, May 20, 1992; Paul M. Fischer, Meyer P. Schwartz, John W. Richards, Jr., Adam O. Goldstein, and Tina H. Rojas, "Brand Logo Recognition by Children Aged 3 to 6 Years," *Journal of the American Medical Association* 266 (1991): 3145–3148. Fischer's concerns about the impact of cigarette marketing were sparked by something his two-year-old son said in his nonsmoking home: "When I grow up, I want to drive fast cars and smoke cigarettes." See http://www.cpcfamilymedicine.com/Physicians/fischer.htm, accessed July 6, 2012.

57. Schwartz, "Research Law Fight"; Jane E. Brody, "Smoking among Children Is Linked to Cartoon Camel in Advertisements," *New York Times,* December 11, 1991, p. D22.

58. Hilts, "Law Opening Research Data"; "Legal Constraints on How Scientists Do Science," *Talk of the Nation,* National Public Radio, February 14, 2003.

59. Schwartz, "Research Law Fight."

60. Hilts, "Law Opening Research Data"; Schwartz, "Research Law Fight"; Gina Kolata, "Heart Attacks May Have Tie to Drug Type," *New York Times,* March 12, 1995, p. A27. Some corporations objected to the bill as written for other reasons, including (1)

costs of collecting, storing, organizing, and sending the information; (2) sensitive commercial information accessible to competitors (e.g., if a pharmaceutical company worked with a university on a clinical trial); and (3) exposure of other nonpatented intellectual property. See also Skrzycki, "Regulators"; Paulette Walker Campbell and Jeffrey Selingo, "Scientists Say U.S. Rules on Access to Research Records Are Better Than They Feared," *Chronicle of Higher Education*, October 22, 1999, p. A40. Some of the opponents recognized and embraced the basic idea that data sharing enhances peer review and replication processes, especially in studies like Pope et al.'s where subjects were interviewed repeatedly over decades. Because of all of the costs and obstacles involved in replicating those kinds of longitudinal studies, data sharing might be appropriate. However, as the president of the American Association of Universities put it, "FOIA is really a blunt instrument when it comes to striking the right balance" between data sharing and confidentiality. See Hilts, "Law Opening Research Data"; Schwartz, "Research Law Fight" (and correction of April 7, 1999), p. A2.

61. Public Law 105-277 (October 21, 1998), 112 Stat. 2681-495 ("Federal awarding agencies to ensure that all data produced under an award will be made available to the public through the procedures established under the Freedom of Information Act"); OMB, "Request for Comments on Clarifying Changes to Proposed Revision on Public Access to Research Data," http://www.whitehouse.gov/omb/fedreg_2ndnotice-a110, accessed August 2, 2011. See also Campbell and Selingo, "Scientists Say"; OMB, "Uniform Administrative Requirements for Grants and Agreements with Institutions of Higher Education, Hospitals, and Other Non-profit Organizations," OMB Circular A–110, *Federal Register* 64, no. 195 (October 8, 1999): 54926–54930, http://www.gpo.gov/fdsys/pkg/FR-1999-10-08/pdf/99-26264.pdf; Sen. Richard Shelby, "Accountability and Transparency: Public Access to Federally Funded Research Data," *Harvard Journal on Legislation* 37 (2000): 369. The EPA soot and particulate regulations were unsuccessfully challenged in court. The Supreme Court eventually unanimously affirmed the EPA's authority to re-evaluate Clean Air regulations. See *Whitman v. American Trucking Associations,* 531 U.S. 457 (Supreme Court, 2001).

62. Jeff Brazil and Mark Platte, "Tower Warnings Ordered on 757s' Turbulence: FAA Order Follows Santa Ana Crash That Killed Five People," *Los Angeles Times,* December 23, 1993, http://articles.latimes.com/1993-12-23/news/mn-4820_1_wake-turbulence; Associated Press, "F.A.A. Reportedly Knew of Jet-Wake Peril," *New York Times,* January 5, 1994, p. A11; Jeff Brazil, "News Analysis: FAA's Policy Collision: Industry or Safety First?," *Los Angeles Times,* January 9, 1994, http://articles.latimes.com/1994-01-09/news/mn-10180_1_wake-turbulence; Brazil, "Officials Warned Years Ago of 757 Turbulence Danger," *Los Angeles Times,* February 13, 1994, http://articles.latimes.com/1994-02-13/news/mn-22544_1_wake-turbulence; Brazil, "U.S. to Probe FAA's Handling of Jet Turbulence," *Los Angeles Times,* June 11, 1994, http://articles.latimes.com/1994-06-11/news/mn-2794_1_wake-turbulence/2; Don Phillips, "FAA to Review Safety Order; Action on 757 Wake Turbulence Questioned," *Washington Post,* June 11, 1994, p. A11; Brazil, "Boeing Image a Fac-

tor in Action on 757 Wake: Documents Show FAA Concern Regarding Possible Effects of Safety Measures on Aircraft Maker," *Los Angeles Times,* July 28, 1994, http://articles.la times.com/1994-07-28/news/mn-20874_1_b-757-wake-turbulence. Another common accusation critics made against Clinton-Gore involved Dr. Andrew Keeler, an economist who worked with the White House's Council of Economic Advisers. Keeler accused the administration of deliberately adjusting economic models so that the predicted costs of greenhouse gas regulations would appear less expensive ("by taking every assumption that would bias them down"). If true, the charge should certainly deflate anyone's perception that the administration had a mostly unblemished, proscience approach. However, Keeler's accusation was tempered by an important caveat: the administration "made available all of the assumptions that went into its analysis." Anyone who wanted to could wade through them. See Revkin, "Bush vs. the Laureates."

63. Jeff Brazil, "FAA Ignored Warnings on 757 Jet Turbulence," *Los Angeles Times,* June 5, 1994.

64. Examining only an administration's violations misses the ways it has positively contributed to making government more transparent. For example, we might also point to Clinton-Gore's information-sharing initiatives in the Department of the Interior, the Department of Health and Human Services, and the EPA. See, e.g., Lawrence K. Altman, "U.S. Data on AIDS to Be Free," *New York Times,* January 25, 1994, p. C6; Bill Shapr and Elaine Appleton, "The Information Gap," *National Parks* 67, no. 11-2 (November–December 1993): 33–37.

65. Cass Peterson, "Experts, OMB Spar on Global Warming," *Washington Post,* May 9, 1989, p. A1; Philip Shabecoff, "Scientist Says Budget Office Altered His Testimony," *New York Times,* May 8, 1989, p. A1; Shabecoff, "White House Admits Censoring Testimony," *New York Times,* May 9, 1989, p. C1.

66. Peterson, "Experts, OMB Spar"; Shabecoff, "Scientist Says"; Shabecoff, "White House Admits."

67. Senate Commerce Subcommittee on Science, Technology, and Space Hearing on "Climate Surprises,"May 8, 1989, 101st Congress; "White House Alters Scientist's Conclusions," *Federal Times,* May 22, 1989; American Library Association (ALA), *Less Access to Less Information by and about the U.S. Government: A 1988–1991 Chronology* (Washington, DC: ALA Washington Office, 1992); Peterson, "Experts, OMB Spar"; Shabecoff, "Scientist Says"; Shabecoff, "White House Admits."

68. Steven T. Taylor, *Sleeping with the Industry: The U.S. Forest Service and Timber Interests* (Washington, DC: Center for Public Integrity, 1994); ALA, *Less Access.* On the hundreds of anonymous whistle-blowers, see Taylor, *Sleeping with the Industry,* p. 12.

69. Taylor, *Sleeping with the Industry*; Marynell Oechsner, Testimony before the House Committee on Government Operations, Subcommittee on Environment, Energy and Natural Resources, March 31, 1992; "Grizzly Bear Recovery," http://www.fws.gov/mountain -prairie/species/mammals/grizzly/, accessed July 9, 2012; Scott Sonner, "Scientists Do Battle with Their Bosses," *Associated Press,* April 7, 1992; Tom Kenworthy, "Voice in the

Wildnerness; Forestry Official Replies—7 Months Later," *Washington Post,* October 8, 1992, p. A19.

70. Taylor, *Sleeping with the Industry*; Oechsner, Testimony; Sonner, "Scientists Do Battle"; Kenworthy, "Voice in the Wilderness."

71. ALA, *Less Access*; Taylor, *Sleeping with the Industry*.

72. The timber industry still held sway over the FS, and the Congress, under Clinton-Gore, in part due to the influence of timber-state Democratic leaders like Tom Foley (D-WA). Taylor, *Sleeping with the Industry*; Brad Knickerbocker, "Endangered Species Act Faces Its Own Dangers," *Christian Science Monitor*, March 8, 1995, p. 3.

73. United Nations Security Council Resolution, 1991, 687 S-RES-687.

74. William Winkenwerder, Jr., "Case Narrative: US Demolition Operations at Khamisiyah; Final Report," U.S. Department of Defense, sec. D1, April 16, 2002, http://www.gulflink.osd.mil/khamisiyah_iii/, accessed August 6, 2012.

75. Sen. Donald W. Riegle and Sen. Alfonse M. D'Amato, "U.S. Chemical and Biological Warfare–Related Dual Use Exports to Iraq and Their Possible Impact on the Health Consequences of the Gulf War," Report of the Senate Committee on Banking, Housing and Urban Affairs with Respect to Export Administration, May 25, 1994, http://www.gulfweb.org/bigdoc/report/riegle1.html, accessed July 10, 2012; Philip Shenon, "Something in the Air; Gulf War Veterans in Navy Unit Tell of an Iraqi Chemical Attack," *New York Times,* September 20, 1996, p. A1; Simon Tisdall, "Iraq 'Used US Biotoxins in Gulf War'; Senate Report Says Evidence Shows Allied Troops Did Come under Chemical Weapons Attack," *Guardian* (London), February 11, 1994, p. 13. The National Security Archive obtained in 2002 a heavily redacted top secret CIA report from March 1991 (containing information up to January 15) saying, "We have strong indications that Iraq is prepared to use chemical weapons in any conflict with US forces over Iraq's invasion of Kuwait." See CIA, "Prewar Status of Iraq's Weapons of Mass Destruction," released December 2002, http://www.gwu.edu/~nsarchiv/NSAEBB/NSAEBB80/wmd04.pdf, accessed August 11, 2012.

76. Philip Shenon, "Range Is Expanded in Federal Search for Victims of Gas," *New York Times*, October 23, 1996, p. A1; Ian Urbina, "Troops' Exposure to Nerve Gas Could Have Caused Brain Damage, Scientists Say," *New York Times,* May 17, 2007, p. A20; Simon Tisdall, "US Launches Study of Gulf War Illness," *Guardian* (London), January 22, 1994, p. 13; Shenon, "Something in the Air"; Urbina, "Troops' Exposure"; Reuters, "Gulf War Syndrome Symptoms Linked to Brain Damage," *CNN.com*, November 27, 2000, http://archives.cnn.com/2000/HEALTH/11/27/gulfwar.brain.reut/.

77. Shenon, "Something in the Air."

78. Philip Shenon, "Report Is Sharply Critical of the Pentagon Inquiry into Troop Exposure to Nerve Gas," *New York Times,* September 6, 1996, p. A22; Shenon, "Deaf to Alarms; Czechs Say They Warned U.S. of Chemical Weapons in Gulf," *New York Times*, October 19, 1996, p. A1; Riegle and D'Amato, "U.S. Chemical"; Urbina, "Troops Exposure"; Persian Gulf War Illnesses Task Force, "Khamisiyah: A Historical Perspective on Related

Intelligence," April 9, 1997, http://www.gulflink.osd.mil/khamisiyah_ii/khamisiyah_ii_refs/n15en003/cia_wp.htm, accessed July 10, 2012. The Veterans Administration offers a "Gulf War Registry health exam, health care, and disability compensation for diseases related to military service," apparently for Khamisiyah victims. See http://www.public health.va.gov/exposures/gulfwar/medically-unexplained-illness.asp, accessed July 10, 2012.

79. CIA, "Khamisiyah: A Historical Perspective on Related Intelligence: Persian Gulf War Illnesses Task Force," 1997, http://www.fas.org/irp/gulf/cia/970409/cia_wp.html, accessed July 11, 2012; Research Advisory Committee on Gulf War Veterans' Illnesses, *Gulf War Illness and the Health of Gulf War Veterans: Scientific Findings and Recommendations*, Report by Department of Veterans Affairs advisory committee (Washington, DC: Government Printing Office, 2008), p. 146, http://www.va.gov/gulfwaradvisorycommittee/docs/GWIandHealthofGWVeterans_RAC-GWVIReport_2008.pdf.

80. Shenon, "Deaf to Alarms"; Ed Timms, "US Had Warning before Blowing Up Weapons; Log Cited Danger of Chemical Cache," *Dallas Morning News*, October 9, 1996, p. 1A. Jon Palfreman, "Was Khamisiyah a Cover-Up?," *Last Battle of the Gulf War*, PBS Frontline film, January 20, 1998, http://www.pbs.org/wgbh/pages/frontline/shows/syndrome/closer/khamisiyah.html, accessed September 7, 2011; Bill McAllister, "CIA Suspected in 1986 Iraqi Site Held Chemicals; Panel Probes Lack of Warning in Gulf War Action," *Washington Post*, March 19, 1997, p. A10. Yasuhiro Nakasone, "Avoiding the Pitfalls of a Perfect Victory," *Los Angeles Times,* April 3, 1991. Larry E. Cable, "Playing in the Sandbox: Doctrine, Combat, and Outcome on the Ground," in *The Eagle in the Desert: Looking Back on U.S. Involvement in the Persian Gulf War,* ed. William Head and Earl H. Tilford, Jr. (Westport, CT: Praeger, 1996), p. 175; Shenon, "Records Gap on Gulf War under Scrutiny," *New York Times,* October 9, 1996, p. A14.

81. The US government approved dual-use exports to Iraq through February 1989—well after Hussein's attacks on Iranians and Kurds. "U.S. Covertly Aided Iraq Despite Use of Gas," *New York Times,* August 18, 2002, p. A2; Jarrett Murphy, "U.S. and Iraq Go Way Back," *CBS News,* August 2, 2002; PBS Frontline, "The Arming of Iraq," September 11, 1990, http://www.pbs.org/wgbh/pages/frontline/shows/longroad/etc/arming.html. Before the Gulf War, many "hawks" argued the so-called Vietnam syndome had permeated American political culture since the United States left Saigon in defeat in 1975. For example, candidate Reagan in 1980 argued the dark collective memory of Vietnam had prevented the United States from using its military to do what was necessary in global politics. Ronald Reagan, "Peace: Restoring the Margin of Safety," speech to the Veterans of Foreign Wars Convention, Chicago, August 18, 1980, http://www.reagan.utexas.edu/archives/reference/8.18.80.html.

82. National Research Council, Committee on Gulf War and Health, *Gulf War and Health,* vol. 8, *Update of Health Effects of Serving in the Gulf War* (Washington, DC: National Academies Press, 2009).

83. Kim I. Mills, "Consumers Get Chicken 'We Wouldn't Feed to Our Dogs,'" *Associ-*

NOTES TO PAGES 241–246

ated Press, November 16, 1989; Judy Mann, "Hard Times at Perdue's Plant," *Washington Post,* March 10, 1989, p. B3.

84. Lamar James, "Chances Are 1 in 3 Chickens Bought at Store Contaminated, Report Says," *Arkansas Democrat-Gazette,* March 30, 1987; Lamar James, "Poultry Firms Cry Foul over TV News Program," *Arkansas Democrat-Gazette,* April 19, 1987; Food Integrity Campaign, "History of FIC," a program of the Government Accountability Project, http://foodwhistleblower.org/about/history-of-fic,accessed July 9, 2012; Arthur S. Brisbane, "Health, Safety Charges Put Poultry Industry under Broiler," *Washington Post,* July 26, 1989, p. A2.

85. Don Kendall, "Groups Say Too Many Dirty Birds Reaching Consumers," *Associated Press,* June 29, 1989; Patricia Picone Mitchell, "Can USDA Inspectors Do More with Less? Controversy Follows Plans to Revamp," *Washington Post,* January 9, 1991, p. E1; ALA, *Less Access.*

86. Kendall, "Groups Say"; Brisbane, "Health, Safety Changes."

87. Martin Tolchin, "Clinton Orders Hiring of 160 Meat Inspectors," *New York Times,* February 12, 1993, p. A23.

Chapter 8: Secret Science

1. Jeanne Mager Stellman, Steven D. Stellman, Richard Christian, Tracy Weber, and Carrie Tomasallo, "The Extent and Patterns of Usage of Agent Orange and Other Herbicides in Vietnam," *Nature* 422 (2003): 681–687; William A. Buckingham, Jr., *Operation Ranch Hand: The Air Force and Herbicides in Southeast Asia, 1961–1971* (Washington, DC: Office of the US Air Force History, 1982); Richard Severo and Lewis Milford, *The Wages of War: When American Soldiers Came Home—From Valley Forge to Vietnam* (New York: Simon & Schuster, 1989); William Booth, "Agent Orange Study Hits Brick Wall," *Science* 237 (1987): 1285–1286. On the question of whether the United States can be blamed for "state terrorism" with the use of Agent Orange (and other chemicals), see, e.g., Mark Selden and Alvin Y. So, eds., *War and State Terrorism: The United States, Japan, and the Asia-Pacific in the Long Twentieth Century* (Lanham, MD: Rowman & Littlefield, 2003). If it was indeed state terrorism, the goal would have been to minimize support for the Viet Cong, although the chemicals' horrific effects probably drove at least as many Vietnamese into the arms of the nationalist Communists.

2. Severo and Milford, *Wages of War,* pp. 360–361, 364–365; Mary McGrory, "Justice for Vietnam Veterans," *Washington Post,* May 9, 1989, p. A2.

3. Severo and Milford, *Wages of War*; Stellman et al., "Extent and Patterns of Usage"; National Research Council Committee on the Effects of Herbicides in Vietnam, *The Effects of Herbicides in South Vietnam: Part A—Summary and Conclusions* (Washington, DC: National Academies of Sciences Press, 1974). Congress in 1970 ordered the NAS to complete the study.

4. Wilbur J. Scott and John Sibley Butler, *Vietnam Veterans since the War: The Politics*

of PTSD, Agent Orange, and the National Memorial (Norman: University of Oklahoma Press, 2004), p. 105; Severo and Milford, *Wages of War,* p. 377. Some leading figures in the debate included journalists Bill Kurtis and Richard Severo, environmentalists like Barry Commoner, attorneys like Hy Mayerson and Victor Yannacone, and veterans themselves. The government did claim to have studied the matter, but no analyses examined a representative sample of the veteran population, and none examined how many veterans were exposed to the chemicals. It is also notable that Max Cleland, a disabled Vietnam War veteran, was at the helm of the VA during this period in the Carter-Mondale administration.

5. Dr. Young's July 22, 1980, testimony was cited in Severo and Milford, *Wages of War*, p. 379; testimony before the EPA Suspension Hearings on 2,4,5-T, 1980, pp. 9937, 10,014, 10,034.

6. Severo and Milford, *Wages of War,* pp. 383–386; Richard Severo, "Furor Looms at Herbicide Hearing," *New York Times*, November 18, 1981, p. A25. Though Congress had ordered the study in 1979, it was not until 1981 that the VA awarded $133,951 to Dr. Spivey and a colleague, Dr. Roger Detels, to begin the process.

7. Severo, "Furor Looms"; Severo and Milford, *Wages of War,* pp. 391–392; Richard Severo, [news brief], *New York Times*, May 8, 1980, p. A16.

8. Richard Severo, "V.A. Assailed on Delaying Agent Orange Study," *New York Times,* September 16, 1982, p. A25.

9. McGrory, "Justice"; Severo and Milford, *Wages of War*; Paula Yost, "Agent Orange Study Called Botched or Rigged," *Washington Post*, July 12, 1989, p. A6.

10. Yost, "Agent Orange Study." On the practice of cynically highlighting scientific uncertainty for political ends, see Michaels, *Doubt Is Their Product*; Oreskes and Conway, *Merchants of Doubt.*

11. Elmo Zumwalt, Jr., and Elmo Zumwalt III, "Agent Orange and the Anguish of an American Family," *New York Times Magazine,* August 24, 1986, pp. 32–40; Associated Press, "Elmo R. Zumwalt 3d, 42, Is Dead; Father Ordered Agent Orange Use," *New York Times,* August 14, 1944, p. A40. As the AP story indicates, Zumwalt IV's disorder may have been caused in part by a congenital defect.

12. Bill McAllister, "Ex-Admiral Zumwalt Claims Manipulation on Agent Orange," *Washington Post*, June 27, 1990, p. A2, emphasis added.

13. Bill McAllister, "U.S. Revises Agent Orange Stance; Veterans Affairs Chief Acknowledges Link to Some Cancers," *Washington Post,* May 19, 1990, p. A6. The VA now recognizes links between Agent Orange and a number of diseases. See http://www.public health.va.gov/exposures/agentorange/diseases.asp, accessed January 22, 2014.

14. Robert Emmet Hernan, *This Borrowed Earth: Lessons from the Fifteen Worst Environmental Disasters around the World* (New York: Palgrave Macmillan, 2010), pp. 45–71.

15. Ibid.; US Department of Justice (DOJ), *"U.S. v. Bliss* (Times Beach)," http://www .justice.gov/enrd/4397.htm, accessed April 4, 2012; Marilyn Leistner [former mayor of Times Beach], "The Times Beach Story," *Synthesis/Regeneration* (1995): 8, http://www .greens.org/s-r/078/07-09.html, accessed January 19, 2014.

16. Hernan, *This Borrowed Earth*; Brian Tokar, "Monsanto: A Checkered History," *Ecologist* 28, no. 5 (September–October 1998): 254–261; DOJ, *"U.S. v. Bliss* (Times Beach)."

17. Hernan, *This Borrowed Earth*; Tokar, "Monsanto."

18. Hernan, *This Borrowed Earth*; Tokar, "Monsanto"; Craig Collins, *Toxic Loopholes: Failures and Future Prospects for Environmental Law* (Cambridge: Cambridge University Press, 1998). NEPACCO was part of the larger Hoffman-Taff chemical company.

19. Hernan, *This Borrowed Earth*.

20. Ibid.; *US v. Northeastern Pharmaceutical and Chemical Company* 579 F. Supp. 823 (Western Missouri District Court, 1984). The official name of the Superfund law is Comprehensive Environmental Response, Compensation, and Liability Act.

21. It is worth noting that Nixon's reputation as a stalwart environmentalist is often overblown, and it is historically inaccurate. For example, even though he launched the EPA, he vetoed the Clean Water Act.

22. Hernan, *This Borrowed Earth*; David Burnham, "1965 Memos Show Dow's Anxiety on Dioxin," *New York Times,* April 19, 1983, p. A1; MacNeil/Lehrer Report, "Dioxin," *PBS's The MacNeil/Lehrer Report,* June 7, 1983.

23. Leistner, "Times Beach Story"; Collins, *Toxic Loopholes*; Hernan, *This Borrowed Earth.* The leaked document showed Reagan officials were quite dismissive toward career government scientists. Also, despite the CDC's determination that anything over 1 ppb demanded attention, the document showed the EPA only planned to act on sites over 100 ppb, including Times Beach.

24. DOJ, *U.S. v. Bliss*; Hernan, *This Borrowed Earth*; Tokar, "Monsanto."

25. DOJ, *U.S. v. Bliss*; Hernan, *This Borrowed Earth*; Tokar, "Monsanto." Lavelle was also charged with obstruction of justice. She ultimately was fined $10,000 and went to jail for six months. See Collins, *Toxic Loopholes.*

26. Rozell, *Executive Privilege,* p. 102. According to the White House, "Sensitive documents found in open law enforcement files should not be made available to the Congress or to the public except in extraordinary circumstances" (p. 102). Therefore, the administration argued the EPA should reject Congress's requests and defy their subpoenas.

27. Ibid.; U.S. Congress, *Investigation of the Role of the Department of Justice in the Withholding of Environmental Protection Agency Documents from Congress in 1982–1983,* House of Representatives, Committee on the Judiciary, 99th Congress, 1st session (Washington, DC: Government Printing Office, 1985); U.S. Congress, *Contempt of Congress,* Committee on Public Works and Transportation, House of Representatives, 97th Congress, 2nd Session (Washington, DC: Government Printing Office, 1982). The administration's lawsuit was *US v. The House of Representatives*, 556 F. Supp. 150 (DC District Court, 1983). Representative Levitas led the Subcommittee on Investigations and Oversight Committee on Public Works and Transportation.

28. Collins, *Toxic Loopholes,* p. 95; Mary McGrory, "This Stuff about Shredders at EPA Smells, in a Creepy Way; FUMES," *Washington Post,* February 15, 1983, p. A3; Mary

Thorton, "FBI Investigating Use of Shredders at Environmental Agency," *Washington Post,* February 16, 1983, p. A2.

29. *US v. Russell M. Bliss,* 667 F. Supp. 1298 (Eastern Missouri District Court, 1987).

30. World Health Organization, "Dioxins and Their Effects on Human Health," Fact sheet #225, May 2010, http://www.who.int/mediacentre/factsheets/fs225/en/, accessed January 22, 2014.

31. Donald Barnes, Alex McBride, Norbert Jaworski, Robert Harless, and Aubry Dupuy, "Status Report on the U.S. National Dioxin Study," *Chemosphere* 15, no. 9–12 (1986): 1401–1404; EPA Office of Research and Development, Office of Health and Environmental Assessment, "Health Assessment Document for Polychlorinated Dibenzo-P-Dioxins," EPA/600/8-84/014F, 1985, http://cfpub.epa.gov/ncea/cfm/recordisplay.cfm ?deid=38484; John S. Stanley et al., "PCDDs and PCDFs in Human Adipose Tissue from the EPA FY82 NHATS Repository," *Chemosphere* 15, no. 9–12 (1986): 1605–1612. The EPA by 1982 had also commenced its National Human Monitoring Program to analyze human tissue samples. See Environmental Working Group (EWG), "Dioxin—Timeline," http://www.ewg.org/dioxin/timeline, accessed January 13, 2014.

32. Maureen Smith, *The U.S. Paper Industry and Sustainable Production: An Argument for Restructuring* (Cambridge, MA: MIT Press, 1997); Associated Press, "Judge Backs Charges on Dioxin Report," *Spokesman-Review* (Spokane, WA), November 12, 1987, p. A7; *Carol Van Strum v. EPA,* 892 F.2d 1048 (Ninth Circuit Court of Appeals, 1990), ¶3.

33. "Opaque" is the government's own description, as of 2004. See DOJ Office of Information Policy, "Exemption 5," FOIA Guide, May 2004, http://www.justice.gov/oip/exemption5.htm, accessed October 9, 2013. The threshold standard was set in *NLRB v. Sears, Roebuck & Co.,* 421 U.S. 132 (Supreme Court, 1975), p. 149 (Exemption 5 should "exempt those documents, and only those documents that are normally privileged in the civil discovery context"). *Van Strum v. EPA*; Carol Van Strum and Paul Merrell, *No Margin for Safety: A Preliminary Report on Dioxin Pollution and the Need for Emergency Action in the Pulp and Paper Industry* (Washington, DC: Greenpeace, USA, 1987); James V. Hillegas, "Dioxin and Willamette River Pollution: A First Step into the Toxic Waters," *Historical Threads* (blog), May 18, 2011, http://wwwhistoricalthreads.blogspot.com/2011/05/dioxin -and-willamette-river-pollution.html. On business power, see Lindblom, *Politics and Markets*; Lindblom, "Market as Prison." Also see Hacker and Pierson, "Business Power."

34. Peter von Stackelberg, "White Wash: The Dioxin Cover-Up," *Greenpeace* 14, no. 2 (March–April 1989): 7–11.

35. Ibid.

36. *Van Strum v. EPA,* 680 F. Supp. 349 (Oregon District Court, 1987), 351; von Stackelberg, "White Wash"; *Van Strum v. EPA,* 892 F.2d 1048; *Van Strum v. EPA,* 972 F.2d 1348; Associated Press, "Judge Backs Charges." The discovery process yielded many more details about the collusion. For example, Alexander McBride, then chief of the EPA's water quality analysis branch, admitted in a sworn statement on May 2, 1988, that the industry specifically asked the EPA to stonewall Van Strum. The EPA finally published the

NDS on September 24, 1987, which environmentalists and many scientists believed had been watered down. Laurent Belsie, "Contaminant Traces: Sizing Up the Risk of Dioxin in Paper," *Christian Science Monitor,* September 25, 1987, p. 1.

37. Ann Mariano, "Proposal to Curb Data Elicits Strong Criticism; OMB Accused of Stifling Information," *Washington Post*, July 18, 1985, p. A21.

38. Associated Press, "V.A. Acts on Miami Hospital," *New York Times*, December 16, 1984, p. A30; Fred Schulte, "VA to Make Public Heart Surgery Report," *Fort Lauderdale Sun Sentinel*, April 30, 1985, http://articles.sun-sentinel.com/1985-04-30/news/8501160945_1_va-heart-surgery-ditzler-va-department, accessed July 18, 2012.

39. Joel Brinkley, "V.A. to Reduce Hospitals' Units in Heart Surgery," *New York Times,* August 12, 1986, p. A1; Margaret Engel, "Heart Death Rate High at District VA Hospital; Mortality at Such Facilities Nationally above Average," *Washington Post*, August 13, 1986, p. D1.

40. Brinkley, "V.A. to Reduce"; Engel, "Heart Death Rate High"; Margaret Engel, "VA Medical Director Quits amid Probe," *Washington Post*, August 9, 1987, p. A6; David Hasemyer, "Dr. John Ditzler, 88; Headed VA Hospitals," *San Diego Union-Tribune*, September 29, 2007, http://www.utsandiego.com/uniontrib/20070929/news_1m29ditzler.html, accessed July 18, 2012.

41. Brinkley, "V.A. to Reduce"; Engel, "Heart Death Rate High"; Engel, "VA Medical Director Quits"; Hasemyer, "Dr. Ditzler."

42. Associated Press, "V.A. Hospitals' Deaths Are Traced to Mistakes," *New York Times*, May 3, 1987, p. A26; Stewart Powell, "Veterans' Care: Condition Critical," *U.S. News & World Report,* June 2, 1986, p. 20.

43. In particular, he urged them to adjust the statistical confidence levels after the apparently unacceptable results, which was a departure from standard practice. See Bill McAllister, "VA Researchers Ordered to Report Fewer Problem Hospitals; Top Medical Officer Feared Unfavorable Comparison with Death Rate at Private Institutions," *Washington Post*, October 11, 1988, p. A1; Mariano, "Proposal to Curb Data."

44. McAllister, "VA Researchers Ordered to Report."

45. United States Government Accounting Office, "VA Health Care: Allegations Concerning VA's Patient Mortality Study," Report to the Chairman, Committee on Veterans' Affairs, US Senate, HRD-89-80, May 18, 1989, available at http://archive.gao.gov/d25t7/138789.pdf, accessed September 12, 2011; Barbara Vobejda, "GAO Finds No Evidence VA Medical Official Acted Improperly," *Washington Post*, June 6, 1989, p. A3.

46. McAllister, "VA Researchers Ordered to Report"; Associated Press, "Francis E. Conrad, V.A. Official, 51," *New York Times,* April 11, 1988, p. D13; News Services and Staff Report, "Arlington Man Fatally Stabbed at Chicago Apartment Complex," *Washington Post,* April 8, 1988, p. B6; Joan Cook, "John Gronvall, V.A. Official, Is Dead at 59," *New York Times,* August 7, 1990, p. B6.

47. Susan Okie, "VDT Study Endangered by OMB," *Washington Post,* June 4, 1986, p. A21; Okie, "Modified VDT Study to Proceed; OMB's Changes Draws Criticism," *Wash-*

ington Post, December 26, 1986, p. A21. It is not clear whether the proposed study would have looked at 4,000 women who had been pregnant or simply 4,000 women in general, some of whom had recently been or currently were pregnant. The study mentioned in Okie's piece was probably Marilyn K. Goldhaber, Michael R. Polen, and Robert A. Hiatt, "The Risk of Miscarriage and Birth Defects among Women Who Use Visual Display Terminals during Pregnancy," *American Journal of Industrial Medicine* 13, no. 6 (1988): 695–706. See also Suzanne Fournier, "Changes in VDTs Recommended by Study," *Globe and Mail* (Toronto), March 12, 1983; Philip J. Hilts, "Women's Groups Cite VDTs in Pregnancy Ills Clusters," *Washington Post,* March 3, 1984, p. A9; William D. Marbach and Jennet Conant, "Are VDT's Health Hazards?," *Newsweek,* October 29, 1984, p. 122; Don Colburn, "Eight Hours at a Desk; From Lighting to Pollution to VDTs, Office Health Issues Spark New Concerns," *Washington Post,* March 13, 1985, p. A13.

48. Okie, "VDT Study"; Okie, "Modified VDT Study"; Fournier, "Changes in VDTs"; Hilts, "Women's Groups"; Marbach and Conant, "Are VDT's Health Hazards?"; Colburn, "Eight Hours."

49. Okie, "VDT Study."

50. Ibid.

51. Okie, "Modified VDT Study."

52. Ibid.

53. Paperwork Reduction Act (44 U.S.C. § 3501–3521); John Shattuck and Muriel Morisey Spence, "The Dangers of Information Control," *Technology Review* 91, no. 3 (1988): 62–73; General Accounting Office, "Paperwork Reduction Act: New Approach May Be Needed to Reduce Government Burden on Public," GAO-05-424, 2005, p. 11; U.S. Senate Committee on Governmental Affairs, *Paperwork Reduction Act of 1995, Report to Accompany S. 244,* 104th Congress, 1st session, Senate Report 104-8 (Washington, DC: Government Printing Office, 1995), pp. 10, 21. President Reagan's Executive Order 12291 offered guidelines for the OMB, rules that would help officials review scientific proposals and regulations. EO 12291 was particularly controversial because of its emphasis on cost-benefit analysis for regulatory review, no matter the policy domain. Curtis W. Copeland, Congressional Research Service (CRS), "Changes to the OMB Regulatory Review Process by Executive Order 13422," Order Code RL33862, 2007, p. 2, http://www.fas.org/sgp/crs/misc/RL33862.pdf, accessed August 4, 2011.

54. "GAO Investigating OMB Meddling with Data Collection," *Library Journal* 112, no. 1 (January 1987): 28; Steven Waldman, "Watching the Watchdogs," *Newsweek,* February 20, 1989, p. 34.

55. Waldman, "Watching the Watchdogs"; OMB, "OMB Puts Children's Health at Risk with Data Quality Act," *OMB Watch,* April 4, 2005, http://www.ombwatch.org/node/2365; Alan B. Morrison, "OMB Interference with Agency Rulemaking: The Wrong Way to Write a Regulation," *Harvard Law Review* 99, no. 5 (1986): 1059–1074n28; Philip J. Hilts, *Protecting America's Health: The FDA, Business, and One Hundred Years of Regulation* (Chapel Hill: University of North Carolina Press, 2004), p. 222.

56. Waldman, "Watching the Watchdogs"; Philip Shabecoff, "Judge Bids U.S. Act on Gas Carcinogen," *New York Times,* January 7, 1983, p. A10; Pete Earley, "OSHA," *Washingon Post,* October 11, 1983, p. A13; Howard Kurtz, "OSHA Official Blocked Efforts to Restrict Chemical," *Washington Post,* November 1, 1983, p. A9; "OSHA Rejects Stiffer Rule on a Chemical," *Washington Post,* December 25, 1984, p. A17; David Burnham, "Suit Challenges U.S. in Revision of a Safety Rule," *New York Times,* April 10, 1985, p. A19; Burnham, "5 in Congress Assail Budget Office Role," *New York Times,* June 29, 1985, p. A8.

57. President Ronald Reagan, "Executive Order 12498—Regulatory Planning Process," January 4, 1985, http://www.archives.gov/federal-register/codification/executive-order/ 12498.html; David Burnham, "Budget Office Role in Reviewing New Rules Expanded by Reagan," *New York Times,* January 5, 1985, p. A7; Mary Thornton, "New Reagan Order Grants OMB Expanded Authority; Agency to Screen Proposed Regulations in Draft," *Washington Post,* January 5, 1985, p. A2; Waldman, "Watching the Watchdogs"; Nicholas Askounes Ashford and Charles C. Caldart, *Environmental Law, Policy, and Economics: Reclaiming the Environmental Agenda* (Cambridge, MA: MIT Press, 2008), p. 269.

58. Interview with James Hansen for "Hot Politics," *PBS Frontline,* April 24, 2007, http://www.pbs.org/wgbh/pages/frontline/hotpolitics/interviews/hansen.html.

59. To be sure, criticisms about excessive nuclear secrecy did occasionally arise. For instance, universities complained when the government forced them to discriminate against foreign academics who planned to collaborate with US scientists working on classified research. See, e.g., David A. Wilson, "Consequential Controversies," *Annals of the American Academy of Political and Social Science* 502, no. 1 (1989): 40–57 (esp. pp. 55–56); Wilson, "National Security Control of Technological Information," *Jurimetrics* 25 (1985): 109–129; Ruth Greenstein, "National Security Control of Scientific Information," *Jurimetrics* 23 (1982): 50; Edward Gerjuoy, "Controls on Scientific Information," *Yale Law and Policy Review* 3 (1985): 447–478.

60. Fred Jerome, "Gagging Government Scientists: A New Administration Policy?," *Technology Review* (August–September 1986): 24–26; David M. Rubin, "How the News Media Reported on Three Mile Island and Chernobyl," *Journal of Communication* 37, no. 3 (1987): 42–56; Dorothy Nelkin, "Risk Reporting and the Management of Industrial Crises," *Journal of Management Studies* 25, no. 4 (1988): 341–351. Because of the government's denial, it was never clear exactly why officials clamped down so aggressively after Chernobyl, and it remains unclear when they rescinded the gag order. Readers might be tempted to draw a comparison with Mikhail Gorbachev's handling of the disaster. One common historical interpretation, for instance, suggests his reformist *glastnost* (openness) policy was initiated in the midst of the crisis to facilitate information flows. However, the evidence indicates Gorbachev's government was even more restrictive after Chernobyl. Eventually, and after pressure, he did loosen the reins, but it was not as if the United States clammed up while the Soviets opened up. See, e.g., David Remnick, *Lenin's Tomb: The Last Days of the Soviet Empire* (New York: Vintage, 1994).

61. U.S.C. 2168(a)(1), emphasis added; Shattuck and Spence, "Dangers of Information Control."

62. The final regulations can be accessed at http://law.justia.com/cfr/title10/10-4.0.3.5 .13.html, accessed September 19, 2011. See, e.g., § 1017.6 (4–10), for some of the added exceptions. See also "Identification and Protection of Unclassified Controlled Nuclear Information," *Federal Register* 48 (April 1, 1983): 13988–13994; "Identification and Protection of Unclassified Controlled Nuclear Information," *Federal Register* 50 (April 22, 1985): 15818–15829; David Burnham, "Plan on Restricting Nuclear Data Arousing Wide Array of Protests," *New York Times*, August 16, 1983, p. A1.

63. Keith Schneider, "The Government Health Data That So Many Want to See," *New York Times*, July 23, 1989, p. D5; Robin Johnston, "How Safe Are US Nuclear Weapons Sites for Workers?," *Christian Science Monitor*, October 14, 1988, p. 3; Arthur C. Upton, "The Biological Effects of Low-Level Ionizing Radiation," *Scientific American* 246, no. 2 (1982): 41–49; Fred Tasker, "How Harmful Is Low-Level Radiation?," *Seattle Times*, March 31, 2011, http://seattletimes.com/html/health/2014636549_webradiate01.html.

64. Schneider, "Government Health Data." Eventually (in 1990), the Three Mile Island Public Health Fund agreed to an out-of-court settlement with the DOE. The fund gained exclusive access to data about 270,000 nuclear workers (less than the estimated 300,000 total). Thus, more citizens gained access to *some* of the data, and the data remained off limits to most. Stephen E. Fienberg, "Sharing Statistical Data in the Biomedical and Health Science: Ethical, Institutional, Legal, and Professional Dimensions," *Annual Review of Public Health* 15 (1994): 1–18, at 15.

65. George C. Wilson, "18 Injected in 1945 Plutonium Testing," *Washington Post*, February 2, 1976, p. A1; Arthur Kranish, "Plutonium Experiment," *Science Trends*, February 3, 1976, p. 128; Howard L. Rosenberg, "Informed Consent," *Mother Jones*, September–October 1981, pp. 31–44; Keith Schneider, "Severe Accidents at Nuclear Plant Were Kept Secret up to 31 Years," *New York Times*, October 1, 1988, p. A1; Eric Alterman, "The Plutonium Files," *Nation*, February 11, 2000, http://www.thenation.com/article/ plutonium-files. By 1994, the GAO uncovered the fact that "over 200 radiation tests and experiments have been identified involving over 210,000 test participants." See Frank C. Conahan, Assistant Comptroller General, National Security and Internal Affairs Division, GAO, Testimony on "Human Experimentation: An Overview on Cold War Era Program" before the Legislation and National Security Subcommittee, House Committee on Government Operations, GAO/T-NSIAD-94-266, 1994, http://archive.gao.gov/t2pbat2/ 152601.pdf. See also "American Nuclear Guinea Pigs: Three Decades of Radiation Experiments on U.S. Citizens," Report prepared by the Subcommittee on Energy Conservation and Power, House Committee on Energy and Commerce, 65-0190, November 1986; DOE, "Human Radiation Experiments: The Department of Energy Roadmap to the Story and the Records," 1995, http://www.hss.doe.gov/healthsafety/ohre/roadmap/index.html, accessed June 4, 2011; DOE, "Human Radiation Experiments Associated with the U.S. Department of Energy and Its Predecessors," Assistant Secretary for Environment, Safety,

and Health, http://www.hss.doe.gov/healthsafety/ohre/roadmap/experiments/index.html, accessed May 18, 2011. The accidents at Savannah included "[1] Fuel rods melted in 1970 after three attempts to restart a reactor following an automatic shutdown. [2] A reactor part melted in 1970, resulting in the exposure of 900 cleanup workers to contamination on and off for a three-month period. [3] In 1965, workers failed to respond properly to a cooling-water leak, taking actions that might have led to the release of reactor-core radiation. [4] A chain reaction almost went out of control in 1960 when technicians tried to restart a reactor." Johnston, "How Safe."

66. Michael D'Antonio, *Atomic Harvest: Hanford and the Lethal Toll of America's Nuclear Arsenal* (New York: Crown, 1993); Keith Schneider, "U.S. Studies Health Problems near Weapon Plant," *New York Times,* October 17, 1988, p. A1; Kathleen Kenna, "Living in the Shadow of Death," *Toronto Star,* January 3, 1991, p. A15; M. O'Neill, "Human Fallout as US Drops the Bomb," *Sunday Herald* (Scotland), March 25, 1990; Rick Bass, "Nuclear Secrets, Toxic Toll," *Washington Post,* December 30, 1993, p. C2; Andrew Goliszek, *In the Name of Science: A History of Secret Programs, Medical Research, and Human Experimentation* (New York: St. Martin's Press, 2003). Mark Pitzke, "Hanford Nuclear Waste Still Poses Serious Risks," *Der Spiegel,* March 24, 2011, http://www.spiegel.de/international/world/0,1518,752944,00.html.

67. O'Neill, "Human Fallout"; D'Antonio, *Atomic Harvest*. Investigative reports were featured in the *Spokesman Review* (Spokane, WA), the *Seattle Times,* the *Albuquerque Tribune,* and later the *New York Times.*

68. Matthew L. Wald, "Nuclear Panel Sees Deep '86 Cuts in Research," *New York Times,* April 18, 1985, p. A19.

69. Mark Crawford, "NRC Tries to Reduce Public Access," *Science* 10, no. 4700 (1985): 697.

70. Ibid.; "NRC Delays Action on Closed Hearings," *Washington Post,* January 21, 1986, p. A13. See Title 10, Code of Federal Regulations § 9.104, http://www.nrc.gov/reading-rm/doc-collections/cfr/part009/part009-0104.html, accessed August 7, 2011. Section (a) states, "Except where the Commission finds that the public interest requires otherwise, Commission meetings shall be closed."

71. Herbert Foerstel, speech delivered at the Secrecy in Science: Exploring University, Industry, and Government Relationships Conference, MIT, Cambridge, MA, March 29, 1999; Rep. John Conyers, "Uncle Sam Is Watching You," *Washington Post,* March 27, 1990, p. A27; Robert L. Park, "Restricting Information: A Dangerous Game," *Issues in Science and Technology* 5, no. 1 (1988): 62.

72. Pozen, "Mosaic Theory"; David Burnham, "Reagan Orders Action on Eavesdropping," *New York Times,* October 15, 1984, p. A20; The White House, "National Policy on Telecommunications and Automated Information Systems Security," NSDD 145, September 17, 1984, http://www.fas.org/irp/offdoc/nsdd145.htm, accessed June 4, 2011.

73. John M. Poindexter, "National Policy on Protection of Sensitive, but Unclassified Information in Federal Government Telecommunications and Automated Informa-

tion Systems," NTISSP No. 2, October 29, 1986, http://www.princeton.edu/~ota/disk2/ 1987/8706/870611.PDF, accessed June 27, 2011; CRS, 2003, [RL31845], p. 12, emphases added; Ross Gelbspan, "Reagan Seeks Controls on Database Access," *Boston Globe,* April 20, 1987; Robert Pear, "Washington Feeling Insecure about Non-secret Information," *New York Times,* August 30, 1987, sec. 4, p. 5; U.S. Congress Office of Technology Assessment, *Defending Secrets, Sharing Data: New Locks and Keys for Electronic Information,* OTA-CIT-310 (Washington, DC: Government Printing Office, 1987); Shattuck and Spence, "Dangers of Information Control."

74. David Burnham, "Pentagon Acts to Curb Science Parley Papers," *New York Times,* April 8, 1985, p. A15; Michael Schrage, "Scientists Defy Pentagon on Research Restrictions," *New York Times,* September 21, 1985, p. A11.

75. Gelbspan, "Reagan Seeks Controls"; Pear, "Washington Feeling Insecure"; U.S. Congress Office of Technology Assessment, *Defending Secrets*; Shattuck and Spence, "Dangers of Information Control."

76. Gelbspan, "Reagan Seeks Controls"; EPIC (Electronic Privacy Information Center), Computer Security Act of 1987, http://epic.org/crypto/csa/, accessed August 13, 2011. Efforts by scientists, librarians, and some in the information technology industry to resist the Reagan-Bush administration's efforts were becoming increasingly common before the CSA—for example, by refusing to disclose client names. The CSA's passage subdued the uncoordinated resistance movement.

Chapter 9: When All Else Fails

1. Larry Martz, Thomas M. DeFrank, and Howard Fineman, "The Road Back," *Newsweek,* May 19, 1986, p. 26; Sandy Grady, "Nixon Ran for Ex-President—and Won," *Montreal Gazette,* May 20, 1986, p. B3; Marvin L. Kalb, *The Nixon Memo: Political Respectability, Russia, and the Press* (Chicago: University of Chicago Press, 1994), p. 31. The "Who's Hot" issue of *Rolling Stone* (no. 474) was published on May 22, 1986. From 1948 to 2004, Nixon made the annual Gallup list twenty-one times, beating President Harry Truman and Winston Churchill and only trailing people like Pope John Paul II and President Dwight Eisenhower by a few points. See Frank Newport, Jeffrey M. Jones, and Lydia Saad, "Ronald Reagan from the People's Perspective: A Gallup Poll Review," Gallup Organization, 2004, http://www.gallup.com/poll/11887/Ronald-Reagan-From-Peoples-Perspective-Gallup -Poll-Review.aspx. See also Michael Schudson, *Watergate in American Memory: How We Remember, Forget, and Reconstruct the Past* (New York: Basic Books, 1993).

2. David Greenberg, *Nixon's Shadow: The History of the Image* (New York: W. W. Norton, 2004), p. 290; Bill Moyers, *The Secret Government: The Constitution in Crisis* (Santa Ana, CA: Seven Locks Press, 1988); "Nicaragua Policy Endorsed by Nixon," *New York Times,* April 22, 1986, p. A17; Carroll Kilpatrick, "Nixon Tells Editors, 'I'm Not a Crook,'" *Washington Post,* November 18, 1973, p. A1. There are many examples of document destruction during the Nixon presidency (and before). For example, as Nixon's team

in 1970 began initial preparations for the 1973 coup d'état in Chile against newly elected President Salvador Allende, Secretary of State William Rogers told Kissinger in 1970, "Whatever we do . . . we want to be sure the paper record doesn't look bad. . . . So our paper work should be done carefully"—in essence, avoid obviously incriminating language, just in case. Although the CIA apparently did not get the message, as its (inexplicably unshredded and unburned) documents years later directly implicated Nixon's White House in the coup, Kissinger was careful enough to destroy the audiotape of his conversation with Rogers. But he forgot to do the same with the transcript, perhaps assuming, in the closed government environment of 1970, it would never see the light of day. Audio transcript of telephone conversation ("Telecon") between Rogers and Kissinger, September 14, 1970, http://www.gwu.edu/~nsarchiv/NSAEBB/NSAEBB255/19700912-1215-Rogers3 .pdf, accessed June 11, 2012. Other examples from the period include: the CIA's 1973 destruction of documents related to its now infamous MKULTRA program, in which it conducted "behavior modification experiments" on people without their knowledge or consent; the CIA's destruction of original documents that detailed the US government's role in the 1953 coup d'état in Iran that overthrow Mohammad Mosaddegh, the democratically elected prime minister; and the Joint Chiefs of Staff's efforts in 1974 to destroy all of its meeting records from 1947 on. See Doyle, "End of Secrecy."

3. Nancy Benac, "Trouble Can Lead to Shredding Impulse," *Associated Press,* January 22, 2002; Ellsberg, *Secrets,* pp. 37–38, 446–447. Burn bags are still commonly used in government and are perfectly legitimate for destroying reproduced classified documents. Indeed, regulations require staffers in some agencies to make frequent use of burn bags.

4. Nixon did order H. R. Halderman, the White House chief of staff, to destroy the tapes on April 18, 1973, immediately after they learned White House counsel John W. Dean III began cooperating with prosecutors. ("I'd like for you to take all these tapes, if you wouldn't mind. . . . I'd like to—there's some material in there that's probably worth keeping. . . . Most of it is worth destroying. Would you like—would you do that?") Halderman agreed to do it but then did not follow the order. He resigned later that month at Nixon's request, apparently for his central role in the Watergate operation. See George Larnder, Jr., and Walter Pincus, "Nixon Ordered Tapes Destroyed," *Washington Post,* October 30, 1997, p. A1; Ken Hughes, "Why Didn't Nixon Burn the Tapes?," Miller Center, University of Virginia, n.d., http://millercenter.org/presidentialclassroom/exhibits/why-didnt-nixon-burn -the-tapes, accessed June 21, 2013. See also Benac, "Trouble"; Ken Hughes, "The Tapes That Destroyed Nixon," *Washington Post,* December 6, 1997, p. A25.

5. "Highlights of Testimony by Hall and Sciaroni," *Washington Post,* June 9, 1987, p. A14; "The Iran-Contra Hearings: The Eighth Week," *Washington Post*, July 10, 1987, p. A16; Tom Blanton, ed., *White House E-mail: The Top Secret Computer Messages the Reagan-Bush White House Tried to Destroy* (New York: W. W. Norton, 1995); Lawrence E. Walsh, *Final Report of the Independent Counsel for Iran/Contra Matters,* vol. 1, *Investigations and Prosecutions,* U.S. Court of Appeals for the District Court of Columbia Circuit, Division No. 86-6, chap. 2 ("United States v. Oliver L. North"), August 4, 1993, http://www

.fas.org/irp/offdocs/walsh/chap_02.htm, accessed September 16, 2012. North came up with the phrase *shredding party* when discussing what happened with former national security adviser Robert McFarlane (1983–1985). Finally, the White House decided to fund the Contras covertly and illegally because the Boland Amendment, passed in Congress from 1982 to 1984, forbade the president from assisting the human rights–abusing paramilitary group.

6. "Highlights of Testimony"; "The Iran-Contra Hearings"; Blanton, *White House E-Mail*; Walsh, *Final Report.*

7. Walsh, *Final Report*; Oliver L. North and William Novak, *Under Fire: An American Story* (New York: HarperCollins, 1991), p. 15; Curt Suplee, "North and Our Hunger for a Hero: A Fading Camelot Seeks Shining Knights and Mythic Salvation," *Washinton Post,* July 19, 1987, p. C1.

8. Andrew Rosenthal, "The North Trial Papers: A Window on the Effort to Circumvent Congress," *New York Times*, April 14, 1989, p. A16; Peter Frier, "Poindexter Denies Conspiracy Cover-Up," *Christian Science Monitor*, July 17, 1987, p. 32; Larry Martz, Robert Parry, Thomas M. Defrank, and Eleanor Clift, "Taking Blame," *Newsweek*, July 27, 1988, p. 14; Dan Morgan and Walter Pincus, "Roots of the Cover-Up Remain Unexplored; Iran Probers Fail to Press Poindexter," *Washington Post*, July 20, 1987, p. A1. The president's professed innocence and isolation was called into question not only by Poindexter but also by North just a few years later: "Ronald Reagan knew of and approved a great deal of what went on with both the Iranian initiative and private efforts on behalf of the contras and he received regular, detailed briefings on both. . . . I have no doubt that he was told about the use of residuals for the Contras, and that he approved it. Enthusiastically." Presumably, Reagan at that point regretted he called North a "national hero" in the thick of the scandal. See David Johnston, "North Says Reagan Knew of Iran Deal," *New York Times,* October 20, 1991, p. A1.

9. President Bush in 1992 pardoned Weinberger, McFarlane, Elliott Abrams (State), Duane Clarridge (CIA), Alan Fiers (CIA), and Clair George (CIA). For details about the immunity deals and the consequences in the criminal cases, see Walsh, *Final Report.* On the problem of elite immunity for constitutional democracy, in this and other cases, see Glenn Greenwald, *With Liberty and Justice for Some: How the Law Is Used to Destroy Equality and Protect the Powerful* (New York: Metropolitan Books, 2011).

10. "THE PARDONS; Independent Counsel's Statement on the Pardons," *New York Times,* December 25, 1991, p. A22.

11. Blanton, *White House E-mail*; Thomas S. Blanton, "Information Ethics and Government Power: From the White House E-mail to the Stasi Files," in *Libraries and Democracy: The Cornerstones of Liberty,* ed. Nancy C. Kranich (Chicago: ALA Editions, 2001).

12. Blanton, *White House E-mail*; Blanton, "Information Ethics."

13. Blanton, *White House E-mail*; Blanton, "Information Ethics."

14. Blanton, *White House E-mail*; Blanton, "Information Ethics."

15. Blanton, *White House E-mail*, p. 8; George Lardner, Jr., "White House Barred from

Destroying NSC Files," *Washington Post,* January 20, 1989, p. A4; Michael York, "Court Bars Destruction of Records; White House Plan on Its Computer Data Ruled to Be Illegal," *Washington Post,* January 7, 1993, p. A1.

16. Blanton, *White House E-mail;* Barilleaux and Rozell, *Power and Prudence,* pp. 81–83.

17. Bush's son, future president George W. Bush, first offered Wilson the job in mid-December 1992. Wilson told the younger Bush he was not interested. Apparently, "no" was not an option: Bush responded by saying Wilson would likely hear from the president directly, since "the President was interested" in hiring him. Associated Press, "Archivist Says He Talked to Bush about Job before Deal on Tapes," *New York Times,* May 3, 1993, p. A22. Also see Blanton, *White House E-mail;* Blanton, "Information Ethics"; Barilleaux and Rozell, *Power and Prudence,* pp. 81–83; "Losing the Paper Chase," *New York Times,* July 9, 1993, p. A12; Michael Precker, "A Legacy and a Library," *Dallas Morning News,* August 8, 1993, p. 1F. The packing operation on inauguration eve was so rushed and harried that they ran out of bubble wrap and did not have time to buy more, violating NARA rules for proper record storage. Finally, the Bureau of Labor Statistics's "CPI Inflation Calculator" estimated 1993 to 2012 dollars. See http://www.bls.gov/data/ inflation_calculator.htm, accessed August 24, 2012.

18. George Lardner, Jr., "White House, Archivist Held in Civil Contempt; Judge Threatens Fines over Handling of Records," *Washington Post,* May 22, 1993, p. A3; Blanton, *White House E-mail.*

19. Blanton, *White House E-mail.*

20. Memorandum from William J. Clinton to Anthony Lake and William H. Itoh, "Access to NSC Records," March 24, 1994, http://www.gwu.edu/~nsarchiv/nsa/DOCU MENT/940411.htm, accessed September 6, 2012; Blanton, *White House E-mail;* Douglas Jehl, "White House Curbs Access to Security Council's Data," *New York Times,* March 26, 1994, p. A6; Jim McGee, "Clinton Tries to Limit Access to NSC Data," *Washington Post,* March 26, 1994, p. A7; Toni Locy, "NSC Not Subject to Information Act, Court Rules," *Washington Post,* August 3, 1996, p. A3; Althan Theoharis, *A Culture of Secrecy: The Government versus the People's Right to Know* (Lawrence: University Press of Kansas, 1998).

21. Toni Locy, "Judge Orders Opening of NSC E-mail Records; Agency Ruled Subject to Access Guidelines," *Washington Post,* February 15, 1995, p. A6; Blanton, *White House E-mail.*

22. Locy, "NSC Not Subject"; *Armstrong v. Executive Office of the President,* 90 F.3d 553 (DC Appeals Court, 1996). Clinton-Gore probably took some inspiration from Reagan-Bush, which in 1985 convinced the same appeals court to grant the president's Council of Economic Advisers similar protections from FOIA. See *Rushforth v. Council of Economic Advisers,* 762 F.2d 1038 (DC Appeals Court, 1985).

23. Jerry Seper, "Watchdog Group Seeks Records of Brown's Travel; Court Asked to Order Compliance," *Washington Times,* January 20, 1995, p. A3; Bill Miller, "Judge Assails Shredding in Commerce Case," *Washington Post,* December 23, 1998, p. A4.

24. George Archibald, "Papers on Fund Raising Trashed, Note Taker Says," *Wash-*

ington Times, December 6, 1996, p. A1; Toni Locy, "Ex-Aide Says She Discarded Notes on Brown's Trade Trips," *Washington Post,* December 7, 1996, p. A11; Archibald, "Judge Seizes Computers of Huang, 3 Others; Search Planned for Erased Notes," *Washington Times,* December 7, 1996, p. A1.

25. Archibald, "Papers on Fund Raising"; Locy, "Ex-Aide Says She Discarded Notes"; Locy, "NSC Not Subject"; Archibald, "Judge Seizes Computers."

26. E-mail from Nina Wilson to author, March 5, 2013, MLIS, Howard University Libraries. The Library of Congress, however, acquired the Ronald Harmon Brown Papers from his wife and children between 2006 and 2010. See http://international.loc.gov/service/mss/eadxmlmss/eadpdfmss/uploaded_pdf/ead_pdf_21_february_2013/ms012197.pdf, accessed March 5, 2013. Miller, "Judge Assails Shredding"; *Judicial Watch v. Dept. of Commerce,* Civ.A. 95-133(RCL) (DC District Court, 1998) [Judge Lamberth's Memorandum Opinion], http://www.judicialwatch.org/cases/2/113.asp, accessed October 21, 2012.

27. *Judicial Watch v. Dept. of Commerce*; Thomas Fitton [Judicial Watch president], "Public Service Denied" (letter to the editor), *Washington Post,* January 23, 1999, p. A20.

28. Savage, *Takeover,* p. 9; Bob Woodward, "Cheney Upholds Power of the Presidency," *Washington Post,* January 20, 2005, p. A7.

29. Mayer, *Dark Side,* p. 74; Frank Lindh, "America's 'Detainee 001'—The Persecution of John Walker Lindh," *Observer* (London), July 9, 2011, p. 9; USA Today/CNN/Gallup Poll results, *USA Today,* January 28, 2002, http://www.usatoday.com/news/poll008.htm, accessed July 12, 2012.

30. Lindh's request for a lawyer was documented in a navy medic's official cable, written immediately after their first meeting. Mayer, *Dark Side*; Lindh, "America's 'Detainee 001.'"

31. Mayer, *Dark Side.*

32. Ibid.; Lindh, "America's 'Detainee 001.'"

33. Mayer, *Dark Side*; Jesselyn Radack, "Whistleblowing in Washington," *Reform Judaism* (Spring 2006), http://reformjudaismmag.org/Articles/index.cfm?id=1104; Laurie Abraham, "Anatomy of a Whistleblower," *Mother Jones,* January–February 2004, http://www.motherjones.com/politics/2004/01/anatomy-whistleblower; Scott Horton, "Justice's Vendetta against a Whistleblower: Six Questions for Jesselyn Radack," *Harper's Magazine,* February 23, 2010, http://harpers.org/archive/2010/02/hbc-90006592; Anthony D. Romero and Dina Temple-Raston, *In Defense of Our America: The Fight for Civil Liberties in the Age of Terror* (New York: HarperCollins, 2009); "Examining the Emails," *Newsweek* (web exclusive), June 15, 2002, http://www.msnbc.msn.com/id/3067190/t/examining-e-mail/#.TrqzhPQr1tM; Attorney General John Ashcroft, "John Walker Lindh Press Conference," Attorney General Transcript, DOJ Conference Center, January 15, 2002, http://www.fas.org/irp/news/2002/01/ag011502.html, accessed July 15, 2012.

34. Mayer, *Dark Side*; Radack, "Whistleblowing in Washington"; Abraham, "Anatomy of a Whistleblower"; Horton, "Justice's Vendetta."

35. Mayer, *Dark Side*; Radack, "Whistleblowing in Washington"; Abraham, "Anatomy of a Whistleblower"; Horton, "Justice's Vendetta."

36. Mayer, *Dark Side*; Radack, "Whistleblowing in Washington"; Abraham, "Anatomy of a Whistleblower"; Horton, "Justice's Vendetta."

37. Mayer, *Dark Side*; Radack, "Whistleblowing in Washington"; Abraham, "Anatomy of a Whistleblower"; Horton, "Justice's Vendetta."

38. Bybee, "Standards of Conduct for Interrogation under 18 U.S.C. §§ 2340-2340A." The administration did "scrub" the Bybee memo once Jack Goldsmith took control of the OLC. However, because many of the Bush-era OLC memos remain secret, we cannot know whether the newer ones granted the president similar types of authority. Priest and Smith, "Memo Offered Justification"; Department of Justice Office of Professional Responsibility [OPR], "Investigation into the Office of Legal Counsel's Memoranda Concerning Issues Relating to the Central Intelligence Agency's Use of 'Enhanced Interrogation Techniques' on Suspected Terrorists," OPR report, July 29, 2009, https://www.aclu.org/files/pdfs/natsec/opr20100219/20090729_OPR_Final_Report_with_20100719_declassifications_annotated.pdf, accessed April 16, 2014; White House Daily Briefing (2004 WLNR 2608695), June 22, 2004, cited in OPR, "Investigation"; Toni Locy and Joan Biskupic, "Interrogation Memo to Be Replaced," *USA Today*, June 23, 2004, p.2A. On Yoo's comments, see Nat Hentoff, "Don't Ask, Don't Tell," *Village Voice*, January 24, 2006, http://www.villagevoice.com/2006-01-24/news/don-t-ask-don-t-tell/. On criticism of the memo, see Scott Higham, "Law Experts Condemn U.S. Memos on Torture," *Washington Post*, August 5, 2004, p. A4; Mike Allen and Dana Priest, "Memo on Torture Draws Focus to Bush," *Washington Post*, June 9, 2004, p. A3; cf. Eric Posner and Adrian Vermeule, "A 'Torture' Memo and Its Tortuous Critics," *Wall Street Journal*, July 6, 2004, p. A22; all cited in OPR, "Investigation."

39. OPR, "Investigation"; Letter from Wolf to H. Marshall Jarrett, Counsel, OPR, June 21, 2004, and letter from Wolf to Glenn Fine, inspector general, http://wolf.house.gov/uploads/Interrogation_Letters.pdf, accessed November 14, 2011. Goldsmith was an influential internal (and later external) opponent of the OLC memos written by Bybee, Yoo, and some of their colleagues. See Goldsmith, Testimony. See also Thrall and Cramer, *American Foreign Policy and the Politics of Fear*.

40. OPR, "Investigation," pp. 1–5, esp. note 3.

41. The missing e-mail situation was not a factor in the OPR's recommendations. OPR, "Investigation"; Glenn Greenwald, "When Presidential Sermons Collide," Salon.com, March 25, 2010, http://www.salon.com/2010/03/25/obama_134/; Sam Stein, "Obama on Spanish Torture Investigation: I Prefer to Look Forward," HuffingtonPost.com, May 17, 2009, http://www.huffingtonpost.com/2009/04/16/obama-on-spanish-torture_n_187710.html.

42. Letter from Paul M. Wester, Jr., to Jeanette Plante, DOJ Office of Records Management Policy, February 24, 2010, http://www.fas.org/sgp/news/2010/02/nara022410.pdf, accessed November 4, 2011; Letter from Anne L. Weismann, Chief Counsel of

CREW, to Paul M. Wester, April 19, 2010, http://crew.3cdn.net/a5a3e73b83b5e56f21_
ram6y93q4.pdf, accessed November 14, 2011. NARA's obligation, 36 CFR 1230.16(b),
http://www.archives.gov/about/regulations/part-1230.html; David Luban, "David Margolis Is Wrong," Slate.com, February 22, 2010, http://www.slate.com/articles/news_and_
politics/jurisprudence/2010/02/david_margolis_is_wrong.html, accessed November 9,
2011; Michael Isikoff, "Archives Demands DOJ Explain Missing E-mails," Newsweek
.com, February 25, 2010, http://www.thedailybeast.com/newsweek/blogs/declassified/
2010/02/25/exclusive-archives-demands-doj-explain-missing-e-mails.html, accessed November 9, 2011; Carrie Johnson, "Inquiry Sought into Disappearance of E-mails in Interrogations Case," *Washington Post,* February 27, 2010, p. A4. The first news story on the
missing e-mails, which only reports them in passing, appears to be Kasie Hunt, "Justice:
No Misconduct in Bush Interrogation Memos," Politico.com, February 19, 2010, http://
www.politico.com/news/stories/0210/33206.html, accessed November 14, 2011.

43. Senator Leahy, questioning of Gary G. Grindler for the Senate Judiciary Committee Hearing, "The Office of Professional Responsibility Investigation into the Office
of Legal Counsel Memoranda," Hearing 111-786, 111th Congress, Second Session, Serial no. j-111-75, http://www.gpo.gov/fdsys/pkg/CHRG-111shrg63193/content-detail
.html; Marcy Wheeler, "Yet Another Letter Asking about Lost Bush Emails," *Emptywheel,*
February 26, 2010, http://emptywheel.firedoglake.com/2010/02/26/archives-writes-
more-letters-asking-about-lost-bush-era-emails/, accessed November 9, 2011.

44. Letter from DOJ to NARA, (February 4, 2011, http://blogs.archives.gov/records
-express/wp-content/uploads/2011/02/2011-02-04-fnl-paul-wester-nara-signedwpd.
pdf, accessed November 14, 2011; Letter from Wester to Plante, February 15, 2011,
http://blogs.archives.gov/records-express/wp-content/uploads/2011/02/national-
archives-and-records-administration-feb-15-2011_2.pdf, accessed November 14, 2011;
Johnson, "Inquiry Sought"; Michael Isikoff and Daniel Klaidman, "A Slap on the Wrist,"
Newsweek February 8, 2010, p. 10; "The Torture Lawyers," *New York Times,* February
25, 2010, p. A32. No one who participated in destruction of government documents or
who helped the president contravene statutes with secret legal memos was ever punished.
Despite the OPR's conclusions, Yoo and Bybee were not punished. David Margolis, an
associate deputy attorney general, decided, in his January 5, 2010 "memorandum of decision," that the years-in-the-making OPR's conclusions about the OLC attorneys were
baseless. The conclusion that Yoo and Bybee were probably guilty of "intentional professional misconduct" would have required their state bar associations to initiate a formal
review of their status. Margolis's memo effectively overruled the OPR, downgrading the
charges against Yoo and Bybee to "poor judgment," which cleared the accused.

45. Office of the Inspector General [OIG], DOJ, *The September 11 Detainees: A Review of the Treatment of Aliens Held on Immigration Charges in Connection with the Investigation of the September 11 Attacks,* 2003, p. 40, http://www.fas.org/irp/agency/doj/oig/
detainees.pdf, accessed November 14, 2011; Peter Slevin and Mary Beth Sheridan, "Jus-

tice Dept. Uses Arrest Powers Fully; Scope of Jailings Stirs Questions on Detainees' Rights to Representation and Bail," *Washington Post*, September 26, 2001, p. A10.

46. OIG, *September 11 Detainees*, p. 111; Dan Eggen, "Audio of Attorney-Detainee Interviews Called Illegal," *Washington Post*, December 20, 2003, p. A2.

47. OIG, *September 11 Detainees*, pp. 149–150; Alan Feuer and Benjamin Weiser, "Translation: 'The How-To Book of Terrorism,'" *New York Times*, April 5, 2001, p. B1; Eggen, "Tapes Show Abuse of 9/11 Detainees; Justice Department Examines Videos Prison Officials Said Were Destroyed," *Washington Post*, December 29, 2003, p. A1.

48. OIG, *September 11 Detainees*, pp. 153–154; Eggen, "Tapes Show Abuse." One detainee, Javad Iqbal, challenged the conditions of his confinement in *Iqbad v. Hasty*, 490 F.3d 143 (Second Circuit Appeals Court, 2007). Iqbal's case eventually went to the Supreme Court as *Ashcroft v. Iqbal*, 556 U.S. 662 (Supreme Court, 2009). The cases mainly involved claims of qualified immunity by senior government officials. Investigators also identified many problems at the Passaic County Jail in Paterson, New Jersey. But only at the MDC did officials destroy videotapes. See, again, OIG, *September 11 Detainees*.

49. OIG, *September 11 Detainees*; Eggen, "Tapes Show Abuse"; Eggen, "Audio of Attorney-Detainee Interviews."

50. OIG, *September 11 Detainees*, pp. 149–150.

51. OIG, *September 11 Detainees*; Eggen, "Tapes Show Abuse."

52. OIG, *September 11 Detainees*; Eggen, "Tapes Show Abuse"; Eggen, "Audio of Attorney-Detainee Interviews"; Julian Borger, "Videos Prove Guards Abused 9/11 Prisoners: Cameras in a New York Detention Centre Recorded Officers Slamming Arabs and Asians against Walls," *Guardian* (London), December 20, 2003, p. A14.

53. Before the CBS and *New Yorker* pieces, other outlets reported on abuse at the prison. They did not present photographs, however. See, e.g., Thom Shanker, "Six G.I.'s in Iraq Are Charged with Abuse of Prisoners," *New York Times*, March 21, 2004, p. A14. See also Seymour M. Hersh, "Torture at Abu Ghraib," *New Yorker*, May 10, 2004 [this was available to online readers on April 30]; *60 Minutes 2*, "Abuse of Iraqi POWs by GIs Probed," April 29, 2004 , CBS News; for evidence showing the abuse was not simply the work of "bad apples," see Mayer, *Dark Side*; Karen J. Greenberg and Joshua L. Dratel, eds., *The Torture Papers: The Road to Abu Ghraib* (New York: Cambridge University Press, 2005).

54. The report, now widely available, is at http://www.npr.org/iraq/2004/prison_abuse_report.pdf, accessed November 18, 2011. Tabuga recognized Sanchez put him into an impossible position, with huge risks to his professional career: "I knew I was already in a losing proposition. If I lie, I lose. And, if I tell the truth, I lose." Hersh's 2004 report suggested the abuses were perpetrated by the 372nd Military Police Company. As the Taguba report notes, the "372nd MP Company, 320 MP Battalion in Iraq . . . are part of the 800th MP Brigade." See also Seymour M. Hersh, "The General's Report," *New Yorker*, June 25, 2007, pp. 58–69.

55. Timothy J. Burger and Douglas Waller, "Closing in on Tenet," *Time*, May 22, 2004,

http://www.time.com/time/magazine/article/0,9171,641078,00.html; Tony Capaccio, "Pentagon Promises Senate Panel 'Complete' Copy of Taguba Report," *Bloomberg*, May 26, 2004, http://www.bloomberg.com/apps/news?pid=newsarchive&sid=aUwJfqBxVqvk& refer=us; Steven Aftergood, "Torture Report May Have Broken Classification Rules," *Secrecy News*, May 5, 2004, http://www.fas.org/sgp/news/secrecy/2004/05/050504.html; Glenn Greenwald, "The Bush Administration's Terrible Luck with Finding Documents," Salon.com, April 12, 2007, http://www.salon.com/2007/04/12/lost_documents/.

56. Burger and Waller, "Closing in on Tenet"; Capaccio, "Pentagon Promises"; Aftergood, "Torture Report"; Greenwald, "The Bush Administration's Terrible Luck."

57. Capaccio, "Pentagon Promises"; Defense Department Operational Update Briefing news transcript, May 26, 2004, http://www.defense.gov/transcripts/transcript.aspx? transcriptid=3103, accessed November 24, 2011.

58. Sumana Chatterjee, "Key Documents Missing in Version of Abuse Probe Given to Congress," *McClatchy Washington Bureau*, June 14, 2004, http://www.mcclatchydc.com/ 2004/06/14/v-print/10408/key-documents-missing-in-version.html; "Chairman Warner Issues Statement on Taguba Report Certification," *US Fed News*, June 8, 2004; "Abu Ghraib, Stonewalled," *New York Times*, June 30, 2004, p. A22. The DOD also told the SASC that the Red Cross was still collecting information in the field, something that was irrelevant to the request for all Taguba-related documents.

59. The ACLU's archive of documents is available at http://www.aclu.org/torturefoia/ released/101904.html, accessed November 21, 2011. See also the University of Minnesota's Human Rights Library, which somehow obtained three of the "missing" annexes: http:// www1.umn.edu/humanrts/OathBetrayed/general-investigations.html, accessed November 21, 2011. On the media's disinterest in Abu Ghraib and torture before the election, see W. Lance Bennett, Regina G. Lawrence, and Steven Livingston, "None Dare Call It Torture: Indexing and the Limits of Press Independence in the Abu Ghraib Scandal," *Journal of Communication* 56 (2006): 467–486, esp. fig. 1 on p. 477. On how the scandal affected Bush's performance ratings, see Eric Voeten and Paul R. Brewer, "Public Opinion, the War in Iraq, and Presidential Accountability," *Journal of Conflict Resolution* 50, no. 6 (2006): 809–830, esp. table 2 on p. 822. On the other stonewalling, see National Security Archive, *The Interrogation Documents: Debating U.S. Policy and Methods*, July 13, 2004, http://www.gwu.edu/~nsarchiv/NSAEBB/NSAEBB127/.

60. Mayer, *Dark Side*, chap. 7; Michael R. Gordon, "A Nation Challenged: Bin Laden Lieutenant; A Top Qaeda Commander Believed Seized in Pakistan," *New York Times*, March 31, 2002, p. A12 (including "big fish"). On "smok[ing] them out," see R. W. Apple, Jr., "After the Attacks: Assessment; President Seems to Gain Legitimacy," *New York Times*, September 16, 2001, p. A6.

61. Mayer, *Dark Side*; Dana Priest, "CIA Holds Terror Suspects in Secret Prisons; Debate Is Growing within Agency about Legality and Morality of Overseas System Set Up after 9/11," *Washington Post*, November 2, 2005, p. A1; George Tenet, with Bill Harlow, *At the Center of the Storm: The CIA during America's Time of Crisis* (New York: HarperPe-

rennial, 2009), pp. 240–241; Frontline/World, "Mapping the Black Sites," *Extraordinary Rendition*, November 4, 2007, http://www.pbs.org/frontlineworld/stories/rendition701/map/; Committee on Legal Affairs and Human Rights, Council of Europe (Dick Marty, reporter), "Secret Detentions and Illegal Transfers of Detainees Involving Council of Europe Member States: Second Report," Document #11302 revised, Third-Part Session, June 11, 2007, http://www.assembly.coe.int/ASP/Doc/XrefDocDetails_E.asp?File ID=11555, accessed November 17, 2011.

62. Mayer, *Dark Side*; Scott Shane, "Waterboarding Used 266 Times on 2 Suspects," *New York Times,* April 20, 2009, p. A1. Government interrogators seemed to think repeated plays of Red Hot Chili Peppers songs would aggravate Zubaydah enough to force him to start talking. About a decade earlier, they blasted Van Halen to rattle Manuel Noriega. Aiming for something more disturbing, the government inflicted "death metal" upon Guantanamo prison detainees—certainly scarier than "When It's Love" and "Suck My Kiss." On the issue of waterboarding, as of early July 2002 CIA lawyers were instructing interrogators they could employ "all forms of psychological pressure discussed [at a Joint Personnel Recovery Agency training session in Survival Evasion Resistance and Escape (SERE) techniques] and all of the physiological pressures *with the exception of the water board.*" The lawyers had met with Ashcroft, Rice, Gonzales, and other White House officials back in May to discuss waterboarding and other EIMs, but it was not until July 26, 2002, that the OLC told the CIA it was about to release (on August 1) a secret legal memo that approved the technique for select detainees, including Zubaydah, despite the laws against torture. On waterboarding and the other EIMs, see Senate Intelligence Committee, "Declassified Narrative: OLC Opinions on the CIA Detention and Interrogation Program," April 17, 2009, http://intelligence.senate.gov/pdfs/olcopinion.pdf, accessed October 24, 2011; Senate Armed Services Committee, "Inquiry into the Treatment of Detainees in U.S. Custody," November 20, 2008, p. 21, http://armed-services.senate.gov/Publications/Detainee%20Report%20Final_April%2022%202009.pdf [released April 22, 2009], accessed October 25, 2011; Marcy Wheeler, "Torture Timeline," *Emptywheel,* http://emptywheel.firedoglake.com/timeline-collection/torture-tape-timeline/, accessed November 21, 2011; Shane and Mazzetti, "Tapes by C.I.A." The SERE techniques had previously been offered in training for US soldiers to prepare them for capture by hostile forces. The Bush-Cheney administration took the unprecedented step of adopting the feared enemy techniques for its own interrogations.

63. Inspector General, CIA, "Special Review: Counterterrorism Detention and Interrogation Activities (September 2001–October 2003)," Report #2003-7123-IG, May 7, 2004, p. 36 [Section 77]; Shane and Mazzetti, "Tapes by C.I.A"; Douglas Cox, "Burn after Viewing: The CIA's Destruction of the Abu Zubaydah Tapes and the Law of Federal Records," *Journal of National Security Law and Policy* 5 (2011): 131–177, at p. 135; Peter Taylor, "'Vomiting and Screaming' in Destroyed Waterboarding Tapes," *BBC News,* May 9, 2012, http://www.bbc.co.uk/news/world-us-canada-17990955.

64. Shane and Mazzetti, "Tapes by C.I.A."

65. Ibid.; Human Rights First, *Command's Responsibility: Detainee Deaths in U.S. Custody in Iraq and Afghanistan* (New York: Human Rights First, 2007), pp. 1, 18, http://www.humanrightsfirst.org/wp-content/uploads/pdf/06221-etn-hrf-dic-rep-web.pdf. Glenn Greenwald, "The Suppressed Fact: Deaths by U.S. Torture," Salon.com, June 30, 2009, http://www.salon.com/2009/06/30/accountability_7/. For an excellent political thriller about the tapes, see Barry Eisler, *Inside Out* (New York: Ballantine Books, 2010).

66. See the denied and partially released ACLU requests for a range of documents, including the CIA cable, "Risks of indefinite retention of videotapes" (8/20/2002) and the CIA cable, "Disposition of videotapes" (10/25/2002), http://www.aclu.org/files/assets/20091120_Govt_Para_4_55_Hardcopy_Vaughn_Index.pdf, accessed March 4, 2013. See also Cox, "Burn after Viewing"; CIA Director Michael Hayden, "Director's Statement on the Taping of Early Detainee Interrogations," December 6, 2007, https://www.cia.gov/news-information/press-releases-statements/press-release-archive-2007/taping-of-early-detainee-interrogations.html.

67. Shane and Mazzetti, "Tapes by C.I.A."; Cox, "Burn after Viewing"; Inspector General, CIA, "Special Review"; Mark Mazzetti and Scott Shane, "Bush Lawyers Discussed Fate of C.I.A. Tapes," *New York Times,* December 19, 2007, p. A1; CIA, "Timeline Regarding Destruction of Abu Zubayda Videotapes" (declassified), available at the National Security Archive website, http://nsarchive.files.wordpress.com/2010/05/torture-addington.pdf, accessed August 12, 2012; Mark Hosenball and Michael Isikoff, "Tracking a Paper Trail," *Newsweek,* December 24, 2007, p. 9.

68. Priest, "CIA Holds Terror Suspects"; Mazzetti and Shane, "Bush Lawyers"; Michael Isikoff and Mark Hosenball, "Fresh Questions about the CIA's Interrogation Tapes" *Newsweek,* May 18, 2009; Dan Eggen and Joby Warrick, "CIA Destroyed Videos Showing Interrogations," *Washington Post,* December 7, 2007, p. A1; Wheeler, "Torture Timeline." A heavily redacted version of the Rodriguez memo approving destruction can be found at http://nsarchive.files.wordpress.com/2010/05/torture-permission-to-destroy.pdf, accessed August 14, 2012. See also *Amnesty International et al. v. CIA,* FOIA document request, request #F-05-00498, F-06-01014, F-06-00994, http://ccrjustice.org/files/2008-4-21%20Declaration%20of%20Ralph%20Dimaio%20-%20Exh%20A3%20-%20CIA%20docs%20released.pdf, accessed July 24, 2012. According to the OIG report (p. 36), twelve of the ninety-two tapes contained EIM applications.

69. Priest, "CIA Holds Terror Suspects"; Mazzetti and Shane, "Bush Lawyers Discussed"; Wheeler, "Torture Timeline"; Isikoff and Hosenball, "Fresh Questions"; Eggen and Warrick, "CIA Destroyed Videos"; CIA Inspector General, "Special Review: Counterterrorism"; Dana Priest, "Former CIA Spy Boss Made an Unhesitating Call to Destroy Interrogation Tapes," *Washington Post,* April 24, 2012, http://www.washingtonpost.com/lifestyle/style/former-cia-spy-boss-made-an-unhesitating-call-to-destroy-interrogation-tapes/2012/04/24/gIQAkdTXfT_story.html.

70. Priest, "CIA Holds Terror Suspects"; Mazzetti and Shane, "Bush Lawyers Discussed"; Wheeler, "Torture Timeline"; Isikoff and Hosenball, "Fresh Questions"; Eggen

and Warrick, "CIA Destroyed Videos"; CIA Inspector General, "Special Review: Coun-terterrorism"; Priest, "Former CIA Boss."

71. See the ACLU's archive of released documents, April 2010, http://www.aclu. org/national-security/torture-foia-torture-documents-released-4152010, accessed July 5, 2012, and in particular the two e-mails to Dusty Foggo, featured on the National Security Archive website: http://nsarchive.files.wordpress.com/2010/05/torture-email-1. pdf and http://nsarchive.files.wordpress.com/2010/05/torture-email-2.pdf, both accessed July 5, 2012. See also Nate Jones, "CIA Agent Who Explained, 'The Heat from Destroy-ing [The Torture Videos] Is Nothing Compared to What It Would Be If the Tapes Ever Got into the Public Domain' Will Not Be Charged," *Unredacted*, November 10, 2010, http://nsarchive.wordpress.com/2010/11/10/document-friday-%E2%80%9Cthe-heat -from-destroying-the-torture-videos-is-nothing-compared-to-what-it-would-be-if-the -tapes-ever-got-into-the-public-domain-%E2%80%9D/#more-1588.

72. Jones, "CIA Agent"; Cox, "Burn after Viewing"; Mark Mazzetti and Charlie Sav-age, "No Charges Filed in Tape Destruction: C.I.A. Officers Let off Despite Wrecking Proof of Brutal Interrogations," *International Herald Tribune,* November 10, 2010, p. 7; Jerry Markon, "No Charges in Destruction of CIA Videotapes, Justice Department Says," *Washington Post,* November 9, 2010, p. A1; David Kravetz, "Judge Refuses to Sanction CIA for Destroying Torture Tapes," *Threat Level* (blog), October 6, 2011, http://www .wired.com/threatlevel/2011/10/cia-dodges-contempt; Jose A. Rodriguez, Jr., with Bill Harlow, *Hard Measures: How Aggressive CIA Actions after 9/11 Saved American Lives* (New York: Threshhold Editions, 2012), p. 193; Priest, "Former CIA Spy Boss." One of the stated justifications for not prosecuting Rodriguez and others was because the statute of limitations had expired, even though the investigation began in January 2008.

73. Thomas H. Kean and Lee H. Hamilton, "Stonewalled by the C.I.A.," *New York Times,* January 2, 2008, p. A17; Susan Schmidt and Dana Priest, "Alleged USS Cole Plotter Caught," *Washington Post,* November 22, 2002, p. A1; Inspector General, CIA, "Special Review," pp. 41–42; Joby Warrick and R. Jeffrey Smith, "CIA Used Gun, Drill in Interrogation; IG Report Describes Tactics against Alleged Cole Mastermind," *Wash-ington Post*, August 22, 2009, p. A1.

74. Dan Eggen and Susan Schmidt, "'Dirty Bomb' Plot Uncovered, U.S. Says; Sus-pected Al Qaeda Operative Held as 'Enemy Combatant,'" *Washington Post,* June 11, 2002, p. A1; Department of Justice, "Summary of Jose Padilla's Activities with Al Qaeda," June 1, 2004, http://www.fas.org/irp/news/2004/06/padilla060104.pdf, accessed August 6, 2011; *Rumsfeld v. Padilla,* Justice John Paul Stevens's dissenting opinion, June 28, 2004, No. 03-1027, available at http://www.law.cornell.edu/supct/html/03-1027.ZD.html, ac-cessed June 14, 2012.

75. *Rumsfeld v. Padilla*; Memorandum from President Bush to Defense Secretary Don-ald Rumsfeld, June 9, 2002, http://www.pbs.org/wgbh/pages/frontline/shows/sleeper/ tools/docprespadilla.html, accessed January 29, 2014; Curt Anderson, "Tape of Padilla Interrogation Is Missing," *USA Today,* March 9, 2007, http://www.usatoday.com/news/

washington/2007-03-09-padilla-tapes_N.htm. Despite strong support for the president, as well as the serious accusations about Padilla, 35 percent polled in an August 2002 national survey indicated they agreed with Bush's actions. About a year after the 9/11 attacks, 58 percent believed that "all American citizens are entitled to be represented by a lawyer and have their day in court." NPR, Kaiser Family Foundation, and Harvard Kennedy School of Government, "NPR/Kaiser Kennedy School Poll; Civil Liberties Update: Combined Results," August 2002, http://www.npr.org/news/specials/civillibertiespoll2/combinedtoplines.pdf, accessed January 29, 2014.

76. *Rumsfeld v. Padilla.* The court majority essentially concluded that Padilla's lawyer filed the petition in the wrong location (i.e., it should have been filed in a South Carolina court, where the brig was located, and against the brig commander). See the Virginia ACLU's summary of *Padilla v. Hanft* at http://www.acluva.org/docket/padilla.html, accessed July 28, 2011.

77. "The Fourth Circuit v. Mr. Bush," *Washington Post,* January 2, 2006, p. A12; Linda Greenhouse, "Justices Let U.S. Transfer Padilla to Civilian Custody," *New York Times,* January 6, 2006, p. A22.

78. James Risen and Philip Shenon, "U.S. Says It Halted Qaeda Plot to Use Radioactive Bomb," *New York Times,* June 11, 2002, p. A1; Alberto Gonzales, "Prepared Remarks of Attorney General Alberto R. Gonzales at the Press Conference Regarding the Indictment of Jose Padilla," November 22, 2005, http://www.justice.gov/archive/ag/speeches/2005/ag_speech_051122.html.

79. Michael Isikoff, "The Missing Padilla Video," *Newsweek,* February 27, 2007, http://www.thedailybeast.com/newsweek/2007/02/27/the-missing-padilla-video.html.

80. Ibid.; Letter from Laurence Brewer to DIA's Office for Information and Special Services, May 16, 2007, and Letter from DIA's Principal Deputy General Counsel to Paul Wester, December 6, 2007, available at http://www.fas.org/sgp/othergov/intel/padilla.pdf.

81. Rep. Henry A. Waxman, Opening Statement of the House Committee on Oversight and Government Reform Hearing on Electronic Records Preservation at the White House, http://oversight-archive.waxman.house.gov/documents/20080226102056.pdf; "Electronic Records: Clinton Administration's Management of Executive Office of the President's E-mail System," GAO-01-446, April 2001, http://www.gao.gov/new.items/d01446.pdf.

82. National Security Archive, "White House E-mail Chronology," April 17, 2008, http://www.gwu.edu/~nsarchiv/news/20080417/chron.htm.

83. Ibid.; NARA, "Summary of Jan 6, 2004, meeting with EOP re ECRMS at Archives II," n.d., http://www.gwu.edu/~nsarchiv/news/20080417/Summary%20of%20Jan%206,%202004%20meeting%20with%20EOP.pdf.

84. Microsoft Premier Support, "Post-mortem for Email Search," report prepared for the White House, February 2004, http://www.gwu.edu/~nsarchiv/news/20080417/20040200.pdf; National Security Archive, "White House E-mail Chronology." Although Cheney's chief of staff, I. Lewis "Scooter" Libby, was originally the main suspect

in the leak to *Washington Post* columnist Robert Novak, it later emerged that Deputy Secretary of State Richard Armitage was Novak's source. However, Libby did discuss Plame's identity with a reporter (Judith Miller of the *New York Times*). But he was convicted on obstruction of justice, perjury, and making false statements charges, which compelled him to resign.

85. Microsoft Premier Support, "Post-mortem for Email Search"; National Security Archive, "White House E-mail Chronology."

86. Subpoena to Office of the Vice President to Testify before Grand Jury (DC District Court, January 30, 2004), http://www2.gwu.edu/~nsarchiv/NSAEBB/NSAEBB215/govt_ex/GX05601.PDF; Memorandum from David Addington, Counsel to the Vice President, to Deputy Special Counsel Ronald Roos, February 2, 2004, http://www.justice.gov/archive/osc/exhibits/0129/GX05601.TXT; Marcy Wheeler, "Plame Investigation and Missing Emails: Analysis on Emails," *Emptywheel* (blog), January 21, 2008, http://emptywheel.firedoglake.com/2008/01/21/plame-investigation-and-missing-emails-analysis-on-emails/.

87. Memo from Addington to Roos; Wheeler, "Plame Investigation"; E-mail from Catherine Martin to Matt Cooper, July 11, 2003, http://static1.firedoglake.com/28/files/2008/01/us-v-libby-dx1639-martin-cooper-emails.pdf; Howard Kurtz, "Jeff Gannon Admits Past 'Mistakes,' Berates Critics," *Washington Post,* February 19, 2005, p. C1.

88. National Security Archive, "White House E-mail Chronology."

89. Libby was the one individual convicted of perjury and obstruction of justice as a result of Plamegate. Bush commuted his sentence. Dana Milbank and Susan Schmidt, "Justice Dept. Launches Criminal Probe of Leak," *Washington Post,* October 1, 2003, p. A1; Charlie Savage, "Ashcroft Steps Aside in Probe into CIA Leak," *Boston Globe,* December 31, 2003, p. A12; Wheeler, "Plame Investigation"; National Security Archive, "White House E-mail Chronology," 2008; Citizens for Responsibility and Ethics in Washington [CREW], *Without a Trace: The Story behind the Missing White House E-mails and the Violations of the Presidential Records Act* (Washington, DC: CREW, 2007); CREW, *The Untold Story of the Bush White House Emails* (Washington, DC: CREW, 2010). The OA study was eventually released to the public in early 2008 by Rep. Henry Waxman (D-CA). The "red" and "yellow" days were determined from this OA analysis: http://www.gwu.edu/~nsarchiv/news/20080417/20051100.pdf, cited in National Security Archive, "White House E-mail Chronology," and by Waxman.

90. National Security Archive, "White House E-mail Chronology."

91. Ibid.; Letter from Fitzgerald to William Jeffress, Theodore V. Wells, and Joseph A. Tate,, January 23, 2006, http://www.gwu.edu/~nsarchiv/news/20080417/fitz012306.pdf; Pete Yost, "Fitzgerald Suggests White House May Be Missing Records," *Associated Press,* February 2, 2006; NARA, "Chronology of White House Meetings," http://www.gwu.edu/~nsarchiv/news/20080417/NARA%20Chronology%20of%20White%20House%20Meetings.pdf.

92. Payton became CIO in May 2006. National Security Archive, "White House

E-mail Chronology"; E-mail from [redacted name] to [redacted name], Office of the CIO, "ECRMS into Production Plan," May 15, 2006, http://www.gwu.edu/~nsarchiv/ news/20080417/20060515.pdf.

93. National Security Archive, "White House E-mail Chronology"; [Redacted name], "ECRMS into Production Plan"; CREW, *Without a Trace*.

94. NARA, "Chronology"; Daniel Schulman, "Re: Those Missing White House Emails," *Political Mojo*, April 13, 2007, http://motherjones.com/mojo/2007/04/re-those -missing-white-house-emails; Michael Abramowitz, "Explaining Missing E-mails, Attorney Says Rove Thought RNC Saved Them," *Washington Post*, April 14, 2007, p. A2; "White House E-mail Mystery," *Washington Post*, April 14, 2007, p. A18; Press briefing by White House Deputy Press Secretary Dana Perino, April 12, 2007.

95. CREW, "CREW Sues White House Office of Administration over Refusal to Respond to FOIA on Missing Emails," May 23, 2007, http://www.citizensforethics.org/ index.php/press/entry/crew-sues-white-house-office-of-administration-over-refusal-to -respond-to-f; *CREW v. Office of Administration*, 1:07-CV-00964 (CKK) (DC District Court, 2007) ["Defendant's Motion for Judgment on the Pleadings and Memorandum Support"], http://www.scribd.com/doc/48128233/CREW-v-Office-of-Administration -Regarding-Lost-White-House-Emails-8-21-2007-OA-s-Motion-for-Judgement-on-the -Pleadings, accessed January 23, 2014.

96. *CREW v. Office of Administration*, p. 19; Dan Eggen, "White House Declares Office Off-Limits," *Washington Post*, August 23, 2007, p. A4.

97. Waxman, Opening Statement; National Security Archive, "White House E-mail Chronology," 2008.

98. Tony Fratto [(White House Spokesperson], "The White House Regular Briefing," *Federal News Service*, January 17, 2008; National Security Archive, "White House E-mail Chronology."

99. National Security Archive, "White House E-mail Chronology"; National Security Archive, "White House Admits No Back-Up Tapes for E-mail before October 2003, January 16, 2008, http://www.gwu.edu/~nsarchiv/news/20080116/index.htm; Del Quentin Wilber, "White House May Keep Documents in E-mail Flap Private," *Washington Post*, June 17, 2008, p. A3; Wilber, "Documents about Lost E-mail Can Stay Secret," *Washington Post*, May 20, 2009, p. A3.

100. The district attorney scandal, which ultimately led to White House counsel Alberto Gonzales's resignation, involved the White House's decision to fire seven federal district attorneys on December 7, 2006 (right after the 2006 midterm elections). The Bush-appointed attorneys were either investigating allegations of corrupt Republican officials or unwilling to begin investigations of Democratic officials. There was a curious "gap" in archival coverage from mid-November until early December 2006, which was the time when the White House discussed the firings and planned a public relations campaign ahead of the expected criticisms. See Mike Allen and John Bresnahan, "GOP Braces

for Testimony Fight, Likely Gonzales Exit," Politico.com, March 20, 2007, http://www .politico.com/news/stories/0307/3227.html. See also Stein, "Obama on Spanish Torture."

101. Michael Isikoff, "Archives Demands DOJ Explain Missing E-mails," *Declassified* (*Newsweek* blog), February 25, 2010, http://www.thedailybeast.com/newsweek/blogs/ declassified/2010/02/25/exclusive-archives-demands-doj-explain-missing-e-mails.html.

102. Paul Bedard and the *U.S. News* Staff, "E-mail Controversy Prompts Many Aides to Stop Usage," *News Desk (US News)*, March 27, 2007, http://www.usnews.com/news/ blogs/news-desk/2007/03/27/e-mail-controversy-prompts-many-aides-to-stop-usage; Letter from Rep. Henry Waxman to White House Counsel Fred Fielding, March 29, 2007, http://oversight-archive.waxman.house.gov/documents/20070329130758-87640 .pdf; Francine Kiefer, "With White House E-mail, It's Click Now and Repent Later," *Christian Science Monitor,* April 7, 2000, p. 1; Neely Tucker, "E-mail Searches Skip Private Clinton, Gore Accounts," *Christian Science Monitor,* August 18, 2000, p. A09. Of course, the fact that no evidence ever emerged of Clinton-Gore wrongdoing in this context does not prove its innocence.

103. 110th House Committee on Oversight and Government Reform, "White House Use of Private E-mail Accounts," http://oversight-archive.waxman.house.gov/investiga tions.asp?ID=251; Letter from Waxman to Mike Duncan (chairman of the Republic National Committee), April 18, 2007, http://oversight-archive.waxman.house.gov/docu ments/20070418161112.pdf; CREW, *Without a Trace* (see "Exhibits"); R. Jeffrey Smith, "GOP Groups Told to Keep Bush Officials' E-mails," *Washington Post,* March 27, 2007, p. A3. In addition to violating records laws, the e-mails potentially violated the Hatch Act, which prohibits officials from doing explicitly partisan business: most "federal employees are prohibited from taking an active part in partisan political management or partisan po-litical campaigns. Specifically, these employees may not campaign for or against candidates or otherwise engage in political activity in concert with a political party, a candidate for partisan political office, or a partisan political group." See http://www.osc.gov/haFederal FurtherRestrisctionandActivities.htm.

104. Letter from Waxman to Fielding; Letter from Waxman to Mike Duncan, Chair-man, Republican National Committee, March 26, 2007, http://oversight-archive.waxman .house.gov/documents/20070326110802-38974.pdf, accessed February 4, 2014; Letter from Waxman to Governor Marc Racicot (Bush-Cheney campaign director), March 26, 2007, http://oversight-archive.waxman.house.gov/documents/20070326110723-80643 .pdf, accessed February 4, 2014; CREW, *Without a Trace* ("Exhibits"), p. 99; Sheryl Gay Stolberg, "Advisers; E-mail Accounts May Have Mixed Politics and Business, White House Says," *New York Times,* April 12, 2007, p. A17.

105. Michael Abramowitz and Dan Eggen, "White House E-mail Lost in Private Ac-counts," *Washington Post,* April 12, 2007, p. A4.

106. Letter from Waxman to Duncan, April 18, 2007; Marcy Wheeler, "Two Re-minders: Not an Agency and Search Terms," *Emptywheel* (blog), January 22, 2008, http://

emptywheel.firedoglake.com/2008/01/22/two-reminders-not-an-agency-and-search-terms/.

107. Doyle, "End of Secrecy," p. 36; E-mail from Stasia Hutchinson [ARS FOIA officer, USDA] to author, February 21, 2013. Specifically, Hutchinson, after speaking with the ARS Office of the Administrator, wrote: "As the electronic version of the list was periodically updated, the content of the previous version was replaced and a hard copy was not maintained. Therefore, the list that was provided to you on July 19, 2012, is the only version still maintained."

108. Shirley Anne Warshaw, *The Co-presidency of Bush and Cheney* (Stanford, CA: Stanford University Press, 2009), p. 159; PBS Frontline, *Cheney's Law*, October 16, 2007, http://www.pbs.org/wgbh/pages/frontline/cheney/etc/script.html (Charlie Savage: "He himself doesn't write things down"); Spencer Ackerman, "How The Pentagon's Top Killers Became (Unaccountable) Spies," *Danger Room,* February 13, 2012, http://www.wired.com/dangerroom/2012/02/jsoc-ambinder/all/1.

109. CREW, *Without a Trace.* For one more example of unexplained and probably illegal document destruction, see Ross Gelbspan, *Break-ins, Death Threats, and the FBI: The Covert War against the Central America Movement* (Boston: South End Press, 1991), p. 119.

Chapter 10: "The Most Open and Transparent Administration in History"?

1. Scott Shane, "U.S. Approves Targeted Killing of American Cleric," *New York Times,* April 7, 2010, p. A12; Tabassum Zakaria, "Spy Agencies Can Target Americans: Official," *Reuters,* February 3, 2010, http://www.reuters.com/article/2010/02/03/us-usa-security-intelligence-idUSTRE61251Z20100203; Jeremy Scahill, *Dirty Wars: The World Is a Battlefield* (New York: Nation Books, 2013). It is worth mentioning that many also criticize extrajudicial killings of noncitizens.

2. *Nasser Al-Aulaqi v. Barack H. Obama,* 727 F. Supp. 2d 1 (DC District Court, 2010); Leon E. Panetta [Director, CIA], "Declaration and Formal Claim of State Secrets Privilege and Statutory Privileges," Civ.A. No. 10-cv-1469, September 25, 2010, http://www.fas.org/sgp/jud/statesec/aulaqi-panetta-092510.pdf; James R. Clapper [Director of National Intelligence], "Unclassified Declaration in Support of Formal Claim of State Secrets Privilege," Civ.A. No. 10-cv-1469, September 25, 2010, http://www.fas.org/sgp/jud/statesec/aulaqi-clapper-092510.pdf; Robert M. Gates [Secretary of Defense], "Public Declaration and Assertion of Military and State Secrets Privilege," Civ.A. No. 10-cv-1469, September 25, 2010, http://www.fas.org/sgp/jud/statesec/aulaqi-gates-092510.pdf; DOJ, "Opposition to Plaintiff's Motion for Preliminary Injunction and Memorandum in Support of Defendants' Motion to Dismiss," Civ. A. No. 10-cv-1469, September 25, 2010, http://www.fas.org/sgp/jud/statesec/aulaqi-opp-092510.pdf. The administration moved to dismiss the case on five "threshold grounds," including a broad assertion

of the SSP. Other grounds for dismissal included the "political question doctrine, the Court's exercise of its 'equitable discretion', [and] the absence of a cause of action under the Alien Tort Statute." See *Al Aulaqi v. Obama*, pp. 1–2, 83; *Mohamed v. Jeppesen Dataplan*, 614 F.3d 1070 (Ninth Circuit Appeals Court, 2010), p. 1080, http://www.fas.org/sgp/jud/statesec/aulaqi-120710.pdf; Robert F. Worth, "Cleric in Yemen Admits Meeting Airliner Plot Suspect, Journalist Says," *New York Times*, January 31, 2010, p. A7. See also Lara Jakes, "Liberal in Domestic Issues, Obama a Hawk on War," *Associated Press*, February 9, 2013; Peter Baker, "Obama's Turn in Bush's Bind," *New York Times*, February 10, 2013, p. A1.

3. Sudarsan Raghavan, "Anwar al-Aulaqi, U.S.-Born Cleric Linked to al-Qaeda, Killed in Yemen," *Washington Post*, October 1, 2011, p. A1; Alice Fordham, "25-Year-Old American Dies alongside Mentor in Drone Strike," *Washington Post*, October 1, 2011, p. A10; Craig Whitlock, "After Yemen Attack, Little Comment," *Washington Post*, October 23, 2011, p. A3. The administration's critics included prominent figures such as Noam Chomsky, Amy Goodman, and Glenn Greenwald. However, left-wing critics of Democrats do not frequently appear in mainstream media sources. The administration announced Jude Kenan Mohammad's death for the first time in May 2013 and claimed it did not specifically target him. See Attorney General Eric H. Holder, Letter to Sen. Patrick J. Leahy, Scott Shane, and Eric Schmitt, May 22, 2013; "One Drone Victim's Trail from Raleigh to Pakistan," *New York Times*, May 23, 2013, p. A12; "The Story of Jude Mohammad: Why Was a U.S. Citizen Secretly Killed by U.S. Drone in Pakistan?," May 24, 2013, *Democracy Now!*, http://www.democracynow.org/2013/5/24/the_story_of_jude_muhammad_why.

4. Peter Finn, "In Secret Memo, Justice Department Sanctioned Strike," *Washington Post*, October 1, 2011, p. A9; Charlie Savage, "Secret US Memo Made Legal Case to Kill a Citizen," *New York Times*, October 8, 2011, p. A1; *Nasser Al-Aulaqi v. Leon C. Panetta*, Case 1:12-cv-01192-RMC [Complaint] (DC District Court, 2012), http://www.aclu.org/files/assets/tk_complaint_to_file.pdf. John Yoo, a leading unitary executive theorist, was indeed supportive. See Yoo, "From Gettysburg to Anwar al-Awlaki," *Wall Street Journal*, October 3, 2011, http://online.wsj.com/article/SB10001424052970204226204576603114226847494.html; cf. Yoo, "The Administration's Strange Reasoning on al-Awlaki," *The Corner*, October 9, 2011, http://www.nationalreview.com/corner/279613/administrations-strange-reasoning-al-awlaki-john-yoo. The secret OLC memo allegedly stripped citizenship status from those on the kill list.

5. "Seymour Hersh: Secret US Forces Carried Out Assassinations in a Dozen Countries, Including in Latin America," March 31, 2009, *Democracy Now!*, http://www.democracynow.org/2009/3/31/seymour_hersh_secret_us_forces_carried; Senator Wyden, Letter to Eric Holder, February 8, 2012, http://www.wyden.senate.gov/news/press-releases/wyden-continues-to-press-justice-department-to-explain-the-extent-of-its-authority-to-kill-americans; Ellen Nakashima, "Democrat Balks over Secrecy on Awlaki Killing," *Checkpoint Washington*, February 8, 2012, http://www.washingtonpost.com/blogs/checkpoint-

washington/post/democrat-balks-over-secrecy-on-awlaki-killing/2012/02/08/gIQA-WTOpzQ_blog.html. See also Glenn Greenwald, "Repulsive Progressive Hypocrisy," *Salon*, February 8, 2012, http://www.salon.com/2012/02/08/repulsive_progressive_hypocrisy/.

6. Macon Phillips [(Director of New Media], "Change Has Come to WhiteHouse. gov," January 20, 2009, http://www.whitehouse.gov/blog/change_has_come_to_white house-gov; President Obama, Memorandum for the Heads of Executive Departments and Agencies: Transparency and Open Government, January 21, 2009, http://www.white house.gov/the_press_office/Transparency_and_Open_Government; Obama, "Remarks at Swearing-In Ceremony," January 21, 2009, http://www.fas.org/sgp/news/2009/01/obama012109.html. For an argument about the autonomous secrecy system, see Aftergood, "Is the Secrecy System an Autonomous Entity?"

7. "Interview with Jacob Lew," *State of the Union with Candy Crowley, CNN,* July 1, 2012, http://transcripts.cnn.com/TRANSCRIPTS/1207/01/sotu.01.html; Abby Phillip, "Shh! Obama Gets Anti-secrecy Award," *Politico*, March 30, 2011, http://www.politico.com/politico44/perm/0311/not_a_secret_anymore_a00ccd98-0d9e-4822-8936-168f3a51b959 .html; The White House/Google+, "President Obama Participates in a Fireside Hangout on Google+," February 14, 2013, http://www.youtube.com/watch?v=kp_zigxMS-Y.

8. National Security Archive, "Glass Half Full," Report about the NSA's Knight Open Government Survey, March 14, 2011, http://www2.gwu.edu/~nsarchiv///NSAEBB/NSAEBB338/index.htm.

9. President Obama, Executive Order 13489: Presidential Records, January 21, 2009, http://www.gpo.gov/fdsys/pkg/FR-2009-01-26/pdf/E9-1712.pdf; President Bush, Executive Order 13233: Further Implementation of the Presidential Records Act, November 1, 2001, http://www.gpo.gov/fdsys/pkg/FR-2001-11-05/pdf/01-27917.pdf; Obama, "President Obama Delivers Remarks"; Peter R. Orszag [(OMB Director], Memorandum for Heads of Executive Departments and Agencies: Open Government Directive," December 8, 2009, http://www.whitehouse.gov/sites/default/files/omb/assets/memoranda_2010/m10-06.pdf; Dan Vergano, "Obama Team Launches Its Interactive 'Openness' Policy with Online Access," *USA Today,* December 7, 2009, p. 2A.

10. Peter Baker, "White House to Open Visitor Logs to Public," *New York Times,* September 5, 2009, p. A11; White House Visitors Database, http://apps.washingtonpost .com/svc/politics/white-house-visitors-log/, accessed October 4, 2012; White House/Google+, "President Obama Participates." The visitor logs policy change also excluded anyone who could automatically bypass White House security, such as members of Congress and executive branch officials. The policy change was sparked by two lawsuits brought by Citizens for Responsibility and Ethics in Washington (CREW), which had pushed the Obama-Biden and earlier administrations to disclose their White House visitors.

11. President Obama, Executive Order 13526: Classified National Security Information, December 29, 2009, http://www.whitehouse.gov/the-press-office/executive-order -classified-national-security-information.

12. There were stirrings of a renewed declassification effort at the very end of Obama-Biden's first term. In October 2012, the National Archives announced a new online source for declassified materials. The archives also announced it would collaborate with the National Declassification Center, the Public Interest Declassification Board, the Presidential Libraries, and the Interagency Security Classification Appeals Panel. See National Archives, "NARA and Declassification," http://www.archives.gov/declassification/, accessed August 2, 2013; Steven Aftergood, "New Declassification Portal at the National Archives," *Secrecy News*, October 4, 2012, http://www.fas.org/blog/secrecy/2012/10/declass_portal.html.

13. Obama, Executive Order 13526; Obama, "Presidential Memorandum: Implementation of the Executive Order, 'Classified National Security Information,'" December 29, 2009, http://www.fas.org/sgp/obama/wh122909.html; National Declassification Center, "Bi-annual Report on Operations of the National Declassification Center," National Archives and Records Administration, http://www.archives.gov/declassification/ndc/reports/2012-biannual-january1-june30.pdf, accessed August 7, 2013; Steven Aftergood, "Agencies Are Likely to Miss 2013 Declassification Deadline," *Secrecy News*, January 30, 2012, http://www.fas.org/blog/secrecy/2012/01/miss_deadline.html; Nate Jones, "'Declassification-as-Usual' Mindset Responsible for the National Declassification Center's Languid Pace," *Unredacted*, February 1, 2012, http://nsarchive.wordpress.com/2012/02/01/declassification-as-usual-mindset-responsible-for-the-national-declassifcation-centers-lanugid-pace/; National Defense Authorization Act for Fiscal Year 2000, Sec. 1068, http://www.fas.org/sgp/news/1999/02/lottamend.html; Nate Jones, "Document Friday: The Department of Defense Needs Only One Paragraph to Illustrate Why the Declassification System Is Broken," *Unredacted*, February 17, 2012, http://nsarchive.wordpress.com/2012/02/17/document-friday-the-department-of-defense-needs-only-one-paragraph-to-illustrate-why-the-declassification-system-is-broken/.

14. Adam Goldman, "AP Exclusive: The CIA and a Secret Vacuum Cleaner," *Associated Press*, July 11, 2013, http://bigstory.ap.org/article/ap-exclusive-cia-and-secret-vacuum-cleaner.

15. Obama, Executive Order 13526; Information Security Oversight Office (ISOO), *Report to the President for Fiscal Year 2011* (Washington, DC: National Archives and Records Administration, 2012), http://www.archives.gov/isoo/reports/2011-annual-report.pdf; Ben Rhodes, "The President Signs H.R. 553, the Reducing Over-Classification Act," *The White House Blog*, October 7, 2010, http://www.whitehouse.gov/blog/2010/10/07/president-signs-hr-553-reducing-over-classification-act.

16. The number of OCAs also substantially decreased. During Bush-Cheney, the number was generally stable around 4,000. In 2009, the number declined to 2,557 and then to 2,378 and 2,372 in 2010 and 2011. See ISOO, *Report to the President for Fiscal Year 2011*. Finally, the ISOO changed its methodology once again in 2009, adding additional potential reliability problems.

17. ISOO, *Report to the President for the Fiscal Year 2011*, p.1; ISOO, *Report to the*

President for Fiscal Year 2009 (Washington, DC: National Archives and Records Administration, 2010), p. 1, http://www.archives.gov/isoo/reports/2009-annual-report.pdf; Mike German, "Memorandum to Interested Persons: ISOO Report for Fiscal Year 2009 and Derivative Classification," April 15, 2010, http://www.aclu.org/files/assets/Inerested_Persons_Memo_re_ISOO_Report_for_FY_2009_and_Derivative_Classification.pdf; Laura W. Murphy and Michael W. Macleod-Ball (ACLU), Written Statement for the ACLU, House Judiciary Committee Hearing on "The Espionage Act and the Legal and Constitutional Issues Raised by WikiLeaks," December 16, 2010, p. 4, http://www.aclu.org/files/assets/ACLU_Statement_for_House_Judiciary_Committee_Hearing_on_WikiLeaks_and_the_Espionage_Act.pdf.

18. President Obama, Memorandum for the Heads of Executive Department and Agencies; Subject: Freedom of Information Act," January 21, 2009, http://www.gwu.edu/~nsarchiv/news/20090121/2009_FOIA_memo.pdf, accessed July 5, 2012.

19. Agencies under Obama-Biden also made strides in reducing FOIA backlogs. In 2009, there was an overall reduction of 40 percent (from 133,295 to 77,377). The positive trend continued through 2010 (to 69,526). Whether the 2011 increase back up to 83,490 occurred only as a result of the spike in FOIA requests remains to be seen. It is also unclear whether the progress had much to do with Obama's memo. Backlogs under Bush-Cheney were, on average, quite high (about 185,000). But in 2008, there was a sharp decrease in the backlog, to 133,295 (from 217,237 in 2007). It is possible that the decrease under Obama-Biden was a continuation of the 2008 decrease under Bush-Cheney. See OpenTheGovernment.org, 2012, Secrecy Report: Indicators of Secrecy in the Federal Government, p. 14, http://www.openthegovernment.org/sites/default/files/Secrecy2012_web.pdf; National Security Archive, 2011, "Glass Half Full"; Chief of Staff Rahm Emanuel and Counsel to the President Bob Bauer, Memorandum for Agency and Department Heads regarding FOIA, March 16, 2010, http://www.gwu.edu/~nsarchiv/NSAEBB/NSAEBB338/foia_memo_3-16-10.pdf, accessed July 21, 2012; OMB Watch, "Assessing Progress toward a 21st Century Right to Know," March 18, 2011, http://dev.ombwatch.org/21strtkrecsassessment; OpenTheGovernment.org, "Agencies Not Meeting Administration's Sunshine Week Commitments," July 8, 2011, http://www.openthegovernment.org/node/3161.

20. Gary Bass (OMB Watch Director), "A Face-to-Face with the President about Transparency," March 29, 2011, http://www.ombwatch.org/node/11570.

21. Ed O'Keefe, "Obama Finally Accepts His Transparency Award . . . behind Closed Doors," *Federal Eye*, March 31, 2011, http://www.washingtonpost.com/blogs/federal-eye/post/obama-finally-accepts-his-transparency-award-behind-closed-doors/2011/03/31/AFRplO9B_blog.html; *The Daily Show* with Jon Stewart, "Victory Lapse," *Comedy Central* (television channel), 2011, http://www.thedailyshow.com/watch/mon-april-4-2011/victory-lapse—obama-transparency-award.

22. Open Letter, "Rescind President Obama's 'Transparency Award' Now," *Guardian* (Lon-

don), 2011, http://www.guardian.co.uk/commentisfree/cifamerica/2011/jun/14/rescind
-barack-obama-obama-transparency-award.

23. Associated Press, "Promises, Promises: Little Transparency Progress," *Washington Post,* March 14, 2011, http://www.washingtonpost.com/wp-dyn/content/article/2011/03
/14/AR2011031400630_pf.html; Charles Ornstein and Hagit Limor, "Where's the Openness, Mr. President?," *Washington Post,* April 1, 2011, p. A15.

24. Viveca Novak and Fred Schulte (Center for Public Integrity), "White House Visitor Logs Leave Out Many," *Politico,* April 13, 2011, http://www.politico.com/news/stories/
0411/53072.html; Eric Lichtblau, "Across Street from the White House, Coffee and a Chat with Lobbyists," *New York Times,* June 25, 2010, p. A18. Another popular location for off-the-books meetings with lobbyists was a set of townhouses near the White House in the Jackson Place complex. Chris Frates, "White House Meets Lobbyists Off Campus," *Politico,* February 24, 2011, http://www.politico.com/news/stories/0211/50081.html. According to Obama's rules, the (e.g.) court nominees' names would appear on the list once the need for secrecy subsided. Also see Josh Gerstein, "Obama's Not-So-Public Schedule," *Politico,* September 12, 2012, http://www.politico.com/news/stories/0912/81085.html.

25. Novak and Schulte, "White House Visitor Logs"; *Judicial Watch v. U.S. Secret Service,* 1:09-cv-02312 [Complaint] (DC District Court, 2009), https://www.judicialwatch
.org/files/documents/2009/jw-v-usss-complaint-12072009.pdf; *Judicial Watch v. U.S. Secret Service,* 1:09-cv-02312-BAH (DC District Court, 2011), p. 3, https://www.judicia
lwatch.org/files/documents/2011/jw-v-usss-opinion-08172011.pdf; Tom Fitton [(Judicial Watch President], "Judicial Watch Historic Victory! Court Slaps Down Obama Administration Secrecy, Rules White House Visitor Logs Subject to FOIA," August 19, 2011, http://www.judicialwatch.org/press-room/weekly-updates/33-jw-beats-obama-court-wh
-visitor-logs/; White House, "Visitor Access Records," http://www.whitehouse.gov/briefing
-room/disclosures/visitor-records, accessed July 28, 2013.

26. President Obama, "Executive Order 13556: Controlled Unclassified Information," November 4, 2010, https://www.federalregister.gov/articles/2010/11/09/2010-28360/
controlled-unclassified-information; Steven Aftergood, "Pentagon Tightens Grip on Unclassified Information," *Secrecy News,* July 11, 2011, http://www.fas.org/blog/secrecy/2011/
07/pentagon_tightens.html.

27. Aftergood, "Pentagon Tightens Grip"; ISOO, "About Controlled Unclassified Information [CUI]," *National Archives,* n.d., http://www.archives.gov/cui/, accessed October 3, 2012; CUI Office, "Controlled Unclassified Information (CUI) Office Notice 2011-01: Initial Implementation Guidance for Executive Order 13556," June 9, 2011, http://www
.archives.gov/cui/documents/2011-cuio-notice-2011-01-initial-guidance.pdf; CUI Office, *Report to the President,* 2011, http://www.archives.gov/cui/reports/report-2011.pdf; John P. Fitzpatrick and Melanie Ann Pustay, Memo for Senior Agency Officials for Executive Order No. 13556, 'Controlled Unclassified Information,'" November 22, 2011, http://www
.archives.gov/cui/documents/2011-doj-oip-cui-joint-issuance-on-foia.pdf.

28. Aftergood, "Pentagon Tightens Grip"; DOD, "Defense Acquisition Regulations System" (proposed rule), *Federal Register* 76, no. 125 (June 29, 2011): 38089–38095, http://www.fas.org/sgp/news/2011/06/dfars-unclass.html; DOD, "Instruction: Security of Unclassified DoD Information on Non-DoD Information Systems," Number 8582.01, June 6, 2012, http://www.dtic.mil/whs/directives/corres/pdf/858201p.pdf.

29. U.S. Code of Federal Regulations, Title 28, vol. 1, 16.6(c), http://www.gpo.gov/fdsys/pkg/CFR-2011-title28-vol1/xml/CFR-2011-title28-vol1-part16.xml; 5 U.S.C. sec. 552(c); Jennifer LaFleur, "Government Could Hide Existence of Records under FOIA Rule Proposal," *ProPublica*, October 24, 2011, https://www.propublica.org/article/government-could-hide-existence-of-records-under-foia-rule-proposal; Marcy Wheeler, "DOJ's 'New' FOIA Rule Just Attempt to Formalize Practice They've Been Following for Years," *Emptywheel*, October 26, 2011, http://www.emptywheel.net/2011/10/26/dojs-new-foia-rule-just-attempt-to-formalize-practice-theyve-been-following-for-years/.

30. *Islamic Shura Council of Southern California et al. v. FBI*, SACV07-1088-CJC(ANx) (Central California District Court, 2011), pp. 3, 18 [Amended Order Regarding Plaintiffs' Request under the Freedom of Information Act], http://www.mainjustice.com/files/2011/04/Cormac-Carney-Order.pdf. The federal appeals court agreed with the district court about the lying but sided with the government about the confidentiality of the records in question. See *Islamic Shura Council v. FBI*, 635 F.3d 1160 (Ninth Circuit Court of Appeals, 2011), http://www.ca9.uscourts.gov/datastore/opinions/2011/03/30/09-56035.pdf. ACLU, CREW, and OpenTheGovernment.org, Letter to Caroline A. Smith, Office of Information Policy, DOJ, "Re: Docket No. OAG 140; AG Order No. 3259-2011; RIN 1105-AB27," October 19, 2011, http://www.openthegovernment.org/sites/default/files/FOIA%20552c%20Comment%20-%2010-19-11%20-%20FINAL.pdf. DOJ, "Freedom of Information Act Regulations," *Federal Register*, 28 CFR pt. 17, vol. 76, no. 54, pp. 15236–15244, March 21, 2011, http://www.gpo.gov/fdsys/pkg/FR-2011-03-21/html/2011-6473.htm; LaFleur, "Government Could Hide"; Wheeler, "DOJ's 'New' FOIA Rule."

31. *Islamic Shura Council v. FBI*, SACV07-1088-CJC(ANx); *Islamic Shura Council v. FBI*, 635 F.3d 1160; Letter from ACLU, CREW, and OpenTheGovernment.org to Caroline A. Smith; DOJ, "Freedom of Information Act Regulations"; LaFleur, "Government Could Hide"; Wheeler, "DOJ's 'New' FOIA Rule." An earlier effort to institutionalize lying in FOIA administration, in a memo written by Reagan-Bush attorney general Edwin Meese, also failed. EFF, "History of FOIA,", https://www.eff.org/issues/transparency/history-of-foia, accessed February 10, 2014.

32. Jennifer Lynch (EFF), "DHS Singles Out EFF's FOIA Requests for Unprecedented Extra Layer of Review," *Deeplinks*, October 29, 2010, https://www.eff.org/deeplinks/2010/10/dhs-singles-out-eff-s-foia-requests-unprecedented; The Identity Project, "DHS Privacy Office Ordered TSA Not to Answer Our FOIA Request,"PapersPlease.org, October 29, 2010, http://papersplease.org/wp/2010/10/29/dhs-privacy-office-ordered-tsa-not-to-answer-our-foia-request/; EPIC, "EPIC Urges Investigation of White House FOIA Re-

view Policy," December 8, 2010, http://epic.org/2010/12/epic-urges-investigation-of-wh
.html; Eric Lipton, "Republican Congressman Proposes Tracking Freedom of Information Act Requests," *New York Times,* January 29, 2011, p. A14.

33. Steven Aftergood, "In Drake Leak Case, Govt Seeks to Block Unclassified Info,"
Secrecy News, May 12, 2011, http://www.fas.org/blog/secrecy/2011/05/drake_unclassified
.html; *USA v. Thomas Andrews Drake,* 10 CR 00181 RDB (Northern Maryland District
Court, 2011) ["Government's Memorandum of Law Regarding Application of Legal Privileges under CIPA"], http://www.fas.org/sgp/jud/drake/050911-cipa.pdf.

34. In addition to Johnsen, Obama chose Marty Lederman, David Barron, Neil
Kinkopf, and Harold Koh to fill key legal positions at the DOJ and the State Department.
All had been critical of Bush-Cheney arguments about executive power and secrecy. Eric
Lichtblau, "Obama Names 4 for Justice Jobs in Break from Bush Path," *New York Times,*
January 6, 2009, p. A16; Evan Perez, "Fierce Critic Is Picked for a Top Job in Justice,"
Wall Street Journal, January 6, 2009, p. A3; Johnsen, Testimony; Charlie Savage, "Long
after Nomination, an Obama Choice Withdraws," *New York Times,* April 20, 2010, p.
A16. In December 2008, the Obama-Biden transition team asked the Bush-Cheney DOJ
for private access to a collection of classified DOJ secret legal memos—including several
that earlier had drawn controversy (e.g., the torture memos). Like legislators and advocacy
groups before them, transition officials encountered a resolutely uncooperative DOJ, unwilling to hand over even redacted OLC legal analyses for private consumption. The DOJ
officials claimed they could not because the CIA and NSA had their "own equity or interest in the information." The matter was left unresolved, at least publicly. Joe Palazzolo,
"Obama Transition Team Pushing for Secret Legal Memos," *The BLT: The Blog of Legal-
Times,* December 9, 2008, http://legaltimes.typepad.com/blt/2008/12/obama-transition
-team-pushing-for-secret-legal-memos.html.

35. Neil A. Lewis, "Memos Reveal Scope of Power Bush Sought in Fighting Terror," *New York Times,* March 3, 2009, p. A1; Mike Allen, "Obama Consulted Widely
on Memos," *Politico,* April 16, 2009, http://www.politico.com/news/stories/0409/21338
.html.

36. Finn, "In Secret Memo"; Savage, "Secret US Memo"; Wyden, Letter to Eric Holder;
Nakashima, "Democrat Balks"; Karen DeYoung, "U.S. Sticks to Secrecy as Drone Strikes
Surge," *Washington Post,* December 20, 2011, p. A1; Charlie Savage, "Obama Team Split
on Tactics against Terror," *New York Times,* March 29, 2010, p. A1. The plaintiffs (ACLU
et al.) in the FOIA cases against the DOJ were dealt a blow at the very end of Obama-
Biden's first term. On January 2, 2013, Judge Colleen McMahon on the U.S. District
Court of the Southern District of New York ruled against the plaintiffs, arguing, "I can
find no way around the thicket of laws and precedents that effectively allow the executive branch of our government to proclaim as perfectly lawful certain actions that seem
on their face incompatible with our Constitution and laws while keeping the reasons for
their conclusion a secret." Judge McMahon acknowledged the serious problems with her
decision: "The Alice-in-Wonderland nature of this pronouncement is not lost on me; but

after careful and extensive consideration, I find myself stuck in a paradoxical situation in which I cannot solve a problem because of contradictory constraints and rules—a veritable Catch-22." *New York Times v. DOJ,* 915 F. Supp. 2d 508 (Southern New York District Court, 2013); Adam Liptak, "Secrecy of Memo on Drone Killing Is Upheld," *New York Times,* January 2, 2013, p. A17; J. F., "Transparency and Secrecy: Score One for the Thicket," *Democracy in America,* January 3, 2013, http://www.economist.com/blogs/democracyinamerica/2013/01/transparency-and-secrecy.

37. Attorney General Eric Holder, Speech at Northwestern University School of Law, March 5, 2012, http://www.justice.gov/iso/opa/ag/speeches/2012/ag-speech-1203051.html; Charlie Savage, "A Not-Quite Confirmation of a Memo Approving Killing," *New York Times,* March 8, 2012, p. A16; Sari Horwitz and Peter Finn, "Holder to Offer Rationale for Killing U.S. Citizens Abroad," *Washington Post,* March 5, 2012, p. A1; Charlie Savage, "U.S. Law May Allow Killings, Holder Says," *New York Times,* March 6, 2012, p. A18; Pozen, "Deep Secrecy." The Fifth Amendment does not guarantee protections only for citizens: "*No person* shall be . . . deprived of life, liberty, or property, without due process of law." See, e.g., Glenn Greenwald, "Susan Collins Spreads Central Myth about the Constitution," *Salon,* February 1, 2010, http://www.salon.com/2010/02/01/collins_5/.

38. Assistant Attorney General Virginia A. Seitz, "Unconstitutional Restrictions on Activities of the Office of Science and Technology Policy in Section 1340(a) of the Department of Defense and Full-Year Continuing Appropriations Act, 2011," Office of Legal Counsel, September 19, 2011, p. 3, http://www.justice.gov/olc/2011/conduct-diplomacy.pdf; Charlie Savage, "Meeting with Chinese, Official Tests Limits Set by Congress," *New York Times,* November 3, 2011, p. A21; Savage, *Takeover* ("Supreme Court in the executive branch").

39. Sec. 215 allows the FBI to obtain "any tangible things" from the lives of targeted individuals without their knowledge.

40. Sen. Ron Wyden, "Statement of Senator Wyden on Patriot Act Reauthorization, May 26, 2011," May 26, 2011, http://www.wyden.senate.gov/news/press-releases/in-speech-wyden-says-official-interpretations-of-patriot-act-must-be-made-public; Sen. Mark Udall, "Udall Votes to Protect Constitutional Freedoms, Opposes Extension of Most Controversial PATRIOT Act Provisions," May 28, 2011, http://www.markudall.senate.gov/?p=press_release&id=1098; Charlie Savage, "Senators Say Patriot Act Is Being Misinterpreted," *New York Times,* May 27, 2011, p. A17; Mark Benjamin, "Democrats Describe Secret Justice Department Spying Opinion," *Time,* May 27, 2011, http://nation.time.com/2011/05/27/democrats-describe-secret-justice-department-spying-opinion/.

41. Paul P. Colborn [(DOJ Special Counsel], Letter to Jameel Jaffer (ACLU), March 15, 2012, http://images.politico.com/global/2012/03/section215letter.pdf; Sen. Ron Wyden and Sen. Mark Udall, Letter to Attorney General Holder, March 15, 2012, http://www.scribd.com/doc/85512347/Senators-Ron-Wyden-Mark-Udall-Letter-to-Attorney-General-Holder, accessed January 4. 2014; Assistant Attorney General Ronald Weich, Letter to Sen. Ron Wyden, October 19, 2011, http://images.politico.com/global/2012/03/

dojltrwyden.pdf; Charlie Savage, "Democratic Senators Issue Strong Warning about Use of the Patriot Act," *New York Times,* March 16, 2012, p. A12; Alexander Abdo, "Government Confirms That It Has Secret Interpretation of Patriot Act Spy Powers," *ACLU Blog of Rights,* March 16, 2012, http://www.aclu.org/blog/national-security/government-con firms-it-has-secret-interpretation-patriot-act-spy-powers; Emily Miller, "Federal Judge Denies Request to Make Government Report on PATRIOT Act Public," Reporters Committee for Freedom of the Press, May 21, 2012, http://www.rcfp.org/browse-media-law -resources/news/federal-judge-denies-request-make-government-report-patriot-act-publ . In September 2013, the FISC released a portion of a July 2013 ruling about the court's secret PATRIOT Act interpretation. However, the heavily redacted document revealed very little, especially about earlier secret interpretations from FISC and OLC from 2001 to 2013. Mike Masnick, "Court Reveals 'Secret Interpretation' of the Patriot Act, Allowing NSA to Collect All Phone Call Data," *TechDirt,* September 17, 2013, http:// www.techdirt.com/articles/20130917/13395324556/court-reveals-secret-interpretation -patriot-act-allowing-nsa-to-collect-all-phone-call-data.shtml.

42. The Intelligence Resource Program at the Federation of American Scientists (FAS) collects information about the NSC memos (and beyond). See FAS, Presidential Policy Directives, Barack Obama Administration, http://www.fas.org/irp/offdocs/psd/index .html, accessed October 9, 2012; FAS, Presidential Study Directives, Barack Obama Administration, http://www.fas.org/irp/offdocs/psd/index.html, accessed October 9, 2012.

43. *US v. Pulungan,* 569 F.3d 326 (Seventh Circuit Appeals Court, 2009), http:// www.fas.org/sgp/jud/pulungan.pdf; Steven Aftergood, "Court Rebukes Government over 'Secret Law,'" *Secrecy News,* July 20, 2009, http://www.fas.org/blog/secrecy/2009/07/ secret_law-3.html.

44. The *re*nomination of Dawn Johnsen in early 2010 to head the OLC suggests a real tension within the administration. She again withdrew her nomination, for unknown reasons.

45. Barack Obama 2008 Campaign website (http://www.barackobama.com/issues/ ethics/) is archived here: http://web.archive.org/web/20080731083937/http:/www .barackobama.com/issues/ethics/, accessed February 5, 2014; Glenn Greenwald, "The 180-Degree Reversal of Obama's State Secrets Position," Salon, February 10, 2009, http:// www.salon.com/2009/02/10/obama_88/.

46. DOJ Office of Public Affairs, "Attorney General Establishes New State Secrets Policies and Procedures," *Justice News,* September 23, 2009, http://www.justice.gov/opa/ pr/2009/September/09-ag-1013.html; DOJ, Office of the Assistant Attorney General, "State Secrets Privilege Report," April 29, 2011, http://www.fas.org/sgp/jud/statesec/doj -ssp.pdf; Steven Aftergood, "Justice Department Defends Use of State Secrets Privilege," *Secrecy News,* July 24, 2012, https://www.fas.org/blog/secrecy/2012/07/doj_ssp.html.

47. The Clinton-Gore cases were *Crater Corp. v. Lucent Technologies; In re Grand Jury Subpoena Dated Aug. 9, 2000; Virtual Def. & Dev. Int'l, Inc. v. Republic of Moldova; DTM Research, LLC v. AT&T Corp;* and *Monarch Assurance P.L.C. v. United States.*

NOTES TO PAGES 350–351

48. Panetta wrote, "It is my belief that my declarations adequately explain why this case cannot be litigated without risking or requiring the disclosure of classified and privileged intelligence information that must not be disclosed." CIA Director Leon Panetta, "Declaration and Formal Claim of State Secrets Privilege and Statutory Privileges," No. 1:10cv01469(JDB) (DC District Court, 2010), http://www.fas.org/sgp/jud/statesec/aulaqi-panetta-092510.pdf; DNI Director James R. Clapper, "Unclassified Declaration in Support of Formal Claim of State Secrets Privilege," Civ. A. No. 10-cv-1469 (JDB) (DC District Court, 2010),, http://www.fas.org/sgp/jud/statesec/aulaqi-clapper-092510.pdf; DOD Secretary Robert M. Gates, "Public Declaration and Assertion of Military and State Secrets Privilege," Civ. A. No. 10-cv-1469 (DC District Court, 2010),, http://www.fas.org/sgp/jud/statesec/aulaqi-gates-092510.pdf. Also see *Aulaqi v. Obama*, Opposition to Plaintiff's Motion for Preliminary Injunction and Memorandum in Support of Defendants' Motion to Dismiss," Civ. A No. 10-cv-1469 (JDB) (DC District Court, 2010), http://www.fas.org/sgp/jud/statesec/aulaqi-opp-092510.pdf.

49. *Mohamed v. Jeppesen Dataplan,* Acting Assistant Attorney General Michael F. Hertz, "Petition for Rehearing or Rehearing *En Banc,*" No. 08-15693 (Ninth Circuit Appeals Court, 2009), p. 10, http://www.aclu.org/files/pdfs/safefree/mohamedvjeppesen_enbanc.pdf. ("Not only are these unprecedented holdings wrong, but they also conflict with decisions of the Supreme Court, this Court, and other courts of appeals, all of which recognize that a case should be dismissed whenever continued litigation threatens the disclosure of state secrets, regardless of the stage of the proceedings or where those secrets are contained.")

50. Josh Gerstein, "Obama Admin Asserts State Secrets Privilege to Dismiss Muslims' Suit," *Under the Radar,* August 1, 2011, http://www.politico.com/blogs/joshgerstein/0811/Obama_admin_asserts_state_secrets_privilege_to_dismiss_Muslims_suit.html.

51. Kate Zernike, "McCain and Obama Split on Justices' Ruling," *New York Times,* June 13, 2008, p. A23; Bob Egelko, "Obama Criticizes Prosecution of 6 Detainees," *San Francisco Chronicle,* February 13, 2008, http://www.sfgate.com/news/article/Obama-criticizes-prosecution-of-6-detainees-3294598.php; "The Candidates on Military Tribunals and Guantanamo Bay," *Council on Foreign Relations*, August 24, 2008, http://www.cfr.org/world/candidates-military-tribunals-guantanamo-bay/p14751#11603; Peter Finn and Carrie Johnson, "Alleged Sept. 11 Planner Will Be Tried in New York," *Washington Post,* November 14, 2009, p. A1; William Fisher, "Back to Military Commissions," *Inter Press Service (IPS) News,* May 13, 2009, http://www.ipsnews.net/2009/05/politics-us-back-to-military-commissions/; Warren Richey, "Obama Endorses Military Commissions for Guantanamo Detainees," *Christian Science Monitor,* October 29, 2009; Scott Shane, "Site for Terror Trial Isn't Its Only Obstacle," *New York Times,* January 31, 2010, p. A18; Scott Shane and Mark Landler, "Obama, in Reversal, Clears Way for Guantanamo Trials to Resume," *New York Times,* March 8, 2011, p. A19; Jennifer K. Elsea, "The Military Commissions Act of 2009: Overview and Legal Issues," Congressional Research Service Report #R41163, at pp. 46–47, April 6, 2010, http://www.fas.org/sgp/crs/natsec/R41163.pdf/.

52. Ed Pilkington, "Obama Resumes Military Trials for Terror Suspects Detained at Guantanamo Bay," *Guardian* (London), March 8, 2011, p. 24; CNN Wire Staff, "Obama Orders Resumption of Military Commissions at Guantanamo," *CNN,* March 7, 2011, http://articles.cnn.com/2011-03-07/politics/obama.guantanamo_1_guantanamo -detainees-guantanamo-bay-facility-military-commissions; Peter Finn, "Sept. 11 Suspects Will Be Tried by a Military Panel," *Washington Post,* April 5, 2011, p. A1; Carol Rosenberg, "Obama Gives up on Plan for 9/11 Civilian Trials," *McClatchy DC,* April 4, 2011, http://www.mcclatchydc.com/2011/04/04/111531/obama-gives-up-on-plan-for-911 .html; William Glaberson, "U.S. May Revive Guantanamo Military Courts," *New York Times,* May 2, 2009, p. A1; Peter Finn, "Taking on 9/11 Case, and Public Opinion," *Washington Post,* May 5, 2012, p. A1.

53. *Kaur v. Holder,* 561 F.3d 957 (Ninth Circuit Appeals Court, 2009); Bob Egelko, "Court: No Secret Evidence in Asylum Case," *San Francisco Chronicle*, April 3, 2009, p. B3; Egelko, "Court Orders Jailed Sikh Activist Freed," *San Francisco Chronicle*, December 3, 2003, p. A23; Camille T. Taiara, "Harpal Singh Cheema Chose 'Voluntary' Deportation," *Sikh Times,* August 7, 2007, http://www.sikhtimes.com/news_080706a.html.

54. *Kaur v. Holder;* Egelko "Court: No Secret Evidence"; Egelko, "Court Orders Jailed Sikh"; Taiara, "Harpal Singh Cheema."

55. GSA, "Increasing the Transparency of Federal Advisory Committee Act (FACA) Information," http://www.gsa.gov/portal/category/101111, accessed February 7, 2014; Lichtblau, "Across Street"; Michael Smallberg, "Lobbyists in Fight-or-Flight Mode after Getting Booted from Advisory Committees," *Project on Government Oversight (POGO) Blog,* February 22, 2012, http://pogoblog.typepad.com/pogo/2012/02/lobbyists-in-fight -or-flight-mode-after-getting-booted-from-advisory-committees.html; Federal Advisory Committee Act, Sec. 5(a)(3), http://epic.org/open_gov/faca.html, accessed February 3, 2014; Dan Eggen, "Lobbyists Pushed Off Advisory Panels," *Washington Post,* November 27, 2009, p. A1; American League of Lobbyists, "Statement of American League of Lobbyists in Response to the Issue of Final Regulation on the Appointment of Lobbyists to Federal Boards and Commissions," October 5, 2011, http://www.alldc.org/pdfs/10-5 -11statement.pdf; Letter from Boeing Company, et al., to President Barack Obama, October 19, 2009, http://www.whitehouse.gov/assets/documents/Chairs_ITAC_letter_to_ Obama_%282%29.pdf; Michael Smallberg, "It's Final—No More Lobbyists on Federal Advisory Committees," *POGO Blog,* October 6, 2011, http://pogoblog.typepad.com/ pogo/2011/10/its-final-no-more-lobbyists-on-federal-advisory-committees.html.

56. FACA Database, http://fido.gov/facadatabase/, accessed February 7, 2014.

57. *Freedom Watch v. Obama,* 807 F. Supp. 2d 28 (DC District Court, 2011), p. 1; Paul Bedard, "Group Sues Obama over Healthcare," *US News,* USNews.com, December 23, 2009, http://www.usnews.com/news/washington-whispers/articles/2009/12/23/group -sues-obama-over-healthcare.

58. *Freedom Watch v. Obama,* "Declaration of Kimberley Harris in Support of Defendants' Supplemental Memorandum," September 26, 2011; "Bringing Everyone to the Ta-

ble: White House Health Care Stakeholder Discussions," http://www.healthreform.gov/forums/stakeholderdiscussions/index.html, accessed April 12, 2012; White House Forums on Health Reform, http://www.healthreform.gov/forums/whitehouseforums/index.html, accessed April 12, 2012; Jesse Lee, "Full Videos: The Health Care Stakeholder Discussions," July 29, 2009, http://www.whitehouse.gov/blog/Full-Videos-The-Health-Care-Stakeholder-Discussions, accessed April 14, 2012.

59. *Freedom Watch v. Obama*, 859 F. Supp. 2d 169 (DC District Court, 2012); *Association of American Physicians and Surgeons v. Clinton*, 997 F.2d 898 (DC District Court, 1993), p. 915.

60. Interestingly, Obama's FACA charter request came six days before the legislators' letter . . . probably without their knowledge. For the charter, the minutes, etc., see NCFRR's website at http://www.fiscalcommission.gov, accessed February 7, 2014. President Obama, "Executive Order 13531—National Commission on Fiscal Responsibility and Reform," February 18, 2010, http://www.whitehouse.gov/the-press-office/executive-order-national-commission-fiscal-responsibility-and-reform; Letter from Speaker John Boehner, March 3, 2010, http://www.speaker.gov/press-release/boehner-calls-president%E2%80%99s-debt-commission-open-all-meetings-public-report-final; Letter from Rep. John Conyers et al. to Chairmen Bowles and Simpson, April 28, 2010, http://conyers.house.gov/_files/042810ConyersFiscalCommissionTransparencyLetter.pdf; Eric Laursen, "Washington behind Closed Doors," *Campaign for America's Future*, April 30, 2010, http://www.ourfuture.org/progressive-opinion/2010041730/washington-behind-closed-doors, accessed May 17, 2012.

61. *Freedom Watch v. Obama*, Civil Action No. 5:13-CV-26-OC-22PRC (Middle Florida District Court, 2013), http://www.freedomwatchusa.org/pdf/130130-FACA%20Amended%20Complaint.pdf. Inside the government, there was disagreement about whether the task force fell under FACA's purview. E-mail from Maggie Weber, GSA Committee Management Secretariat, to author, January 10, 2013. Weber wrote: "Thus far, the form of the interactions we have seen and know about do not intrude into FACA territory and we have not seen a draft of the expected EO formally establishing the task force. We expect and suspect that the task force will take the form of an all government (federal, state, and local) inter agency committee that will operate within the FACA principles of openness and transparency and will hear from non-government interests but will not include those representatives on the task force, and will not be subject to FACA's meeting notice requirements. However, we do not know that for certain. We are waiting and watching as well." By August 2013, it was clear the administration defied FACA completely. E-mail from Maggie Weber, GSA Committee Management Secretariat, to author, August 21, 2013 ("the administration did not ever cross the line into FACA with the operations of the gun control task force managed by Mr. Biden"). The FACA-defiant behavior continued into the second term. Michelle Obama, for example, invited to the White House about 100 private sector individuals from the food industry, entertainment corporations (e.g., Disney), business associations, and advocacy groups (e.g., NAACP, MomsRising).

The quasi task force met with government officials from the Federal Trade Commission. After a brief opening session with public statements by Michelle Obama and Senior Policy Adviser for Nutrition Policy Sam Kass, White House officials showed journalists the door, leaving the public-private sector group to have a "a candid conversation," as a "press aide" put it. Helena Bottemiller Evich, "Michelle Obama to Industry: Promote Broccoli," *Politico*, September 19, 2013, http://www.politico.com/story/2013/09/michelle-obama-to-industry-promote-broccoli-97061.html; Josh Gerstein, "White House Hosts Closed-Door Food Talks," *Politico,* September 19, 2013, http://www.politico.com/blogs/under-the-radar/2013/09/white-house-hosts-closeddoor-food-talks-173093.html.

62. Senate Judiciary Committee, Hearing on "Examining the History and Legality of Executive Branch 'Czars,'" October 6, 2009, http://www.judiciary.senate.gov/hearings/hearing.cfm?id=e655f9e2809e5476862f735da150eff4; Michael A. Fletcher and Brady Dennis, "Obama's Many Policy 'Czars' Draw Ire from Conservatives," *Washington Post,* September 16, 2009, p. A6. (Sen. Robert Byrd [D-WV]: "As presidential assistants and advisers, these White House staffers are not accountable for their actions to the Congress, to Cabinet officials, and to virtually anyone but the president.") Given that the concept of "czars" is not explicitly and officially recognized, no official or even comprehensive journalistic list exists. Take the estimate of forty-two with caution, as it came from Wikipedia ("List of U.S. Executive Branch Czars," http://en.wikipedia.org/wiki/List_of_U.S._executive_branch_czars, accessed October 25, 2013). For a comprehensive treatment of the czar phenomenon, see Mitchel A. Sollenberger and Mark J. Rozell, *The President's Czars: Undermining Congress and the Constitution* (Lawrence: University Press of Kansas, 2012).

63. Colin Sullivan (Greenwire), "Vow of Silence Key to White House–Calif. Fuel Economy Talks," *New York Times,* May 20, 2009, http://www.nytimes.com/gwire/2009/05/20 / 20greenwire-vow-of-silence-key-to-white-house-calif-fuel-e-12208.html. Judicial Watch filed a complaint about the matter but concentrated on FOIA, rather than FACA. See *Judicial Watch v. Department of Energy and Environmental Protection Agency*, No. 10-246, http:// www.judicialwatch.org/press-room/press-releases/judicial-watch-sues-records-climate-czar-carol-browners-role-crafting-policy/; Michael James, "White House Climate Change Czar Carol Browner Departing," *Political Punch,* January 24, 2011, http://abcnews.go.com/blogs/politics/2011/01/white-house-climate-change-czar-carol-browner-departing/.

64. Mathew D. McCubbins and Thomas Schwartz, "Congressional Oversight Overlooked: Police Patrols versus Fire Alarms," *American Journal of Political Science* 28 (1984): 165–179.

65. In most years, three units—DOD, Department of Health and Human Services, and National Science Foundation—account for most of the closed meetings. See, e.g., G. Martin Wagner (GSA), Statement before the Subcommittee on Government Management, Information and Technology, Committee on Government Reform and Oversight, U.S. House of Representatives, July 14, 1998, http://www.gsa.gov/portal/content/100919, accessed April 18, 2014.

66. President Obama, "Memorandum for the Heads of Executive Departments and

Agencies, Subject: Scientific Integrity," March 9, 2009, http://www.whitehouse.gov/the_
press_office/Memorandum-for-the-Heads-of-Executive-Departments-and-Agencies-3-9-
09/. In October 2010, the nonprofit group Public Employees for Environmental Responsibility (PEER) sued the OSTP for its failure to respond to its August FOIA request.
Curtis Brainard, "Transparency Watch: Closed Door," *Columbia Journalism Review*, September–October 2011, http://www.cjr.org/feature/transparency_watch_a_closed_door
.php?page=all.

67. Director of the Office of Science and Technology Policy John P. Holdren, "Memorandum for the Heads of Executive Departments and Agencies; Subject: Scientific Integrity," December 17, 2010, http://www.whitehouse.gov/sites/default/files/microsites/ostp/
scientific-integrity-memo-12172010.pdf; Brainard, "Transparency Watch."

68. Brainard, "Transparency Watch."

69. Director of the Office of Science and Technology Policy John P. Holdren, "Next
Steps to Ensuring Scientific Integrity," *The White House Blog*, October 31, 2011, http://
www.whitehouse.gov/blog/2011/10/31/next-steps-ensuring-scientific-integrity; Union of
Concerned Scientists, "Press Release: Obama Administration Calls for Final Scientific In-
tegrity Policies," November 1, 2011, http://www.ucsusa.org/news/press_release/holdren
-SI-policies-0568.html; Holdren, "Scientific Integrity Policies Released," *The White House
Blog*, April 6, 2012, http://www.whitehouse.gov/blog/2012/04/06/scientific-integrity
-policies-released; Brainard, "Transparency Watch."

70. Brainard, "Transparency Watch."

71. Ibid.; Tom Hamburger and Kim Geiger, "Scientists Expected Obama Administration to Be Friendlier," *Los Angeles Times,* July 10, 2010, http://articles.latimes.com/2010/
jul/10/nation/la-na-science-obama-20100711; Jonathan H. Adler, "The 'War on Science'
Continues," *The Volokh Conspiracy*, July 11, 2010, http://www.volokh.com/2010/07/11/
the-war-on-science-continues/.

72. Justin Gillis, "Doubts Are Raised on Accuracy of Government's Spill Estimate," *New
York Times*, May 14, 2010, p. A1; Craig Pittman, "USF Says Feds Tried to Squelch Oil Findings," *St. Petersburg (FL) Times,* August 10, 2010, p. 1B; Lea Winerman, "Report: Government Underestimated, Underreported Oil Spill Size," *PBS News Hour,* October 6, 2010,
http://www.pbs.org/newshour/rundown/2010/10/report-federal-government-under
estimated-underreported-oil-spill-size.html; John M. Broder, "Report Faults Administration on Spill," *New York Times,* October 7, 2010, p. A20; Jonathan H. Adler, "Suppressing Oil Spill Science," *Volokh Conspiracy,* October 6, 2010, http://www.volokh.com/
2010/10/06/suppressing-oil-spill-science/; Ornstein and Limor, "Where's the Openness?"

73. Ornstein and Limor, "Where's the Openness?"; Gillis, "Doubts Are Raised"; Pittman, "USF Says"; Winerman, "Report"; Broder, "Report Faults Administration"; Adler,
"Suppressing Oil Spill Science."

74. Ornstein and Limor, "Where's the Openness?"; Gillis, "Doubts Are Raised"; Pittman, "USF Says"; Winerman, "Report"; Broder, "Report Faults Administration"; Adler,
"Suppressing Oil Spill Science."

75. Ornstein and Limor, "Where's the Openness?"; Gillis, "Doubts Are Raised"; Pittman, "USF Says"; Winerman, "Report"; Broder, "Report Faults Administration"; Adler, "Suppressing Oil Spill Science."

76. DOI Inspector General, "Investigative Report of Federal Moratorium on Deepwater Drilling," November 8, 2010, http://www.politico.com/static/PPM152_101109_oig_report.html; Dan Berman, "Interior Inspector General: White House Skewed Drilling-Ban Report," *Politico,* November 9, 2010, http://www.politico.com/news/stories/1110/44921.html.

77. Elizabeth Souder, "Parker County Water Contamination Case Stokes Debate over Natural Gas Drilling," *Dallas Morning News,* December 9, 2010, http://www.dallasnews.com/business/headlines/20101209-parker-county-water-contamination-case-stokes-debate-over-natural-gas-drilling.ece; Brantley Hargrove, "How One Man's Flaming Water Fired Up a Battle between Texas and the EPA," *Dallas Observer,* April 26, 2012, http://www.dallasobserver.com/2012-04-26/news/fire-in-the-hole/full/; Ramit Plushnick-Masti, "EPA's Water Contamination Investigation Halted in Texas after Range Resources Protest," *Associated Press,* January 16, 2013.

78. Hargrove, "How One Man's"; Plushnick-Masti, "EPA's Water Contamination"; Neela Banerjee, "Internal EPA Report Highlights Disputes over Fracking and Well Water," *Los Angeles Times,* July 28, 2013, http://www.latimes.com/news/nationworld/nation/la-na-epa-dimock-20130728,0,4847442.story; Kate Sinding, "Why Would EPA Hide Info on Fracking & Water Contamination in Dimock?," *Switchboard: Natural Resources Defense Council Staff Blog,* July 28, 2013, http://switchb oard.nrdc.org/blogs/ksinding/why_would_epa_hide_info_on_fra.html.

79. EPA, "Range Resources Imminent and Substantial Endangerment Order, Parker County, TX," http://www.epa.gov/region6/region-6/tx/tx005.html, accessed July 29, 2013; Hargrove, "How One Man's"; Plushnick-Masti, "EPA's Water Contamination"; Banerjee, "Internal EPA Report"; Sinding, "Why Would EPA Hide"; *US v. Range Production Co.,* 793 F. Supp. 2d 814 (Northern Texas District Court, 2011). In the January 2011 complaint, the EPA argued that "even if a State has obtained primary responsibility for administering and enforcing EPA's standards, EPA retains the authority to issue emergency administrative orders pursuant to the emergency powers provision." *US v. Range Production Co.,* 3:11-cv-00116-F, http://www.scribd.com/doc/47111636/EPA-v-Range-Resources-Jan-18-2011, p. 3, accessed July 29, 2013. See also Steve Horn, "Breaking: Obama EPA Shut Down Weatherford, TX Shale Gas Water Contamination Study," *DeSmogblog,* January 16, 2013, http://www.desmogblog.com/2013/01/16/breaking-obama-epa-shut-down-weatherford-tx-shale-gas-water-contamination-study; Mike Lee, "EPA Agrees to Dismiss Well Contamination Case against Range," *Bloomberg Businessweek,* March 30, 2012, http://www.businessweek.com/news/2012-03-30/epa-agrees-to-dismiss-well-contamination-case-against-range.

80. Plushnick-Masti, "EPA's Water Contamination"; Sinding, "Why Would EPA Hide." The RRC continued its countersuit against Lipsky and his wife after the EPA

withdrew its order and lawsuit. See Tony Korosec, "Range Resources Frack Suit Should Be Reheard, Court Says," *Bloomberg,* April 2, 2013, http://www.bloomberg.com/news/2013 -04-02/range-resources-frack-suit-should-be-reheard-appeals-court-says.html.

81. EPA, "EPA Completes Drinking Water Sampling in Dimock, Pa.," news release, July 25, 2012, http://yosemite.epa.gov/opa/admpress.nsf/0/1A6E49D193E 1007585257A46005B61AD; Michael Rubinkam, "Dimock, Pennsylvania: EPA to Send Water to Town with Tainted Wells," *Associated Press,* January 19, 2012; Banerjee, "Internal EPA Report."

82. Banerjee, "Internal EPA Report."

83. Plushnick-Masti, "EPA's Water Contamination"; Sinding, "Why Would EPA Hide"; EPA, "Wyoming to Lead Further Investigation of Water Quality Concerns outside of Pavillion with Support of EPA," news release, June 20, 2013, http://yosemite .epa.gov/opa/admpress.nsf/20ed1dfa1751192c8525735900400c30/dc7dcdb471dcfe17 85257b90007377bf!OpenDocument.

84. Another somewhat prominent case involved EPA economist Alan Carlin. See Kimberley A. Strassel, "The EPA Silences a Climate Skeptic," *Wall Street Journal,* July 3, 2009, http://online.wsj.com/news/articles/SB124657655235589119; Jonathan Adler, "A War on Science?," *Volokh Conspiracy,* http://www.volokh.com/posts/1246220386.shtml; Declan McCullagh, "E-mails Indicate EPA Suppressed Report Skeptical of Global Warming," *CNET News,* June 27, 2009, http://news.cnet.com/8301-13578_3-10274412-38 .html; Roger Pielke, Jr.), "Who Cares about Integrity of Process When There Are Political Points to Score?," *Roger Pielke Jr.'s Blog,,* June 28, 2009, http://rogerpielkejr.blogspot .com/2009/06/who-cares-about-integrity-of-process.html. For an opposing view (i.e., that Carlin's science was not suppressed), see Gavin Schmidt (NASA Goddard Institute), "Bubkes," *RealClimate,* June 26, 2009, http://www.realclimate.org/index.php/archives/ 2009/06/bubkes/langswitch_lang/pl. For a case about Obama-Biden *surveillance* of FDA scientists, see Eric Lichtblau and Scott Shane, "Vast F.D.A. Effort Tracked E-mails of Its Scientist," *New York Times,* July 15, 2012, p. A1.

85. As of July 2013, the audit report had not been released, and a congressional investigation about private e-mail accounts more broadly continued. Melissa M. Heist, Assistant Inspector General for Audit, Memorandum to EPA Administrator et al., "Audit of Certain EPA Electronic Records Management Practices," EPA Office of Inspector General, Project No. OA-FY13-0113, December 13, 2012, http://www.epa.gov/oig/reports/ notificationMemos/newStarts_12-13-2012_Audit_of_Records_Managements_Practices .pdf; Mark Schleifstein, "EPA Investigating Lisa Jackson's Agency's Use of Private Email Accounts," *Times-Picayune,* December 17, 2012, http://www.nola.com/environment/index .ssf/2012/12/epa_inspector_general_to_inves.html; Tom Kludt, "EPA Administrator Lisa Jackson under Investigation for Use of Private Email Accounts," *Talking Points Memo,* December 17, 2012, http://livewire.talkingpointsmemo.com/entry/epa-administrator-lisa -jackson-under-investigation-for-use; Michael Bastasch, "EPA Chief's Secret 'Alias' Email Account Revealed," *Daily Caller,* November 12, 2012, http://dailycaller.com/2012/11/12/

epa-chiefs-secret-alias-email-account-revealed/; John M. Broder, "E.P.A. Chief Set to Leave; Term Fell Shy of Early Hope," *New York Times,* December 28, 2012, p. A14; Stephen Dinan, "Fictitious Email ID Honored by EPA; Former Chief's Alias Lauded for Good Job," *Washington Times,* June 3, 2013, p. A1. See also Jack Gillum, "Top Obama Appointees Using Secret Email Accounts," *Associated Press,* June 4, 2013, http://bigstory. ap.org/article/emails-top-obama-appointees-remain-mystery; Josh Gerstein, "HHS, Labor Officials Also Had Secret Accounts," *Politico,* June 4, 2013, http://www.politico. com/blogs/under-the-radar/2013/06/hhs-labor-officials-also-had-secret-email-accounts-165332.html.

86. DOJ Inspector General Michael E. Horowitz, Letter to Senators Joseph I. Lieberman and Susan Collins, December 20, 2012, http://msnbcmedia.msn.com/i/msnbc/sections/news/130110_Justice_IG_Letter.pdf; Marcy Wheeler, "Shorter DOJ: It's No Big Deal If DEA Agents Destroy Evidence," *Emptywheel,* January 10, 2013, http://www .emptywheel.net/2013/01/10/shorter-doj-its-no-big-deal-if-dea-agents-destroy-evidence /?utm.

87. On some of the conceptual differences between whistle-blowing and other kinds of "leaking," see Jesselyn Radack, "Whistleblowing (in the Public Interest) vs. Leaking ("Authorized" Leaks for Political Gain)," *Whistleblogger* (Government Accountability Project), June 7, 2012, http://www.whistleblower.org/blog/42/2034; C. Fred Alford, *Whistleblowers: Broken Lives and Organizational Power* (Ithaca, NY: Cornell University Press, 2002); Myron P. Glazer, *Whistleblowers* (New York: Basic Books, 1991); Brian Martin, "Whistleblowing and Nonviolence," *Peace and Change* 24, no. 1 (1999): 15–28.

88. *Times* editors held Risen and Lichtblau's story for thirteen months—through the 2004 election cycle—to placate the Bush-Cheney administration (among other reasons). See Margaret Sullivan, "Lessons in a Surveillance Drama Redux," *New York Times,* November 9, 2013, http://www.nytimes.com/2013/11/10/public-editor/sullivan -lessons-in-a-surveillance-drama-redux.html. James Risen and Eric Lichtblau, "Bush Lets U.S. Spy on Callers without Courts," *New York Times,* December 16, 2005, p. A1; Risen and Lichtblau, "Spying Program Snared U.S. Calls," *New York Times,* December 21, 2005, p. A1; Michael Isikoff, "The Fed Who Blew the Whistle," *Newsweek,* December 22, 2008, pp. 32–40; Electronic Frontier Foundation, "Timeline of NSA Domestic Spying," https://www.eff.org/nsa-spying/timeline, accessed November 13, 2013; US Senate Select Committee to Study Governmental Operations with Respect to Intelligence Activities [Church Committee], October 29 and November 6, 1975, *The National Security Agency and Fourth Amendment Rights*, vol. 3, #07-522 (Washington, DC: Government Printing Office, 1975). This epilogue limits its attention to NSA-related leaks. See, especially, the *Guardian* for reporting about Britain's signals intelligence agency, Government Communications Headquarters (GCHQ).

89. Later, we learned the NSA had even targeted Sen. Frank Church, whose committee investigated the NSA. Also, as of late 2013, the extent to which the official story about 9/11 as a huge turning point in surveillance policy was true remained unclear (i.e., the

clean pre-9/11 and post- 9/11 break). James Bamford, *The Shadow Factory: The Ultra-secret NSA from 9/11 to the Eavesdropping on America* (New York: Anchor Books, 2008), p. 108. FISA is formally the Foreign Intelligence Surveillance Act of 1978, 50 USC § 1801 (e)(2), http://www.law.cornell.edu/uscode/text/50/1801; Select Committee to Study Governmental Operations [Church Committee], Intelligence Activities and the Rights of Americans, Final Report of the Select Committee to Study Governmental Operations with Respect to Intelligence Activities [Church Committee Report], Report 94-755, http://www.intelligence.senate.gov/pdfs94th/94755_II.pdf, accessed April 18, 2014; *First Unitarian Church of Los Angeles v. National Security Agency,* 3:13-cv-03287 JSW, Amicus Curiae Brief in Support of Plaintiffs' Motion for Partial Summary Judgment, "Experts in the History of Executive Surveillance: James Bamford, Loch Johnson, and Peter Fenn" (Northern California District Court, 2013), https://www.eff.org/files/2013/11/15/history nsaexpertsamicusbrief.pdf, accessed November 22, 2013; Conor Friedersdorf, "Experts on the NSA's History of Abuses: There They Go Again," *Atlantic,* November 21, 2013, http://www.theatlantic.com/politics/archive/2013/11/experts-on-the-nsas-history-of -abuses-there-they-go-again/281703/; Peter Fenn, "When the NSA Was Spying on the Congress," *U.S. News & World Report,* September 27, 2013, http://www.usnews.com/ opinionlblogs/Peter-Fenn/2013/09/27/when-the-nsa-spied-on-the-congress.

90. Trevor Timm, "NSA's Vast Surveillance Powers Extend Far Beyond Counterter-rorism, Despite Misleading Government Claims," *Deeplinks* (Electronic Frontier Foun-dation), November 11, 2013, https://www.eff.org/deeplinks/2013/11/nsas-surveillance -powers-extend-far-beyond-terrorism-despite-governments; James Ball and Spencer Ack-erman, "NSA Loophole Allows Warrantless Search for US Citizens' Emails and Phone Calls," *Guardian* (London), August 9, 2013, http://www.theguardian.com/world/2013/ aug/09/nsa-loophole-warrantless-searches-email-calls#; Cyrus Farivar, "Judge: 'NSA Ex-ceeded the Scope of Authorized Acquisition Continuously," *Ars Technica,* November 19, 2013, http://arstechnica.com/tech-policy/2013/11/judge-nsa-exceeded-the-scope-of-authorized-acquisition-continuously/. The "gloves" comment was immortalized by the CIA's Cofer Black, who said this in 2002: "All I want to say is that there was 'before' 9/11 and 'after' 9/11. After 9/11 the gloves come off." See Dana Priest and Barton Gellman, "U.S. Decries Abuse but Defends Interrogations," *Washington Post,* December 26, 2002, p. A1; *First Unitarian Church of Los Angeles v. NSA* (Bamford, Johnson, and Fenn brief); Barton Gellman and Ashkan Soltani, "NSA Infiltrates Links to Yahoo, Google Data Cen-ters Worldwide, Snowden Documents Say," *Washington Post,* October 30, 2013, p. A1. Bamford, Johnson, and Fenn (p. 9) describe the "three-hop" program this way: "Once the agency identifies a suspect, it reviews all of that person's contacts, then all of these first-hop people's contacts, and finally all of those people's contacts. The NSA thus routinely examines the calling records of Americans with no direct relationship to an investigation's target. By targeting a single person whose call history includes 40 contacts, it can sweep the phone records of roughly 2.5 million people into the review." The MUSCULAR program, reported in Gellman and Soltani, "NSA Infiltrates Links," revealed covert NSA

actions against its erstwhile corporate collaborators Google and Yahoo. MUSCULAR operatives somehow tapped into the companies' internal links between global data centers. Analysts were apparently allowed to "presume that anyone using a foreign data link is a foreigner."

91. The NSA's understanding of its "threatening activities" mission statement includes a range of operations: "support for US military in the field; gathering information about military technology; anticipating state instability; monitoring regional tensions; countering drug trafficking; gathering economic, political and diplomatic information; ensuring a steady and reliable energy supply for the US; and ensuring US economic advantage." Ewen MacAskill and James Ball, "Portrait of the NSA: No Detail Too Small in Quest for Total Surveillance," *Observer* (UK), November 2, 2013, p. 18, available at http://www.the guardian.com/world/2013/nov/02/nsa-portrait-total-surveillance; President Obama, The President's News Conference (transcript), August 9, 2013, http://www.presidency.ucsb.edu/ ws/?pid=104008; Scott Shane, "No Morsel Too Minuscule for All-Consuming N.S.A.," *New York Times,* November 3, 2013, p. A1; Jonathan Watts, "NSA Accused of Spying on Brazilian Oil Company Petrobras," *Guardian* (London), September 9, 2013, http://www. theguardian.com/world/2013/sep/09/nsa-spying-brazil-oil-petrobras. On FISC-ignoring behavior as of November 2013, see, e.g., Farivar, "Judge"; Brendan Sasso, "Snowden Leaks Help NSA Critics in Government Surveillance Lawsuits," *The Hill,* September 21, 2013, http://thehill.com/blogs/hillicon-valley/technology/323793-snowden-leaks-help-nsa -critics-in-legal-fights; James Glanz and Andrew W. Lehren, "N.S.A. Spied on Allies, Aid Groups and Businesses," *New York Times,* December 20, 2013, p. A1; Luke Harding, "State Surveillance: Staff at Human Rights Groups Have Been NSA Targets, Says Snowden," *Guardian* (London), April 8, 2014, p. 2.

92. James Ball, Julian Borger, and Glenn Greenwald, "Revealed: How US and UK Spy Agencies Defeat Internet Privacy and Security," *Guardian* (London), September 5, 2013, http://www.theguardian.com/world/2013/sep/05/nsa-gchq-encryption-codes-security.

93. After Snowden's leaks, Senate Intelligence Committee members Ron Wyden and Mark Udall suggested the bulk phone data programs were less than effective, given the costs and alternatives: "We have yet to see any evidence that the bulk phone records collection program has provided any *otherwise unobtainable* intelligence." Senators Wyden and Udall, in their June 2013 statement, also wrote: "It may be more convenient for the NSA to collect this data in bulk, rather than directing specific queries to the various phone companies, but in our judgment convenience alone does not justify the collection of the personal information of huge numbers of ordinary Americans if the same or more information can be obtained using less intrusive methods." Senator Wyden and Senator Udall, "Wyden, Udall Issue Statement on Effectiveness of Declassified NSA Programs," press release, June 19, 2013, http://www.wyden.senate.gov/news/press-releases/wyden-udall-issue-statement -on-effectiveness-of-declassified-nsa-programs, emphasis added. See also *First Unitarian Church of Los Angeles v. NSA* (Bamford, Johnson, and Fenn brief), p. vi (the "preoccupation with secrecy . . . thwarts an effective evaluation of these programs' effectiveness").

94. Glenn Greenwald, "NSA Collecting Phone Records of Millions of Verizon Customers Daily," *Guardian* (London), June 5, 2013, http://www.theguardian.com/world/2013/jun/06/nsa-phone-records-verizon-court-order. The Supreme Court ultimately decided against Amnesty in *Clapper v. Amnesty International*, 133 S. Ct. 1138 (Supreme Court, 2013). See also *Jewel v. NSA*, 673 F.3d 902 (Ninth Circuit Court of Appeals, 2011).

95. Glenn Greenwald, "Members of Congress Denied Access to Basic Information about NSA," *Guardian* (London), August 4, 2013, http://www.theguardian.com/commentisfree/2013/aug/04/congress-nsa-denied-access. The leaked documents also provided evidence of lies senior officials told to the intelligence committees. See, e.g., Scott Shane and Jonathan Weisman, "Disclosures on N.S.A. Surveillance Put Awkward Light on Previous Denials," *New York Times,* June 12, 2013, p. A18. A brief note about MUSCULAR: one of the first stories in June 2013 revealed the PRISM program, which involved cooperation between NSA and the major technology firms—including Google, Yahoo, Microsoft, Apple, and Facebook. In short, the NSA used FAA Section 702 authority to demand information about citizens. Eventually, the NSA decided PRISM's "front-door access" to the companies' servers was insufficient. It therefore devised a "back door" plan—MUSCULAR—and hacked into Google and Yahoo's international fiber-optic cables linking their "data centers." This time, they proceeded without the companies' cooperation or knowledge. The backdoor access, apparently rationalized with a loose reading of President Reagan's Executive Order 12333, offered a convenient way around the already permissive FISA and FAA. Tapping the cables outside US territory gave the NSA free rein to operate outside US laws, letting it siphon information at "high volume." MUSCULAR's warrantless domestic spying appeared to far surpass PRISM's, and it included metadata as well as message content. Unlike FISA/FAA-related activities, the NSA enjoyed little to no oversight from the relevant congressional committees due to its basis in Executive Order 12333 ("United States Intelligence Activities," amended by orders 13284, 13355, and 13470); Gellman and Soltani, "NSA Infiltrates Links"; *First Unitarian Church of Los Angeles v. NSA* (Bamford, Johnson, and Fenn).

96. *First Unitarian Church of Los Angeles v. NSA* (Bamford, Johnson, and Fenn), pp. 13–14.

97. A former senior Obama-Biden intelligence official assured me that the problem is different now compared with the Church Committee era because the people in charge are not characters like Nixon or former FBI director J. Edgar Hoover. See *First Unitarian Church of Los Angeles v. NSA* (Bamford, Johnson, and Fenn), p. 3; Friedersdorf, "Experts on the NSA's History"; Glenn Greenwald, Ryan Gallagher, and Ryan Grim, "Top-Secret Document Reveals NSA Spied on Porn Habits as Part of Plan to Discredit 'Radicalizers,'" *Huffington Post,* November 26, 2013, http://www.huffingtonpost.com/2013/11/26/nsa-porn-muslims_n_4346128.html.

Chapter 11: Conclusion

1. The Partnership for Civil Justice Fund, "Occupy Crackdown FOIA Requests," December 21, 2012, http://www.justiceonline.org/our-work/ows-foia.html; "The FBI vs. Occupy: Secret Docs Reveal 'Counterterrorism' Monitoring of OWS from Its Earliest Days," *Democracy, Now!*, December 27, 2012, http://www.democracynow.org/2012/12/27/the_fbi_vs_occupy_secret_docs. Earlier document releases showed the involvement of the Department of Homeland Security and the National Parks Service.

2. Michael Evans, *Lifting the Veil on Colombia's "Emerald Czar,"* National Security Archive Electronic Briefing Book No. 408, December 21, 2012, http://www.gwu.edu/~nsarchiv/NSAEBB/NSAEBB408/.

3. Todd Shields, "U.S. to Study Staffing at Air-Traffic Control Facilities," *Bloomberg News,* December 21, 2012, http://www.bloomberg.com/news/2012-12-21/u-s-to-study-staffing-at-air-traffic-control-facilities.html.

4. Department of the Interior, "Secretary Salazar Appoints Members to the U.S. Extractive Industries Transparency Initiative Committee," December 21, 2012, http://www.doi.gov/news/pressreleases/secretary-salazar-appoints-members-to-the-us-extractive-industries-transparency-initiative-committee.cfm; Department of the Interior, U.S. Extractive Industries Transparency Initiative (USEITI) Advisory Committee, Secretary Appointed Members, 2012, December 21, 2012, http://www.doi.gov/eiti/upload/members.pdf.

5. Philip Zelikow, Tarek E. Masoud, Richard Betts, and James H. McCall, March 16–17, 2000, Interview with Richard B. Cheney, George H. W. Bush Oral History Project, Miller Center, University of Virginia.

6. Aftergood, "Is the Secrecy System an Autonomous Entity?"

7. Ibid.; James C. Scott, *Two Cheers for Anarchism: Six Easy Pieces on Autonomy, Dignity, and Meaningful Work and Play* (Princeton, NJ: Princeton University Press, 2013), p. xii.

8. See the end of chapter 4 for a discussion of important elements of a FACA reform bill. The Whistleblower Protection Enhancement Act does not solve some of the enforcement, implementation, and coverage problems that bedeviled earlier whistle-blower protection laws. See Jesselyn Radack, "House Unanimously Passes Whistleblower Protection Bill," *The Whistleblogger* [Government Accountability Project blog], October 1, 2012, http://www.whistleblower.org/blog/42-2012/2276-house-unanimously-passes-whistleblower-protection-bill; Radack, "Whistleblower Protection Enhancement Act Passes: Guess Who's Left Out?," *Daily Kos,* November 15, 2012, http://www.dailykos.com/story/2012/11/15/1161890/-Whistleblower-Protection-Enhancement-Act-Passes-Guess-Who-s-Left-Out#.

9. Garfinkel, Presentation.

10. Senator Lieberman, Opening Statement of Chairman Lieberman, Senate Committee on Homeland Security and Governmental Affairs, Ten Years after 9/11, Hearing 112-403, Washington, DC, October 12, 2011, http://www.gpo.gov/fdsys/pkg/CHRG-112

shrg67123/html/CHRG-112shrg67123.htm; Zoë Baird Budinger and Jeffrey H. Smith, "Ten Years after 9/11: A Status Report on Information Sharing," Senate Committee on Homeland Security and Governmental Affairs, Ten Years after 9/11, Hearing 112-403, Washington, DC, October 12, 2011, p. 1. It is important to emphasize how problematic this remains. See, e.g., Michael Kranish, Bryan Bender, Sean P. Murphy, and Noah Bierman, "Data-Sharing Troubles Raise Questions in Marathon Case," *Boston Globe,* April 25, 2013, http://www.bostonglobe.com/news/nation/2013/04/24/govern ment-terrorism-information-sharing-program-rated-high-risk-despite-years-effort-since/ 3ImcHIZOaPKfeeBYTAXRHN/story.html. The programs' problems also involve privacy violations and high costs. See, e.g., Matt Apuzzo and Eileen Sullivan, "Intelligence Effort Named Citizens, Not Terrorists," *Associated Press,* October 2, 2012.

11. On horizontal accountability, see, e.g., Guillermo O'Donnell, "Delegative Democracy," in *Counterpoints: Selected Essays on Authoritarianism and Democratization,* ed. O'Donnell (Notre Dame, IN: University of Notre Dame Press, 1999), pp. 159–174.

12. Ed Pilkington, "Bradley Manning's Treatment Was Cruel and Inhuman, UN Torture Chief Rules," *Guardian* (London), March 12, 2012, http://www.guardian.co.uk/ world/2012/mar/12/bradley-manning-cruel-inhuman-treatment-un.

13. Daniel Ellsberg and Harry Kreisler (moderators), High School Students' E-mail Exchange with Daniel Ellsberg, Institute for International Studies, University of California, Berkeley, May 14, 1999, http://globetrotter.berkeley.edu/people/Ellsberg/ells.QA99.leak .html. On the complicated relationship between Ellsberg and Kissinger—complicated even before the Pentagon Papers conflict—see Ellsberg, *Secrets*; Walter Isaacson, *Kissinger: A Biography* (New York: Simon & Schuster, 2003), pp. 329–331.

INDEX

ABA. *See* American Bar Association

Abductions, extraterritorial, 143, 144

Abdulmutallab, Umar Farouk, 325, 351

Abraham, Spencer, 173, 440n21

Abramoff, Jack, 320, 321

Abrams, Elliott, 474n9

Abubakr, Ali, 60, 405n10

Abu Dhabi Welfare Organization, 175, 177

Abu Ghraib prison, 134, 302–304, 479n53, 480n59

Accountability, 3, 19, 23, 32, 76, 93–94, 133, 164, 196, 198, 262, 285, 309, 321, 328, 335, 341, 376, 380, 383, 399n43, 510n11

Accuracy in Media, 157

ACLU v. Clapper (2013), 371

ACLU v. NSA (2008), 148, 193

Act of June 21, 1941, 170

Adair County (Iowa) Board of Health, 211

Adams, John, 31, 32

Adams, Robert H., 123

Addington, David, 45, 94, 98–101, 106, 113, 137, 139, 148, 191, 307, 314, 322, 358

Administrative Procedures Act, 136

Advisory Committee on Gulf War Veterans, 240

Aftergood, Steven, 7, 8, 15, 39–40, 115, 138, 193, 336

Agent Orange, 200, 258, 279, 382, 464n13
concealing government information about, 245–252
health effects of, 5, 239, 246–247, 250–252, 377

Agricultural Research Service (ARS), 211–213, 220, 322

Ahmed, Nasser, 172

Al-Aulaqi, Abdulrahman, 325, 342

Al-Aulaqi, Anwar, 324–327, 342–343, 348

Al-Aulaqi, Nasser, 325, 350

Algerian Armed Islamic Group (GIA), 175, 176, 177

Algerian Six, 176, 178, 442n35

Al-Haramain Islamic Foundation, Inc. v. Bush (2007), 193

Al-Haramain Islamic Foundation v. Obama et al. (2012), 350

Alien and Sedition Acts, 31

Alien Terrorist Removal Court (ATRC), 168, 438n9

Allende, Salvador, 82, 413n54, 473n2

Allison, Graham, 43

Al-Maqtari, Ali, 60

Al-Najjar, Mazen, 172

Al-Nashiri, Abd al-Rahim, interrogation of, 310

Al Qaeda, 15–16, 52–53, 56, 57, 64, 80, 172, 175, 176, 177, 180, 195, 197

Álvarez Machain, Humberto, 142–143, 144, 146

Amer, Bashar, 172

American Anti-terrorism Committee, 157

American Association of Universities, FOIA and, 459n60

American Bar Association (ABA), 125–126, 424n63

American Cancer Society, 227, 457n48

American Civil Liberties Union (ACLU), 33, 61, 93, 148, 304, 340, 342, 345, 350, 371, 405n12, 406n17, 433n42, 482n66, 483n71
al-Aulaqi and, 324–325

American Council for Health Care Reform, 419n32